THE LITERARY CHURCHILL

JONATHAN ROSE is William R. Kenan Jr Pro
University. Well known as a historian of the book
many specialist publications. His 2001 book, *The*
Working Classes, published by Yale, was a spe
Britain, and won the Longman-History Today Historical Book of the Year Prize, the Jacques Barzun Prize in Cultural History, the British Council Prize, the SHARP Book History Prize, the Bela Kornitzer Prize, and the New Jersey Council for the Humanities Book Prize. It was named a Book of the Year by *The Economist*.

THE LITERARY CHURCHILL

AUTHOR, READER, ACTOR

Jonathan Rose

YALE UNIVERSITY PRESS
NEW HAVEN AND LONDON

Cover images:
Front: Winston Churchill by Sir William Orpen, 1916. Lent by the Churchill Chattels Trust © National Portrait Gallery, London
Back: Churchill at his writing desk at Chartwell, 25 February 1939. Photo by Kurt Hutton/Picture Post/Hulton Archive/Getty Images

First published in paperback in 2015

For information about this and other Yale University Press publications, please contact:

U.S. Office: sales.press@yale.edu yalebooks.com
Europe Office: sales@yaleup.co.uk www.yalebooks.co.uk

Set in Minion Pro by IDSUK (DataConnection) Ltd
Printed in Great Britain by TJ International Ltd, Padstow, Cornwall

Rose, Jonathan, 1952
The literary Churchill: author, reader, actor / Jonathan Rose.
pages cm
ISBN 978-0-300-20407-0 (cl : alk. paper)
1. Churchill, Winston, 1874–1965—Literary art. 2. Great Britain—History—20th century. I. Title.
DA566.9.C5R649 2014
941.084092—dc23

2013041979

A catalogue record for this book is available from the British Library.

ISBN 978-0-300-21234-1 (pbk)

10 9 8 7 6 5 4 3 2 1

Contents

Illustrations

Acknowledgments

The superbly organized Churchill Archives Centre at Churchill College Cambridge was, of course, indispensable to this project. But no less important were the Interlibrary Loan staff at Drew University Library, whom I ran ragged. I thank the Churchill Estate, Firestone Library at Princeton University, the Special Collections Library at the University of Illinois at Urbana-Champaign, and the John F. Kennedy Presidential Library and Museum for permission to quote from unpublished documents. Quotations from Churchill's published and unpublished writings are reproduced with permission of Curtis Brown, London on behalf of the Estate of Sir Winston Churchill, © Winston S. Churchill.

I am equally grateful for access to the book and manuscript collections at the British Library, the New York Public Library, the Seeley G. Mudd Manuscript Library at Princeton University, Columbia University Library, Yale University Library, the Library of Congress, the Wilson Library at the University of North Carolina at Chapel Hill, the Harry Ransom Center at the University of Texas at Austin, the Carl A. Kroch Library at Cornell University, Syracuse University Library, Ball State University Library, the Guildhall Library, the Archive of British Publishing and Printing at the University of Reading, and the Forbes Collection. Images were supplied by the Churchill Archives Centre, the John F. Kennedy Presidential Library and Museum, Getty Images, the National Portrait Gallery, the National Trust, the British Cartoon Archive, Argenta Images, Solo Syndication/Associated Newspapers Ltd., the Max Beerbohm estate, and the Thomas Fisher Rare Book Library at the University of Toronto.

My research was supported by the Presidential Initiatives Fund at Drew University and by a Visiting Fellowship with the Victorian Studies Group at Cambridge University. One tremendous asset was Norman Tomlinson's collection of Churchilliana – some of it donated to Drew University Library, and some given directly to me.

Parts of this book were published earlier as articles in the *Sewanee Review* and *Historically Speaking*. They are reproduced here, with some revisions, with the kind permission of the editors.

I must thank Jan-Pieter Barbian, James Brophy, Luis Campos, David Cannadine, James Carter, Ronald I. Cohen, James J. Connolly, Robert Darnton, Donald G. Davis, Jr., Frank Felsenstein, Simon Frost, Edith Hall, Barbara Hochman, James R. Kelly, Dane Kennedy, Mark Samuels Lasner, Jon Lawrence, Peter Logan, Kate Longworth, Peter Mandler, Cary Mazer, Alistair McCleery, Matthew Rubery, Christopher Rundle, Andrew Scrimgeour, Mark Sheridan, Ronald Tetreault, Anders Toftgaard, Michele Troy, Ine van Linthout, Robert Weisbuch, and James L. W. West III for their advice and commentary. Beyond that, every academic study is fertilized by informal conversations with colleagues, and in that respect I owe much to a host of friends in the Society for the History of Authorship, Reading and Publishing. And it was a privilege to work (once again) with Robert Baldock and his team at Yale University Press, who are scholars as well as editors. My careful copy-editor, Richard Mason, and my proofreader, Loulou Brown, saved me from a number of embarrassments.

More than I can say, I have been aided and comforted by Gayle, my partner in life in every way. It always helped to talk through issues at home – not necessarily about Churchill specifically, but more broadly about the business of literature and cultural analysis. Here we are both fortunate to have a professional author in the family, so this book is rightfully dedicated to Jennifer.

Jonathan Rose
September 2013

Preface: A Literary History of Politics

In February 2002, when the world was debating what should be done about Iraq, Europeans reached for a metaphor they like to apply to Americans. President George W. Bush and his advisors, they protested, were behaving like Hollywood cowboys. Writing in the *Wall Street Journal*, R. James Woolsey, the former director of Central Intelligence, accepted that label as a badge of pride. Yes, he agreed, you could compare us to Gary Cooper in *High Noon* (his favorite movie). When evildoers descended on the marshal's town, only he was willing to stand up to them. His neighbors all turned out to be appeasers or pacifists or cowards or potential collaborators, but the marshal wouldn't "give up doing his duty just because everyone else found excuses to stay out of the fight."[1]

Meanwhile, Dominique de Villepin, Secretary General to the President of France, and soon to become French Foreign Minister, spun out a parallel but different narrative. He had just published *Le Cent Jours ou l'Esprit de Sacrifice*, his account of Waterloo, another legendary gunfight. In his review, Denis MacShane, Britain's Minister for Europe, called it "simply a thrilling read . . . His description of characters is as good as any popular historian and his sense of narrative pace carries the reader along," though the book might leave one with the impression that Napoleon won the battle. Waterloo, wrote de Villepin, "glows with the aura worthy of a victory," for as a diplomat and a prolific author, he always insisted that France could not be France unless she pursued "epic collective adventures."[2]

So here we have two nations following two narratives on a diplomatic collision course, an episode that illustrates the power of stories to steer politics. You may object that politics is really a matter of national interests, however this begs the question: what are nations interested in? Of course they want power, wealth, trade, land, and security. But political actors also act out stories, which can have a force and a momentum of their own, and which may not always serve the more material national interests. Foreign policies inspired by Napoleon or Gary Cooper do not necessarily benefit France or the United States, and they may not have served the personal interests of M. Chirac or Mr. Bush. All politicians, however, tell stories, whether they are grand Bonapartist myths or homey Reaganesque anecdotes, and these stories can drive policy. After all, a few years ago Americans catapulted an obscure politician into the White House largely because they loved reading his life story.

All politicians are authors. Very few of them write anything like an 800-page critique of French poetry, as Dominique de Villepin has, but they all create and publish texts: oral texts, printed texts, filmed texts, broadcast texts. Most politicians, like most authors, are hacks who simply recycle clichés; a few are genuinely creative visionaries. But either way, what they write (or have others write) sets politics in motion. And obviously all politicians are actors, usually performing from a crafted script, but occasionally improvising.

Therefore, we can write political history as literary history. That is, we gain a deeper understanding of politics if we employ the methods developed by literary historians, especially theatre historians and historians of the book. We can ask of politicians the same questions that these scholars ask of authors. What did they read? When they wrote, what were their generic models? How were their writings refashioned by editors, publishers, literary agents, researchers, co-authors, lawyers, and censors? How were their political careers made and unmade by the sociology and economics of authorship, print technology, the structure of media ownership, the machinery of publicity and distribution, book reviewers, and the demands of the literary marketplace? How did they achieve the kind of dramatic effects that are so important in politics? Which literary circles did these political actors move in? Which audiences did they appeal to? How did readers respond to what they wrote, and did that feedback cause them to revise their methods of composition? What can we discover by comparing the successive drafts and editions of their works? And how were those writings translated into other languages and other media, especially film and television? (This study defines "literature" broadly, to include journalism, historical writing, movies, and broadcasting.) When we address these issues, we delve into a mostly unexplored dimension of politics, and we may be able to explain certain kinds of political behavior that might otherwise seem baffling.

Winston Churchill is an ideal subject for experimenting with this new methodology. Winner in 1953 of the Nobel Prize in Literature, a tremendously successful middlebrow author, he clearly could have made a handsome living from his pen even if he had never been elected to public office. In the Churchill Archives at Cambridge, one out of eight boxes is devoted to his literary affairs. And yet scholars have scarcely touched on that side of his life. He may be one of the most intensively studied individuals of modern times, according to Historical Abstracts, but he has only a handful of entries in the MLA Bibliography. Some entries refer to an altogether different Winston Churchill, an American novelist (1871–1947) of the Progressive era. Manfred Weidhorn and Paul Alkon wrote appreciative literary criticism of the British Churchill, and perceptive analyses of the composition of *The Second World War* and *A History of the English-Speaking Peoples* have been produced by David Reynolds and Peter Clarke.[3] But this volume has a different and broader objective: it surveys all of Churchill's important writings, reconstructs (as far as we can) his reading and theatre-going experiences, and assesses their impact on his politics. For Churchill, politics and literature were two sides of the same career, impossible to prise apart. His political goals and methods were shaped by what he read in books and saw on the stage. In turn, he recast his political experiences as literature, inevitably with some artistic license. In fact he made important policy decisions and composed memoranda with a view toward how they would appear on the page, in the grand story that he spent his life composing. He was an artist who used politics as his creative medium, as other writers used paper.

Like most radical ideas, this method of writing history is not entirely new. We have studies of the literary diets of Thomas Jefferson,[4] William Gladstone,[5] Adolf Hitler,[6] Harold Macmillan,[7] John F. Kennedy,[8] and Barack Obama,[9] not to mention *Nixon at the Movies*.[10] But they are still only a handful: we are only beginning to grasp how far politics and literature overlap. Like Churchill, Douglas Hurd, Jeffrey Archer, Anne Widdecombe, Edwina Currie, Iain Duncan Smith, Jimmy Carter, Barbara Boxer, Newt Gingrich, Barbara Milkulski, William Weld, William S. Cohen, and Gary Hart have all published novels – and that only counts recent British and American politicians. If we look to France, the list of political *littérateurs* becomes practically endless.

And Churchill was clearly not the only statesman of his generation to treat politics as performance art. In the grand drama of the Second World War, he played opposite an unforgettable cast. An earlier dull grey cadre of bourgeois politicians had by then given way to Hitler, Mussolini, Roosevelt, De Gaulle, and Churchill, all of them dazzling actors who played off each other and exploited their own personal charisma. This book, then, is not only a literary biography: it explores the crucial and under-appreciated role of theatre in both politics and armed conflict, by placing Churchill and his contemporaries in the context of theatre history.

Every historical study should begin with these cautious words: "This does not explain everything." I emphasize here the literary and theatrical dimensions of politics because they are neglected and important, but certainly not all-important. The everyday business of government is, by and large, an inartistic routine of nudging bureaucracies, negotiating deals, balancing competing interests, and serving constituents. Political historians should not stop doing psephological analyses and research in diplomatic archives. But they should recognize that literature can illuminate political behavior in ways that more conventional methodologies cannot. If the trajectory of an atomic particle follows no known laws of physics, then it is probably in the grip of an unknown force, something we need to understand and work into our calculations. And the political orbit of Winston Churchill could be breathtakingly eccentric.

CHAPTER 1

The Theatre Rage

Everyone knows that as a boy he loved playing with toy soldiers, but biographers do not often mention an equally significant fact: he was no less fond of his miniature theatre. Churchill was thirteen when his aunts Leonie and Clara presented him with a toy stage, which at the time he called "a source of unparalleled amusement." He had the evident approval of his tutor, James Theodore Best, who "told me that the Theatre Rage is very great." His letters to his mother are filled with breathless demands for accessories, as well as a promise "to give a grand performance when I come home."[1] As Churchill recalled many years later, "I certainly remember visiting Mr [W. J.] Webb of Old Street" – the great Victorian impresario of toy theatres – "and also purchasing from him from time to time some of his plays. The one I remember best is 'The Miller and His Men.' For three or four years of my life a model theatre was a great amusement to me." This suggests that he continued playing with it to the advanced age of sixteen or seventeen. Webb's son remembered his frequent patronage and his enthusiasm: "He was a jolly and impulsive lad, and I shall never forget the way he would vault over my counter."[2]

Churchill was throughout his life a passionate theatregoer. Several files in his archives are stuffed with ticket receipts from booking agencies, but unfortunately the receipts do not reveal what plays he attended.[3] However, from other sources we can reconstruct much of that record, which is essential to understanding his political career. More than most politicians, he was a public performer, always on stage and in character. His prose was distinguished by a lifelong addiction to dramatic metaphors. Many of his most crucial political decisions were essentially acts of theatre, and some of them only make sense when placed in the context of theatre history.

In the late Victorian upper-class milieu of his childhood, the theatre had become respectable, fashionable, and ubiquitous. Churchill once alluded to his youthful "infatuation" with private dramatic performances, and he was enthusiastic about school theatricals, performing Robin Hood in an operetta and Martine in Molière's *Le Médecin Malgré Lui*. He enjoyed Gilbert and Sullivan and Christmas pantomimes. He made a point of memorizing Shakespeare at Harrow for a prize competition, in which he placed fourth out of about twenty-five boys.[4] He may have even tried his hand as a playwright: in October 1887 his brother Jack reported to their father that Winston "is going to write a Greek play for Christmas."[5]

His mother Jennie had grown up in a Manhattan mansion equipped with a 600-seat private theatre.[6] Throughout their marriage, she and Lord Randolph exchanged notes about the latest plays.[7] In 1909 she would write and produce her own play, *His Borrowed Plumes*. It had a short run but a fair share of clever epigrams, including: "Is there so much difference between politicians and actors? Both are equally eager for popular applause and both equally doubtful whether they will get it."[8] She probably had in mind both Winston and Lord Randolph. The son learned political theatre at first hand from the father, whom Beatrice Webb considered a dazzling public performer:

> Surely we shall look back on the last fifty years of the nineteenth century as the peculiar period of political artists: we have no statesmen – all our successful politicians, the men who lead the parties, are artists and nothing else: Gladstone, Disraeli, Randolph Churchill, Chamberlain, and the unsuccessful Rosebery, all these men have the characteristics of actors – personal charm, extraordinary pliability and quick-wittedness.[9]

As a drama critic Max Beerbohm proclaimed that in or around 1880 human nature changed. He identified at that point in time a "great change in the constitution of English society," which cast off Victorian reserve and became flamboyantly theatrical: "The sphere of fashion converged with the sphere of art, and a revolution was the result." The Aesthetic movement permeated everything, including parliamentary politics, now enlivened by the "incomparable" performances of Liberal tribune W. E. Gladstone, Irish firebrand Charles Stewart Parnell, and militant atheist Charles Bradlaugh. In that company Randolph Churchill, "despite his halting speech, foppish mien and rather coarse fibre of mind, was yet the greatest Parliamentarian of his day."[10]

He led a small circle of upstart Tory MPs, the "Fourth Party," which succeeded in winning plenty of sympathetic publicity in the *Morning Post* and *Vanity Fair*. In July 1880 the latter identified Lord Randolph as the group's most brilliant actor, even if he did not attach great importance to being earnest:

> He does not care much for facts, it is true, and his blows are not always perfectly legitimate; while he scarcely pretends to be too much in earnest; but

> surely after all he is therein right. . . . The House of Commons should really be taken to be what it is – that is to say, a club of gentlemen who for the most part have a fair amount of money and no particular occupation in life but that of finding an escape from being bored. If men in that frame of mind come down to the House after their dinners, they want to be made to laugh, and have a profound dislike of heroics, unless when really well acted, and recalling memories of Modjeska or Bernhardt. Lord Randolph Churchill has grasped this fact, and *il ira loin.*[11]

Lord Randolph's favorite theatrical device was the political coup, a stroke so unexpected that it shocked even his cronies in the Fourth Party. During the First Boer War he suggested that, "like a thunderbolt in a clear sky," they should call for an end to British military operations and peace talks with the Boers. He proposed to set off "political dynamite" with an amendment to limit the 1881 Irish Coercion Bill to one year.[12] These stands were hardly consistent with mainstream Conservatism, but he conceded that his Tory Democracy was "chiefly opportunism," which succeeded brilliantly in garnering public attention.[13] His public speeches were marked by melodramatic hand gestures and walking "about the platform as though it were really a stage," the *Pall Mall Gazette* observed.[14] He dispatched his opponents with facile catchphrases that journalists liked to pick up and repeat: Gladstone was "the Moloch of Midlothian," Joseph Chamberlain "this pinchbeck Robespierre."[15] One of his most famous (and self-revealing) assaults on Gladstone came in Blackpool, on 24 January 1884:

> Gentlemen, we live in an age of advertisement, the age of Holloway's pills, of Colman's mustard, and of Horniman's pure tea; and the policy of lavish advertisement has been so successful in commerce that the Liberal party, with its usual enterprise, had adapted it to politics. The Prime Minister is the greatest living master of the art of personal political advertisement. Holloway, Colman, and Horniman are nothing compared with him. Every act of his, whether it be for the purposes of health, or of recreation, or of religious devotion, is spread before the eyes of every man, woman and child in the United Kingdom on large and glaring placards.

At Hawarden Castle, his Flintshire estate, Gladstone conspicuously chopped down trees as staged media events. Once he hosted a delegation of workmen:

> One would have thought that the deputation would have been received in the house, in the study, in the drawing-room, or even in the dining room. Not at all. That would have been out of harmony with the advertisement "boom." Another scene had been arranged. The working men were guided through

> the ornamental grounds, into the wide-spreading park . . . [where] the Prime Minister . . . in scanty attire and profuse perspiration, engaged in the destruction of a gigantic oak, just giving its last dying groan. They are permitted to gaze and to worship and adore and, having conducted themselves with exemplary propriety, are each of them presented with a few chips as a memorial of that memorable scene . . . .

Likewise Gladstone's celebrated Midlothian campaigns, first staged in 1880 and reprised over the next few years, were ridiculed by Lord Randolph as play-acting: "The old stage properties have been brought out at every station: all the old scenery, all the old decorations, the old troupe, they have all been brought forward in a sadly tarnished and bedraggled condition. . . ."[16] This was perfect hypocrisy: no politician was more ruthless at self-publicity than Lord Randolph Churchill. He fully grasped that the enfranchisement of a broad electorate, the creation of a mass-circulation press, and the rise of the advertising industry, had transformed the ground rules of politics. Delivering Olympian speeches in Parliament was no longer enough: one had to exploit the new culture of celebrity, which placed a premium on flamboyant public performance. Lord Randolph had an advertising agent's talent for inventing catchy slogans, either rhyming jingles ("Ulster will fight, Ulster will be right") or clichés with an unexpected twist (Gladstone was an "old man in a hurry").[17] He strategically positioned himself as President of the Conservative News Agency. The Central News Agency (a competitor of Reuters) reported his speeches in their entirety: only Gladstone, Joseph Chamberlain, and Lord Salisbury (the Conservative Party leader) enjoyed the same level of coverage.[18]

More conventional politicians might distrust and resent Lord Randolph, but for the time being they had to do business with him. By 1885 *Punch* was portraying him as a prima donna dictating terms to impresario Lord Salisbury.[19] J. B. Crozier, an early and unfriendly biographer, found Lord Randolph a dull public speaker whose reputation for verbal fireworks had been puffed up by the press. His clever catchphrases, which would now be called "sound bites," oversimplified issues and caricatured opponents, but were endlessly repeated by the newspapers. They might denounce him in editorials, but they gave him the coverage he craved in their news columns.[20] "The best thing that can happen to a politician is to be abused by the press," Lord Randolph cheerfully observed. "It does him some good to be praised. But when he's ignored altogether, it's the devil!"[21]

Young Winston was paying attention and learning his lessons. As he put it in the 1906 biography of his father, "Instead of that paragraph of mutilated misrepresentation with which so many eminent Ministers and ex-Ministers have to remain dissatisfied, column after column of the *Times* was filled with the oratory of an unproved stripling of thirty-two." His speeches upheld no consistent principles and advocated no coherent policies, but they attracted attention because

> they were entirely fresh and original. Wit, abuse, epigrams, imagery, argument – all were "Randolphian." No one could guess beforehand what he was going to say nor how he would say it. No one else said the same kind of things, or said them in the same kind of way. He possessed the strange quality, unconsciously exerted and not by any means to be simulated, of compelling attention, and of getting himself talked about. Every word he spoke was studied with interest and apprehension. Each step he took was greeted with a gathering chorus of astonished cries.

Winston had revolted against his classical education and rarely resorted to Latin tags, but now he deployed a quotation from Tacitus: *Omnium quae dixerat, feceratque quadam ostentator* ("He had the showman's knack of drawing attention to everything he said or did").[22] And if that aroused the suspicions of stodgy Tories, Winston quoted first Pope, and then Machiavelli:

> Sworn to no master, of no sect am I,
> As drives the storm, at any door I knock.[23]

> Of this, however, I am well persuaded, that it is better to be impetuous than cautious. For Fortune is a woman who to be kept under must be beaten and roughly handled; and we see that she suffers herself to be more readily mastered by those who treat her so, than by those who are more timid in their approaches. And always, like a woman, she favours the young, because they are less scrupulous and fiercer, and command her with greater audacity.[24]

In this culture of celebrity, the distinction between fiction and reality dissolved. One could never know whether Lord Randolph had any real core convictions or was simply playing to the gallery. Was he an actual person, or a theatrical persona created by himself? In fact he appeared as a character in several literary and stage works, at least some of which were familiar to Winston. Lord Randolph was thinly disguised in Justin McCarthy's novel *The Rebel Rose* (1887) and W. F. Rae's *An American Duchess* (1890), and not disguised at all in Rae's *Miss Bayle's Romance* (1887) and J. M. Barrie's first novel, *Better Dead* (1888). In the last of these, Lord Randolph invents an ingenious quantitative method for "calculating fame," an early form of media research. He haunts tobacconists' shops and counts the celebrities' faces appearing on matchboxes, anxiously comparing his totals to those of Gladstone, Chamberlain, and Lily

Langtry.[25] In 1883 Jennie took Winston to a pantomime that starred a poodle named Lord Randolph Churchill.[26] Early in 1885 Jennie saw another play, *The Candidate*, which mentioned her husband.[27] In February 1890 Winston's Aunt Frances wrote to him about a burlesque of Victor Hugo's play *Ruy Blas* (1838), that including satiric topical songs "with allusions to your Father!" In the same letter she reported that Lord Randolph also starred in that week's full-page cartoon in *Punch*, which twitted him for introducing temperance legislation.[28] In 1891 Randolph was spoofed on stage once again, in the political extravaganza *Joan of Arc*, until the Lord Chamberlain ordered the satire to be toned down. In his turn, Winston too would be incarnated as a character in a number of novels.

In August 1886 Lord Randolph became Chancellor of the Exchequer under Lord Salisbury, but then his hunger for publicity finally did for him. He wanted to score yet another political coup by cutting income tax, but that would require both the Army and Navy to cut costs, usually not a policy favored by Conservative governments. When it was clear that the Cabinet would not agree to those reductions, Lord Randolph resigned in December, without discussing the matter with his wife beforehand. Probably it was yet another act of political theatre: as Chamberlain explained, it was "only the classical annual resignation of a Chancellor of the Exchequer" designed to pressure the government to trim the budget. But Salisbury outmaneuvered Lord Randolph by accepting his resignation. The result was a public relations disaster: Lord Randolph was denounced by all major newspapers except the *Morning Post*, and his career never recovered.[29] And yet, even if he was a political failure and a cold father, his son saw in his life "a great and vivid drama."[30] Winston was keenly aware that Lord Randolph had successfully fashioned himself into a media phenomenon, and studied carefully how he had done it:

> We saw as children the passers-by take off their hats in the streets and the workmen grin when they saw his big moustache. For years I had read every word he spoke and what the newspapers said about him. Although he was only a private member and quite isolated, everything he said even at the tiniest bazaar was reported verbatim in all the newspapers, and every phrase was scrutinized and weighed.[31]

By 1930, when he published *My Early Life*, Winston had come to understand why his father's theatrical style of politics had ended in failure. He had posed as "the daring pilot in extremity," and that did not play well in an era of political calm and retrenchment – as Churchill the son discovered in the early 1930s. But Winston nevertheless insisted that Lord Randolph's greatness had to be measured by the persona he created, "not by his words and actions, but by the impression which his personality made upon his contemporaries. This was intense, and had circumstances continued favourable, might well have manifested itself in decisive episodes. He embodied that force, caprice and charm which so often springs from genius."[32]

By age fifteen, when he was probably still playing with his toy stage, Winston was attending legitimate theatres in London. Often he saw melodramas, with titles such as *A Million of Money*. Churchill's rhetoric and politics would be profoundly shaped by melodrama – a connection between low literature and high statecraft that is more common than we might imagine. When George W. Bush said "Bin Laden: Dead or Alive," we all saw the allusion, because we all know the clichés of the American Western. We don't easily recognize that Churchill's prose was saturated with allusions to melodrama, because melodramatic conventions are today forgotten by everyone except a handful of theatre historians. But Churchill's contemporaries knew those conventions well and saw that he was in thrall to them. Even for his bodyguard, "melodramatic" was the word that summed up the great man.[33] Therefore a brief tutorial on the essentials of melodrama is necessary before proceeding further.

Melodrama dominated British popular culture in the century between Waterloo and the Somme, just as the Western dominated American popular culture between Appomattox and the Tet Offensive. It pervaded the theatre, novels (especially Scott and Dickens), journalism, and historical writing. Political rhetoric often employed the themes and language of melodrama, as in popular protests against the 1834 Poor Law.[34] Michael Booth, the leading scholar of the genre, defined melodrama as "a world of certainties where confusion, doubt, and perplexity are absent; a world of absolutes where virtue and vice coexist in pure whiteness and pure blackness; and a world of justice where after immense struggle and torment good triumphs over and punishes evil, and virtue receives tangible material rewards." Good people suffer terrible ordeals, but:

> The shootings, strangling, hangings, poisonings, drowning, stabbings, suicides, explosions, conflagrations, avalanches, earthquakes, eruptions, shipwrecks, train wrecks, apparitions, tortured heroines, persecuted heroes, and fearsome villains are only a lengthy prelude to inevitable happiness and the apotheosis of virtue. Audiences could enjoy crime and villainy and horror in the full knowledge that the bright sword of justice would always fall in the right place, and that bags of gold would always be awarded to the right people. Evil can only destroy itself, no matter how hard it tries.

Melodramatic characters are therefore stereotyped and entirely predictable. The plot is driven by the villain: he "thinks, chooses, initiates action, alters his plans, makes new ones." And in asides to the audience, he explicitly reveals those plans. The hero, however, must be unaware of the villain's machinations, otherwise he would take appropriate countermeasures, and there would be no play. Necessarily, Booth concedes, "The basic hero is really rather stupid."[35] But the ideology of melodrama was radically and rousingly libertarian: yeomen denounce noblemen, workers resist capitalists, sailors stand up to officers, rebels fight tyrants, virtuous women defy sexual predators, and (a favorite theme) innocent men are imprisoned but ultimately set free.[36] The hero always resists evil, never surrenders, forgives his defeated enemies, and deals honestly and charitably with everyone. Or, as Churchill formulated it:

> *IN WAR:* RESOLUTION
> *IN DEFEAT:* DEFIANCE
> *IN VICTORY:* MAGNANIMITY
> *IN PEACE:* GOOD WILL

Melodrama relied on "sensational and rapid action" shifting from scene to scene, though this was difficult and expensive to produce on the stage. It often climaxed with spectacular explosions, whether of boilers, railway locomotives, or kegs of gunpowder. This was something that children could try at home with a miniature theatre and the right accessories, before there were tiresome regulations governing toy safety. Isaac Pocock's *The Miller and His Men*, young Winston's favorite play, concluded with an unforgettable pyrotechnic display.[37] And melodramatic diction was typically exaggerated and histrionic, often relying on rolled r's[38] – even when there were no r's to roll, as when Churchill rallied his countrymen to resist "the Narzis."

London's Adelphi Theatre specialized in this genre, to the point where "Adelphi melodrama" was a universally recognized brand. In September 1890 one such new work electrified the fifteen-year-old Winston: George R. Sims and Robert Buchanan's "ripping piece," *The English Rose*. "Well acted – well put on – excellently carried out – beautiful scenery – capital songs," he gushed to his mother. Already Winston understood melodramatic stagecraft, noting that *The English Rose* had its three essential elements: "Capital girl – good old hero – splendid villain."[39] *The English Rose* was an Irish melodrama, but in some ways it departed from the conventions of that popular genre. The critic of *The Times*[40] applauded Sims and Buchanan for resisting the temptation to portray Ireland as

> a land of kneebreeches and brimless hats, sprigs of shillelagh, wakes, jigs, shebeens, and jaunting cars, with a population of black-eyed and short-skirted

> colleens, "bhoys" who are always "spoiling for a fight," shovel-hatted priests, familiarly addressed as "your riverince," and soldiers wearing the uniform of the Georges. . . . They have brought the Ireland of the stage up to date. They have swept away the comic opera *personnel* which has hitherto represented the Irish character.

In fact *The English Rose* was a hybrid of melodrama and "problem play" – that is, a theatre piece addressing a contemporary social or political issue. It portrayed

> not the Ireland of Mr. Boucicault or Charles Lever, but that of the daily newspapers or the Parnell Commission—the Ireland of judicial rents, threatening letters, police protection, moonlight outrage, and murder, side by side with a fund of law-abiding sentiment and a fair sprinkling of the heroic virtues. It may be thought that these are dangerous elements to juggle with in a popular entertainment.

This was indeed treacherous terrain. A decade earlier, in *The O'Dowd*, Dion Boucicault had attempted to address Irish grievances on the stage, but the ensuing controversy compelled him to cancel the run. Irish nationalism could be fueled by Irish melodrama, and for that reason the Lord Chamberlain often censored inflammatory stage rhetoric.[41] As *The Times* recognized, Sims and Buchanan therefore took great "care to hold the scale so evenly between all parties, to be so unbiased in their views, so unpolitical, in a word, that *The English Rose* can be applauded by Unionists and Home Rulers alike, if indeed under the spell of a strongly dramatic theme all political partisanship is not forgotten." In his 1968 essay "The Affirmative Character of Culture," Herbert Marcuse argued that "problem plays" served to contain political dissent by addressing social ills without resolving them, but the same principle was well understood in late Victorian West End theatres.

The plot of *The English Rose* involves an English gentleman, Sir Philip Kingston, who purchases Connemara land from impoverished Irish gentry, the Knight of Ballyreeny and his handsome son Harry O'Mailley. Inevitably, romance blossoms between O'Mailley and Kingston's fetching niece, Ethel. There is some grumbling among the tenants about paying rent to an Englishman, but the only real villain in the play is Sir Philip's agent, Macdonnell, who has embezzled from his employer and who covets Ethel's affections. To cover up his fraud and eliminate his rival, Macdonnell incites some tenants to murder Sir Philip and plans to pin the crime on O'Mailley. When he discovers the plot, O'Mailley gallops off on horseback to save Kingston, but he wrenches the murder weapon from the actual perpetrator a moment too late, and is discovered with the smoking gun in his hands. Tried and convicted of murder, O'Mailley is rescued by a righteously indignant mob, eventually vindicated, and affianced to Ethel.[42]

The Times shrewdly recognized why the play succeeded: London audiences could flatter themselves that they were enjoying something more serious than the usual Irish romance, when in fact "the authors have not diverged as widely from the beaten track of melodrama as would at first sight appear." With the exception of the nefarious agent, all the characters were essentially well intentioned. Sims and Buchanan reduced seven hundred years of Anglo-Irish conflict to "a mere misunderstanding."

Churchill's views on Ireland, as they evolved, agreed entirely with the easy political optimism of *The English Rose*. He even-handedly presumed that both Unionists and Home Rulers (but not Republicans) had legitimate concerns and grievances, which could be reconciled. The Irish had been the victims of injustices, which, however, could be corrected by British justice, and Ireland should be allowed greater autonomy within (but not outside) the British Empire. Writing to the Irish-American politician Bourke Cochran in 1896, Churchill granted that "England has treated Ireland disgracefully in the past," but he considered "it unjust to arraign the deeds of earlier times before modern tribunals & to judge by modern standards." Centuries ago Irish Catholics had been cruelly oppressed, but no more so than the French Huguenots or the Russian serfs, and it would be unfair to hold Queen Victoria answerable for the sins of Oliver Cromwell. The Irish problem "is nearly solved. . . . There is no tyranny in Ireland now. The Irish peasant is as free and as well represented as the English labourer. Everything that can be done to alleviate distress and heal the wounds of the past is done," in spite of troublemakers who were striving "to keep the country up to the proper standard of indignation." He predicted that Ireland would eventually achieve a measure of Home Rule, but within some kind of greater imperial federation.[43]

Some years later Churchill would see a send-up of Irish melodrama in the form of Bernard Shaw's play *John Bull's Other Island*, which took a much more jaundiced view of Irish underdevelopment and provinciality than *The English Rose*. Shaw decisively rejected the project of "making St. George's Channel a frontier and hoist[ing] a green flag on College Green. . . . I want Ireland to be the brains and imagination of a big Commonwealth, not a Robinson Crusoe island." As Churchill later recalled the performance, "We are no sooner captivated by Irish charm and atmosphere than we see the Irish race liveried in humbug and strait-jacketed in infirmity of purpose. The Liberal Home Ruler, who so hopefully expected from Bernard Shaw, justification and approval for his cause, found himself in a trice held up as an object of satire rarely equaled upon the stage."[44] Shaw did not oppose Home Rule, but his play sent the message that Ireland could only escape poverty and backwardness through integration with the larger Anglophone world.

Indirectly, *The English Rose* might have also engaged Churchill in Jewish issues. The play never mentions Jews or Judaism, but the plot strikingly parallels the Dreyfus affair, which erupted four years later in 1894: a gallant representative of a dispossessed race is villainously condemned for a crime he did not commit, but in the end is proved innocent. The first record of Churchill's commitment to a Jewish cause is a letter he wrote to his mother from Omdurman on 8 September 1898: "Bravo Zola! I am delighted to witness the complete debacle of that monstrous conspiracy."[45] He was still obsessed with the controversy as late as 1929,[46] and it was precisely the political theatrics that always fascinated him. "The developments of the Dreyfus case are wonderful," he told his mother. "Never since gladiatorial combats were abolished has the world witnessed such a drama – with real flesh & blood for properties."[47] The Dreyfus affair gripped the European imagination largely because it had all the elements of melodrama – a sensational trial scene, a man unjustly accused and imprisoned, the hero shouting "Vive la République" after he is stripped of his uniform, the long righteous speeches in his defense. An 1895 Adelphi melodrama by Seymour Hicks and George Edwardes, *One of the Best*, reset the scandal in England – not very convincingly, in Bernard Shaw's opinion. "The French govern by melodrama, and give everybody a part in the piece," whereas the English preferred "breaking and getting rid of our Dreyfuses in the quietest possible manner, instead of advertising them by regimental *coups de théâtre*."[48]

The *coup de théâtre* was a perennial melodramatic device: a stunning reversal of fortune. It might work against the hero (as when O'Mailley is caught with the murder weapon) or in his favor (for instance, the last-minute rescue of Dick Dudgeon in Bernard Shaw's *The Devil's Disciple*).[49] But either way it should be wholly unexpected and leave the audience gasping. It could as well be a political maneuver, often deployed by Lord Randolph Churchill, not always successfully: notably his resignation from the Exchequer. As we will see, the *coup de théâtre* would be one of Winston's favorite literary and political strokes, with very mixed results.

Imperialist melodrama was another staple of the Adelphi and Empire Theatres, both of which young Winston frequently patronized.[50] In his writings he often alluded generally to the genre, if not to particular plays. The heroes were usually British (and occasionally French) soldiers in Africa or India, while the natives fell into three distinct categories. There were good natives: loyal, childlike, incapable of self-government, and properly grateful for British rule. They were oppressed or misled by wicked natives, defined as those who took up arms against the British. Then there was usually a treacherous character, who might be a native or a European: either way, he was inevitably unmasked as a traitor. A wicked native might be respected as a brave enemy, the familiar example being Rudyard Kipling's "Fuzzy Wuzzy" ("You're a pore benighted 'eathen but a first-class fightin' man"), but the treacherous character was always beneath contempt. In 1885 two London plays offered fanciful portrayals of General Gordon's defeat that same year, spinning it as a British victory, and in both treacherous Machiavels played key roles: in *Khartoum!* he tries to plant a bomb on a British troopship, and in *Human Nature* he opens the city gates to the Mahdi's assault. *Khartoum!* also features a good native, a glamorous "Queen of the Desert" who warns the Mahdi (the wicked one) that "The race you war against, though alien to ours, is destined yet to fill this land with faith and freedom that *you* cannot give because you know it not!"[51] We may laugh, but there were colonized people who talked like that. One of them, encouraging Indians to fight for the British Empire in 1918, assured his listeners that the English "love justice.... The liberty of the individual is very dear to them. They have shielded men against oppression.... To sacrifice sons in the war ought to be a cause not of pain but of pleasure to brave men."[52] The recruiting agent was Mohandas Gandhi. Imperial melodrama faded from the stage after the Boer War (1899–1902), but it enjoyed a second life in the movies. For a lesson in the conventions of this genre, see *Lives of a Bengal Lancer* (1935), *Gunga Din* (1939), based on a poem of that name by Kipling and *North West Frontier* (as late as 1959, starring Kenneth More as the hero and Herbert Lom as a treacherous half-breed).

There is no direct evidence that Churchill ever saw *Khartoum!* or *Human Nature*, but imperial melodrama was a highly standardized product,[53] and he definitely was in the audience for a very similar play. In December 1891 he saw *Michael Strogoff*, a dramatization of Jules Verne's 1876 novel.[54] Nominally set in Russia, it is for all practical purposes a celebration of British imperialism, substituting *Czar* and *Siberia* for *Queen* and *India*. Tartar insurgents led by the Emir of Bokhara have invaded Asian Russia, and from there plan to attack Europe. The Russians have dispatched a relief column to besieged Irkutsk, but the telegraph line has been cut, so Captain Michael Strogoff is sent ahead on horseback to alert the garrison that help is on the way. Strogoff is captured by the Emir, who (following the instructions of the Koran) orders him to be blinded with a red-hot saber, an act simulated in plain view of the audience. The Tartars use incendiary weapons against Irkutsk, an opportunity for spectacular stage pyrotechnics. A turncoat Russian officer almost delivers the city to the invaders, but is foiled by Strogoff, who, it turns out, was not blinded after all. As he explains the miracle to his mother, "When I thought I was looking on you for the last time, mother, my eyes were so filled with tears that the hot iron only dried my tears without destroying my sight."[55]

That last touch helps to explain why melodrama was eventually laughed off the stage. With adolescent enthusiasm, Churchill had embraced a form of drama that metropolitan audiences increasingly regarded as tired, creaky, and ridiculous. *The English Rose* was a hit among plebeians but provoked yawns in quality papers such as *The Times* and the *Pall Mall Gazette*: for the latter it offered only "cut-and-dried melodramatic conventionalities . . . the old bill of fare with an Irish dressing."[56] In 1895 George Bernard Shaw alluded to "the hostility of that sceptical spirit which is now growing among first-night audiences in a very marked degree. This is an inevitable reaction against the artificialities, insincerities, and impossibilities which form about three-fourths of the stock-in-trade of those playwrights who seek safety and success in the assumption that it is impossible to underrate the taste and intelligence of the British public."[57] Most London audiences could no longer stomach such clichés as "the thrashing of the villain, or the 'Just before the battle, mother' episode, otherwise than with its tongue in its cheek. The minority who are affected by these devices are disparaged as sentimentalists and greenhorns; it is a point of honour with the seasoned playgoer to grin cynically at such things as 'rot,' whilst affecting much connoisseurship in the cleverness with which they are contrived."[58] Shaw would appeal to those sniggering sophisticates with *Captain Brassbound's Conversion* (1900), which systematically lampooned all the traditions of imperialist melodrama. Something similar would be done to the American Western in *Cat Ballou* (1965), *Little Big Man* (1970), and *Blazing Saddles* (1974). Parody is the final illness of a dying literary form. But Churchill, to the end of his life, never accepted that melodrama was dead: he loved it and constantly performed it in politics. The Victorian stage offered numerous species of melodrama, in addition to Irish and imperialist versions: political melodrama, revolutionary melodrama, military melodrama, prison melodrama, capitalist melodrama, and temperance melodrama.[59] Churchill would act out all of these subgenres except (of course) the last.

In fact, Churchill's first act of political theatre was an anti-temperance burlesque. At Sandhurst military academy he enjoyed weekend leave twice a month, during which he and his friends frequented the Empire Theatre, congregating in the promenade behind the dress circle. There (he recalled in *My Early Life*) "young people of both sexes . . . not only conversed together during the performance and its intervals, but also from time to time refreshed themselves with alcoholic liquors." In summer 1894 Laura Ormiston Chant, a suffragist on the London County Council, "made a number of allegations affecting both the sobriety and the morals of these merrymakers; and she endeavoured to procure the closing of the Promenade and above all of the bars which abutted on it." The *Daily Telegraph* counter attacked with such leaders as "Prudes on the Prowl," and other newspapers joined in the debate, which stirred Winston to action. He volunteered to become an activist for a libertarian organization, the Entertainments Protection League, until he discovered that it had no members other than the founder. But he succeeded in publishing a philippic in the *Westminster Gazette*:

> The improvement in the standard of public decency is due rather to improved social conditions and to the spread of education than to the prowling of the prudes. . . . State intervention, whether in the form of a statute or by the decision of licensing committees, will never eradicate the evil. . . . The State should protect each member as far as possible from harm, and must govern men as they are and not as they ought to be. . . . Whereas the Vigilance Societies wish to abolish sin by Act of Parliament, and are willing to sacrifice much of the liberty of the subject into the bargain, the "anti-prudes" prefer a less coercive and more moderate procedure.[60]

Mrs. Ormiston Chant ultimately had to accept what Churchill called "a characteristically British compromise. It was settled that the offending bars were to be separated from the promenade by light canvas screens." Even this was too restrictive for the young bloods at the theatre, who tore down the barricade, whereupon Churchill delivered the first political speech of his career, congratulating the mob for striking a blow for British freedom. "It reminded me of the death of Julius Caesar when the conspirators rushed forth into the street waving the bloody daggers with which they had slain the tyrant." (Always reticent about discussing sex in print, Churchill did not explicitly mention what really outraged the purity campaigners: the promenade was a haunt for prostitutes, and the dancers on stage were scantily clad.)[61]

In his debut, Churchill introduced several themes that he would develop throughout his political life, particularly his libertarianism and anti-puritanism. What is especially significant is that he made his first political speech and fought his first political battle in a theatre. For Winston, politics was performative, as it had been for Lord Randolph. He adopted his father's tricks for attracting newspaper attention, including the cliché with a twist: if Gladstone was an "old man in a hurry," Mrs. Ormiston Chant and her sister vigilantes were "old women in a hurry". The results were highly satisfactory: Winston showed off his newspaper clippings to his mother and brother, and sought applause from his difficult-to-please father ("I am sure you will disapprove of so coercive and futile a measure").[62]

It is possible that Churchill was inspired here by a celebrated anti-puritan dramatist. According to Vyvyan Holland, "Winston Churchill was once asked whom he would like to meet and talk with in after life, and he replied, without hesitation: 'Oscar Wilde'."[63] We might write off this remark as apocryphal, but there is more evidence, neither conclusive nor dismissable, of Oscar's influence on Winston. Churchill never produced an extended and explicit discussion of Wilde, as he did for Shaw and many other writers, but he may have written homages to Wilde without actually mentioning his name.

Wilde and Jennie Churchill were friends and mutual admirers. They corresponded as early as 1888,[64] and she liked to quote *The Importance of Being Earnest*. He considered her "both beautiful and brilliant," and she returned the compliment: "A more brilliant talker did not exist."[65] Winston clearly endorsed Oscar's enlightened hedonism: his bodyguard, Walter Thompson, once "heard him say he wished he might at one time have had the opportunity to see whether he could carry as much as Oscar Wilde who could drink three bottles of brandy in a day, so it was said."[66] And Winston occasionally quoted Wilde's epigrams: he compared Lord Curzon's proposal to hang Kaiser Wilhelm to "The English country gentleman galloping after a fox—the unspeakable in full pursuit of the uneatable" (*A Woman of No Importance*, 1893).[67] Of course, it is possible that he picked up these quips from the newspapers or dinner conversations, without actually reading or seeing the plays. But in a retrospective on Bernard Shaw, Churchill wrote this sentence: "Into the void left by the annihilation of Wilde he stepped armed with a keener wit, a tenser dialogue, a more challenging theme, a stronger construction, a deeper and more natural comprehension."[68] If Churchill was not familiar with Wilde's work, how could he have known that it was less clever than Shaw's?

If Churchill was a fan of Wilde, he had a motive for concealing the fact. In 1895 a group of young officers in the 4th Hussars, including Churchill, allegedly tried to prevent another new officer, Allan Bruce, from joining the regiment. In February 1896 Bruce's father, A. C. Bruce-Pryce, claimed that his son knew that Churchill had committed "acts of gross immorality of the Oscar Wilde type" at Sandhurst. Like Wilde, Churchill sued for libel. Unlike Wilde, he won, securing an apology and £500 in an out-of-court settlement.[69] However, that was not the end of the controversy. Henry Labouchere's *Truth* – a weekly journal devoted to denouncing Army scandals, miscarriages of justice, and Jews – pursued a vendetta against Winston, labeling him the ringleader of a conspiracy against Bruce.[70] The 25 June 1896 issue vaguely alluded to Bruce-Pryce's charges but professed to disbelieve them, slyly publicizing the accusation while avoiding the risk of another defamation suit.[71] (Labouchere had authored Section 11 of the Criminal Law Amendment Act of 1885 that outlawed all male homosexual acts and which had been used to prosecute Wilde in 1895.) In the following months, *Truth* continued to pursue the Bruce case,[72] attacking and insinuating ("A Subaltern in a Cavalry regiment does anything that he pleases. Penalty: *nil*"),[73] all the while protesting that the journal would not be intimidated by threats of libel action.[74] In 1899 *Truth* reported Churchill's capture by the Boers with ill-concealed *Schadenfreude*, reminding its readers once again of the three-year-old scandal.[75]

There is evidence that Churchill identified with Wilde, given that they had both faced the same accusation. By the standards of his times Winston was remarkably broadminded about homosexuality, which he occasionally had to deal with as a policy issue. His long and warm working relationship with his secretary Edward Marsh suggests that he enjoyed the company of homosexual aesthetes. But given his political ambitions, he had to tread very carefully. On 11 September 1912 he gave a speech in Dundee defending the achievements of the Liberal government, and at one point he offered this quip: "Sir George Reid, a brilliant writer, whose life ended in tragedy, once said, 'I can resist everything except temptation.' (Laughter.)"[76]

Sir George Reid was neither a writer nor dead. He was an eminent Scottish painter who, as far as we know, never said anything about surrendering to the delectable. It may be that Churchill intended to give proper credit for the epigram, but at the last minute decided that to mention Wilde was politically risky in Presbyterian Dundee, and substituted the name of a more respectable figure. (Or perhaps it was a scandalized reporter who made the switch. At any rate, in a 1948 Commons debate Churchill attributed the quotation correctly.)[77]

Like Wilde, young Winston wrote dissertations on aesthetics. In his 1897 unpublished essay "The Scaffolding of Rhetoric"[78] he laid out the rules for public speaking that we have come to call "Churchillian." It was clearly written by a student of the drama, applying to politics the techniques he had observed on stage. Short Anglo-Saxon words have more impact than multisyllabic Greek or Latinate terms (one is tempted to scribble in the margin "e.g. blood, sweat, tears"). Naturally "a clear and resonant voice" carries, though "sometimes a slight and not unpleasing stammer or impediment" – like his own lisp – "has been of some assistance in securing the attention of the audience." Pay attention to rhythm, producing "a cadence which resembles blank verse rather than prose": in fact, Churchill often wrote out his speeches not in continuous paragraphs, but in a form like *vers libre*. Strive to evoke "a rapid succession of waves of sound and vivid pictures. The audience is delighted by the changing scenes presented to their imagination." Here the model was once again melodrama, which was distinguished by rapidly changing scenes, however cumbersome and expensive they might be. Melodrama also indulged in "a tendency to wild extravagance of language – to extravagance so wild that reason recoils," which, Churchill advised, could be very effective in a peroration. Such hyperbolic statements "become the watchwords of parties and the creeds of nationalities," and Churchill would deploy them against not only Hitler, but also Lenin, Gandhi, and (in the 1945 General Election) the Labour Party.

So far it might seem that "The Scaffolding of Rhetoric" offers only a bag of tricks to manipulate audiences, but Churchill takes his argument to a higher philosophical plane. Rhetoric, he insists, is more than an "artificial science." Although the arts of rhetoric must be acquired through training:

> The peculiar temperament and talents of the orator must be his by nature. Their development is encouraged by practice. The orator is real. The rhetoric is partly artificial. Partly, but not wholly; for the nature of the artist is the spirit of his art, and much that appears to be the result of study is due to instinct. If we examine this strange being by the light of history we shall discover that he is in character sympathetic, sentimental and earnest: that he is often as easily influenced by others as others are by him. Indeed the orator is the embodiment of the passions of the multitude. Before he can inspire them with any emotion he must be swayed by it himself. When he would rouse their indignation his heart is filled with anger. Before he can move their tears his own must flow. To convince them he must himself believe. His opinions may change as their impressions fade, but every orator means what he says at the moment he says it. He may often be inconsistent. He is never consciously insincere.

Rhetoric, then, is performative but not phony, at once aesthetic and authentic. To be an effective actor, the speaker must become the part he is playing. Being "earnest" is important, even if it is a matter of artifice. Churchill deconstructed and collapsed the distinction between theatre and reality, between melodramatic gesture and sincerity. In "The Scaffolding of Rhetoric" he was thinking along lines parallel to Oscar Wilde's "The Decay of Lying." Both essays presume that "acting naturally" is either impossible or a bore: the human personality must be consciously constructed as a work of dramatic art. Although there is no direct evidence that Churchill had read "The Decay of Lying," in places his essay sounds very much like it, especially where Wilde argues that the blank verse of Elizabethan drama

> created an entirely new race of beings, whose sorrows were more terrible than any sorrow man has ever felt, whose joys were keener than lover's joys, who had the rage of the Titans and the calm of the gods, who had monstrous and marvellous sins, monstrous and marvellous virtues. To them she gave a language different from that of actual use, a language full of resonant music and sweet rhythm, made stately by solemn cadence, or made delicate by fanciful rhyme, jewelled with wonderful words, and enriched with lofty diction. She clothed her children in strange raiment and gave them masks, and at her bidding Caesar stalked through the streets of risen Rome, and with purple sail and flute-led oars another Cleopatra passed up the river to Antioch. Old myth and legend and dream took shape and substance. History was entirely re-written, and there was hardly one of the dramatists who did

> not recognize that the object of Art is not simple truth but complex beauty. In this they were perfectly right. Art itself is really a form of exaggeration; and selection, which is the very spirit of art, is nothing more than an intensified mode of over-emphasis.[79]

Churchill insisted that "There is no more important element in the technique of rhetoric than the continual employment of the best possible word. Whatever part of speech it is it must in each case absolutely express the full meaning of the speaker." It seems a banal truism, but then Churchill gave it a Wildean twist: "So powerful indeed is the fascination of correct expression that it not only influences the audience, but sometimes induces the orator, without prejudice to his sincerity, to adapt his principles to his phrases." Or as Wilde put it, "Life imitates Art far more than Art imitates Life." When Wilde wrote "Literature always anticipates life. It does not copy it, but moulds it to its purpose," he anticipated Churchill's political ideology. Life "is simply the desire for expression, and Art is always presenting various forms through which this expression can be attained. . . . Think of what we owe to the imitation of Christ, of what we owe to the imitation of Caesar."[80] Churchill would imitate the latter more than the former, but substitute "Politics" for "Art" in that statement, and we have his philosophy of life and government.

In October 1897 Winston made plans to publish "The Scaffolding of Rhetoric." He suggested to his mother that the "most appropriate" venue would be the *Nineteenth Century*, the intellectual monthly that had published Wilde's "The Decay of Lying" (January 1889) and "The Critic as Artist" (July and September 1890). "It will make me enemies," he told Jennie, "but they are inevitable in any case."[81] It is difficult to see anything in this essay on aesthetics that would make enemies – unless readers associated the author with Oscar Wilde. In the end, Churchill never published it.

The downfall of Wilde had been universally applauded in the popular press, and scholars have assumed that no one spoke up in his defense after his conviction for homosexual offenses in May 1895. But Margaret Stetz, reading between the lines, has identified a number of fin-de-siècle writers who published "a set of covert and coded, yet easily decipherable, statements about Wilde that would serve to convey their anguish or outrage over his fate and their undiminished admiration for his artistic accomplishments." They included Ella D'Arcy's story "The Death Mask," Richard Le Gallienne's *Yellow Book* essays, George Egerton's defense of *Salome*, as well as "The Happy Hypocrite," Max Beerbohm's gentle spoof of *The Picture of Dorian Gray*.[82] As an aspiring politician, Churchill had more to lose than these late Victorian aesthetes, but it may be that "The Scaffolding of Rhetoric" was his coded homage to Oscar Wilde – and not necessarily the only one he wrote.

CHAPTER 2

An Uneducated Man

In 1912, on the Admiralty yacht *Enchantress*, Churchill toured Greek and Roman ruins in the Mediterranean with the Prime Minister Herbert Asquith and his daughter Violet. "My father was a voracious sight-seer," she recalled:

> . . . scouring museums and lingering in ruined temples. Winston showed some impatience with his absorption in the classical past. "Those Greeks and Romans," he protested, "they are so overrated. They only said everything *first*. I've said just as good things myself. But they got in before me."

And, Violet added, Churchill could never quite forget his responsibilities as First Lord of the Admiralty:

> As we leaned side by side against the taffrail, gliding past the lovely, smiling coast line of the Adriatic, bathed in sun, and I remarked "How perfect!" he startled me by his reply: "Yes – range perfect – visibility perfect" – and details followed, showing how effectively we could lay waste the landscape and blow the nestling towns sky-high.[1]

In a sense, that was something he had wanted to do to the Greeks and Romans at Harrow. His hostility to classical education is legendary. As he wrote in *My Early Life*:

> Where my reason, imagination or interest were not engaged, I would not or I could not learn. In all the twelve years I was at school no one ever succeeded in making me write a Latin verse or learn any Greek except the alphabet. . . . Even as a schoolboy I questioned the aptness of the Classics for the prime structure of our education. So they told me how Mr. Gladstone read Homer for fun, which I thought served him right. . . .[2]

"To the vast majority of boys who attend our public schools a classical education is from beginning to end one long useless, meaningless rigmarole," he protested in 1908. The ancient Greeks conducted education in their vernacular, and English moderns should follow their example.[3] Only in old age, in 1948, did he reconsider: the classics had been "a great unifying force in Europe," though he still noted that the "Greek and Latin philosophers ... seemed often quite unconscious that their society was based on slavery."[4]

Except for his mastery of English, he dismissed his twelve years of formal schooling as a waste and a trial, "the only barren and unhappy period of my life."[5] That was an exaggeration. At Harrow he performed well in history and science. He loved illustrated lectures on these subjects, because they brought a rare element of drama to the routine of public school: "These made a great impression on me. To have an exciting story told you by someone who is a great authority, especially if he has a magic lantern, is for me the best way of learning. Once I had heard the lecture and had listened with great attention, I could have made a very fair show of delivering it myself."[6]

Churchill hated not just classical education, but any kind of structured classroom environment. In that realm he could be as anarchistic as A. S. Neill of Summerhill or the "deschooling" movement of the 1970s. He once said, with sincerity, that he would have rather been a bricklayer's apprentice: "It would have been real; it would have been natural; it would have taught me more; and I should have done it much better. Also I should have got to know my father, which would have been a joy to me." He seriously suggested that the sons of the upper classes should be trained in manual labor rather than force-fed dead languages: "And then perhaps in the evenings a real love of learning would come to those who were worthy – and why try to stuff it into those who are not? – and knowledge and thought would open the 'magic casements' of the mind."[7] This closely resembles the libertarian educational philosophy laid out in William Morris's *News from Nowhere*, though there is no evidence that Churchill ever read this book. But we can say that both men generated astonishing creative energies that burst out in all directions. Where Morris mastered the arts of painting, architecture, tapestries, furnishings, wallpapers, fine printing, poetry, socialist polemics, and utopian fiction, Churchill expressed his artistic drives in politics, history, biography, social reform, war, military technology, painting, voracious reading, novel writing – and bricklaying.

John Charmley, then, was seriously wrong to conclude that young Winston's "literary interests were confined to a few classics."[8] In fact he read few of the ancient classics and some of the Victorian classics, but his literary tastes were mainly contemporary: he read books as they were published and saw plays in their first runs. Churchill was always a fervent autodidact and a relentlessly self-directed reader. His distinctive literary diet certainly shaped his politics, but it also set him apart from Britain's political class, producing a mind that did not fit easily into conventional ideological categories. That helps to explain why Churchill was such a powerful communicator. Whereas other politicians of his generation weighted down their speeches with Latin tags that baffled most voters, Churchill alluded to the modern authors that common readers were actually reading: Rudyard Kipling, Bernard Shaw, H. G. Wells, John Galsworthy, Upton Sinclair, Rupert Brooke, Siegfried Sassoon, T. E. Lawrence, Pearl S. Buck, Sinclair Lewis, Margaret Mitchell, C. S. Forester. In an age when critics were anxiously classifying everything as high-, low-, or middlebrow, Churchill was what would now be called a "nobrow," a cultural omnivore who enjoyed what he enjoyed regardless of its intellectual level. As Dwight Eisenhower recalled, he "drew on everything from the Greek classics to Donald Duck for quotation."[9]

Of course as a schoolboy Winston indulged in much unrequired reading, and one of his favorite subjects, then and for the rest of his life, was the American Civil War. On that subject he was one of the most expert Englishmen of his generation. He drew inspiration from his ancestor, the Duke of Marlborough, but on the other side of his family he also found a model in his maternal grandfather Leonard Jerome. As part-owner of the *New York Times*, Jerome staunchly supported Abraham Lincoln in a city where anti-war feelings were vehement. During the Draft Riots of 1863 the Union Army loaned the paper three Gatling guns, two of which were personally commanded by Jerome himself, even though he never had to fire them.[10] Winston's own account was more melodramatic than accurate ("When in 1862 the war party in New York was discredited by the disasters of the campaign, and riotous mobs attacked the *Times* office, Mr. Jerome – having purchased a battery of cannon and armed his staff with rifles – beat them off, not without bloodshed"[11]), but it illustrates that, in Churchill's mind, there was no clear boundary between war and journalism.

He was first introduced to the Civil War at age seven, when he discovered in his Brighton prep school library bound volumes of *Punch*, which regularly published cartoons about the American conflict. Clearly, he later recalled, "Mr. Punch was against the South, and we had a picture of a fierce young woman, Miss Carolina, about to whip a naked slave, a sort of Uncle Tom, with a kind of scourge which, not being yet myself removed out of the zone of such possibilities, I regarded as undoubtedly severe. I was all for the slave." Later *Punch* took a more jaundiced view of Lincoln, portraying him as a bumpkin who dressed like a scarecrow and ruled like a tyrant. But at a time when schools did not teach contemporary history, Winston learned "the story of what had happened in recent history" from these cartoons, including the last and most memorable, where a conscience-stricken Britannia laid a wreath on the bier of the murdered Emancipator.[12]

For his thirteenth birthday Winston requested an illustrated edition of the *Personal Memoirs of U. S. Grant*, which would have a real impact on his literary and political careers.[13] The book was published in 1885 in the United States and shortly thereafter in Britain, where it had obvious and immediate relevance. In 1886 Gladstone tried and failed to secure Home Rule for Ireland. A bloc of Liberal MPs broke with him and eventually merged with the Conservative Party, which Randolph Churchill rechristened the Unionist Party, explicitly equating his cause with the cause of Lincoln.[14]

For Winston, this was the beginning of a lifelong romance. At sixteen, given a choice of topics for his Army Preliminary Examination essay, he chose the American Civil War.[15] At twenty-one he read and recommended Stephen Crane's 1895 novel *The Red Badge of Courage*.[16] At twenty-three he made plans to write "A short & dramatic History of the American Civil War."[17] (Eventually, he would.) Later in life he loved Civil War novels like Mary Johnston's *Long Roll* (1911) and *Cease Firing* (1912),[18] as well as Margaret Mitchell's *Gone with the Wind* (1936). As First Lord of the Admiralty during the opening phase of the First World War, he revived what was thought to be obsolete naval technology, constructing four "monitors" (single-turret shallow-draft gunboats) for the Royal Navy. They were christened *HMS General Grant, HMS Admiral Farragut, HMS Robert E. Lee*, and *HMS Stonewall Jackson*, though the names were changed in deference to American neutrality. On his visits to the United States he made a point of visiting Civil War battlefields, wrote about them with Lincolnesque eloquence, and knew enough about them to correct tour guides. In 1930 he published in *Scribner's Magazine* an exercise in counterfactual history, speculating about the results of a Confederate victory at Gettysburg. In that case, he suggested, the United States would have split in two, but the North and South would have eventually joined Britain in an English-speaking alliance strong enough to prevent Germany from launching the First World War. The idea of an Anglophone union, which became Churchill's most visionary political project, may have been first inspired by Ulysses Grant's memoirs. Certainly Churchill would have agreed enthusiastically with Grant when Grant wrote:

> England and the United States are natural allies, and should be the best of friends. They speak one language and are related by blood and other ties. We together, or even either separately, are better qualified than any other people to establish commerce between all the nationalities of the world.
>
> England governs her own colonies, and particularly those embracing the people of different races from her own, better than any other nation. She is just to the conquered, but rigid. She makes them self-supporting, but gives

> the benefit of labor to the laborer. She does not seem to look upon the colonies as outside possessions which she is at liberty to work for the support and aggrandizement of the home government.[19]

Churchill was enthralled by the War Between the States because he saw it as a successful struggle to preserve the American Empire – a model to be followed when fighting to preserve the British Empire. In the Sudan War of 1898 he approved when the British allowed a wounded Arab, "in something of the spirit of Grant's proclamation to the Confederates, to depart and plough his native sands."[20] He cited Grant at Appomattox again when he urged lenient peace terms to end the Boer War.[21] But when Liberals charged British troops with using "methods of barbarism" in that conflict, Churchill, in his maiden parliamentary speech on 18 February 1901, argued that they could use "any methods of warfare which are justified by precedents set by . . . American generals during the last fifty or sixty years."[22] He insisted that the Afrikaaners, like the Confederates, could only be defeated through vastly superior numbers and attrition.[23] And when the New York politician Bourke Cockran criticized British dominion over Ireland, Churchill played his trump card: "shd the United States accede to the demand for Confederate independence?"[24] In April 1922, faced with the possibility of an IRA coup in Ireland and the proclamation of a republic, Churchill, as Secretary of State for the Colonies, recommended that Britain treat the Irish as the Union had treated the Confederacy, even to the point of imposing a blockade on the rebellious counties.[25] After the attack on Pearl Harbor in 1941 he called for the rapid improvisation of aircraft carriers, "a field for invention and ingenuity similar to that which called forth the extraordinary fleets and flotillas which fought on the Mississippi in the Civil War."[26] And when, in November 1944, Franklin Roosevelt suggested that a conciliatory message addressed to the German people might bring the war to an earlier end, Churchill insisted that they had "to fight it out on this line, if it takes all summer."[27]

It is not unusual for a schoolboy to be enraptured by a book, to dream of writing something like it, and then, later in life, to write it. But this case presents a special problem: to write a book like the memoirs of Ulysses Grant one must advance oneself to a position of high command in some great conflict. Churchill did that twice: in both world wars he directed combat operations and then published major histories of those conflicts. That is why he so much admired T. E. Lawrence, as a fellow "author and commander." Lawrence understood the compliment, and returned it: "What a subject for a book you would have been, if you had not written it yourself!"[28]

As a young cavalry officer in Bangalore, Winston was well aware of his serious educational deficits. When someone once alluded to "Ethics" he realized that he had never encountered that word before, an indication of the breadth of his schooling at Harrow and Sandhurst. Therefore, in the winter of 1896, he began a program of self-education. For all his hostility to the ancient classics, he studied Plato's *Republic* and Aristotle's *Politics*. He also read *The Decline and Fall of the Roman Empire*: he copied its style, he adopted Gibbon's anti-Christian attitudes, and, like many statesmen of his generation, he found the huge book a useful guide to how not to run an empire. He also read Macaulay's *History of England* and essays, Schopenhauer on pessimism, Malthus on population, Lecky's *Rise and Influence of Rationalism* and *History of European Morals*, and Darwin's *The Origin of Species*.

If all this sounds like the promiscuous self-improving literary diet of a working-class autodidact, in fact Churchill followed the lead of his nanny's brother-in-law, a prison warder who had bought Macaulay's *History of England* in installments and read it worshipfully. Churchill described himself as "an uneducated man" who taught himself from compendia like Bartlett's *Familiar Quotations*.[29] He was "impressed" by Hardy's *Jude the Obscure*, which he read in 1897.[30] And in 1952 he embarrassed his own Minister of Education, Florence Horsbrugh, by grandiloquently objecting to her modest budget cut for continuing education: "The appetite of adults to be shown the foundation and processes of thought will never be denied by a British Administration cherishing the continuity of our Island life."[31]

What Churchill read in Bangalore, in a colonial setting, reinforced and fleshed out the imperial attitudes that he had already picked up from plays and novels. The influence of Gibbon is obvious. There he read, in the first few pages, that the Romans "preserved peace by a constant preparation for war."[32] More than the native regimes they supplanted, they gave their subject peoples the blessings of order and tranquility over a vast part of the globe, and they gave their slaves real legal protection.[33]

Churchill was already familiar with Macaulay. At Harrow he had written a 30,000-word essay on the great historian and, rereading it in 1933, he was "astonished to find how well I was taught and what a number of points were made." Churchill would come to view the whole imperialist project through the lens of Macaulay's classic 1841 essay on Warren Hastings, the first governor-general of India. Macaulay was among the most self-assured and self-righteous of the Victorians, but this particular sketch contained some of the most lacerating criticisms of colonialism ever written. In the present day the British Raj was benevolent, Macaulay assured his readers, but in the mid-eighteenth century it had been criminally exploitative:

> On one side was a band of English functionaries, daring, intelligent, eager to be rich. On the other side was a great native population, helpless, timid, accustomed to crouch under oppression. ... The master caste, as was

> natural, broke loose from all restraint; and then was seen what we believe to be the most frightful of all spectacles, the strength of civilisation without its mercy. . . . During that interval the business of a servant of the Company was simply to wring out of the natives a hundred or two hundred thousand pounds as speedily as possible, that he might return home before his constitution had suffered from the heat, to marry a peer's daughter, to buy rotten boroughs in Cornwall, and to give balls in St. James's Square.[34]

Macaulay presumed that Indians were children who could not govern themselves. Thus the British had a right and a responsibility to rule them – but by the same logic, any violation of that trust was a horror comparable to child abuse. And one episode in particular "has left a lasting stain on the fame of Hastings and of England." Rohilcund was practically an independent province governed by Afghan warriors, the Rohillas, and governed well: "Agriculture and commerce flourished among them; nor were they negligent of rhetoric and poetry." This territory was coveted by Surajah Dowlah, the Nabob Vizier of Oudh. To conquer it he hired from Hastings a brigade of troops from the East India Company for £400,000 (plus expenses). "England now descended far below the level even of those petty German princes who, about the same time, sold us troops to fight the Americans." The Hessians at least fought "in conformity with the humane rules of civilised warfare," whereas Hastings was aware that the Nabob would respect no such rules, and made no attempt to rein him in. In a division of labor, British troops fought and defeated the Rohillas, while the Nabob assumed responsibility for plundering them:

> Then the horrors of Indian war were let loose on the fair valleys and cities of Rohilcund. The whole country was in a blaze. More than a hundred thousand people fled from their homes to pestilential jungles, preferring famine, and fever, and the haunts of tigers, to the tyranny of him, to whom an English and a Christian government had, for shameful lucre, sold their substance, and their blood, and the honour of their wives and daughters. . . .
>
> The finest population in India was subjected to a greedy, cowardly, cruel tyrant. Commerce and agriculture languished. The rich province which had tempted the cupidity of Sujah Dowlah became the most miserable part even of his miserable dominions.

Even within the East India Company's territories, the imposition of English law proved disastrous. Macaulay did have some understanding of the principle of cultural relativism, and he recognized that imposing an unmodified Western legal system on India would grossly violate Indian cultural values and sensitivities.

And yet Macaulay concluded that, even if he had been responsible for "the great crime of England," Hastings did more good than harm in India.[35] Like Robinson Crusoe, he had built a society from the ground up. He had replaced anarchy with order, creating practically from scratch a functioning bureaucratic and judicial system. That regime was far from perfect, but it represented a great step forward. Macaulay's Whig vision of history was consummately progressive. Well before *On the Origin of Species* (which Churchill also read at Bangalore) he argued that English society had evolved ever more advanced political and legal systems, to the point where England in 1841 represented the acme of human achievement. Whatever the past crimes of imperialism, it was in the long view an unequalled and indispensable force for human uplift.

This optimistic teleology was reinforced by Winwood Reade's *The Martyrdom of Man*, a Victorian bestseller now largely forgotten. Churchill cited it as a favorite of his commander at Bangalore, Colonel John Brabazon: "He had read it many times over and regarded it as a sort of Bible."[36] *The Martyrdom of Man* was a universal history, starting with the origins of the cosmos and ultimately projecting into the far future. Its world view was a militantly secular religion of progress: through a Darwinian struggle for survival, man conquers nature and builds ever greater empires. The Egyptians, the Persians, the Greeks, the Romans, and the Muslims each in their turn were in the vanguard of progress. Eventually, each succumbed to decadence and gave way to new and more progressive empires. In the nineteenth century it was Europeans, and the British in particular, who were leading the world. Imperialism was clearly a good thing, which would eventually civilize all the non-European peoples. Except for an anachronistic Established Church, Victorian Britain was practically perfect. Like Churchill, Reade supported the Union in the American Civil War, but not because he objected to slavery or favored racial equality. Reade believed that the North deserved to win because it was a progressive industrial society; he had only contempt for the feudal, backward Confederacy. (Churchill found this point reinforced by Alexis de Tocqueville, who compared "the relative prosperity in the free and slave states of America before the Civil War.")[37] But forced labor had been a motor for economic progress in the ancient empires, Reade argued, and might prove necessary again in modern European colonies.

The future, Reade predicted, would see the development of new energy sources to replace coal and oil, air transport, and artificial food (which he thought far preferable to real food). There would be a world state run along technocratic lines, which would eradicate poverty and send out starships to colonize other planets, carrying forward the imperialist project on a galactic scale. Medicine and science would advance to the point where man would become immortal and practically omnipotent. At that point, Reade concluded, "Man will then be perfect; he will then be a creator; he will therefore be what the vulgar worship as a god."[38] And he envisioned all this in 1872.

In 1937 Churchill still had complete confidence in this world view, as he wrote in a preface to a never-published *Biographical Dictionary of the British Empire*. Egypt, Assyria, Persia, Macedonia, Rome, Spain, Portugal, Austria-Hungary all rose to power only to "fall back into ruin and confusion, leaving nothing but memories of grandeur and a crumbling milestone or two beside the dusty path of progress." The British Empire alone had survived, for two reasons. First, it was progressive, constantly adapting to modern conditions: "In this world, everything must change which would persist. The might of Macedon, of Spain, of Portugal vanished because it built too much on authority at the centre, aloof, unpliant, immovable." Second, the British seemed to have a talent for resolving apparent contradictions – "deconstructing binaries," as we might put it today – which ideologically rigid foreigners did not share. The British Empire had uniquely

> succeeded in reconciling the rights of the individual citizen with the duties of government, the privileges of the individual state with the claims of Imperial unity. It has reconciled the irreconcilable, sought union in disunity, found strength in concession and compromise. Authority and liberty: personal rights and public duty: monarchy and democracy – we have found the way, by inquiry, trial and error, to build on foundations and with materials which alien philosophers have declared to be incompatible.[39]

Young Winston had been a regular, believing, utterly conventional churchgoer. But if he had gone to university, and had been invited into the Cambridge Apostles by Bertrand Russell, he would not have found greater freedom of belief than he encountered among his fellow officers in Bangalore, who debated the existence of God, life after death, and reincarnation in a perfectly friendly and open-minded spirit. "Religious toleration in the British Army had spread till it overlapped the regions of indifference," he recalled in *My Early Life*. "In India the deities of a hundred creeds were placed by respectful routine in the Imperial Pantheon" in the interest of keeping the peace among these sects. "There was general agreement that if you tried your best to live an honourable life and did your duty and were faithful to friends and not unkind to the weak and poor, it did not matter much what you believed or disbelieved. . . . Among natives especially, fanaticism was highly dangerous and roused them to murder, mutiny or rebellion." But mainstream religion of any kind had "a disciplinary value," insofar as it kept women well behaved and the masses content with their station in life. "From this standpoint ceremonies and ritual ceased to be of importance. They were merely the same idea translated into different languages to suit different races and temperaments."[40] This was probably the thrust of Churchill's favorite quotation from Disraeli:

> "Sensible men are all of the same religion."
> "And pray, what is that?"
> "Sensible men never tell."[41]

In this respect cultural relativism and equality were perfectly compatible with imperialism, indeed essential to its smooth operation. In an 1896 letter to J. E. C. Welldon, the headmaster of Harrow, Churchill argued that Christian missionaries only upset the colonial status quo and created unrest among the natives – a very common anxiety among British Army men in India.[42] It was a philosophy reinforced by his reading of Gibbon, Darwin, Winwood Reade, and Lecky's *Rise and Influence of Rationalism* and *History of European Morals*. Then (just as he was approaching the end of *The Decline and Fall of the Roman Empire*) Winston wrote a second letter to Welldon, but it was so subversive that he sent it only to his brother Jack and asked him to burn it. Here Winston explained human spirituality in materialist, almost Darwinian terms. "Religion was originally evolved in process of time – by the influence of material forces – climate & physical – acting on the *innate upward* striving by which all human beings are impelled – and which, I am told, is inherent in an elementary proto-plasmic cell." Thus "Religion is natural to man," but only in the anthropological sense. It takes on different expressions among different cultures and races: Islam, Buddhism, and Confucianism suit the temperaments of Asians, whereas Christianity is for Europeans. ("The sole exception is the somewhat florid Christianity of Abyssinia.") Therefore, any attempt to introduce a new and foreign religion into a culture already adapted to an older spiritual tradition was bound to cause serious turmoil, and should be avoided. Churchill was willing to follow this logic to its ultimate conclusion:

> Had I lived in the days when the influence of Buddha – of Christ – or of Mahomet began to disturb these primitive forms of worship – I should probably have opposed – though I would not have impeded – the great movements they initiated. And this would have been my reason – that though these religions were in every case more worthy of God and man – than those they superseded – yet the change would be attended with deluges of blood and floods of theological controversy – extending over hundreds of years – during which period the sum of human happiness and prosperity would be appreciably diminished. The event would have justified these anticipations.[43]

In *My Early Life* Churchill claimed that "I passed through a violent and aggressive anti-religious phase,"[44] but his surviving letters do not entirely bear that out. *The Martyrdom of Man*, read alongside Plato's *Republic*, represented the succinct "crystallization of much that I have for some time reluctantly believed." But Reade was not (Winston wrote to his mother) a true philosopher, merely "an excellent precis writer. . . . He may succeed in proving Christianity false. He completely fails to show that it is wise or expedient to say so. '*Toute verité n'est pas bon à dire*' – is the criticism I have saddled his book with." Humanity might eventually evolve to the point where

> Christianity will be put aside as a crutch which is no longer needed, and man will stand erect on the firm legs of reason . . . & we shall go out into the fields to seek God for ourselves. The great laws of Nature will be understood – our destiny and our past will be clear. We shall then be able to dispense with the religious toys that have agreeably fostered the development of mankind. Till then – anyone who deprives us of our illusions – our pleasant hopeful illusions – is a wicked man & should – (I quote my Plato) – "be refused a chorus."[45]

As a matter of personal belief, he later privately affirmed, "I expect annihilation at death. I am a materialist – to the tips of my fingers."[46] But in England as in India he respected native religions (as long as they were not too zealous) and recognized that they could be an effective form of moral policing. He therefore argued that English state schools should offer some broadly Christian instruction (essentially the Bible and some hymns) that would be acceptable to all denominations. Following the example of Disraeli, he was prepared to suppress ritualism within the Established Church, as he promised in a June 1899 election speech at Oldham.[47] But here Churchill (like Disraeli) may have been adjusting his views to suit the passions of the Conservative Party. The previous January he had advised his cousin Ivor Guest to avoid getting involved with the anti-ritualist Protestant League, which Guest's mother had founded. As a rationalist Churchill considered all religions superstitious, the English Church only somewhat less so than the Roman Church. But, assuming a position widely held in the Aesthetic Movement and the High Church, he argued that Catholicism could be defended on aesthetic grounds:

> I can see a poor parish – working men living their lives in ugly white-washed factories, toiling day after day amid scenes & surroundings destitute of the element of beauty. I can sympathise with their aching longing for something not infected by the general squalor & something to gratify their love of the mystic, something a little nearer to the "all-beautiful" – and I find it hard to

> rob their lives of this one ennobling aspiration – even though it finds expression in the burning of incense, the wearing of certain robes and other superstitious practices.

True, Catholicism is "a delicious narcotic," but (he argued) to some extent so is every religion.[48]

If this theology seems soft and contradictory, a matter of believing whatever one wants to believe at any given moment, Churchill cheerfully agreed. His secularism never prevented him from praying for divine intervention on the battlefield:

> I even asked for lesser things than not to be killed too soon, and nearly always in these years, and indeed throughout my life, I got what I wanted. This practice seemed perfectly natural, and just as strong and real as the reasoning process which contradicted it so sharply. Moreover the practice was comforting and the reasoning led nowhere. I therefore acted in accordance with my feelings without troubling to square such conduct with the conclusions of thought.
>
> . . . . It seemed to me that it would be very foolish to discard the reasons of the heart for those of the head. Indeed I could not see why I should not enjoy them both. I did not worry about the inconsistency of thinking one way and believing the other. It seemed good to let the mind explore so far as it could the paths of thought and logic, and also good to pray for help and succour, and be thankful when they came. I could not feel that the Supreme Creator who gave us our minds as well as our souls would be offended if they did not always run smoothly together in double harness. After all He must have foreseen this from the beginning and of course He would understand it all.[49]

That is how Churchill resolved a dilemma faced by every thinking member of his generation: in a post-Darwinian age, how could one reconcile religion with secular rationalism? More than a few scientists and churchmen approached the problem by joining the Society for Psychical Research: conducting controlled experiments with table-rapping and mediumism, they tried to find scientific evidence for the existence of an immortal human soul. University philosophy faculties were taken over by neo-Hegelian Idealists, who saw the universe happily evolving toward a perfect Absolute, a teleology consistent with both liberal Christianity and *The Origin of Species*. "There can be no conflict between matters of faith and the conclusions of knowledge," proclaimed the Anglican Bishop Charles Gore, affirming that Jesus was both human and divine, historical and holy. Bernard Shaw invented his own vitalist theology of the "Life Force," James Joyce transmuted Roman Catholicism into an all-embracing religion of literary art, and D. H. Lawrence sacralized sex. All of them were searching for what Lawrence termed a "religious Agnosticism," what the dramatist Harley Granville-Barker called "the prose for God."[50]

One could say that Churchill was a part of this movement to reconcile rationalism and religion, except that the word "reconcile" would imply that he made some intellectual effort to work out the contradictions between the two. Churchill granted that, if he had attended university, "my difficulties might have been resolved by the eminent professors and divines who are gathered there." He arrived instead at a kind of utilitarian flexidoxy, opportunistically adopting any religious or irreligious beliefs that maximized human happiness, however inconsistent they might be. "I have always been surprised to see some of our Bishops and clergy making such heavy weather about reconciling the Bible story with modern scientific and historical knowledge," he wrote:

> Why do they want to reconcile them? If you are the recipient of a message which cheers your heart and fortifies your soul, which promises reunion with those you have loved in a world of larger opportunity and wider sympathies, why should you worry about the shape or colour of the travel-stained envelope; whether it is duly stamped, whether the date on the postmark is right or wrong? These matters may be puzzling, but they are certainly not important. What is important is the message and the benefits to you of receiving it. . . . The idea that nothing is true except what we comprehend is silly, and that ideas which our minds cannot reconcile are mutually destructive, sillier still. . . . I therefore adopted quite early in life a system of believing whatever I wanted to believe, while at the same time leaving reason to pursue unfettered whatever paths she was capable of treading.[51]

This habit of happily embracing apparent contradictions went far beyond religion. Although we associate the word "Churchillian" with adamant resistance, he had an exceptional predilection for compromise. He was confident that seemingly irrepressible conflicts could be resolved: conflicts between the British and the Boers, Irish Catholics and Protestants, Arabs and Jews, a nuclear-armed USA and USSR. He was an imperialist democrat, in love with tradition and technology, who believed in individualism and social welfare, waged war ruthlessly and offered generous peace terms, and crossed party lines twice. His mind was extraordinarily supple, capable of jettisoning preconceived notions and collapsing opposites in a manner that we now might call "deconstructive."

Thus Churchill rarely experienced the angst that comes from grappling with painful questions. An exception was his encounter with *An Essay on the Principle of Population* (1798): in Bangalore, Churchill not only read it but saw the Reverend Malthus's projections in operation. His letters home frequently dwelled on plagues and famines. "I don't like this plague spreading as it is doing & what with the famine India seems in a bad way," he wrote on 15 January 1897, and two weeks later, "The Indian news looks very black – the plague & the famine."[52] This was not the response of a heartless man, though it was difficult not to fall in with the fatalism shared by Britons and Indians alike. As he wrote to his mother on 29 December 1898, "The Plague of which I heard plenty coming up is here unnoticeable." Of course Churchill noticed it, but apparently no one else did:

> We have about 60 deaths a day – but nobody cares a rap & you never hear a word about it. Two of my best Syces have died and you will be sorry to hear that Sambo [Winston's carrier] returned from the wars only to find his old mother & his young wife dead & buried. He now declares that he does not wish to stay any longer in the world. And I fear he means what he says. I promised to try and help him to a new life – but that wd cost about Rs 400 and as for the mother – she is of course irreplaceable.[53]

How far Churchill embraced Malthusianism is questionable. In a letter sent on 18 February 1898 to Algernon West he wrote, commenting on a plague that had killed 70,000 Indians, "Nature applies her own checks to population, and a philosopher may watch unmoved the destruction of some of those superfluous millions, whose life must of necessity be destitute of pleasure."[54] This passage is often quoted as evidence of Churchill's indifference to the plight of the natives,[55] but in the context of his other letters (where he was clearly moved by dying Indians) it takes on a very different meaning. Churchill appears to have been distancing himself from the dismal theories of "a philosopher" – Malthus – with dark existential irony, mourning humanity's fate in an indifferent universe. He was not so much echoing *An Essay on the Principle of Population* as anticipating Albert Camus's *The Plague*. A year after witnessing the pestilence in Bangalore, Churchill was much more optimistic, arguing that the British Raj had in fact broken the Malthusian curse: "The rice crop [has] been more abundant, the number of acres under cultivation greater, the population larger and the death rate lower, than at any period in the history of India."[56]

This is not to say that Churchill entirely rejected Malthus. In two *News of the World* articles, published in the shadow of the Munich crisis of 1938, he would cite Malthus in warning about the decline of the British birth rate. He condemned the "disastrous effect" of contraception: "the more civilized peoples are utilizing it and jeopardizing their chances of survival in a world in which the barbarian is breeding against them."[57] Such eugenic anxieties were widely shared among British intellectuals and politicians on both the left and the right: Marie Stopes, Bertrand Russell, John Maynard Keynes, Julian Huxley, Havelock Ellis, George Bernard Shaw, Dean William Inge, Cyril Burt, J. Arthur Thomson, J. B. S. Haldane, William Beveridge, and even the bohemian weekly *The New Age*.[58] Yet it would be too simple to call Churchill a Malthusian: his reading of *The Principle of Population* was balanced by other countervailing views. The kind of imperialism he absorbed from Macaulay and the Victorian stage presumed that Britain could and should raise the living standards of the colonized masses. But what he read in India and elsewhere profoundly shaped his views of India, ultimately with very serious consequences for the Indians. The business of tracking down literary influences is often dismissed as a purely academic exercise, but sometimes the lives of millions depend on what their rulers read.

CHAPTER 3

A Pushing Age

"You see, Charles, it all began at Harrow," he told his doctor, Lord Moran, in 1943:

> Sitting at the bottom of the school, under something of a cloud, he discovered that he could do what other boys could not do – he could write. And when, as a subaltern in India, he began to read Gibbon, already he knew what he wanted to do in life. He confessed that from the beginning "personal distinction" was his goal, and he knew, too, that it could only be achieved by cultivating this inborn aptitude. . . .

In fact, according to Moran, "few men have stuck so religiously to one craft – the handling of words. In peace it made his political fortune, in war it has won all men's hearts. Without that feeling for words he might have made little enough of life. For in judgment, in skill in administration, in knowledge of human nature, he does not at all excel."[1]

Lord Randolph considered his son a wretched writer, and was happy to say so. "I am awfully sorry that Papa does not approve of my letters," Winston wrote to his mother in September 1893. "I take a great deal of pains over them & often re-write entire pages. If I write a descriptive account of my life here [at Sandhurst], I receive a hint from you that my style is too sententious & stilted. If on the other hand I write a plain and excessively simple letter—it is put down as slovenly. I can never do anything right." Lord Randolph was that destructive and painful thing, the parent who cannot be pleased. "It is no use my trying to explain to Papa," Winston sighed, "& I suppose I shall go on being treated as 'that boy' till I am 50 years old."[2] In June 1894 Randolph returned a letter to Winston so "that you may from time to time review its pedantic & overgrown schoolboy style. . . . If you are going to write letters to me . . . so ridiculously expressed I would rather not receive them."[3]

Lord Randolph died in January 1895. The following October Winston departed to report on the Cuban insurrection for the *Daily Graphic*, a newspaper his father had written for just four years earlier. Before his tenth birthday Winston had "devoured" *Treasure Island*, and now (as he recalled in *My Early Life*):

> When first in the dim light of early morning I saw the shores of Cuba rise and define themselves from dark-blue horizons, I felt as if I sailed with Captain Silver and first gazed on Treasure Island. Here was a place where real things were going on. Here was a scene of vital action. Here was a place where anything might happen. Here was a place where something certainly would happen. Here I might leave my bones.[4]

Though Lord Randolph had earned £2100 for his *Daily Graphic* dispatches,[5] they were generally panned in the press: the *Harrow Gazette* ranked him considerably lower than "a second-rate American reporter."[6] In contrast, Winston was not only published in London, his adventures in Cuba were covered in the *New York Times*. When he returned to New York harbor in December, he was besieged at the pier by a clutch of American reporters eager for his views on the Cuban war.

This episode would be significant for Churchill's future career, on several planes. After his father had bent every effort to rip through his self-confidence, Winston found himself validated as an author – and validated by Americans. During his visit to New York, he was befriended by the democratic politician Bourke Cockran, who became his antifather, offering everything that his actual father had refused to give. Where Lord Randolph had been chilly, remote, stiff, censorious, and English, Cockran was warm, close, relaxed, encouraging, and Irish-American. Cockran praised Winston's writing and was a strong influence on his literary style. Winston had found his identity and his mission, as a writer whose body of work, over a lifetime, would deal primarily with war. He had not merely reported on Cuba: he had become the story. Like Caesar, he would be at once a reporter, a fighter, and the leading character in his own narrative. And he would write for American as well as British audiences.

He also learned something about handling the media, when the *New York World* communicated to its readers one of the first distinctively Churchillian witticisms on record. "The most remarkable fact seems to be that two armies will shoot at each other for hours and no one will get hit," the paper quoted him as saying. "I believe that statisticians say that in a battle it takes 2,000 bullets to kill a man. When the calculations are arranged I think it will be found that in the Cuban war it took 2,000 bullets to miss each individual combatant." It may be that Churchill did not say that exactly: the *New York Herald* reported a different and less clever version of his remarks.[7] But it would not have been the first time that an American reporter juiced up the words of a UK visitor. When he sailed to the United States in 1882, Oscar Wilde's offhand remark about an uneventful voyage was transmuted by journalists into a high-handed aesthetic dismissal of the Atlantic Ocean ("The roaring ocean does not roar").[8] "Many a clumsy sentence has been put right" by obliging journalists, Churchill told the London Press Club in 1938.[9] In New York both Oscar Wilde and Winston Churchill learned what Randolph Churchill had discovered earlier: the press was eager for quotable material, and one could enhance one's celebrity by manufacturing a steady supply of witticisms. By the turn of the century the demand was so great that some authors produced essays consisting wholly of epigrams: for example, Oscar Wilde's "Phrases and Philosophies for the Use of the Young" (1894) and Bernard Shaw's "Maxims for Revolutionists" (1903).

Both Wilde and Shaw offered Churchill models for self-advertisement. "Almost my first literary effusion, written when I was a subaltern in India in 1897 (it never saw the light of day), was a ferocious onslaught upon [Shaw], and upon an article which he had written disparaging and deriding the British Army in some minor war." A few years later his mother brought them together over lunch, and over the next half-century they spoke and corresponded at intervals. As journeymen authors, Shaw was poor and Churchill was not, but they were both unsuccessful novelists, and they both launched their careers in the New Journalism of the 1890s. And Churchill realized that each of them succeeded by means of ruthless self-publicity. "I leave the delicacies of retirement to those who are gentlemen first and literary workmen afterwards," Winston quoted GBS. "The cart and trumpet for me." For both, a favorite means of publicity was the memorable epigram, such as this from Shaw's *The Quintessence of Ibsenism*: "There are just as good reasons for burning a heretic at the stake as for rescuing a shipwrecked crew from drowning; in fact, there are better." Churchill found this one shockingly subversive, but of course that was precisely the point.[10]

In the last two decades of the nineteenth century, the New Journalism created what we would now recognize as "the culture of celebrity." The invention of the interview focused media attention on personalities. New methods of photomechanical reproduction facilitated the use of photographic portraits, sketches, and caricatures in newspapers and magazines. Daily newspapers expanded their coverage of literature and literary gossip. Penny papers reached out to a new and much wider audience, which wanted news about people and their clever sayings rather than oceans of gray type about high politics.[11] Lord Randolph had been among the first politicians to exploit personality-driven journalism successfully, but writers also used it to advertise themselves, starting with Oscar Wilde: he played the flamboyant aesthete because he knew that a complicit media would broadcast that image to an amused reading public. Likewise, George Bernard Shaw would play the Mephistophelean socialist; Max Beerbohm, the dandy caricaturist; H. G. Wells, the technocrat leaping into the future; G. K. Chesterton, the jolly rotund traditionalist pilgrimaging toward Rome. Churchill observed their triumphs and errors and, in a similar way, constructed a dual persona: the military adventurer dashing into battle, and the visionary statesman who (at one point or another) filled nearly every job in the British Cabinet. In either role, everything he did was transformed into reportage, memoir and history. There was no clear distinction between Churchill the soldier, Churchill the politician, and Churchill the author – all three were engaged in performing and publicizing a common narrative.

In that culture, journalists themselves could become celebrities. Late nineteenth-century newspapers drew a distinction between "reporters," who were supposed to be self-effacing transcribers of events, and "correspondents," who were dramatically visible in their own stories, which they told from a highly personal point of view. Examples of the latter include Stephen Crane and Rudyard Kipling (both of whom Churchill read), as well as W. T. Stead and Richard Harding Davis. Their style of journalism was participatory and autobiographical. A reporter merely reports the story; a correspondent is himself the story.[12]

Or herself: think of Nellie Bly's round-the-world trip of 1889–90. A stunt staged by the *New York World*, it was advertised as a better-than-fiction race against Jules Verne's novel – and Bly, an intrepid, unescorted woman, completed her circumnavigation in just seventy-two days.[13] Again and again, Churchill likewise would follow a fictional model (*Treasure Island*, in the case of Cuba) to perform a real-life adventure and then publish the story, in which the correspondent was inevitably at the center of the narrative. Not incidentally, this kind of personal journalism offered excellent publicity for politicians: for example, Theodore Roosevelt's 1899 book *The Rough Riders*, which, as Finley Peter Dunne's "Mr. Dooley" noted, should have been entitled "Alone in Cubia."

This approach to journalism inevitably involved an element of fiction, freely employing all the literary devices available to novelists and playwrights. There had to be a gripping plot, unforgettable characters, gorgeous settings, cleverly constructed dialogue, memorable turns of phrase, a strong and opinionated authorial voice, impressionistic commentary, and a fine sense of dramatic timing. To achieve these artistic goals, facts could be rearranged, embellished, and used selectively, though the main outline of the story was still supposed to conform (more or less) to reality.[14] Journalists often cast their stories in the styles of popular literary genres, such as mysteries, thrillers, or melodramas. As Karen Roggenkamp concludes, "What reporters manufactured was something that looked a lot like fiction, read like fiction, and entertained like fiction but that was ultimately, they argued, better than fiction, because it was, after all, 'real.' "[15] This was the template that Churchill followed throughout his authorial life – not just in what he wrote for publication, but also in his correspondence and government memoranda.

On 4 August 1896 he laid out plans to parlay his self-publicizing journalism into a future political career. As Winston explained to his mother, he would have himself assigned to a cavalry regiment in southern Africa, where a conflict with the Matabele seemed to be brewing. There he could find "scenes of adventure and excitement . . . where I could gain experience and derive advantage." He planned to win a decoration or two, then a couple more in Egypt, and then "beat my sword into an iron dispatch box."[16] Disappointingly, the Matabele surrendered to Cecil Rhodes without much of a fight, so the following April Winston asked Jennie to find a newspaper (any newspaper) that would send him to cover the Greek-Turkish war (on either side): "Of course my sympathies are entirely with the Greeks, but on the other hand the Turks are bound to win," and coverage of the war from the latter perspective would be "less glorious but much more safe."[17] Again, the war ended before he could reach it.

Later that year he covered the fighting on India's Northwest Frontier, publishing fifteen dispatches in the *Daily Telegraph* (6 October–6 December 1897). These became the basis of his first book, *The Story of the Malakand Field Force* (1898). On 29 August 1897, the day he left Bangalore for the combat zone, he wrote to his mother admitting that he was seeking publicity: "It might not have been worth my while, who am really no soldier to risk so many fair chances on a war which can only help me directly in a profession I mean to discard. But I have considered everything and I feel that the fact of having seen service with British troops while still a young man must give me more weight politically – must add to my claims to be listened to and may perhaps improve my prospects of gaining popularity with the country."[18] In a letter of 2 October he told Jennie that he was embroiled in serious combat, "the hardest fighting on the frontier for forty years. . . . Still it means the medal and also that next time I go into action I shall command a hundred men – and possibly I may bring off some 'coup.' "[19] He had instructed his mother to make sure that his letters to the *Daily Telegraph* had bylines: "It may help me politically to come before the public in this way."[20] But Jennie published them anonymously, on the advice of Lord Minto: "He said it was very unusual and might get you into trouble."[21] But, as Winston protested, anonymity defeated the purpose of publishing the dispatches: "I had written them with the design, a design which took form as the correspondence advanced, of bringing my personality before the electorate. I had hoped that some political advantage might have accrued. . . . I will only add that if I am to avoid doing 'unusual' things it is difficult to see what chance I have of being more than an average person" – and averageness was Winston's worst nightmare. He baldly scolded his mother for not doing enough to make him a celebrity: "Never was there such modesty as yours for me. If I am to do anything in the world, you will have to make up your mind to publicity and also to my doing unusual things. . . . I regard an excellent opportunity of bringing my name before the country in a correct and attractive light – by means of graphic & forcible letters, as lost." Disgusted that the *Daily Telegraph* offered him only £5 per column, he insisted on twice that, quoting Samuel Johnson, "No one but a blockhead ever wrote except for money."[22] He resolved to write *The Story of the Malakand Field Force* "as a means [of] repairing the non signature of my letters" and enhancing his earnings. "It is a great undertaking but if carried out will yield substantial results in every way, financially, politically, and even, though I do care a damn, militarily."[23]

All this compelled Winston to admit that "I am more ambitious for a reputation for personal courage than [for] anything else in the world. . . . As to deserving such an honour – I feel that I took every chance and displayed myself with ostentation whenever there was danger."[24] In effect, he had transformed himself into a character in a non-fiction drama, much as his father and Oscar Wilde had done. In Winston's mind, the boundary between reality and theatre had dissolved. He appeared fearless on the battlefield because that was his role. And he did not expect to be killed, because then there would be no play: "I do not believe the Gods would create so potent a being as myself for so prosaic an ending. . . . 'Fame' sneered at, melodramatised, degraded, is still the finest thing on earth."[25]

But what if war was boring – as war is more often than not? Churchill's quip about the breathtaking inaccuracy of Spanish and Cuban riflemen illustrated a problem with his first adventure as a professional author: nothing much was happening in Cuba. His dispatches from the island were so uneventful that one collection of his war journalism did not even bother to reprint them.[26] As he complained in the *Saturday Review*:

> When an insurrection which ceases to present novel and original features or great and stirring situations is unduly prolonged, it no longer excites the interest of peoples whose welfare it does not intimately reflect. The rebellion in Cuba, being remarkable for its monotonous duration, is for this reason almost ignored by the Press and entirely unnoticed by the public. Other questions more important, more dramatic, more remarkable, fill the pages of the newspapers and the minds of their readers. The Cretan insurgents have

> ousted those of Cuba; the filibusters of Greece are found to be more attractive than those of the United States. . . . Yet events in Cuba have pursued the dreary, tedious, and unprofitable tenor of their way. The same tales of barren victories and of equally desultory defeats, the same successful filibustering expeditions and the same ruthless destruction of property and loss of human life, have been remorselessly repeated until the world at large is heartily sick of the whole subject, and war correspondents are tired of copying out their telegrams of a year ago.[27]

In *The Times* Churchill explained that the brushfire wars fought on the fringes of the Empire were not so dramatic as conflicts between great European powers. "When civilized forces collide one side or the other wins the battle. . . . The peculiar difficulty which attends mountain warfare is that there are no general actions on a large scale, no brilliant successes, no important surrenders, no chance for *coups de théâtre*."[28] Clearly Churchill understood how useful that melodramatic contrivance could be in war reportage, even if it involved embellishing the mundane. In the *Malakand Field Force* he acknowledged that the newspaper public wanted to read about thrilling battles, "Yet he who would obtain a clear idea of a soldier's life on service, must mentally share the fatigues of the march and the monotony of the camp."[29] Therefore, when he recast his dispatches as a book, he enlivened them with theatrical devices. He began with a quotation from Shakespeare's *King John*:

> According to the fair play of the world,
> Let me have an audience.

The author then took that audience "behind the scenes" to explain his stagecraft.[30] He described, with the eye of a director, "the scenery of the theatre of war,"[31] and then re-enacted "the great drama of frontier war."[32] A peaceful sector of the Empire is suddenly plunged into armed combat: "Never was transformation scene more complete, or more rapid."[33] (On the Victorian stage, a "transformation scene" was a total change of setting in full view of the audience.) With a flourish from *Julius Caesar* ("Cry Havoc and let slip the dogs of war") the book erupts in violence that "was to know no intermission."[34] Thus he made a gripping tale out of a minor borderland conflict. *The Story of the Malakand Field Force* is the source of one of his most famous epigrams: "Nothing in life is so exhilarating as to be shot at without result."[35] If the book reads like melodrama, Churchill admitted that "it is very 'blood and thunder' – but that is the usual style for such literature."[36]

Paul Fussell called attention to the habit of theatrical metaphors in First World War literature,[37] but Glenn Wilkinson has since shown that late

Victorian and Edwardian newspapers had earlier presented war "as a 'stage play' or 'comic entertainment' with 'scenes', 'curtains', 'actors' and an 'audience'."[38] Churchill did what other contemporary war correspondents did, only more deliberately and frequently, with greater attention to artistic affect, and he continued to do it throughout his working life, long after the theatrical style had gone out of fashion.

In the *Malakand Field Force*, Churchill grasped an insight that would govern his entire career as a war leader: he recognized that all successful warfare is theatre. As he asked his readers: why don't soldiers under fire run for safety? Most of them admit that they experience fear and do not recklessly seek death:

> It appears to be this. The courage of the soldier is not really contempt for physical evils and indifference to danger. It is a more or less successful attempt to simulate these habits of mind. Most men aspire to be good actors in the play. There are a few who are so perfect that they do not seem to be actors at all. This is the ideal after which the rest are striving. It is one very rarely attained.[39]

War correspondents are also actors, except that they perform before a much larger audience. In a letter to his mother Winston described a bloody engagement in which he and a subaltern "carried a wounded Sepoy for some distance and might perhaps, had there been any gallery, have received some notice. . . . Foolish perhaps but I play for high stakes and given an audience there is no act too daring or too noble. Without the gallery things are different."[40]

But Churchill pointed to a modern development that threatened to leach the drama from war. Until the late nineteenth century war reportage could only be written by battlefield participants who ran all the attendant risks. Electronic communication – first telegraph, then wireless, then radar – changed that forever, allowing generals and admirals to monitor warfare remotely from London, Paris, Berlin, or Washington. The central nervous system of the British Empire was a vast telegraph network running overland and under the seas, a Victorian internet that permitted command and control from the metropolis. But there were still some remote regions where the wires did not reach, and as the Malakand force advanced beyond the last telegraph station, Churchill reflected:

> We were at the end of the wire. I have often stood at the other and watched the tape machine click off the news as it arrives; the movement of the troops; the prospects of action; the fighting; the causalities. How different are the scenes. The club on an autumn evening – its members grouped anxiously

> around, discussing, wondering, asserting; the noise of the traffic outside; the cigarette smoke and electric lights within. And, only an hour away along the wire, the field, with the bright sunlight shining on the swirling muddy waters; the black forbidding rocks; the white tents of the brigade a mile up the valley; the long streak of vivid green rice crop by the river; and in the foreground the brown-clad armed men. I can never doubt which is the right end to be at. It is better to be making the news than taking it; to be an actor rather than a critic.[41]

As both actor and critic, Churchill had nothing but praise for the Sikh regiment that fought by his side:

> It is difficult to convey the impression that these splendid Indian troops make on an impartial spectator. Their strength, their patience, their skill with the weapons are shown by a thousand incidents of march, camp, and picket. Their bravery has been attested on many occasions. Their discipline may be gauged by anyone who takes the trouble to watch them. . . .
>
> Nothing is so remarkable as the ascendancy which the British officer maintains over the native soldier. The dark sowars follow the young English subaltern who commands them with a strange devotion. He is their "bucha" – the best in the regiment – as brave as a lion. None rides so straight as he; no one is so confident. Things seem to be going wrong; men and horses are rolling over. But looking to him they feel it is all right. He is "in the know", and will pull them out of any difficulty. To save his life they will sacrifice their own. Nor could a squadron face its comrades if their officer's body had been left in the hands of the enemy. The military history of England – a long and diverse volume – does not record an instance of their confidence being misplaced.[42]

The Sikh soldiers comported themselves exactly like the "good natives" of the theatre. Today imperialist melodrama strikes us as absurdly false, idealizing the English and infantilizing the colonized. But in 1897 British theatregoers (most of whom had never set foot in India) had no reason to doubt what they saw on the stage, which was consistent with everything they read in the newspapers and all that they had heard from missionaries lecturing to Sunday School classes. Imperialist melodrama often strived for the trappings of documentary, a kind of pre-cinematic newsreel that portrayed recent events with claims of authenticity. *Khartoum!* boasted real camels and "Soudanese Natives" onstage; while *Human Nature* was accompanied, in the Grand Saloon at Drury Lane, by an exhibition of maps and a reconstruction of the cell in which Ahmad Urabi, the Egyptian nationalist, had been incarcerated.[43]

Youth (1881) used actual Gatling guns and Martini-Henry rifles to stage a battle in Afghanistan.[44] In both *Khartoum!* and *Michael Strogoff* there are characters who blur the roles of war correspondent and combatant, as Churchill did. And at this point he perceived no dissonance between combat on the frontier and combat in the theatre, where some natives were hostile but most were wonderfully loyal.

Of course, native loyalty depended on maintaining British prestige, and that too was largely a matter of stagecraft. "Remember," Churchill advised his readers, "that the great drama of frontier war is played before a vast, silent but attentive audience, who fill a theatre that reaches from Peshawar to Colombo, and from Kurrachee to Rangoon."[45] It was a point that George Orwell would make, more sardonically, in his 1936 essay "Shooting an Elephant," when the natives were no longer playing their Victorian roles.

Like Winwood Reade, Churchill assumed that imperialism – the impulse to dominate other human beings – was normal and universal. As he put it in his next book, *The River War*, it was a Darwinian manifestation "of the spirit of competition, the condition of our continued existence. All the vigorous nations of the earth have sought and are seeking to conquer."[46] In the *Malakand Field Force* he illustrated this anthropological theory by sketching "the rise and fall of an ambitious Pathan" who begins in a state of nature and then buys a rifle:

> He becomes a man to be feared. Then he builds a tower to his house and overawes those around him in the village. Gradually they submit to his authority. He might now rule the village; but he aspires still higher. He persuades or compels his neighbours to join him in an attack on the castle of a local khan. The attack succeeds. The khan flies or is killed; the castle is captured. The retainers make terms with the conqueror. The land tenure is feudal. In return for their acres they follow their new chief to war. Were he to treat them worse than the other khans treated their servants, they would sell their strong arms elsewhere. He treats them well. Others resort to him. He buys more rifles. He conquers two or three neighbouring khans. He has now become a power.
>
> Many, perhaps all, states have been founded in a similar way, and it is by such steps that civilization painfully stumbles through her earlier stages. . . .

But because the Pathans were so fiercely independent, no warlord could long gain ascendancy over the others. Inevitably the ambitious Pathan is brought down by a general revolt, "the victors quarrel over the spoil, and the story closes, as it began, in bloodshed and strife."[47] Obviously, Churchill concluded, a Pax Britannica was far preferable to the anarchy of petty squabbling native tyrants. He considered the Muslim tribesmen he was fighting to be hopelessly degraded, especially in their treatment of women. The Mullahs had incited a revolt against the British because "Contact with civilisation destroys the superstition and credulity on which the wealth and influence of the 'Mullah' depends. A combination of the religious forces of India against that civilising, educating rule which unconsciously destroys the faith in idols of brass and stone is one of the dangers of the near future. Here it is Mohammedanism that is threatened, and resists." On several fronts throughout the Empire, Churchill observed, "civilisation is confronted with militant Mohammedanism," which, on more than one occasion, he compared with rabies.[48] "The forces of progress clash with those of reaction. The religion of blood and war is face to face with that of peace. Luckily the religion of peace is usually the better armed."[49] Following Winwood Reade, Churchill defended imperialism as the vanguard of the relentless advance of civilization.

But it did not follow that Europeans would always be in that vanguard. His reading of Reade and Gibbon taught him that in the fifth century AD, when the Roman world was disintegrating into barbarism, "the wild mountains of Northern India, now overrun by savages more fierce than those who sacked Rome, were occupied by a placid people, thriving, industrious, and intelligent; devoting their lives to the attainment of that serene annihilation, which the word *nirvana* expresses." If the positions of Europe and India were now reversed, that was because "the sun of civilisation can never shine all over the world at once."[50] Neither Gibbon nor Reade anticipated the decline and fall of the British Empire. But Churchill, observing the ruins of an ancient Buddhist civilization at the Valley of Sarai, could not help but wonder whether a "traveller shall some day inspect, with unconcerned composure, the few scraps of stone and iron which may indicate the British occupation of India." From that far future perspective, the British Raj would be defensible only on progressive grounds: if "the rice crop had been more abundant, the number of acres under cultivation greater, the population larger and the death rate lower, than at any period in the history of India—we should not be without a monument more glorious than the pyramids."[51]

"Public relations" did not yet exist as a recognized profession in 1897, when the term was first used in print.[52] But Lord Randolph had understood the concept perfectly, and Winston was now a media-savvy twenty-something, wise to cutting-edge methods of publicity, which he used ruthlessly to promote the *Malakand Field Force*. On the recommendation of Arthur Balfour, Jennie Churchill employed the literary agency of A. P. Watt. The literary agent was such a new phenomenon that Balfour did not quite know what to call it: he used the term "publishing 'broker'."[53] Watt would handle all of Winston's early books, while Jennie was put to work as his publicist. "You must see that all efforts are made to launch it well," he instructed his mother. "Reviews & editorial notes must be arranged & carefully worked up. . . . I made it my business to lunch with the Editor of the *Pioneer* at Calcutta and he will do all he can out here."[54] Jennie would solicit positive reviews from G. E. Buckle (editor of *The Times* and an old friend of Lord Randolph's), Frank Harris (editor of the *Saturday Review*), and Henry Norman (assistant editor of the *Daily Chronicle*).[55] And Winston, of course, asked her to "send me all cuttings etc that may gratify or offend my vanity."[56]

"The publication of the book will certainly be the most noteworthy act of my life. Up to date (of course)," he told Jennie. "By its reception – I shall measure the chances of my possible success in the world." Winston understood that publicity is itself a form of theatre, but in his mind there was nothing phony about it. Advertisements for himself were an expression of his authentic persona. Following the prescriptions laid out in "The Scaffolding of Rhetoric," he insisted that the politician must become the part he is playing. There can be no gap between his real self and his public self:

> In Politics a man, I take it, gets on not so much by what he *does*, as by what he *is*. It is not so much a question of brains as of character & originality. It is for these reasons that I would not allow others to suggest ideas and that I am somewhat impatient of advice as to my beginning in politics. Introduction – connections – powerful friends – a name – good advice well followed – all these things count – but they lead only to a certain point. As it were they may ensure admission to the scales. Ultimately – every man has to be weighed – and if found wanting nothing can procure him the public confidence.
>
> Nor would I desire it under such circumstances. . . . I should never care to bolster up a sham reputation and hold my position by disguising my personality. Of course – as you have known for some time – I believe in myself.[57]

In spite of gross misprints, the *Malakand Field Force* was an intoxicating success.[58] According to the *Athenaeum*, "it suggests in style a volume by Disraeli, revised by a mad printer's reader," which the author took as high praise.[59] Even the Prince of Wales sent a complimentary note.[60] "When the first bundle of reviews reached me together with the volume as published, I was filled with pride and pleasure at the compliments, and consternated with the blunders," Churchill recalled in *My Early Life*. "The reader must remember that I had never been praised before. The only comments which had ever been made upon my work at school had been 'Indifferent,' 'Untidy,' 'Slovenly,' 'Bad,' 'Very bad,' etc." (He did not mention his father's comments on his writing.) "Now here was the great world with its leading literary newspapers and vigilant erudite critics, writing whole columns of praise! . . . I was thrilled.

I knew that if this would pass muster there was lots more where it came from, and I felt a new way of making a living and of asserting myself, opening splendidly out before me." He noted well that the book had generated royalties equivalent to two years' salary. Through a literary career "I would free myself from all discipline and authority, and set up in perfect independence in England with nobody to give me orders or arouse me by bell or trumpet."[61] It was the fulfillment of an adolescent's wish-dream, the death of his father having relieved him of any necessity for Oedipal rebellion.

Churchill now brainstormed ideas for more books: a collection of journalistic short stories, a life of Garibaldi, a "dramatic History of the American Civil War," and biographies of Marlborough and Lord Randolph.[62] (Eventually he would write the latter three.) And another opportunity for reportage presented itself: Churchill tried to attach himself to Sir Herbert Kitchener's expedition to reconquer the Sudan. Once again he enlisted his mother to pull strings, but Kitchener quite reasonably preferred to work with dedicated career officers. He realized that Churchill was only using the Army to promote himself and would leave as soon as he was ready to jump to another profession.[63] But the Prime Minister, Lord Salisbury, had been impressed with the *Malakand Field Force*, and invited Churchill to meet him at the Foreign Office. They chatted for more than half an hour, and at the end Salisbury said, "If there is anything at any time that I can do which would be of assistance to you, pray do not fail to let me know."[64] It may have been merely a polite offer, but Churchill took him up on it. He asked to be sent to the Sudan, and laid out his motives with alarming frankness: "It is not my intention, under any circumstances to stay in the army long. I want to go, first, because the recapture of Khartoum will be a historic event: second, because I can, I anticipate, write a book about it which will from a monetary, as well as from other points of view, be useful to me."[65]

Salisbury may have been taken aback by the young man's pushfulness: at any rate his reply was not encouraging. He did ask Lord Cromer to write to Kitchener, but warned Churchill not "to rely too confidently on the result of his letter."[66] Again, Kitchener refused, but after more string-pulling the War Office assigned Churchill to the 21st Lancers, which was based in Cairo and preparing to advance up the Nile. As he remembered in *My Early Life*, he was anxious to observe "the final phase of the long drama of the Soudan," but now he noticed:

> that there were many ill-informed and ill-disposed people who did not take a favourable view of my activities. On the contrary they began to develop an adverse and even a hostile attitude. They began to say things like this: "Who the devil is this fellow? How has he managed to get to these different campaigns? Why should he write for the papers and serve as an officer at the

same time? Why should a subaltern praise or criticise his senior officers? Why should Generals show him favour? How does he get so much leave from his regiment? Look at all the hard-working men who have never stirred an inch from the daily round and common task. We have had quite enough of this – too much indeed. He is very young, and later on he may be all right; but now a long period of discipline and routine is what 2nd Lieutenant Churchill requires." Others proceeded to be actually abusive, and the expressions "Medal-hunter" and "Self-advertiser" were used from time to time in some high and some low military circles in a manner which would, I am sure, surprise and pain the readers of these notes. It is melancholy to be forced to record these less amiable aspects of human nature, which by a most curious and indeed unaccountable coincidence have always seemed to present themselves in the wake of my innocent footsteps, and even sometimes across the path on which I wished to proceed.[67]

So Churchill disarmed his critics by archly advertising the fact that he was a self-advertiser – a brilliant maneuver in any culture of celebrity. The Sudan campaign was a much-desired assignment for career-minded army officers, with 2,500 of them on a waiting list, and Churchill had jumped the queue.[68] As he told his mother, "It is a pushing age and we must shove with the best."[69]

In his eagerness to produce a popular celebration of imperial adventure, Churchill had suppressed serious private reservations about the Malakand expedition. "Financially it is ruinous," he confided to Lady Randolph. "Morally it is wicked. Militarily it is an open question, and politically it is a blunder."[70] He was horrified when Sikhs burned a wounded man alive,[71] and when British troops used dum-dum bullets. But these, he admitted, were things "to which one does not allude in print." As he wrote to his grandmother, "I wonder if people in England have any idea of the kind of warfare that is being carried on here. It is so different from all one has been led to expect" – certainly nothing like anything he had seen on the stage:

> I do not doubt there are many people who do not realise for instance that no quarter is ever asked or given. The tribesmen torture the wounded & mutilate the dead. The troops never spare a single man who falls into their hands – whether he be wounded or not. The field hospitals and the sick convoys are the especial targets of the enemy and we destroy the tanks by which alone [water] for the summer can be obtained.[72]

In his next book, he would be less discreet.

CHAPTER 4

War of the Worlds

Churchill published three very different accounts of the Sudan War. The first draft consisted of his fifteen dispatches to the *Morning Post*, filed between 8 August and 20 September 1898. They would be greatly expanded in the first printing of *The River War* in 1899, which was in turn substantially abridged in a 1902 edition. Subsequent editions generally followed the 1902 text, but the palimpsests of the earlier versions reveal Churchill's evolving attitudes towards imperialism, which could be much more critical than we usually imagine.

Long before he ever touched a brush to canvas, Churchill was an artist. In the first paragraph of his first report to the *Morning Post* he notified readers that his war journalism would aspire to the condition of painting and theatre: "I shall try in this and following letters to paint you a picture of the war, and shall hope to raise in your mind a lively impression of the scenes and characters of the last act in the great drama of Khartoum."[1] Or, shifting his metaphors, he described the Nile as "a sort of subdued *motif* that recurs throughout the whole opera."[2] Usually the river was simply muddy and dull:

> Yet there is one hour when all is changed. Just before the sun sets towards the western rocks a delicious flash brightens and enlivens the landscape. It is as though some titanic artist in the hour of inspiration was retouching the picture, painting in dark purple shadows among the rocks, strengthening the lights on the sand, gilding and beautifying everything, and making the whole scene live. The river, whose windings give the impression of a lake, turns from muddy brown to silver grey. The sky from a dull blue deepens into violet in the west. Everything under that magic touch becomes vivid and alive. And then the sun sinks altogether behind the rocks, the colours fade out of the sky, the flush off the sands, and gradually everything darkens and grows grey like a man's cheek when he is bleeding to death. We are left sad and sorrowful in the dark, until the stars light up and remind us that there is always something beyond.[3]

The New Journalism placed a premium on impressionistic reporting, and some of Churchill's descriptions strikingly resembled an Impressionist painting: "The great army of the Dervishes was dwarfed by the size of the landscape to mere dark smears and smudges on the brown sand of the plain."[4] As Churchill advised his readers, "You must not look on this correspondence as an attempt to tell the story, much less record the history of the campaign." His objective was to convey only his own "impressions of the moment," which were meant to illuminate dry battlefield communiqués with "some dashes of local colour."[5] In a description of the Battle of Omdurman, his impressionism becomes cinematic, perhaps the earliest use of that metaphor in the history of literature:

> The whole scene flickered exactly like a cinematograph picture; and, besides, I remember no sound. The event seemed to pass in absolute silence. The yells of the enemy, the shouts of the soldiers, the firing of many shots, the clashing of sword and spear, were unnoticed by the senses, unregistered by the brain.[6]

"Everyone describes an action from his own point of view," Churchill explained. "Indeed, it is thence that we look at most things, human or divine. Why should I be or make an exception?"[7] One could classify young Winston as a late member of the Aesthetic movement, in the company of Walter Pater, James McNeill Whistler, Dante Gabriel Rossetti, and Oscar Wilde. But Churchill, uniquely, was an aesthete of war.

He granted that "war, disguise it as you may, is but a dirty, shoddy business, which only a fool would play at." But all the same, it could be wonderful theatre. The conquest of the Sudan made possible the liberation of Karl Neufeld, a German explorer imprisoned in chains for eleven years, and this convinced Churchill "that there are some things that have to be done, no matter what the cost may be." Releasing an innocent man from prison was the classic melodramatic climax: it reminded Churchill of the freeing of the Bastille prisoners in Dickens's *A Tale of Two Cities*.[8] And the final act was straight out of imperial melodrama: "The hoisting of the British flag amid the ruins of Khartoum" (along with a much smaller Egyptian flag), while soldiers saluted and the band played "God Save the Queen." "We are a sober and phlegmatic stock," Churchill noted, "yet the dramatic appeals to most of us at times."[9]

That last report was filed on 9 September. In his next dispatch, dated 10 September, there is a startling change. At this point Churchill abruptly abandons his aestheticism and turns to expose the hollow artifice of this imperial drama. He had been present when the 21st Lancers successfully charged a much larger body of Dervishes at Omdurman. He knew how much courage and initiative it involved, and for exactly that reason he felt keenly a soldier's impatience with sensation-seeking newspaper-reading civilians, who cheered on the cavalry without understanding what such a battle involved:

> The glamour of a cavalry charge impresses a wide public. Thousands of people who care little, and know less, of the more intricate and delicate operations of war are attracted by the dramatic aspect which such an incident presents. This keen interest will perhaps call forth a great deal of unmeasured eulogy and of extravagant expression. It is not fitting that those sentiments of duty and patriotism which rise from the altar and the hearth should descend to the music hall and the pothouse.

In the Sudan Churchill at last understood what he had failed to see (or failed to admit) on the Northwest Frontier: that real war was not like the theatre. The dissonance between what he saw on the stage and on the desert battlefield was finally too much for him. Now he cast off his earlier pose of aesthetic subjectivity and announced that he would henceforth "write with both knowledge and impartiality."[10] One day after he celebrated saluting the Union Jack, he forced his readers to look squarely at the horror of combat. Even after more than a century of global conflict and mass murder, his account is still difficult to read. In photographic detail, he described what happened to the thousands of Dervishes who were mowed down by British Maxim guns and left in the desert, piled two or three deep. After three days, some were still barely alive. At their breakfast tables, readers of the *Morning Post* were forced to gaze upon "a man that had crawled a mile in three days, but was yet two miles from the river. He had one foot. The other remained behind. I wonder if he ever reached the water he had struggled so hard to attain." For the British wounded there were anaesthetics, proper medical care, and a pension; for the British dead, burial with full military honors:

> But there was nothing *dulce et decorum* about the Dervish dead. Nothing of the dignity of unconquerable manhood. All was filthy corruption. Yet these were as brave men as ever walked the earth. The conviction was borne in on me that their claim beyond the grave in respect of a valiant death was as good as that which any of our countrymen could make.[11]

Back home, he sardonically observed, all this was reduced to an amusing theatrical spectacle. For the British public, the various African and Asian peoples they had conquered were merely semi-comic characters in the newspapers, the music halls, and *Punch*:

> . . . how strange and varied are the diversions of an Imperial people. Year after year, and stretching back to an indefinite horizon, we see the figures of

> the odd and bizarre potentates against whom the British arms continually are turned. They pass in a long procession. The Akhund of Swat, Cetewayo brandishing an assegai as naked as himself, Kruger singing a Psalm of Victory, Osman Digna, the Immortal and the Irrepressible, Theebaw with his umbrella, the Mahdi with his banner, Lobegula gazing fondly at the pages of *Truth*, Prompeh abasing himself in the dust, the Mad Mullah on his white ass and, latest of all, the Khalifa in his Coach of State. It is like a pantomime scene at Drury Lane. These extraordinary foreign figures, each with his complete set of crimes, horrible customs and "minor peculiarities," march one by one from the dark wings of Barbarism up to the bright footlights of Civilisation. For a space their names are on the wires of the world and the tongues of men. The Sovereign on his Throne, the Minister in his Cabinet, the General in his tent pronounce or mispronounce their styles and titles. A thousand compositors make the same combination of letters. The unusual syllables become household words. The street-boy bellows them in our ears. The artisan laughs over them at night in his cottage. The child in the nursery is cajoled into virtue or silence by the repetition of the dread accents. And the world audience clap their hands, amused yet impatient, and the Potentates and their trains pass on, some to exile, some to prison, some to death – for it is a grim jest for them – and their conquerors, taking their possessions, forget even their names. Nor will history record such trash.[12]

In 1885 the Mahdi had vanquished General George Gordon at Khartoum and established a militant Muslim Empire in the Sudan. One would expect Churchill to welcome the destruction of that regime. But he was revolted when British forces desecrated the Mahdi's tomb:

> This place had been for more than ten years the most sacred and holy thing that the people of the Sudan knew of. Their miserable lives had perhaps been brightened, perhaps in some way ennobled, by the contemplation of something which they did not quite understand, but which they believed exerted some protecting influence. It had gratified that instinctive desire for the mystic which all human creatures possess, and which is perhaps the strongest reason for believing in a progressive destiny and a future state. And we had deliberately destroyed and profaned it.

This reaction reflected the secularism that Churchill had absorbed from Gibbon and Winwood Reade, along with the pragmatic respect for all religions he had adopted in British India. Was the Mahdi a "false prophet"? No more so than any of the others. "That only means, my dear . . . that *you* do not believe him. 'False' is the epithet which all religious sects have applied to all others since the beginning of all things."[13] In the *Malakand Field Force* he had blandly assured his readers "that no European can gauge the motives or assume the points of view of Asiatics."[14] Now he was doing precisely that, with some genuine understanding. "Perhaps to these savages with their vile customs and brutal ideas we appear as barbarous aggressors," he wondered. "The British subaltern, with his jokes, his cigarettes and his soda water, may seem to them a more ferocious creature than any Emir or fanatic in Omdurman. The Highlanders in their kilts, the white loop-holed gunboats, the brown-clad soldiery and the lyddite shells are all elements of destruction which must look ugly when viewed from the opposite side."[15]

Churchill still believed that the conquest of the Sudan was justified by the imperative of progress, because it brought closer the day "when a mighty stream of irrigation has changed the desolate plain of Omdurman into a fertile garden, and the mud hovels of the town have given place to the houses, the schools and the theatres of a great metropolis." Progress is relentless and holds no favorites: someday the turn of the British Empire would come. "The Dervish host was scattered and destroyed. Their end, however, only anticipates that of the victors, for Time, which laughs at Science, as Science laughs at Valour, will in due course contemptuously brush both combatants away."[16] This was the moment of Kipling's poem "Recessional" (1897), when, amidst the vainglory of Victoria's Diamond Jubilee, there was a troubling sense that Britain had passed the pinnacle of global power. Politicians and journalists worried about imperial decline, and especially about the growing military and commercial challenge emerging from Germany.[17] The charge of the 21st Lancers was widely celebrated by the British people as proof that they still possessed "those intrinsic fighting virtues without which no race can long continue to rule" – but as Churchill recognized, the fact that they needed that reassurance only highlighted the underlying fears: "All great empires have been destroyed by success and triumph. No empire of the past has enjoyed so great a measure of that fatal glory as the British. The patriot who boasts his faith in our destiny may often anxiously look back, fearing, almost expecting, to discover signs of degeneration and decay."[18]

In *The River War*, nearly a thousand pages in length, his newspaper observations would be greatly expanded and become, if anything, more sarcastic on the subject of imperialism:

> What enterprise that an enlightened community may attempt is more noble and more profitable than the reclamation from barbarism of fertile regions and large populations? To give peace to warring tribes, to administer justice where all was violence, to strike the chains off the slave, to draw the richness from the soil, to plant the earliest seeds of commerce and learning, to

> increase in whole peoples their capacities for pleasure and diminish their chances of pain – what more beautiful ideal or more valuable reward can inspire human effort? The act is virtuous, the exercise invigorating, and the result often extremely profitable. Yet as the mind turns from the wonderful cloudland of aspiration to the ugly scaffolding of attempt and achievement, a succession of opposite ideas arise. Industrious races are displayed stinted and starved for the sake of an expensive Imperialism which they can only enjoy, if they are well fed. Wild peoples, ignorant of their barbarism, callous of suffering, careless of life but tenacious of liberty, are seen to resist with fury the philanthropic invaders, and to perish in thousands before they are convinced of their mistake. The inevitable gap between conquest and dominion becomes filled with the figures of the greedy trader, the inopportune missionary, the ambitious soldier, and the lying speculator, who disquiet the minds of the conquered and excite the sordid appetites of the conquerors. And as the eye of thought rests on these sinister features, it hardly seems possible for us to believe that any fair prospect is approached by so foul a path.[19]

Imperialist ideology supersaturated all aspects of late Victorian popular culture, not just the stage, and Churchill had absorbed it at every hand from a very early age. He recalled visiting his nanny's brother-in-law when he was four, and the newspapers were reporting the Zulu War:

> There were pictures in the papers of the Zulus. They were black and naked, with spears called "assegais" which they threw very cleverly. They killed a great many of our soldiers, but judging from the pictures, not nearly as many as our soldiers killed of them. I was very angry with the Zulus, and glad to hear they were being killed; and so was my friend, the old prison warder. After a while it came to an end and there were no more pictures of Zulus and nobody worried any more about them.[20]

The headmaster of Harrow, J. E. C. Welldon, preached a benevolent paternalistic imperialism which emphasized that the British were superior to, and responsible for, their subject races. In fact those assumptions were embedded in almost everything young Winston read about the Empire, including George Chesney's handbook *Indian Polity* and the works of Rudyard Kipling.[21] But as suggested by his ironic comments on Zulus as depicted in the newspapers, Churchill was not incapable of distinguishing between media representations of the Empire and reality.

Churchill's paradoxical attitudes toward the Sudan may have been shaped by H. Rider Haggard's novel *King Solomon's Mines* (1885). Winston first read it at age eleven and sent the author a letter of congratulation.[22] He went on to perform several close readings of the text and interrogate the author (literally). "He believed it was true," his cousin Shane Leslie recalled.[23] "He read it twelve times, and once drove its author *haggard* in the course of a cross-examination. 'What did you mean?' he insisted on one disputed point, and the author confessed he did not know himself."[24] In 1932 Churchill still considered it Haggard's best book.[25]

King Solomon's Mines is today often classified as an imperialist novel, but if one reads it as carefully as Churchill did, a more complicated message emerges. The narrator is Allan Quatermain, who lives young Winston's wish-dream: he gives up school to pursue a life of adventure in South Africa, "trading, hunting, fighting, or mining." He forswears the word "nigger," insisting that he has known many Africans who were better gentlemen than rich Englishmen. As warriors he equates the Aryan Danes with the Zulus, who speak "a language as beautiful and sonorous as the old Greek."[26] Quatermain possesses a map pointing the way toward King Solomon's legendary mines, and joins an English expedition traveling in that direction. An imposing native, Umbopa, volunteers to join the trek as a porter, though his carriage and manner suggest that he is much more than a servant. The expedition reaches Kakuanaland, a formidable kingdom in the interior ruled by the tyrant Twala and his evil henchwoman Gagool. They base their power on terror, ordering periodic "witch-hunts" in which hundreds of their subjects are arbitrarily and gruesomely executed. Umbopa turns out to be Ignosi, the rightful king of Kakuanaland, who leads a rebellion and overthrows Twala, with the help of the Englishmen. They only ask that he replace witch-hunts with the rule of law, which Ignosi considers an odd white men's custom, but he agrees, if only to humor his English friends. They will always be welcome in Kakuanaland, he proclaims, but the borders of his kingdom will be closed to all other Europeans: no traders, no soldiers, no missionaries.

King Solomon's Mines, then, affirms African independence and racial equality, and was therefore enormously popular among African readers.[27] Haggard even permits a romance between a white man and a black woman, though she is conveniently killed off. The witch-hunt, the most chilling episode in the novel, may have also had a deep and lasting impact on Churchill's political consciousness, for here he read a study in the anthropology of holocausts. The spectacle of Africans carrying out mass murder might have reinforced racist attitudes among some readers, but only if they presumed that white men were incapable of such crimes, and Churchill was never under any such illusion.

In Churchill's writings, Africans and Asians almost always play very minor roles, as extras in the background. But there is one fully realized and sympathetic character among them: the Mahdi. Far from treating him as the Other, Churchill insisted that he resembled no one so much as his adversary, General George Gordon:

> Both were earnest and enthusiastic men of keen sympathies and passionate emotions. Both were powerfully swayed by religious fervour. Both exerted great personal influence on all who came in contact with them. Both were reformers. The Arab was an African reproduction of the Englishman; the Englishman a superior and civilised development of the Arab. In the end they fought to the death, but for an important part of their lives their influence on the fortunes of the Soudan was exerted in the same direction.[28]

And as literary characters they were equally unforgettable. As Gordon's "wild and varied fortunes lead him from Sebastopol to Pekin, from Gravesend to South Africa, from Mauritius to the Soudan, the reader follows fascinated. Every scene is strange, terrible, or dramatic. Yet, remarkable as are the scenes, the actor is the more extraordinary; a type without comparison in modern times and with few likenesses in history." Impetuous when he should have been diplomatic, enthusiastic to the point of fanaticism, courageous to the point of recklessness, "his daring and resource might turn the tide of war. His energy would have animated a whole people."[29] And always he was "sustained by that belief in personality which too often misleads great men and beautiful women."[30] At a young age, Winston Churchill saw clearly in General Gordon all the strengths and weaknesses of Winston Churchill.

In the late 1870s Gordon had combated the slave trade in the Sudan. Performing the classic heroic role of an imperialist melodrama:

> he scattered justice and freedom among the astonished natives. He fed the infirm, protected the weak, executed the wicked. To some he gave actual help, to many freedom, to all new hopes and aspirations. Nor were the tribes ungrateful. The fiercest savages and cannibals respected the life of the strange white man. The women blessed him. He could ride unarmed and alone where a brigade of soldiers dared not venture.

He was also the prime mover of a revolution. His attack on slavery "undermined the whole social system" and spread a subversive ideology: "Oppressed yet ferocious races had learned that they had rights." Gordon set in motion the upheaval that would ultimately lead to the triumph of the Mahdi. This historical irony led Churchill to the conclusion that the Mahdi's rebellion was motivated not so much by Muslim fanaticism (as conventional wisdom had it) as by an entirely understandable hunger for freedom from Egyptian domination:

> Those whose practice it is to regard their own nation as possessing a monopoly of virtue and common-sense, are wont to ascribe every military enterprise of savage peoples to fanaticism. They calmly ignore obvious and legitimate motives. The most rational conduct is considered mad. . . . Rebellions of natives goaded to fury by brutal oppression are airily set down to their fanaticism, and the question is dismissed as unworthy of further reflection.

In his last book Churchill himself had attributed the 1897 Northwest Frontier rebellion to Islamic zealotry, but now he recognized that the Pathans, "having seen the forts and roads being made in their territory . . . rightly thought their liberties were threatened by annexation." Likewise:

> there exists no record of a better case for rebellion than that which presented itself to the Soudanese. Their country was being ruined; their property was plundered; their women were ravished; their liberties were curtailed; even their lives were threatened. Aliens ruled the inhabitants; the few oppressed the many; brave men were harried by cowards; the weak compelled the strong. Here were sufficient reasons.

Churchill did not suggest that Islam played no important role in these two rebellions. He believed that injustice was a necessary but not sufficient cause of revolution. Something more was needed to motivate the oppressed to rebel, something that we would now call ideology. Churchill called it:

> the desire, which most men and all communities manifest at all times, to associate with their actions at least the appearance of moral right. . . . No community embarks on a great enterprise without fortifying itself with the belief that from some points of view its motives are lofty and disinterested. . . . The sufferings of a people or a class may be intolerable, but before they will take up arms and risk their lives some unselfish and impersonal spirit must animate them.

For the French revolutionaries of 1789, this spirit was supplied by the Declaration of the Rights of Man; for the tribesmen of the Northwest Frontier and the Sudan, it was the Koran. "In countries where there is education and mental activity or refinement, this high and often ultra-human motive is found in the pride of glorious traditions, in a keen sympathy with surrounding misery, or in a philosophical recognition of the dignity of the species" – precisely the oratorical themes Churchill would use in 1940 to mobilize the British people.[31]

If Churchill saw himself in General Gordon, he also identified with the Mahdi, born Mohammed Ahmed. Their fathers had died relatively young: "Solitary trees, if they grow at all, grow strong: and a boy deprived of a father's care often develops, if he escape the perils of youth, an independence and vigour of thought which may restore in after life the heavy loss of early days." (Churchill quoted that sentence in a letter to his mother, effectively underscoring its importance to him.)[32] That independence ultimately led Mohammed to rebel against his elders and mentors: "Although the scene is laid in the wilds of Africa, and the actors differ from us in colour, faith, and custom, the story will recall the personal experiences of many readers, and enable them to sympathise." Mohammed was a reformer, a patriot, a prophet, a brilliant publicist, a "widely read" author, a charismatic military leader who demanded great sacrifices from his people and led them to victory – everything that Churchill aspired to be, and became. "Whatever is set to the Mahdi's account," he concluded:

> it should not be forgotten that he put life and soul into the hearts of his countrymen, and freed his native lands of foreigners. The poor miserable natives, eating only a handful of grain, toiling half-naked and without hope, found a new, if terrible magnificence added to life. Within their humble breasts the Mahdi roused the fires of patriotism and religion. Life became filled with thrilling, exhilarating terrors. They existed in a new and wonderful world of imagination. While they lived there were great things to be done. . . .[33]

Is it far-fetched to suggest that here Churchill found one of his prime models for war leadership? His sketch of the Mahdi reads like something out of Joseph Conrad: where the hero penetrates to the heart of Africa, looks into the face of a "savage," and sees himself. *Heart of Darkness* was serialized in *Blackwood's Magazine* between February and April 1899, while Churchill was writing *The River War*, but beyond that there is no evidence that he ever read anything by Conrad. What is certain is that he had read several times over *King Solomon's Mines*, which, like *The River War*, tells a story about a charismatic native leader who topples an oppressive regime in the African interior. Much of *The River War* sounds astonishingly postcolonial, dismissing European pretensions to cultural superiority. Churchill acknowledges that the Mahdi's successor, the Khalifa Abdullahi, was "an evil man" who once again reduced the Sudan to misery. However:

> No execution which he ordered at Omdurman was more terrible than those which, with the approval of the British Government, accompanied the

> suppression of the Indian Mutiny. His chastisement of rebellious tribes was less brutal than the massacres of Armenians, and far more rational than the anti-Semitism from which even the most polite nations have not purged themselves. . . . And his treatment of the European captives was . . . not much worse than the methods of keeping French prisoners of war practised in England within the present century.[34]

Given that, what justified the British conquest? Once again Churchill points to progress and good government: whereas the Egyptians and the Khalifa tyrannized over the Sudan, British administrators had restored law and order in Egypt, reformed the native army, promoted irrigation projects, and generated a budget surplus. But this time a sardonic undercurrent appears in Churchill's prose, something like the "Bloomsbury snigger" we associate with Lytton Strachey – who used *The River War* as a source for the General Gordon chapter in *Eminent Victorians*. Churchill assumes that arch tone when he discusses the popular belief that British imperialism was a charitable enterprise much like the Toynbee Hall settlement house, except that it operated in Egypt rather than Whitechapel: "The interest of the British people in the work of regeneration grew continually. The fascination of doing good began to appeal to men of many classes. Each new reform was hailed with applause." Churchill compared the colonial venture to a transformation scene in a pantomime ("It was as though at the touch of an angel the dark morasses of the Slough of Despond had been changed to the breezy slopes of the Delectable Mountains"), suggesting that it was more theatre than reality. It was also a matter of clever publicity, which took shape in the form of Sir Alfred Milner's 1893 book *England in Egypt*:

> His skilful pen displayed what had been overcome, no less than what was accomplished. By explaining the difficulties he enhanced the achievement. He showed how, while Great Britain was occupied elsewhere, her brilliant, persevering sons had repeated on a lesser scale in Egypt the marvelous evolution which is working out in India. . . . Such was the wonderful story, and it was told in a happy moment. The audience were eager and sympathetic. The subject was enthralling. The story-teller had a wit and a style that might have brightened the dullest theme. In these propitious circumstances the book was more than a book. The words rang like the trumpet-call which rallies the soldiers after the parapets are stormed, and summons them to complete the victory.[35]

The publication of two sensational narratives of escape from the Sudanese Muslims, Father Joseph Ohrwalder's *Ten Years of Captivity* (1892) and Rudolf

Carl von Slatin's *Fire and Sword in the Sudan* (1896), added fuel to the fire. And bound up with these paternalistic and philanthropic impulses was a primitive desire to avenge General Gordon:

> The personal character of "The Christian hero" had produced a profound impression upon the people of Great Britain. His death at the hands of infidel savages transformed him into something like a martyr. There was an earnest desire on the part of a pious nation to dissociate his name from failure. The idea of revenge, ever attractive to the human heart, appeared to receive the consecration of religion. What community is altogether free from fanaticism? The spirit of the Crusaders stirred beneath the surface of scientific civilisation; and as the years passed by, there continued in England a strong undercurrent of public opinion which ran in the direction of "a holy war."[36]

With that last phrase, Churchill delivered his most telling satiric thrust: Who, then, was waging jihad? But when he described the Battle of Omdurman, his tone shifted from irony to outright censure. After the Dervishes were clearly defeated, one final suicide attack was launched by their remaining horsemen, none of whom survived:

> "Mad fanaticism" is the depreciating comment of their conquerors. I hold this to be a cruel injustice. Nor can he be a very brave man who will not credit them with a nobler motive, and believe that they died to clear their honour from the stain of defeat. Why should we regard as madness in the savage what would be sublime in civilised men? For I hope that if evil days should come upon our own country, and the last army which a collapsing Empire could interpose between London and the invader were dissolving in rout and ruin, that there would be some – even in these modern days – who would not care to accustom themselves to a new order of things and tamely survive the disaster.[37]

That last sentence too may have been inspired by Churchill's recent reading. Probably his favorite contemporary author was H. G. Wells, whose books he habitually read almost as soon as they appeared in print. *The War of the Worlds* was published in January 1898; in November Churchill signed his publication contract for *The River War* and began writing, finishing by 2 October 1899.[38] The Wells novel was a Swiftian allegory of imperialism: this time Britain is the native society overrun by a colonizing power armed with more advanced weaponry. Lest that point escape his readers, Wells reminded them, in his first chapter, that "The Tasmanians, in spite of their human likeness, were entirely swept out of existence in a war of extermination waged by

European immigrants, in the space of fifty years." The novel portrays a frantic and unsuccessful defense of London – and an artilleryman who, rather than submit to the new order of things, plots to commandeer the Martian fighting machines and turn them on the invader. *The River War* includes a long section that describes the construction of a British military railway along the Nile, paralleling Wells's description of Martian interplanetary transport. And in 1908, after visiting Uganda, Churchill would make the analogy explicit: the British were, "in all that constitutes fitness to direct, as superior to the Baganda as Mr. Wells's Martians would have been to us."[39]

In melodrama, Churchill observed, "The sentiment that the British soldier is incapable of brutality, is one which never fails to win the meed of popular applause; but there are in fact a considerable proportion of cruel men in every army."[40] He revealed that some Dervish prisoners were killed after surrendering, mostly by the Sudanese and Egyptians but in a few cases by British troops,[41] and that British shells had killed a number of women and children in Omdurman.[42] And in language even more scathing than his original dispatches, he condemned at length the deliberate destruction of the Mahdi's tomb:

> By Sir H. Kitchener's orders the Tomb has been profaned and razed to the ground. The corpse of the Mahdi was dug up. The head was separated from the body, and, to quote the official explanation, "preserved for future disposal" – a phrase which must in this case be understood to mean, that it was passed from hand to hand till it reached Cairo. Here it remained, an interesting trophy, until the affair came to the ears of Lord Cromer, who ordered it to be immediately reinterred at Wady Halfa. The limbs and trunk were flung into the Nile. Such was the chivalry of the conquerors!
>
> Whatever misfortunes the life of Mohammed Ahmed may have caused, he was a man of considerable nobility of character, a priest, a soldier, and a patriot. He won great battles; he stimulated and revived religion. He founded an empire. To some extent he reformed public morals. Indirectly, by making slaves into soldiers, he diminished slavery.

He also treated prisoners well and protected Christian priests who refused to convert to Islam. Vandalizing his tomb violated any standard of morality, whether Christian, Islamic, or secular. A pragmatic imperialist would consider it the worst possible blunder: in India there was an absolute taboo against offending any religious group. "If the Soudan is to be administered on principles the reverse of those which have been successful in India," Churchill thundered, ". . . then it would be better if Gordon had never given his life nor Kitchener won his victories."[43] Such atrocities, he pressed home, were the inevitable result of demonizing the enemy: "the Dervishes, from the Mahdi and the Khalifa downwards, have been loaded with every variety of abuse and charged with all conceivable crimes. This may be very comforting to philanthropic persons at home; but when an army in the field becomes imbued with the idea that the enemy are vermin who cumber the earth, instances of barbarity may very easily be the outcome." The Khalifa was no doubt a tyrant, "But he must be judged by other codes than ours; and so judged, he need not fear comparison with several potentates with whom the Imperial Government has not scrupled to establish intimate and cordial relations."[44]

"I do not think the book will bring me many friends," he confided to his cousin Ivor Guest in January 1899. "But . . . after all in writing the great thing is to be honest."[45] In fact the reviews of *The River War* were mixed but not as negative as he expected, suggesting, as Richard Toye has argued, that Churchill's criticisms of this imperial adventure did not "stray outside the limits of acceptable discourse." He was not quite as vitriolic as Macaulay on Warren Hastings, and no more so than Sir Henry Campbell-Bannerman, leader of the Liberal Party, who a few years later would denounce British "methods of barbarism" in the Boer War. Queen Victoria also objected to the desecration of the Mahdi's tomb, and Lord Salisbury allowed Churchill to dedicate *The River War* to him.[46] Sharp critiques of British imperialism were voiced by contemporary intellectuals such as J. A. Hobson, G. K. Chesterton, Henry Labouchere, and Wilfrid Scawen Blunt – the last would become quite friendly with Churchill.[47] Nevertheless, the dominant tone of the press coverage of Khartoum was sensationally patriotic. There had been a two-year build-up as the campaign had been planned and carried forward, culminating in total victory with minimal British casualties. Headlines screaming "Gordon Avenged!" set off months of national celebration. Amidst that imperial triumphalism, Churchill offered a rare voice of dissent.[48]

When *The River War* was republished in 1902, Churchill shortened it by a third. Every chapter was revised, if not omitted altogether, and all criticisms of Kitchener and the British Army were cut out. Now, as a Conservative MP, he found it prudent to tone down his questioning of the imperialist adventure. As he explained in his new preface, "What has been jettisoned consists mainly of personal impressions and opinions, often controversial in character, which, however just, were not essential to the narrative or a permanent record, and which some indeed may think to have been not the most valuable part of the book." Subsequent editions used this text but omitted the new preface, thus erasing any evidence of abridgment.[49] When he retold the story a fourth time in *My Early Life*, it was once again a gorgeous Impressionist painting:

> Nothing like the Battle of Omdurman will ever be seen again. It was the last link in the long chain of those spectacular conflicts whose vivid and majestic

> splendour has done so much to invest war with glamour. Everything was visible to the naked eye. The armies marched and manoeuvered on the crisp surface of the desert plain through which the Nile wandered in broad reaches, now steel, now brass. Cavalry charged at full gallop in close order, and infantry or spearmen stood upright ranged in lines or masses to resist them. From the rocky hills which here and there flanked the great river the whole scene lay revealed in minute detail, curiously twisted, blurred and interspersed with phantom waters by the mirage. The finite and concrete presented itself in the most keenly-chiselled forms, and then dissolved in a shimmer of unreality and illusion. Long streaks of gleaming water, where we knew there was only desert, cut across the knees or the waists of marching troops. Batteries of artillery or long columns of cavalry emerged from a filmy world of uneven crystal on to the hard yellow-ochre sand, and took up their positions amid jagged red-black rocks with violet shadows. Over all the immense dome of the sky, dun to turquoise, turquoise to deepest blue, pierced by the flaming sun, weighed hard and heavy on marching necks and shoulders.[50]

Churchill now remembered Omdurman as the last romantic battle of the nineteenth century. But when one reads his early drafts, it looks more like the first infernal battle of the twentieth century.

In 1907, as Under-Secretary of State for the Colonies, Churchill would come back to Africa, touring Kenya and Uganda and then returning to Khartoum. The memoir he produced, *My African Journey*, is on one level an advertisement for the blessings of imperialism, but on another level Churchill repeatedly subverts that message with the implication that Africans might be capable of managing their own affairs. At several points he offers unsettling suggestions of cultural relativism. Missionaries were anxiously promoting European dress among the natives, but Churchill pointed to the Kavirondo people, who considered clothing taboo but who nevertheless "are said to be the most moral of all the tribes" in the region. Their example, he puckishly remarked, might have compelled Thomas Carlyle to rethink *Sartor Resartus*.[51] More seriously, he argued:

> to compare the life and lot of the African aboriginal – secure in his abyss of contented degradation, rich in that he lacks everything and wants nothing – with the long nightmare of worry and privation, of dirt and gloom and squalor, lit only by gleams of torturing knowledge and tantalizing hope, which constitutes the lives of so many poor people in England and Scotland, is to feel the ground tremble under foot. "It would never do to have a lot of 'mean whites' in this country," I heard one day a gentleman say. "It would destroy the respect of the native for the white man, if he saw what miserable

> people we have got at home." So here, at any rate, the boot is on the other leg, and Civilization is ashamed of her arrangements in the presence of a savage, embarrassed lest he should see what lies behind the gold and purple robe of State, and begin to suspect that the all-powerful white man is a fraud.[52]

Churchill naturally tried to put these doubts aside, assuring his readers and himself that British rule was a force for economic development in East Africa. On his second visit to Khartoum, he indeed found peace and order, railways and tramways, schools and colleges, increased agricultural production, the abolition of slavery, electricity, and "excellent European shops."[53] But when he turned to the autonomous Kingdom of Uganda, he discovered a very real "fairy tale. You climb up a railway instead of a beanstalk, and at the end there is a wonderful new world" – a world remarkably like England, reassuringly hierarchical. "Under a dynastic King, with a Parliament, and under a powerful feudal system, an amiable, clothed, polite, and intelligent race dwell together in an organized monarchy. . . . There is a Court, there are Regents and Ministers and nobles, there is a regular system of native law and tribunals; there is discipline, there is industry, there is culture, there is peace," as well as a high literacy rate. Churchill attributed all these good things largely to selfless missionaries and the Colonial Office's willingness to "work through and by the native Government," but he specifically warned against the imposition of direct British rule.[54] Uganda looked very much like a sequel to *King Solomon's Mines*, the happy kingdom that Ignosi etsablishes in Kakuanaland after the novel ends.

Churchill never changed his view of the Mahdi, whom he always admired as a superb antihero. In a preface to a 1931 biography of the Muslim leader by Richard Bermann, Churchill began with a Shavian quip: "It is always interesting to know what kind of book the devil would have written – but the theologians never gave him a chance." The British reading public needed "to learn the Mahdi's point of view," and this book made clear that he was motivated by "a religious enthusiasm as sincere and philanthropic as that which inspired Saint Dominic or General Booth. . . . The life of the Mahdi is a romance in miniature and wonderful as that of Mohammed himself." But for his untimely death and the Maxim gun, his empire might have extended throughout the Middle East. "The balance between East and West depends on the advance of knowledge of arms. When arms were equal, the East as often won, as in the Crusades." Above all, the Mahdi was one of the central characters of an enthralling drama: "Literature will not be weary of re-telling the story of General Gordon. He is a treasure trove for the romancers of history like Lytton Strachey."

Strachey had in fact treated the Mahdi with bemused contempt. He was merely the latest in a long line of "imposters" worshiped by credulous orientals, just one more example of "the drunkenness, the madness, of religion." With "barbaric zeal" he imposed a rigidly puritanical form of Islam on his followers, punishing infractions with floggings or death. And yet, Strachey insinuated, "There were rumours of debaucheries in high places; of the Mahdi, forgetful of his own ordinances, revelling in the recess of his harem, and quaffing date syrup mixed with ginger out of the silver cups looted from the church of the Christians."[55] This was a conventional caricature of a native rebel, which would have found favor in any British Army officers' club. It was Churchill who painted an appreciative, humane, multidimensional portrait of the Mahdi – and it was Churchill who delivered a truly scathing indictment of the praxis of British imperialism. The first edition of *The River War* was far more subversive than *Eminent Victorians*. "One day," Churchill concluded:

> a Gibbon will summarize England's work in Egypt and discover splendid material for a ruthless and unrestricted pen. It is too close for the final word, for the shaping of the scenes of that Drama, for the weaving of the appropriate Chorus, but the dumb-show which in Greek Tragedy was wheeled into the orchestra (as when the body of Agamemnon was displayed in the theatre of Aeschylus), the part of the Egyptian Drama is irrevocably fixed on the stairs outside the Palace of the Governor-General of Khartoum.

This was one of the most arresting climaxes in theatre history, "the moment when the last Christian hero met the last insurgence of Islam." Churchill could treat the Mahdi indulgently for two reasons: because he played a magnificent role on the world stage, and because his rebellion seemed to represent the final burnout of Muslim fury. The allusion to Gibbon suggests that Britain's empire would one day lie in ruins, but for the time being it represented progress, and the Mahdi's regime was a romantic anachronism. Churchill and his fellow officers at Bangalore had no prejudices whatsoever against cooperative Muslims. And today, in 1931 (Churchill concluded with Stracheyesque irony), "The son of the Khalifa is an ADC to the Governor-General of the Sudan, while, stranger still, the posthumous son of the Mahdi is Sir Abderrahman El Mahdi, knighted for his services to King and Empire, [residing] in a villa on Gordon Avenue in Khartoum."[56]

CHAPTER 5

A Portrait of the Artist

On 24 August 1897 Churchill reported to his mother that he had written eighty manuscript pages of a novel. He entertained a high opinion of his literary talents: "It is far and away the best thing that I have ever done. . . . I find a fertility of ideas that surprises me. . . . I am quite enthusiastic about it. All my philosophy put into the mouth of the hero. . . . It is full of adventure."[1] "Affairs of State" was the working title, and it was set "somewhere in the Balkan Peninsula."[2] *The Malakand Field Force* would be marred by numerous misprints, but that only strengthened the author's resolve "to write something that will take its place in permanent literature."[3] The novel, published as *Savrola*, is now almost completely forgotten. Churchill's biographers devote little attention to it, perhaps because it arguably ranks among the worst novels of the nineteenth century. But bad books can be wonderfully revealing, and this one in particular offers remarkable insights into the author's core political convictions and methods.

Savrola was a knock-off of Anthony Hope's *The Prisoner of Zenda*, a best-selling novel of 1894. (Churchill was never ashamed to pursue lucrative trends in the literary marketplace.) *The Prisoner of Zenda* is a tale of romance and political intrigue set in the mythical Balkan kingdom of Ruritania (it introduced the term "Ruritanian" into the language), and Churchill christened his fictional republic "Laurania." Like many young and clumsy writers, he made himself the hero of his first book. Savrola is an author/politician who agitates to overthrow Molara, the tyrant ruler of Laurania. In his oratory, Savrola draws on the same literary models that Churchill followed: the grand historical narratives of Gibbon, Lecky, and Macaulay. Or perhaps not so grand in the larger scheme of things: for Savrola is also an amateur astronomer and, gazing at the planets and stars, he puts aside these brief and trivial human histories. His imagination, "overleaping space and time, carried the story to periods still more remote. . . . The whole solar system, the whole universe itself, would one day be cold and lifeless as a burned-out firework."[4] The problem alluded to here is entropy. The second law of thermodynamics seemed to promise that eventually all the energy in the universe would dissipate, and the grandest narrative of all, the story of the cosmos, would come to an end. That was a commonplace anxiety of the *fin-de-siècle*, expressed a few years earlier in H. G. Wells's *The Time Machine*, which Churchill had read. (Nearly fifty years later he called it "a wonderful book, in the same class as *Gulliver's Travels*. It is one of the books I would like to take with me to Purgatory.")[5]

Now, if everything and everyone in the universe will inevitably assume room temperature, what is the point of politics or any other human activity? Wells had a classic answer to that existential question: "If that is so, it remains for us to live as though it were not so." Churchill's answer was similar, but more specific, and something one would expect from a dedicated theatregoer: if "the universe dies and is sepulchered in the cold darkness of ultimate negation . . . I can imagine that the drama would not be an uninteresting one to watch."[6] Whatever may happen, the essential thing is to have "played my part."[7] The novel is saturated with these theatrical tropes: "played their part,"[8] "the play is growing high,"[9] "the drama of the night,"[10] "the world's stage."[11] When fighting breaks out in the streets and rebels rush to the barricades, "The scene . . . suggested the stage of a theatre viewed from the gallery."[12] Even the revolutionary placards resemble "theatrical advertisements."[13] With operatic gestures Savrola is able to control the mob, "to whom the dramatic always appeals with peculiar force."[14] In the end, though we are all mortal, we must "leave life's stage with dignity,"[15] for life is essentially performative. Savrola does not assign a high value to authenticity: he admits that his philosophy is "a pious fraud."[16] His oratorical methods follow the outline of "The Scaffolding of Rhetoric,"[17] and he uses them to rouse the masses of Laurania to revolt, but he knows that it is all theatre, all manipulation of the audience. For example, he gives the impression that his speeches are extemporaneous, sometimes groping for *le mot juste* and always finding it, but in fact they are all scripted beforehand and very carefully staged: this was a trick that Churchill himself used all his life, and which he admitted to using.[18] "What a game it was!" Savrola thinks to himself, but "whatever the game, he would play it to his amusement, if not to his advantage."[19]

Given his theatrical proclivities, Churchill would have found *The Prisoner of Zenda* an intriguing literary model on several levels. In 1896 it was staged as a West End melodrama. The Hope novel indulges in the same kind of stage metaphors found in *Savrola*: "play the part," "underground drama," "farce."[20] And the plot revolves around an audacious act of political theatre: Englishman Rudolf Rassendyll impersonates the King of Ruritania to save him from a palace coup. He is, in a word, a "play-actor."[21]

In addition to borrowing from Anthony Hope, *Savrola* incorporated elements of another popular subgenre, the revolutionary melodrama. Churchill once alluded to seeing a Russian nihilist drama, without naming the play.[22] A possible candidate is *The Red Lamp*, a favorite vehicle for Herbert Beerbohm Tree, first performed in 1887 and revived repeatedly through the 1890s. In any case, Savrola is a good revolutionary – moderate, democratic, constitutional. But there is also a cabal of wicked revolutionaries, anarchists "of foreign aspect" who aim at the collective ownership of women, as well as the means of production.[23]

The revolution erupts after the Lauranian fleet is dispatched to confront the British navy over an African colonial dispute, and no longer able to support Molara. After more than three hundred pages, the dictator and his remaining followers are forced to surrender. At this point, the conventions of melodrama dictated that the tale should be wrapped up with one or more *coups de théâtre*. For example, the Anarchists could have seized power from Savrola's provisional government, Bolshevik-style. Or the Lauranian navy might have suddenly returned and restored Molara to his throne under their guns. And then, with Savrola facing a firing squad, the British fleet, in pursuit of the Lauranian squadron, could have appeared on the horizon, landed the Royal Marines, arrested all the bad characters, and restored democracy to Laurania. Last-minute rescues by bluejackets arriving in gunboats were almost inevitable in imperialist melodramas, and this kind of ending would have made for a clichéd but well-constructed novel with the usual multiple surprises and thrilling climaxes.

But Churchill wrote no such neat ending. In the final pages, the Lauranian revolution – and with it the novel – spins out of control. After surrendering, Molara is assassinated by an anarchist. Then the Lauranian fleet arrives, too late to save the dictator, and pointlessly shells the capital. The revolutionaries retaliate by threatening to execute their prisoners. Horrified by all this, Savrola decides that he cannot cope with the revolution he set in motion and flees the country with Molara's lovely widow Lucile. At this point the novel is a tangle of loose ends, so Churchill ended it the only way he could: he stopped writing. In a brief postscript, he assured his (no doubt exasperated) readers that the Lauranians eventually came to their senses, re-established peace, and welcomed Savrola home. As the *New York Times* complained, in an otherwise favorable review, "With the flight of Savrola the tale suddenly collapses, as if the author, grown weary of complications and bloodshed, had abruptly resolved to come to an end."[24]

Churchill failed as a novelist on several counts. As his grandmother Fanny told him frankly, he was incapable of handling love scenes.[25] More seriously, he could not construct a plot. Like many journeyman writers, he fell in love with a literary device but did not know how to use it effectively. In this case it was the *coup de théâtre* (the term is specifically mentioned in *Savrola*.)[26] Such dramatic bombshells cannot simply be dropped on an audience without forethought. The author must have a clear plan for taking the plot in a new direction, or he will write himself into a dead end – as Churchill did. Maurice Ashley, who later assisted Churchill in researching his biography of Marlborough, put his finger on the problem when he noted that "his books were all written at frantic speed. . . . His first two books had to be written quickly, because he was afraid lest some other war correspondent would get in first and spoil the market." He also needed large and steady earnings to support an expensive style of living. "Thus, it became a habit with him to write quickly and even to jump the gun; that is to say, his propensity for starting to dictate a chapter before he had fully mastered the detail meant that he was pretty well committed to a particular way of presenting his story, even before he knew how the story would develop; it was not all that easy to modify a chapter afterwards, although there were a few occasions when a chapter would be entirely scrapped."[27] This was a serious enough handicap when writing reportage, history or biography, where the outlines of the story were more or less given. But in the case of *Savrola*, where the plot had to be composed from scratch, the results were disastrous.

Churchill ultimately recognized that *Savrola* was an artistic failure, which he did not care to repeat. In 1916 he turned down an offer to write stories for *Strand Magazine*: "I am extremely doubtful of my ability to write fiction."[28] In 1929 a reporter for the *Toronto Daily Star* dredged up what was obviously a painful memory:

> "Do you ever think, Mr. Churchill, of writing fiction?"
> "Not much – I wrote a novel once."
> "What happened to it?"
> "I don't know," in the tone of voice people employ when they say "lost at sea."[29]

He devoted only one paragraph in *My Early Life* to *Savrola*, concluding: "I have consistently urged my friends to abstain from reading it." Revealingly, he characterized the novel's muddled conclusion as "a sort of Dardanelles."[30] The assault of the Lauranian navy does uncannily anticipate Churchill's plan for attacking Constantinople: both presumed that a fleet could somehow capture and secure a major city with no ground forces to speak of. And that raises a troubling question: Did Churchill habitually resort to *coups de théâtre* in military and political matters as well as in literature – without thinking them through to a workable conclusion? Later in *My Early Life* Churchill suggested such an analogy:

> Writing a book is not unlike building a house or planning a battle or painting a picture. The technique is different, the materials are different, but the principle is the same. The foundations have to be laid, the data assembled, and the premises must bear the weight of their conclusions. Ornaments or refinements may then be added. The whole when finished is only the successful presentation of a theme. In battles however the other fellow interferes all the time and keeps upsetting things, and the best generals are those who arrive at the results of planning without being tied to plans.[31]

But in politics, literature, and war, how can one succeed without some kind of plan? Was Churchill too improvisational, too impulsive, too keen (like his father) to score a great dramatic stroke?

In its review of *Savrola*, the *Star* recognized what other critics had already noted: that "Mr Churchill follows the Disraelian tradition. He is ambitious; he is a perfect poseur; and he is adept in the arts of notoriety. He has turned war correspondence into a gigantic advertisement of his modest personality. The novel is a sideshow which, as Disraeli knew, is an excellent means of keeping up public interest."[32] At this point Winston defined himself as a third-generation Tory Democrat, carrying forward the political tradition established by Beaconsfield and Lord Randolph. His course of self-education in Bangalore included ploughing through the *Annual Register*, starting with Disraeli's government of 1874–80. In his writings one finds his first allusions to *Coningsby* and *Sybil* as early as 1903,[33] *Endymion* in 1906,[34] *The Young Duke* in 1926,[35] *Tancred* in 1930.[36] In 1906 he was invited to write an introduction for the Everyman's Library edition of *Coningsby*.[37] It is not clear which of Disraeli's novels he had read before he wrote *Savrola*, but when he began work on it, he asked his mother for an edition of Disraeli's speeches.[38] It seems likely that, following Disraeli's example, Churchill hoped to publicize his politics and himself through novels, and thus launch his parliamentary career. As he told his grandmother in February 1898, Beaconsfield's youthful years offered a model to "a man who really means to rise."[39]

In 1916 Churchill read his cousin Shane Leslie's memoir *The End of a Chapter*, and was enthralled. "It is a literary treasure & by itself entitles him to a place in the world of letters," he wrote to Shane's mother.[40] He did not specifically say what he admired in that volume, but therein he would have read Shane's defense of Wilde as "a literary Dreyfus,"[41] as well as a sketch of another statesman whose politics followed literature:

> Disraeli's career was a romance such as no Eastern vizier or Western plutocrat could tell. He began as a pioneer in dress and an aesthete of words. It was Disraeli, and not Oscar Wilde, who wrote: "I like a sailor's life much, though

> it spoils the toilette!" Wilde wrote his life into plays, but Disraeli was his own actor. Wilde accused nature of copying literature, but Disraeli actually made his novels come true. In *Tancred*, written in the thirties, he described the military occupation of Cyprus which he carried out as a prime minister forty years later.[42]

Two sections of *Savrola* may reflect the influence of that other great Victorian self-advertiser, Oscar Wilde, though he is never mentioned in the text. Churchill wrote a brief preface to the book, which reads like a mild attempt to reproduce Wilde's insouciant hedonism, his amoral aestheticism, and his insistence that a true artist writes only for himself:

> Books are frequently written with an ulterior object; to plead some cause or to teach some great moral lesson. The object of these pages is only to amuse. Like the perfect dinner they should be agreeable at the time and never cause a thought afterwards. . . . I have written what would please me to read.[43]

If those maxims were likely to remind readers of Wilde, that danger may explain why this section was cut from the published version. *Savrola* retained a sub-Wildean dialogue on aesthetic theory, in which Molara argues that art is socially constructed and historically contingent: "Beauty depends on human caprice, and changes with the times." Savrola counters that standards of beauty are eternal: men make more or less unsuccessful attempts to realize that ideal, and call the result "art."[44] Churchill considered this exchange "clever & very thoughtful."[45] Actually it is digressive and irrelevant, doing nothing to advance the plot, illuminate the characters, or enhance the political message. In fact it serves no apparent purpose at all – except, possibly, as a covert homage to Wilde.

For all the shortcomings of *Savrola*, in some respects it was fairly successful. *Macmillan's Magazine* serialized it from May to December 1899, paying the author £100.[46] Published as a book by Longmans on both sides of the Atlantic in February 1900, it had sold roughly 8,000 copies by 31 July, not a bad record for a first novel. Newnes brought out a sixpenny paperback in 1908, for which Churchill received a £275 advance.[47] In June 1915 Hodder and Stoughton printed 25,000 copies of a sevenpenny edition and within two years sold 24,270 of them. In Churchill's lifetime it would be translated into Danish, Finnish, French, German, Spanish, and Swedish.[48]

There was even a Chinese version, serialized in a magazine from October 1912 to February 1913, published in one volume in Shanghai in November 1914, and reprinted in 1915. It was produced by Lin Shu, who pioneered the publication of Western literature in China. Evidently he ranked Churchill with Charles Dickens, Walter Scott, Robert Louis Stevenson, Daniel Defoe, Jonathan

Swift, Harriet Beecher Stowe, Washington Irving, Henrik Ibsen, Leo Tolstoy, and William Shakespeare, whose works he also adapted. (To say that he "translated" them might be stretching a point, since he did not know English or any other Western language. Assistants selected and orally translated books, which he then rendered into classical Chinese.) Significantly, this *Savrola* was Lin Shu's first Western publication after the Qing dynasty was overthrown in the 1911 Revolution. The theme would naturally resonate with Chinese readers, and Lin Shu made the connection explicit in his preface to the volume.[49]

Despite its obvious artistic blunders, *Savrola* offers a revealing summary of Churchill's political ideology and his cosmic philosophy, which could be called ethical Darwinism. As Savrola explains it, evolution is driven forward by "the will to live, and the eternal ideal; the great author and the great critic." Here Churchill seems to be alluding to two turn-of-the-century responses to Darwinism. The first was vitalism, as expressed in the *élan vital* of Henri Bergson and the "Life Force" posited by George Bernard Shaw. The second was the Neo-Hegelianism of T. H. Green, Edward Caird, and F. H. Bradley. The vitalists saw evolution as a conscious and deliberately creative process toward ever higher planes of intelligence and ethics, rather than a series of accidents with no connection to morality. Likewise, the Neo-Hegelians posited an "absolute" or "ideal" as the ultimate goal of history, with humanity constantly striving toward this state of social perfection. Both these philosophies were consistent with evolution, as observed in the natural world, without the amoral ruthlessness of natural selection and social Darwinism. Both reflected Victorian confidence in human progress. And both offered the emotional satisfactions of traditional Christianity in a post-Darwinian world, without contradicting modern science. Even if God is redundant, we will eventually arrive at His Kingdom. As Savrola puts it, "It is pleasant to think that such a Being exists to approve our victories, to cheer our struggles, and to light our way; but it is not scientifically or logically necessary to assume one after the two factors I have spoken of are once at work."[50]

Savrola goes on to argue that human morality is a product of natural selection. "The survival of the fittest" is not ensured by an individualistic war of all against all, which would result in the self-destruction of the species. Rather, the capacity for altruism and mutual assistance gave some packs of human ancestors an evolutionary advantage over other packs. "Thus man became a social animal," Savrola explains. "Gradually the little societies became larger ones. From families to tribes to nations the species advanced, always finding that the better they combined, the better they succeeded." The clear implication was that, in 1899, the biggest and most successful combination was the British Empire, and it enjoyed supreme power because it practiced supreme morality. "It depended on the members keeping faith with each other, on the practice of honesty, justice, and the rest of the virtues."[51] In short, right makes might.

Lucile raises two possible objections to this happy equation. What of empires, like Rome, that exercised power without ethical scruples? Savrola grants that the Romans were undone by their moral poverty: "They had only their swords to fall back upon as an ultimate appeal; and when they became effete they could no longer wield them." And he suggests that modern imperialism may suffer the same fate: "When we have degenerated, as we must eventually degenerate, when we have lost our intrinsic superiority, and other races, according to the natural law, advance to take our place, we shall fall upon these weapons. Our morals will be gone, but our Maxims will remain. The effete and trembling European will sweep from the earth by scientific machinery the valiant savages who assail him." But such victories (and here Churchill seems to allude to Omdurman) will be temporary. In the end, if it abandons ethical superiority, the West will go under.[52]

Savrola has a simple formula for averting imperial decline: "The evolutionist would not hesitate to affirm that the nation with the highest ideals would succeed." "Unless," Lucile suggests, "some other nation with lower ideals, but stronger arms, intervenes." Savrola grants that brute force has triumphed over civilization and reversed the march of progress "many hundred times" in history, but he insists that in the very long run "the upward tendency" will prevail, not "always" but "ultimately." Despotism, then, is "an anachronism."[53] On a philosophical plane, Churchill had already worked out the problem that would confront him in 1940, when Britain faced an adversary with far lower ideals and much stronger arms.

There *Savrola* turned out to be a remarkable prophecy. It tells the story of a brilliant author and public speaker who uses his wonderful oratorical powers to defeat the evil dictator of a Middle European country, a dictator who tears up treaties, stabs his political rivals in the back, murders prisoners of war, does not hesitate to use torture, and recklessly seeks an armed confrontation with the British Empire. Historians have long struggled to explain why Churchill, who was wrong about so many things, was right about Hitler from the very beginning. Once again, Churchill's politics followed his literary imagination. He recognized and resisted Hitler largely because the Führer so closely resembled the fictional villain he had created years before. In a July 1940 essay George Orwell discussed several early prophecies of fascism, such as Jack London's *The Iron Heel*.[54] He was apparently unaware that the Prime Minister had published his own anti-fascist melodrama well before the invention of fascism. The difference, as Shane Leslie might have put it, was that Churchill actually made his novels come true. In *Savrola*, as Disraeli had done in *Tancred*, he described a political crusade that he carried out as Prime Minister forty years later.

CHAPTER 6

Publicity Capital

Churchill's next newspaper assignment – and his most celebrated – was the Boer War. On 18 September 1899 the *Morning Post* agreed to send him to South Africa as a war correspondent for £250 a month plus expenses and retention of copyright.[1] At the time it was probably the most lucrative contract ever negotiated by a British journalist, but Churchill understood that publicity was itself a valuable commodity that could be brokered. In the Sudan War he had proposed a trade to Lionel James, a fellow correspondent: Churchill would share with James his eyewitness record of the charge of the 21st Lancers if James would highlight Churchill in his dispatch to Reuters. G. W. Steevens, another star war reporter, was impressed: "His method of exploiting his publicity capital suggests at any rate considerable business capacity."[2] Churchill, Steevens predicted, possessed "qualities which might make him, almost at will, a great popular leader, a great journalist, or the founder of a great advertising business"[3] – and in a sense, he became all three. For the South African War he worked out a plan to invest in new media: £700 for a film camera and cameraman.[4] Significantly, he referred to the cinematographers as "artists."[5] As Churchill put it in his autobiography, his life had become "An endless moving picture in which one was an actor."[6]

He arrived in Cape Town at the end of October 1899. On 15 November an armored train was sent out from Estcourt to reconnoitre in the direction of Boer occupied Colenso. Captain Aylmer Haldane, in charge of the train, invited Churchill along for the ride, though he warned that it was a risky and ill-conceived enterprise. "Nothing looks more formidable and impressive than an armoured train," Churchill explained in *My Early Life*, "but nothing is in fact more vulnerable and helpless. It was only necessary to blow up a bridge or culvert to leave the monster stranded far from home and help, at the mercy of the enemy. This situation did not seem to have occurred to our commander." In that case, why did Churchill agree? "I thought it was my duty to gather as much information as I could for the *Morning Post*," he explained, and besides "I was eager for trouble."[7] He correctly foresaw that there was a potential story here. He invited J. B. Atkins of the *Manchester Guardian* to join him, but Atkins pointed out that his employer would be unhappy if he ended up as a prisoner of war. "That is perfectly true," Winston granted. "I can see no fault in your reasoning. But I have a feeling, a sort of intuition, that if I go something will come of it. It's illogical, I know." So Churchill went and ended up with the greatest scoop of the war, leaving Atkins to ask himself, "Is this man accompanied by a daemon who tells him things? Perhaps; but on the whole I think the explanation is that he manages events."

"Keep cool, men," Churchill said when the train was ambushed. "This will be interesting for my paper." Given that, Churchill was not entirely displeased to be captured by the Boers. His strategy, as Atkins put it in his next dispatch to the *Manchester Guardian*, was "On to success through notable performances; and if not through notability, then through notoriety; but, anyhow, on to success."[8] Churchill himself assured Haldane (who had also been captured) "that what had taken place, though it had caused the temporary loss of his post as war correspondent, would help considerably in opening the door for him to enter the House of Commons."[9]

"Again and again, watching his life and fortunes, it has seemed to me that Winston had a private wire with Fate," observed Violet Bonham Carter. His actions were "always unpredictable, sometimes inexplicable in terms of reason," and yet somehow he repeatedly triumphed. Was it "intuition" or "destiny" or "instinct" that drove him?[10] In fact it was literature, the desire to frame a thrilling story in real life. Once we understand that as his life goal, then Churchill's impulsive courtship of danger becomes predictable, explicable, and eminently reasonable.

Though Churchill protested that he was a non-combatant, Boer General P. J. Joubert noted that, according to the newspapers, he had taken an active role in defending the armored train. Even as a journalist, "he can still do us a lot of harm." Accordingly, Churchill was sent to the State Model School in Pretoria, which had been converted to a prisoner-of-war camp. On 26 November he appealed his detention, arguing that the South African Republic would reap a windfall of good publicity if he were released ("My case while under detention as a prisoner of war has doubtless attracted a great deal of attention abroad and my release would be welcomed as a graceful act of correct international behaviour by the world's press"), or bad publicity if he were not ("My further detention as a prisoner will most certainly be attributed in Europe and America to the fact that being well known I am regarded as a kind of hostage; and this will excite criticism and even ridicule"). But the local Boer commander, Captain Danie Theron, maintained that "Churchill is one of the most dangerous prisoners in our hands," because "The Natal papers are making a big hero of him." The South African Republic decided to keep him under wraps.[11]

The artist in prison: Wilde and Churchill both knew that ordeal. True, Churchill's incarceration was less onerous, more justified, and much briefer (less than a month). But the wound was still painful thirty years later: "I certainly hated every minute of my captivity more than I have ever hated any other period in my whole life." Beyond the loss of personal freedom, the aesthetic deprivation was oppressive:

> Meanwhile the war is going on, great events are in progress, fine opportunities for action and adventure are slipping away. Also the days are very long. Hours crawl like paralytic centipedes. Nothing amuses you. Reading is difficult, writing, impossible. Life is one long boredom from dawn till slumber.

Churchill's detention would later drive him, as Home Secretary, to introduce sweeping reforms in the prison system. And the specific improvements he focused on in his autobiography were literary: "I did my utmost consistent with public policy to introduce some sort of indulgence into the life of their inmates, to give to educated minds books to feed on, to give to all periodical entertainments of some sort to look forward to and to look back upon. . . ."[12] In the State Model School he read two inspirational books, one a biography of an audacious war leader, the other a great philosophical testament to human freedom: Thomas Carlyle's *Frederick the Great* and John Stuart Mill's *On Liberty*.[13]

Churchill's reputation as a publicity-seeking journalist did not endear him to his fellow inmates. As Aylmer Haldane recalled, by 9 December Churchill had concluded that he would not be released:

> and knowing that Sergeant Brockie and I intended to escape, he suggested coming with us. When he approached me on the subject I did not hide from him how greatly, in my opinion, his presence with us would add to the risk of capture. At this time no roll-call nor other means of checking the number of prisoners had been instituted, and I felt confident that neither Brockie nor I would be missed, the more so because we had taken care to avoid in any way drawing upon ourselves – as some officers had succeeded in doing – the special attention of our jailors. On the other hand the absence of Churchill, who was regarded by the Boers as a valuable hostage, was certain to be noticed within twelve hours, a limit of time which would not allow a sufficient interval to elapse in order to give us a chance of reaching the Portuguese frontier. . . .

> In pressing me to allow him to accompany me Churchill held out as bait that he would take care that, if successful, my name was not hid under a bushel. In other words I should share "in a blaze of triumph" such as, according to the account of his escape in the *Strand Magazine*, he enjoyed on reaching Durban. But advertisement has never appealed to me.

For Haldane, an attempt to escape a prison camp was simply a soldier's duty, not a newspaper stunt. Though he worried that Churchill was too "talkative," he agreed to include him in his plans. (Brockie was more skeptical.)[14] Churchill's motive, as he boldly proclaimed in a later dispatch to the *Morning Post*, was not only a desire for personal liberation: he also wanted to strike a blow in the publicity war. The Afrikaaner paper *Volksstem* was regularly publishing reports "of Boer victories and of the huge slaughters and shameful flights of the British." Even if it was all propaganda, it undermined the morale of the prisoners. Like his fellow inmates, Churchill was driven by an "earnest desire to do something, however small, for the British cause," with one important difference: "Of course, I am a man of peace. I do not fight. But swords are not the only weapons in the world. Something may be done with a pen."[15] Of course, that confirmed Boer suspicions and contradicted Churchill's insistence that he was a genuine non-combatant. Moreover, on 8 December he had proposed to the Boers to lay down his pen in exchange for his freedom. He promised, if released, not "to give any information affecting the military situation" – that is, to cease his activities as a war correspondent and go home to England. General Joubert wondered whether Winston could be trusted – he was surely "a chip off the old block" – but on 12 December he telegraphed his government that he was willing to free the young man on those terms.[16]

That evening Churchill broke out of the State Model School. The escape plan devised by Haldane and Brockie was extremely risky, but as he affirmed in *My Early Life*, "the history of war – and I must add, crime – contains many equally unexpected and audacious strokes." The other prisoners were concocting a still more daring plan: to overcome their guards, free all British POWs (more than 2,000) in Pretoria, and seize control of the capital – "a great and romantic enterprise."[17] Churchill clambered over the wall surrounding the camp, but before Haldane could follow he was spotted by a sentry. That meant Churchill was on his own, without Haldane or Brockie (who could speak Afrikaans) to rely on. As he put it in an unpublished 1912 memorandum, "How was I alone, without any local knowledge, without even a compass or a map, or any fixed plan what to do except to walk by night and hide by day, to cover 300 miles of wild and hostile country to the frontier?"[18]

It was certainly the stuff of melodrama, where daring jailbreaks were a favorite theme both on the stage and in the press. In 1897 William Randolph

Hearst's *New York Journal* had scored a legendary journalistic coup by sending a reporter to engineer the escape of Evangelina Cossío y Cisneros, who had been imprisoned in Havana for conspiring to kill a Spanish colonel.[19] And the fugitive soldier in flight was a perennial figure in theatrical melodrama, from Thomas Morton's *The Angel in the Attic* (1843) to Tom Taylor's *Lady Clancarty* (1874) to Bernard Shaw's *Arms and the Man* (1894).[20] The *Standard and Digger's News* described Churchill as "the melodramatic descendant of the great Marlborough," though it assured Transvaal readers that, since he would inevitably be recaptured, "There is really nothing to be gained by Mr. Churchill from this latest journalistic exploit save 'copy'."[21] Churchill was directly inspired by F. Anstey's comically Oedipal novel *Vice Versa*, where Paul Bultitude, a prosperous businessman, magically exchanges bodies with his son and is packed off to a dreadful public school. Unsuccessful in his efforts to get himself expelled, he finally escapes by hiding under a seat in a railway compartment.[22] And while he hid out from the Boers and prepared for his final dash to Lourenço Marques, Churchill read Robert Louis Stevenson's *Kidnapped*: "Those thrilling pages which describe the escape of David Balfour and Alan Breck in the glens awakened sensations with which I was only too familiar."[23] Meanwhile, as he later boasted in the *Morning Post*, Churchill had brilliantly achieved his goal of becoming a celebrity – in the Boer press:

> The newspapers made so much of the affair that my humble fortunes and my whereabouts were discussed in long columns of print, and even in the crash of the war I became to the Boers a topic all to myself. The rumours in part amused me. It was certain, said the *Standard and Digger's News*, that I had escaped disguised as a woman. The next day I was reported captured at Komarti Poort dressed as a Transvaal policeman. There was great delight at this, which was only changed to doubt when other telegrams said that I had been arrested at Bragsbank, at Middleburg and at Bronkerspruit. But the captives proved to be harmless people after all. Finally it was agreed that I had never left Pretoria. I had – it appeared – changed clothes with a waiter, and was now in hiding at the house of some British sympathiser in the capital. On the strength of this all the houses of suspected persons were searched from top to bottom, and these unfortunate people were, I fear, put to a great deal of inconvenience. A special commission was also appointed to investigate "stringently" (a most hateful adjective in such a connection) the causes "which had rendered it possible for the war correspondent of the *Morning Post* to escape."[24]

But Churchill's primary aim was publicity in the British press, and there he succeeded beyond all expectations. Once he reached Lourenço Marques and had a hot bath at the British Consulate, he "devoured" the newspapers and "found that during the weeks I had been a prisoner of war my name had resounded at home." If the reports took some liberties with reality, so much the better: "The part I had played in the armoured train had been exaggerated by the railway men and the wounded who had come back safely on the engine. The tale was transmitted to England with many crude or picturesque additions by the Press correspondents gathered at Estcourt. The papers had therefore been filled with extravagant praise of my behaviour." And then his successful flight from Boer territory "provoked another outburst of public eulogy. Youth seeks Adventure. Journalism requires Advertisement. Certainly I had found both. I became for the time quite famous."[25]

Churchill soon resumed his work as a war correspondent and his theatrical style of reportage. By 8 January 1900, British forces had advanced to within a few miles of Ladysmith: "The long interval between the acts has come to an end. The warning bell has rung. Take your seats, ladies and gentlemen. The curtain is about to rise. 'High time, too,' say the impatient audience. . . ."[26] The capture of Pretoria on 5 June ended the campaign magnificently – and confirmed once again that Churchill was entirely at home with the clichés of imperial melodrama. Alone, he and his cousin "Sunny" (the 9th Duke of Marlborough) rode to the prison camp for British officers:

> I raised my hat and cheered. The cry was instantly answered from within. What followed resembled the end of an Adelphi melodrama. We were only two, and before us stood the armed Boer guard with their rifles at the "ready." Marlborough, resplendent in the red tabs of the staff, called on the Commandant to surrender forthwith, adding by a happy thought that he would give a receipt for the rifles. The prisoners rushed out of the house into the yard, some in uniform, some in flannels, hatless or coatless, but all violently excited. The sentries threw down their rifles, the gates were flung open, and while the last of the guard (they numbered 52 in all) stood uncertain what to do, the long-penned-up officers surrounded them and seized their weapons. Someone produced a Union Jack, the Transvaal emblem was torn down, and amidst wild cheers from our captive friends the first British flag was hoisted over Pretoria. Time: 8.47, June 5. Tableau![27]

But in March, just a few weeks after the relief of Ladysmith and well before he reached Pretoria, Churchill had already been making plans to capitalize on his notoriety. He told his mother that for his next book (which would be *London to Ladysmith via Pretoria*) he would accept an advance of no less than £2,000. He began to plan an American lecture tour, insisting on a minimum of "*at least* a thousand pounds a month for three months and I should expect a good deal more. £5,000 is not too much for such a labour and for making oneself so cheap."[28] Writing to his close friend Pamela Plowden, he even considered a career as a playwright: "I will write a play: scene South Africa: time: the war. A play of the Drury lane autumn drama class. . . ." For a producer, he wanted the great actor-manager Herbert Beerbohm Tree, a friend of his mother. Imperialist melodramas often strove for spectacular and documentary effects, and Churchill had exactly that in mind:

> It will be perfectly true to life in every respect and the scenic effects should be of such a novel and startling character that the audience will imagine themselves under fire. Local colour will be perfect throughout and I should hope to show several of the real Dutch & Colonial types. Of course the piece would have to be largely spectacular but I believe that with my name, and a good deal of assistance from a skilful playwright a great success might be obtained. Ask Tree about this and if he likes the idea, I will get to work. Of course I should want a great deal of help in plot and execution: but given the various situations I can make the people talk and act as they would do in real war: and in detail the work could be made quite perfect.[29]

But on 12 May his mother scotched the idea: "Pamela spoke to me about yr idea of a play – but I discourage it. *Honestly* it would not do. People won't stand any war play – you forget how it wd harrow their feelings & it wd be thought bad taste. Even a year after the A. Civil War nothing cd be given of that kind. The Princess wd not allow a show of the armoured train at Olympia when she went."[30] As a stage genre, imperialist melodrama would not survive the Boer War. The morality of the conflict was too ambiguous to celebrate in the Victorian fashion, the price of victory was too high, and audiences were becoming more sophisticated.

In any case, there were other possibilities. The South African financier Abe Bailey invited him on a Cape Town to Cairo expedition, which Winston found appealing, "for what with a series of letters to a London newspaper and a good sized book to be published later I should be able to earn a good deal of money."[31] That did not materialize, but by 31 July 1900 *London to Ladymith* had sold 10,000 copies in Britain and 3,000 in America – far more than *The Malakand Field Force* or *The River War*, though Churchill had hoped for still better sales. As he reported to his brother Jack, *Savrola* was still selling "tolerably well and even the poor little *Malakand Field Force* has sold 600 copies in the last year." He had earned from his books about £1,500, plus another £2,050 from the *Morning Post*.[32] All told he was making £5,000 a year from his writings alone, about what Robert Louis Stevenson had earned in his best years. In purely monetary terms he was among the most successful authors of his day, at age twenty-six. (H. Rider Haggard earned more than £10,000 a year, Anthony Hope £70,000 over a decade.)[33]

On his way to deliver a magic-lantern lecture on the war in Windsor, Churchill was awestruck when he saw, for the first time in his life, his name in capital letters on a poster. "Fame! Fame!" he shouted.[34] G. W. Steevens was promoting him in Harmsworth's popular paper, the *Daily Mail*, a still Newer Journalism enterprise whose publicity strategy was summed up in the slogan "Boom the Boomsters."[35] As Andrew Horrall has shown, the Edwardian music hall was a publicity industry that created and magnified fame,[36] and here too the celebrated young war reporter was promoted:

> You've heard of Winston Churchill;
> This is all I need to say,
> He's the latest and the greatest
> Correspondent of the day.[37]

When a *Times* journalist claimed that most British soldiers in South Africa were brave but "stupid," *Reynolds's Newspaper* interjected that this "out-Churchills Mr Winston Churchill."[38] Note that both the music-hall singer and *Reynolds's* presumed that their respective audiences were familiar with Churchill's distinctive style and crochets. He had achieved the classic definition of celebrity: he was famous for being famous.

Around the turn of the century it was by no means uncommon for writers to be parliamentary candidates, some successful (Hilaire Belloc, A. E. W. Mason, Gilbert Parker, John Buchan), some not (Anthony Hope, Rider Haggard, Silas Hocking, Arthur Conan Doyle).[39] In July 1899 Churchill had stood for a seat at Oldham and lost by more than a thousand votes. He tried again for the same seat on 1 October 1900, and this time he swept home, increasing his vote by almost 1,500. It all showed, as he told Lord Salisbury, that "nothing but personal popularity arising out of the late South African War, carried me in."[40] And as he wrote to Bourke Cochran a few days later, "I have suddenly become one of the two or three most popular speakers in this election, and am now engaged on a fighting tour, of the kind you know – great audiences (five and six thousand people) twice & even three times a day, bands, crowds and enthusiasm of all kinds."[41]

Churchill would rely on the publicity skills he had developed and refined in his journalistic career throughout his political life, practically from the day he entered Parliament. As early as 1901 he proposed a historic innovation in media management, suggesting that each Army division should have an officer assigned to public relations who would write up dispatches that the War Office could release to the press.[42] And in the same year he asked Joseph

Chamberlain to help him get "some sort of military mention or decoration" for the armored train affair, in which he was ostensibly a non-combatant. "As it is I suspect the authorities think the whole thing purely a piece of journalistic humbug: which it was not. Of course," he assured Chamberlain, in a faintly sardonic tone, "in common with all the other members of Parliament I care nothing for the glittering baubles of honour *for my own sake*," but there was the publicity value to consider. "I have like others – as you know – to 'think of my constituents'. . . ."[43]

CHAPTER 7

Things to Come

Lord Randolph Churchill was willing to tell the Conservative Party an unpleasant truth: "Politics is the science of the future. . . . Politics is not a science, it is not a profession, which consists in looking back; it is not a profession which consists in standing still; it is in this country essentially a science and a profession of progress."[1] His son was no less a Tory Futurist. Embracing ideas that more plodding minds would consider irreconcilable, Winston was simultaneously enthralled with tradition and technology, history and innovation, poetry and science. Though he twice flunked the entrance examination for Sandhurst, he performed remarkably well on the chemistry section.[2]

This was partly a function of his disdain for classical education, which set him apart from other politicians of his generation and his class. As Violet Asquith recalled:

> My father and his friends were mostly scholars, steeped in the classical tradition, deeply imbued with academic knowledge, erudition and experience. Their intellectual granaries held the harvests of the past. On many themes they knew most of the arguments and all the answers to them. In certain fields of thought there was to them "nothing new under the sun." But to Winston Churchill everything under the sun was new – seen and appraised as on the first day of Creation. His approach to life was full of ardour and surprise. Even the eternal verities appeared to him to be an exciting personal discovery. (He often seemed annoyed to find that some of them had occurred to other people long ago.) And because they were so new to him he made them shine for me with a new meaning. However familiar his conclusion it had not been reached by any beaten track. His mind had found its own way everywhere.[3]

In the nineteenth century a classical education, focused on the remote past, usually inculcated a certain pessimism about the future, which often manifested itself as an Arnoldian disdain for Huxleyan science. It also suggested inevitable cultural decline: there were once great civilizations, they were now in ruins, and ultimately the same fate would overtake the British Empire. Churchill too worried about imperial decline, but he saw a way to prevent it: the Empire could survive as long as it maintained a technological edge. That was the lesson he learned at Omdurman, where the British had the Maxim gun and the Dervishes had not. Churchill was not entirely ignorant of the ancient classics, but he read much more science fiction. He was "thrilled" by Olaf Stapledon's 1930 vision of the far future, *Last and First Men*, awestruck by its grand narrative sweep: "The great value of this book is its power to impart a sense of the vast scale of world history." He specifically compared it to Winwood Reade's *The Martyrdom of Man*, which looked forward to space travel and other technological marvels.[4] *The Martyrdom of Man* was profoundly inspirational for both Churchill and H. G. Wells, and that common reading ultimately brought them together, even if they drew different lessons from it.

In 1931 Churchill claimed to have read all of Wells's books twice over: "I could pass an examination in them."[5] They launched their literary careers simultaneously, in 1895, with the publication of Wells's *The Time Machine* and Churchill's war dispatches covering guerrillas in Cuba. In January 1898 Churchill recommended *The Invisible Man* to his mother.[6] The year 1899 saw the publication of Wells's *When the Sleeper Wakes* and Churchill's *Savrola*: they were both revolutionary melodramas, in many ways similar, except that Wells's story was set two hundred years in the future. The two men finally made contact in November 1901, when they were both hugely successful authors. Churchill wrote to Wells saying that he had read *Anticipations* (a volume of prognostications for the new century) and everything else Wells had written up to that point, except for *The First Men in the Moon*. In *Anticipations* Wells looked forward to the development of a "new republic—a republic that must ultimately become a world state of capable, rational men," in effect government by experts.[7] At some length, Churchill explained that:

> There is a great deal in the present volume with which I agree: but there is also a great deal which I cannot accept.
>
> Nothing would be more fatal than for the government of states to get into the hands of the experts. Expert knowledge is limited knowledge: and the unlimited ignorance of the plain man who knows only what hurts is a safer guide, than any vigorous direction of a specialised character. Why should you assume that all except doctors, engineers etc are drones or worse? Surely

> outside scientific spheres there are vast regions of human thought. Is not government itself, both an art and a science. To manage men, to explain difficult things to simple people, to reconcile interests, to weigh the evidence of disputing experts, to deal with the clamorous emergency of the hour; are not these things in themselves worth the consideration and labour of a lifetime. If the Ruler is to be an expert in anything he should be an expert in everything; and that is plainly impossible. Wherefore I say from the dominion of all specialists (particularly military specialists) good Lord deliver us. The mere administration of public affairs is so vast and complicated a business that it precludes the specialized study of anything else. I quite agree with you that it is vy badly done at present. But like all other sciences, government is progressive. Year after year we get a little less corruption, a little less chatter, a little broader basis, a more delicate and perfected machinery. . . .

They were both progressives, but they had divergent conceptions of progress. For Wells, who would join the Fabian Socialists, it meant rigorous scientific planning by technocrats. For Churchill it meant muddling through by aristocrats, and he was far less willing to sacrifice human freedom for the sake of a better future. Mankind, he advised Wells, "has no intention of putting himself in the hands of amiable but pitiless philosophers to be regulated and uniformed as if he were a breed of shorthorns. Plato felt the same desire to mold and shape; and perished under somewhat painful circumstances. And the 'men of the New Republic' should be warned by his fate."[8]

Wells appreciated Churchill's comments on *Anticipations*, up to a point, but this first exchange of letters, like all their subsequent dealings, was irritated by open class resentment. "That you should find my estimate of the rapidity of development excessive is simply due to the difference in our social circumstances," Wells responded:

> You belong to a class that has scarcely altered internally in a hundred years. If you could be transported by some magic into the Household of your ancestors of 1800, a week would make you at home with them. In that time the tailor, hairdresser & the atmosphere of different manners only have done all that was needed. But of the four grandparents who represented me in 1800 it's highly probable two could not read & that any of them would find me and that I should find them as alien as contemporary Chinese. I really do not think that your people who gather in great country houses realize the pace of things.[9]

In response, Churchill pleaded sympathy for the poor bloody governing classes: "You must not be too impatient with the politician. He has his own necessary function; it is in the immediate future by makeshifts and compromises to protect millions of imperfect people who merely wish to remain comfortable against those who on the one hand would make them perfect and those who on the other would make them drudges."[10]

In 1906 Wells sent Churchill *A Modern Utopia*, in which the latter found much to admire. He praised Wells for tackling controversial eugenic and marriage issues, and acknowledged that "there is so much in your writing that stimulates my fancy that I owe you a great debt." But again Churchill had an important reservation: "You have certainly succeeded in making earth a heaven; but I have always feared that heaven might be a vy dull place *à la longue*. . . . Will you think me captious and frivolous when I admit that I wanted more *story*. I am always ready to eat your suet & have eaten all you have ever prepared; but I must have the jam too."[11] Churchill had been and always would be a great nonfiction storyspinner. He was entranced by such gripping tales as *The Time Machine* and *The Invisible Man*, but his eyes glazed over when Wells began sketching blueprints for antiseptic utopias. While Churchill shared Wells's faith in science, he saw it as a means of making the British Empire mightier yet, not creating a World State. If human history was one long narrative of progress, then British power depended on investments in technology. That was the conclusion Churchill drew from Gibbon and Winwood Reade about the fate of the Roman Empire: "If only they had paid a little more attention to mechanics & science they might have survived the barbarian shocks."[12]

Still, in the Edwardian years the two men had enough in common to solidify a political friendship. Churchill was never a socialist, but before the First World War he was a fairly radical social reformer who played a key role in delivering the first installment of Britain's welfare state. Wells therefore endorsed Churchill when he contested a Manchester parliamentary seat in 1908, though there was also a socialist candidate in the race.[13]

In November 1932, when Hitler was on the verge of power and Stanley Baldwin had warned Parliament that "the bomber will always get through," Churchill specifically cited *The War in the Air* (1908), in which H. G. Wells envisioned a world holocaust triggered by a sudden German air strike on New York City.[14] Churchill almost certainly read it shortly after it was published, as was his habit with Wells novels. When he was appointed First Lord of the Admiralty in 1911, he became the driving force behind the development of the Fleet Air Arm, and he enthusiastically took flying lessons himself. He would later profess "to have added the words 'seaplane' and 'flight' (of aeroplanes) to the dictionary."[15] (The first claim might be valid, but the *Oxford English Dictionary* records that an "aërial ship took her first flight" in 1835.)

Churchill was the first head of the Admiralty to think seriously about new weapons technology, and with the outbreak of war in 1914 his passion for

Wellsian gadgetry knew no bounds. He proposed mobile shields to protect advancing infantry in trench warfare,[16] creating artificial islands to serve as naval bases,[17] and equipping a motorized vehicle with a "large steel hammer" or "heavy roller" that could detonate mines in front of it.[18] A satire published in *Town Topics* in July 1917 portrayed him as re-equipping the Army with square shells ("I am thinking also of having square guns to match them"), and inventing a new kind of airplane and ordering a thousand to be produced before it had been tested ("I am quite sure it will go up").[19] In reality, Churchill was soon proposing all kinds of innovations in artillery, including replaceable rifled liners to extend the life of gun barrels ("It is for invention to solve this difficulty").[20]

And then there was the tank, which Wells had anticipated in his 1902 story "The Land Ironclads," and which Churchill then researched and developed during the First World War. By October 1916 he had sent Wells a letter of congratulation: "You will have been interested to see the success with wh yr land battleship idea was at last – after many weary efforts – put into practice."[21] But it would be far too simple to say that Wells inspired Churchill to invent the tank, as Churchill was the first to recognize. In a September 1919 statement to the Royal Commission on War Inventions, he explained the development in terms that even by today's standards would reflect a fairly sophisticated understanding of the motors behind technological innovation. Historians of science recognize that no single inventor invents anything out of the whole cloth. All "new" technology builds on precursors in older technology, and often is imagined beforehand in science fiction, as in the case of robotics and space travel. "Inventions" are usually achieved by combining existing technologies, and hence can only be "invented" when those component technologies have already been developed. Scientific advances, of course, involve solving objective technical problems, but political, economic, and cultural factors provide the impetus behind scientific research: historians of science refer to these as "internal" and "external" influences. Even when all of these factors come together, there are usually several "inventors" pursuing the same goal, working either in collaboration, in competition, or independently. Some of them may reach that goal, but others end up in blind alleys and are forgotten.

Churchill understood all of this perfectly. He stated at the outset that "There was no novelty about the idea of an armoured vehicle to travel across country and pass over trenches and other natural obstacles while carrying guns and fighting men." In addition to Wells's fictional prognostication, "from very early times the history of war is filled with devices of this character for use in the attack of fortresses and fortified positions." And by 1914 the three basic technological components of the tank had already been developed: bulletproof armor, the internal combustion engine, and caterpillar treads.

The question, then, was to determine the external and internal influences that called the tank into existence, or as Churchill put it: "(a) The responsibility for initiating and sustaining the action which led to the tanks being produced and (b) the credit for solving the extremely difficult problems connected with design apart from main principles." Given these premises, it becomes clear that "There never was a moment when it was possible to say that a tank had been 'invented'. There never was a person about whom it could be said 'this man invented the tank'. But there was a moment when the actual manufacture of the first tanks was definitely ordered, and there was a moment when an effective machine was exactly designed as the direct outcome of this authorisation."[22]

As First Lord of the Admiralty, Churchill had set up bases on the Continent from which navy airplanes could attack Zeppelin sheds. To protect these bases, he improvised armored cars, fitting Rolls-Royces with steel plate. These worked well enough until they had to confront impassable lines of trenches. In late October 1914, Churchill therefore authorized the development of a new armored vehicle that could carry its own bridge, which could be laid over a trench, passed over, and then picked up again. A prototype was built, but (as one might expect) it proved impractical. Meanwhile, Colonel Ernest Swinton independently proposed to Sir Maurice Hankey a steam-powered armored personnel carrier on caterpillar treads. On 18 January 1915 Churchill authorized "certain experiments with steam rollers with a view to smashing in by the mere weight of the engine trenches of the enemy," but these too ended in failure. On 17 February he met over dinner Major Gerald Hetherington of his own armored car squadron, who had a plan for an armored vehicle with wheels 40 feet in diameter. Churchill then created the Landships Committee of the Admiralty and (without informing the War Office or the Treasury) gave it £70,000 to develop prototype tanks, some with giant wheels and some with treads. Only the latter proved workable. When Churchill resigned as First Lord in May 1915, the Board of Admiralty appeared ready to discontinue the project, but he persuaded his successor, Lord Balfour, to press ahead with one prototype, which ultimately evolved into the tank first deployed at the Somme in August 1916.[23] Only with those qualifications and complications could it be said that an H. G. Wells story "inspired" the tank, as Churchill acknowledged.

After the war, on 3 March 1920, H. A. L. Fisher (President of the Board of Education) lunched with Churchill, "who tells me that he had read *all* Wells' books & that Wells foresaw the war wonderfully."[24] But by then Wells had become disillusioned with Churchill: he could not forgive the Gallipoli fiasco of 1915–16. They also fell out over Bolshevik Russia, which Churchill regarded as diabolically evil but which Wells considered a deeply flawed but genuine experiment in socialism. In a 5 December 1920 article in the *Sunday Express*

Churchill denounced Wells as an apologist for the Communist regime.[25] As he often did, Wells exacted his revenge in the form of a clumsy didactic novel, *Men Like Gods* (1923), in which a party of twentieth-century Englishmen fall through a time warp and land in a utopia three thousand years in the future. One of the accidental visitors is Winston Churchill, who appears transparently as "Rupert Catskill." This Shangri-La is pretty much what one would expect from Wells: Man has eradicated poverty, disease, ugliness, and half of all animal species. (They were all bugs and pests, and the word "biodiversity" had yet to be invented.) Human beings are now free to devote their lives to scientific research, eating artificial food, and dismally clean sex. It is all too perfect to hold much appeal for Rupert Catskill:

> Life on earth was, he admitted, insecure, full of pains and anxieties, full indeed of miseries and distresses and anguish, but also, and indeed by reason of these very things, it had moments of intensity, hopes, joyful surprises, escapes, attainments, such as the ordered life of Utopia could not possibly afford. "You have been getting away from conflicts and distresses. Have you not also been getting away from the living and quivering realities of life?"[26]

This was not an unfair caricature of Churchill's views about the future: in fact, it was more or less a paraphrase of the first letter he had sent to Wells twenty years earlier.

Having broken with Wells, Churchill found another technological mentor in the Oxford physicist Frederick Lindemann. Outside of his personal staff, no one worked more closely with Churchill during the 1930s and the Second World War. Unlike Wells, Lindemann was a true working scientist, who could and did offer informed advice about all the technological challenges that Churchill and Britain would face over the next three decades: air warfare, radar, the V-2, nuclear weaponry. He also advised Churchill about possible future developments in science and helped him to write essays in pop futurology for mass circulation newspapers and magazines.[27] Churchill's article "Fifty Years Hence" (published 1931–32 in the *Strand Magazine*, *Maclean's*, and *Popular Mechanics*) cited Wells and copied his conviction that scientists were a revolutionary force, "a vast organized united class-conscious army marching forward upon all the fronts towards objectives none may measure or define. It is a proud, ambitious army which cares nothing for all the laws that men have made; nothing for their most time-honoured customs, or most dearly-cherished beliefs, or deepest instincts." Skipping over nuclear fission, he predicted that nuclear fusion would produce enough energy to move Ireland to the mid-Atlantic and melt the icecaps at both poles, without explaining why anyone would want to do that. He foresaw that the poultry of the future would be pumped full of hormones, and that wireless telephones and television would facilitate ex-urban sprawl by making face-to-face human contact unnecessary. Inspired by Karel Capek's play *Rossum's Universal Robots* (which premiered in London in 1923) and by J. B. S. Haldane's paper entitled *Daedalus* (which Lindemann had sent him),[28] Churchill envisioned human beings that would be

> grown under glass. There seems little doubt that it will be possible to carry out in artificial surroundings the entire life cycle which now leads to the birth of a child. Interference with the mental development of such beings, expert suggestion and treatment in the earlier years, would produce beings specialized to thought or toil. The production of creatures, for instance, which have admirable physical development with their mental endowment stunted in particular directions, is almost within the range of human power. A being might be produced capable of tending a machine but without other ambitions.

Churchill was confident that only atheist Russia would embark on such a project: without a spiritual dimension, he warned, all kinds of scientific horrors were possible. He was fascinated by Olaf Stapledon's vast space opera *Last and First Men*, in which humanity is followed by several successive races of higher beings evolved over millions of years, until at last they gain full control over nature, very much like the conclusion of *The Martyrdom of Man*:

> A state was created whose citizens lived as long as they chose, enjoyed pleasures and sympathies incomparably wider than our own, navigated the interplanetary spaces, could recall the panorama of the past and foresee the future. But what was the good of all that to them? What did they know more than we know about the answers to the simple questions which man has asked since the earliest dawn of reason – "Why are we here? What is the purpose of life? Whither are we going?" No material progress, even though it takes shapes we cannot now conceive, or however it may expand the faculties of man, can bring comfort to his soul.[29]

Science, then, had unlimited potential for expanding human powers, but without some kind of moral and spiritual foundation it could be horrifically dangerous. "I have undertaken to write on the future possibilities of war and how frightful it will be for the human race," Churchill wrote to Lindemann on 3 April 1924. "On this subject I have a good many ideas" – and the source of many of them, evidently, was H. G. Wells. Apocalyptic future warfare had been a theme of *The War in the Air, The World Set Free, The Salvaging of Civilization*, and Wells's just-published novel *The Dream*, which Churchill considered "quite good."[30] The article Churchill produced offered frightening predictions of guided missiles, chemical and biological warfare, and worse:

> May there not be methods of using explosive energy incomparably more intense than anything heretofore discovered? Might not a bomb no bigger than an orange be found to possess a secret power to destroy a whole block of buildings – nay to concentrate the force of a thousand tons of cordite and blast a township at a stroke?

If both sides possessed such weapons, the mutual destruction of civilization was assured. But there was another terrifying possibility: "The possession by one side of some overwhelming scientific advantage would lead to the complete enslavement of the unwary party. Not only are the powers now in the hands of man capable of destroying the life of nations, but for the first time they afford to one group of civilized men the opportunity of reducing their opponents to absolute helplessness." Churchill was all too aware of these apocalyptic threats when he confronted first Nazi Germany and then the post-war nuclear arms race between the United States and the Soviet Union. *The Martyrdom of Man* and *The Origin of Species* seemed to promise that "in the hard evolution of mankind the best and fittest stocks would come to the fore. But no such saving guarantee exists to-day." Returning to a troubling question he had first raised in *Savrola*, Churchill concluded that "There is no reason why a base, degenerate, immoral race should not make an enemy far above them in quality, the prostrate subject of their caprice or tyranny, simply because they happened to be possessed at a given moment of some new death-dealing or terror-working process and were ruthless in its development."[31]

He wrote that in 1924, well before the atomic bomb, before he had even heard of the Nazi Party. But H. G. Wells had imagined just such a scenario in *The Time Machine*. Churchill had speculated about future bacteriological weapons as early as 1899, in *The River War*.[32] Possibly he had been inspired by *The War of the Worlds*, where there is no deliberate germ warfare, but the Martians are done in by a lack of resistance to terrestrial infections.

Wells famously said that civilization was a race between education and catastrophe: enlightened science could offer us utopia, but perverted science would lead to the nightmare futures described in *The Time Machine, When the Sleeper Wakes*, and *The War in the Air*. Likewise, even at its most dismal, Churchill's vision of the future was never fatalistic: nothing was predetermined. For him, as for Wells, history was an infinite series of forks in the road, and men always had the opportunity to choose between alternative futures. As he wrote in *The River War*, "every incident is surrounded by a host of possibilities, any one of which, had it become real, would have changed the whole course of events. . . . In the flickering light of conflict the outlines of solid fact throw on every side the vague shadows of possibility. We live in a world of 'ifs.' "[33] Churchill was therefore fascinated with counterfactual history.[34] Even in his massive biography of Marlborough, he not only described the battles that were actually fought but also endlessly speculated about what might have happened if certain commanders had sent their troops off in another direction.[35] And then there was his 1930 article imagining the results if General Robert E. Lee had won at Gettysburg. In this speculation the Confederates proceed to capture Washington, where Lee proclaims the abolition of slavery, even if that seems to defeat the whole purpose of secession. (Actually, Lee's army captured and re-enslaved free Northern blacks.) In any case, Churchill assures us, the end of slavery does not lead to "some idiotic assertion of racial equality": the Confederacy sensibly governs its black population with the same benevolent paternalism that has worked so well for non-whites in the British Empire. Having lost both the war and the moral high ground, the North is forced to recognize Southern independence. This is a fortunate result for Great Britain: rather than face an increasingly powerful United States, she can dominate two more manageable halves of a divided nation.[36] When he composed *The Second World War*, Churchill once again toyed with alternative histories, as in this 1949 note:

> What would have happened if the Germans had not attacked Russia?
> ? The air war over Germany in such circumstances.
> US + GB against Germany.
> Bomb in Canada.
> I still believe that we (US + GB) could have won single-handed.[37]

Some critics of Churchill have noted that, as late as October 1937, he still held out the possibility that Adolf Hitler might "go down in history as the man who restored honour and peace of mind to the great Germanic nation, and brought them back serene, helpful and strong, to the European family circle," but this was entirely consistent with his belief in the indeterminacy of history. At this point Hitler had not yet committed aggression against any other nation, and it was still possible to hope that his anti-Jewish campaign, which had been toned down somewhat during the 1936 Olympics, might be a passing phase. In this article, entitled "Hitler and His Choice," Churchill denounced the crimes the Chancellor had already committed, and warned that he could "let loose upon the world another war in which modern civilization will irretrievably succumb." But only an undecided future could "determine whether he will rank in Valhalla with Pericles, with Augustus and with Washington, or welter in the inferno of human scorn with Attila and Tamerlane. It is enough to say that both possibilities are open at the present moment."[38]

Churchill would drive home the same point in a 1937 series of futurology speculations published in *News of the World*. Science could give us power generated by nuclear fission and fusion, space travel, teleconferencing, artificial food, safe and non-addictive recreational drugs, and preserving and resuscitating human bodies by means of cryogenics. It could also lead to mass brainwashing through scientific propaganda techniques, the creation through genetic engineering of a race of helots programmed to work but not think, and terrifyingly destructive weapons of war.[39] Jules Verne, Churchill once noted, "delighted the Victorians" by showing them the wonderful potentialities of science; but Wells painted "a far more complex scene; and Wells saw the bloody accomplished fact, illustrating his pages while the ink was still wet."[40]

In the Second World War Churchill would once again seek victory in futuristic Wellsian inventions. One striking example was a kind of land submarine, a monstrous trench-digging machine that was supposed to burrow through the Siegfried Line. If it had gone into full production, it would have absorbed a large fraction of Britain's total output of steel and diesel engines. The German conquest of France in 1940 rendered the project pointless, but Churchill nevertheless pressed ahead with the development of a few working models.[41] Geoffrey Shakespeare, who worked with Churchill as Parliamentary Secretary to the Admiralty, recalled that he had the open-mindedness of a creative scientist: "If he summoned anyone to discuss a problem he would throw out a number of alternative solutions. . . . Though he had an inflexible purpose, he had no rigidity of mind. He was, in fact, an empiricist. If one experiment proved unsuccessful, another was suggested. The only unpardonable sin was to sit back and accept the seemingly inevitable. . . ."[42]

Probably his favorite wartime department was MD1, charged with developing new and unorthodox weapons. Its detractors called it "Winston Churchill's Toyshop," and one of its officers recalled that he enjoyed watching weapons demonstrations "like a small boy on holiday."[43] But Churchill's interest in technology was limited to weapons of war: in stark contrast with Wells, he was mostly indifferent to advances in medicine, nutrition, hygiene, or space flight. And, also in a boyish way, he insisted that scientific innovation had to have a gripping story line. In *The Second World War* he related how Dr. R. V. Jones, a scientist at the Air Ministry, cracked the secret of *Knickebein*, the German system of guiding bombers to their targets with intersecting radio beams: "For twenty minutes or so he spoke in quiet tones, unrolling his chain of circumstantial evidence, the like of which for its convincing fascination was never surpassed by tales of Sherlock Holmes or Monsieur Lecoq."[44] As he wrote in April 1938, "you have always got to be thinking about something new and something unexpected. Especially this is true in an age when science is moving forward so fast. Once a conjuring trick has been explained or exposed, it is no longer entertaining."[45] That argument would be persuasive if war technology were judged by its entertainment value – and the Martian weaponry in *The War of the Worlds* is certainly mesmerizing. As Robert Rhodes James grasped, Churchill was fascinated by Professor Lindemann's science because it was so much like science fiction: "There was in it a strong element of daring and adventure, of impatience with practical difficulties, and of fascination with those things not yet achieved which professional scientists usually disliked and distrusted, yet which Churchill found refreshing and invigorating."[46] For this very reason, Lindemann was (with Churchill's full backing) a distracting and disruptive force on the Committee for the Scientific Study of Air Defence, founded in 1935 and chaired by Sir Henry Tizard. Tizard wanted to concentrate on the development of radar. To him:

> Lindemann's schemes appeared irrelevant and even lunatic. Lindemann . . . put forward proposals for aerial mines (to be dropped by high-altitude aircraft in the path of bomber formations, whose pilots would presumably fly obediently into them), infra-red detection of night-flying aircraft, and the placing of "a cloud of substance in the path of an aeroplane to produce detonation". The aerial-mine project, it has been rightly remarked, "was a completely blind alley for research on which valuable time and money were wasted". The "cloud of substance" proposal was based upon no practical basis whatever, and smacked more of casual reading in bad futuristic fiction than the proposal of a serious professional scientist. The proposal for research into infra-red detections was considerably more interesting, but, again, there was nothing of any serious evidence that Lindemann could produce that remotely compared with the RDF researches.[47]

In 1957 a Fellow of the Royal Society who had worked with Lindemann during the war confirmed that he again and again persuaded Churchill to "not allow the expert to kill new ideas or technical innovations. . . . No project was too far-fetched, too novel."[48] Summing up the views of the Labour politician Stafford Cripps and two RAF commanders (Charles Portal and Arthur Tedder), Lord Moran concluded that

> the Prime Minister's mind was ingenious rather than scientific. . . . It was true that he would always welcome any new idea; even if it did not sound plausible, he would insist that it be given a fair trial. He played, too, a considerable part in initiating some of our more fruitful inventions – such as the Mulberry Harbours used in the invasion of France in 1944 – but the scientific habit of mind was wholly foreign to his mental processes.[49]

Churchill was always passionately interested in the newest weapons, but once they passed the research and development stage, once science fiction became mundane reality, he lost interest. Before and during the First World War he had the foresight to authorize experiments with torpedoes launched from seaplanes, urging that "intense efforts should be made to organize a powerful force and deliver an overwhelming surprise attack upon the capital ships of the enemy as they lay in their harbours."[50] But throughout the 1930s he remained confident that the Royal Navy was secure from air attack, an illusion shattered by the sinking of the *Repulse* and the *Prince of Wales* just days after Pearl Harbor. And in contrast to the First World War, Churchill did little to prepare for tank warfare in the Second World War, relying on the French Army and the Maginot Line to hold off the Germans. Two years before the fall of France, he had predicted that static fortifications would be practically invulnerable: "The idea that enormous masses of mechanical vehicles and tanks will be able to overrun these fortifications will probably turn out to be a disappointment."[51] Three years before "the Battle of the Atlantic" nearly strangled Britain (March 1938), he assured his readers that "the undoubted obsolescence of the submarine as a decisive war weapon, should give a feeling of confidence and security so far as the seas and oceans are concerned, to the western democracies."[52] And in the 14 January 1939 *Collier's*, sixteen months before German dive-bombers assisted panzer divisions in breaking through Allied defenses and overrunning France, he asserted that "an air attack on trench lines and fortified points is incomparably less effective than the bombardment of artillery."[53]

But this much must be said for Churchill: with him there was no gap between "the two cultures." In 1949, a decade before C. P. Snow delivered his classic warning, Churchill told an audience at the Massachusetts Institute of Technology (MIT) that "We have suffered in Great Britain by the lack of colleges of university rank in which engineering and the allied subjects are taught." Immediately after he retired from his second premiership, he began discussing plans for a British MIT with Lindemann and John Colville. The result was Churchill College at Cambridge University, which admitted its first students in 1960.[54] Modern British conservatism – the conservatism of Lord Salisbury, Arthur Balfour, Stanley Baldwin, Neville Chamberlain, and Harold Macmillan – has generally taken a pessimistic view of the future. The working assumptions have been that British power will inevitably decline, the best we can do is to manage that decline, and no "slick salesman of synthetic science" (as Alec Douglas-Home put it) will save us. But Churchill was more in line with the optimistic, progressive conservatism of that professional chemist, Margaret Thatcher – not to mention the Star Wars conservatism of Ronald Reagan.

CHAPTER 8

Comédie Anglaise

Young Winston absolutely loathed the authoritarian atmosphere of his first school, St. George's at Ascot. When Maurice Baring was sent there he found that "Dreadful legends were told about Winston Churchill, who had been taken away from the school. His naughtiness appeared to have surpassed anything. He had been flogged for taking sugar from the pantry, and so far from being penitent, he had taken the Headmaster's sacred straw hat from where it hung over the door and kicked it to pieces. His sojourn at this school had been one long feud with authority."[1] At his next school in Brighton, his conduct would earn him a place at the absolute nadir of the class.[2] And at Harrow his housemaster judged him "so regular in his irregularity, that I really don't know what to do. . . . As far as ability goes he ought to be at the top of his form, whereas he is at the bottom."[3]

Most rebels start as student rebels. According to Shane Leslie, Winston never forgave the St. George's headmaster who birched him, having "realized in later years that he had been disciplined by a sadist."[4] The dystopia of *Nineteen Eighty-Four* resembles an English public school blown up to monstrous proportions (as a number of English public school graduates have testified), and Churchill's hatred of dictators may have had the same psychological roots as Orwell's. In a September 1936 speech on the totalitarian threat, Churchill revealingly asked: "How could we bear to be treated like schoolboys when we are grown-up men; to be turned out on parade by tens of thousands to march and cheer for this slogan or that; to see philosophers, teachers and authors bullied and toiled to death in concentration camps; to be forced every hour to conceal the natural workings of the human intellect and the pulsations of the human heart? Why, I say that rather than submit to such oppression, there is no length we would not go to. . . ."[5]

Churchill was congenitally ornery, an inborn individualist who kicked against any kind of restrictions. His reading informed, refined, and mobilized his instinctive libertarianism to political action. It also enabled him to identify and combat what he considered the three greatest threats to human freedom. Two of them, obviously, were Nazism and Communism, but it is not widely appreciated that, especially before 1917, Churchill was no less hostile to monopoly capitalism. He studied the free market economics of Adam Smith, John Stuart Mill, and Frédéric Bastiat, and he acquired a deep suspicion of what Smith called "mercantilism."[6] (Today we call it "industrial policy," "public-private partnership," or "crony capitalism," depending on your choice of words.) While imprisoned in Pretoria in 1899, Churchill wrote to Bourke Cockran that he wanted to take up

> the struggle against vast combinations of capital, which I am told will be the feature of the next Presidential election. . . . Capitalism in the form of Trusts has reached a pitch of power which the old economists never contemplated and which excites my most lively terror. . . . The new century will witness the great war for the existence of the Individual. Up to a certain point combination has brought us nothing but good: but we seem to have reached a period when it threatens nothing but evil. I do not want to see men buy cheaper food & better clothes at the price of their manhood. Poor but independent is worth something as a motto. . . ."[7]

Churchill was never within hailing distance of poverty, but he cherished independence and saw that, in the twentieth century, it was under threat. In November 1901 he warned a Liverpool audience: "One aspect of modern life which strikes me very much is the elimination of the individual. In trade, vast and formidable combinations of labour stand arrayed against even vaster and more formidable combinations of capital, and, whether they war with each other or cooperate, the individual in the end is always crushed under." Party machines were rendering obsolete the independent MP. One of the last of that breed was his father, and in 1886 he had paid dearly for that independence. As Winston proclaimed, "I believe in personality" – especially his own.[8]

And yet for a maverick and flamboyantly performative politician like Churchill, 1900 was an ideal moment to start a parliamentary career. Party discipline was increasing but not yet stifling, dramatic oratory was very fashionable, and newspapers reviewed parliamentary speeches like West End plays. The *Manchester Guardian* found in Winston's maiden effort "a literary flavour" that his father had lacked. The *Yorkshire Post* reported that:

> When sitting in the House or moving about the Lobby he has been eyed as a new actor is eyed on the stage during rehearsals, and of whom a great deal is expected. . . . And when he rose to speak what a magnificent audience he

> had – the Chamber overflowing, a crowd of men about the bar, Lords and Bishops up in the Peers' Gallery, and many women's faces pressed against the grille of the Ladies' Gallery. And in that packed assembly, everybody a critic, watching to see what sort of a start he would make in politics, Winston Churchill made his debut.[9]

In 1939 Churchill recalled that before 1914 politics was Britain's favorite spectator sport:

> This Party strife was very exciting. Millions of people in the country followed it, as they now follow the football pools. All the "stars" were known, and their values and performances appraised from week to week.
>
> When one addressed a large meeting in the country, there were, perhaps, a dozen or a score of women present; but the whole body of the hall was filled with a mass of male voters deeply interested in politics, knowing all the moves of the game, and responsive to every point.[10]

As the American expatriate Chips Channon would put it, Parliament was then "the world's greatest play house, 'La Comédie Anglaise.' "[11] And as Lloyd George observed of Churchill in 1907, "The applause of the House is the very breath of his nostrils. He is just like an actor. He likes the limelight and the approbation of the pit."[12] That passion for grandstanding was very common among Edwardian politicians. Joseph Chamberlain, wrote G. K. Chesterton, was a "romantic actor. He has one power which is the soul of melodrama – the power of pretending, even when backed by a huge majority, that he has his back to the wall."[13]

This particular actor set off Churchill's first great libertarian crusade. In April 1902 Chamberlain dined with the "Hughligans," young Tory rebels grouped around Lord Hugh Cecil. Churchill was present, and he recorded Chamberlain's first-act curtain line:

> As he rose to leave he paused at the door, and turning said with much deliberation, "You young gentlemen have entertained me royally, and in return I will give you a priceless secret. Tariffs! They are the politics of the future, and of the near future. Study them closely and make yourself masters of them, and you will not regret your hospitality to me."[14]

Chamberlain's tariff scheme proposed to end a half-century of Free Trade, taxing imports from other nations but not from the colonies. Thus it would promote imperial unity by turning the British Empire into a kind of Common Market. Domestic industries would be protected from foreign (especially

German) competition, and customs revenues could be used to fund a system of Old Age Pensions. But tariffs would mean higher prices for food, which consumed a large section of working-class budgets.

With Churchill, that hit a raw literary nerve. In 1898, while writing *Savrola*, he had also composed a short story, "Breaking Strain," about a fantastically wealthy American trust baron and senator, a "modern Dictator," a "Napoleon of Commerce." Having bought up newspapers and politicians, he corners the wheat market, driving up prices and creating hunger in London's East End.[15] The story closely resembles D. W. Griffith's 1909 short film *A Corner in Wheat*: both cross-cut between the gloating plutocrat and an increasingly restive proletariat. The similarities between the story, the movie, and Frank Norris's 1903 novel *The Pit* probably reflect a common source of inspiration: Joseph Leiter's attempt in 1897–98 to corner the Chicago wheat market. All three works were rooted in a species of Victorian melodrama where apparently respectable businessmen are revealed to be swindlers, such as Dion Boucicault's *The Streets of London* (1864) and Tom Taylor's *The Ticket-of-Leave Man* (1863).[16] (Churchill was apparently familiar with the latter.) And in 1917, while Griffith was in London, Lloyd George suggested that he encourage Churchill to write movie scripts, recognizing the stylistic affinities between the two artists.[17]

Churchill recoiled so vehemently against Chamberlain's campaign for food tariffs because he was convinced that it would promote "the great development of the Trust system, which we have seen with such striking results in the United States."[18] In the Army he had read *Wealth Against Commonwealth* (1894), in which the muckraking American journalist Henry Demarest Lloyd exposed the crimes of the Standard Oil Company. As he recalled in 1936:

> It made a profound impression on me. It roused me to anger against the oil magnates and against great trusts. There was set out in scathing argument the methods by which the Standard Oil attained a monopoly position. The ruthless war that Rockefeller waged against his rivals, the callousness with which he exploited the producers of the oil he turned into gold, are all recounted. I read how the railroads were cajoled or browbeaten or blackmailed into playing Standard's game of illegal rebates and drawbacks; how they were forced to become the Standard's spies, I read how, cynically and systematically, politicians, public officials and the trusted employees of other companies were corrupted and debauched. Behind all this lay the trail of businesses ruined, homes wrecked, lives broken and the ever-swelling power of Standard Oil.[19]

Churchill had also read *When the Sleeper Wakes*, in which H. G. Wells envisioned a future where one behemoth corporation literally owns half the world.

And in 1906, for the first issues of T. P. O'Connor's journal *P. T. O.*, Churchill would write a lengthy two-part review of Upton Sinclair's *The Jungle*. He hailed it as a devastating exposé, written in "exquisite detail and with a ruthlessness of purpose which certainly leave nothing to be desired from an artistic point of view," and he quoted at length Sinclair's most stomach-churning passages. True, the author was "a thorough and unshrinking Socialist," and Churchill was not: he believed that incremental liberal factory legislation would spare Britain the worst abuses of American capitalism. But all the same, *The Jungle* was a "really excellent and valuable piece of work. . . . It pierces the thickest skull and the most leathery heart. It forces people who never think about the foundations of society to think and wonder."[20]

The British Cabinet discussed Chamberlain's tariff proposal on 21 October 1902 and was mostly favorable towards it, despite the opposition of the Chancellor of the Exchequer, Charles Thomson Ritchie. Just two days later, Churchill launched a pre-emptive strike in a speech at Oldham. Tariffs, he warned, were an invitation to political corruption. Various industries would demand special protection for themselves and would work to elect MPs who would secure those favors for them. "The lobbies of the House of Commons would be crowded with touts and concession-hunters. . . . Rivers of money would flow into the war chest of the ministers who were prepared to protect certain great, important, well organized and progressive trades. We would grow millionaires throughout the country just as we grew hothouse flowers."[21] That last sentence was a dig at Chamberlain, whose hobby was raising orchids. In subsequent speeches, Churchill continued to hammer away at the theme that Protectionism was a swindle promoted by a cabal of big landowners, plutocrats, and bought-and-paid-for journalists.[22]

In 1901 he had reviewed Seebohm Rowntree's pioneering sociological study *Poverty: A Study of Town Life*, arguing that the condition of the poor was a moral disgrace: "Although the British Empire is so large, they cannot find room to live in it; although it is so magnificent, they would have had a better chance of happiness if they had been born cannibal islanders of the Southern seas; although its science is so profound, they would have been more healthy if they had been subjects of Hardicanute."[23] Churchill used Rowntree to demonstrate that even modest taxes on food would starve those living on the margins of destitution.[24] He further warned that Chamberlain's scheme of tariffs would betray Britain's obligations to the Indian people, who owed their well-being to free trade with the mother country. "That [India's] markets should be free and her people prosperous and contented is absolutely vital to Lancashire trade," he proclaimed. "India is a great trust for which we are responsible. . . . The lives, liberties, and progress towards civilization – towards a better and happier life – of nearly 300 million souls are in our hands."[25]

Churchill was no Malthusian, at least not at this point. He sincerely (if melodramatically) argued that Free Trade could raise living standards for King Edward VII's poorest subjects, at home and in the colonies. Primarily for that reason, on 31 May 1904 he crossed the floor of the House of Commons to join the Liberal Party. The Conservatives, he proclaimed, had become "a party of great vested interests, banded together in a formidable confederation; corruption at home, aggression to cover it up abroad; the trickery of tariff juggles, the tyranny of a party machine . . . dear food for the million, cheap labour for the millionaire."[26]

"Many people are frightened at the Independent Labour Party," he told a Scottish Liberal rally in November 1904. "There is much more to fear from the Independent Capitalist Party. (Cheers)" He charged that of fifty-five ministers in the current government, thirty-one held a total of sixty-eight company directorships, and that a protectionist cabal was buying up independent newspapers and converting them to Tariff Reform organs. Great Britain was becoming a nation where "Nothing is esteemed except money, nothing accounted except a bank account. Quality, education, civic distinction, public virtue, are valued less and less. We have in London an important section of people who go about preaching the gospel of Mammon advocating 10 per cent commandments – who raise each day the inspiring prayer 'give us cash in our time, O Lord.' "[27]

Churchill warned that a socialist government in Britain would restrict individual rights, including the right to strike. But he also affirmed (in 1904) that "If I were in Germany I would be a socialist myself," because there socialism represented a protest against militarism and imperial despotism.[28] His 1906 speech "Liberalism and Socialism" was a classic manifesto of the "New Liberalism," which steered a middle course between collectivism and pure laissez-faire, advocating civil liberties accompanied by state welfare measures, municipal services, and public ownership of monopolies.[29] In 1908 he defended trade unions on the ground that they represented "the antithesis of Socialism. They are undoubtedly individualistic organizations, more in the character of the old Guilds, and much more in the direction of the culture of the individual, than they are in that of the smooth and bloodless uniformity of the masses."[30] Churchill always hated the bureaucratic, regimented, controlling aspects of socialism; he was far more open-minded when socialists proposed to redistribute wealth and protect workers. In 1908 Sidney and Beatrice Webb found him gratifyingly receptive, even "obsequious," when they laid out their proposals for addressing unemployment.[31] He later favorably cited the works of Sidney Webb on factory legislation.[32] Even his notorious 1945 election broadcast, where he warned that a Labour government could only rule through "some kind of Gestapo," also promised that the Conservatives would control or break up monopolies.

If Churchill's melodramatic rhetoric provoked eye-rolling in sophisticated circles, it still had popular appeal among the masses. Long after it went out of fashion in the West End, melodrama continued to draw audiences in more plebeian venues. Melodrama is the theatre of crisis, and for the comfortable and affluent, who live lives largely insulated from real crises, it seems overwrought and divorced from reality. But for the Edwardian working classes, melodrama was documentary. Factory explosions, grinding employers, drunken fathers, dying children, and gentlemanly sexual adventurers were all part of their everyday experience. They had sons or mates who were languishing in prison or fighting colonial wars. As G. K. Chesterton explained in 1909, compared with modernist realism:

> melodrama is much more like life. It is much more like man, and especially the poor man. It is very banal and very inartistic when a poor woman at the Adelphi says, "Do you think I will sell my own child?" But poor women in the Battersea High Road do say, "Do you think I will sell my own child?". . . . It is very stale and weak dramatic art (if that is all) when the workman confronts his master and says, "I'm a man." But a workman does say "I'm a man" two or three times every day. . . . And if we wish to lay a firm basis for any efforts to help the poor, we must not become realistic and see them from the outside. We must become melodramatic, and see them from the inside. The novelist must not take out his notebook and say, "I am an expert." No; he must imitate the workman in the Adelphi play. He must slap himself on the chest and say, "I am a man."[33]

That was Churchill's method. And in the 1906 General Election, when he stood as a Liberal for North West Manchester, he established himself as a star political performer. He even drew media attention away from the Prime Minister, Arthur Balfour, who was defending another seat in the same city. Churchill had become the kind of celebrity who is recognized by his first name alone, as the *Daily Mail* reported:

> "WINSTON"
> MORE INTERESTING THAN FREE TRADE
> MANCHESTER FASCINATED
> HIS JU-JITSU
> HE SETS A FASHION IN HATS
>
> There is no question about it; the public interest of Manchester in the General Election is centred and focussed on the personality of Mr. Winston Churchill. You can hardly see the rest of the political landscape for this dominant figure. . . . You hear more talk in Manchester of "Winston" than

> of Free Trade. . . . He appeals to their sporting sense. "It isn't so much his politics, it's his Ju-Jitsu that I like", said a citizen today. . . . They discuss his various attributes; his mammoth posters with "Winston Churchill" in letters five feet high, his alliterative habit . . . his book, his clothes. He is wearing a new old-fashioned hat, a flat-topped sort of felt hat and already the hatters are having inquiries for articles of that pattern.[34]

Turn-of-the-century writers and artists advertised themselves through eccentric costumes and props: Oscar Wilde's green carnation, Mark Twain's brilliant white suit, Robert Louis Stevenson's velvet jacket, Aubrey Beardsley's floppy ties, George Bernard Shaw's Jaeger suit, G. K. Chesterton's swordstick and flamboyant hats, Augustus John's capes.[35] Even in the gray 1930s and 1940s, Churchill dressed like an Edwardian dandy, with his polka-dot bow tie, Homburg hat, silver-tipped walking stick, and cigars. In his 1931 essay "Cartoons and Cartoonists" he argued that "One of the most necessary features of a public man's equipment is some distinctive mark which everyone learns to look for and recognize." Joseph Chamberlain had his monocle, Stanley Baldwin his pipe, and (he might have added) Lord Randolph his handlebar moustache. Winston professed to be above resorting to such props – but, he sighed, the media had invented one for him. During an election campaign he once borrowed an ill-fitting hat, and:

> Ever since, the cartoonists and paragraphists have dwelt on my hats; how many they are; how strange and queer; and how I am always changing them; and what importance I attach to them, and so on. It is all rubbish, and it is all founded on a single photograph. Well, if it is a help to these worthy gentlemen in their hard work, why should I complain? Indeed, I think I will convert the legend into a reality by buying myself a new hat on purpose![36]

The difficulty was that portraying Churchill in an array of silly hats conveyed the wrong image. It suggested flippancy and inconsistency, flitting from ministry to ministry – and from party to party. For communicating bulldog resolution, the cigar was far more effective.

Ju-jitsu is the martial art of turning an attacker's energy against himself, and Churchill certainly deployed that strategy against the Conservatives. His opponent, William Joynson-Hicks, distributed a pamphlet listing statements Churchill had made when he was still following the Tory party line. Churchill disposed of that with a striking melodramatic gesture. He produced the pamphlet at a rally, admitted that the quotations were accurate, scathingly repudiated his former views, and then (to hearty cheers) tore up the pamphlet and threw it away.[37] He won with a handsome majority. Nationwide the

Conservatives were smashed, saving just 157 seats to 377 for the Liberals, 53 for the new Labour Party, and 83 Irish Nationalists. The Liberal government now had a clear mandate to enact social reform. Free Trade had been saved (for the time being). And Churchill's celebrity grew apace: by November 1907 *Punch* was running a "Winston day by day" column.

In November 1930, following the success of *My Early Life*, Churchill seriously proposed to Charles Scribner, his American publisher, that he write a sequel about his battle with the Tory Party over Free Trade. Though it would offer readers "no violent adventures in action," Churchill was sure that it would be every bit as thrilling as his accounts of colonial wars or his hair-breadth escape from the Boers. One might well wonder why Americans would take any interest in an ancient British political controversy, especially as they had just enacted the staggeringly high Smoot-Hawley Tariff. Why, for that matter, would Churchill want to reopen old wounds with the Conservative Party, which he had since rejoined? The answer may lie in his proposed title: *A Parliamentary Drama*. It had been one of his most glorious performances, even if Free Trade, as a political script, was no longer stageworthy.[38]

The Liberal Party was Churchill's natural home. Not only was it the party of Free Trade, freedom of the press, and freedom in general: it was the party of literature. A small host of authors, critics, public intellectuals, and "men of letters" served with Churchill as Liberal MPs: Hilaire Belloc, James Bryce, R. B. Haldane, John Morley, A. E. W. Mason, C. F. G. Masterman, Augustine Birrell, Herbert Paul, J. M. Robertson.[39] In his early life Herbert Asquith had written criticism for the *Spectator*, and as Prime Minister (in summer 1911) he did something unprecedented: he staged plays at 10 Downing Street. The occasion was a party for the new King and Queen, and both dramas were highly relevant to the politics of the day: J. M. Barrie's feminist one-acter *The Twelve-Pound Look* and the final act of Shaw's *John Bull's Other Island*. (The King asked whether the latter had been "written for the occasion" – and Shaw, who was present, was too polite to correct him.)[40]

In October 1907 a campaign against theatrical censorship was launched with a revival of *The Devil's Disciple* starring Harley Granville-Barker, whose own play *Waste* had recently been blocked by the Lord Chamberlain's Office. Churchill lent his name to a published petition supporting that campaign, along with his mother, Max Beerbohm, Roger Fry, H. Rider Haggard, Bertrand Russell, and Sidney and Beatrice Webb.[41] In 1910 he even proposed to find a parliamentary seat for Granville-Barker.[42] For Churchill, authorship was the highest expression of liberalism. With most other important twentieth-century writers, from James Joyce to Allen Ginsberg, he was convinced that in an increasingly mechanized, bureaucratized, standardized, regimented, and conformist society, the literary artist defends liberty in its purest form. Wilfred

Scawen Blunt saw in him a bohemian "*gaminerie* and contempt of the conventional" that was rare in politicians.[43] "A syndicate may compile an encyclopaedia, only a man can write a book," Churchill affirmed. "Once the human element in a book is destroyed by unsympathetic or foreign alterations, it cannot be of any real literary excellence."[44] As he told the Author's Club in February 1908:

> . . . is not the author free, as few men are free? Is he not secure, as few men are secure? The tools of his industry are so common and so cheap that they have almost ceased to have commercial value. He needs no bulky pile of raw material, no elaborate apparatus, no service of men or animals. He is dependent for his occupation upon no one but himself, and nothing outside him that matters. He is the sovereign of an empire, self-supporting, self-contained. No one can sequestrate his estates. No one can deprive him of his stock in trade; no one can force him to exercise his faculty against his will; no one can prevent him exercising it as he chooses. The pen is the great liberator of men and nations. No chains can bind, no poverty can choke, no tariff can restrict the free play of his mind. . . . Whether his work is good or bad, so long as he does his best he is happy. I often fortify myself amid the uncertainties and vexations of political life by believing that I possess a line of retreat into a peaceful and fertile country where no rascal can pursue and where one need never be dull or idle or even wholly without power. It is then, indeed, that I feel devoutly thankful to have been born fond of writing. It is then, indeed, that I feel grateful to all the brave and generous spirits who, in every age and in every land, have fought to establish the now unquestioned freedom of the pen.[45]

Having affirmed radical freedom, Churchill turned to the second great existential question: Death. One difficulty with individualism is that individuals eventually cease to exist. Churchill's secularism ruled out the possibility of personal immortality – except through the vehicle of literature. "Words are the only things which last forever," he declaimed. "The most durable structures raised in stone by the strength of man, the mightiest monuments of his power, crumble into dust, while the words spoken with fleeting breath, the passing expression of the unstable fancies of his mind, endure not as echoes of the past, not as mere archaeological curiosities or venerable relics, but with a force and life as new and strong, and sometimes far stronger than when they were first spoken, and leaping across the gulf of three thousand years, they light the world for us today."[46] Those who submerge themselves in some larger organization (a Church, a nation, a party, an ideology, a regiment) can take comfort in the fact that the collective will outlive them. Those who value their own autonomy must realize that someday their freedom will end forever – unless they use that freedom to create something permanent. Every word Churchill wrote, and every battle he fought for free expression, was a blow struck against personal annihilation.

In the new government, Churchill became Under-Secretary of State for the Colonies (in December 1905), serving the Colonial Secretary, the Ninth Earl of Elgin. The Ninth Earl sent Churchill the memoirs of his father, the Eighth Earl, which illustrated how Canada had been guided toward self-government, following the recommendations of Lord Durham (the Ninth Earl's maternal grandfather).[47] Of course only "white" colonies were meant to have that kind of independence, but during his tenure at the Colonial Office Churchill was genuinely (and, from Elgin's perspective, unsettlingly) protective of non-white peoples, in the spirit of Macaulay and any number of stage heroes.

Churchill was more critical than Elgin of the use of indentured Chinese laborers in South Africa. He was particularly outraged when they were flogged, while Elgin was inclined to think that the practice was "in the interest of the coolies." Given that there were few Chinese women in South Africa, the floggings were often administered for what one MP called "systematic unnatural vice." Churchill responded to that charge with a mischievousness that can only be called Wildean. He granted that some of the Chinese were "catamites" – a term never before used in Parliament, according to the word-searchable *Hansard*. (The shorthand recorder, out of ignorance or shock, wrote it down as "Amalekite.") But where other MPs warned against the moral "contamination of the native population, who were learning to look lightly upon this class of offence," Churchill reassured them that these "particular forms of vice had long prevailed among the native tribes in South Africa . . . even to a greater extent than it prevailed among the Chinese coolies." At any rate, how could one recognize a practitioner of "sodomy" (another word rarely spoken in the House of Commons)? The clues were "perhaps only of a character to be understood by those who dealt in such matters and not by others who had no sympathy or agreement with them."[48] It was all probably a wicked allusion to the accusations he had faced a decade earlier.

In 1906, when the government of Natal cracked down severely on native unrest, it was Churchill who came to the natives' defense. He scathingly denounced the imposition of martial law ("preposterous") and censorship ("pure folly"). The Natal Cabinet came close to resigning, protesting that Whitehall was meddling in the internal affairs of a self-governing colony. By the end of the year they had killed 3,000 Africans, imprisoned 4,000, and made plans to deport 25 ringleaders. When the latter were sent to St. Helena, Churchill made sure that they were fed properly, though Elgin questioned whether the dietary standards maintained for English prison inmates should apply to Africans. And when Churchill minuted that the "disgusting butchery of natives" illustrated "the kind of tyranny against which these Zulus have been struggling," Elgin urged him to be more charitable: "Where there are small white communities in the midst of large coloured populations, the former are liable to panics. But that does not mean the Government is tyrannous."[49]

Sometimes Churchill's interventions approximated the theatre of the absurd. Sekgoma, the despotic chief of the Batawana in Bechuanaland, had been jailed and replaced with a more legitimate claimant to the throne, as most of his tribe wished. To avoid further trouble, it was proposed to deport Sekgoma, prompting Churchill to pen a rare tour de force among bureaucratic memoranda:

> We cannot imprison him or deport him without flat violation of every solid principle of British justice. As at present advised I could not undertake even to attempt a defence of the lawless deportation of an innocent man upon an informal *lettre de cachet*. If we are going to embark on this sort of law-breaking and autocratic action, where are we going to stop? What kind of injustice is there that would not be covered by precedents of this kind?

Then the satire shifted to a high Swiftian plane:

> If we are going to take men who have committed no crime, and had no trial, and condemn them to life-long imprisonment and exile in the name of "State policy" why stop there? Why not poison Sekgoma by some painless drug? No argument, that will not justify his deportation to the Seychelles, will not also sustain his removal to a more sultry clime. If we are to employ medieval processes, at least let us show medieval courage and thoroughness. Think of the expense that would be saved. A dose of laudanum, costing at the outside five shillings, is all that is required. There would be no cost of maintenance, no charges for transportation, no legal difficulties, no need to apply to the Portuguese, no fear of habeas corpus. Without the smallest money or expense the peace of the Protectorate would be secured, and a "dangerous character" obnoxious to the Government, removed.

If this was meant as a joke, it escaped Lord Elgin. Everyone in the Colonial Office knew that native troublemakers sometimes had to be disposed of – especially when, as in this case, their fellow natives wanted them out of the way. And here was Churchill pounding the table on behalf of this scoundrel, as if he were an African Dreyfus. Historian Ronald Hyam was astonished by this episode, and struggled to explain it. "It is doubtful whether there could be found anywhere in the history of British government a more audacious minute than this," he began. "It is a splendidly written piece of prose," he granted, even if it irresponsibly whipped up a storm over a very petty tyrant. In fact it sounds like a speech ripped from a melodrama. *The English Rose*, after all, was also about an unjustly condemned colonial subject. And that was a consistent pattern: Churchill would use memoranda as a stage for acting out, and Elgin would try to rein him in. Most Colonial Office business was routine, but Churchill tended to treat even minor questions as deeply dramatic. As Hyam concluded: "Churchill exaggerated the importance of everything he touched. Every speck on the horizon, he assumed, would turn out to be a Cunarder, not a cockleshell. As a result of historical instincts and histrionic tendencies, he treated too many issues indiscriminately as matters of fundamental concern or historic significance. If important issues did not exist he would invent them." The results could sometimes be farcical, but "Nobody ever contrived to get so much fun out of official business as Churchill."[50]

For all his histrionics, Churchill worked honestly and effectively to help those at the bottom of the social pyramid, in the colonies and at home. As President of the Board of Trade (from April 1908) he promoted three key pieces of legislation. The Trade Boards Act created joint labor-management panels to establish minimum wages in sweated industries. The Labour Exchange Act founded what became a hallowed British institution, local bureaux matching unemployed workers with potential employers. Churchill would also play a major role in creating the 1911 National Insurance Act, which provided unemployment benefits and medical insurance to many (but by no means all) workers, paid for by contributions from the government, employers, and the employees it covered. Together with Lloyd George, Churchill was a prime mover behind the foundation of Britain's welfare state. Here there was no gap between political theatre and political reality. And yet, in December 1905, when he wandered into the slums of Manchester with Eddie Marsh, he was struck above all by the aesthetic poverty: "Fancy living in one of these streets – never seeing anything beautiful – never eating anything savoury – *never saying anything clever!*"[51]

Churchill moved to the Home Office on 19 February 1910. On the 21st he attended the opening night of John Galsworthy's prison play *Justice*, together with Evelyn Ruggles-Brise. As chairman of the Prison Commission, Ruggles-Brise had overseen some important penal reforms. He thought that Galsworthy's denunciation of solitary confinement was too sweeping,[52] but Churchill wrote to thank the playwright

> for the excellent valuable support you have given me in the public Press. There can be no question that your admirable play bore a most important

> part in creating that atmosphere of sympathy and interest which is so noticeable upon this subject at the present time. So far from feeling the slightest irritation at newspaper comments assigning to you the credit of prison reform, I have always felt uncomfortable at receiving the easily-won applauses which come to the heads of great departments whenever they have ploughed with borrowed oxen and reaped where they have not sown. In this case I can only claim a personal interest which has led me to seek the knowledge of others.[53]

Justice was certainly not the sole factor that impelled Churchill to reform the prisons. His own experiences as a prisoner of war had implanted a keen sensitivity to the issue. His predecessor at the Home Office, Herbert Gladstone, had already reduced terms of solitary confinement, and public opinion was clearly moving in the direction of reform. But Churchill knew that public opinion was shaped by writers like Galsworthy,[54] and he took full advantage of the more liberal climate: making it easier for persons convicted of minor offenses (mainly drunkenness) to avoid prison by paying fines; dramatically reducing imprisonment of adolescents for misdemeanors (offenses, as Churchill noted, which were usually treated much more leniently when committed by Oxford and Cambridge students); improving supervision and assistance of released convicts; and further limiting solitary confinement.[55] That last issue, he told the House of Commons on 20 July 1910, "has been brought before our notice by various able writers in the Press, and exponents of the drama, who have with force and feeling brought home to the general public the pangs which the prisoner may suffer in long months of solitude." And then, summing up his reforms, he turned on the assembled honorable gentlemen:

> We must not forget that when every material improvement has been effected in prisons, when the temperature has been rightly adjusted, when the proper food to maintain health and strength has been given, when the doctors, chaplains, and prison visitors have come and gone, the convict stands deprived of everything that a free man calls life. We must not forget that all these improvements, which are sometimes salves to our consciences, do not change that position. The mood and temper of the public in regard to the treatment of crime and criminals is one of the most unfailing tests of the civilisation of any country. A calm and dispassionate recognition of the rights of the accused against the State, and even of convicted criminals against the State, a constant heart-searching by all charged with the duty of punishment, a desire and eagerness to rehabilitate in the world of industry all those who have paid their dues in the hard coinage of punishment, tireless efforts towards the discovery of curative and regenerating processes, and an

> unfaltering faith that there is a treasure, if you can only find it, in the heart of every man – these are the symbols which in the treatment of crime and criminals mark and measure the stored-up strength of a nation, and are the sign and proof of the living virtue in it.[56]

Would any politician today dare say that? Convinced that literature could rehabilitate, Churchill improved prison libraries and introduced theatrical performances and lectures. "Books, lectures, entertainments, help a prisoner to feel that he is still a man," he wrote in a 1938 retrospective. "They remind him, not only of what he has forfeited by crime, but also of what he may regain by honesty."[57] Churchill told Violet Asquith that those reforms were driven by the literary deprivation he suffered in a Boer prison. "I asked what books he thought they would enjoy," she recalled, "and he trotted out several old favorites from his first days of self-education at Bangalore, headed by Gibbon and Macaulay." Violet was naturally skeptical: "If you had just committed murder would you feel inclined to read Gibbon?" Churchill granted that if he was to be hanged in the morning he would probably not embark on *The Decline and Fall of the Roman Empire*. "But for robbery with violence, arson, rape," Gibbon might be just the ticket.[58]

Churchill also reformed probation for prisoners released early for good behavior. Now they would report regularly to prisoners' aid societies rather than to the police, a policy that carried less stigma for ex-convicts trying to reintegrate into society. This issue, he noted in a 1938 memoir, had been addressed in the Victorian melodrama *The Ticket-of-Leave Man*.[59] And it is just possible that one other literary work drove Churchill to reform the prisons, a work which, in 1910, he might have hesitated to mention in a parliamentary speech. Throughout his career Churchill received unsolicited books from well-wishers, and normally his thank-you notes were perfunctory, but one of them, sent in January 1945, stands out as exceptionally effusive. Evidently donated by a French bibliophile, Churchill called the volume "exquisite . . . illustrated with such skill and discernment," a gift of "the highest value. . . . In sending you my warmest thanks, I should like to say how honoured I feel that you should have thought the presentation of this book to me a sufficient justification for robbing yourself of what must surely be one of the most treasured works in your collection." It was Oscar Wilde's *The Ballad of Reading Gaol*.[60]

Churchill tried unsuccessfully to include a provision for sterilization of the "feeble-minded" in the Mental Deficiency Act of 1913. He was influenced by a pamphlet praising a program for involuntary sterilization of "degenerates" in Indiana, which, in 1907, had become the first American state to adopt such a policy. This was another example of Churchill's eagerness to embrace new technologies, in this case profoundly misguided. But he counterintuitively argued for sterilization on libertarian grounds. It could, he insisted, permit the de-institutionalization of those mental inmates who

> are abnormal only in the weakness of their self-control. . . . For my part I think it is cruel to shut up numbers of people in institutions, to them at any rate little better than prisons, for their whole lives, if by a simple surgical operation they could be permitted to live freely in the world without causing much inconvenience to others. I certainly do not look forward to that millennium for which some scientists appear to hanker when the majority of the human race will be permanently confined within the walls of state-maintained institutions, attended by numerous doctors, and guarded by legions of warders.[61]

Churchill played a star role in the escalating series of political crises of 1910–14 – and in George Dangerfield's classic account of those feverish years, *The Strange Death of Liberal England* (1935). In 1909, to pay for expanding welfare measures and an accelerating naval arms race with Germany, Lloyd George introduced his "People's Budget". It increased inheritance taxes, added an income supertax in the higher brackets, and created some modest taxes on land. All of these taxes targeted the wealthy: the British central government, for the first time, was deliberately redistributing wealth from the rich to the poor. The House of Lords rejected the budget, an act of dubious constitutionality. Asquith fought two general elections, in January and December 1910, the first to pass the budget, the second to enact the Parliament Bill, under which the House of Lords would have the power only to delay (not block) legislation approved by the House of Commons. Both elections resulted in a virtual dead heat between the Liberals and Conservatives, with the Labour and Irish parties holding the balance. The Irish Nationalists agreed to support the Parliament Bill in return for a Home Rule bill. The Conservatives saw an immediate threat to their three most cherished principles: the power of the aristocracy, the wealth of the wealthy, and the union with Ireland. Heretofore they could always rely on the House of Lords to serve as a brake on reform: now, however, that safeguard against democracy might be disabled. The resulting panic enflamed parliamentary politics to a degree never seen during the Victorian "age of equipoise."

If necessary, Asquith was prepared to insist that the King create more than four hundred new Liberal peers, who would pack the House of Lords and vote to approve the Parliament Bill. Faced with the alternative of opening up the world's most exclusive club, Balfour advised the Conservative leadership to give way. Those "die-hard" peers who were determined to "fight to the last ditch" were indulging in melodrama, though he conceded that their posturing might have some publicity value:

> I regard the policy which its advocates call "fighting to the last" as essentially theatrical, though not on that account necessarily wrong. It does nothing, it can do nothing; it is not even intended to do anything, except advertise the situation. . . . Their policy may be a wise one, but there is nothing heroic about it; and all the military metaphors which liken the action of the "fighting" Peers to Leonidas at Thermopylae seem to me purely for Music Hall consumption.
>
> I grant that the Music Hall attitude of mind is too widespread to be negligible. By all means play up to it, if the performance is not too expensive. If the creation of X Peers pleases the multitude, and conveys the impression that the Lords are "game to the end", I raise no objection to it, *provided it does not swamp the House of Lords. . . .*[62]

The Lords finally capitulated, by a vote of 131 to 119. The margin of victory might have been larger if the peers had known that Asquith planned to ennoble J. M. Barrie, Anthony Hope, Bertrand Russell, and Thomas Hardy.[63] Churchill went so far as to propose a peerage for arch-anti-imperialist Wilfrid Scawen Blunt.[64] Desperate times called for desperate measures.

Lloyd George had described his budget as "a war budget . . . to wage implacable war on poverty and squalidness." Like another "war on poverty", in another country in another decade, it was followed by an irruption of social unrest. Militant suffragettes heckled MPs, smashed shop windows, slashed paintings in public galleries, firebombed letterboxes, went on prison hunger strikes, and (clearly crossing the line) poured acid on golf links. An unprecedented crescendo of strikes – conducted by South Wales miners, London dockers, Dublin transport workers, Southampton seamen, Bermondsey women jam workers, and railwaymen nationwide – at times threatened to paralyze the national economy. To block Home Rule, Ulster Protestants organized a private army of 100,000 men, backed by the Conservative Party. In response, Irish nationalists recruited a still larger volunteer force, and by 1914 Ireland was on the verge of civil war.

Churchill was neither opposed in principle to women's suffrage nor an enthusiastic supporter, and was never much interested in the subject. On this issue he did not challenge Asquith, who stalled and resisted the suffragettes as much as he could. Christabel Pankhurst disrupted one of Churchill's rallies, and two suffragists (one female, one male) tried to attack him with whips. His ambivalence is manifest in what was practically his only written commentary on feminism, a 1934 essay on John Stuart Mill's *On the*

Subjection of Women. He granted that we need only compare Mill's "prescient thoughts with what we see around us every day to realize how gigantic has been the enfranchisement which has occurred." However, the entry of women into the professions and the factories contributed to high unemployment among men, and it was having a "grave and far-reaching" impact on sex, marriage, and the family. "Nevertheless one must regard it as one of the greatest enrichments and liberations that have ever taken place in the whole history of the world."[65]

Given the frenzied political climate of the pre-war years, what is remarkable is how far Churchill was able to keep his head. More often than not he was a focused and sensible leader who enacted valuable legislation and managed crises well. Robert Rhodes James gave him credit for coolly handling strikes in the South Wales coalfields in 1910 and the London docks in 1911. But Churchill misread the rail strike of 1911 as an insurrectionary threat, mobilizing 50,000 armed troops. "The important point was Churchill's instruction that the military commanders were to ignore the regulation that forbade the use of the military unless it was specifically requested by the civil authority," James objected. "This was a very serious abrogation of control by the Home Secretary, whose consequences could have been alarming."[66]

On more than one occasion, Churchill was carried away by the revolutionary spirit of the times. During their battle over the "People's Budget," he dined with C. F. G. Masterman and Lloyd George, and (Masterman's wife recalled):

> . . . they began talking wildly, absolutely in fun, of the revolutionary measures they were proposing next: the guillotine in Trafalgar Square; and nominating for the first tumbrel. Winston, whose sense of humour is not very quick, became more and more indignant and alarmed, until they suggested this would give him a splendid opportunity of fighting as the second Napoleon of the revolutionary forces, when, still perfectly serious, Winston, as George put it, seemed to think there was something in it. "If this is what it leads to, you must be prepared for me to leave you!" Churchill emoted. "You are at the bottom of all this revolutionary talk, Masterman!"[67]

A more notorious episode began 16 December 1910, when police surprised anarchist burglars who were tunneling into a Houndsditch jewelry shop. In the ensuing battle three police officers were killed and two wounded, a truly shocking event in the tranquil Edwardian era, when homicides were extremely rare. Not until 1966 would the police again suffer such casualties. The perpetrators were later pursued to 100 Sidney Street in the East End, where they barricaded themselves and once again shot at the police, fatally wounding one of the officers. Alerted by telephone, Churchill interrupted copying a long letter to Asquith on strategies for overthrowing the House of Lords and the Conservative Party. He sent in Scots Guards from the Tower of London and authorized the deployment of the Horse Artillery, though the latter were not used. In fact the police, who had only revolvers and were under automatic pistol fire, needed more weaponry. Churchill proceeded to Sidney Street to observe the confrontation himself. He did not interfere with the police, though when the house caught fire he supported their decision to let it burn. After the blaze burned out, the police entered the ruins and found just two dead bodies, one shot and one asphyxiated.

"It was a striking scene in a London street," Churchill excitedly told Asquith immediately afterwards, "firing from every window, bullets chipping the brickwork, police & Scots Guards armed with loaded weapons, artillery jingling up etc." A newsreel of the incident was made and shown to London audiences, who roundly jeered Churchill.[68] He was not displeased with the publicity, though some of his political colleagues certainly were. "What the hell have you been up to, Winston?" shrieked Charles Masterman. "*Now* Charlie," Churchill lisped. "Don't be croth. It was such fun."[69] It was a lark because Churchill had a chance to act out a melodrama that he had written: *Savrola* is a novel of revolution, anarchists, and dramatic urban street fighting. At Sidney Street, it seemed for an uncanny moment that reality was paralleling the fictional narrative that Churchill had created years before: on cue, he leapt into his role and followed his script. He was proud enough of the affair to rehearse the story in a 1924 magazine article, retelling it as a terrorism thriller. He conceded that there was no good reason for him to leave his desk at the Home Office, where he could have received all the information he needed and dispatched any necessary instructions, but he was eager to watch "the closing scenes of the drama."[70]

When politics is theatre, the substance matters less than the script. Often Churchill was a prisoner of his own rhetoric, willing to adopt almost any ideological stance as long as it offered an opportunity for a great solo performance. In 1910 he was inclined to favor the Conciliation Bill (Women's Suffrage), though it would have only enfranchised some property-owning women, who were likely to vote Conservative. Then Charles Masterman ran past him the "rhetorical points" against the bill. "Winston began to see the opportunity for a speech on these lines, and as he paced up and down the room, began to roll off long phrases," recalled Lucy Masterman. "By the end of the morning he was convinced that he had always been hostile to the Bill and that he had already thought of all these points himself."[71] As Charles Masterman explained it, Churchill arrived at policy decisions not through any ploddingly rational process, but through something more like artistic inspiration:

> In nearly every case an *idea* enters his head from outside. It then rolls round the hollow of his brain, collecting strength like a snowball. Then, after whirling winds of *rhetoric*, he becomes convinced that it is *right*; and denounces everyone who criticizes it. He is in the Greek sense a Rhetorician, the slave of the words which his mind forms around ideas. He sets ideas to Rhetoric as musicians set theirs to music. And he can convince himself of almost every truth if it is once allowed thus to start on its wild career through his rhetorical machinery.[72]

In 1913 the journalist A. G. Gardiner recognized that Churchill was a revolutionary leader in a revolutionary era:

> He is the unknown factor in politics. . . . His orbit is not governed by any known laws, but by attractions that deflect his path hither and thither. It may be the attraction of war or of peace, of social reform or of a social order – whatever it is he will plunge into it with all the schoolboy intensity of his nature. His loves may be many, but they will always have the passion of a first love. Whatever shrine he worships at, he will be the most fervid in his prayers.[73]

Like 1789, 1848, 1968, and 1989, the year 1913 was a moment when history abruptly accelerated, and anything seemed possible. Militant labor, unstoppable feminists, armed Irishmen, various schools of socialists and avant-garde artists, the young Bloomsbury Group, the bohemian eruptions reported in the *New Age* – all launched a general insurrection against Victorian certainties. In *The Strange Death of Liberal England*, George Dangerfield identified Churchill as one of the most audacious rebels of the period: "He had brought impudence to a fine art, so that his most spectacular effects in the world of politics were always achieved with an air of having thumbed his nose at all that was tardy and tedious in human affairs."[74] Gardiner considered him

> the typical child of his time. It is a time of feverish activity, of upheaval and challenge, of a world in revolt. The dams have broken down and the waters are flooding the land. The old continents are submerged, and new and strange worlds are shaping themselves before our eyes. . . . We might in these times ask daily what ancient fabric has fallen, what venerable tradition has been jettisoned, what new gospel has leapt into the saddle. . . . Labour is marching, the women are marching. Religion, politics, journalism, literature – all are seething with a new and unintelligible life. Harmony has gone out of music and beauty out of art. The Ten Commandments are challenged and the exploitation of self is elevated into a religion. . . . "Let us do something – never mind what it is, but do it." . . . Don't reflect: Act. That is the gospel.

> Into this vast turmoil Mr. Churchill plunges with the joy of a man who has found his natural element. A world in transition is a world made for him. Life is a succession of splendid sensations, of thrilling experiences. . . . He is reckless of his life and of his money, indifferent to consequences. All that matters is this magic world of which he has become the momentary possessor, and which he must devour ere the curtain is rung down on the drama and the dream.

The operative word here is "drama." In this cultural revolution politics had become performance art, to which Churchill brought

> an unusual melodramatic instinct. He is always unconsciously playing a part – an heroic part. And he is himself his most astonished spectator. He sees himself moving through the smoke of battle – triumphant, terrible, his brow clothed with thunder, his legions looking to him for victory, and not looking in vain. He thinks of Napoleon; he thinks of his great ancestor. Thus did they bear themselves; thus, in this rugged and awful crisis, will he bear himself. It is not make-believe, it is not insincerity; it is that in that fervid and picturesque imagination there are always great deeds afoot with himself cast by destiny in the Agamemnon rôle. Hence that tendency to exaggerate a situation which is so characteristic of him – the tendency that sent artillery down to Sidney Street and, during the railway strike, despatched the military hither and thither as though Armageddon was upon us. "You've mistaken a coffee-stall row for the social revolution," said one of his colleagues to him as he pored with knitted and portentous brows over a huge map of the country on which he was marking his military dispositions. . . . His mind once seized with an idea works with enormous velocity round it, intensifies it, enlarges it, makes it shadow the whole sky. In the theatre of his mind it is always the hour of fate and the crack of doom.[75]

Gardiner concluded that Churchill's core ideology was neither Liberalism or Conservatism. It was Impressionism, the expression of his own aesthetic personality:

> He flashes through life taking impressions, swift, searching, detached. He absorbs a moral or an intellectual atmosphere as another man absorbs the oxygen of the air, and he gives it out as if it were his own vital breath. He is what the Spiritualists call a "medium" – a vehicle through which some vision, some doctrine, some enthusiasm finds temporary utterance apart from himself. No one has stated the principles of Liberalism with such breadth as he has done; no one has preached peace with more fervour, economy with

> more conviction, and social reform with a more thrilling break in the voice; or, on the other hand, presented an unexampled naval expenditure with such an adroit and disarming appearance of sad necessity. Each task, however subversive of former tasks, finds him perfectly equipped, for he always knows his subject, and convinces himself first.[76]

Churchill later confessed that he had always been a partisan of self-expression: "I have mostly acted in politics as I felt I wanted to act. When I have desired to do or say anything and have refrained therefrom through prudence, slothfulness or being dissuaded by others, I have always felt ashamed of myself at the time; though sometimes afterwards I saw that it was lucky for me I was checked." As he explained it, his repudiation of the Conservative Party was not just a matter of tariff policy, it was a healthy and vital Oedipal revolt: "The flood tides of a new generation long pent-up flowed forward with the breaking of the dikes upon the low-lying country. Of course it is a lamentable thing to leave the party which you have been brought up in from a child, and where nearly all your friends and kinsmen are. Still, I am sure that in those days I acted in accordance with my deepest feeling and with all that recklessness in so doing which belongs to youth and is indeed the glory of youth and its most formidable quality."[77]

Every Edwardian suffragette, modern poet, radical socialist, and experimental artist shared those fervors. In that restive age Churchill acquired great power and responsibility without shedding anything of the schoolboy rebel. He always hated the authoritarian left and despised the puritanical left, but at this point he was a prophet of the lyrical libertarian left. He denounced robber barons, ridiculed prudes, and battled censors. He fought to better the lives of workers and convicts. He championed oppressed Africans, Chinese laborers, and Jewish immigrants. He coolly discussed homosexuality in Parliament, as if he were addressing a Bloomsbury soirée. He adored poetry and the theatre. He proposed to elect an avant-garde director to the House of Commons and elevate an anti-imperialist intellectual to the House of Lords. At Sidney Street he was a better anarchist than the anarchists, a daring provocateur who cast aside bureaucratic protocol to hurl himself into street theatre with unforgettable éclat. As a Cabinet-level bohemian, he performed the politics of ardor and lived life as a work of art.

However, with a sudden turn in the tides of history, those same creative passions could be directed into a very different channel. "Keep your eye on Churchill," Gardiner advised his readers. "Remember, he is a soldier first, last, and always. He will write his name big on our future. Let us take care he does not write it in blood."[78]

CHAPTER 9

On the Stage of History

In the eighteenth century British naval inspections were, in fact, inspections: the King personally examined his ships to make sure they were in working order. But by the early twentieth century they had become spectacular public rituals. When the Fleet visited London between 17 and 24 July 1909, all 150 ships (except submarines) were open to civilians, and the total audience was nearly four million. Navy men frankly labeled these events "theatre" or "shows." Newspapers covered them as they might review a new play or ballet, as "spectacles" or "pageants" performed in an "amphitheatre." Attending the 1909 review "was like watching a cinematograph" exulted the *Daily Express,* and the *Daily News* thought it better than anything one could have seen "at the old Adelphi." It was all "naval theatre" sniffed the *Frankfurter Zeitung,* though the German Navy staged similar performances. And they were accompanied by a blaze of publicity: 267 journalists were accredited for the 1911 naval review, and by 1912 one cinematographer listed 371 naval films in his catalogue. As Great Britain and Germany raced to build more dreadnoughts, showmen staged miniature naval battles using model ships and dazzling special effects. The Admiralty encouraged such publicity – shrewd public relations at a time when it was requesting ever greater appropriations. And like any other form of drama, naval theatre was inevitably burlesqued. In February 1910 a young Virginia Woolf and her friends, in blackface and fake beards, impersonated an Abyssinian prince and his retinue and secured a royal tour of HMS *Dreadnought.*[1]

This context is necessary to understanding an extraordinary German diplomatic report filed 18 November 1911 by Wilhelm Widenmann, a naval attaché in London. Widenmann evidently thought it important enough to send not only to the Foreign Office and Admiral Tirpitz, but even to the Kaiser himself:

> A most reliable source tells me about the following incident which took place in the house of an influential London banker at the end of August.

> After dinner the invited ladies and gentlemen reconvened [in another room], but Mr. Churchill, who was one of the guests, abstained and read the evening news instead. A lady known for her quick-wittedness was evidently annoyed by this lack of politeness. She asked Mr. Churchill if he found politics even in the presence of ladies so interesting that he preferred the newspaper to a conversation with them. – Mr. Churchill answered very sharply that he had indeed no time for chit-chat with ladies at such a serious hour; and pointing to an article which dealt with the approaching naval review at Kiel, he continued: *Let them come, they can have war, if they want.*

The Kaiser underscored that last line and (quite reasonably) scribbled words to the effect that he had no intention of going to war.[2] Fleet reviews were regular rituals in both countries. They were a form of muscle-flexing, an arena to show off new naval hardware, but hardly equivalent to a declaration of hostilities. However, the Agadir crisis (the Second Moroccan Crisis), which in late August was still unresolved, had heightened international tensions. "Perhaps the time is coming when decisive action will be necessary," Churchill warned the Foreign Secretary, Sir Edward Grey, on the 30th.[3]

To explain his overreaction to this piece of naval theatre, we must look once again to the legitimate theatre. Military melodramas commonly opened with a ball or dinner party, to establish the calm before the storm. Then word would arrive of an impending conflict, and the officers would retire to plot strategy, a device evidently modeled on the Duchess of Richmond's ball on the eve of Waterloo. One can find such scenes in the first act of Jules Verne's *Michael Strogoff* and the seventh chapter of Churchill's *Savrola*, where the hero is explicitly compared to the Iron Duke.

As early as 1900 Churchill had warned in a speech that the Army had to prepare for a possible attack on England.[4] His apprehensions about a coming conflict were fed by a new popular literary genre that emerged in the first years of the twentieth century: fictional anticipations of an invasion of Britain. There was A. C. Curtis's *A New Trafalgar* (1902), Erskine Childers's *The Riddle of the Sands* (1903), E. Phillips Oppenheim's *A Maker of History* (1905), William Le Queux's *The Invasion of 1910* (1906), and Guy du Maurier's drama *An Englishman's Home* (1909). Occasionally the invaders were from an imaginary country, but usually they were Germans. If these stories are studied in chronological order, a clear trend emerges: they became progressively more pessimistic. In the best known of these tales, *The Riddle of the Sands*, two Englishmen in a yacht single-handedly foil the German attack. But in Captain Henry Curties's *When England Slept* (1909) the Germans conquer Britain literally overnight, assisted by what would later be called Fifth Columnists. In Saki's *When William Came* (1914), published just before the actual war, Britain has already been defeated and occupied when the story opens.[5]

Churchill knew at least a few of these novels. A couple of references suggest that he was probably familiar with *The Riddle of the Sands*.[6] He certainly read H. G. Wells's *The War in the Air*, where a German air raid against New York City triggers a global war and ultimately plunges humanity into a new Dark Age. And while it proves nothing conclusively, the similarity in titles between *When England Slept* and Churchill's own volume *While England Slept* (1938) is striking. Churchill recalled reading in 1913 "one of those nightmare novels that used to appear from time to time before the war . . . in which, to the amazement of the defeated British Fleet, the German new vessels opened fire with a terrible, unheard-of 15-inch gun." It is difficult to pin down the title of this invasion novel, simply because so many of them were published. In fact when he became First Lord of the Admiralty the largest German naval gun was just 12 inches, against 13.5 inches for the largest British gun, and Churchill initiated the successful development of a 15-inch weapon.[7]

Before Franz Ferdinand's assassination in Sarajevo, Churchill wrote two fictional future war stories. As First Lord, he was responsible for anticipating possible war scenarios. The second of these stories, drafted in April 1913 for the benefit of the Admiralty War Staff had the lurid title "The Time Table of a Nightmare". It correctly predicted that Germany would attack France through Belgium and that, in response, a British expeditionary force of six divisions would be dispatched to the Continent, but from that point on the story becomes progressively more sensational. Less than twenty-four hours after the commencement of hostilities, the Germans begin landing 45,000 infantry and supplies at Harwich, escorted by a fleet that somehow manages to carry out the invasion and return to Germany with only minor losses. Meanwhile, another German squadron sails unmolested into Scapa Flow, blocks the Pentland Firth, and then establishes a base in the Shetlands. Five zeppelins bomb the Chatham dockyards, destroying some of the naval workshops, setting off general panic among civilians, seriously disrupting war mobilization, and sinking the battleships *Canopus*, *Flory*, and *Ocean*. (Ironically, two years later two of these ships would actually be sacrificed at the Dardanelles.) British cruisers try to blockade the beachhead at Harwich but suffer heavy losses at the hands of German destroyers. Out of loyalty to its ally, the government continues to dispatch the expeditionary army to France, but with disastrous results. When (on D-plus 2) the German invasion force strikes south in the direction of London, it is opposed only by a disorganized body of territorials and a handful of regular army troops, who are scattered with devastating losses. By D-plus 6 mobs are rioting in Westminster, protesting the departure of troops to France. The

Guards are forced to fire upon the crowds, and elsewhere civilians "prevent the departure of troop trains by invading the lines, tearing up the rails, or laying themselves in front of the engines." On D-plus 8 the House of Commons votes no confidence in the government by 617 votes to 22 (evidently only the front-benchers oppose the motion), and a new ministry immediately halts the dispatch of British forces to France. By this point there is already fighting in the streets of Waltham Abbey, Romford, and Woolwich. British troops deployed to the Continent are called back, but the French refuse to provide transport. By D-plus 10 German forces in the London suburbs have been surrounded, but a few days later another invasion force slips past the British fleet and seizes Newcastle. On D-plus 14 allied armies in France, fighting on the Meuse, suffer a catastrophic defeat because much of the British expeditionary force has been held back on the other side of the Channel. And on D-plus 18 the commander of the surrounded German force in London offers to cease fighting on condition of safe passage back to Germany; otherwise he will execute the 10,000 British prisoners he holds. Facing disaster on several fronts, the British accept these terms.

Admiral Sir Henry Jackson, Chief of the War Staff, found all this "sensational," "satirical," and "alarmist."[8] It does read like one of the more laughable invasion novels. For the past decade British and German military planners had known that a German invasion of Britain was not a real possibility. A British naval exercise in the summer of 1912 had demonstrated that the Germans could have landed a force of at most 12,000 men, hardly sufficient to conquer the island, though Churchill nevertheless concluded that such raids might be attempted.[9] Reinforcing and resupplying such an invasion would have required continuous and secure control of the North Sea, which was far beyond the capacity of the German Navy.[10]

However, two years before the 1913 scenario, in response to the 1911 Agadir crisis, Churchill had sketched out, in a memorandum, sobery entitled "Military Aspect of Continental Problem," a much more realistic and accurate forecast. He predicted that the German army would advance swiftly to the gates of Paris, but then, with their supply lines over-extended and increasing Russian strength on the Eastern Front, they would be vulnerable to an Allied counterattack. Shortly after the actual war broke out, on 2 September 1914, as events on the Western Front moved to their climax, Churchill had his 1911 memorandum (but not his 1913 memorandum) reproduced and distributed to the men who were organizing the war effort. Their relief was overwhelming, and Churchill was hailed as a seer by R. B. Haldane ("extraordinarily accurate"), Arthur Balfour ("a triumph of prophecy"), Sir Ian Hamilton ("All the way down you hit the nail bang on the head as if you were a historian recapitulating rather than a statesman risking prophecies!"), and, soon to resume his duties as commander of the Royal Navy, Lord Fisher ("*It makes one trust your further forecast!*").[11] Here Churchill was a beneficiary of what has been termed the "Jeanne Dixon effect": like many clairvoyants, stock market analysts, political pundits, and military intelligence officers, he made multiple and contradictory prophecies, and then took credit when one of them proved correct.

These two scenarios illuminate three critically important points about Churchill as a warlord. First, the 1911 memo proved that he was capable of rational and farsighted military planning. Second, the 1913 memo proved that he could also fall under the spell of cheap thrillers, imagining audacious offensive strokes that kept his listeners at the edge of their seats but which had no strategic logic whatsoever. And third, when he predicted that Turkey could be knocked out of the war by an assault on the Dardanelles, the 1911 memo greatly enhanced his credibility in the War Cabinet.

In many invasion tales the attackers are assisted by resident aliens, the working assumption being that German waiters in London restaurants were all agents of the Kaiser. This was a source of the paranoia directed against Germans in Britain before and (much more so) during the war.[12] It led to the creation (in 1909) of the Secret Service Bureau, a counter-intelligence agency that later evolved into MI5. The bureau briefed Churchill (in his capacity as Home Secretary) on its counter-espionage work, and he was sufficiently enthralled to expand greatly the powers and reach of the fledgling cloak-and-dagger office. He secured measures to register aliens in peacetime and relocate or deport them in time of war. He strengthened the Official Secrets Act to outlaw any unauthorized sending or receipt of official information, and make it very easy for the prosecution to prove guilt. He expanded postal surveillance, which could now be used against political dissidents as well as suspected spies. (His successor as Home Secretary, Reginald McKenna, intercepted telegrams sent to and received by the suffragettes of the Women's Social and Political Union.) After Churchill moved to the Admiralty, he helped to set up a joint committee representing the Navy, the Army, and the newspapers to administer a system of voluntary censorship, where the press agreed not to publish sensitive information related to national security. Throughout most of his career Churchill was sincerely committed to the preservation of personal freedoms, but this spy scare, fomented largely by bad novels, also impelled him to construct the foundations of a national security establishment.[13] Too often, *When England Slept* would trump *On Liberty*.

Well after the War, in "My Own True Spy Story", Churchill conceded that "Spy-mania" had gripped the country: "No suspicions were too outrageous to be nourished, no tale too improbable to be believed, and the energies of thousands of amateur and irregular detectives reinforced at every moment and in every district the stern and unsleeping vigilance of the public authorities." And yet, he added, "In the higher ranges of Secret Service work the actual facts in many cases were in every respect equal to the most fantastic inventions of romance or melodrama. Tangle within tangle, plot and counter-plot, ruse and treachery, cross and double-cross, true agent, false agent, double agent, gold and steel, the bomb, the dagger and the firing party were interwoven in many a texture so intricate as to be incredible and yet true." Once again, Churchill was blurring the distinction between fact and fiction, which can be dangerous when powerful men read spy thrillers.[14]

Churchill greeted the outbreak of the actual war with indecent enthusiasm. Asquith wrote to Venetia Stanley that on 27 July 1914, when it momentarily appeared that the conflict might be averted, Winston "exclaimed moodily that it looked after all as if we were in for a 'bloody peace'!"[15] At midnight on 28 July Churchill wrote to his wife, Clementine, "Everything tends towards catastrophe & collapse. I am interested, geared up & happy. Is it not horrible to be built like that? The preparations have a hideous fascination for me. I pray to God to forgive me for such fearful moods of levity."[16] At 11 p.m. on 4 August, when Britain declared war, Asquith, Lloyd George, McKenna, and Grey sat in gloomy silence. Then, Lloyd George recalled, "Winston dashed into the room radiant, his face bright, his manner keen and he told us, one word pouring out on the other how he was going to send telegrams to the Mediterranean, the North Sea, and God knows where! You could see he was a really happy man. I wondered if this was the state of mind to be in at the opening of such a fearful war as this. . . ."[17] Asquith told Venetia on 14 September, "I am inclined almost to shiver when I hear Winston say that the last thing he would pray for is Peace."[18] As Winston explained to his brother Jack, they were all performing in a magnificent drama: "After all this is a gt moment in the history of the world & of our small country & we must all try to act so as to make them like to read about it in the years that will follow."[19]

As early as 21 August, Charles Hobhouse (the Postmaster General) described the First Lord's wildly impulsive behavior in the Cabinet. "Churchill jumping about from consideration to consideration, 'backing and filling' without rhyme or reason, but with incessant talk." He was already proposing war with Turkey – and even more bizarre schemes. "Greece having made us an offer of 250,000 men, her fleet and harbours, W.S.C. propounded a Napoleonic plan of forcing the Danish passage with the help of the Greeks, and convoying Russian troops to the coast off Berlin and making a *coup de théâtre*."[20] This plan presumed that the Russian Army was capable of launching a hastily improvised amphibious assault, that the Greek Army was amenable to occupying Copenhagen, and that the Danes were agreeable to hosting them. Then on 8 September Hobhouse noted that Churchill "proposed to take the Dutch Govt. 'by the throat' and force them to allow us to use the Scheldt to revictual and rearm Antwerp, to which violation of the neutrality of Dutch waters, he assured us the Dutch would not object." It was left to Hobhouse to point out that (1) there was no moral difference between the German invasion of Belgium and Churchill's proposed incursions into various other neutral countries and (2) such an act would probably bring the Netherlands into the war on the German side.[21] Later, in the context of justifying the Dardanelles operation, Churchill explained that it was precisely the maddest military schemes that had true method:

> Nearly all the battles which are regarded as masterpieces of military art, from which have been derived the foundation of states and the fame of commanders, have been battles of manoeuvre in which very often the enemy has found himself defeated by some novel expedient or device, some queer, swift, unexpected thrust or stratagem. In many such battles the losses of the victors have been small. There is required for the composition of a great commander not only massive common sense and reasoning power, not only imagination, but also an element of legerdemain, an original and sinister touch, which leaves the enemy puzzled as well as beaten.[22]

That kind of ingenious plotting is often found in unrealistic war novels, but in actual combat the results can be disastrous, farcical, or both. In order to play a role in the land war, Churchill cobbled together the Royal Naval Division from Navy personnel and enthusiastic but green recruits, and equipped them with a uniform of his own design. Captain Herbert Richmond, Assistant Director of Operations at the Admiralty, concluded "I really believe Churchill is not sane. . . . What this force is to do, Heaven only knows. . . . These men who are thus to be employed in soldiering know nothing about the business. They are all amateurs of the most marked kind. They are mostly undisciplined. . . . The whole thing is so wicked that Churchill ought to be hanged before he should be allowed to do such a thing."[23]

When German forces were on the verge of capturing Antwerp, the Royal Naval Division made its dramatic entrance. On 3 October the British Legation in the city was already burning its papers, so the war correspondent E. Alexander Powell was naturally surprised when:

> At one o'clock that afternoon a big drab-colored touring-car filled with British naval officers tore up the Place de Meir, its horn sounding a hoarse warning, took the turn into the narrow Marché aux Souliers on two wheels, and drew up in front of the hotel. Before the car had fairly come to a stop the door of the tonneau was thrown violently open and out jumped a smooth-faced, sandy-haired, stoop-shouldered, youthful-looking man in the undress

> Trinity House uniform. There was no mistaking who it was. It was the Right Hon. Winston Churchill. As he darted into the crowded lobby, which, as usual at the luncheon hour, was filled with Belgian, French, and British staff-officers, diplomatists, Cabinet Ministers, and correspondents, he flung his arms out in a nervous, characteristic gesture, as though pushing his way through a crowd. It was a most spectacular entrance and reminded me for all the world of a scene in a melodrama where the hero dashes up, bareheaded, on a foam-flecked horse, and saves the heroine or the old homestead or the family fortune, as the case may be.

The Burgomaster tried to convey the gravity of the situation to Churchill, as he dashed past. "I think everything will be all right now, Mr. Burgomaster," he said halfway up the stairs. "You needn't worry. We're going to save the city." Most of those present were reassured, "because we took it for granted that Mr. Churchill would not have made so confident and public an assertion unless ample reinforcements in men and guns were on the way," but Powell noticed that the roar of the German guns was growing ever closer.[24] He could not help but admire the courage of Churchill (who repeatedly exposed himself to enemy fire) and the Royal Naval Division. However, the men obviously lacked the necessary training and materiel: "They were, in fact, equipped very much as many of the American militia organizations were equipped when suddenly called out for strike duty in the days before the reorganization of the National Guard."[25] About 1,500 of them retreated across the Dutch border, unaware that they would then be interned for the duration. When Powell tried to warn them, "They looked at me as though I had walked into their club in Pall Mall and had spoken to them without an introduction." One Wodehousian monocled officer asked, "Why should the bally Dutchmen want to trouble us?"[26] Asquith, whose son Arthur was in the unit, complained that Churchill had hurled into battle "a callow crowd of the rawest tiros, most of whom had never fired off a rifle, while none of them had ever handled an entrenching tool." He noted that the division was manned by an exceptionally high proportion of artistic types, including Rupert Brooke and his friend, the composer William Denis Browne, "who had respectively served 1 week . . . & 1 day. It was like sending sheep to the shambles. . . . I trust that Winston will learn by experience, and now hand over to the military authorities the little circus which he is still running 'on his own'."[27]

Though the Antwerp escapade now looks like *opera bouffe*, on 7 October it generated notes of congratulation from Lloyd George ("brilliant effort") and Edward Grey ("I cant tell you how much I admire his courage & gallant spirit & genius for war"). From Lord Haldane came exactly the words that Winston wanted to hear: "A great and heroic episode – you are a figure for history."[28]

The next day the situation in Antwerp deteriorated badly, and the city had to be evacuated. But the operation delayed the German advance for a week, allowing the British time to secure the Channel ports. And sometimes sheer éclat may have real military value. According to Charles Hobhouse, hardly a friendly diarist, Lord Grey "said that a Belgian officer of some standing called on him chiefly to tell him that the visit of W.S.C. to Antwerp had been the means of reviving the spirit of the Belgian troops and inducing them to renew a struggle they had determined to abandon."[29]

However, by 23 October Lloyd George (as his secretary Frances Stevenson recorded) was "rather disgusted with Winston still about Antwerp, and thinks that the P.M. is too. Having taken untrained men over there, he left them in the lurch. He behaved in a rather swaggering way when over there, standing for photographers & cinematographers with shells bursting near him, & actually promoting his pals on the field of action."[30] Earlier that month Asquith had had a long telephone conversation with Churchill:

> who, after dilating in great detail on the actual situation, became suddenly very confidential, and implored me not to take a "conventional" view of his future. Having, as he says, "tasted blood" these last few days, he is beginning like a tiger to raven for more, and begs that sooner or later, & the sooner the better, he may be relieved of his present office & put in some kind of military command. I told him that he could not be spared from the Admiralty, but he scoffs at that, alleging that the naval part of the business is practically over, as our superiority will grow greater & greater every month. His mouth waters at the sight & thought of K[itchener]'s new armies. Are these "glittering commands" to be entrusted to "dug-out trash", bred on the obsolete tactics of 25 years ago – "mediocrities, who have led a sheltered life mouldering in military routine &c &c." For about ¼ of an hour he poured forth a ceaseless cataract of invective and appeal, & I much regretted that there was no short-hand writer within hearing – as some of his unpremeditated phrases were quite priceless. He was, however, quite three parts serious, and declared that a political career was nothing to him in comparison with military glory. ... He is a wonderful creature, with a curious dash of schoolboy simplicity ... and what someone said of genius – "a zigzag streak of lightning in the brain"....[31]

Asquith was beguiled by Churchill's poetic audacity, a fact that goes far to explain why he supported the Dardanelles operation. Andrew Bonar Law (the Leader of the Opposition) was, however, less enchanted: he granted that Churchill had "very unusual intellectual ability, but at the same time he seems to have an entirely unbalanced mind, which is a real danger at a time like this."[32]

As for Captain Richmond, on 24 October he found Churchill depressed by inaction and casting about for some scheme to bring him once again into the thick of combat: "He wanted to send battleships – old ones – up the Elbe, but for what purpose except to be sunk I did not understand."[33] That same day Asquith told Venetia Stanley that he had a "really interesting" tête-à-tête with Winston, plotting a daring and risky seaplane raid on Cuxhaven and the Kiel Canal on the north German coast. "As Winston grimly says, a lot of them will never be able to use the second half of their return tickets. But this is far the most romantic & adventurous side of modern war. . . . I like this: it is inventive & resourceful, & shows both originality and dash."[34] His wife Margot agreed:

> What is it that gives Winston his preeminence? It is certainly not his mind. I said long ago and with truth Winston has a noisy mind.
>
> Certainly not his judgment – he is constantly very wrong indeed. . . . It is of course his courage and colour – his amazing mixture of industry and enterprise. He can and does always – all ways put himself in the pool. He never shirks, hedges, or *protects* himself – though he thinks of himself perpetually. *He takes huge risks.* He is at his very best just now; when others are shrivelled with grief – apprehensive, silent, irascible and self-conscious morally; Winston is intrepid, valourous, passionately keen and sympathetic, longing to be in the trenches – dreaming of war, big, buoyant, happy, even. It is very extraordinary, he is a born soldier.[35]

Churchill and his defenders justified the Dardanelles assault as a sensible strategy for bypassing the stalemate on the Western Front, an operation that could have worked if it had been better executed. In fact it was a product of Churchill's lifelong obsession with scoring a wartime *coup de théâtre*, which (as he half admitted) can be traced back to *Savrola*. It did not really matter where the blow fell, as long as it was astonishingly unexpected. Well before the war, in early 1913, Churchill ordered the Admiralty to prepare contingency plans for amphibious assaults against Norway, Sweden, Denmark, or the Netherlands, with the objective of securing bases for a war against Germany. Later that year he proposed an assault on the German islands of Borkum, Sylt, and Heligoland. He apparently did not think seriously about the resources necessary to conduct such hazardous operations, or about the consequences of violating the neutrality of various neighboring countries, or about the dangers shore batteries posed to warships.[36] Just days after the outbreak of war Churchill talked seriously about capturing a base in the Dutch Frisian islands. "I saw that no words could check his vivid imagination & that it was quite impossible to persuade him both of the strategical & tactical futility of such an operation," recorded an exasperated Captain Richmond.[37] When that idea was scotched, Churchill's mind flitted to a scheme for a destroyer raid straight into the Heligoland Bight, Germany's backyard. "I'm unable to see what object this operation serves," protested Richmond. "It is not a reconnaissance, for there is nothing one can reconnoiter. It is not an attack, for the most it can do is cut off some isolated detachments of the enemy. It is far more likely to bump into a superior force & be cut off itself. It serves no purpose and merely loses men & ships – an amateur piece of work of a mediaeval type." Two days later that plan was dropped: "Apparently some other brilliant conception has entered into the mind of our War Lord. . . . It makes me sick to see war managed in this manner. There is not a glimmering of the main principles of employment of naval force. . . ."[38]

Churchill first proposed to invade the Dardanelles as early as late August 1914, before the Western Front had stalemated, even before Turkey entered the war. On 1 September, when the battle in France was still very much in motion and every soldier was needed to meet the German attack, he asked the General Staff to prepare a plan for capturing Gallipoli, employing a Greek army and British naval forces. He was not deterred by a discouraging response filed by Sir Charles Callwell, Director of Military Operations. "Mr. Churchill was very keen on attacking the Dardanelles from a very early stage," Callwell later testified before the Dardanelles Commission. "He was very keen to get to Constantinople somehow." Churchill argued tirelessly for the scheme, despite the skepticism of high-ranking naval advisors. Admiral Sir Percy Scott dismissed it as "an impossible task." Sir Henry Jackson, the Third Sea Lord, found that his attempts to dissuade Churchill were "not welcomed and had no effect." Fisher had profound doubts, but complained that Churchill "always out-argues me."[39] And Churchill did not allow the War Council to see an Admiralty report sharply criticizing his plans.

On 28 December, when the Western Front had deadlocked, Maurice Hankey, Secretary of the War Council, proposed to seize the straits and Constantinople, though he envisioned that Britain, France, and Russia would all pounce on Turkey with the collaboration of the Serbs, Greeks, and Bulgarians.[40] Churchill at this point preferred to attack Germany from the north, occupying Borkum and then Schleswig-Holstein, bottling up the German fleet in its ports, drawing Denmark into the war on the Allied side, interdicting the Kiel Canal, gaining naval control of the Baltic, and finally landing Russian troops within 90 miles of Berlin.[41] Admiral Sir Henry Oliver, Chief of the Admiralty War Staff, recalled that "Churchill would often look in on his way to bed to tell me how he would capture Borkum or Sylt. If I did not interrupt to ask questions he could capture Borkum in twenty minutes"[42] – disregarding the forts, minefields, torpedo boats, and submarines in the vicinity. Asquith, frustrated with the stalled Western Front, was now ready "to devise, in concert with the French & the Russians, a diversion on a great & effective scale."[43] On 31 December Lloyd George argued that an attack on Turkey would "give us a chance of winning a dramatic victory, which would encourage our people at home, whilst it would be a corresponding discouragement to our enemies. . . . It would be a great advantage from this point of view if it were in territory which appeals to the imagination of the people as a whole." But he favored landing 100,000 men in Syria to cut off Turkish forces advancing towards the Suez Canal.[44]

Increasingly dismal news from all battlefronts gave Churchill his dramatic opening. On 13 January 1915, as Hankey recalled the scene:

> The War Council had been sitting all day. The blinds had been drawn to shut out the winter evening. The air was heavy and the table presented that rather dishevelled appearance that results from a long session. I was looking forward to release from the strain of following and noting the prolonged and intense discussion. I suppose the councillors were as weary as I was. At this point events took a dramatic turn, for Churchill suddenly revealed his well-kept secret of a naval attack on the Dardanelles! The idea caught on at once. The whole atmosphere changed. Fatigue was forgotten. The War Council turned eagerly from the dreary vista of a "slogging match" on the Western Front to brighter prospects, as they seemed, in the Mediterranean. The Navy, in whom everyone had implicit confidence and whose opportunities so far had been few and far between, was to come into the front line. Even French [Sir John French, Commander-in-Chief of the British Expeditionary Force] with his enormous preoccupations caught something of the general enthusiasm.
>
> Churchill unfolded his plans with the skill that might be expected of him, lucidly but quietly and without exaggerated optimism.[45]

On 3 September 1914 General Callwell had warned Churchill "that an attack on the Gallipoli Peninsula from the sea side (outside the Straits) is likely to prove an extremely difficult operation of war." In 1906 the Committee of Imperial Defence had considered this option and rejected it as impractical, as had Churchill himself in a March 1911 Cabinet memorandum, and since then Turkish forces in the area had been considerably strengthened. Callwell concluded that an amphibious assault would require at least 60,000 men.[46] But on 6 September Churchill confidently told Edward Grey that the Ottomans could be knocked out of the war with just 50,000 troops, either Greeks or, failing that, Russians.[47] Churchill was still convinced that a purely naval assault would not work. But it soon became clear that something had to be done to support the beleaguered Russians, and the War Secretary, Lord Kitchener, insisted that he had no troops to spare. So, writes Martin Gilbert,

"Under the pressure of unforeseen events and dire possibilities Churchill took up the very plan which until then he had believed to be impossible. A naval demonstration had to be made on Russia's behalf."[48]

On 3 January 1915 Churchill had sent a telegram to Admiral Sir Sackville Carden, commander of the Allied fleet near the Straits, asking whether an assault on the Dardanelles would be feasible. Carden's guardedly affirmative reply turned the discussions of the War Council in that direction. However, Churchill pitched his query so that it would have been difficult to refuse ("Importance of results would justify severe loss"), and Carden's 5 January response was highly qualified and dubious: "I do not consider Dardanelles can be rushed. They might be forced by extended operations with large number of ships."[49] What degree of probability did "might" represent? Extended for how long? And how many ships and sailors was the First Lord prepared to lose?

With extraordinary deficits of attention, Churchill's mind continued to flit from one peripheral attack to another. On 4 January he was still arguing for an attack on Borkum, and Captain Richmond was still incredulous: "It is *quite mad*. The reasons for capturing it are NIL, the possibilities about the same. I have never read such an idiotic, amateur piece of work as this outline in my life."[50] Before the War Council on 7 January Churchill supported Sir John French's proposal for an assault on Zeebrugge. When Kitchener blocked that, Churchill reverted to his scheme to capture an offshore German island. The following day he suggested bringing the Netherlands into the war, a coup that certainly would have surprised the Germans, not to mention the Dutch.

On 11 January Carden sent Churchill a plan for gradually putting the forts out of action. It would take twelve battleships, three battlecruisers, and twelve minesweepers, plus destroyers, submarines, and an enormous supply of shells. (The fleet that was actually sent was seriously deficient in minesweepers and ammunition.) Carden estimated that this force "might do it all in a month about," first destroying the outer forts and then moving up the Straits. As Robin Prior observed, "On examination, Carden's 'plan' is seen to be hardly a plan at all but merely a statement of the order in which the Dardanelles defenoes were to be reduced." The ships would bombard the forts from beyond the range of Turkish artillery. Shot from old and worn gun barrels, only one in fifty shells would hit their targets from that distance. The Straits were also honeycombed with minefields protected by coastal batteries, and there was no clear plan for dealing with these.

Nevertheless, Churchill seized upon the proposal and presented it to the War Council on 13 January. Admiral Sir John Jellicoe (in command of the Grand Fleet) had by then discouraged any attack on Borkum, the Council decided against an assault on Zeebrugge, and no one had figured out how to persuade the Dutch to invade Germany. That left the Dardanelles. Churchill breezily assured the Council that "once the forts were reduced the minefields would be cleared and the Fleet would proceed up to Constantinople." He did not explain how, with no ground troops, the Fleet would occupy one of the largest cities in Europe. Nevertheless, the War Council warmly embraced the scheme. Planners at the Admiralty may not have been happy with it, but none of them unequivocally spoke out against it – victims of the kind of groupthink that often leads to military disaster. As Prior concluded, "They enabled Churchill, the only real enthusiast for the plan, to say to the War Council on January 13th that the Admiralty believed that Carden's proposals could lead to success." But that begs a question that baffled Prior: "Whether Churchill needed a success to salvage his flagging reputation, whether his inability to contemplate a further period of inactivity at sea led him to ride roughshod over the doubts of his naval advisers, or whether in his enthusiasm for the Carden plan he grasped only those positive aspects of their advice is not clear."[51]

The explanation may be revealed in an 8 January 1915 letter to Sir John French, in which Churchill uses a telling metaphor: "We are on the stage of history."[52] The meaning was made clear in conversation shortly thereafter with Margot Asquith. "My God!" he exclaimed, "This, this is living History. Everything we are saying and doing is thrilling – it will be read by a thousand generations – think of *that*!! Why I would not be out of this glorious delicious war for anything the world could give me." Then it occurred to him that such gushing might not read well in the history books, and he hastened to add an editorial note: "I say don't repeat that I said the word 'delicious' – you know what I mean."[53] Churchill was aiming at a literary and naval coup in one blow. At last he had the chance to play Ulysses S. Grant, and already he was framing the memoir that he would write after the war.

According to Frances Stevenson's diary, Lloyd George protested that the Cabinet only agreed to bombard the Straits forts if no public announcement was made: then if anything went wrong they could withdraw without losing face. But Churchill was so eager for a publicity splash that "on the very first day that the bombardment commenced [19 February], he broke faith with his colleagues & caused the announcement to be made in the Press with great éclat that we had begun the bombardment of the Dardanelles forts, & intended to force the Straits. Thenceforth it was of course impossible for the Government to withdraw."[54]

On 26 February Churchill demanded that two Anzac divisions, the elite 29th Division, the Royal Naval Division, and French and Russian troops stand ready to be redeployed to the Straits – a total of 115,000 men. Such a large force could invade and secure the Gallipoli peninsula, though it amounted to a tacit admission that a naval assault by itself might not be sufficient. When the War Cabinet refused, he warned that "If a disaster occurred in Turkey owing to the insufficiency of troops, he must disclaim all responsibility." But given that he agreed to attack without ground forces, Churchill was fully responsible for a battle plan that, as he now belatedly acknowledged, could end in catastrophe.[55]

However, on 25–26 February Carden managed to destroy the outer forts, and victory for the Allies seemed within grasp.[56] Violet Asquith dined with the Churchills at the Admiralty on 2 March. Though struggling with influenza, Winston was jubilant, anticipating the imminent capture of Constantinople. "That will make them sit up – the swine who snarled at the Naval Division!" he gloated. As Violet noted in her diary, "This reflection seemed to afford him even more satisfaction than the prospect of the impending downfall of the Ottoman Empire!" But finally his high spirits gave way to a more somber insight into his own motives: "I think a curse should rest on me because I am so happy. I know this war is smashing and shattering the lives of thousands every moment, and yet – I cannot help it – I enjoy every second I live."[57] Shortly thereafter Violet found that the attack on Dardanelles had inspired a yet more passionate expression of romantic ecstasy, in a letter from Rupert Brooke:

> Oh Violet – it's too wonderful for belief! I had not imagined Fate could be so benign. . . . I'm filled with confident and glorious hopes. I've been looking at the maps. Do you think *perhaps* the fort on the Asiatic corner will want quelling, and we'll land and come at it from behind, and they'll make a sortie and meet us on the plains of Troy? . . . Will Hero's Tower crumble under the 15-inch guns? Shall I loot mosaics from St. Sophia and Turkish Delight and carpets? Shall we be a Turning Point in History? Oh God! I've never been quite so happy in my life I think. Not quite so pervasively happy; like a stream flowing entirely to one end. I suddenly realize that the ambition of my life has been – since I was two – to go on a military expedition against Constantinople. And when I thought I was hungry or sleepy or aching to write a poem – *that* was what I really, blindly wanted.[58]

The prospect of fighting on (or just across from) the plains of Ilium was poetically intoxicating, and not only for Brooke and Churchill. Even the prosaic Captain Clement Attlee rhapsodized about "Ulysses' wanderings and Circe's wile, / Achilles and his armour, Helen's smile" – and as a veteran of the battle, he always defended "Churchill's fine strategic conception."[59]

When the War Council met on 3 March, the discussion focused on following up the anticipated victory and carving up the Ottoman Empire: only Asquith warned that the Turks and the Germans "would not give in easily."[60] In *The World Crisis* Churchill described the main naval attack on the straits of 18 March as a moment of high drama and dazzling aesthetics:

> The spectacle at this period is described as one of terrible magnificence. The mighty ships wheeling, manoeuvering and firing their guns, great and small, amid fountains of water; the forts in clouds of dust and smoke pierced by enormous flashes; the roar of the cannonade reverberating back from the hills on each side of the Straits, both shores alive with the discharges of field guns; the attendant destroyers, the picket-boats darting hither and thither in their perilous service – all displayed under shining skies and upon calm blue water, combined to make an impression of inconceivable majesty and crisis.[61]

That was before five Allied battleships were sunk or crippled by Turkish mines and gunfire. After such heavy losses the Allied commanders on the spot, Admiral Sir John de Robeck and General Sir Ian Hamilton, agreed that no further attacks should be undertaken until ground forces were ready to be landed on 14 April, though Churchill argued forcefully and unsuccessfully for a renewed attack.

After the failure of 18 March Churchill and Fisher fell out. "You are just simply eaten up with the Dardanelles and cant think of anything else!" Fisher wrote to Churchill on 5 April. "D—n the Dardanelles! they'll be our grave!"[62] On 8 April Churchill replied with a message consisting of two quotations:

> And thus the native hue of resolution
> Is sicklied o'er by the pale cast of thought,
> And enterprises of great pith & moment
> With this regard their currents turn awry
> And lose the name of action.

> We are defeated at sea because our Admirals have learned – where I know not – that war can be made without running risks.

The first was from *Hamlet*, and Napoleon is supposed to have made the second comment after Trafalgar.[63] "The vital thing is not to break off because of losses but to persevere," Winston wrote on 19 April to his brother Jack, who was serving on Ian Hamilton's staff. "This is the hour in the world's history for a fine feat of arms and the results of victory will amply justify the means."[64]

Poetry would once again intervene just before the assault on the Gallipoli peninsula began. The obituary for Rupert Brooke that Churchill wrote for *The Times* deployed all of his favorite literary strategies.[65] The circumstances of his death were banal (an infected mosquito bite while he was en route to Gallipoli), but the timing (23 April) was poetic: "His life has closed at the moment when it seemed to have reached its springtime." Churchill assumed that the epic drama of the Great War was about to climax: for a gallant, handsome hero to die at this point in the play was a stroke of melodrama. But in this case it was not a solo performance: Churchill made sure to involve his audience in the drama. He revealed this rhetorical device in *Savrola*, where the protagonist makes sure to speak of "events in which the audience had participated, and they liked having them recalled to their memories."[66] Churchill suggested that every British soldier and sailor was a war poet. Brooke voiced what they all felt:

> The thoughts to which he gave expression in the very few incomparable war sonnets which he has left behind will be shared by many thousands of young men moving resolutely and blithely forward into this, the hardest, the cruelest, and the least-rewarded of all the wars that men have fought. They are a whole history and revelation of Rupert Brooke himself. Joyous, fearless, versatile, deeply instructed, with classic symmetry of mind and body, ruled by a high undoubting purpose, he was all that one would wish England's noblest sons to be in days when no sacrifice but the most precious is acceptable, and the most precious is that which is most freely proffered.

Brooke was not merely a poet: he had lived poetically, he inspired poetry, he looked like a poem. Like Churchill, he was a life artist, celebrated perhaps more for his persona than for his "very few incomparable war sonnets." According to Violet Asquith, he and Winston only had one genuine conversation, after an Admiralty dinner, but Winston's "imagination was caught by Rupert's eagerness and beauty and by his romantic sense of dedication."[67]

Before Gallipoli, it was still possible to describe the Great War in such flowery terms. If anything, the first response to the conflict was a revival of melodramatic language. Paul Fussell quotes a personal advertisement that one early volunteer placed in *The Times* ("PAULINE—Alas it cannot be. But I will dash into the great venture with all that pride and spirit an ancient race has given me. . . .") and then offers a glossary of the histrionic idiom commonly used by soldiers:

Friendship is	*comradeship*, or *fellowship*
A horse is a	*steed*, or *charger*
Danger is	*peril*
To conquer is to	*vanquish*
To attack is to	*assail*
To be earnestly brave is to be	*gallant*
To be cheerfully brave is to be	*plucky*
To be stolidly brave is to be	*staunch* . . .[68]

When the world is in crisis, it is natural to model everyday speech on the theatre of crisis. Gilbert Murray – Regius Professor of Greek at Oxford, successful playwright, internationalist Liberal, friend of George Bernard Shaw – explained that:

> We are living now [October 1915] in a great age . . . in which the language of romance and melodrama has now become true. It is becoming the language of our normal life. The old phrase about "dying for freedom," about "Death being better than dishonour"—phrases that we thought were fitted for the stage or for children's stories—are now the ordinary truths on which we live. A phrase which happened to strike me was recorded of a Canadian soldier who went down, I think, in the [SS] Arabic after saving several people; before he sank he turned and said, "I have served my King and country and this is my end." It was the natural way of expressing the plain fact. I read yesterday a letter from a soldier at the front about the death of one of his fellow soldiers, and the letter ended quite simply: "After all he has done what we all want to do—die for England." The man who wrote it has since then had his wish. Or, again, if one wants a phrase to live by which would a few years ago have seemed somewhat unreal, or high-falutin, he can take those words of Miss Cavell that are now in everybody's mind, "I see now that patriotism is not enough; I must die without hatred or bitterness towards any one." Romance and melodrama were a memory, broken fragments living on, of heroic ages in the past. We live no longer upon fragments and memories; we have entered ourselves upon a heroic age.[69]

On 25 April 1915 the amphibious attack on Gallipoli was launched. "Remember every minute of this is history," Churchill wrote on 26 April, "and every attack requires backing."[70] By 29 April, when it was becoming clear that Allied troops had not reached their initial objectives, he proclaimed, "This is one of the great campaigns of history."[71] But as the *Morning Post* warned, "Mr. Churchill's instinct for the melodramatic has blossomed into megalomania."[72] On 11 May he admitted to Lord Fisher that "We are now in a vy difficult position," indeed a melodramatic cliffhanger: "A great army hanging on by its eyelids to a rocky beach & confronted with the armed power of the Turkish Empire under German military guidance." Nevertheless, "We are now committed to one of the greatest amphibious enterprises of history."[73] Three days later, with the Gallipoli front stymied and the Cabinet growing pessimistic, Churchill lectured the Prime Minister: "Through all this with patience & determination we can make our way to one of the gt events in the history of the world."[74] A disturbing pattern was emerging: as the military situation deteriorated, Churchill's language was becoming ever more grandiose. As reality diverged from the narrative he had planned, he insisted ever more shrilly that the climax was approaching and there could be no deviation from the plot line. The next day, 15 May, a disgusted Admiral Fisher resigned as First Sea Lord, and Churchill histrionically warned him that he would "be very harshly judged by history on whose stage we now are."[75] But that evening Lloyd George told Frances Stevenson that Fisher's resignation would force Churchill out of the government: "It is the Nemesis of the man who has fought for this war for years. When the war came he saw in it the chance of glory for himself, & has accordingly entered on a risky campaign without caring a straw for the misery and hardship it would bring to thousands, in the hope that he would prove to be the outstanding man in this war."[76] On 20 May Churchill confessed to newspaper magnate Sir George Riddell: "I am finished . . . in respect of all I care for – the waging of war; the defeat of the Germans."[77] Asquith had to reconstitute his government as a coalition with the Conservatives. On 27 May Churchill had to resign from the Admiralty, and on 1 June he was compelled to admit to Admiral Jellicoe that the Dardanelles had become "a Greek tragedy."[78]

Greek tragedy is immortal art, and on that level Churchill tried to transform a military disaster into an aesthetic triumph. According to Cynthia Asquith (the Prime Minister's daughter-in-law), "he said he was experiencing the 'austerity of changing fortune' and congratulated himself on being able to extract some epicurean enjoyment from it." Even the death in combat of his friend Francis Grenfell was an occasion for a dramatic monologue, eliciting from Churchill "an eloquent melodramatic outburst."[79] He continued to hope (on 18 June) that Constantinople could be captured by the end of summer, a triumph "unparalleled in the history of nations,"[80] but that kind of incredible reversal of fortunes rarely happened outside of Victorian plays. As he told Sir Ian Hamilton on 7 July, even defeat could be aesthetically wonderful: "The superb conduct & achievements of the soliders wd redeem even a final failure." And the reward of an unexpected victory would be literary immortality, "a military episode not inferior in glory to any that the history of war records."[81]

Churchill was more right than he knew to see in *Savrola* an anticipation of Gallipoli. In both cases he constructed a ripping war story, full of sound and fury, but was unable to plot a satisfactory conclusion. As Margot Asquith put it, he had "a lot of suggestion and young ideas, elastic vital youthful military ideas but he is very dangerous because he has no real imagination in the sense of seeing deeply into events and probabilities."[82] Churchill admitted to Ian Hamilton, "I never look beyond a battle. It is a culminating event, & like a brick wall bars all further vision." But rather than question his strategy, he urged Hamilton forward with yet another burst of stirring but vaporous histrionics: "Your daring spirit and the high qualities of your nature, will enable you to enjoy trials and tests under wh the fleshly courage of commonplace commanders wd quail."[83] Churchill again deployed the rhetoric of adversity in a speech to munitions workers at Enfield Lock on 17 September 1915, when the news from Gallipoli was particularly bleak:

> We cannot understand the inscrutable purposes which have plunged these evils upon the world and have involved all the nations of Europe in a catastrophe measureless in its horror. We only know in this time of crisis and strain that if we do our duty we shall have done all that it is in human power to do.
>
> We, all of us, whatever part we play upon the stage of the world's history, shall bear ourselves so that those who come after us when we are gone, and, amid the signs and scars of this great struggle, find that the liberties of Europe and of Great Britain are still intact and inviolate – then those, looking back upon our efforts, such as they have been, will say of this generation – this unhappy but not inglorious generation placed in a position of extraordinary trial – "They did not fail under the test, and the torch which they have preserved lights the world today."[84]

It sounds like a first draft of the "Finest Hour" speech of 1940, and in a sense it is: the same structure is used, the same chords are played. The 1940 version is, of course, much pithier, more blunt, stripped of all qualifications and throat-clearing, and hence far more gripping. But the basic message is identical. We are all of us actors on the stage of history, all of us collective authors of the grand narrative of British history, and any reverses we suffer only enhance the drama. As Eddie Marsh told Archibald Sinclair on 13 October, "the worse things go, the braver and serener he gets – it was the feeling of being condemned to inactivity that was so terribly *depressing* to him."[85]

A 15 October memorandum represented Churchill's last-ditch attempt to dissuade the Cabinet from evacuating Gallipoli. It was a question of history and drama: the worst British defeat since Yorktown, and "one of the most shocking tragedies of war," whereas "History will no doubt also dwell on the extraordinary valour and tenacity of the Turkish resistance." Certainly the Anzacs were no less courageous, but what kind of historical memories would they take home? "Anzac is the greatest word in the history of Australasia. Is it for ever to carry to future generations of Australians and New Zealanders memories of forlorn heroism and of sacrifices made in vain at the incapable bidding of the British Government?" In parallel columns, Churchill then sketched out two alternative future histories, like two opposing war prophecy novels. In the event of an evacuation, there would be widespread unrest among Britain's Muslim subjects; the Turks would renew their attacks on Egypt; the Germans would take over Rumania, northern Italy, and even

Persia; and the Western Front would be deadlocked. But if a victory could be secured, Constantinople would fall, Greece and Rumania would join the Allies, Bulgaria would make peace, Allied forces would advance to Belgrade by 15 March 1916, and by 1 May there would be a general Allied offensive on both the Western and Eastern Fronts.[86] Neither of these fictions became reality: the Allied evacuation began on 7 December and was completed (with astonishingly few casualties) by 9 January 1916.

Having suffered defeat on the seas and on the ground, Churchill resolved to achieve victory in the history books. On 1 October 1915, C. P. Scott of the *Manchester Guardian* found him obsessed with self-justification: "He longed for the day when he could publish the whole of the facts."[87] "The tale has yet to be told to its conclusion," he wrote to Eddie Marsh on 15 December, even as the evacuation was under way. He placed his faith in "an underlying instinct that all will be well and that my greatest work is to hand."[88] On the 17th he sent Clementine two letters written in a state of depression, but then, mindful that they might blemish his historical record, he had her burn them.[89] On 14 January 1916, five days after the evacuation was completed, Winston assured his brother Jack that "History will vindicate the conception, & the errors in execution will on the whole leave me clear."[90] Eleven days later he told Lloyd George that, with proper backing, his assault on the Dardanelles "could have altered the history of the world."[91] He grasped at vindication when, on 27 January, *The Times* reported that Enver Pasha, the Ottoman War Minister, conceded that the Allies had nearly succeeded in forcing the Straits the previous March – though Enver went on to say that "even had the British ships got to Constantinople, it would not have availed them much. Our plan was to repair our army to the surrounding hills and to Asia Minor."[92]

Churchill was also cheered by the publication of two flattering biographical sketches. One was Alexander MacCallum Scott's *Winston Churchill in Peace and War*. "What a tale it is!" he exulted, and he began compiling notes "to put on record a full & complete account of this gt series of war events."[93] Soon thereafter he secured MacCallum Scott's assistance and advice in preparing his testimony before the Dardanelles Commission.[94] By September 1916 he had also read a memoir by his cousin Shane Leslie, *The End of a Chapter*, and was enthralled by it.[95] "His career is the most brilliant in recent politics," Leslie wrote. He particularly praised Churchill's work at the Admiralty, climaxing with the declaration of war in 1914. "If Winston had died on the day the fleet was mobilized, he would have fulfilled his ambition, which had been to enjoy a decade of power and achievement."[96] On 8 September Churchill drafted a defense of his Gallipoli strategy, arguing that the Turkish forts had nearly exhausted their artillery shells when the Allied naval bombardment was called off.[97]

He could also justify (not to mention enrich) himself by returning to journalism. In July 1916 he predicted that he would be "able quite easily to earn ten or twelve thousand pounds in the next six months. . . . I get four or 5 shillings a word for everything I write."[98] For a series of five articles on the war, published in the *London Magazine* from October 1916 to February 1917, he received £5,000.[99] He told C. P. Scott that if the newspapers (other than the *Manchester Guardian*) would not report his parliamentary speeches, he could bypass them by publishing his own articles. A piece for the *Sunday Pictorial* required no more work than a speech and earned him £250.[100]

A few weeks after leaving the Admiralty, Churchill took up painting, which was not entirely new to him. One school subject he was fairly good at was drawing, which he studied in preparation for his Sandhurst entrance examination.[101] Prior to his Cuban trip of 1895 he read a handbook, *Making Sketches*, and his dispatches were accompanied by his own drawings.[102] In "The Scaffolding of Rhetoric" he had analogized that, just as in "painting partly mechanical arrangements of colour give pleasure to the eye," so "the art of oratory also had its 'values' and its 'thorough base',"[103] and he had painted gorgeous word pictures in his reports from the Sudan in 1898. He always conducted politics as an artist, and now that his political universe was spinning apart, the canvas offered him an alternative world where he could exercise complete creative control. As Churchill explained in his essay, "Painting as a Pastime," art was therapy, a treatment for his Gallipoli trauma. The most painful dimension of his departure from the Admiralty was the loss of power. He was still in the Cabinet and the War Council, but:

> In this position I knew everything and could do nothing. The change from the intense executive activities of each day's work at the Admiralty to the narrowly-measured duties of a counsellor left me gasping. Like a sea-beast fished up from the depths, or a diver too suddenly hoisted, my veins threatened to burst from the fall in pressure. I had great anxiety and no means of relieving it; I had vehement convictions and small power to give effect to them. I had to watch the unhappy casting-away of great opportunities, and the feeble execution of plans which I had launched and in which I heartily believed. I had long hours of utterly unwonted leisure in which to contemplate the frightful unfolding of the War. At a moment when every fibre of my being was inflamed to action, I was forced to remain a spectator of the tragedy, placed cruelly in a front seat. And then it was that the Muse of Painting came to my rescue. . . .

In fact "painting a picture is like fighting a battle," he observed. "It is a proposition which, whether of few or numberless parts, is commanded by a single unity of conception." J. M. W. Turner planned his vast canvases with attention to detail and proportion "equal in quality and intensity of the finest achievements of warlike action, of forensic argument, or of scientific or philosophical adjudication." Like a general, a landscape painter had to make a "thorough reconnaissance of the country." He had to study art history for the same reason military commanders study military history. And proportion and relation in art were analogous to reserves in warfare, without which "The pictorial battlefield becomes a sea of mud mercifully veiled by the fog of war."[104]

"A striking characteristic of his pictures is their quite extraordinary decisiveness," the critic Thomas Bodkin once observed:

> Each is a clear and forcible pronouncement. He does not niggle nor retouch. His paint is laid once and for all with no apparent hesitation or afterthought. It is never fumbled or woolly in texture. Spaces are filled with obvious speed. His colours are bright, clean and well-harmonized. His drawing makes factual statements, though these may not always be quite accurate in detail. . . . But were he more scientific, it is likely that he would lose some of the spontaneity which is one of his most potent attractions.[105]

"I rejoice in the highest lights and the brightest colours," Churchill explained to Sir John Rothenstein (director of the Tate Gallery) shortly after he left the premiership in 1955. "If I have been of any service to my fellow men, it has never been by self-repression, but always by self-expression. . . . If it weren't for painting, I couldn't live; I couldn't bear the strain of things."[106] That remark points to the crashing despair that art usually kept at bay, except in two post-Gallipoli portraits. One, by William Orpen (1916), reveals what we almost never see in Churchill: self-doubt. The other, a self-portrait (1919–20), is almost unrecognizable, a study in dismal brown. His jaunty determination is gone. The face is thinned, gaunt, half eclipsed in shadow. It delivers the shock we feel when we find a normally robust friend in hospital, shrunken by disease. Churchill was often a candybox impressionist, but occasionally he was a modern artist.

He served a few months (November 1915–March 1916) on the Western Front, where he could recover his spirits, salvage his military reputation, and once again be an aesthete of war. He observed a German barrage at a Ploegsteert farm near the front lines as a study in pure color: "Some were white shrapnel, other big black HE [High Explosive] 'crumps': others 'woolly bears' & some make a tremendous cloud of yellowy white smoke – or even plum & black, 30 in all. Having luckily wandered down the right turn, Archie [Sinclair, his second-in-command] & I had a fine view of this exhibition without being at all inconvenienced." One of his officers, Lieutenant Hakewill Smith, was astonished when:

> Winston started painting the second or third time he went up to the farm. Each time we were in the line he spent some time on his paintings. Gradually, too, the courtyard became pitted with shellholes. As his painting came nearer to completion, he became morose, angry, and exceedingly difficult to talk to. After five or six days in this mood, he suddenly appeared cheerful and delighted, like a small boy at school. I asked him what had happened, and he said "I have been worried because I couldn't get the shell-hole right in the painting. However I did it, it looked like a mountain, but yesterday I discovered if I put a little bit of white in it, it looked like a hole after all."[107]

Meanwhile, just across no-man's-land, on the German side, another soldier-artist was sketching a ruined church: Adolf Hitler.[108]

Churchill painted as he practiced politics and wrote history: supremely confident, impulsive, gorgeously vivid, but not ploddingly photographic, and quite willing to rearrange and embellish reality to achieve an artistic effect. "I remember once in his early painting days," wrote Violet Asquith:

> when we were both staying in a country house, set in a monochrome of dull, flat, uneventful country, I went out to watch him paint, half wondering what he would make of it. Looking over his shoulder I saw depicted on his canvas range upon range of mountains rising dramatically behind the actual foreground. I searched the skies for a mirage and then enquired where they had come from, and he replied, "Well – I couldn't leave it quite as dull as all that." No landscape and no age in which he lived could ever be consigned to dullness.[109]

As Field Marshal Harold Alexander recalled much later, "He loved colours, and used far too many. That's why his paintings are so crude. He couldn't resist using all the colours on his palette."[110] That generalization could apply to all of Churchill's efforts to transmute life into art, whether on canvas or on the printed page.

By July 1917 Churchill once again had his hands on the levers of power, as Minister of Munitions. In August 1918 he dined with his pilot, Lieutenant Gilbert Hall, who recalled that "Churchill started to tell us about the preparation of his speeches," which he rehearsed like an actor. "Apparently he went through a routine, even to making gestures with his arms and hands, and I believe before a mirror, in the seclusion of his study at home." As a self-publicist, Churchill was naturally fascinated by a new bit of slang: "During a lull he suddenly, without any warning, uttered the word 'stunt'. 'Stunt' he repeated, 'that is a remarkable word, and it has come to stay'. He then asked each of us . . . to define this wonderful new word 'stunt' that had come over to us from America." Hall also recalled that Churchill liked to recite Siegfried Sassoon:

> It was obvious that the Minister held the greatest admiration for Sassoon as a man, as a soldier and as a poet. We quickly realized that the main theme of the poems was anti-war, the futility of war and the misery war brought. We heard that Generals were seriously worried at the damage to morale these poems might inflict on the troops, and that it would be preferable for Sassoon to remain in England, out of harm's way. Mr. Churchill then stated that . . . he intended to get in touch with Sassoon and to make some amends to him, possibly I believe by offering him a job in the Ministry of Munitions. I feel sure it was Winston's brother John who thereupon exclaimed "I should leave that man alone if I were you. He might start writing a poem about *you*," to which Mr. Churchill immediately replied "I am not a bit afraid of Siegfried Sassoon. That man can think. I am afraid only of people who cannot think."[111]

He actually invited Sassoon to his London office, and offered the anti-war poet a post in the Ministry of Munitions. As Sassoon remembered:

> His manner was leisurely, informal, and friendly. Almost at once I began to feel a liking for him. . . . He then made some gratifying allusions to the memorable quality of my war poems, which I acknowledged with bashful decorum. Having got through these preliminaries, he broached – in a good-humoured and natural way – the subject of my attitude to the war, about which – to my surprise – he seemed interested to hear my point of view. Still more surprising was the fact that he evidently wanted me to "have it out with him." Overawed though I was, I spotted that the great man aimed at getting a rise out of me, and there was something almost boyish in the way he set about it.

Sassoon was too diffident to rise to the bait, but Churchill was setting up a dramatic dialogue. A general concerned merely with winning the war might consider Sassoon dangerous, but as a student of the theatre Churchill knew that there could be no drama without conflict. He welcomed and needed someone to be his foil. When it became clear that Sassoon found Churchill too likable to engage him in debate:

> our proceedings developed into a monologue. Pacing the room, with a big cigar in the corner of his mouth, he gave me an emphatic vindication of militarism as an instrument of policy and stimulator of glorious individual achievements, not only in the mechanism of warfare but in spheres of social

> progress. The present war, he asserted, had brought about inventive discoveries which would ameliorate the condition of mankind. For example, there had been immense improvements in sanitation. Transfixed and submissive in my chair, I realized that what had begun as a persuasive confutation of my anti-war convictions was now addressed, in pauseful and perorating prose, to no one in particular. From time to time he advanced on me, head thrust well forward and hands clasped behind his back, to deliver the culminating phrases of some resounding period. . . . He now spoke with weighty eloquence of what the Ministry was performing in its vast organization and output, and of what it might yet further achieve in expediting the destruction of the enemy.

War, then, is a creative act, a collective work of art that included both the poems of Siegfried Sassoon and the artillery shells rolling out of the factories. "It had been unmistakable that for him war was the finest activity on earth," Sassoon concluded. Even when Edward Marsh announced that Churchill's next appointment, Lord Fisher, had arrived, "The Winstonian exposition continued until Eddie reappeared with an apologetic intimation that Lord Fisher was growing restive."[112]

There is a logical explanation for this incredible scene. Churchill was re-enacting George Bernard Shaw's *Major Barbara* (1905), where Andrew Undershaft, the master of a vast weapons-making empire, recruits the peace-loving poet Adolphus Cusins to work with him. Churchill saw the play during its initial run, and again with his children twenty years later. In the interval the world had been transformed by social revolutions and global war, but, he recalled, "in *Major Barbara* there was not a character requiring to be re-drawn, not a sentence nor a suggestion that was out of date. My children were astounded to learn that this play, the very acme of modernity, was written more than five years before they were born."[113] Shaw ultimately reconciles Undershaft and Cusins in a neo-Hegelian dialectic that somehow points to a better future,[114] and Churchill had a similar propensity for bringing together polar opposite ideas in a paradoxical synthesis. For Churchill, war was poetry, and the horrors of war were inevitably part of the poetry. He was always receptive to pacifist writers like Sassoon, whose verses he could recite by heart.[115] In an introduction to A. P. Herbert's anti-war novel *The Secret Battle*, he called it "a work of art" that, "like the poems of Siegfried Sassoon, should be read in each generation, so that men and women may rest under no illusion about what war means."[116]

The language of melodrama, which was momentarily revived in the early enthusiastic phase of the war, was killed by general disillusionment that had set in by the time of the Armistice. "Abstract words such as glory, honor, courage, or hallow were obscene beside the concrete names of villages, the numbers of roads, the names of rivers, the numbers of regiments and the dates": everyone quotes that from Ernest Hemingway's *A Farewell to Arms*.[117] The modernist sensibility – already developing before 1914 – that emerged from the war, defined itself in opposition to melodrama: a shift from moral absolutes to moral ambiguities, from idealism to disenchantment, from patri otism to cosmopolitanism, from histrionics to understatement, from earnestness to irony, from passion to dispassion, from crisis to ennui, from action to futility, from purity to eros, from obviousness to subtlety, from the populist to the esoteric, from simplicity to difficulty, from military glory to shell shock. But Churchill, for the rest of his life, continued to speak and act in a melodramatic idiom that, for sophisticated metropolitans, seemed increasingly anachronistic and absurd. When the discouraging news of the Battle of Jutland was received at the beginning of June 1916, Cynthia Asquith sighed: "Winston very melodramatic, brooding and scowling. 'They're a terrible foe'. . . . He gave me one of his most purple, metaphorical, period-talking of his impotent watching of the mismanagement of his Dardanelles scheme after he was out of office. 'It was like being bound hand and foot, and watching one's best girl being – well, I won't say what.' "[118] In May 1917 Lord Esher (chief of the British Mission in Paris) had warned Douglas Haig about Churchill in very similar terms: "He handles great subjects in rhythmical language, and becomes quickly enslaved by his own phrases," Esher wrote. "He appeals to L George, because he can strike ideas into colour and imagery. But his ideas are 'Transpontine'. . . ."[119] That last term meant "across the bridges," in South London, where the theatres specialized in cheap swashbuckling melodrama, and where no one with any sense of taste ever ventured.

CHAPTER 10

What Actually Happened

One of the first historical accounts of the Gallipoli fiasco was the Interim Report of the Dardanelles Commission, filed in April 1917, which faulted Churchill and nearly everyone else connected with the expedition. In his response, on 1 May, Churchill charged that the commissioners

> assembled a mass of extracts and quotations which though they tell the story, do not tell it fully or evenly. . . . Sentences extracted from . . . documents, apart from the context, are built into the narrative in a manner which is in some cases actually misleading. . . . The Commissioners have a right and a duty to state their opinion, and to lay emphasis on this or that set of facts; but the narrative so constructed, however impartial in its intention, can be no substitute for the . . . elementary right of persons whose conduct is impugned to state their own case with as much publicity as is given to the judgment of the Tribunal.[1]

So Churchill, in 1917, suggested that (1) historical narratives are constructed; (2) it is possible, through selective and partial quotation, and the arrangement and contextualization of facts, to create any narrative one wishes; and (3) the narrative which receives the greatest publicity is most likely to win general acceptance. It all sounds uncannily like postmodern historiography, and in fact there is a connection. Although he is never mentioned in Hayden White's postmodern manifesto *Metahistory*, Churchill was a metahistorian. That is, he thought seriously and creatively about the questions that later engaged postmodern historians, questions of epistemology (How do we know what happened?); narrativity (Do we necessarily distort reality when we tell a story?); objectivity (Is it possible?); fiction (Does it have any place in historical writing?); the archive (What does it include or not include?); selectivity (What do historians choose to include or not include?); teleology (Where is history headed?); mediation (How do the media affect our perception of the past?); causation (How do we know that X was caused by Y and not Z?); and poetics (Is history a science or an art?). Though the postmodernists revived interest in such issues, they were by no means the first to engage with them: earlier such topics fell under the rubric of "the philosophy of history." Churchill brought to this subject a mind undisciplined by conventional university-level historiography. He was a habitually innovative thinker, who loved to sweep away assumptions and examine problems with a fresh eye. One could say that he engaged in "defamiliarization" *avant la lettre*. Because he was a naive (i.e. non-academic) historian, he asked questions that most professional historians would not have thought to ask.

Although Churchill liked to portray himself as a dismal student, he received good marks for history at St. George's School in Ascot, which he attended 1882–84.[2] At his next school, in Brighton, he studied Herodotus and ranked at the top of the class in Biblical, Ancient, and English history.[3] His Harrow housemaster admitted that, in spite of his "phenomenal slovenliness," history was one area where he performed well and won a prize.[4] Along with Gibbon's *Decline and Fall* and Hallam's *Constitutional History of England*, Macaulay's "crisp and forcible" prose and his patriotic Whiggism were an early and lasting influence.[5] As Churchill told his brother Jack in 1897, "I believe you have the same affection for reading the records of our glorious past as I have. A good knowledge of history is a quiver full of arrows in debate."[6] And in 1901 he summed up Macaulay's Whig interpretation of history in one exultant sentence: "Many and varied are the events of English history; but there is one story running through it all. Free institutions developing manhood and commerce; commerce impatient of island limits going down to the sea in ships and breeding fleets; sea-power preserving us from Continental tumult, stimulating manufacture anew, and enabling vast but distant possessions to be conquered and kept by comparatively little armies."[7]

But already Winston was venturing beyond simple Whiggism to grapple with troubling epistemological issues. No one can work as a journalist – especially a war correspondent – without coming to question the reliability of newspaper articles and other historical sources. In a 30 March 1898 letter to *The Times*, Churchill complained that anti-imperial prejudice and the resentments of junior officers regarding "the vices and blunders of their superiors" had created a fog of reportage regarding a recent frontier war in India's Tirah Valley, aired in "the widest and most powerful press the world has yet seen. . . . In such a 'climate of opinion' the rumours and reports from the frontier have raised a tempest of pettish irritation. The wildest statements have been accepted as indisputable. Falsehood brazenly repeated has become fact. Accusations have been treated as verdicts. Gossip is passing into history.

. . . For my part I cannot forget the description of Brussels on a memorable Monday morning when the Belgian Chasseurs galloped madly through the streets with the news that the duke was slain and Waterloo was lost."[8] No less baffling was the problem of historical causation, as he explained in *The Story of the Malakand Field Force*:

> The historian of great events is always oppressed by the difficulty of tracing the silent, subtle influences, which in all communities precede and prepare the way for violent outbursts and uprisings. He may discover many causes and record them duly, but he will always be sensible that others have escaped him. The changing tides of public opinion, the undercurrents of interest, partisanship and caprice, the whirlpools of illogical sentiment or ignorant prejudice, exert forces so complex and numerous, that to observe and appreciate them all, and to estimate the effect of each in raising the storm, is a task beyond the intellect and industry of man.[9]

As a practitioner of the New Journalism, Churchill knew that reporters used fictional devices to enhance their "stories." "It is quite true," he admitted to his mother when he was just twenty-three, "I do not care so much for the principles I advocate as for the impression which my words produce & the reputation they give me. This sounds vy terrible. But . . . I vy often yield to the temptation of adapting my facts to my phrases."[10] Many years later he would growl at Maurice Ashley, his research assistant, "Give me the facts, Ashley, and I will twist them the way I want to suit my argument."[11]

In the age of Carlyle and Macaulay, there had been much scope for that kind of personal bias. It was generally accepted that history was a literary art produced by literary men who were licensed to introduce literary embellishments into their narratives, addressing the same lay public that read Thackeray, Dickens, and Trollope. And that public loved that kind of history. Between 1870 and 1919, 12 to 15 percent of all books published in Britain were history titles, and some of them were bestsellers. Macaulay famously collected £20,000 in royalties for his *History of England* (1855–61), and ever since publishers and authors had hoped to repeat that success. However, toward the end of the nineteenth century, as academic history became professionalized, university-based historians turned to producing thesis-driven specialized monographs written for other academics.[12] That meant abandoning "narrative" for "problems," as J. R. Seeley explained in *The Expansion of England*:

> So long as you think of history as a mere chronological narrative, so long you are in the old literary groove which leads to no trustworthy knowledge, but only to that pompous conventional romancing of which all serious men are

> tired. Break the drowsy spell of narrative; ask yourself questions; set yourself problems; your mind will at once take up a new attitude; you will become an investigator; you will cease to be solemn and begin to be serious.[13]

The mandarinization of academic history left open a vast market for middlebrow history – grand syntheses with a strong narrative line and aimed at a popular audience. That gap would be filled by non-academic writers like H. G. Wells, Hilaire Belloc, Will Durant, Arthur Bryant, and Churchill. In 1929, when G. N. Clark was planning the *Oxford History of England* series and looking for a "really potent star" to write the 1870–1914 volume, he entertained "envious thoughts of Winston." But Churchill would have had trouble working within the constraints of the series, and no university press could afford to pay him what he could earn from a trade publisher.[14] The job ultimately went to R. C. K. Ensor, a journalist turned academic, whose volume outsold every earlier installment of the series.[15]

As the example of Ensor illustrates, the secular trend from literary history to "scientific" history was gradual and uneven, and the transition was far from complete in the 1920s and 1930s. Herbert Butterfield's first book, published in 1924, was *The Historical Novel*, which in a rather postmodern way explored the borderlands between history and fiction. Archival records, he argued, offered only scattered fragments of the past, and the process of arranging these shards in a narrative and an explanatory framework inevitably involved an element of fiction.[16] Later he moved, with the rest of his profession, in the direction of scientific history, though he was never entirely comfortable with rigid structuralism and the abandonment of narrative.[17] Historians continued to refine their methodologies to the point where, by the 1970s, they were striving to make their discipline a rigorous social science, modeled on economics (cliometrics), psychology (psychohistory), anthropology (ethnohistory), sociology (the "new social history"), or demography (Peter Laslett and the Cambridge Group for the History of Population and Social Structure). Then the postmodernists, led by Hayden White, objected that historians, for all their scientific pretensions, were actually prisoners of their own tropes and metaphors. Though scholars might profess that they first did research and then created a narrative, usually they did the reverse.

But that had been Churchill's method all along. As Maurice Ashley explained it, "First he decides his subject and his broad theme. He envisages the grandeur of the story, the qualities and weaknesses of the men whom he characterizes; he sets the scene." Only then does he begin doing research. He does not fabricate data (well, not much), "but he ensures that it fits into the broad framework of his narrative."[18] Or in Churchill's own words, "My habit is to dictate in the first instance what I have in mind on the subject and a body of argument which I believe is substantially true and in correct proportion," and then verify the facts.[19]

As Robin Prior has shown, it was Churchill who selected and arranged facts to construct a misleading narrative about Gallipoli. His history of the Great War, *The World Crisis*, insisted that the Dardanelles attack came very close to succeeding, when in reality it was deeply flawed and probably unworkable from the very beginning. Churchill also redistributed blame by leaving the impression that the War Council and the Navy broadly supported the invasion plan, though Churchill himself promoted it in the face of widespread skepticism. Applying the methods of literary history to military history, Prior compared successive drafts of *The World Crisis* to show how Churchill progressively covered his tracks and put increasingly positive glosses on some very questionable policy decisions. In one version Churchill conceded that he had been wrong to strongarm Fisher into suppressing his growing doubts, but that passage did not make it into the final text. Churchill further claimed that if the fleet had reached Constantinople, Greece, Bulgaria, and Russia would have likely provided the ground troops needed to secure the area – "an extreme degree of optimism," comments Prior. Finally, Churchill asserted that, thanks to the attack, Italy joined the war on the Allied side, Bulgaria held back from joining the Central Powers, and a Turkish army was destroyed. But Italy was an ally of doubtful value, the stalemate at Gallipoli may have actually encouraged Bulgaria to enter the conflict, and Turkish casualties have to be balanced against the very serious Allied losses on land and at sea. Churchill used Admiralty statistics to argue that Carden's fleet had plentiful ammunition, but the figures refer to the inventory of shells for the whole Navy: the ships in the Straits were actually ill-supplied. At one point Churchill wrote a paragraph admitting that the ammunition was insufficient, the minesweepers were inadequate, the seaplanes used to spot the accuracy of Allied fire were ineffective, and he accepted personal responsibility for all these failures – and then he discarded the passage. In *The World Crisis* and, indeed, in all his military writings, Churchill said little about all-important logistical issues, simply because they lacked drama. An early draft of the final sentence of the Gallipoli section read weakly: "The pity was that we did not persevere," but Churchill ultimately changed it to a melodramatic applause line: "Not to persevere – that was the crime."[20]

A favorite cliché of Victorian melodrama was to have the hero rescued or the villain foiled just in the nick of time, as in George Bernard Shaw's *The Devil's Disciple*:

> ANDERSON: Thank God, I was in time!
> BURGOYNE *(calm as ever, and still watch in hand)* Ample time, sir. Plenty of time. I should never dream of hanging any gentleman by an American clock.

In late 1914, when Admiral Maximilian von Spee's cruiser squadron was wreaking havoc in the southern seas, Churchill sent two battlecruisers to intercept the Germans. According to *The World Crisis*, a dockyard admiral protested that the ships would not be ready to sail until 13 November, but Churchill manfully dispatched them two days earlier. As a result, they arrived at the Falklands on the same day as von Spee, just "in the nick of time" to destroy the Germans. What this ripping yarn obscures is the fact that Churchill's speedy dispatch of the battlecruisers hardly affected the outcome: once they were at sea, they meandered down to the Falklands at a maddeningly leisurely pace, and only intercepted von Spee by dumb luck. Still, as the thriller-writer John Buchan affirmed, Churchill had taken a messy reality, "a war of many scattered campaigns," and forged "a real, artistic whole" arranged in a "brilliant and exciting narrative."[21]

He used much the same method – starting with a narrative outline and then researching facts to fit it – when he composed *The Second World War*. There Churchill worked with a team of assistants, and the primary ghostwriter, F. W. Deakin, recalled that

> Winston and I would discuss together, alone, a sort of synopsis, which he would think out in his head and discuss with me. I would work into that frame. I would look up what happened. He then would dictate away what he remembered about people. He would also send me to talk to people, as a kind of interpreter. He sent me to talk to General Georges, to discuss the state of the French Army in 1940.
>
> When I would produce a memorandum, this would provoke his personal memory. He would stop completely. No more documents. He would dictate his feelings (when he became First Lord, when he became Prime Minister).[22]

Churchill, Deakin emphasized, always insisted on "remaining autobiographical and not writing a history."[23] In November 1941 Thomas North Whitehead, the United States expert at the Foreign Office, suggested that the most effective propaganda the British could produce for Americans would outline "the broad picture" of the war, full of concrete information, yet written more like a historical novel than a work of journalism.[24] That more or less describes *The Second World War*.

One could say that Churchill wrote history "from the top down," except that he never ventured far down the social scale. Social history, history "from the bottom up," had been pioneered by R. H. Tawney and Eileen Power, whose work Churchill did not know, and by Macaulay and G. M. Trevelyan, whom Churchill knew very well, but he made no attempt to adopt their methodology. In writing *A History of the English-Speaking Peoples*, he drew a bit on

J. R. Green's *A Short History of the English People* (which he read as early as 1905) and those wonderful documents of life in fifteenth-century England, the Paston family letters.[25] On the nineteenth anniversary of the outbreak of the First World War, he affirmed that "Everyone in however humble a station has a tale to tell of how the event struck him, what he noticed, what he heard, what he said, where he went and, above all, what he left. There are millions of unwritten dramas that need only to be recorded to command sympathy and interest."[26] But Churchill never recorded them. Some of his 1940 speeches would celebrate the People's War, but his history of the Second World War only briefly acknowledges the sacrifices made by the aircraft workers, the infantrymen, the housewives struggling with ration books, the bombed-out East Enders. It tells us next to nothing about their finest hour.[27]

For *A History of the English-Speaking Peoples*, he did ask Alan Bullock to "write two or three thousand words on the social history and institutional development of this period, showing the life of the people, their houses, their foods, their troubles, their habits, with quotations from contemporary authorities." He admitted "It is quite true that in the first instance going over this long story I do dwell on battles and kings, but I am most anxious that the other side should be represented so far as it lends itself to narration. Of course people were living and dying all the time."[28] Bullock supplied information on Australia, but Churchill complained that it conveyed "inevitably a somewhat drab picture. There are so many convicts and penal settlements." He asked for more on "the unique character of her animals, the kangaroo, the platypus, etc.," and of course the "Australian love of sport; horse-racing; the Melbourne cup; Adam Lindsay Gordon's poems about all these," not to mention "Something about the very fine type of manhood developing there. An exceptionally handsome race, with virile and martial qualities proved in the Great War. An equal land; a happy land; climate lovely apart from droughts, which water-storage should eventually cure. Kipling wrote some fine verses about Australia." And as an afterthought, "We should have a page or so on New Zealand."[29] The hard reality, replied Bullock, was that "life in a 19th century Australian town was crude, & monotonous and only relieved by the rather tawdry orgies of the gold diggers," though he promised to send "a fuller account of the exploration of central Australia, an epic story in its way & one which might do something to relieve the dullness."[30]

At this time there was already a public debate, by no means limited to academics, over whether history was driven by great men or broad social forces, and Churchill came down on the side of the great men. He acknowledged "the decisive part which accident and chance play at every moment" in all of our lives. "And if this be true of the daily experience of ordinary average people," he reasoned, "how much more potent must be the deflection which the Master Teachers – Thinkers, Discoverers, Commanders – have imparted at every stage. True, they required their background, their atmosphere, their opportunity; but these were also the leverages which magnified their power."[31] "War has always fascinated him," Lord Moran noted in 1943, but only the conventional generals-and-battles history of war: ". . . he knows in surprising detail about campaigns of the great captains; he has visited nearly all the battlefields and he can pick out, in a particular battle, the decisive move that turned the day. But he has never given a thought to what is happening in the soldier's mind, he has not tried to share his fears. If a soldier does not do his duty, the P.M. says that he ought to be shot. It is as simple as that." Moran showed him the manuscript of his behavioral study of combat, *The Anatomy of Courage*, but Churchill, like any Blimpish colonel, brushed aside "all this psychological nonsense" and warned that it might depress morale.[32] The history of science, industry, literature, and philosophy are likewise mostly ignored in *A History of the English-Speaking Peoples*.

Of course Churchill also overlooked millions of Anglophone Africans, Asians, and West Indians. At only one point in his historiographical career – in 1937, when Japan was making a bid for global power – did he perceive the shortcomings of this approach:

> To the English-speaking nations history is mainly the story of the white races. We remember the Persian Empire because its hordes broke themselves in vain against the Greeks; Carthage because for a time she challenged the power of Rome; the Mongols because they nearly conquered Europe. We forget that civilization existed in Asia centuries before it reached the Mediterranean, and that for many centuries more, white supremacy, even in Europe – that "little peninsula of the Asiatic continent" – hung precariously in the balance. It is, therefore, perhaps difficult for us to realize that we are in the presence of claims to world leadership by peoples of another colour.[33]

However, as with any author, if we fixate on what Churchill did not do, we may lose sight of what he did accomplish, which was remarkable. In effect, he leapfrogged the "new social history," which was fashionable in the mid-twentieth century, and anticipated the postmodern historiography that superseded it in the late twentieth century.

F. W. Deakin claimed that "Churchill never posed to himself the problem of the nature of history,"[34] and Gordon Craig asserted that he never read Leopold von Ranke.[35] They were both wrong. Churchill developed a sophisticated theoretical approach to history, laid out in, of all places, his biography of Marlborough. That may seem counterintuitive, since at first glance it looks like that Victorian dinosaur, the celebratory multivolume life of a great man.

But this work, as well as *A History of the English-Speaking Peoples*, relies importantly on Ranke's *A History of England*.[36] For postmodernists, Ranke is the great epistemological naïf, who thought that trawling the archives would unproblematically tell us *wie es eigentlich gewesens* – usually translated as "what actually happened," as if we could ever know that. But here the postmodernists forgot their own cardinal insight, that all texts are open to multiple readings, and Churchill's reading of Ranke was quite different. Here is the key passage that Churchill quotes from Ranke's *History of England*:

> Some years ago I was reproved with writing history out of scraps. Certainly I do not, so long as detailed informants hold out. But when the originals were either lost, or kept concealed, it is absolutely necessary to make use of less perfect accounts and fragmentary communications. It is just at such points that cases are wont to occur, which are purposely kept dark and which are among the most important.

So here is Ranke, whom Churchill calls the "most pregnant and fairest of historians," admitting that history is fraught with uncertainty. As the postmodernists should have recognized, translation involves tricky nuances, and it has been suggested that Ranke meant to discover not "what actually happened" but "what essentially happened," a more achievable goal. Churchill did once use the phrase "in essentials what had happened," in *The World Crisis*, though he did not attribute it to Ranke.[37] "History cannot proceed by silences," Churchill wrote, picking up Ranke's argument:

> The chronicler of ill-recorded times has none the less to tell his tale. If facts are lacking, rumour must serve. Failing affidavits, he must build with gossip. Everything is relative. One doubtful fact has to be weighed against another. A rogue's testimony is better than no evidence. A forged letter, if ancient, is at least to be preferred to mere vacuity. Authentic documents and credible witnesses may be sought with perseverance; but where they do not exist the less trustworthy understudies who present themselves must be suffered, often without the proper apologies and reserves, to play the major parts, if the drama is to be presented at all. . . . But when the process is complete, when every vestige of knowledge, such as it is, has been gathered, sifted, weighed, and fitted into the story, it may be well to ask whether the result corresponds at all with what actually happened.[38]

Note, in that last sentence, Churchill's skepticism regarding positivist history. Note his assertion that "Everything is relative," three little words that sum up postmodernism. He uses all the unconventional sources that postmodernists would use: testimonies of the marginalized, gossip, even forgeries may tell us something about the past. Churchill understood as well as the postmodernists that archives are fragmentary: "these written fragments, luckily preserved, represent only a tiny part of all that happened."[39] Therefore no written work of history can hope to include, in a few hundred pages, the whole of human experience over many years: "To understand history the reader must always remember how small is the proportion of what is recorded to what actually took place, and above all how severely the time factor is compressed."[40] Where records did not exist, Churchill was quite willing to concoct dialogue.[41] University of Manchester historian Lewis Namier did not care for this habit of creating "imaginary pictures of what *may* have happened or what some people *must* have felt," and said so in no uncertain terms.[42] In response, Churchill granted that his invented conversations "were a weak indulgence on my part, but they sometimes make the ordinary reader realise the position," and they were rendered necessary by the incompleteness of archives:

> One of the most misleading factors in history is the practice of historians to build a story exclusively out of the records which have come down to them. These records in many cases are a very small part of what took place, and to fill in the picture one has to visualize the daily life—the constant discussions between ministers, the friendly dinners, the many days when nothing happened worthy of record, but during which events were nevertheless proceeding.[43]

Churchill's fictive historiographic methods were very similar to those used by Natalie Zemon Davis in *The Return of Martin Guerre*, which (in her words) she constructed "like a detective story."[44] If this blurring of history and fiction suggests we have come full circle, Michael Bentley has observed that "the post-modern world has in some ways encouraged the rubber ball to resume its bouncing in the direction of history as meaning, story-telling, communicating with a wide general audience."[45] In fact, "Among the younger historians now known to the public for their skills in communication we detect nothing so much as a new whiggery. Stories have returned, footnotes have thinned or disappeared, history has relocated itself as a literary and visual medium."[46] Arguably, one common weakness of whiggish history is presentism. Churchill and other Whig historians were criticized for projecting their Whig ideology on past historical actors – just as Natalie Davis has been faulted for projecting her twentieth-century feminism onto a sixteenth-century French peasant woman.[47]

Churchill devoured historical novels throughout his life, and believed that historical fiction could be more truthful than historical monographs. Josephine Tey's novel *The Daughter of Time* convinced him that Richard III had been framed for the murder of the princes in the Tower, no matter what those "goddam dons" said.[48] He explicitly denied that his histories of the First and Second World Wars were histories at all: the words he repeatedly used to describe them were *story, tale*, and *narrative*.[49] Manny Shinwell was not far wrong when, in a *Daily Herald* review, he characterized *The Second World War* as "a novel with Winston Churchill as the hero."[50] If this meant treating useful myths as if they were facts, Churchill was quite willing to do that, as Deakin recalled:

> I remember on one occasion just before the War an argument conducted with energetic brutality and disarming kindliness as to whether or not King Alfred ever burnt the cakes. Churchill explained that, at times of crisis, myths had their historical importance: that the cakes symbolized a myth of resistance in their sternest hour against the foreign invader, and were the source of inspiration to those dim distant figures, the Counts of the Saxon shore, striving to defend the island. I was duly chastened, and shortly afterwards, with inexorable historical logic, Churchill was to find himself the lineal and supreme successor of those Counts of the Saxon shore, and the leader of the most decisive British resistance in her history—at Dunkirk.
>
> Myths have their poetic place in history in epic times. . . .[51]

More scientific historians generally hoped that at some point in the future, after enough research had been done, a definitive interpretation of events would be arrived at, and that this would be "the verdict of history." M. M. Postan thought this moment of finality had actually arrived in 1939, when he proclaimed that the economic historian J. H. Clapham had created "a structure of facts as hard and certain as granite. On his ground in his manner nothing else remains to be done."[52] Postmodern historians have pointed out one of the several fallacies in that assumption: because history never ends, it will forever be reinterpreted. We always judge the past in the light of the present, and as present conditions are always changing, so must our view of the past. To take an obvious example, in the placid 1950s, the "consensus school" of American historians seemed to make reasonably good sense – until the tumultuous 1960s hit. Again, the postmodernists were not the first to realize this. The same point had been wryly made in that classic 1931 treatise on metahistorical theory, *1066 and All That*: "History is now at an end . . . this History is therefore final." Churchill often wrote and spoke publicly of "the verdict of history," and usually seemed quite sure that it would favor him, but in private, according to Maurice Ashley, "he seldom thought that a final verdict could be reached which might not have to be modified in the light of later knowledge." That agnosticism even applied to his biography of his father:

"Ah!" he told Ashley, "if I had known then what I know now I should have written it very differently."[53] In one famous speech (November 1940) he offered a kind of uncertainty principle for historians:

> It is not given to human beings, happily for them, for otherwise life would be intolerable, to foresee or to predict to any large extent the unfolding course of events. In one phase men seem to have been right, in another they seem to have been wrong. Then again, a few years later, when the perspective of time has lengthened, all stands in a different setting. There is a new proportion. There is another scale of values.

That was from his generous eulogy for Neville Chamberlain. We don't often associate Churchill with the quality of humility, but he was modest enough to admit that "History with its flickering lamp stumbles along the trail of the past, trying to reconstruct its scenes, to revive its echoes, and kindle with pale gleams the passion of former days."[54]

Churchill also anticipated a historical method even more modern than postmodernism: the history of print culture. Like Adrian Johns, he recognized that technologies of print could lead to the perpetuation of myths, as mistakes were reproduced from text to text: "Thus easily do chains of error trail link after link through history."[55] More importantly, as a journalist, Churchill well understood the role of print in making a historical reputation. Clearly, he wrote, Marlborough was a greater military genius than either Louis XIV or Napoleon: after all, he won his wars. Why then were the two Frenchmen immortalized in a way that the Englishman had not been? Churchill concluded that the victories Marlborough won on the battlefields of Europe were then lost on the printed page, where his reputation was savaged by deceptive "word-spinners" like Thomas Babington Macaulay.[56] Louis XIV may have been a mediocre general, but he was excellent at handling the media, and not just print media: he marched into battle with "a personal retinue . . . of painters, poets, and historians," so that everything he did "was duly immortalized in the French poetry, tapestries, pictures, and engravings of the age."[57] Marlborough made no effort to publicize himself, and never wrote any memoirs. "I do not love to see my name in print," he confided to his wife Sarah, "for I am persuaded that an honest man must be justified by his own actions, and not by the pen of a writer."[58] His descendant would bend every effort to avoid that mistake. Where Marlborough merely made history, Winston both made it and wrote it, racing to produce the first comprehensive histories of both world wars.

Churchill himself had endured some fairly savage newspaper attacks during the First World War. In May 1915 a sympathetic journalist, Edward Bell of the

Chicago Daily News, warned him that "The Germans in America are making valiant use of the attacks of Northcliffe and the Morning Post on the Government in general and you in particular. They have strewn handbills broadcast over Chicago & put them into every home – representing the 'great newspaper of London' as accusing you of having 'overruled Lord Fisher' and brought upon England the 'gigantic and fatal blunder' of the assault upon the Dardanelles." The only reply Bell received was from Eddie Marsh: "Mr. Churchill asked me to thank you very much for the courtesy of your letter, but to say that he has made up his mind that it is best to ignore the attacks to which you refer, and to leave events to speak for themselves."[59] Painfully, Churchill learned that events never speak for themselves: they are filtered and refashioned by the media. After his ejection from the Admiralty, he made much greater efforts to cultivate friendly journalists such as J. L. Garvin, C. P. Scott, and Lord Rothermere.[60] He blamed the Northcliffe press when Lloyd George (who became Prime Minister in December 1916) kept him out of the Cabinet.[61] As he complained to the Dardanelles Commission, the Somme had cost nearly 600,000 British casualties, far more than Gallipoli, but "Nevertheless with a good Press sedulously manipulated & employed and the effective support of the governing forces, these operations have been represented as a long series of famous and memorable victories and the initial disaster of the 1st of July has been established in the public mind as a brilliant triumph."[62] In *The World Crisis* he asserted that no history of the war would be complete without an account of the press and its often irresponsible influence,[63] and *Marlborough* was based on the same premise. Winston understood that the English press under Queen Anne, newly freed from the constraints of pre-publication censorship, had suddenly become a very potent factor in politics. Both Whig and high Tory papers assaulted Sidney Godolphin, Sarah Churchill, and even the great commander himself, to the point where they limited his freedom of action on the battlefield. As long as Godolphin remained in power, his government could prosecute the most virulent anti-Marlborough papers for seditious libel (the press was not yet completely free), but once he was gone, there was nothing to prevent Jonathan Swift, Daniel Defoe, and Mary Manley from going for the jugular.[64]

Along with C. V. Wedgwood, A. L. Rowse, and G. M. Trevelyan, Churchill was trying to bridge the growing gap between academics and the mass reading public. They all wrote "crossover" history, founded on serious archival research that might win the respect of scholars, while deploying a literary flair that appealed to the common reader. In *Marlborough* Churchill identified himself with this "new school of writers who are reconciling scientific history with literary style and popular comprehension."[65] Violet Barbour, the prize-winning Vassar College historian, was duly impressed by his ability to combine solid scholarship with the "stormy eloquence" of Thomas Carlyle and the "ironic disdain" of Lytton Strachey.[66] As G. M. Trevelyan told him, "Professional historians most of them haven't the art of getting themselves read, and the unprofessional ones, like Wells and Belloc, usually have a bee in their bonnet. So you fill a gap."[67] (There might have been a tinge of jealousy in that comment: Trevelyan's *England under Queen Anne* was published almost simultaneously with *Marlborough*, and these two great, fat, and very similar books may have cut into each other's sales.)

Besides earning royalties (an important consideration), Churchill wrote history with three prime objectives in mind. Of course it was a means of self-dramatization and self-justification, especially in his accounts of the two world wars. (Arthur Balfour characterized *The World Crisis* as "Winston's brilliant autobiography, disguised as a history of the universe.")[68] He was also sending a political message, whiggishly exalting English traditions of liberty and warning against the threat of foreign dictatorships. On 4 October 1933, upon the publication of the first installment of *Marlborough*, he addressed his publishers, the firm of George G. Harrap: "All over the world you see Governments springing into power—power based on force—force derived from the suppression of public opinion," but strong and growing public interest in Britain's history "will enable us still to hold the light of civilization —of a free and cultivated society which will stand, I believe, like a barrier against the extremes either of Communism or Fascism."[69]

As the story of a heroic English military leader who managed a coalition of powers to contain an aggressive continental despot, *Marlborough* had obvious relevance in the 1930s, though the target (at least in the first volume) was Stalin as much as Hitler. (After the revocation of the Edict of Nantes, Louis XIV pursued a policy of "expropriation, imprisonment, and death," enforcing ideological conformity, commanding a sycophantic cult of personality, wasting the nation's wealth and the lives of thousands of workmen on vast showcase construction projects. "Flight from tyranny across the frontiers was forbidden, as it is at the present time from Russia.")[70] *A History of the English-Speaking Peoples* would have much the same thrust, as Churchill explained to Maurice Ashley in April 1939:

> In the main, the theme is emerging of the growth of freedom and law, of the rights of the individual, of the subordination of the State to the fundamental and moral conceptions of an ever-comprehending community. Of these ideas the English-speaking peoples were the authors, then the trustees, and must now become the armed champions. Thus I condemn tyranny in whatever guise and from whatever quarter it presents itself. All this of course has a current application.[71]

Thirdly, Churchill believed that nations were validated by history: the longer the history, the greater the nation. He was enthralled by grand narratives, and by any country that could offer a big story, preferably running for at least a millennium. England was great because her history extended back two thousand years (as chronicled in *A History of the English-Speaking Peoples*) and would continue for at least another thousand (as promised in the "Finest Hour" speech). Likewise, when Churchill discussed the German invasion of Norway, he hearkened back to the Vikings,[72] and when Japan was about to enter the war, he contrasted that fatal decision with her "long, romantic history."[73] Ethiopia had "thousands of years" of history, at least when Mussolini threatened her.[74] (For some reason he never said that about India.) Australia had a relatively short history, if one overlooked the aborigines (as Churchill did), but he got around that by insisting that the idea of Australia had "a long history in the realms of human imagination. From the days of Herodotus mankind has had its legends of distant lands, seen for a moment on the horizon, inhabited by strange monsters and rich with the fabulous wealth of Solomon's Ophir and Tarshish."[75]

The peacemakers at Versailles in 1919 created Czechoslovakia, a nation that had never before existed, but it too was justified by a long narrative history: "The ancient kingdom of Bohemia and Moravia, where the Czechs lived, stirred popular memories of King Wenceslas on the Feast of Stephen, of blind King John of Bohemia at the Battle of Crécy, of the Prince of Wales's feathers with its German motto 'Ich Dien,' and perhaps of John Huss of Prague. Here were time-honoured tales." Churchill realized that including the Sudeten Germans would create another Ulster, burdening the new state with a discontented minority and violating the idea of self-determination. But he supported the decision "to adhere to the ancient frontiers of Bohemia, well defined by mountain ranges, and consecrated by five hundred years of tradition."[76] Czechoslovakia and Poland would be wiped off the map after barely twenty years of independent existence, but the Czechs were still "a nation famous and recognizable as a distinct community for many centuries past in Europe," and Poland was an "ancient country . . . with a history extending back far beyond anything that Germany can boast."[77]

This enchantment with long historical narratives helps to explain Churchill's lifelong attachment to the Greeks and the Jews, nations far older than England. Each, he explained, was a

> famous ancient race, whose stormy and endless struggle for life stretches back to the fountain springs of human thought. No two races have set such a mark upon the world. Both have shown a capacity for survival, in spite of the unending perils and sufferings from external oppressors, matched only

> by their own ceaseless feuds, quarrels, and convulsions. The passage of several thousand years sees no change in their characteristics and no diminution of their trials or their vitality. They have survived in spite of all the world could do against them, and all they could do against themselves, and each of them from angles so different have left us the inheritance of their genius and wisdom. No two cities have counted more with mankind than Athens and Jerusalem. Their messages in religion, philosophy, and art have been the main guiding lights of modern faith and culture. Centuries of foreign rule and indescribable, needless oppression leave them still living, active communities and forces in the modern world, quarrelling among themselves with insatiable vivacity. Personally I have always been on the side of both, and believed in their invincible power to survive internal strife and the world tides threatening their extinction.[78]

Everyone who thinks about history has a historical horizon, which determines how far backward and forward we look. Up to a point we consider the past relevant and important, and up to a point we plan for the future; everything beyond those boundaries we dismiss as ancient history or unforseeable. Winwood Reade and H. G. Wells had the farthest possible horizons, from the origins of the cosmos to interplanetary voyages. Churchill's sweep of history was not quite so broad, but he still thought in terms of millennia rather than years. In March 1940 Sumner Welles and Joseph P. Kennedy (the US Under Secretary of State and ambassador to the UK) visited him at the Admiralty, and he orated to them as to a large audience, vowing total victory over Nazi tyranny. It would "cost us dear," he admitted, but "that is the only hope for civilization." The American diplomats raised an objection that others have raised since: even a victorious war would bankrupt Britain. But Churchill had a ready answer: "That is taking the short view of it."[79] Given that vision of history, his logic was impeccable.

CHAPTER 11

Revolutionaries

In Czarist Russia, Boris Savinkov was a leader of the terrorist wing of the Social Revolutionary Party. He successfully plotted two important assassinations: in 1904 V. K. Plehve, Minister of the Interior, and in 1905 the Grand Duke Sergei, uncle of the Czar. Arrested and condemned to death, Savinkov escaped from prison and enjoyed a glamorous exile among Paris bohemians. In the First World War he fought with the French Army. After the February 1917 Revolution he returned to Russia and served for a few weeks as Deputy War Minister in Alexander Kerensky's Provisional Government. He then supported General Kornilov's unsuccessful revolt against that regime: for that he was expelled from the Social Revolutionary Party. After the Bolsheviks seized power he worked for White Army leaders, first Admiral Kolchak and then General Denikin. When their armies disintegrated he set up his own army corps based in Poland, until the Poles made peace with the Soviets. Then he organized guerrillas inside Russia, working with the legendary spy Sidney Reilly, and again had little success. In 1924 Leon Trotsky and Lev Kamenev enticed Savinkov back to the Soviet Union with the promise that they would work together to create a more humane regime, but of course it was a trap: he either killed himself or was executed in prison.[1]

If this dossier sounds like a revolutionary melodrama, that is how it struck Winston Churchill. He first met Savinkov when he was an agent for Kolchak: "I had never seen a Russian nihilist except on the stage, and my impression was that he was singularly well cast for the part."[2] In important ways, Churchill's responses to five major revolutionary movements of his era – Bolshevik, Zionist, Arab, Irish, and Nazi – were powerfully conditioned by literary influences.

In the case of Savinkov, one of those influences was that Nihilist melodrama, whose title Churchill never mentioned. Another was Savinkov's own autobiographical novel, *The Pale Horse*, published in English in 1919, which according to Churchill "depicts with an accuracy that cannot be doubted the methods, the daily life, the psychological state and the hair-raising adventures" of a revolutionary cell.[3] Savinkov reminded him as well of Cimourdain in Victor Hugo's *Ninety-Three*, a novel of an uprising against the Jacobins in Brittany.[4] Cimourdain is an intensely dedicated revolutionary, but eventually he is sickened by the Terror: after condemning a decent man to the guillotine, he commits suicide. According to Hugo's biographer, the character of Cimourdain also "made a deep impression on a young Georgian seminarian named Dzhugashvili, who was confined to his cell for reading *Ninety-Three* and later changed his name to Stalin."[5] And a fourth influence was Churchill's own *Savrola*, whose plot uncannily anticipated the trajectory of the Russian Revolution: an Eastern European despot is overthrown by a liberal revolution, which is then hijacked by extremists, who assassinate the fallen tyrant, whereupon reactionary armed forces counterattack and plunge the country into a chaotic civil war. In an extraordinary act of wishful thinking, Churchill apparently saw the wildly unreliable Savinkov as the incarnation of Savrola, quite possibly because the names were similar. Savinkov, he insisted, was "that extraordinary product – a Terrorist for moderate aims. A reasonable and enlightened policy – the Parliamentary system of England, the land tenure of France, freedom, toleration and good will – to be achieved whenever necessary by dynamite at the risk of death."[6]

Churchill reacted to the Bolsheviks just a few months after they seized power. On 23 February 1918 he urged Lord Beaverbrook, as Minister of Information, "that there can be no more valuable propaganda in England at the present time than graphic accounts of the Bolshevik outrages and ferocity, of the treacheries they have committed, and what ruin they have brought upon their country and the harm they have done to us and to our fighting men."[7] In 1919–20 he repeatedly proclaimed that "Of all tyrannies in history, the Bolshevik tyranny is the worst, the most destructive, the most degrading."[8]

> Was there ever a more awful spectacle in the whole history of the world than is unfolded by the agony of Russia? This vast country, this mighty branch of the human family, not only produced enough food for itself, but before the war, it was one of the great granaries of the world, from which food was exported to every country. It is now reduced to famine of the most terrible kind, not because there is no food – there is plenty of food – but because the theories of Lenin and Trotsky have fatally, and it may be finally, ruptured the means of intercourse between man and man, between workman and peasant, between town and country; because they have scattered the systems of scientific communication by rail and river on which the life of great cities depends; because they have raised class against class and race against race in

> a fratricidal war; because they have given vast regions where a little while ago were smiling villages and prosperous townships back to the wolves and the bears; because they have driven man from civilization to a barbarism worse than the Stone Age, and have left him the most awful and pitiable spectacle in human experience, devoured by vermin, racked by pestilence, and deprived of hope.
>
> And this is progress, this is liberty. This is Utopia! What a monstrous absurdity and perversion of the truth it is to represent the communistic theory as a form of progress, when, at every step and at every stage, it is simply marching back into the dark ages. . . .[9]

On that final point Churchill and Savinkov thought alike. They last met at Chequers, where Lloyd George discussed the Russian situation and offered the standard Liberal diagnosis and prognosis:

> The Prime Minister argued that revolutions like diseases run a regular course, that the worst was already over in Russia, that the Bolshevik leaders confronted with the responsibilities of actual government would quit their Communistic theories or that they would quarrel among themselves and fall like Robespierre and St. Just, that others weaker or more moderate would succeed them, and that by successive convulsions a more tolerable regime would be established.
>
> "Mr. Prime Minister," Savinkov replied, "you will permit me the honor of observing that after the fall of the Roman Empire there ensued The Dark Ages."[10]

The Victorian world view that Churchill had absorbed from Winwood Reade's *The Martyrdom of Man* envisioned a future of endless human progress. For anyone who grew up with that comfortable assurance, the radical breakdown of the European economy and political order in the aftermath of the First World War was an unimaginable shock. Russia during the Civil War collapsed into famine, anarchy, and terror conducted by both Reds and Whites. The catastrophe resembled what H. G. Wells had envisioned in *The War in the Air*, and would later imagine in *Things to Come*. Many British liberals and socialists had profound misgivings about the Bolshevik regime, but they generally viewed it as "progressive" – an attempt at making a better world, however misguided it might be. But Churchill saw it as an atavism, dismantling centuries of civilization. Hence the lurid, overwrought language he used against the Soviets, which only ruined his credibility. "You don't sum up Russia by calling Lenin a traitor," said the literary critic John Squire, after meeting Churchill in September 1918. "That is melodrama."[11] Churchill's portrait of the horrors of

"War Communism" was not much exaggerated, but regarding the alternatives he was hopelessly unrealistic. Neither the Cabinet nor the general public had much stomach for prolonging British military intervention in Russia or assisting the White armies. Churchill's efforts to prevent the Whites from staging their own terror and attacking Jews were both sincere and wholly naive, as was his backing for a rogue like Boris Savinkov.[12]

For an election speech delivered in Dundee on 11 November 1922 Churchill, as was his habit, laid out his notes in poetic cadence:

What a disappointment the Twentieth Century has been
How terrible & how melancholy
is long series of disastrous events
wh have darkened its first 20 years.
We have seen in ev country a dissolution,
a weakening of those bonds,
a challenge to those principles
a decay of faith
an abridgement of hope
on wh structure & ultimate existence
of civilized society depends.
We have seen in ev part of globe
one gt country after another
wh had erected an orderly, a peaceful
a prosperous structure of civilized society,
relapsing in hideous succession
into bankruptcy, barbarism or anarchy.

It was, in effect, *The Waste Land* written by a middlebrow, in the same year as T. S. Eliot's poem, and cast in *vers libre*. Everywhere the march of progress had been abruptly reversed. In Ireland there was "enormous retrogression of civilization & Christianity," in Egypt and India "we see among millions of people hitherto shielded by superior science & superior law a desire to shatter the structure by which they live & to return blindly & heedlessly to primordial chaos."

Can you doubt, my faithful friends
as you survey this somber panorama,
that mankind is passing through a period marked
not only by an enormous destruction
& abridgement of human species,
not only by a vast impoverishment

& reduction in means of existence
but also that destructive tendencies
have not yet run their course?[13]

That kind of post-war cultural despair often produced a backlash against the Jews, who were widely viewed as agents of corrosive modernity. On 29 November 1919 Archibald Sinclair suggested that Churchill read *The Protocols of the Elders of Zion*. Sinclair meant to warn against the dangers of anti-Semitism, dismissing the screed as "sheer, wild nonsense," comparable to *Alice through the Looking Glass*.[14] But Churchill apparently read it differently. On 2 January 1920 he delivered a speech in Sunderland denouncing the Bolsheviks in the usual vitriolic terms, but adding that their leaders were mainly Jews.[15] This last allegation elicted a protest from Claude Montefiore, a leader of the Liberal Jewish movement. In response, Churchill produced a list of Soviet leaders that included six Jews (Trotsky, Lev Kamenev, Grigory Zinoviev, Maxim Litvinov, Leonid Krassin, Karl Radek) and three gentiles (Lenin, Georgi Chicherin, Felix Dzerzhinski). He cited a report that claimed that proportions of Jews in various Petrograd Commissariats ranged from 25 to 93 percent. "I cannot help thinking that the Jews in this country would be better advised to admit the facts more openly than they do, to denounce the renegades in Russia and Poland who are dishonouring their race and religion, and to rally to the support of such forces in Russia as offer some project of restoring a strong, democratic and impartial Government."[16]

Then on 8 February Churchill published in the *Illustrated Sunday Herald* an article that has baffled and troubled his biographers. The polemic was a bizarre concoction, two parts philo-Semitism to one part anti-Semitism. The Jews, he began, "are beyond all question the most formidable and the most remarkable race which has ever appeared in the world. . . . We owe to the Jews in the Christian revelation a system of ethics which, even if it were entirely separated from the supernatural, would be incomparably the most precious possession of mankind, worth in fact the fruits of all other wisdom and learning put together." Released from the ghetto, modern Jewry was now moving in three divergent political directions: assimilation, Zionism, and Marxism. The first two Churchill warmly endorsed, but in Bolshevism, he insisted, the same Jewish genius that in other realms had done so much good was now promoting unspeakable evil. Leon Trotsky, Bela Kun, Rosa Luxemburg, and Emma Goldman were the agents of a "world-wide conspiracy for the overthrow of civilization and for the reconstitution of society on the basis of arrested development, of envious malevolence, and impossible equality." And this conspiracy of "International Jews" had been at work for some time: "It played . . . a definitely recognizable part in the tragedy of the

French Revolution. It has been the mainspring of every subversive movement during the Nineteenth Century; and now at last this band of extraordinary personalities from the underworld of the great cities of Europe and America have gripped the Russian people by the hair of their heads and have become practically the undisputed masters of that enormous empire."[17] He identified as his source of inspiration Nesta Webster, whose book *The French Revolution: A Study in Democracy* argued that revolutionary upheavals in Europe, from 1789 to 1917, had all been fomented by a Jewish-Masonic conspiracy. She claimed that the authenticity of *The Protocols of the Elders of Zion* was "an entirely open question," though she often cited it as if it were true.[18]

One can only explain this temporary insanity in terms of Churchill's lifelong passion for grand narratives. In modern times two such narratives, diametrically opposed, have attached themselves to the Jews: in one they are a light unto the nations, in the other the agents of diabolical global conspiracy. Churchill always held to the first of these narratives, but for a brief interval, panicked by the Bolshevik Revolution, he somehow managed to believe in both of them simultaneously, yet another example of his capacity for embracing contradictions. He apparently shook off this paranoia when he himself became its target. In 1923 Lord Alfred Douglas publicly accused him of aiding a Jewish bankers' plot, manipulating stock market prices by filing misleading reports about the Battle of Jutland.[19] Churchill must have realized that with all his Jewish friends and connections he was more vulnerable to this kind of attack than any other important gentile politician.

This episode is all the more puzzling because Churchill was otherwise a fierce champion of the Jews. He had cheered on Captain Dreyfus and vociferously opposed the 1905 Aliens Bill, Britain's first immigration restriction legislation. Though it did not specifically target Jews, it was a response to a surge of Jewish immigration from Russia, and Churchill warned that it could be enforced arbitrarily by "an intolerant or anti-Semitic Home Secretary." Happily, he added, English workmen "do not respond in any marked degree to the anti-Semitism which has recently darkened recent Continental history." The "opposition of wealthy and influential Jews" to such a bill was to be applauded: "That men like Lord Rothschild and others of his faith should earnestly strive to preserve a free asylum in England for their co-religionists who are driven out from foreign countries by religious persecution, although the expense must fall upon themselves, is an honourable fact in thorough accordance with the traditions of the Jewish people."[20] As he told Cheetham Jews in October 1906, "Remember that no Jew who is not a good Jew can ever really be a good Englishman."[21] He denounced pogroms, and not only in Russia. In August 1911, when anti-Jewish rioting and looting broke out in the South Wales mining valleys, Churchill swiftly dispatched troops to the area and apprehended the perpetrators. In 1913 he quit the Reform Club when it blackballed Baron de Forest, a Jewish MP.[22]

As early as 1906 he expressed sympathy in principle with the idea of a Jewish homeland somewhere within the British Empire, though he was aware of "the numerous and serious difficulties involved."[23] He himself dated his conversion to Zionism in 1909.[24] In the Great War, as First Lord of the Admiralty, he would engage the chemist and Zionist leader Chaim Weizmann to synthesize acetone. (Acetone was necessary for the production of cordite, an explosive used in naval ammunition.) A Zion Mule Corps, recruited from Palestinian Jews, fought with distinction at Gallipoli, and Jews inside Palestine gave vital assistance to invading British forces. As Minister of Munitions Churchill worked closely with his Director-General of Tank Production Sir Albert Stern, an active Zionist. The Balfour Declaration – which committed Britain to support "the establishment in Palestine of a national home for the Jewish people" – was approved by the War Cabinet on 31 October, dispatched to Baron Rothschild on 2 November, and published 9 November. It was motivated in part by the hope that Russian Jews would rally to keep their country in the war, and Weizmann was preparing to travel to Russia to encourage them. That plan was forestalled on 7 November, when the Bolsheviks seized power in Petrograd. But all of this reinforced Churchill's conviction that the Balfour Declaration was a just reward for meritorious service during the war.[25]

In March 1921, as Colonial Secretary, Churchill visited Palestine. He was duly impressed by the vineyards and orange groves of Rishon le-Zion – and noted that "all round the Jewish colony, the Arab houses were tiled instead of being built of mud." The Jewish community, he enthused, "is transforming waste places into fertile; it is planting trees and developing agriculture in desert lands; it is making for an increase in wealth and of cultivation; it is making two blades of grass grow where one grew before." And the Arab majority was "deriving great benefit, sharing in the general improvement and advancement." He repeatedly thumped that last point when speaking to skeptical Arabs, and however sincere he was, he sometimes assumed the tone of a nanny dispensing medicine to a stubborn child. "You can see with your own eyes in many parts of this country the work which has already been done by Jewish colonies," he lectured one Arab audience, "how sandy wastes have been reclaimed and thriving farms and orangeries planted in their stead." Once he returned home he repeatedly gushed over Zionist achievements: "They have not only created wealth for themselves but for the Arabs around them. Wherever the footprints of the Jew in Palestine are found you have prosperity, progress and scientific methods of cultivation."[26] It all seemed to confirm what he had read in Macaulay and Winwood Reade: that imperialism was a force for progress that benefited colonized peoples. (And strictly speaking,

Palestine was not a colony: from 1923 it was administered by Britain under a League of Nations mandate, which included instructions to carry out the Balfour Declaration.)

Apart from the economic benefits, the magazine *Palestine* concluded, Churchill's "historical imagination has been touched by the grandeur of the idea of endowing Jewry with nationhood in its old home of Palestine."[27] His Zionism was largely a function of his predilection for taking a very long view of history. Meeting with an Arab delegation in London on 22 August 1921, he argued that "This is a country where they have great historic traditions, and you cannot brush that aside as though it was absolutely nothing. They were there many hundreds of years ago. They have always tried to be there."[28] Churchill had earlier tried to convey that grand narrative to Palestinian Arabs on 30 March 1921: "It is manifestly right that the Jews, who are scattered all over the world, should have a national centre and a National Home where some of them may be reunited. And where else could that be but in this land of Palestine, with which for more than 3000 years they have been intimately and profoundly associated?" This the Arabs found unpersuasive. Churchill then asked them to think of the future as well as the past in terms of a long arc. Eventually the British would prepare Palestine for full democratic self-government, but "All of us here to-day will have passed away from the earth and also our children and our children's children before it is fully achieved." That probably did not reassure either the Arabs or the Jews.[29]

Today, after a century of conflict between Jews and Arabs, we tend to think of them as natural adversaries, on the front lines in the battle between West and East. But Jews were generally classified as "Oriental" before 1880, when most of them lived in Eastern Europe or the Middle East, and the most fashionable style of synagogue architecture was Moorish. In his proto-Zionist novel *Tancred* (1847) Disraeli argued that the Jews belonged in Palestine because they were, in fact, "an Arabian tribe" – or to put it another way, "The Arabs are only Jews upon horseback." At the time Jews and eastern Mediterranean Arabs were often subsumed under the category "Levantine," a term sometimes applied to Disraeli himself: for example when Gladstone called him "a clever Levantine manipulator."[30] For Disraeli, Europe represented a decadent, materialistic civilization: the spiritual renewal of the world could only come from the East, when the Jews had returned to their true home. "God has never spoken to a European," he proclaimed, indeed "God never spoke except to an Arab."[31] *Tancred* was no doubt an influential book, preparing British public opinion for the Balfour Declaration.[32] When Herbert Samuel proposed a Jewish homeland in a January 1915 Cabinet memorandum, Asquith said "It reads almost like a new edition of *Tancred* brought up to date," even if he was not enamored of the idea.[33] But Disraeli's Zionism was not exactly the Zionism that Churchill and other Englishmen embraced after 1917. By then the Jews were perceived as more Westernized, and hence a possible bridge between East and West, as well as a force for progress in an impoverished region. Disraeli (at least in *Tancred*) glorified the ancient civilizations of the East and scoffed at European notions of progress: "Progress to what?"[34] In any case, Churchill only made one passing allusion to *Tancred*, in *My Early Life*.[35] As we will see, another literary work, more widely read, probably had a more powerful impact on Churchill's Zionism.

Tancred did promote the idea that Arab nationalism and Jewish nationalism were reconcilable, even synergistic. As the Conservative MP Leo Amery recalled, he and other young men in Churchill's orbit who embraced the idea of a Jewish homeland were "pro-Arab as well as pro-Zionist, and saw no essential incompatibility between the two ideals."[36] T. E. Lawrence believed that Zionism would actually be essential to the success of an Arab awakening. "Speaking entirely as a non-Jew," he said one year after the Balfour Declaration, "I look on the Jews as the natural importers of western leaven so necessary for countries of the Near East." In the months following the Armistice he had brought Emir Feisal and Chaim Weizmann together for meetings to find a path toward (in Lawrence's words) "the lines of Arab and Zionist policy converging in the near future." Feisal agreed that "We Arabs, especially the educated among us, look with the deepest sympathy on the Zionist movement. . . . We are working together for a reformed and revived Middle East, and our two movements complete one another." As Lawrence argued in a 1920 article in the *Round Table*, Zionism represented "a conscious effort, on the part of the least European people in Europe, to make head against the drift of the ages, and return once more to the Orient from which they came." Because they were an Eastern people endowed with Western "skill and capital", they were ideally equipped to fuse the two cultures and modernize the Middle East, raising "the present Arab population to their own material level. . . . The consequences might be of the highest importance for the future of the Arab world. It might well prove a source of technical supply rendering them independent of industrial Europe, and in that case the new confederation might become a formidable element of world power." Thus Zionism would incite what we might today call an "Arab Spring." (And that suggests a mind-reeling counterfactual: Where would the Arabs be today if they had embraced the Zionists as allies?) At the Cairo Conference in May 1921, Lawrence noted Churchill's assurance that, after Palestine had been ruled "under the influence of a just policy" for a few years, Arab anti-Zionism "would have decreased, if it had not entirely disappeared."[37]

If that seems dangerously naive, remember that at this point Arabs and Jews had not yet fought a war. The British and the Boers had fought, and now (as

Churchill liked to point out) they were living together peacefully in a Union of South Africa that was free and democratic (for whites, at any rate). Ireland was wracked by violence, but by May 1921 Churchill was urging a truce with Sinn Fein and a negotiated settlement, which did come about. In both Irish and Middle Eastern contexts, Churchill quoted his Irish-American mentor Bourke Cockran: "The earth is a generous mother, and will provide for all her children if they will cultivate her soil in justice and in peace."[38] At this time there was not much awareness that the Muslim world had its own history of anti-Semitism. Sir Henry Wilson (Chief of the Imperial General Staff) saw Churchill's Zionism as yet another creation of his literary imagination, and a costly one at that:

> Yes, in a vague sort of way Winston appears to think that he is going to govern Palestine as he is going to try and govern Mesopotamia, by his hot air, aeroplanes and, Jews this time. This experiment, like those of holding Antwerp with men in plain clothes who have never carried a rifle, or those of forcing the Dardanelles by ships without soldiers . . . are experiments which cost this country hundreds of millions, thousands of lives, and the loss not only of territory but of prestige. . . . I admire Winston in many ways but in truth he is too expensive for any purpose that I can see that he can serve.[39]

When he became Colonial Secretary in 1921, Churchill was not unaware of the danger of an explosion in the Middle East:

> We had recently suppressed a most dangerous and bloody rebellion in Iraq, and upwards of forty thousand troops at a cost of thirty million pounds a year were required to preserve order. This could not go on. In Palestine the strife between the Arabs and the Jews threatened at any moment to take the form of actual violence. The Arab chieftains, driven out of Syria with many of their followers – all of them our late allies – lurked furious in the deserts beyond the Jordan. Egypt was in ferment. Thus the whole of the Middle East presented a most melancholy and alarming picture.

Churchill formed a special department staffed with experts familiar with the area, including T. E. Lawrence, in whom he had unlimited faith. Ultimately, they recommended making Emir Feisal King of Iraq, Emir Abdullah (his elder brother) King of Transjordan, and using the RAF rather than ground troops to police Iraq. For all this, Churchill assigned much of the credit to Lawrence, and he asked him, "What would you like to do when all this is smoothed out." "In a very few months my work here will be finished," Lawrence replied. "The job is done, and it will last." It was still possible to believe this when Churchill wrote that, one year before the Arab Revolt of 1936. Confident that he and Lawrence had solved the Middle Eastern problem, Churchill hailed *Seven Pillars of Wisdom* as one of "the greatest books ever written in the English language," ranking it with *Pilgrim's Progress, Robinson Crusoe*, and *Gulliver's Travels*. But in this case the work was not fiction, and "The author was also the commander," a magical combination that Churchill had always aspired to:

> Caesar's *Commentaries* deal with larger numbers, but in Lawrence's story nothing that has ever happened in the sphere of war and empire is lacking. When most of the vast literature of the Great War has been sifted and superseded by the epitomes, commentaries and histories of future generations, when the complicated and infinitely costly operations of its ponderous armies are the concern only of the military student, when our struggles are viewed in a fading perspective and truer proportion, Lawrence's tale of the revolt in the desert will gleam with immortal fire. . . .
>
> Here we see Lawrence the soldier. Not only the soldier but the statesman: rousing the fierce peoples of the desert, penetrating the mysteries of their thought, leading them to the selected points of action and as often as not firing the mine himself. Detailed accounts are given of ferocious battles with thousands of men and little quarter fought under his command on these lava landscapes of hell. There are no mass-effects. All is intense, individual, sentient – and yet cast in conditions which seemed to forbid human existence. Through all, one mind, one soul, one will-power. An epic, a prodigy, a tale of torment, and in the heart of it – a Man.

It's all about Lawrence then. In the actual *Seven Pillars of Wisdom* the Arabs, the Turks, and the rest of the British Army are all prominent players, but in Churchill's reading of the book they are only background, and play no active role, not even as "mass-effects." Churchill spotlights Lawrence as a pure artist, "not in complete harmony with the normal," a creative genius radically free of all social trammels:

> The world feels, not without a certain apprehension, that here is someone outside its jurisdiction . . . someone strangely enfranchised, untamed, untrammeled by convention, moving independently of the ordinary currents of human action; a being readily capable of violent revolt or supreme sacrifice, a man, solitary, austere, to whom existence is no more than a duty, yet a duty to be faithfully discharged. He was indeed a dweller upon the mountain tops where the air is cold, crisp and rarefied, and where the view on clear days commands all the Kingdoms of the world and the glory of them.

Compared with ordinary men, Lawrence was "moving alone on a different plane and at a different speed." Moreover, *Seven Pillars of Wisdom* was not just a literary masterpiece, it was also a brilliant example of the book arts, where "every illustration had been profoundly considered and every incident of typography and paragraphing settled with meticulous care."[40] After his retirement, Churchill was asked whether *Seven Pillars of Wisdom* was reliable factual history, and he brushed the question aside as irrelevant: "No. But it was a remarkable work. He was a stylist."[41]

For Lawrence – who wrote that his Arab liberation campaign was inspired by Malory's *Morte d'Arthur* and Swinburne's "Super Flumina Babylonis"[42] – the admiration was mutual. At the Cairo Conference he wrote, Churchill had, in a matter of weeks, "made straight all the tangle, finding solutions fulfilling (I think) our promises in letter and spirit (where humanly possible) without sacrificing any interest of our Empire or any interest of the peoples concerned."[43] The two adventurers mutually recognized that they were both creating artistic personas and dramatizing themselves. "What a subject for a book you would have been, if you had not written it yourself!" Lawrence told Churchill.[44] He also understood Churchill's audacious habit of reconciling opposites: "surprise, stood on its head, as it were, in Chestertonian paradox."[45] In July 1937, when the Arab Revolt threatened to halt Jewish immigration to Palestine, Churchill complacently asserted, "I am quite sure that the genius of a man like Lawrence of Arabia, if Fate had not swept him from the human scene, would in a few months restore the situation, persuade one side to concede and the other to forbear, and lead both races to bathe their hands together in the ever-growing prosperity and culture of their native land."[46]

Testifying before Lord Peel's Palestine Royal Commission in March 1937, Churchill approached the Palestine issue by again taking a very long view of history. He argued that the Palestinian Arabs had fought for the Turks and lost, so Britain ruled by right of conquest, the same right that had secured Arab rule over the region 1,300 years earlier. It followed that, far from imposing a "foreign race" on Palestine, Britain was facilitating the return of its indigenous people.[47] When asked, "after seventeen years, or fifteen years, is it not time we tried something else?" Churchill replied, "Not at all. What is seventeen years? . . . The time to think about changing our policy is in another fifty or hundred years." Churchill's timeline for the establishment of an independent Jewish state ran to "generations or . . . centuries."[48]

On the Irish issue he was likewise too optimistic, too confident in his ability to reconcile the irreconcilable. After he crossed over to the Liberal Party, he took the consistent position that there were no intractable differences between the British and the Irish, or between Irish Catholics and Protestants, or between Unionists and Home Rulers – the political message of that happy melodrama *The English Rose*. Economic reforms and a measure of Irish autonomy could bring about general peace and brotherhood. The exact form and degree of autonomy was an open question. When he first joined the Liberals Churchill balked at creating an Irish parliament, arguing (unrealistically) that Irish demands for self-government could be satisfied by devolving administrative and legislative power down to the county level. When the Liberal Party embraced Home Rule in 1908, Churchill embraced with them, but here again he resorted to the language of conciliation and enlightened liberal imperialism. If granting self-government to South Africa had united Boers and Britons and kept them both loyal to the King, surely a similar strategy would work for Ireland. "If you want to make the British Empire strong," he told Swansea miners, "work for a national settlement with Ireland on the basis of some generous reconciliation which shall secure them the national rights which they do most deeply deserve. . . . Home Rule." The following year he qualified that commitment by proposing (in the privacy of the Cabinet Room) the exclusion of Ulster from Home Rule, before most British or Irish politicians were willing to consider it. But whereas Randolph Churchill had played the "Ulster card" to block Home Rule, Winston offered exclusion as a compromise designed to make Home Rule acceptable to all parties in Ireland. "It was," as Mary Bromage characterized it, "less a case of divide and rule than divide and pacify."[49]

In March 1911, after the December 1910 General Election left the Liberals dependent on the support of the Irish Party, Churchill proposed in a Cabinet paper to divide the United Kingdom into ten regions – Ireland, Scotland, Wales, and seven in England – each with its own parliament to govern local affairs.[50] The common thread behind this and all of Churchill's other schemes for resolving the Irish issue was a conviction that, if the right formula were found, all the parties to the conflict might shake hands, but he never found a way to square that circle.

On the contrary, Unionist rhetoric escalated to the point where (in June 1912) Bonar Law promised that his party would "not be guided by the restraints which would influence us in an ordinary constitutional struggle. . . . There are things stronger than Parliamentary majorities. . . . I can imagine no length of resistance to which Ulster can go in which I should not be prepared to support them, and in which, in my belief, they would not be supported by the overwhelming majority of the British people." Churchill sternly reminded the leader of the Conservative Party that if he was talking revolution, "There are many millions of very poor people in this island . . . to whom these counsels of violence and mutiny may not be unattractive." In *Savrola* it is the forces of reaction that, in a last-ditch effort to resist necessary reforms, plunge Laurania into civil war.

By spring 1914 the threat of insurrection by the Ulster Volunteers was frighteningly real. On 9 March Asquith moved an amendment to the Home Rule Bill that would have allowed any Irish county to exclude itself from a Dublin parliament for six years. The premise here seemed to be that Ulstermen would eventually come around to Home Rule if they were not pressed too hard and given time to get used to the idea, and as such Churchill supported the amendment. When the Unionist leader Edward Carson contemptuously rejected the compromise ("We do not want a sentence of death with a stay of execution for six years"), Churchill was furious. On 17 March he informed a Cabinet committee that he would dispatch the Royal Navy's Third Battle Squadron to Lamlash, within striking distance of Belfast, to overawe the Ulstermen and secure arms depots. According to H. A. Gwynne, on the 20th he used extraordinarily threatening language with the Chief of the Imperial General Staff, Sir John French: "If Belfast showed fight he would have the town in ruins in twenty-four hours."[51] Sending in the gunboats was a favorite climax in melodrama, including *Savrola*, and at Bradford on 14 March Churchill had delivered one of the most melodramatic speeches of his career. "There are things worse than bloodshed, even on an extended scale," he thundered:

> If the civil and Parliamentary systems under which we have dwelt so long, and our fathers before us, are to be brought to the crude challenge of force, if the Government and the Parliament of this great country and greater Empire are to be exposed to menace and brutality; if all the loose, wanton and reckless chatter we have been forced to listen to, these many months, is in the end to disclose a sinister and revolutionary purpose, then I can only say to you: "Let us go forward together and put these grave matters to the proof!"[52]

Churchill repeated that last sentence when he returned to Bradford on 6 December 1942,[53] and "Let us go forward together" was blazoned over his image in one of the most celebrated posters of the Second World War. But the 1914 Bradford speech and the deployment of the Navy may have been, once again, political theatre. The previous November Churchill had met with Austen Chamberlain on the Admiralty yacht *Enchantress*, and at that time he was quite creative and flexible in seeking a compromise. It might (he suggested) involve excluding Ulster from Home Rule (at least temporarily), or granting Ulster autonomy in a self-governing Ireland ("Home Rule within Home Rule"), or a federal reorganization of the whole United Kingdom ("Home Rule all round"). Churchill thought that party leaders were ready to do a deal, but not their militant followers. Therefore, he proposed to screw up the tension until there was real fear of civil war: then a negotiated solution would be accepted with relief by both sides. As Chamberlain paraphrased it:

> Public opinion had got to have a shock. Both sides had to make speeches full of party claptrap and no surrender, and then insert a few sentences at the end for the wise and discerning on the other side to see and ponder. "A little red blood had got to flow" and then public opinion would wake up, and then–!

Today the term "claptrap" refers generally to any kind of hogwash or bombast, but in 1913 it had a more specific meaning: it was a melodramatic rhetorical device. As the play approaches its climax, the action pauses while the hero delivers a brief but fervent oration, proclaiming what he is fighting for, and hurling defiance in the face of the villain. This performance naturally obliges the audience to applaud furiously: they are fairly trapped into clapping. Then the struggle resumes, inevitably ending with the triumph of the good. It was a trick used in *Michael Strogoff*, hundreds of other deservedly forgotten plays, and several more memorable Churchill speeches. Chamberlain thought it "very dangerous" to talk of blood flowing in an Irish context,[54] but late in life Churchill angrily denied that he would have ever ordered the fleet to bombard Belfast.[55] The dispatch of the Navy was a dramatic shock tactic, designed to bring everyone to their senses. For that reason Churchill declaimed and shook his fist in the face of injustice at Bradford, as Harry O'Mailley had done in *The English Rose*. To head off an Irish civil war, Churchill played to the hilt a stage Irishman.

The Bradford speech was a high-risk tactic that failed. Fifty-eight army officers responded with the Curragh Mutiny, promising to resign rather than take up arms against Ulster. On 24 July 1914, in order to exclude Protestant Ireland from Home Rule, the Cabinet was struggling over the boundaries of Fermanagh and Tyrone, trying to find a line that would be acceptable to both sides. It was hopeless, though everyone knew that failure "meant something very like civil war and the plunge into the depths of which no one could make any measure." In *The World Crisis* Churchill sets up the scene, builds the suspense to breaking point, and then drops the *coup de théâtre* – as he put it, the "all-sufficient shock":

> The discussion had reached its inconclusive end, and the Cabinet was about to separate, when the quiet grave tones of Sir Edward Grey's voice were heard reading a document which had just been brought to him from the Foreign Office. It was the Austrian note to Serbia. He had been reading or speaking for several minutes before I could disengage my mind from the tedious and bewildering debate which had just closed. We were all very tired, but gradually as the phrases and sentences followed one another impressions

> of a wholly different character began to form in my mind. This note was clearly an ultimatum; but it was an ultimatum such as had never been penned in modern times. As the reading proceeded it seemed absolutely impossible that any State in the world could accept it, or that any acceptance, however abject, would satisfy the aggressor. The parishes of Fermanagh and Tyrone faded back into the mists and squalls of Ireland, and a strange light began immediately, but by perceptible gradations, to fall and grow upon the map of Europe.[56]

Here Churchill evokes the fade-out/fade-in device employed by "transformation scenes" in Victorian pantomimes, "dissolving views" in magic lantern shows, and the cinema.[57] The implementation of Home Rule was effectively suspended for the duration of the war – a decision which, as Churchill recognized in retrospect, undid the compromise he had worked so hard to achieve and undermined Irish confidence in British conciliation.[58] The Irish civil war had only been postponed.

But even after 1916, when open revolt erupted in Ireland, Churchill still sought some means of keeping the island united and linked to Great Britain. He supported the 1920 Government of Ireland Act, which created separate legislatures for Northern and Southern Ireland, along with a "Council of Ireland" which would somehow eventually undo the division that the act had created and unite the island under a single Parliament. It did nothing, however, to mollify the rebels. Churchill defended the brutal methods of the Black and Tans (which he shrugged off as no worse than the normal operating procedures of the Chicago police) but resisted the imposition of martial law throughout Southern Ireland. When peace talks began in London in 1921, Churchill's negotiating position was clear and consistent: dominion status, which went a step beyond Home Rule but still kept Ireland in the Empire. The North would remain in the United Kingdom, but Churchill told the House of Commons that he still believed "that some day . . . Ulster will join herself with Southern Ireland and . . . the national unity of Ireland within the British Empire will be attained." With that ultimate (and wholly unrealistic) goal in mind, Churchill warmly endorsed the treaty creating the Irish Free State.[59] As Colonial Secretary, he ordered the withdrawal of British forces from Ireland, predicting that British and Irish Free State soldiers would soon be exchanging salutes. "The optimistic imagination of Mr. Winston Churchill that the acceptance of the treaty would result in cessation of disturbance and a loyal interpretation of its terms was by no means shared by the Crown forces in Ireland," recalled their commander, Sir Nevil Macready.[60]

When violence did break out on both sides of the border, Churchill brought James Craig (the Northern Ireland Prime Minister) and Michael Collins

(Chairman of the Provisional Government of the Irish Free State) together in his office to draft a settlement on a blotting pad. On 30 March 1922 they jointly proclaimed "Peace is today declared" – but there was no peace. On 14 April IRA men occupied the Four Courts in Dublin, and on 28 June Free State forces opened fire on them, with Churchill supplying the ammunition. On 7 July, with Dublin pacified but civil war spreading to southwest Ireland, Churchill wrote to both Craig and Collins urging them to revive their reconciliation agreement. "The events which have taken place since you opened fire on the Four Courts seem to me to have in them the possibilities of a very great hope for the peace and ultimate unity of Ireland," he assured Collins. "As soon as you have established the authority of the Irish Free State throughout the 26 Counties" – and Churchill was confident this could be achieved in short order – "a new phase will begin far more hopeful than any we have hitherto experienced. In this phase the objective must be the unity of Ireland. How and when this can be achieved I cannot tell," but Churchill did not doubt that it was attainable. Granting that Collins was busy "grappling with revolt and revolution," Churchill suggested that in spare moments "you should turn over in your mind what would be the greatest offer the South could make for Northern co-operation. Of course, from the Imperial point of view there is nothing we should like better than to see North and South join hands in an all-Ireland assembly without prejudice to the existing rights of either" – and without specifying how this would be accomplished. Then he added, as an afterthought: "I hope you are taking good care of yourself and your colleagues. The times are very dangerous."[61]

A few weeks later Collins was ambushed and killed by IRA forces in County Cork. "Tell Winston we could have never done without him," he reportedly said shortly before his death. Churchill in fact deserved much credit for working out the treaty and bringing the Irish Free State into existence, focusing single-mindedly on those goals, successfully resisting all attempts to derail the process, in the face of growing violence in Ireland and loud recriminations in Westminster.[62] But he could never let go of his conviction that Ireland's tragedy would end as happily as an Irish melodrama. "Don't confuse the Irish revolutionaries with Russian revolutionaries," he advised his cousin Clare Sheridan. "The Irish all believe in God, uphold the family and love their country."[63] At any rate, that generalization held true on the Victorian stage.

Throughout the 1920s Churchill was no less optimistic about reconciling Britons and Germans. In 1929 he asserted that the disarmament of Germany was an "astonishing" success, "and the whole military caste, that vast vested interest and also type of national virtue which had been the permanent agency of German might must fade in the passage of a generation out of German life."[64] But he reacted swiftly to a new development in German politics. In the election of 14 September 1930 the Nazi Party won its first large bloc of representatives in the Reichstag. On 20 October Prince Bismarck, the German ambassador to London, reported the following conversation: "Churchill, who had apparently been following recent newspaper reports in detail and was extremely well informed . . . expressed himself in cutting terms on National Socialism, which had, he said, contributed towards a considerable deterioration of Germany's external position, in particular vis-à-vis France. . . . Hitler had admittedly declared that he had no intention of waging a war of aggression; he, Churchill, however was convinced that Hitler or his followers would seize the first available opportunity to resort to armed force."[65] In the early 1930s British newspapers across the political spectrum did not take Hitler very seriously, assuming that he would either soon disappear from the political scene or join a coalition government and become more "moderate."[66] But Churchill immediately locked on to his prime target.

In 1932 Ernst Hanfstaengel, known as Putzi, a top public relations man for the Nazi Party, tried to arrange a meeting between Churchill and Hitler at a Munich hotel. Hitler shied away, though Hanfstaengel assured him that Churchill was "the easiest man in the world to talk to," and suggested that they might chat about matters of shared interest, such as art and architecture. Churchill instructed Hanfstaengel to "Tell your boss from me that anti-Semitism may be a good starter, but it is a bad sticker."[67]

Even at this early stage, Churchill anticipated that Hitler was capable of mass murder, as suggested in his arresting essay "Moses: The Leader of a People." It was first printed in the *Sunday Chronicle* on 8 November 1931 and included in *Thoughts and Adventures*, published on 10 November 1932 by Thornton Butterworth – after Churchill became aware of the surging electoral strength of the Nazi Party but before Hitler had become Chancellor. Two themes dominate the essay: the relevance of the Exodus story to contemporary politics, and the author's strong identification with the hero of the piece. Moses was "the greatest of the prophets" and "the national hero who led the Chosen People out of the land of bondage, through the perils of the wilderness," as well as "the supreme law-giver." And he was a bestselling writer: "Tradition . . . ascribed to him the authorship of the whole Pentateuch." The conflict that drives the story of Exodus is the Egyptian perception that the Israelites

> had become a social, political, and industrial problem. There they were in the "Land of Goshen," waxing exceedingly, and stretching out every day long arms and competent fingers into the whole life of Egypt. There must have arisen one of those movements with which the modern world is acquainted. A wave of anti-Semitism swept across the land. Gradually, year by year and inch by inch, the Children of Israel were reduced by the policy of the State

> and the prejudices of its citizens from guests to servants and from servants to almost slaves.

And Churchill drew a further, yet more chilling, analogy. Ultimately, he concluded, the Pharaoh resorted to genocide: the murder of Hebrew male infants. At this time the British press was aware of, and generally repelled by, Hitler's anti-Semitism, but it is difficult to think of anyone else who foresaw that it would end in a holocaust. In many ways Hitler resembled the dictator of *Savrola* and the African despot of *King Solomon's Mines*. The latter organizes monster rallies of warriors who mesmerize themselves with rhythmic chants of "*Death!*" and carry out orgies of mass extermination. Today one cannot read those passages without thinking of the Nazis, and Churchill may have been the first to make that connection, consciously or unconsciously. Yet anti-Semitism plays no role in either novel: that essential element was supplied by Exodus. Churchill immediately recognized his enemy because Hitler seemed to be an amalgamation of his three favorite melodramatic villains, created by Churchill, H. Rider Haggard, and the eminent author of Exodus.

The baby Moses is rescued and raised as an Egyptian prince, but then he witnesses a beating of an Israelite by an Egyptian. It was "no doubt a common spectacle, an episode coming to be accepted as part of the daily social routine," but without hesitation Moses kills the Egyptian

> amid the loud and continuing applause of the insurgents of the ages. . . .
>
> The most cultured and civilized states and administrations of the present day would have felt with Pharaoh that this was going altogether too far. Very likely Egyptian public opinion – and there is always public opinion where there is the slightest pretence of civilization – fixed upon this act of violence as a final proof that the weakness of the government towards these overweening strangers and intruders had reached its limit. At any rate Pharaoh – which is as good a name as any other for the governing classes in any country at any time under any system – acted. He decreed death upon the murderer.

Moses escaped to the Sinai desert, where he found himself in a situation similar to Churchill's in the 1930s:

> Every prophet has to come from civilization, but every prophet has to go into the wilderness. He must have a strong impression of a complex society and all that it has to give, and then he must serve periods of isolation and meditation. This is the process by which psychic dynamite is made.

Then God spoke unto Moses from the Burning Bush. Or more exactly, Churchill paraphrases what God spoke, putting a distinctive spin on His words. In fact the Deity becomes a mouthpiece for Winstonian fortitude. "There is nothing that man cannot do, if he wills it with enough resolution. Man is the epitome of the universe. All moves and exists as a result of his invincible will, which is My Will." It was a distinctively Churchillian theology: God's mission is to do Man's will.

As for Pharaoh, "Across the centuries we feel the modernity of his actions." The plagues at first induced him to make prudent concessions to the Israelites, but the loss of their labor "caused considerable derangement in the economic life of the country. It was very like a general strike." Churchill offered naturalistic explanations for the plagues, the parting of the Red Sea, and all the other miracles of Exodus. And he affirmed one miracle in particular, that the Israelites were in their times an unequaled force for progress:

> This wandering tribe, in many respects indistinguishable from numberless nomadic communities, grasped and proclaimed an idea of which all the genius of Greece and all the power of Rome were incapable. There was to be only one God, a universal God, a God of nations, a just God, a God who would punish in another world a wicked man dying rich and prosperous; a God from whose service the good of the humble and of the weak and poor were inseparable.

Churchill was aware of the deconstructive scholarship of biblical criticism, but he rejected

> with scorn all those learned and laboured myths that Moses was but a legendary figure upon whom the priesthood and the people hung their essential social, moral, and religious ordinances. We believe that the most scientific view, the most up-to-date and rationalistic conception, will find its fullest satisfaction in taking the Bible story literally, and in identifying one of the greatest human beings with the most decisive leap-forward ever discernible in the human story. We remain unmoved by the tomes of Professor Gradgrind and Dr. Dryasdust. We may be sure that all these things happened just as they are set out according to Holy Writ. We may believe that they happened to people not so very different fro-m ourselves, and that the impressions those people received were faithfully recorded and have been transmitted across the centuries with far more accuracy than many of the telegraphed accounts we read of the goings-on of today.[68]

It was a stunningly vivid essay. Cecil B. de Mille once said that it supplied the inspiration for his film *The Ten Commandments*, for which Churchill may deserve a credit line.[69] It was also consistent with the sensible theology Churchill outlined in *My Early Life*: he was an atheist except when he chose to be otherwise, and in the case of Exodus he preferred to be a fundamentalist. In *Beyond the Pleasure Principle* Sigmund Freud identified going forth and returning home (*Fort/Da*) as the first and most basic story that children learn. Churchill always based his politics on stories, and Exodus, the most compelling version of this story ever told, became the foundation of his passionate Zionism. It was reinforced by the fact that Chaim Weizmann reminded him of "an Old Testament prophet."[70] In 1950 Eliahu Elath, Israel's ambassador to Britain, would report that Churchill spoke warmly of how the Jews had organized their survival for millennia around the Old Testament. Churchill urged the new state to "preserve close association with the book"[71] – speaking as someone whose statecraft had always been closely associated with books.

CHAPTER 12

The Chancellor's Star Turn

Neville Chamberlain recorded his entire parliamentary career in a series of letters to his sisters, Hilda and Ida. In the summer of 1919 he gave Hilda his impressions of a speech by Lloyd George, which was well received by the House of Commons, even if the Press Gallery wrote it off as "piffle": "What struck me most was the audacious amount of acting put into the performance. He had every trick of gesture, of voice, of dramatic pause, and of carefully rehearsed passion. He also had the phrases which for some reason, to me mysterious and inexplicable, move the majority of men."[1]

What Chamberlain found contemptible in Lloyd George was what others found ingenious. "What a wonderful man he is!" Churchill exclaimed. "What an actor he would have made!"[2] Lord Beaverbrook was in awe of "his genius for theatrical management, which always makes him withdraw a piece which has failed before it is actually hissed off the stage. He knows that the people see high politics much like a film picture: they will forget that you have fallen down the stairs in the last reel if you are doing something brilliant in the present one."[3] And somewhat like Churchill, Lloyd George performed in politics what he read in literature: he attributed his vision of social justice to Thomas Carlyle, Hugo's *Les Misérables*, and Ibsen's *A Doll's House*.[4]

Looking back on that parliamentary session (his first), Chamberlain expressed satisfaction that he had accomplished something concrete "without having created any sensation, a thing to be avoided like the plague in these days of journalistic stunts" (that new bit of American slang, which Churchill loved).[5] Chamberlain was acutely sensitive to – and contemptuous of – political theatre. For him politics ideally should be a rational science based on hard study, realism, frankness, mastery of detail, objective problem-solving, and reconciling diverse interests with a minimum of melodrama. It was those qualities that ultimately sent him to 10 Downing Street. As one admirer put it, "Mr. Chamberlain is the plain man in politics, his yea is yea and his nay is nay. . . . He would have the business of state carried on in the same orderly manner as Birmingham business. . . . He is the statesman for the counting house."[6] He understood and respected civil servants, usually accepted their advice, and worked within their rules.

In contrast, Churchill loved the company of haute bohemia. The Other Club, the fortnightly dining club he founded with the flamboyant Tory politician F. E. Smith, included the usual roster of MPs, generals, and admirals, but also authors (H. G. Wells, Arnold Bennett, A. E. W. Mason, P. G. Wodehouse), artists (William Orpen, Alfred Munnings, John Lavery, Edwin Lutyens), and actors (Herbert Beerbohm Tree, Laurence Olivier). Through Eddie Marsh, who introduced him to Rupert Brooke, Churchill also had links with "The Souls," the circle of intellectual aristocrats presided over by Lady Desborough. At Taplow Court, the Desborough home in Buckinghamshire, he mixed with Maurice Baring and G. K. Chesterton.[7] Churchill was often a guest of the wealthy aesthete Sir Philip Sassoon, hobnobbing with the artists and authors (George Bernard Shaw, T. E. Lawrence) who frequented Port Lympne, the fantastically gorgeous house Sassoon had built for himself in Kent. Churchill painted the house and gardens, and Sassoon lent him paintings by John Singer Sargent to copy. At Sassoon's enormous mansion in Park Lane, Churchill chatted at length with Lytton Strachey. "Do you know, in spite of everything I couldn't help liking him," Strachey wrote to Dora Carrington. "He was delighted when I said I thought his book [*The World Crisis 1911–1914*] very well done, and hardly seemed to mind when I added that I also thought it very wicked."[8] If anyone had called *Eminent Victorians* "wicked" Strachey would have been flattered. Why could he not see a kindred spirit in Churchill, who subscribed to Sylvia Beach's 1922 edition of James Joyce's *Ulysses*[9] and adored the rule-breaking creativity of the great modern artists? As Churchill wrote in "Painting as a Pastime":

> Have not Manet and Monet, Cézanne and Matisse, rendered to painting something of the same service which Keats and Shelley gave to poetry after the solemn and ceremonious literary perfections of the eighteenth century? They have brought back to the pictorial art a new draught of *joie de vivre*; and the beauty of their work is instinct with gaiety, and floats in sparkling air.[10]

For Chamberlain, however, nothing floated in sparkling air. His aesthetics were high-minded and bourgeois. He played a key role in giving the city of Birmingham Britain's first municipal symphony orchestra. But he disliked any kind of bohemian flash: Augustus John etchings ("mostly repellent"), Jacob Epstein's sculpture of Jesus ("it strikes me as audacious to call it a Christ") and his memorial to W. H. Hudson ("barbarous affected and ugly"), Stanley Spencer ("hideous, distorted, grotesque"), or Mark Gertler ("hideous nudes"). Even "Cézanne is beyond me," he sighed.[11] Except for Mozart, he did not care for opera, that most melodramatic of arts.[12] His literary tastes were conventional, running to Thackeray, Dickens, George Eliot, Mark Twain, Galsworthy's *The Forsyte Saga*, and Conrad's *The Shadow Line*.[13] Chamberlain rarely went to the movies, and never saw a Charlie Chaplin film until 1936.[14] He immersed himself in Shakespeare but was otherwise uninterested in the theatre.[15] He had no time for Shaw's *St. Joan*, who reminded him too much of Nancy Astor.[16] On the whole he much preferred music to drama.[17] He was therefore very good at detecting phony theatrics, as in a June 1920 debate on Army estimates featuring Lloyd George in full flow:

> Ll.G. made a most "eloquent" speech, that is he employed every art of rhetoric in successfully leading the House off the scent and after saying contemptuously to Asquith who had been demanding information "you shall get the information" amid the approving and triumphant cheers of his supporters he quite "forgot" to give it. I suppose I am prejudiced but the little Welshman always leaves me completely cold.

Chamberlain was, however, more impressed with another member of the Government:

> On the other hand Winston who spoke to a very hostile & ugly House on scarlet uniforms had another triumph. With the first sentence he put the House into good humour and then with a mixture of sound reason & good natured chaff he fairly washed his critics out of the field and emerged with an overwhelming majority. In my mind he is far the most attractive speaker on the front bench.[18]

But even this praise was qualified: "With all his genius Ch. has got no judgement and that is why he will never get first place, unless he mends his ways."[19]

Here Chamberlain was more in tune with the national mood than Churchill. The theatrical style of parliamentary oratory, so popular in the Edwardian era, was going out of fashion, and politicians who indulged in it (notably Lloyd George and Churchill) were no longer trusted. With that kind of high rhetoric they had led the country into war, justified bungled military operations, and made unfulfilled promises to veterans ("Homes fit for heroes"). A new style of political discourse was emerging: direct, conversational, grounded in facts, reassuringly tedious, the style of Stanley Baldwin, Clement Attlee, and Neville Chamberlain himself. Churchill stuck to his old melodramatic mode, which seemed increasingly ludicrous in the post-war world. It probably cost him the March 1924 Westminster by-election, as the author Winifred Holtby reported:

> He really and truly points an accusatory finger at the crowd, and cries in sepulchral tones, "I say, that if another war is fought, civilization will perish." (Laughter. A sweeping gesture.) "A man laughs!" (Out goes the finger.) "That man dares to laugh. He dares to think the destruction of civilization a matter for humour!" (Rocking cheers and hoots of laughter from the gallery – in which I joined.) Indeed, he is such a preposterous little fellow, with his folded arms and tufted forelock and his Lyceum Theatre voice, that if one did not detest him one might love him from sheer perversity.[20]

In the October 1924 General Election the Conservatives were swept back into power, and Churchill won a seat at Epping as a "Constitutionalist" running with Conservative support. Baldwin as Prime Minister was ready to appoint Chamberlain to the Exchequer, but Chamberlain preferred the less glamorous Ministry of Health, where he could do much to improve housing and medical services. Therefore Churchill became Chancellor of the Exchequer, though he had no background in either economics or business, and had not quite yet rejoined the Conservative Party. It was a surprising appointment, but shrewd on Baldwin's part: Churchill might bring some fellow discouraged Liberals into the Tory ranks, and in any case he would be less trouble inside the tent.

Like his father, Winston aimed to score a coup as Chancellor. According to Thomas Jones, the Deputy Cabinet Secretary, he confided: "I want this Government not to fritter away its energies on all sorts of small schemes; I want them to concentrate on one or two things which will be big land-marks in the history of the Parliament. . . . I was all for the Liberal measures of social reform in the old days, and I want to push the same sort of measures now."[21] In fact Churchill's term at the Exchequer was notable for lots of small schemes to balance budgets: diverting money from the Road Fund, accelerating the collection of beer duties, a betting tax that brought in much less revenue than he estimated, and, to safeguard Britain's vital match industry, a tariff on cigarette lighters. "Churchill was certainly a dramatic chancellor, and his budget speeches were memorable for their style, vigor, and unfailing sense of occasion," observed Robert Rhodes James. But "it is very difficult, with the best will in the world, to regard his record as anything more than economic and fiscal opportunism."[22]

Churchill did have an early opportunity to press for the kind of dramatic social reforms that would have riveted public attention. He had been a Keynesian before Keynes: in the 1909 battle over the People's Budget, he had proposed "that the State should increasingly assume the position of the reserve employer of labour," carrying out public works projects to counteract recessions. "There is nothing economically unsound in increasing temporarily and artificially the demand for labour during a period of temporary and artificial contraction," he insisted.[23] After 1919 he suspected that the cause of long-term unemployment was the government's deflationary policies, designed to return the pound to its pre-war value. Then he read a 21 February 1925 article in the Liberal weekly the *Nation*, where Keynes argued against a return to the Gold Standard. Churchill now shot a challenging memorandum to his Controller of Finance, Otto Niemeyer:

> The Treasury has never, it seems to me, faced the profound significance of what Mr. Keynes calls "the paradox of unemployment amidst dearth". The Governor [of the Bank of England, Montagu Norman] shows himself perfectly happy in the spectacle of Britain possessing the finest credit in the world simultaneously with a million and a quarter unemployed. Obviously if these million and a quarter were usefully and economically employed, they would produce at least £100 a year a head, instead of costing us at least £50 a year a head in doles. We should have at least £200 millions a year healthy net increase. . . .
>
> The community lacks goods, and a million and a quarter people lack work. It is certainly one of the highest functions of national finance and credit to bridge the gulf between the two. This is the only country in the world where this condition exists. The Treasury and Bank of England policy has been the only policy consistently pursued. It is a terrible responsibility for those who have shaped it.

Churchill concluded (prophetically) that under the Gold Standard the unemployed would "hang like a millstone round the neck of industry and on the public revenue until they become permanently demoralised." It sounds like pure Keynesianism, but the memorandum also contained some fatal qualifications. Churchill conceded that "I do not pretend to see even 'through a glass darkly' how the financial and credit policy of the country could be handled so as to bridge the gap between a dearth of goods and a surplus of labour; and well I realise the danger of experiment to that end. The seas of history are full of famous wrecks." And he granted that Niemeyer and Montagu Norman "know more about [British fiscal policy] than anyone else in the world," a concession that effectively delivered him into their hands. Niemeyer responded that the Gold Standard was necessary to prevent inflation, and pointed to the recent examples of Russia and Germany as a warning against the dangers of fiscal irresponsibility.[24]

Churchill then staged a dinner party debate, with Niemeyer and Sir John Bradbury (a Treasury official) defending the Gold Standard, and Keynes and Reginald McKenna rebutting the policy. Even McKenna ultimately threw in the towel, concluding that there was no politically realistic alternative to gold.

For once, Churchill chose conventional wisdom over maverick experimentalism. As he admitted, the Chancellor of the Exchequer simply lacked the economic literacy to challenge the experts, nearly all of whom endorsed the return to gold.[25] In September 1945, however, he told Lord Moran that "The biggest blunder in his life had been the return to the gold standard."[26]

By April 1925 Chamberlain had concluded that:

> Winston is a rather trying person to work with for he never sticks to anything for two minutes together and when you have had a conference in order to arrive at a final decision on doubtful points your one certainty is that the agreement arrived at will be thrown overboard a few hours afterwards. I must say I think there is something to be said for my method in contrast to his. I always postpone my decisions to the very last moment possible, but once taken I very seldom go back upon them, because I have generally been pretty well all around the subject and new considerations therefore seldom arise.[27]

Chamberlain's method sounds more methodical, but once he arrived at a decision, he could easily lock himself into it. And he was not above resorting to theatrical coups himself. With Ramsay MacDonald vowing to "fight and fight" for widows' and orphans' pensions, Chamberlain and Churchill plotted to upstage Labour by including those very proposals in the next budget: "Indeed the secret has been well kept and Winston is looking eagerly forward to a *Sensation*."[28] The Budget Speech of 28 April was in fact "a great triumph for Winston who enjoyed himself thoroughly and treated the subject with masterly skill, relating every part of the whole abounding in witticisms and overflowing with spirits & good humour." True, he could be a prima donna, taking credit that should have been shared with Chamberlain, but the latter did not mind terribly, especially when Labour and Liberals MPs complained that their parties might be put out of business.[29] In a letter to George V, Baldwin praised the Budget Speech without ever mentioning questions of economics: instead, he offered dramatic criticism. It was, he reported:

> a first-rate example of Mr. Churchill's characteristic style. At one moment he would be expounding quietly and lucidly facts and figures relating to the financial position during the past and current years. At another moment, inspired and animated by the old political controversies on the subject of tariff reform, he indulged in witty levity and humour which comes as a refreshing relief in the dry atmosphere of a Budget speech. At another moment, when announcing the introduction of a scheme for widows and mothers pensions, he soared into emotional flights of rhetoric in which he

has few equals; and throughout the speech he showed that he is not only possessed of consummate ability as a parliamentarian, but also all the versatility of an actor.

In the case of such a masterly performance criticism would seem to be superfluous and almost unfair, but, if a critic wished to assail any weak points in the speech, it . . . might perhaps be suggested that the prosaic nature of the Budget does not present a suitable background for some of the rhetorical flights which Mr. Churchill undertook. It is doubtful whether these dramatic declarations, impressive as they were from the purely oratorical point of view, were such as to carry conviction in the minds of the Opposition Members who tend to be more impressed with quiet sincerity than impassioned declamation. . . .

These criticisms, however, are of small account if the speech be looked at as a whole. In its arrangement, in its marshalling of facts and arguments, in the picturesque, dramatic and humorous presentation, it was one of the most striking Budget speeches of recent years.[30]

Two months later, in the course of the Finance Bill debate, Churchill's hand gestures were so melodramatic that he accidentally smacked the face of the Financial Secretary, Walter Guinness.[31] Writing to Baldwin on 30 August 1925, Chamberlain readily admitted that, "Looking back over our final session I think our Chancellor has done very well. . . . He has been a tower of debating strength in the House of Commons . . . [and] a source of increased influence & prestige to the government as a whole." Even if the Chancellor necessarily overshadowed the Minister of Health, by virtue of their powers and their personalities:

I for one have never for a moment regretted the decision I made then or envied Winston his pre-eminence. What a brilliant creature he is! But there is somehow a great gulf fixed between him and me which I don't think I shall ever cross. I like him. I like his humour and his vitality. I like his courage. . . . But not for all the joys of Paradise would I be a member of his staff! Mercurial! a much abused word, but it is the literal description of his temperament.[32]

And by October, Chamberlain happily reported, Churchill was notably orating less in Cabinet and listening more. "[Baldwin] told me that it was beginning to dawn upon him that his new colleagues were not all duds after all!"[33] That would change with a thunderclap during the General Strike of 1926, which gave Churchill an opportunity to return briefly to his old profession of self-dramatizing journalism.

On 1 May 1926 coalminers rejected a proposal by mine owners to cut wages. The employers locked out the miners, and the Trades Union Congress called for a General Strike, to begin just before midnight on 3 May. Earlier that day Churchill called a meeting at his Treasury office to plan the production of "a really powerful readable broadsheet not merely to contain news but in order to relieve the minds of the people." Andrew Caird, managing director of the *Daily Mail*, pointed out that untrained volunteers could not operate the presses without running the risk of wrecking them. Churchill did not see the problem: "Is it quite impossible to teach a highly educated person with a good teacher?" As a matter of fact (Caird replied), yes, it was impossible on short notice. "Are there not at the university people who know how to print?" Churchill demanded to know. Someone confirmed that this skill was not taught much at Oxbridge.[34] The following day Samuel Hoare dropped in at the *Daily Express* offices: "Winston there. Blood and Iron. [Winston in his element]."[35] The strike had shut down all newspapers, and the gap was filled only by the *British Worker*, a TUC organ, and the *British Gazette*, in which Churchill published the government's version of events. On 9 May Thomas Inskip wrote to Lord Irwin: "Winston is enjoying himself in editing the *British Gazette*. His Budget of 820 millions no longer interests him very much. I don't say he is wrong in his instinct for the dominant issue of the moment, but he is entertaining in his absorption in 'publicity'."[36]

Naturally, Churchill micromanaged the *British Gazette*. "The Chancellor occupied the attention of practically the whole of the staff who normally would have been thinking out the details," J. C. C. Davidson (Parliamentary Secretary for the Admiralty) protested to Baldwin. Churchill could now best assist the newspaper by staying away: "He thinks he is Napoleon, but curiously enough the men who have been printing all their life in the various processes happen to know more about their job than he does."[37] "He butts in at the busiest hours and insists on changing commas and full stops until the staff is furious," reported Thomas Jones.[38] Churchill unsuccessfully urged the BBC to broadcast the rolling thunder of the presses churning out the *British Gazette*. In the Cabinet he went so far as to demand that the government commandeer the BBC and make it into a propaganda organ: Baldwin judiciously deferred a decision until the strike ended, on 12 May.[39]

The columns of the *British Gazette* were filled with bombastic denunciations of the strikers, dark warnings of Bolshevik plots, and rousing poetry by Tennyson and Kipling. As Churchill later recalled, it deliciously resembled "the combination of a first-class battleship and a first-class general election." The rival *British Worker* called it "a melodramatic 'stunt' on Sydney Street lines."[40] And James Grigg, Churchill's private secretary, concluded that "Winston always has in mind the doing of things which would impress posterity, that the articles he dictates for *The British Gazette* are conceived with an eye either to his next book, or to his biographer. . . ."[41]

In the wake of the General Strike, Chamberlain concluded, "Winston has decidedly improved his position & is very popular I believe with our side as he is really with the whole House for the wonderful entertainment he gives them." But was he, perhaps, too entertaining to be taken seriously?[42] On 15 August Chamberlain described a hilarious movie that seemed to sum up the public image of the Chancellor:

> . . . at a sort of preparatory blare of trumpets, the words "Winston" appeared on the screen and immediately the letters of which it was composed all separated themselves and, moving about by some jugglery which enchanted me, although I could not understand, finally settled themselves into a caricature of our Chancellor with the well-known beetling brows and bald head.
>
> This was funny without being vulgar and while we were still in a good humour the door flew open and in burst Winston himself (all in the film you understand). By Jove! How things hum in that office. The table groaned under mountains of books, secretaries rushed in and out. . . . Lighting a cigar of Brobdingnagian proportions, Winston grimaced, stormed, graticulated (??!!), and orated until the film man got paralysed or his film burst. . . .
>
> Winston constantly improves his position in the House and in the Party. His speeches are extraordinarily brilliant and men flock in to hear him as they would to a first class entertainment at the theatre. The best show in London, they say, and there is the weak point. So far as I can judge they think of it as a show and they are not prepared at present to trust his character and still less his judgment.
>
> Personally, I can't help liking and admiring him more, the more I see of him, but it is always accompanied by a diminution of my intellectual respect for him. I have noticed that in all disputes of a departmental character that I had with him he has had to give way because his case was not really well founded.[43]

On 5 September Thomas Jones recorded, "W is a most brilliant and incessant talker—his sentences full of colour and alliteration and frequent military metaphor," whether the subject was politics, his 1908 journal to East Africa, or the coal strike. "He is always deploying guns or barrages on the owners or the men."[44] The next day Arthur Steel-Maitland (Minister of Labour) wrote, "Winston is a great study" in the coal industry negotiations, delivering an "awfully good" and well-rehearsed speech. But in his flights of rhetoric he changed the government's agreed-on terms, at various points taking up "an anti-owner position" and then "bullying the miners. . . . He's jolly difficult when he's in a napoleonesque attitude, dictating instructions in military metaphors, and the spotlight full on him."[45] The problem, Steel-Maitland later added, is that "his impulsiveness and combativeness are an awful danger in negotiations. . . . He thinks out industrial policy in terms of making a political speech. . . . He is a most brilliant fellow, but his gifts aren't those of judgement, nor of appreciating industry, nor of a negotiator."[46] As Chamberlain summed it up, "Winston always wants things to be done in a spectacular way with himself in the foreground." And unfortunately, "as he holds the purse I cant get on without him."[47]

Yet the government included another actor who, in his own way, was more subtle and effective than Churchill. Stanley Baldwin liked to portray himself as a stolid, unintellectual, plain-spoken, easygoing countryman. But the politician that emerges from Philip Williamson's biography was a hardworking industrialist who shrewdly used and outfoxed his political colleagues – Churchill especially. Baldwin was well-read, and his reading of Carlyle, Dickens, Arnold, Ruskin, and J. B. Priestley – all of them critics of unbridled capitalism – may well have encouraged him to promote social welfare measures and protective tariffs.[48] But when he was competing for votes with the grandiloquent Lloyd George and shrill socialists, he cultivated what can only be called anti-oratory: a speaking style that was unpolished, undemonstrative, understated to the point of drowsiness. Scrupulously avoiding high political rhetoric, he won over audiences with his apparent authenticity. He disdained the clever cut-and-thrust of traditional parliamentary debates, disarming his opponents by refusing to attack them. Baldwin was "probably . . . the worst speaker of the Prime Ministers of the last thirty years," reported an astonished Charles Masterman, and yet "when he sat down he was received with tumultuous cheers."[49] Even as he harkened back to an earlier England, he used the cutting-edge media of the wireless and talking pictures far more expertly than Churchill. Baldwin understood that the emotive projection of the platform orator would not work with radio, which called for a softer and more intimate mode of speech: in a 1924 election broadcast, long before Franklin Roosevelt, he invented the "fireside chat."[50] In his filmed address for the 1931 General Election he seemed to make every possible mistake. He was hesitant, slow, fiddling with a fountain pen, rolling his tongue in his cheek, often not looking into the camera – but therefore strikingly persuasive.[51]

"Eloquence" and "oratory" were the foulest words in Baldwin's vocabulary. He denounced "stunts," "wizards," "sensations," "demagogues," "spell-binders and fire-eaters," and words of "half a dozen syllables." "If there is any class to be regarded with suspicion in a democracy it is the rhetorician – the man who plays on half-educated people with fallacies which they are incapable of detecting." In fact rhetoric was "one of the greatest dangers of modern civilization." He advised voters that "the art of statesmanship was a very different thing from the art of a cinema star." They should listen instead to "plain, unadorned statements of cases," such as he offered. As Baldwin summed it up in a March 1924 speech, "to tell the truth needs no art at all."[52]

Of course, only the greatest artists can convincingly simulate artlessness. Samuel Hoare, his Secretary of State for Air, compared Baldwin to

> a performer on the stage or the radio . . . [who] had the same signature tune for all his chief appearances. . . . His personality was by no means as simple as it seemed. Although he was born a townsman, his best role was as the lover of England's green and pleasant land. When he broadcast, he gave the impression of an English countryman sitting at the end of the day in a comfortable chair in friendly conversation with two or three of his old friends. As a matter of fact, the talk that seemed to flow so naturally had been very carefully prepared. Sitting, or, as some thought, sleeping over his pipe, he had meditated for hours over what he intended to say, with the result that when he said it, every word had become a part of his own nature.[53]

Baldwin knew well how to use the political theatrics he professed to disdain. He fully appreciated that Churchill was the government's most brilliant performer. And yet, all the while, the Prime Minister was changing Britain's political culture, discrediting the high rhetoric that his Chancellor so brilliantly achieved. In the new climate of plain speaking, Churchill would become something of a dinosaur.

Reporting on the 11 April 1927 Budget Speech to the King, Baldwin described Churchill's performance as a dazzling vaudeville act. Long before it began, the chamber of the House filled up with MPs, peers, the Prince of Wales, and other eager spectators. "The scene was quite sufficient to show that Mr. Churchill as a star turn has a power of attraction which nobody in the House of Commons can excel." And the performance did not disappoint: "It was a masterpiece of cleverness and ingenuity which was only matched by the subtlety and ingenuity of the framework of his Budget proposals." The coal strike had reduced revenue and increased expenditure to the point where the Chancellor had somehow to cover a deficit of more than £36 million. "Nevertheless, this gloomy background only served to enhance his buoyant optimism, just as the severity of his subject served to intensify the flashes of irrepressible gaiety and humour which, at oft-recurring intervals, brought a touch of life and humanity into his soulless theme."

Churchill was not wrong to counter dismal economic news with humor and optimism. In still harder times, Franklin Roosevelt would do the same. But

Baldwin recognized that, with the social wounds of the General Strike still fresh, Wildean wit could easily be perceived as unserious:

> There is in Mr. Churchill an undercurrent of buoyant mischievousness which frequently makes its appearance on the surface in some picturesque phrase or playful sally at the expense of his opponents. Thus, when describing the lamentable effects of the coal stoppage, he represents himself not as an impartial judge but only the public executioner whose task it is to apportion the burden but not the blame. . . .
>
> If there is one criticism that might be levelled against the speech, which was otherwise perfect, it is that some of Mr. Churchill's observations on the subject of national economy and retrenchment were characterised by a slight appearance of flippancy which might have been better dispensed with, having regard to the strong feelings of Members on this subject.

Still, Baldwin added, there was no denying "Mr. Churchill's wonderful sense of the dramatic touch." Even in a Budget Speech, he knew how conjure up a trap from which there seemed no escape, and then make his audience wait before springing a breathtaking *coup de théâtre*:

> In order to maintain interest, all Chancellors have to arrange their speeches so as to keep their most important secrets up their sleeves to the last moment; but nobody could have practised the art of tantalisation better than did Mr. Churchill. Having set before the House the nature of the task with which they were confronted, he showed the most deft manipulation in the order and arrangement of his proposals, so as to keep the Members keyed up to the highest pitch. . . .
>
> His enemies will say that this year's Budget is a mischievous piece of manipulation and juggling with the country's finances, but his friends will say that it is a masterpiece of ingenuity.

"Ingenuity" is a compliment for a dramatist, but highly suspect when applied to an accountant. Baldwin admitted to the King that Churchill had closed the budget gap with gimmicks that could not be repeated: "The hidden reserves have now been exhausted and if any unfortunate events during the current year should lead to increased expenditure, the Chancellor of the Exchequer cannot have recourse to such methods again."[54] As Thomas Jones noted, "Papers full of Winston's Budget speech. *The Times* calls it ingenious, but most of the other papers speak of trickery." At No. 10 Jones encountered the Governor of the Bank of England, Montagu Norman, who, "looking thoroughly ill and disconsolate," compared the Chancellor to Blondin the tightrope walker. Jones found the Prime Minister "horribly tired and once again twitching restlessly. As a work of art he thought Winston's speech as good as it could possibly be," damning it with aesthetic praise. "There was a general sense of bewilderment at the end of it."[55] As for economics, Churchill admitted that he was "quite uneducated on the subject," even though he "had to argue about it all my life."[56]

"Winston's position is curious," Baldwin told Lord Irwin on 15 September. "Our people like him. They love listening to him in the House, look on him as a star turn and settle down in the stalls with anticipatory grins. But for the leadership, they would turn him down every time." Baldwin added that logical successors to the premiership would be Neville Chamberlain or Sir Douglas Hogg, but the following April he effectively took Hogg out of the running by elevating him to the House of Lords.[57]

Meanwhile, Churchill was working out a dramatic new plan for relieving Britain's chronically high unemployment. He proposed to abolish rates (local property taxes) and make up the difference through other taxes. That would relieve industry and agriculture of a heavy financial drain and, he hoped, would encourage these sectors to expand and create jobs. Chamberlain, however, considered the scheme "unwise immoral and dangerous. It is dangerous because as usual it is only the idea he has got. He has nothing worked out but he gets so enamoured with his ideas that he won't listen to difficulties or wait until plans have been made to get over them. Its like Gallipoli all over again. . . . It is not made easier by the fact that all my principal officials are working overtime on Winston's d—d fantasies."[58] Winston's plan, he wrote on 24 March 1928, was no plan at all: "It changes like a kaleidoscope so that even now I don't know what form it will take when it comes before the Cabinet on Thursday."[59] Chamberlain did not look forward to the 1928 Budget: "Winston will do all the prancing and I shall do all the drudgery."[60] And as usual the 24 April Budget Speech was, as Leo Amery commented, "done with Winston's best literary skill."[61]

In a 12 August letter to Lord Irwin, Chamberlain explained that Churchill's "half-baked" plan "involved the complete freedom from rates of all industrial concerns (this vague description was never defined), and the imposition instead of a National Rate of 5 per cent in the £." It looked like another triumph of theatre over substance, but Chamberlain was coming round to recognize that political theatre might have its uses after all. He granted that Churchill's scheme could have real value "for election purposes. It provides an answer to the criticism so often brought against an ageing Government, that it has exhausted its vitality and its ideas and no longer has a policy. Neither of the other parties has any new ideas for dealing with unemployment. Here is a plan which we can advocate as meeting one of the most generally admitted industrial grievances." Chamberlain was now willing to reduce rates for industry somewhat, but not (as Churchill insisted) eliminate them altogether. At the same time he noted that Baldwin habitually fell into the opposite error, "timidity or lethargy when rapid or vigorous action are wanted. . . . [He] fails again and again to make the speech that is wanted."

Chamberlain recognized Churchill's greatest strength and greatest weakness: that he governed with the tools of a poet or playwright. He arrived at policy decisions through a mental process that was more like artistic inspiration than any rational assessment of political and economic realities:

> One doesn't often come across a real man of genius or, perhaps, appreciate him when one does. Winston is such a man and he has *les défauts de ses qualités*. To listen to him on the platform or in the House is sheer delight. The art of the arrangement, the unexpected turn, the master of sparkling humour, and the torrent of picturesque adjectives combine to put his speeches in a class by themselves. Then as you know there is no subject on which he is not prepared to propound some novel theory and to sustain and illustrate his theory with cogent and convincing arguments. So quickly does his mind work in building up a case that it frequently carries him off his own feet.
>
> I have often watched him in Cabinet begin with a casual comment on what has been said, then as an image or simile comes into his mind proceed with great animation, when presently you see his whole face suffused with pink his speech becomes more and more rapid and impetuous till in a few minutes he will not hear of the possibility of opposition to an idea which only occurred to him a few minutes ago.
>
> In the consideration of affairs his decisions are never founded on exact knowledge, nor on careful or prolonged consideration of the pros and cons. He seeks instinctively for the large and preferably novel idea such as is capable of representation by the broadest brush. Whether the idea is practicable or impracticable, good or bad, provided he can see himself recommending it plausibly and successfully to an enthusiastic audience, it commends itself to him. . . .

As Chamberlain concluded, "There is too deep a difference between our natures for me to feel at home with him or to regard him with affection. He is a brilliant wayward child who compels admiration but who wears out his guardians with the constant strain he puts upon them."[62] The contrast was starkly illuminated in November, when Chamberlain introduced his 127-page Local Government Bill, which had cost him months of hard work and negotiations. It took him two and a half hours to explain all the bureaucratic details to a rapt House of Commons, which erupted in energetic and prolonged cheers when he finished. The Bill granted substantial rate relief to agriculture and industry and effected a long-overdue revision of the 1834 Poor Law. It sailed easily through Parliament and demonstrated that the Conservative Party was willing to enact progressive social reforms. It represented a triumph of substance over theatrics.[63]

Churchill deeply regretted the general decline of political theatre, as he wrote to Clementine: "The session opens super-tame. The PM almost mute – a sort of [Calvin] Coolidge or [Herbert] Hoover. It is astonishing what goes down in these days of mass politics. One thing is as good as another. All the old Parliamentary drama & personal clashes are gone – perhaps for ever."[64] As he recalled in 1939, the rise of party discipline meant the governments were now made and unmade not in open debate, but "behind the scenes." The fall of Labour in 1931, for example, was accomplished by "action taken off the stage."[65]

In February 1929 Leo Amery and Neville Chamberlain agreed that it was time to move Churchill to another Cabinet post, but where? Amery suggested the Foreign Office, but (he recorded in his diary) "Neville thought that the PM would not run such a risk and would dread to find himself waking up at nights with a cold sweat at the thought of Winston's indiscretions. I suggested that Winston was not really in fact so rash as picturesque, that there were no really critical situations in foreign policy just now and that a little colour and vivacity would do no harm."[66] That was hardly a ringing endorsement in 1929 – still less so a few years later, when foreign crises were erupting everywhere.

The 15 April 1929 Budget speech, in Chamberlain's opinion:

> was one of the best he has made and kept the House fascinated & enthralled by its wit, audacity, adroitness & power. I think the general public were a little disposed to complain that it was a humdrum Budget; if so, it was because W. has taught them to expect something startling each year, and their anticipations had been aroused accordingly. But frankly it is constructed with both eyes on the Election and from that point of view there is no doubt that it is a very serviceable affair. Indeed it has contributed materially to the marked reaction from the depression in our ranks which was so apparent a few weeks ago but has now largely disappeared.[67]

Others were not so complimentary. The final volume of *The World Crisis* had recently been published, and it was here (Lord Irwin suggested to the Archbishop of Canterbury, Cosmo Lang) that Churchill's true talents lay: "What an astounding thing it is that any man should be able to combine authorship on that scale with being Chancellor of the Exchequer. I suppose his critics would say that, having dissipated all our finance and mortgaged every service, there was nothing more for him to do from the financial side. I cannot help feeling that it would be well for him and for national finance if he found other ministerial activity."[68] Irwin told Chamberlain that Sir Francis Floud, who worked with Churchill as Chairman of the Board of Customs and Excise, "writes to me periodically with complete freedom and indiscretion and evidently regards Winston as a public danger at the Treasury, and according to him Winston has left a very *Damnosa Hereditas* for his successors for many years to come."[69]

The Conservatives were voted out of power on 30 May. "Mr. Churchill presented five consecutive Budgets," a sympathetic economist concluded, "for which as a series, and even individually for the dullest of them, the only epithet is dramatic. New measures of first-rate importance such as contributory pensions and the reform of the system of local taxation, as well as suggestions for new tax experiments and devices of unprecedented ingenuity for balancing the Budget fell in quick succession on the ears of a fascinated House."[70] But others noticed that the tax experiments were makeshift and the Budget was balanced by sleight-of-hand. In his tenure as Chancellor, Churchill had not won more respect from his political colleagues. Many regarded him as a clever *littérateur* who neither focused on his job nor understood money. In 1954 Sir Frederick Leith-Ross, the government's Chief Economic Advisor from 1932 to 1946, told Lord Moran that "Winston was not a bad Chancellor of the Exchequer; only he was not certain of himself. Of course, he was not the easiest Minister to work for, but he was stimulating and full of ideas."

"Good ones?" asked Moran.

"About one in twenty of them were sound," Sir Frederick concluded. "You see Winston is really an artist. . . ."[71]

Even as a literary artist, he was increasingly regarded as a nineteenth-century anachronism. In the American journal *Foreign Affairs*, Sir Frederick Barton Maurice published a point-by-point demolition of *The World Crisis*, arguing that Churchill had seduced readers with his enchantingly antique rhetoric: "In England to-day oratory is almost dead. . . . So, where we find the sonorous periods and the biting invective of the early Victorians applied to descriptions of current events, we experience all the charm of novelty, we are swept along by the exuberance and compelling force of our author, and are little disposed to pause and question his facts."[72] In a February 1929 lecture on "War Books," the author H. M. Tomlinson singled out *The World Crisis* as the worst of the lot. The anthropomorphic images that Churchill used to narrate the mobilization of the Royal Navy on the eve of war – ". . . the Admiralty wireless whispers through the ether to the tall masts of ships . . . torpedoes ripping the bellies of half-awakened ships . . . gigantic castles of steel wending their way across the misty shining sea, like giants bowed in anxious thought" – Tomlinson dismissed as overwrought melodrama. "It gives a reader the fear that the performer may, in his exultation, step right over the footlights and let his eloquence have its way on the big drum." The only light that Churchill cast on the Great War was the "kind which comes in chromatic beams from the wings to give an object on the stage an appearance it does not own."[73] In his influential 1928 guide *English Prose Style*, the critic Herbert Read held up this passage from *The World Crisis* as an example of "ludicrous" writing:

> He is about to be struck down. A dark hand, gloved at first in folly, now intervenes. Exit Czar. Deliver him and all he loved to wounds and death. Belittle his efforts, asperse his conduct, insult his memory; but then pause to tell us who else was found capable. Who or what could guide the Russian State? Men gifted and daring; men ambitious and fierce; spirits audacious and commanding – of these there was no lack. But none could answer the few plain questions on which the life and fame of Russia turned. With victory in her grasp she fell upon the earth, devoured alive, like Herod of old, by worms. But not in vain her valiant deeds. The giant mortally stricken had just time, with dying strength, to pass the torch eastward across the ocean to a new Titan long sunk in doubt who now arose and began ponderously to arm. The Russian Empire fell on March 16; on April 6 the United States entered the war.[74]

For Read this concentrated, in one paragraph, the menagerie of clichés that made up melodrama:

> Such eloquence is false because it is artificial: it is one of the many pits into which a writer may fall if his conception of "fine writing" is not supported by an inner structure of fine thinking. Here the images are stale, the metaphors violent. The whole passage exhales a false dramatic atmosphere, descending to the childish use of the very rubrics of drama with "Exit Czar". There is a volley of rhetorical imperatives, followed by an inevitable ironic question. Then a volley of epithets, high-sounding and redundant. Then the simile of Herod's worms, too familiar to produce the calculated shudder. Then a line ("But not in vain," etc.) and a spate of still staler images – giant, torch and Titan. And to complete the bathos, a plain and very literal statement of the cause of all this false eloquence.[75]

Even in the revised 1952 edition of that book, Read retained all his earlier ridicule of Churchill's prose. Like a severe tutor, he granted that the Prime Minister had recently "done better than this," for example his "Never Surrender" speech, but even that was not quite as good as Edmund Burke on the French Revolution.[76]

As Isaiah Berlin explained in 1949, Read's reaction reflected the post-war revulsion against all things Victorian, the great debunking led by Lytton Strachey, Bertrand Russell, and John Maynard Keynes. "This was the time when rhetoric and, indeed, eloquence were held up to obloquy as camouflage for literary and moral Pecksniffs, unscrupulous charlatans who corrupted artistic taste and discredited the cause of truth and reason, and at their worst incited to evil and led a credulous world to disaster." The younger generation was "painfully reacting against anything which appeared to go beyond the naked skeleton of truth."[77] However, Berlin concluded, in the next war this kind of eloquence was indispensable to victory. Then Britain needed a leader who was at once theatrical and authentic, as only Churchill could be:

> Like a great actor – perhaps the last of his kind – upon the stage of history, he speaks his memorable lines with a large, unhurried, and stately utterance in a blaze of light, as is appropriate to a man who knows that his work and his person will remain the object of scrutiny and judgment to many generations. His narrative is a great public performance and has the attribute of formal magnificence. The words, the splendid phrases, the sustained quality of feeling, are a unique medium which convey his vision of himself and of his world, and will inevitably, like all that he has said and done, reinforce the famous public image, which is no longer distinguishable from the inner essence and the true nature of the author: of a man larger than life, composed of bigger and simpler elements than ordinary men, a gigantic historical figure during his own lifetime, superhumanly bold, strong, and imaginative, one of the two greatest men of action his nation has produced, an orator of prodigious powers, the saviour of his country, a mythical hero who belongs to legend as much as to reality, the largest human being of our time.[78]

This is the classic appreciation of Churchill, as the supreme master of English prose, established in the public mind after the Second World War. But in the interwar years, educated persons were much more likely to agree with Herbert Read's acid critique. Back then, Churchill was trotted out as a lesson in what writers should avoid.

CHAPTER 13

That Special Relationship

Winston Churchill began his authorial career just four years after the United States Congress ratified an international copyright agreement, opening up a vast new market for British writers. The lack of such an agreement had cost Charles Dickens, Thomas Hardy, and Oscar Wilde untold sums in royalties. From the start, Churchill deliberately wrote for audiences on both sides of the Atlantic. In 1901 he proposed the creation of an Anglo-American Academy, along the lines of the Académie Française, which would standardize US and UK English and prevent them from drifting too far apart. After all, he frankly argued, that common language "enables a writer to reach twice as many people – an actor can appeal to two publics."[1] However, for all his efforts, Churchill had very limited success in reaching the American reading public before the Second World War. In literature as well as politics, his lifelong romance with what he called "the Great Republic" was, for some time, unrequited.

He first visited the United States in November 1895, arriving in New York on his way to cover the insurrection in Cuba. "What extraordinary people the Americans are!" he wrote to his (American) mother. "Their hospitality is a revelation to me and they make you feel at home and at ease in a way that I have never before experienced" – that is, never experienced in England.[2] He inspected a manifestation of America's new global power, the battleship *New York*: "I was much struck by the sailors: their intelligence, their good looks and civility and their generally businesslike appearance. These interested me more than [the] ship itself, for while any nation can build a battleship – it is the monopoly of the Anglo-Saxon race to breed good seamen."[3] To his brother he wrote: "This is a very great country my dear Jack. Not pretty or romantic but great and utilitarian. There seems to be no such thing as reverence or tradition. Everything is eminently practical and things are judged from a matter of fact standpoint." There were no silly wigs or robes in the courthouses, just men in business suits, "But they manage to hang a man all the same, and that after all is a great thing." Most American newspapers were hopelessly trashy, but:

> I think mind you that vulgarity is a sign of strength. A great, crude, strong, young people are the Americans – like a boisterous healthy boy among enervated but well bred ladies and gentlemen. . . . Picture to yourself the American people as a great lusty youth – who treads on all your sensibilities perpetrates every possible horror of ill manners – whom neither age nor just tradition inspire with reverence – but who moves about his affairs with a good hearted freshness which may well be the envy of older nations of the earth.[4]

One of Churchill's prime objectives in writing for American readers was to cement an Anglo-American alliance. But it often happens that politicians, before they commit themselves to dubious policies, see all too clearly the potential drawbacks. He supported the United States in its war with Spain in 1898, but conceded that, in this imperial adventure, "America certainly presents its unattractive side to the world." Naturally, "As a representative of both countries – the idea of an Anglo-Saxon *rapprochement* is very pleasant. One of the principles of my politics will always be to promote the good understanding between the English speaking communities. At the same time alliances nowadays are useless. . . . As long as the interests of two nations coincide & as far as they coincide – they are and will be allies. But when they diverge they will cease to be allies." Britain and America might have common interests in the Pacific, but otherwise "I am afraid we have nothing to give the States in return."[5] When Joseph Chamberlain advocated an Anglo-American pact, Churchill was skeptical: "The idea of an Anglo-Saxon alliance may delight or alarm Editors, jingos & idiots of various countries. It will not trouble diplomats who know that no alliance is possible until community of interest is established. Is it likely that the cute Uncle Sam will pick our Asiatic, African & European chestnuts out of the fire for us?"[6]

All the same, New York newspapers had taken an interest in his Cuban exploits, and it was reasonable to assume that his subsequent writings might have an American market. When he published the *Malakand Field Force*, he instructed his mother, "It ought to have some circulation in America – and this should be carefully looked to."[7] Of the first edition, 200 copies were shipped to the United States, but there is no record of actual purchases.[8] Apparently *The River War* had a modest American sale: the first two printings (November 1899 and February 1900) totaled 2,500 copies, nearly all of them sold by 1 June 1900, and 500 of them had been shipped to New York.[9] *London to Ladysmith via Pretoria* performed much better in Britain: published in May

1900, it sold 11,454 copies by 1 June 1901. But though Churchill's Boer War adventures were covered in *Harper's Bazaar* and *Harper's Monthly*, at most 1,850 copies of the American edition were sold overall, and at least 1,000 were ultimately pulped.[10]

No sooner had Churchill participated in the relief of Ladysmith than an American agent, James B. Pond, broached the idea of a North American lecture tour. Dickens, Wilde, and Matthew Arnold had all done triumphant American speaking tours, recouping much of what they had lost in royalties, and Churchill hoped for the same financial success. When he arrived in New York in December 1900, he was met once again by a crowd of journalists, a reassuring sign that his celebrity was intact. But the tour was not very successful. There was much pro-Boer sentiment among Americans, especially Irish-Americans. In Baltimore he spoke to a nearly empty hall, in Chicago and Minneapolis he was loudly heckled, at Ann Arbor his speech was disrupted. Significantly, he enjoyed a far better reception in Montreal, Ottawa, Toronto, and Winnipeg. Overall he earned more than $6,000 from the tour, which Martin Gilbert describes as "an enormous sum of money," but that is all relative. Churchill had expected to earn £5,000, a wildly optimistic estimate. True, Dickens had reportedly earned £20,000 on his 1867–68 American tour, but that was an extraordinary case. Even Wilde grossed only £1,178.[11] Five weeks of lecturing in the United Kingdom netted Churchill £3,782 15s 5d, compared with about £1,300 for two months in North America, with a far more exhausting travel schedule.[12] As an economist would put it, the American tour involved heavy opportunity costs.

All the same, his fierce opposition to Joseph Chamberlain's tariff scheme was partly motivated by a fear that it would spark a trade war with the United States. As Churchill told a Manchester election rally in January 1906:

> Mr. Chamberlain's dream of a united Empire is a famous dream, but a dream of the glories of the British race which leaves out the people of the United States can not be a very wise and complete revelation. (Hear, hear.) And, after all, finer than any dream of a united British Empire is the dream of a great Anglo-Saxon Federation. (Cheers.) It might be a dream, but I think it will come nearer and nearer as the years go by.[13]

Meanwhile, American sales of Churchill's books continued to disappoint him. His biography of Randolph Churchill was published by Macmillan, the same firm that produced John Morley's *Life of Gladstone*. The latter had sold 25,000 copies in its first year, and vastly more in subsequent cheaper editions.[14] *Lord Randolph Churchill*, released on 2 January 1906, had sold nearly 5,000 copies in Britain by 5 February and 6,250 by 15 May 1907, including sales through the Times Book Club.[15] Churchill repeatedly badgered Frederick Macmillan for American sales figures, but these amounted to only 603 by 30 April 1906,[16] earning less than half of his £500 US advance. Why would Americans want to read about a dead British politician known only for his opposition to Home Rule? Paul Revere Reynolds, America's first literary agent, had offered the book to Charles Scribner's Sons for a $10,000 advance. "Winston Churchill is a bright young man and will make the most of his material," concluded an internal Scribner memorandum, "but there is not much of vital interest in the subject."[17] *My African Journey* (1908) was also offered to Scribner's, and again they refused it. Published by Hodder and Stoughton, its sales were 7,870 in Britain and 2,876 in the Empire (including Canada), but just 1,400 in the United States.[18]

In December 1915, when Winston's political fortunes were at their lowest ebb, Lady Randolph shared with him a letter from her nephew, Shane Leslie, then a British intelligence officer serving in the United States. "I must write to tell you how great [Winston] looms in his *mother*-country, America," he gushed. There his speeches were widely read and admired, and sending him to the front in France was regarded as yet another blunder by the British government: "With so many pawns at their disposal they can hardly spare the only effective knight in their control."[19]

Churchill's departure from the Admiralty in 1915 allowed him to resume his second career as a journalist, and for the first time he established a solid beachhead in the American newspaper and magazine market. Between 1916 and 1919 he published in the *New-York Tribune, Collier's,* the *Outlook, Century Magazine*, the *Atlantic Monthly,* the *New York Times*, and the *Los Angeles Times*. By 1924 he was earning 6s. per word from the Americans.[20]

Once the United States entered the war in April 1917, paeans to Anglo-American unity filled the newspaper columns, at least in Britain. On 4 July 1918, speaking to the Anglo-Saxon Fellowship in Westminster, Churchill predicted that the war would bring about the "supreme reconciliation" of the United Kingdom and the United States.[21] Shortly after the Armistice, he warmly thanked his American opposite number, Bernard Baruch, for cooperating so fully with the common effort to build weapons of war, and he went on to offer this counterfactual: "If, in order to secure complete victory, it had been unhappily necessary to prolong the war during 1920 and 1921, I am certain that Anglo-American co-operation would have become so intimate as almost to amount to a fusion in many respects of our war effort." Though peace had arrived before that merger could be completed, Churchill remained "quite certain that those men on either side of the Atlantic who, through their official duties, have been brought into relationship during these years of stress have a special duty laid upon them all their lives to keep in touch in public matters and work with the same aim."[22] Elected President of the English-Speaking Union in 1921, Churchill proclaimed that an Anglo-American alliance would be "an insurmountable barrier against tyranny in every form, whether it was organized on the old Prussian model or according to the new Russian dispensation." But privately, he complained that Americans' stubborn insistence on repayment of war debts, naval parity, and Irish independence was driving a wedge between the two countries.[23]

Between the world wars, Churchill's American publisher was Charles Scribner's Sons, which had rejected two of his earlier books. It was a respected establishment firm, but also receptive to modern writers: in these decades its legendary editor, Maxwell Perkins, was working with F. Scott Fitzgerald, Ernest Hemingway, and Thomas Wolfe. It was the first American publisher to make a major effort to promote Churchill's books, bringing out *The World Crisis, Marlborough*, and *My Early Life* (under the title *A Roving Commission*). In Britain and the dominions Churchill's interwar books sold well, but in America Scribner's was consistently disappointed. And that literary failure would have consequences for Churchill's political agenda.

Thornton Butterworth would be the London publisher of *The World Crisis*, but long before it was finished he was promoting it to Charles Kingsley, the London agent of Scribner's. "Butterworth was extremely anxious that I emphasise the fact that Churchill proposes to make all sorts of revelations," Kingsley reported to Charles Scribner in a 20 December 1920 letter; "that large numbers of unpublished naval, diplomatic, and military papers will be brought to light, and that, in short, it will be a work of sensational character in which Churchill will fully live up to his reputation of being an 'enfant terrible'." Butterworth conceded that Churchill was expensive, frankly "out for all the traffic will bear," but he assured Scribner that the investment would pay off. "Visualise its potentialities," he urged. "Do not I beg you visualise this as a war book in the ordinary sense of the word. It will be something far greater. . . . I cannot help feeling that it is a book that is worth going for with the gloves off."[24] Scribner followed that advice, advancing Churchill $16,000 for the United States and Canadian rights. For the first volume alone he bought $5,000 worth of newspaper advertising and mailed out 30,000 publicity circulars.[25] Ultimately he would invest more than $20,000 in advertising the series. Kingsley said that Scribner's was counting on American sales of 15,000, and Butterworth thought it could sell as many as 40,000.[26]

Thornton Butterworth would make money on every Churchill book he published, but Scribner's experience was far more discouraging.[27] The first volume of *The World Crisis* (covering the origins of the war) was widely and (for the most part) favorably reviewed in America, but sales were weak.

Published on 6 April 1923, it had sold only 2,500 copies by 22 June – "absurdly small numbers," as Scribner told Churchill.[28] By 1 April 1924 sales had not quite reached 4,000, and as late as 1930 no more than 5,000 copies were in print. By comparison, the Paris firm of Payot printed 4,000 copies of a French translation in 1925 and sold them out by 1939, in a much smaller literary market. And by the end of 1923 Butterworth had sold 10,814 copies in Britain alone, plus another 1,034 abroad. The second volume was published on 29 October 1923 in an American edition of 4,040 copies, of which only 2,700 had been sold by 1 February 1924, and no second printing was called for until 1929. Butterworth oversold his entire first printing (7,500 copies) before the publication date, including 6,340 in Britain and 1,415 overseas. The third Scribner volume, published on 1 March 1927, sold only 1,500 copies in its first two weeks. In London, Butterworth had to order a second printing three days before the publication date, and by the end of the year his total sales were 12,894. "I don't know of any book recently published that received more attention from the press. The reviewers have also treated it as one of the outstanding books of the year, and have written about it in a way as should stimulate the sale," Scribner wrote Churchill. He was therefore "at a loss to explain the resistance that we have found in selling this and in the earlier volumes." The next volume, *The Aftermath*, covering the post-war settlement, performed better in America: published on 7 March 1929, the first printing of 4,000 copies had sold out by the end of May and was followed by a second printing (2,085 copies), and, on 29 October, a third (1,170 copies). But by then Butterworth had 11,000 copies in print. *The Unknown War*, the volume dealing with the Eastern front, was published on 10 November 1931 (3,870 copies) and reprinted in December (1,110 copies) and January (990 copies). That was not a bad record in the Great Depression, but still well behind the 9,000 copies that Butterworth had printed.[29] And Scribner's figures overstate US sales by as much as a third, because they include Canadian sales. For example, by August 1929 *The Aftermath* had sold 3,667 copies in the United States and 1,350 in Canada, a ratio of just 2.7 to 1.[30] When one considers that there were only about five million anglophones over the age of ten in Canada, compared with almost 100 million in the United States, Churchill's failure to reach his American audience becomes apparent.

As of June 1930 he had $33,000 in unearned advances from Scribner's.[31] The publisher tried to overcome customer resistance with a cheap abridged edition of *The World Crisis*, cutting out the parts that would not interest American readers. On 6 February 1931, 4,120 copies were printed, but by 25 April only 2,005 had been sold, and no second printing was called for until 1942. Back in Britain, in 1933–34 Newnes published an illustrated version in twenty-six one-shilling installments, selling about 40,000 sets.[32] And on

9 January 1939 Odhams brought out a 7s 6d two-volume edition, which by the end of the month had sold another 40,000.[33]

Although American reviews of the first volumes were mostly positive, there were some telling criticisms. "The layman, especially the admirer of Mr. Churchill's career, will find it a very readable book; but the professional historian, and particularly the professional sailor, will harbor a different opinion," wrote Edward Breck in the *American Historical Review*, where he detailed Churchill's tendency to blame others for his own failures.[34] Some reviewers distrusted the author's electric rhetoric. "His style, always distinguished and often brilliant, tempts the reader to place unwarranted confidence in arguments more plausible than conclusive, and in facts and figures marshaled to support a thesis with greater artistry than accuracy," observed the *American Political Science Review*.[35] "The judgments may not be ultimate – the writing is," was the backhanded compliment offered by Ellery Sedgwick, critic-at-large for the *Atlantic Monthly*.[36] Columbia University historian Carlton J. H. Hayes, writing in the liberal *New Republic*, credited the book with "real literary distinction" as well as "its amazing revelation of the mind of Winston Spencer Churchill." But, he added, "One fact about this important book transcends all others: it bespeaks the mind of a militarist, and militarists are as dangerous now as they were from 1911 to 1914."[37]

With the publication of *The Aftermath*, offering Churchill's opinions on the peace treaty and the Russian Revolution, the reviews took a sour turn. It was "partial and incomplete" (*American Historical Review*), falling "somewhat short of its powerful predecessors" (*New York Herald Tribune*), and reading "like an apologia written after the event" (*Christian Science Monitor*). "Churchill . . . is faced with intangibles that he seems neither to understand nor interpret" (*Survey*). "The book is crowded with passages of resonant absurdity, among which the character sketch of Lenin stands out as unsurpassable bosh" (*Nation*). Many of the reviewers saw Churchill as another wily British imperialist out to humbug Americans: "Colored by the point of view of an English statesman, who [is] not always to be trusted as a historian" (*North American Review*); "Brilliant though he is as a writer and though his imagination is broad and richly furnished by the study of other times, Churchill is not always trustworthy or even sincere" (*Springfield Republican*). *Time* concluded that "Winnie the Poohbah" could only deal with the war "in terms of exasperation, cynicism, vitriolic indignation." The *New York Evening Post* wished the book had never been published: "No one has ever sung a more bitter Hymn of Hate than the Chancellor of the Exchequer in his exposition of the Russian situation; no one has ever been more blandly and bitingly rhetorical than this same gentleman on America's part in the war and peace." "Unfortunately, the incendiary character of some of the opinions here expressed – by a member of the British government – raises a question far more vital than that of style," protested the *New York Times*. "The mere recrimination in which the book abounds, the underlying pessimism which exults over unattained ideals, the sneers, the indifference to diplomatic propriety" could only inject more poison into Anglo-American relations.[38]

Americans readers rejected Churchill for the same reason that their country did not join the League of Nations. Whereas Europeans were keenly interested in what politicians from neighboring European countries were writing, Americans were determinedly isolationist in their politics and their literature. They deeply distrusted British politicians, who (they believed) had lured the United States into the First World War with deceptive propaganda.[39] Naturally, they did not care to read Churchill's multivolume vindication of Britain's conduct (and his own) in that war.

The Aftermath had been written partly as a rebuttal to the most popular American account of the 1919 Versailles Peace Conference, Ray Stannard Baker's *Woodrow Wilson and the World Settlement*. Baker, who had been Wilson's press secretary at Versailles, was an audience-grabbing popular journalist. Even Churchill envied his ability to spin a beguiling story. In *The World Crisis* he compared Baker's history to a manipulative Hollywood movie, pointing to one episode in particular, when the press corps at Versailles demanded access to all negotiation sessions. After all, they argued, "Open covenants of peace openly arrived at" was the first of Wilson's Fourteen Points. "Mr. Wilson was seriously embarrassed at this application of his doctrine," Churchill wryly observed. "He hastened to repeat that he had not intended that every delicate matter must at every state be discussed in the newspapers of the world. Obviously one had to draw the line somewhere." But the assembled journalists would not be put off:

> The great question was, said Mr. Stannard Baker, "What would democracy do with diplomacy." One the one hand, one hundred million strong, stood the young American democracy. On the other cowered furtively, but at the same time obstinately, and even truculently, the old European diplomacy. Here young, healthy, hearty, ardent millions, advancing so hopefully to reform mankind. There, shrinking from the limelights, cameras and cinemas, huddled the crafty, cunning, intriguing, high-collared, gold-laced diplomatists. Tableau! Curtain! Slow music! Sobs: and afterwards chocolates![40]

This Churchill dismissed as pure "Hollywood":

> In conventional film style all the lights are heightened and all the shadows darkened. The apparatus of lurid contrast is lavishly employed. A plot suited

> to the more fruity forms of popular taste is chosen; and the treatment of the facts, events and personalities is compelled to conform to its preconceived requirements. For this purpose the President is represented as a stainless Sir Galahad championing the superior ideals of the American people and brought to infinite distress by contact with the awful depravity of Europe and its statesmen. Mr. Baker's film story is, in short, the oldest in the world. . . . The plot is certainly sensational, but it scarcely represents what actually happened.[41]

It was the complaint of a melodramatic author who had been beaten at his own game.

Churchill did not quite understand that he was failing to reach the American common reader, perhaps because he had won a following among a much more select audience. On his 1929 trip to United States he was hosted lavishly by wealthy Anglophiles, treated to five nights in a luxury Los Angeles hotel by the investment banker James R. Page, and then transported to New York in Bernard Baruch's private railway car. They told him exactly what he wanted to hear: "I met all the leading people & have heard on every side that my speech & talks (to circles of ten or twelve) have given much pleasure. I explained to them all about England & her affairs – showing how splendid & tolerant she was, & how we ought to work together. I gave a dinner & a lunch to the leading men. I liked the best mostly British born, & all keenly pro-England."[42] At San Simeon in California he talked with William Randolph Hearst, who "seems very much set upon the idea of closer and more intimate relations between the English speaking peoples."[43] In his 1932 lecture tour his speeches on Anglo-American cooperation elicited one standing ovation after another. "One feels, at this distance, the solid enduring strength of England and her institutions," he wrote to the newspaper heir Esmond Harmsworth. "I have never seen anything like the friendliness of sentiment towards us in any of my former visits. All classes and both Parties are in an entirely favourable mood.... We are a power respected and considered to be revivified."[44]

That conclusion was based on a tiny, self-selected, and highly unrepresentative sample, but Churchill could point to the fair success of *My Early Life* (published in October 1930). Butterworth sold 11,000 copies of the original 21s. edition and 5,000 copies of a cheaper 1934 reprint. Within a year, Scribner's had sold out two printings totaling almost 8,000 copies, having invested more than $6,000 in advertising.[45] In spite (or perhaps because) of the deepening Depression, readers wanted diverting and gripping stories set in a romantic past era. Churchill won splendid reviews from the *New York Times* ("Besides being a playboy and a politician, he is a born writer"), the *New York World* ("A brilliant book, with a notable style and a graphic tale to tell"), and the *Nation* ("a racy narrative, vividly and at times brilliantly written, abounding in good stories, striking descriptions of personalities, and caustic comments").[46]

British booksellers were pessimistic about the market for *Thoughts and Adventures* (published on 10 November 1932). Collections of previously published articles were not usually strong sellers, especially in a depressed economy. But it swiftly ran through four editions, selling 7,050 copies by the end of the year, with printers and binders working overtime to keep up with demand,[47] and in 1933–34 there were two printings of a cheap reprint. Scribner's, however, printed just 4,000 copies (under the title *Amid These Storms*) and never reprinted. The volume included some of Churchill's most entertaining essays, including "Painting as a Pastime," but nothing on a specifically American topic.[48]

For his vast biography *Marlborough*, Churchill switched London publishers. George Harrap paid £10,000 for British Empire rights, where Butterworth had offered only £5,000. In May 1929 Scribner's agreed to pay a staggering $25,000 for the American rights, one of those heady and ill-conceived investments made just before the stock market crash. The book was planned as a two-volume work, but ultimately expanded to six. When Churchill decided that more volumes would be needed, he secured an additional £3,000 advance from Harrap and asked for similar consideration from Scribner's, in return for producing a much longer and less marketable book.

Scribner's printed and bound 4,000 copies of volumes I and II, which were published on 3 November 1933 and took a full decade to sell out, despite enthusiastic reviews.[49] "It has been treated as one of the most important, if not the most important, biographies of the year," reported Charles Scribner, "but thus far it has not had any great influence on the sale."[50] And buyer interest declined steadily with each successive volume. On 15 March 1935, 3,040 copies of volumes III and IV were released, which did not sell out until the end of 1941. In March 1937 volume V had a print run of 3,000, of which only 2,537 were purchased. And the final volume, printing 2,700 copies in October 1938, sold just 2,481. Not many Americans in the 1930s wanted to buy a very long and expensive biography of a founding father of the British Empire. As late as December 1949 Churchill was still a long way from earning back his advance.[51]

Churchill had a nineteenth-century view of the literary marketplace, when the United States imported more literature from Britain than it exported, and Washington Irving was a postcolonial author. When there was no transatlantic copyright, English literature could be published in America in numerous abysmally cheap editions and achieve astonishing sales. After 1891, when Congress passed the Chace Act, British authors could earn royalties on American sales, but their protected US editions lost their competitive price advantage. After the First World War, the literary balance of trade shifted decisively in favor of the United States, and by the 1930s there were complaints that British bestseller lists were dominated by American books.[52] Some English authors, such as D. H. Lawrence, made an effort to appeal to the American market,[53] but Churchill was slow to adapt. He refused to accept cuts in a cheap American edition of *My Early Life*, though Scribner protested that "the Fenians, High and Low Church, and even Beaconsfield and Gladstone, are I feel likely to mean little to the younger American."[54] In 1937 Churchill offered Scribner's the American rights to his book *Great Contemporaries*, a collection of sketches of eminent people, including Bernard Shaw, Kaiser Wilhelm, Lawrence of Arabia, Trotsky, Clemenceau, and Hitler. He apologetically acknowledged that none of his subjects were Americans, explaining that he planned to publish another volume entitled "American Studies," which never materialized.[55] Scribner promptly refused *Great Contemporaries*,[56] which was instead published in America on 5 November by G. P. Putnam's Sons. It had sold 6,500 copies by the end of the year, compared with 10,871 in Britain.[57]

American tastes in English literature were changing. Before the Great War, the British writers who had scaled the US bestseller lists were middlebrow and conventional: Anthony Hope, J. M. Barrie, Rudyard Kipling, Mrs. Humphry Ward, Arthur Conan Doyle, Hall Caine, Elinor Glyn, Gilbert Parker, W. J. Locke.[58] After the war, Americans were still reading British authors, but they preferred debunkers and anti-establishmentarians. An annual accounting of non-fiction bestsellers by *Publishers Weekly* included John Maynard Keynes's *The Economic Consequences of the Peace* (2nd place, 1920), H. G. Wells's *The Outline of History* (1st place, 1921 and 1922), Lytton Strachey's *Elizabeth and Essex* (8th place, 1922) and *Queen Victoria* (4th place, 1929), Shaw's *Saint Joan* (8th place, 1924), and T. E. Lawrence's *Revolt in the Desert* (3rd place, 1927).[59] Maxwell Perkins realized that readers wanted young rebels like Fitzgerald, Hemingway, and Wolfe. If the House of Scribner continued to rely on authors such as Winston Churchill – English, middle-aged, bumptiously patriotic, with a distinct Victorian odor – it would go bankrupt.

Nevertheless, Perkins thought that Churchill might have one really good book in him. Visiting London in 1927, he saw the Chancellor of the Exchequer, "brilliant with life," performing at the House of Commons, and conceived the idea of inviting him to write a history of the British Empire. Perkins broached the proposal in 1931, when Churchill met him and Charles Scribner in New York. "It was then that he got up and began walking about rapidly, and it seemed as if at that moment he hit upon a project – a history of the English race, which was to include us," Perkins recalled in 1940. "He must truly have thought of it previously, but it was as if he took the idea from the Empire and immediately enlarged and changed it."[60]

Perkins was right to assume that this idea had already occurred to Churchill, who conceived of writing *A History of the English-Speaking Peoples* at the Army-Yale football game.[61] More than a history of the British Empire, this promised to sell handsomely on both sides of the Atlantic. In the 1920s, the two bestselling non-fiction books in America had been H. G. Wells's *The Outline of History* (1920) and Will Durant's *The Story of Philosophy* (1926). The former sold three million copies, and was more lucrative for the author than all of his other books.[62] Scribner editor Roger Burlingame sat up and took notice. "Wells started an epidemic" of similar surveys, he recalled, "a new avidity for 'culture' to be got in quick doses." Popular historians had to write "with more of the novelist's technique, making real people as alive as if they were imagined characters."[63] Both Wells and Durant produced quintessential examples of the middlebrow culture documented by Joan Shelley Rubin, and they offered a simple formula for literary success: take a subject normally handled by academics, and produce a grand synthesis with a strong narrative line and no footnotes, accessible to general readers. As *Punch* quipped, middlebrows were "people who are hoping that some day they will get used to the stuff they ought to like."[64]

Wells's history was truly global, giving due attention to all human cultures; Churchill's, however, would be proudly Anglocentric. His aim in writing it was to make money, of course, but also to propagandize for a permanent alliance of the anglophone nations, which would preserve both world peace and the British Empire. It would tell the grandest narrative of all, "the whole story of the origin, the quarrels and the re-association of the English speaking peoples," with special emphasis on "the birth of those traditions, institutions and ideas which have become characteristic of our common civilisation in all parts of the globe."[65]

Charles Scribner was skeptical. "It is such a tremendous undertaking that it is hard for me to get a clear idea of how it might be done," he told Churchill. "I rather fear that a two-volume work would be apt to appall people and not have a really popular sale." (The finished work ultimately ran to four volumes.) "Another difficulty," he added, "is that unfortunately enough, from my point of view, the American people are becoming less and less of an Anglo Saxon race, and the Nordic tradition with England as the mother country of the USA is less popular in this country than one might expect."[66] Churchill – who liked to refer to Americans as "our cousins, our brothers" – had some difficulty grasping this point.[67]

Scribner was already co-publishing *Marlborough* with Harrap and proposed a similar arrangement for *A History of the English-Speaking Peoples*. But Harrap was losing money on *Marlborough* and declined to throw away more. Then Scribner received a cable from his board of directors, who had reached the same conclusion. In the depths of the Depression, they would have had to advance $30,000 to $40,000 for an unwritten book, which instead went to Dodd, Mead in the United States and (for £20,000) Cassell in Great Britain.[68] (Alexander Korda paid Churchill an astonishing £50,000 for the movie rights,[69] though one can hardly imagine how such a sprawling two-millennia narrative could have been filmed, except as a "1066 and All That" spoof.) Scribner would consider acquiring *The Second World War*, but he was understandably apprehensive, given the painful experience of losing money on every previous book by Churchill, and knowing his habit of overwriting far beyond his contract. In any case, the book that would have recouped all his losses went to Houghton Mifflin.[70]

In a May 1938 newspaper article, Churchill finally seemed to understand the huge differences that separated the two great anglophone nations. He acknowledged that many Americans were German, Swedish, Italian, Irish, or black, and felt no affinity with Great Britain. As he patiently explained to his British readers, they might regard the American War of Independence as ancient history, and the War of 1812 as a minor sideshow in the struggle against Napoleon, but for Americans these conflicts defined them as a nation, and they taught their schoolchildren that the British were the villains in the drama. True, America's elite universities were still anglocentric: more than a third of Yale's history faculty specialized in English history.[71] But Churchill knew – and regretted – that American history was practically untaught in the United Kingdom. He knew that the British people commonly stereotyped "the United States as a land of money-grubbers and multiple divorces" (Wallis Simpson, for instance). And he knew that the war debt issue had driven a wedge between the two nations. But he was still convinced that literature, written in a common tongue, could overcome these differences. "Words are the only things that last forever," he repeated once again:

> It is this power of words – words written in the past; words spoken at this moment; words printed in the newspapers; words sent speeding through the ether in a Transatlantic broadcast; the flashing interchange of thought – that is our principle agency of union. . . . It is encouraging . . . that so many American books are being read in England and so many English books in America. The literature of a nation is the best interpreter of its spirit. Reading each other's books, we come to appreciate more clearly our fundamental kinship, and to see our differences in truer perspective.[72]

Churchill had friends and fans among America's financial and media elites, but not many among the general public. He was misled by Bernard Baruch, Henry Luce, William Randolph Hearst, and Charles Scribner, who flattered him into thinking that he was a household name in the United States. Even when Churchill's sales were dismal, Scribner kept reassuring him that "your name is as well known here as that of any public character outside of America."[73] That was hardly the case: in the 1937 edition of *Bartlett's Familiar Quotations* Churchill did not rate a single entry, whereas Disraeli had fifty-three, and even Mussolini had six.

British views of American society had been shaped largely by James Bryce's *The American Commonwealth* (1888, revised edition 1910). Bryce argued that only 5 percent of Americans – politicians, journalists, intellectuals, and educators – "create and lead opinion" among the other "passive" 95 percent. The British on the whole realized that the United States had become a multiethnic society, but those elite opinion-makers were still almost entirely Anglo-Saxon.[74] "The people who govern America are our people," said Lloyd George in 1921. "They are our kith and kin. The other breeds are not on top."[75] Therefore, British propaganda during the First World War had focused on those elites, with considerable success, but the anti-war reaction following the Versailles Treaty left most Americans profoundly suspicious of British intentions. For them, Churchill's theme of Anglo-American cooperation sounded like yet another ruse to lure the United States into propping up the British Empire. By publishing in mass circulation magazines such as *Collier's*, Churchill was trying to speak directly to that "passive" 95 percent. But the damage had been done.

Today – when Americans warmly associate Britain with adorable rock stars, sexy spies, zany comedians, quality television, and bulldoggish war leaders – it is difficult to remember the intense Anglophobia of the 1920s and 1930s. It was a classic example of what Richard Hofstadter, an American historian, called "the paranoid style in American politics," often resembling a demented parody of the McCarthy hysteria of the 1950s, with Britain rather than the Soviet Union playing the evil empire. Senator John K. Shields of Kentucky denounced the Rhodes Scholarships as a plot to indoctrinate American youth with the insidious ideology of Anglo-American union. Senator Robert La Follette of Wisconsin wanted to investigate British subjects resident in the United States as possible foreign agents working to undermine American independence. Congressman George Holden Tinkman of Massachusetts condemned the Carnegie Endowment for International Peace and the Rockefeller Foundation as part of a "subversive, disloyal, and seditious movement against American independence." In some quarters the English-Speaking Union (which Churchill chaired between 1921 and 1926) was regarded with the kind of suspicions usually reserved for the Communist Party: the peace activist Dorothy Detzer actually wanted ESU members to be registered as foreign agents. Americans resisted joining the League of Nations not because they were opposed to participation in international organizations, but because they feared that the League was controlled by Great Britain.

Anglo-American tensions were exacerbated by numerous other issues. Churchill considered Prohibition (1920–33) a ludicrous policy, and as Colonial Secretary he pointedly refused to crack down on liquor smuggling from the Bahamas (which after all benefited the local economy).[76] He also approved a plan to boost the price of rubber by restricting exports from Ceylon and Malaya, with the explicit goal of making Americans pay more for a British product. In retaliation, US Commerce Secretary Herbert Hoover led a remarkably passionate and successful campaign to reduce American rubber consumption. In the 1920s conflicts over naval construction poisoned relations to the point where some on both sides of the Atlantic – including Churchill[77] – considered the possibility of an Anglo-American war. Though there was plenty of anti-Communist sentiment in the United States, the USSR did not yet have its own empire or the ability to challenge the US Navy, whereas Britain still had both.

While Churchill spoke of anglophone unity, the German-American journalist H. L. Mencken produced a masterpiece of amateur linguistics demonstrating the distinctiveness of *The American Language* (1919, followed by several supplements and updated editions). Immigrant groups – especially Irish-Americans and German-Americans – paraded their Anglophobia to prove that they were more "American" than Anglophile WASP elites. They canonized their own revolutionary war heroes, such as General Friedrich von Steuben and General Kazimierz Pułaski. And in fact many WASPs defined their American identity in opposition to Britain, which they saw as a prime obstacle to US trade and world power. Pressured by a united front of the Knights of Columbus, the Daughters of the American Revolution, the American Legion, and the Veterans of Foreign Wars, schools and libraries purged their shelves of history textbooks that portrayed Britain in a favorable light – as *The World Crisis* did. And where the British establishment regarded Wallis Simpson as a louche adventuress, Americans saw her as a victim of anti-American snobbery.[78]

British-American cooperation unraveled throughout the 1920s and 1930s, and did not begin seriously to improve until 1939. By 1934 Neville Chamberlain had given up on working with the United States to contain aggression,[79] in part because he followed what American journalists actually wrote about Britain, and hence harbored no Churchillian illusions about Anglo-Saxon brotherhood:

> It is perhaps fortunate that the British public is kept in complete & blissful ignorance of the way we are represented to the other "English speaking" people. The messages of course refer to the naval conversations and every

> one is surcharged with venom and hate. Our motives are impugned our methods are denounced and no American could read these accounts without thanking God that he had a 100 per cent honest-to-God he-man American to hold up his end against those smiling treacherous false Britons who are always betraying him behind his back to the common enemy. There is a calm assumption throughout that G.B. has nothing else to do but serve American interests: to think of British interests is to shatter American confidence in our good faith. Of course, with such a calculated distortion of the situation we haven't a chance.[80]

Churchill's literary failure in America was symptomatic of his political failure. In both arenas, he vastly and consistently overestimated his influence in the United States between the wars. Nothing he could have done or written would have persuaded Americans to embrace his utopian project of an Anglo-Saxon reunion. He assumed that any book that succeeded in Britain would succeed in America, failing to realize that the transatlantic literary marketplace had changed radically since Charles Dickens. The market signals in Scribner's royalty statements should have told him that, but he missed the message. Even when the two nations were pushed into a wartime alliance, Churchill again placed too much faith in American willingness to follow Britain's lead. He would not be the last British Prime Minister to make that mistake.

CHAPTER 14

The Apple Cart

In the 1930s Churchill committed two of the worst blunders of his political career. He adamantly resisted greater self-government for India, and he quixotically championed King Edward VIII. The first campaign alienated all MPs except the most right-wing Conservatives; the second exasperated nearly every important politician. At this time, to press for rearmament and meet the threat of Hitler, he should have focused on building alliances. Instead, he drove himself ever deeper into the political wilderness. These actions cannot be explained in rational terms. Most Conservative MPs were rational political actors: therefore they accepted (however reluctantly) that the 1935 Government of India Bill was a necessary concession, and that Edward's abdication was a sensible solution to an embarrassing crisis. Churchill's eccentric trajectory, however, was driven not so much by political considerations as by literature. Only if we look to those sources can we detect the motives behind his actions, which were often self defeating.

On 13 April 1919, following growing unrest and some violence in the Punjab, British authorities placed most of the province under martial law, which included a ban on public meetings. That afternoon there was a large but peaceful meeting of Hindus, Muslims, and Sikhs in an enclosed garden in Amritsar. Brigadier General Reginald Dyer marched his Baluchi and Gurkha soldiers to the meeting and ordered fifty riflemen to fire into the crowd, with no warning or order to disperse. They continued firing until their ammunition was nearly exhausted. The dead numbered 379, according to the British government; about 1,000 according to a separate investigation by the Indian National Congress.

As Secretary for War, Churchill wanted Dyer punished or at least retired. That meant a head-on collision with his own Army Council, who wanted to take no action. After weeks of browbeating, he was only able to persuade them to bar Dyer from further service in India. Even this slap on the wrist was furiously denounced by right-wing Tories in a heated parliamentary debate on 8 July 1920. In response, Churchill was relentless, uncompromising, and damning. "That is an episode which appears to me to be without precedent or parallel in the modern history of the British Empire. . . . It is an extraordinary event, a monstrous event, an event which stands in singular and sinister isolation." After alluding to the "frightfulness" practiced by the Germans in Belgium, and the "bloody and devastating terrorism" of the Bolsheviks, he insisted that "We have to make it absolutely clear, some way or other, that this is not the British way of doing business." And then he quoted Macaulay: Amritsar was "the most frightful of all spectacles, the strength of civilisation without its mercy."

> Our reign in India or anywhere else has never stood on the basis of physical force alone, and it would be fatal to the British Empire if we were to base ourselves only upon it. The British way of doing things . . . has always meant and implied close and effectual co-operation with the people of the country. In every part of the British Empire that has been our aim, and in no part have we arrived at such success as in India, whose princes spent their treasure in our cause, whose brave soldiers fought side by side with our own men, whose intelligent and gifted people are co-operating at the present moment with us in every sphere of government and of industry.[1]

Arthur Herman calls it "his greatest speech," indeed, "his finest hour."[2] But just two years later Churchill urged Pamela Plowden, now married to the Governor of Bengal, to "keep the Flag flying" and preserve "the prestige & authority of the white man undiminished. Our true duty in India lies to those 300 millions whose lives & means of existence wd be squandered if entrusted to the chatterboxes who are supposed to speak for India today."[3] He was probably alluding to Gandhi, who at that moment was in jail for sedition. Starting in August 1921, protests against British rule in India took a violent turn. In November riots in Bombay resulted in fifty-eight deaths. The following February a mob in Chauri Chaura set fire to a police station and massacred twenty-three Indian policemen as they tried to escape. Horrified, Gandhi called off his Non-cooperation Movement, an act that alienated many of his followers. Churchill had once backed the Montagu-Chelmsford reforms, which established limited power-sharing for Indians on the provincial level, while preserving overall British control. Edwin Montagu (Secretary of State for India) intended this to be a first step toward eventual self-government, but now Churchill concluded (and Lloyd George agreed) that further concessions would only feed Indian unrest.[4]

Churchill's ambivalence reflected the imperialism he had absorbed from Macaulay and Victorian melodrama, which mandated a benevolent paternalism.

This ideology held that native populations must be protected from abuse, and that native rebelliousness must be sternly repressed. The potential conflict between these two goals was never quite resolved, neither on the stage nor in Churchill's mind.

Another example of those mixed signals arose in August 1920, when Churchill proposed to Sir Hugh Trenchard, Chief of the Air Staff, that Iraq could be pacified by dropping "gas bombs, especially mustard gas, which would inflict punishment upon recalcitrant natives without inflicting grave injury upon them."[5] In fact the British never used poison gas in Iraq, but how could he think it would not inflict grave injury? When he authorized the deployment of mustard gas against the Germans in September 1918 he called it "a hellish poison,"[6] suggesting he was aware that it caused serious damage to the skin and bronchial tubes, and in large doses could be fatal. And unlike the Germans, the Iraqis had not used the gas first and had no means of protection or retaliation. But then in July 1921 he shifted back to his protective mode, when he read a report of an RAF attack on civilians. "To fire wilfully on women and children taking refuge in a lake is a disgraceful act, and I am surprised you do not order the officers responsible for it, to be tried by Court Martial," he protested to Trenchard. "By doing such things we put ourselves on the lowest level."[7]

Even compared with his contemporaries amongst the British governing classes, Churchill neglected to assign speaking roles to colonized peoples. In June 1921 Neville Chamberlain noted that Churchill had delivered a superb 90-minute parliamentary speech on Mesopotamia ("a brilliant performance . . . great art in delivery") and then ruined the effect the following day at a dinner for Dominion prime ministers. India was represented at the dinner by Srinivasa Sastri, like Churchill a National Liberal politician. But when Churchill spoke:

> He clean forgot about India and talked about "our race" "English speaking peoples" and the "four great Dominions" so that I could not help asking myself What does Mr. Sastri think of all this. Towards the end of the speech someone handed up a card on which "India" was written and Winston then produced an eloquent passage about the day when India would take her place on equal terms with the Dominions. But it was too late and when later on Sastri rose he administered in perfect English and with perfect taste one of the most scathing rebukes I ever heard. W. must have cussed a bit. . . . I never quite know whether most to admire his great gifts or to be alarmed at his impulsiveness and hasty judgment.[8]

By 1927 Churchill had become a passionate admirer of Katherine Mayo's *Mother India*, a denunciation of the treatment of Indian women.[9] The problems

Mayo exposed – child marriage, caste barriers, infant and maternal mortality – were real enough, albeit sensationalized. But she went further, portraying Indian males as physically weak, morally depraved, and impotent in both senses of the term, incapable of real political leadership. Her jeremiad led to the conclusion that Indians could not govern themselves, and that Gandhi would undo whatever progress British rule had brought to the subcontinent. In 1931 Churchill read the proofs of *India Insistent* by Harcourt Butler, formerly Governor of Burma, who likewise insisted that the colony was not ready for self-rule.[10]

Gandhi's agitation for Indian independence finally bore fruit in November 1930 when the Prime Minister, Ramsay MacDonald, convened the first of three Round Table Conferences in London. Representing an array of Indian politicians and princes, it was charged with proposing constitutional reforms in India. The conferences led to the 1935 Government of India Act, which established elected provincial legislatures (ultimately subject to British-appointed governors), and proposed for the whole of India a federal governing structure – which was never implemented. The Act represented an attempt to grant Indians greater autonomy while retaining British control at the center, comporting with Stanley Baldwin's moderate conservatism. For most Indian political leaders it did not go far enough. For Churchill and the hard right wing of the Conservative Party, it represented a capitulation to demands for independence.

In his denunciations of the Round Table Conferences, Churchill alluded to "the decline and fall of the British Empire."[11] One can certainly discern the roots of his imperial ideology in Edward Gibbon's vast book, where he read, in the first few pages, that the Romans "preserved peace by a constant preparation for war."[12] More than the native regimes they supplanted, the Romans gave their subject peoples the blessings of order and tranquility over a vast part of the globe, and they gave their slaves real legal protection.[13] Churchill no doubt had that in mind when he compared the benefits of British rule to precolonial despotisms – and to the new and expansionist totalitarian empires. Gibbon's description of Rome under Emperor Constantine could resonate with anxious Britons in the 1890s, and even more in the 1930s:

> The threatening tempest of barbarians, which so soon subverted the foundations of Roman greatness, was still repelled, or suspended, on the frontiers. The arts of luxury and literature were cultivated, and the elegant pleasures of society were enjoyed, by the inhabitants of a considerable portion of the globe. . . . The sage principles of Roman jurisprudence preserved a sense of order and equity unknown to the despotic governments of the East. The rights of mankind might derive some protection from religion and

> philosophy; and the name of freedom, which could no longer alarm, might sometimes admonish, the successors of Augustus, that they did not reign over a nation of Slaves or Barbarians.[14]

And Gibbon's chapter on Alaric's invasion of Italy (circa AD 401) could be read as a warning against appeasement:

> The incapacity of a weak and distracted government may often assume the appearance and produce the effects of a treasonable correspondence with the public enemy. If Alaric himself had been introduced into the council of Ravenna, he would probably have advised the same measures which were actually pursued by the ministers of Honorius. . . . In the arts of negotiation, as well as in those of war, the Gothic king maintained his superior ascendant over an enemy whose seeming changes proceeded from the total want of counsel and design.[15]

But in an Indian context, Churchill overlooked one of Gibbon's key conclusions – that the empire might have saved itself if it had granted its colonized peoples some kind of parliamentary system:

> If such an institution, which gave the people an interest in their own government, had been universally established by Trajan or the Antonines, the seeds of public wisdom and virtue might have been cherished and propagated in the empire of Rome. The privileges of the subject would have secured the throne of the monarch; the abuses of an arbitrary administration might have been prevented, in some degree, or corrected, by the interposition of these representative assemblies; and the country would have been defended against a foreign enemy by the arms of natives and freemen. Under the mild and generous influence of liberty, the Roman empire might have remained invincible and immortal; or if its excessive magnitude, and the instability of human affairs, had opposed such perpetual continuance, its vital and constituent members might have separately preserved their vigour and independence.[16]

Much of *My Early Life*, published on 20 October 1930, almost simultaneous with the announcement of the first Round Table Conference, was a delicious warm bath of imperial nostalgia, where Indians appeared only as cheerful and efficient servants. Churchill recalled his arrival in Bangalore:

> Daylight brought suave, ceremonious, turbaned applicants for the offices of butler, dressing boy, and head groom, which in those days formed the foundation of the cavalry subaltern's household. All bore trustworthy

> testimonials with them from the home-going regiment; and after brief formalities and salaams laid hold of one's worldly possessions and assumed absolute responsibility for one's whole domestic life. If you liked to be waited on and relieved of home worries, India thirty years ago was perfection. All you had to do was hand over all your uniform and clothes to the dressing boy, your ponies to the syce, and your money to the butler, and you need never trouble any more. Your Cabinet was complete; each of these ministers entered upon his department with knowledge, experience and fidelity. They would devote their lives to their task. For a humble wage, justice, and a few kind words, there was nothing they would not do. Their world became bounded by the commonplace articles of your wardrobe and other possessions. No toil was too hard, no hours were too long, no dangers too great for their unruffled calm or their unfailing care. Princes could live no better than we. . . .
>
> On the whole, after forty-eight hours of intensive study, I formed a highly favourable opinion about India. . . . We certainly felt as we dropped off to sleep the keenest realization of the great work which England was doing in India and of her high mission to rule these primitive but agreeable races for their welfare and our own.[17]

My Early Life won laudatory reviews on both sides of the Atlantic, largely because its boyish enthusiasm and rosy Victorianism offered a relief from modern Stracheyite cynicism. "The Winston Churchill now living in this post-war age of disillusionment and skepticism resuscitates for himself and his reader a Winston Churchill of a day that was brighter and happier, more real and more solid," wrote T. R. Ybarra in the *New York Times*.[18] "Into an age of introspection, Freudian complexes, doubt and despair, Mr. Churchill comes like a great wind blowing through a little window into a musty, overfurnished room," as Duff Cooper put it in the *Spectator*.[19]

Stanley Baldwin fully recognized that Churchill, in his desperate campaign against Indian self-rule, had reverted to the mindset of *My Early Life*: "He has become once more the subaltern of the Hussars of '96."[20] Lord Irwin concurred: Churchill was still a "vigorous Imperialist in the 1890–1900 sense of the word," and his condescension would only inflame Indian sensitivities.[21] As a *Times* leader concluded, however "brilliant" he might be as an author, "the omniscient subaltern is not, after all, so very far removed from the statesman who has nothing to learn in 1930."[22]

Churchill was concerned about the wretched condition of the toiling masses of Asia. He profoundly admired Pearl S. Buck's *The Good Earth* (1931), "which shows the virtues and the sufferings of hard-working Chinese cultivators of the soil, and how happy they would be if they could only have impartial justice and the security for the fruits of their toil instead of being tortured by warlords, Bolshevists, and brigands of all kinds." But from that novel he drew a lesson that the author certainly had not intended: "China is in the same state that India would be if the guiding hand of British rule were withdrawn," and Japanese-occupied China, which enjoyed "orderly government," was the "least unhappy" part of the country.[23]

Churchill drew on another literary source when he warned (again and again) that there were "evil elements" behind Gandhi. If he won independence a "triumphant Brahmin oligarchy" would persecute the Muslims, oppress the untouchables, and exploit the poor masses. "It is our duty to guard those millions from that fate," he insisted.[24] "You cannot desert them, you cannot abandon them," he proclaimed in March 1933. "They are as much our children as any children can be."[25]

Every imperial melodrama had a scene like that. Good but childlike natives are oppressed by a wicked native, or a wicked European, whereupon the hero declaims "You cannot leave these hapless creatures to his mercy!" (an actual line from Henry Pettitt and Augustus Harris's 1885 play *Human Nature*).[26] And there was Churchill's blind spot: he could not see Indians as adults. His concerns were not groundless: B. R. Ambedkar, the leader of the Untouchables, was apprehensive about their position in an independent India and was glad that Churchill had spoken out about the issue.[27] But it was one thing to insist that Indian self-government must include safeguards for her oppressed minorities (as Ambedkar did) and quite another to oppose independence altogether.

The puzzle that needs explaining is why Churchill, who was still writing encomiums to the Mahdi as late as 1931, vilified gentle Gandhi at the same time. A partial reason was that the Mahdi's movement had been crushed and no longer presented a threat. For the time being, jihadism appeared to be an extinct volcano. As Duff Cooper recorded in 1921, Churchill favored conciliating unrest in Egypt, but only after it had been suppressed: "His great line was that you could only make concessions to people you had beaten."[28] In a March 1933 article in *Strand Magazine* he extolled "Great Fighters in Lost Causes," for example, Vercingetorix: "What Europeans have done in Africa in the last two generations Rome did to the Gauls."[29] The message he drew from Margaret Mitchell's *Gone with the Wind* (1936) was that, given the overwhelming power of the North, "the Confederates never had any chance at all. . . . The dramatic point is the wonderful resistance which they made."[30] From a literary perspective, history's losers were always romantic figures, even if they deserved to lose. But by 1933 Gandhi was clearly winning. As early as 1909 Churchill had realized that, whereas the British Army could contain any armed insurrection, it would be powerless against peaceful noncooperation. "If [the Indians] ever unite against us and put us in coventry all round, the game would be up," he admitted to Wilfred Scawen Blunt. "If they could agree to have nothing at all to do with us the whole thing would collapse."[31] Victorian melodrama offered a standard script for dealing with native revolts, but as far as we know, there were no episodes of nonviolent anticolonial resistance on the nineteenth-century stage.

In dramatic terms, the Mahdi was a wicked native, who openly took up arms against the British and could therefore be respected for his "martial virtues."[32] Gandhi was obviously neither an overtly wicked native nor a good native. By a process of elimination, Churchill shoehorned him into the third stage stereotype, the treacherous native, a false friend of the British hero who turns on him when his back is to the wall. This character type was created partly in reaction to the Sepoy Mutiny of 1857, though it was postulated even earlier by Macaulay in his essay on Warren Hastings. Macaulay had argued that a long history of imperial subjugation (which certainly did not begin with the English) had robbed Indian Hindus of any capacity for "manly resistance," so they resorted to deception as their only protection against power:

> All those arts which are the natural defence of the weak are more familiar to this subtle race than to the Ionian of the time of Juvenal, or to the Jew of the dark ages. What the horns are to the buffalo, what the paw is to the tiger, what the sting is to the bee, what beauty, according to the old Greek song, is to woman, deceit is to the Bengalee. Large promises, smooth excuses, elaborate tissues of circumstantial falsehood, chicanery, perjury, forgery, are the weapons, offensive and defensive, of the people of the Lower Ganges.[33]

In various speeches, and with a fine disregard for consistency, Churchill projected onto Gandhi the three forms of tyranny he hated most. Sometimes he was the tool of super-rich Bombay capitalists, sometimes he used "Moscow methods," and sometimes he was an Indian Fascist. (True, Gandhi had paid Mussolini some foolish compliments – but then so had Churchill.)[34] The common thread was that, underneath his veneer of saintliness, Gandhi was a fraud who was working with sinister forces that aimed to destroy the British Empire and exploit the Indian masses. Gandhi could be a wily politician, but most Raj officials trusted and respected him and found that they could do business with him – radically unlike the stage caricature projected by Churchill. "Mr. Gandhi is a philanthropic enthusiast," concluded the Lieutenant Governor of Bihar, "but I regard him as perfectly honest; and he was quite reasonable in his discussions with me."[35]

Significantly, Churchill's first pejorative use of the term "appeasement" was directed against Gandhi: in October 1930 Prince Bismarck reported to the German Foreign Office that "Both Churchill and Lord Reading expressed great anxiety over the forthcoming Indian Round Table Conference and both of them strongly blamed the Viceroy, Lord Irwin, for his policy of appeasement."[36] This same report contained Churchill's first recorded warning against the menace of Hitler. For Churchill, these two threats to the British Empire appeared on the horizon simultaneously, and in the 1930s he sometimes had difficulty distinguishing between them. (Irwin would later, as Lord Halifax, become a prime appeaser of Nazi Germany.)

Churchill began his political life as a Whig, but in this decade he radically revised his Whiggish vision of history. If India (as Macaulay had hoped) was gradually adopting British culture and British institutions, then it made sense that she should evolve toward the same kind of autonomy enjoyed by Canada or Australia. On 4 May 1933 Lord Linlithgow, chair of the Round Table Conference, pointed out to Churchill that the Indian Civil Service was already largely and successfully Indianized. But Churchill replied:

> I think we differ principally in this, that you assume that the future is a mere extension of the past whereas I find history full of unexpected turns and retrogressions. The mild and vague Liberalism of the early years of the twentieth century, the surge of fantastic hopes and illusions that followed the armistice of the Great War have already been superseded by a violent reaction against Parliamentary and electioneering procedure and by the establishment of dictatorships real or veiled in almost every country. Moreover the loss of our external connections, the shrinkage in foreign trade and shipping brings the surplus population of Britain within measurable distance of utter ruin. We are entering a period when the struggle for self-preservation is going to present itself with great intenseness to thickly populated industrial countries.

Under those Darwinian conditions, any colonies freed by Britain would only be swallowed up by the more ruthless and predatory empires of Japan, Italy, and Germany. It was a nightmare future, similar to that later conjured up in George Orwell's *Nineteen Eighty-Four*. Only the preservation of the Raj could prevent that.[37] Churchill agreed with H. G. Wells that a new and aggressive nationalism threatened the future of civilization, yet his answer to that menace was not Wells's dream of a World State, but the reality of the British Empire:

> If from the relaxing hands of Britain the reins of Empire fall,
> others will advance eagerly and hungrily
> to assume our neglected duties,
> to exploit our discarded treasures,
> and to fill our place in the world.

It will not be to any benevolent Utopia
that your inheritance will pass,
but only to a fierce band of rival nationalisms,
who once they know you are weakened and solitary,
will brush you from their path
without even a word of apology or thanks.[38]

In his campaign against Gandhi, Churchill mobilized all his skills as a publicist. On 3 February 1931 he thanked Lord Rothermere for newspaper leaders supporting him on India, but as a journalist he realized that coverage in the news columns had far more impact than anything published on the editorial pages. Though the *Daily Mail* had covered all three of his recent speeches on India, it had not given them sufficient space – in one case (he complained) a mere column and three-quarters. And those speeches incurred real opportunity costs: they involved as much work as writing a newspaper or magazine article, which would earn him between £300 and £400. He offered a deal: "Can you not give me some assurance that if I take the trouble to let the Daily Mail have a copy beforehand they will give me certainly 1,800 to a couple of thousand words on various occasions agreed upon beforehand. Otherwise Baldwin with the Times at his back is master of the fate of India."[39]

In August 1931 Churchill accepted an offer to write weekly articles of 1,500 words for the *Daily Mail*, fifty-two weeks at £150, for a total of £7,800. He made clear that he would not limit his topics to politics: "Sometimes descriptive when I am in America on travel and foreign matters, sometimes on British politics, sometimes on personalities or books or questions apart from the common round." Even in times of high political crisis, he presented himself not just as a politician but as a man of letters, modeling himself after Sainte-Beuve, producing causeries as well as polemics.[40]

In a 6 December 1932 article in the *Daily Mail*, he extolled the achievements of Warren Hastings as "a drama of the highest order." As Macaulay had written, Hastings was willing "to make the choice between innocence and greatness, between crime and ruin," and the Indian Civil Service today had to follow his example. Churchill also quoted the headmaster of Westminster school, Harold Costley-White: "We cannot renounce our trusteeship till the social evils of India are removed: the mortality among young mothers equal in a generation to that of the Allies in the Great War, the horrors of child-marriage, the dreadful treatment of the 26,000,000 widows, the infantile mortality, the stifling system of purdah . . . the 60,000,000 outcasts." And Churchill agreed: "To hand over the helpless hundreds of millions to a Brahmin oligarchy; to allow every public service to deteriorate through lack of control; to open the floodgates alike of corruption and carnage; to let Indians fall back into the conditions from which they were rescued by Warren Hastings, would be to incur charges graver than any preferred against that grand Englishman, and, unlike him, to be found guilty before history."[41]

In another *Daily Mail* article, written in January 1933, Churchill returned once again to the subject of General Gordon, on the centenary of his birth. But this time the Mahdi, that wonderful insurgent, practically disappears from the story. The focus is on the heroic Gordon, who "will be remembered [for] that sense of honour which united him to a helpless native community whose safety and welfare had been committed to his charge."[42]

After the Government of India Bill passed its final reading on 4 June 1935, the conventions of melodrama prescribed a shift to magnanimity, and Churchill again followed the script. He mended fences with his parliamentary opponents, and he invited Gandhi's supporter, the industrialist G. D. Birla, to lunch with him at his country residence, Chartwell. Birla found his host warm, voluble, conciliatory, open-minded, apparently free of racial prejudice, and shockingly ignorant of modern India, unaware that it was becoming an industrial society. Churchill praised Gandhi for his defense of the Untouchables, and he seemed reconciled to (and even relieved by) the prospect of eventual independence for India.[43]

As Samuel Hoare wrote, Baldwin had won the debate because "his speeches on India, like his broadcast talks, were all the more effective for the complete contrast that their simple and direct English made with Churchill's flood of words."[44] The India controversy only enhanced Churchill's bad reputation for oratorical swaggering at the expense of common sense. After a March 1933 speech on the air estimates, the Tory MP Allen Bathurst remarked, "whenever he makes a speech, whenever he writes a book, and, I am told, whenever he paints a picture, he is always able to produce a work of art and not infrequently a masterpiece."[45] It was a backhanded compliment, implying that Churchill was more a beguiling artist than a serious statesman. "Mr. Churchill's carefully composed attitudes as he sits at the corner of the gangway and makes beautiful inflections with his hands when talking to his neighbour tell of the dramatic artist who has nearly ruined a statesman," Harry Boardman observed in the *Manchester Guardian* in 1937.[46] Churchill himself felt compelled to tone down his high rhetoric and move toward the more conversational style of Baldwin and Chamberlain. As he told Clementine in 1935, "At sixty I am altering my method of speaking, largely under Randolph's tuition, and now talk to the House of Commons with garrulous unpremeditated flow. They seem delighted. But what a mystery the art of public speaking is! . . . There is apparently nothing in the literary effect I have sought for forty years!"[47]

The following year he would strive for literary effect in another political controversy, again with disastrous results. In this case his dramatic model was

George Bernard Shaw's *The Apple Cart* (1929), a political burlesque centering on Magnus, a future English King, who tires of being an "indiarubber stamp" for the government and dares to express his own political opinions in public. When he reminds the British people that the royal veto still stands as a bulwark against parliamentary tyranny, the Prime Minister, Proteus, decides to issue an ultimatum. He herds together his fractious Cabinet, and they threaten to resign unless the King submits to his proper role as a figurehead. If necessary they are willing to resort to another kind of blackmail: they know that Magnus, though married, is carrying on an affair with Orinthia, a twice-married woman. Ultimately, Magnus trumps them with a threat of his own: he will first dissolve Parliament, then abdicate, and then, as a commoner, form his own political party to campaign against Proteus. The Cabinet, realizing that Magnus would sweep into office on a wave of popular sympathy, caves in. The play was an astonishing anticipation, seven years before the fact, of Edward VIII and Mrs. Simpson, albeit with a different ending. Certainly Churchill thought that reality closely paralleled

> the kind of situation which Mr. Bernard Shaw has illuminated for modern eyes in the witty scenes and dialogue of *The Apple Cart*. Our Fabian dramatist and philosopher has rendered a service to monarchy which never perhaps could have been rendered from any other quarter. With his unsparing derision he has held up before the Socialists of every land the weaknesses, the meannesses, the vanities and the follies of the trumpery figures who float upwards and are borne forward upon the swirls and eddies of so-called democratic politics. The sympathies of the modern world, including many of its advanced thinkers, are powerfully attracted by the gay and sparkling presentation of a king, ill-used, let-down, manipulated for personal and party ends, yet sure of his value to the mass of his subjects, and striving not unsuccessfully to preserve their permanent interests, and to discharge his duty.[48]

That quotation is taken somewhat out of context: it refers to King Alfonso XIII of Spain. But Shaw's play encouraged Churchill to view Edward through the same romantic lens.

At first Churchill hoped that Edward and Mrs. Simpson would drop the idea of marriage, but in late November 1936 there was some talk of the possibility of a morganatic marriage. That is, the King would remain on the throne, but his wife would assume the title of Duchess of Cornwall rather than Queen, and their children would have no right of succession. Churchill was credited with originating this idea, and he certainly supported it.[49] But on the morning of 27 November, at a hurriedly called meeting, Baldwin told the

Cabinet about his conversations with the King on 18 October, 16 November, and 25 November. Later that day Lord Zetland, the Secretary of State for India, communicated the explosive revelations in a secret letter to Lord Linlithgow:

> The first talk took place after the visit of Mrs. Simpson to Balmoral and the announcement in the Press of the divorce of Mr. Simpson. SB it seems spoke with great frankness and said that the situation was a serious one; that the press of America was commenting freely on the prospect of Mrs. Simpson becoming Queen of England and that serious concern was being displayed in the Dominions at these widespread rumours. He asked the King what his intentions were? It seems that the Monarch replied that he was determined to marry the lady. SB asked him if he realised that this would probably mean abdication? He agreed that this would be a probable consequence and that he was prepared for it. He was willing to abdicate voluntarily and to make things as easy as possible for his successor.
>
> This held good until the talk on the 25th, when his attitude changed. He now said that he believed that he would have the sympathy and support of a very large part of the people, and that while he realised that they might be unwilling to accept her as Queen, they would accept a morganatic marriage if the Government were willing to introduce legislation authorising it. SB told him bluntly that if he thought he was going to get away with it in that way he was making a huge mistake. . . .
>
> It was pointed out at the Cabinet that this might involve the resignation of the Government and that in this case it would give rise to a Constitutional issue of the first magnitude, viz the King *v.* the Government. It seems that the King has been encouraged to believe that Winston Churchill would in these circumstances be prepared to form an alternative Government. If this were true there would be a grave risk of the country being divided into two camps – for and against the King. This clearly would be fraught with danger of the most formidable kind.
>
> . . . I thought it only fair to warn you of a storm of incalculable possibility which is brewing and which, so far as I can see, may at any moment break upon us. Keep it in your most secret repository. What the effect of it may be in India I scarcely dare try to imagine.

"I have seldom listened to a more dramatic narrative," Zetland wrote.[50] Once again, Baldwin had played the steady, responsible pilot of Empire, and cast Churchill as a recklessly ambitious windbag. Churchill only reinforced that impression when, on 30 November, he collared the War Secretary Duff Cooper in the House of Commons lobby and

> . . . delivered himself of an oration. What crime, he asked, had the King committed? Had we not sworn allegiance to him? Were we not bound to that oath? Was he to be condemned unheard? Was he seeking to do anything that was not permitted of the meanest of his subjects? For his own part he would need satisfaction on a great many points before he could consider himself absolved from his oath of allegiance.[51]

On 5 December Churchill wrote a giddily encouraging letter to the King, still hoping for "an ultimate happy ending." And he concluded, "For real wit Bernard Shaw's article in tonight's *Evening Standard* should be read. He is joyous!" Shaw's squib, "The King, The Constitution and The Lady, Another Fictitious Dialogue," was in effect a condensation of *The Apple Cart*, updated to make the relevance more obvious. The cast was reduced to just three characters: over the objections of the Prime Minister and the Archbishop of Canterbury, the King insists on marrying his Lady in a civil ceremony and refuses to abdicate.[52]

That same day Churchill issued a statement to the press. "I plead for time and patience," he began. When he is apparently cornered by the Cabinet, King Magnus likewise pleads for time, which Proteus naively grants – and the King uses that opportunity to plan his countermove. (It also allowed Shaw to insert an interlude where Magnus confronts his mistress in her boudoir, and pad out a one-acter to make a full-length play.) Churchill asserted that the Cabinet was acting "without having previously ascertained at the very least the will of Parliament," which is precisely what the Cabinet does in *The Apple Cart*. He granted that "If the King refuses to take the advice of his Ministers they are of course free to resign," as they threatened to do in Shaw's play. But "They have no right whatever to put pressure upon him to accept their advice by soliciting beforehand assurances from the Leader of the Opposition that he will not form an alternative administration in the event of their resignation, and thus confronting the King with an ultimatum." Of course, the Cabinet had every right to do that, and "ultimatum" is exactly the word that Proteus uses – whereupon King Magnus threatens to form an alternative administration.[53]

Desmond Morton (an intelligence official who was collecting data on German rearmament, and passing it on to Churchill) warmly approved of Churchill's press statement, writing to him that "there is an overwhelming desire in the country that he should remain our King." The public might not be prepared to accept Mrs. Simpson as Queen, but if Edward could

> by any means give her up, his popularity would be so great that he could make himself Dictator of England, if he so chose. The whole of this business would be regarded as forging an unbreakable bond between himself in

person and his subjects. There is nothing, in my opinion, that he could not do with them afterwards.

The belief is, I find, widely held that this is a Baldwin and Parliamentary plot; that Parliament led by SB is determined to reduce the Monarchy to an utterly impotent symbol, lacking even those powers still enjoyed by it and so wisely used on rare occasions by King George. An immense number of people rightly or wrongly believe that although the Monarchy is highly circumscribed, it does, at times, act as a court of disinterested equity, to prevent the rasher acts of no matter what Party being carried through without sufficient consideration, in the heat of political strife and controversy. They believe that SB has with set purpose taken advantage of an unfortunate situation to destroy the last vestige of Kingly power and dignity, in favour of himself and Parliament.[54]

Here Morton looked forward to a denouement similar to that of *The Apple Cart*, and ascribed to Baldwin the nefarious motives that Shaw assigned to Proteus. Whether Morton was familiar with the play is unknown, but Churchill certainly was, and this letter could have only encouraged him to re-enact it on the stage of history. Likewise, a note from Professor J. H. Morgan suggested that, if Baldwin and his Cabinet resigned, the King could ask Churchill to form a new government. Though few MPs would join him, Churchill could immediately call an election, "and on so grave an issue you might 'sweep the country'."[55] According to several recorders of political gossip (Leslie Hore-Belisha, Chips Channon, Victor Cazalet, John Reith, Leo Amery) the air was abuzz with rumors that Churchill might do just that.[56]

However, the journalist J. A. Spender, more firmly grounded in reality, warned Churchill that any attempt to drag out the constitutional crisis would be madness.[57] On 3 December Churchill had participated in a mass meeting at the Albert Hall to launch the Focus, a broad nonpartisan coalition of anti-Nazis and anti-appeasers. Just four days later Henry Wickham Steed, a key figure in the Focus, protested that Churchill was already driving a wedge between himself and the movement he helped to found: "I cannot well see how we can stand up for democracy and parliamentary institutions, if, when the issue is raised, we do not dissociate ourselves from a course calculated to endanger the principle of parliamentary supremacy over the Crown."[58] The letter did not reach Churchill in time and, even if it had, it probably would not have deterred him. According to G. D. Birla, "He had the honesty to admit to me that when he stood up in favour of the ex-King, he did not know that public opinion was so much against him."[59]

But what exactly was "public opinion"? If it meant the people of Britain and the mass-circulation papers, they (as Susan Williams has shown) mostly sided with the King. And the people said so, in an avalanche of letters sent to Churchill, Edward, and the newspapers. Churchill, then, had reason to think that the country was behind him. But at the time "public opinion" was often understood to mean the British establishment and the "quality" papers, and they were mainly opposed to the marriage. In these circles there was widespread suspicion that Churchill would use the crisis to ride back to power at the head of a "King's Party." In reality, neither Churchill nor Edward ever contemplated such a constitutional coup, which never takes place in *The Apple Cart* either. But the governing classes, hanging together in pursuit of an unpopular policy, clearly felt threatened by Churchill, and their response to his defense of the King was vitriolic.[60]

On 7 December Churchill pleaded with the House of Commons to give the King more time, and was howled down for his pains. "He was completely staggered by the unanimous hostility of the House, as well as being called to order by the Speaker," Leo Amery observed.[61] Lord Winterton called it "one of the angriest manifestations I have ever heard directed against a man in the House of Commons."[62] Churchill's protégé Robert Boothby was apoplectic:

> Dear Winston,
>
> I understood last night that we had *agreed* upon a formula, and a course, designed to save the King from abdication, if that is possible. I thought you were going to use all your powers – decisive, as I believe, in the present circumstances – to secure a happy issue, on the lines that were suggested.
>
> But this afternoon you have delivered a blow to the King, both in the House and in the country, far harder than any that Baldwin ever conceived of.
>
> You have reduced the number of potential supporters to the minimum possible – I shd think now about seven in all.
>
> *And you have done it without any consultation with your best friends and supporters.*
>
> I have never in my life said anything to you that I did not sincerely believe. And I never will.
>
> What happened this afternoon made me feel that it is almost impossible for those who are most devoted to you personally to follow you blindly (as they wd like to do) in politics. Because they cannot be sure where the hell they are going to be landed next. . . .[63]

Boothy confided to Harold Nicolson:

> I knew that Winston was going to do something dreadful. I had been staying the weekend with him. He was silent and restless and glancing into corners. Now when a dog does that, you know that he is about to be sick on the

carpet. It is the same with Winston. He managed to hold it for three days, and then comes up to the House and is sick right across the floor.

Nicolson was compelled to agree: "He has undone in five minutes the patient reconstruction work of two years."[64] On 13 December, three days after the abdication, Neville Chamberlain gloated:

Winston did his best to cross us and at one moment had gorgeous visions of a clash between the Sovereign & his Cabinet, the resignation of Ministers, general consternation and then in a flash of glory a champion stepping forth to defend the King in shining armour. I am told he had gone a long way in the formation of his Cabinet and in the plans for action when it was installed. But this pretty picture faded like an unsubstantial pageant last Monday. I saw the Press myself on Sunday, and swept his false inventions out of existence. The Times man told our publicity official that my words were worth their weight in gold. Next morning the whole press had dropped the fiction of a conflict between King & Cabinet & Winston's fulmination was relegated to a back page. Later in the week I heard Austen [Chamberlain] telling a sceptical Editor of the Birmingham Mail that Winston had been moved solely by his affection for the King & his innate chivalry, without a thought for his own fortunes – and I smiled.[65]

In fact Austen Chamberlain was closer to the truth than Neville. As Graham Stewart has noted, Churchill had warned the King that he would have to choose between the throne and Mrs. Simpson.[66] Those who thought Churchill was plotting to lead a King's party in Parliament were wrong to ascribe such rational motives to him. He was once again performing in a drama, without clearly thinking ahead to a conclusion.

Edward remembered having lunch with Churchill on the final day of his brief reign:

As I saw Mr Churchill off, there were tears in his eyes. I can still see him standing at the door; hat in one hand, stick in the other. Something must have stirred his mind; tapping out the solemn measure with his walking-stick, he began to recite, as if to himself:

"He nothing common did or mean
Upon that memorable scene."

His resonant voice seemed to give an especial poignancy to those lines from the ode by Andrew Marvell, on the beheading of Charles I.[67]

As for his potential future in politics, Edward was sandbagged when his brother, now George VI, awarded him the royal title of Duke of Windsor, which barred him from either sitting in the House of Commons or expressing political opinions in the House of Lords.[68]

Churchill could at least find some comfort in comments by his publisher, George Harrap, about the high drama of his third volume of *Marlborough*:

> . . . the dramatic intensity is often so great that at times you compelled an extra beat or two from my pulse.
>
> I read your chapter on the Fall of Harley in the midst of the recent crisis and that historical moment was no more absorbing than the dramatic scene in which Anne was stricken and defeated. One feels that Marlborough in Volume Three is moving like a majestic figure in Greek tragedy to eventual catastrophe. His triumphs contribute to the mesh within which the Fates are encircling him, and you inspire in the reader, after 200 years, emotions which he would feel were he contemplating world-shaking events of which the issue is still in doubt.[69]

And when he completed the biography, Churchill told Eddie Marsh that he hoped it would "bring home to modern readers the life and drama of that great age. How like their forerunners the modern Tories are!"[70]

In these two controversies Churchill earned – or rather, enhanced – his reputation for recklessly upsetting the apple cart. His actions were often irrational, and like many twentieth-century writers he rebelled against the kind of rationality that erases personality. He shared with D. H. Lawrence, Evgeny Zamayatin, Aldous Huxley, George Orwell, W. H. Auden, and the Beat Poets the defining fear of the literary modernists – that a mechanized society might abolish the individual. His 1925 essay "Mass Effects in Modern Life" conceded that the welfare state, mammoth corporations, cheap consumer goods, and the mass-circulation press had spread affluence and knowledge more broadly, but they had also produced "enormous numbers of standardized citizens, all equipped with regulation opinions, prejudices or sentiments, according to their class or party." War was no longer a matter of individual heroism, where commanders were on the front line leading their troops. Now a general typically sat at a teletype machine calmly dispatching hundreds of thousands of men to their deaths, much like a financier trading securities from his office: "He is the manager of a stock-market, or stock-yard." The process was most advanced in the Soviet Union, where "No one is to think of himself as an immortal spirit, clothed in the flesh, but sovereign, unique, indestructible."[71] Even at home (he observed in 1934) the independent MP was nearly extinct, a victim of party discipline. "Everywhere, in every country, in every sphere of human activity, as civilisation has spread its multiplying complications, the power of the machine has grown greater, the power of the man grown less; combinations, organisations of all kinds flourish and increase; individuals sink into insignificance." But "those who think – as opposed to those who follow, shout, or obey – must make it their care, unwearying, bold, intelligent, to assert the individual life of the man who is only a man, as against the man who controls some powerful engine and the men who have become merely some part of its mechanism."[72] Throughout his political life – and not always wisely – Churchill raged against the machine.

One key to understanding Churchill's decade in the political wilderness is a recent psychological study of more than five thousand subjects, which found two common responses to ostracism.[73] Many will strive ever harder to conform to group expectations in the hope of being readmitted: this was the course chosen by most Conservative MPs under Baldwin, and even more so under Chamberlain. But those who conclude that they will never be accepted may engage in increasingly aggressive and provocative action directed against the group. They want to be noticed rather than liked – and Churchill's attacks on the government's Indian policies certainly got him noticed in the press, particularly Rothermere's *Daily Mail*. Because the ostracized have been shut out of the group's decision-making processes, they feel vulnerability and a loss of control (themes that pervaded Churchill's speeches on India and Czechoslovakia), and boldly expressing radical views may be a desperate attempt to reassert mastery over a threatening situation. This strategy naturally appeals to individuals with a strong sense of psychological, economic, or intellectual independence – and Churchill enjoyed all three. It usually involves overstatement for dramatic effect, as Churchill admitted in the context of his claims about German aircraft production in the 1930s. "I strove my utmost to galvanise the Government into vehemence and extraordinary preparation, even at the cost of world alarm," he wrote in *The Gathering Storm*, the first volume of *The Second World War*. "In these endeavours I no doubt painted the picture even darker than it was."[74]

Of course, the contrarian who habitually challenges the consensus often backs himself into extreme and untenable positions, such as opposing Indian self-government or championing King Edward VIII. But sometimes the threat is real and the cranks are right.

CHAPTER 15

The Producer

Speaking at an opening of the New Burlington Galleries in London on 27 July 1937, Churchill briefly alluded to the work of another artist:

> The other day, across the North Sea or German Ocean, a very great man, who is certainly a master of propaganda, favoured us with his views on art. They were very drastic and formidable pronouncements. I would feel it a very hazardous employment in some countries to be an amateur artist. If you had only the alternatives of being hung if your picture were accepted or hanged if it were rejected, it might put a great damper on individual enthusiasm.[1]

Eight days earlier, in an attempt to hold nearly every important modern artist up to public ridicule, the Nazi exhibition of *Entartete Kunst* – "Degenerate Art" – had opened in Munich. The above represents practically the only comment Churchill ever made on the artistic side of Adolf Hitler. It is surprising that he did not say more, for in aesthetic terms Hitler was a photographic negative of Churchill, identical yet opposite, using similar techniques for diametrically opposed political goals.

In May 1940 the Second World War became a duel between two artists. The significance of that fact should be better appreciated by political and military historians, because aesthetics contributed importantly to deciding the outcome of that conflict. Hitler enjoyed amazing success up to 1942, thanks very largely to his artistic talents. Applied to the fine arts, those talents could only produce submediocre paintings and ludicrous plans for hypertrophied neoclassical buildings. But applied to the political realm, they produced a mass movement that conquered most of Europe. He might have won the war if he had not been opposed by an equally brilliant political artist.

It is difficult to think of any important political leader in history who scored a greater literary success at an early age than Winston Churchill – or who failed so miserably at art than the young Adolf Hitler. He scraped a living as a painter, first in Vienna and then in Munich. As far as he could afford to, he indulged in the theatre and opera and (at least according to his own account) read widely in the history of art and architecture. Hopeless at sketching the human form, he did have a knack for architectural drawing.

When Hitler joined the tiny German Workers' Party in September 1919, it was only one of dozens of ultra-nationalist political and paramilitary groups that emerged in post-war Germany, most of them ephemeral. And it was largely on the strength of his artistic abilities that the party (which he rebranded as the National Socialist German Workers' Party) emerged from the pack to become a mass movement. He designed the party's banners, uniforms, stationery, and insignia. The swastika had been used previously by other extreme right movements, but Hitler's sense of graphic coordination created the hypnotic Nazi flag: a black swastika in a white disc on a red background. The mass political rallies were son et lumière shows, employing the spectacular effects of torchlight and floodlight. (Searchlight displays had been pioneered in the pre-war naval reviews conducted by both Britain and Germany.)[2]

Although *Triumph of the Will* (1934) is usually classified as a documentary, it was more like an elaborately staged grand opera, with Hitler delivering arias to an adoring responsive chorus against a background of swelling orchestral music. And although Leni Riefenstahl was the director, Hitler was a scriptwriter, set designer, and choreographer as well as the lead performer.[3] Throughout the nineteenth century, Prussia and then Imperial Germany had used military spectacles as nationalist propaganda. The disarmed Weimar Republic could not employ this kind of political theatre – but the Nazi Party did, with mesmerizing effect.[4]

In contrast to Churchill's playful Impressionism and passion for contemporary writing, Hitler's tastes were conservative, running to Greek sculpture, Roman architecture, nineteenth-century German romantic painting, and Wagnerian opera. He reviled all forms of modernist art as "Jewish" and "Bolshevik." In the summer of 1937 Nazi authorities confiscated about seventeen thousand works of modernist art from German museums, a statistic which reveals that those institutions had heretofore led the world in collecting and exhibiting the avant-garde.[5]

Frederic Spotts illustrated in depth what Albert Speer (the chief Nazi architect) grasped: that Hitler's prime aim was to reconstruct Germany according to his own aesthetic principles. He began in November 1933 with the creation of the Reich Culture Chamber, which established absolute state control over all the arts and all creative artists. Even in the midst of war, he would interrupt vital military discussions to talk about the arts. In May 1943, after the disastrous

German losses at Stalingrad and in Tunisia, he met his propaganda minister Joseph Goebbels in Berlin to discuss at length the governance of art galleries and the encouragement of individual art collectors, the talents of certain sculptors and architects, and the management of theatres and orchestras. "I became a politician against my will," he once told his staff. "For me politics are only a means to an end" – the creation of a German Empire devoted to great works of art, music, and architecture. "If someone else had been found, I would never have gone into politics; I would have become an artist or a philosopher."[6] "It's a pity," he said in March 1942, "that I have to wage war on account of a drunken fellow [Churchill], instead of serving the works of peace, like art," when, he protested, he really preferred to indulge in the theatre and "be human again."[7]

"Art is the clearest and most immediate reflection of the spiritual life of a people," Hitler proclaimed.[8] Ultimately he planned to demolish central Berlin and construct an array of gargantuan government buildings (the basic designs were mainly his rather than Speer's), and he projected similar redevelopment schemes for dozens of other German cities. Such titanic structures were absurdly out of proportion for a midsized country like Germany: they only made sense as monuments to a great world empire. And they could only have been built by an estimated three million slave laborers working for ten years. In 1941, when he should have been concentrating everything on the invasion of Russia, Hitler diverted scarce resources to his monumental construction projects. Even in the desperate final months of the war he assigned a high priority to keeping open galleries, theatres, concert halls, and opera houses.[9] As in any modern state, the bureaucratic machinery was kept running by armies of banal functionaries, but the Third Reich could only have been created by an artist.

Bertolt Brecht recognized that Hitler was a master of "Politik des Bluffs und Theatercoups," which he used to thrill his followers and demoralize his enemies.[10] Modeled on Mussolini's March on Rome in 1922, the Beer Hall Putsch of November 1923 was distinguished by hopelessly inept planning, an absurdist melodrama that began with Hitler waving a pistol in the air and promising to shoot himself if he failed. But taking the long view, the coup was by no means entirely a failure. Hitler's audacious stroke and his bravura performance at his subsequent trial established him as the leading man on the far right, and would eventually attract ultra-nationalists to the Nazi banner.[11]

Once in power, rather than rearm Germany by stealth, Hitler announced his repudiation of the Versailles Treaty during a spectacular military ceremony on 16 March 1934 at the State Opera House.[12] He probably could have secured British and French assent to the remilitarization of the Rhineland through negotiation, but he preferred to act with dramatic éclat.[13] The reintroduction of conscription, the Anschluss with Austria, the extinction of

Czechoslovakia, the Nazi-Soviet Pact, the strike against France and the Low Countries in May 1940, the invasion of the Soviet Union, the declaration of war against the United States, and the final 1944 offensive in the Ardennes were all attempts to seize the dramatic initiative and transform the world stage with a thunderclap. Even more than Churchill, Hitler was addicted to the *coup de théâtre*. The high-risk stakes only heightened the drama. "He was above all a consummate actor," Ian Kershaw concludes:

> This certainly applied to the stage-managed occasions – the delayed entry to the packed hall, the careful construction of his speeches, the choice of colourful phrases, the gestures and body-language. Here, his natural rhetorical talent was harnessed to well-honed performing skills. A pause at the beginning to allow the tension to mount; a low-key, even hesitant, start; undulations and variations of diction, not melodious certainly, but vivid and highly expressive; almost staccato bursts of sentences, followed by well-timed *rallentando* to expose the emphasis of a key point; theatrical use of the hands as the speech rose in crescendo; sarcastic wit aimed at opponents: all were devices carefully nurtured to maximize effect.

He could assume whatever role the occasion called for: Austrian gallantry with ladies, "manly" eye contact with Party comrades, sensitive in his artistic moods, reasonable when he had to appear statesmanlike, and (notoriously) insanely enraged when he aimed to intimidate.[14] And the Beer Hall Putsch was just one of several occasions where, as the ultimate dramatic gesture, Hitler threatened suicide.[15]

"The Fuehrer," Churchill recognized, had a "theatrical sense of history."[16] Hitler had developed his performance skills by practicing gestures in front of a mirror. Lloyd George's playacting might be ridiculed by the post-war generation in Britain, but Hitler admired his "psychological masterpieces in the art of mass propaganda," especially "the primitiveness of his language, the primordiality of its forms of expression, and the use of easily intelligible examples of the simplest sort."[17] His legendary rants for the benefit of foreign leaders and diplomats were usually staged. General Edmund Ironside summarized a report by the director of British military intelligence on the heavy-handed but effective theatrics used to bring about the Anschluss with Austria in March 1938:

> He described most dramatically the scene in the ante-room at Berchtesgaden, when [Kurt von] Schuschnigg was summoned to meet Hitler. Apparently, the Austrian Chancellor was kept waiting an hour. During this time he was left in full view of a map showing the disposition of the German troops in

> South Germany. All the time he was waiting German Generals came in and loudly reported that their various commands were ready to march. . . .
>
> When Hitler eventually received Schuschnigg he [Hitler] was in a highly neurotic and excited state. He raved at Schuschnigg. . . . Our Ambassador, [Nevile] Henderson, saw Hitler and was treated to a diatribe upon the behavior of the British Press. Hitler told Henderson that Germany would act like lightning and that Germany would know how to fight. . . .[18]

As late as 10 July 1939, Neville Chamberlain still believed that Hitler's tirades were spontaneous and sincere.[19]

Richard Wagner's Ring cycle could even shape Hitler's political strategy, much as Victorian melodrama shaped Churchill's. On 17 July 1936 the Spanish Army launched a coup against the Republic, but within a few days it was clear that workers' militias had secured control of the major cities. The Nationalist General Francisco Franco, who needed to move his army from Morocco to the mainland, requested transport aircraft from the Germans. The German Foreign Office, diplomat Joachim von Ribbentrop, Aviation Minister Hermann Göring, and Goebbels were all more or less opposed, and they had compelling arguments for staying out. Intervention might antagonize Britain and France. Germany needed all her weapons production to build up her own armed forces, and could ill afford the quagmire of an extended civil war. But on 25 July – just after seeing *Siegfried* at Bayreuth – Hitler ordered the dispatch of twenty Junkers JU-52 transports, twice what Franco had requested. This was *Unternehmen Feuerzaber*, Operation Magic Fire: Hitler would rescue Spain from Bolshevism, just as Siegfried had braved the ring of fire to rescue Brünnhilde in *Götterdämmerung*.[20]

Where Churchill crafted memoranda with an eye toward eventual publication, Hitler had a bohemian disdain for bureaucratic paperwork. After February 1938, Nazi Germany became the only state in modern history that never held Cabinet meetings, simply because Hitler could not be bothered. But he worked tirelessly to write and rewrite his speeches and endlessly rehearsed their performance. He once called himself "the greatest actor in Europe."[21] In fact his regime was a "theatocracy," a term invented by Plato, denounced by Nietzsche, and embraced by Nazi "philosopher" Alfred Rosenberg.[22] Spectacular rallies, mass processions, rhythmic chants, operatic speeches delivered from balconies, uniforms worn as costumes, monumental buildings that served as backdrops, acts of aggression as *coups de théâtre* – these methods were pioneered by the proto-fascist poet Gabriele D'Annunzio, perfected by Mussolini, and adopted by all fascist regimes. Such performances served to celebrate leaders, mobilize followers, and enforce participatory conformity.[23]

Nazi Germany and Fascist Italy developed theatocracy in its most advanced form, but other striking examples may be found in diverse human cultures. In Bali, the anthropologist Clifford Geertz located and described such a regime:

> a theatre state in which the kings and princes were the impresarios, the priests the directors, and the peasants the supporting cast, stage crew, and audience. The stupendous cremations, tooth filings, temple dedications, pilgrimages, and blood sacrifices, mobilizing hundreds and even thousands of people and great quantities of wealth, were not means to political ends: they were the ends themselves, they were what the state was for. Court ceremonialism was the driving force of court politics; and mass ritual was not a device to shore up the state, but rather the state, even in its final gasp, was a device for the enactment of mass ritual. Power served pomp, not pomp power.[24]

The Soviet Union was in its own way a theatre state propped up by public performance, which often veered widely from reality. These spectacles could take the form of mass rallies and processions, propaganda films, Potemkin village construction projects (which resembled stage sets more than working factories), and the Bolshevik catchphrases that citizens were obliged to utter. The most terrifying dramas of all were the show trials: fully scripted melodramas where absolutely good heroes unmasked absolutely evil villains.[25]

"That politics is an art there is no doubt," Mussolini proclaimed in a 1926 speech. "The artist creates with inspiration, the politician with decision." On more than one occasion he declared his mission to "make a masterpiece" of his life and to mold the Italian people like so much clay. His invasion of Abyssinia in October 1935 would be cast as a classic imperialist melodrama, in which the virtuous hero (Mussolini) overcame a thoroughly evil villain (the League of Nations) and battled a wicked native (Haile Selassie) to protect good natives (those Ethiopian tribal groups that sided with the Italians).[26]

Hitler's favorite books included Cervantes's *Don Quixote* (tellingly), the works of Shakespeare (he regretted that no German romantic had ever written anything to match *The Merchant of Venice*), and the Wild West stories of Karl May (a German author who never ventured west of Buffalo, New York). He had in his collection a 1931 booklet on poison gas, including a chapter on prussic acid, which was sold under the trade name Zyklon B. In the formative years 1919–21 he borrowed from a far-right lending library Montesquieu, Rousseau, Kant's *Metaphysical Elements of Ethics*, Oswald Spengler's *The Decline of the West*, and a host of anti-Semitic tracts, including *The Foundations of the Nineteenth Century* by Houston Stewart Chamberlain (Wagner's son-in-law) and Henry Ford's *The International Jew*. He possessed about fifty volumes, many well-thumbed and filled with marginalia, published by J. F. Lehmann Verlag, a house that specialized in scientific racism. One Lehmann book was a translation of Madison Grant's *The Passing of the Great Race*, an American treatise arguing the superiority of the "Nordic race," which Hitler once called his "Bible." (It had been published in 1916 by Scribner's, later Churchill's publisher, which had a number of other eugenic works on its list.)[27] Hitler also owned numerous weird tracts on spiritualism, the occult, alchemy, and pseudo-science, which probably influenced his world view more than Schopenhauer or Nietzsche. And he avidly read military history, including Carl von Clausewitz's *On War*.[28]

Both Italian Fascism and German Nazism relied on dramatic coups (such as the March on Rome) to intimidate and overwhelm the gray, plodding bourgeois politicians of interwar Europe. Such dramas could only be understood and effectively resisted by someone with the same talent for political theatre. Churchill's classic analysis of Hitler and methods was included in his 1937 volume *Great Contemporaries*. At first glance the book looks like a miscellaneous collection of potted biographies, but it does have a unifying theme: to spotlight the most dramatic political personalities of the modern era, to "present both the actors and the scene."[29] George Bernard Shaw, T. E. Lawrence, Boris Savinkov, and Franklin Roosevelt[30] were the most obvious examples, but there was also Lord Rosebery, "an actor on the political stage" who "often seems to march out of the pages of *Coningsby* – the aristocrat-champion of the poor and depressed classes."[31] Joseph Chamberlain likewise aimed "to play upon the world's stage" as a great reformer.[32] In 1914 "the first shock of the War was drama at the highest pitch of intensity," with Sir John French playing a lead role.[33] Marshal Foch performed "in the center of this drama,"[34] and Douglas Haig's "Backs to the Wall" order of April 1918 showed that "he was not insensitive and indurated to the torment and drama in the shadow of which he dwelt."[35] In parliamentary debates the Liberal politician John Morley "loved the pageantry as well as the distinction of words,"[36] F. E. Smith's spontaneous wit "would be held brilliant in a carefully-written play,"[37] and Arthur Balfour languidly offered Wildean epigrams.[38] "One of the strangest, most baffling personalities that ever trod the world's stage" was Charles Stewart Parnell, whose story "comprised all the elements of a Greek tragedy. Sophocles or Euripides could have found in it a theme sufficient to their somber taste."[39] In India, at an amateur entertainment for British Army officers, Churchill had seen Robert Baden-Powell perform a song and dance "which certainly would have held its own on the boards of any of our music halls," and he later came to admire the General's "theatrical" popularity among the masses.[40] And in France, in the fascinatingly corrupt age of General Boulanger, the Dreyfus Affair, and the Panama Scandal:

> All the elements of blood-curdling political drama were represented by actual facts. The life of the French Chamber, hectic, fierce, poisonous, flowed through a succession of scandals and swindles, of exposures, of perjuries, forgeries, and murders, of plottings and intriguings, of personal ambitions and revenges, of crooking and double-crossing, which find their modern parallel only in the underworld of Chicago. But here they were presented upon the lime-lit stage of the most famous of the nations before an audience of all the world. The actors were men of the highest ability, men of learning and eloquence, men of repute and power; men who proclaimed the noblest sentiments, who lived in the public eye; men who directed armies, diplomacy and finance. It was a terrible society, grimly polished, loaded with explosives, trellised with live electric wires. Through the center of it, turning to make a front now here, now there, and beating down opponents with his mace, Clemenceau long strode, reckless, aggressive and triumphant.[41]

This was the Clemenceau who, as the Germans advanced toward Paris in 1918, told Churchill to his face, "I will fight in front of Paris; I will fight in Paris; I will fight behind Paris," words that the latter would save and adapt for a later occasion.[42] Churchill saw no such drama in the figures of Stalin and his cronies:

> For all its horrors, a glittering light plays over the scenes and actors of the French Revolution. The careers and personalities of Robespierre, of Danton, even of Marat, gleam luridly across a century. But the dull, squalid figures of the Russian Bolsheviks are not redeemed in interest even by the magnitude of their crimes. All form and emphasis is lost in the vast process of Asiatic liquefaction. Even the slaughter of millions and the misery of scores of millions will not attract future generations to their uncouth lineaments and outlandish names.

A possible exception was Trotsky: "He lingers on the stage." But he had become a mere *littérateur*, reduced to justifying himself in "chatty newspaper articles" produced for the capitalist press.[43]

Then there was the former Kaiser. The photograph chosen to illustrate his biographical sketch is astonishingly banal. Instead of the scowling warlord we have come to expect, here Wilhelm resembles a burger enjoying retirement, relaxing with a cigarette. Once he sported a ludicrously waxed moustache, now he doesn't seem to mind that his hair is mussed. The eyes almost twinkle. He looks like a man who is happy because, at last, he no longer has to put on an act. Churchill insists that Wilhelm probably never wanted to play his assigned part, and certainly lacked the talent for it. It was the generals, admirals, bankers, diplomats, professors, and colonialists who pressed him to assume the role of "warrior-king". Until 1914 he was content to "Just strut about and pose and rattle the undrawn sword. All he wished was to feel like Napoleon, and be like him without having had to fight his battles." He assumed, with obvious relief, that the Serbian response to Austria's ultimatum would render war unnecessary, but real power lay with the General Staff, which led Germany into catastrophe. The All-Highest was merely

> a picturesque figurehead in the center of the world stage, called upon to play a part far beyond the capacity of most people. He had little in common with the great princes who at intervals throughout the centuries have appeared by accident of birth at the summit of states and empires. . . . He knew how to make the gestures, to utter the words, to strike the attitudes in the Imperial style. He could stamp and snort, or nod and smile with much histrionic art; but underneath all this posing and its trappings, was a very ordinary, vain, but on the whole well-meaning man, hoping to pass himself off as a second Frederick the Great.

That illusion was happily shattered by Wilhelm's own published memoirs: "No more disarming revelation of inherent triviality, lack of understanding and sense of proportion, and, incidentally, of literary capacity, can be imagined." Lloyd George might have called for hanging the Kaiser, but Lloyd George was "himself an actor." A public execution would have been double-edged theatre, serving "to gratify the passions of victorious crowds," but also, in the eyes of the German people, elevating a very plain man into Valhalla. Churchill pleaded for clemency on grounds of mediocrity. In November 1918 some diehard officers urged the Kaiser to lead one last suicide attack, but he was humane enough to end the war anticlimactically: "He would not sacrifice the lives of more brave men merely to make a setting for his own exit."[44] The finale of the next war, of course, would be more Wagnerian.

To accommodate the British Foreign Office, Churchill toned down his profile of Hitler, but when it was juxtaposed with Wilhelm's biography in the same volume, it became obvious which leader was a true threat to peace. Churchill did not rule out the possibility that Hitler might choose to become more statesmanlike, but his final paragraphs, read carefully, suggest that the Führer's affection of reasonableness was an actor's ruse:

> Those who have met Herr Hitler face to face in public business or on social terms have found a highly competent, cool, well-informed functionary with an agreeable manner, a disarming smile, and few have been unaffected by a subtle personal magnetism. Nor is this impression merely the dazzle of

> power. He exerted it on his companions at every stage in his struggle, even when his hopes were in the lowest depths. Thus the world lives on hopes that the worst is over, and that we may yet live to see Hitler a gentler figure in a happier age.
>
> Meanwhile, he makes speeches to the nations, which are sometimes characterized by candor and moderation. Recently he has offered many words of reassurance, eagerly lapped up by those who have been so tragically wrong about Germany in the past. Only time can show, but, meanwhile, the great wheels revolve; the rifles, the cannon, the tanks, the shot and shell, the air-bombs, the poison-gas cylinders, the airplanes, the submarines, and now the beginnings of a fleet flow in ever-broadening streams from the already largely war-mobilized arsenals and factories of Germany.[45]

Neville Chamberlain first recognized Nazism as a threat not long after Churchill did, in December 1931, when he complained to his sister Hilda that French stubbornness over reparations was "precipitating the advent of Hitler to power."[46] But as soon as Hitler became Chancellor, Chamberlain fell into the habit of giving him the benefit of every doubt. "I must say that so far as Hitler is concerned he has really been the best of the bunch since he has been in office," he wrote on 16 April 1933,[47] apparently thinking he was a moderate restraining radicals such as Göring. This was after the Enabling Act invested Hitler with dictatorial powers, after the official boycott of Jewish businesses, after a law banning Jews from the civil service. In early 1934 Chamberlain found Hitler's response to British arms control proposals "conciliatory & pacific."[48] The assassination of the Austrian Chancellor Engelbert Dollfuss by local Nazis in July 1934 made him "hate Nazi-ism and all its works with a greater loathing than ever," but he gave Hitler credit for "keeping his head" during the crisis.[49] "Hitler's Germany is the bully of Europe," he wrote when it reintroduced conscription in March 1935. "Yet I don't despair."[50] On 21 March 1936, two weeks after the remilitarization of the Rhineland, Chamberlain confided to Hilda that Ribbentrop was a man he could do business with, suggesting a negotiating tactic he often used in Parliament, "trying to get criticism focused on the point on which I have something to give away."[51] His strategy was to deal with German threats through negotiation and gradual rearmament, as opposed to Churchill's insistence on rapid rearmament. "By careful diplomacy I believe we can stave [a German attack] off, perhaps indefinitely," he wrote to Hilda in November 1936, "but if we were to follow Winston's advice and sacrifice our commerce to the manufacture of arms we should inflict an injury upon our trade from which it would take generations to recover, we should destroy the confidence which now happily exists and we should cripple the revenue."[52]

Again relying on literary sources, Churchill took *Mein Kampf* seriously, and publicly recommended it as a guide to Hitler's plans.[53] He once compared it to the Koran: "turgid, verbose, shapeless, but pregnant with its message."[54] He also continued to cite H. G. Wells, who had anticipated "the bombing of undefended cities and wholesale slaughter of men, women and children. . . . He saw from the beginning of this new discovery that it would lead the twentieth century to accept with a helpless shrug barbarities of which Marius and Julius Caesar would have been ashamed, and which even Genghis Khan would have thought unbecoming."[55] In a 28 November 1934 speech to Parliament, Churchill discounted "the sweeping claim of the extreme votaries of the air," but he still predicted that a few days of intense bombing would kill or injure at least 30,000–40,000 Londoners, drive three or four million refugees from the capital, and, by taking out the docks and fuel storage facilities, "might actually paralyze the Fleet, with consequences which no one can fail to perceive."[56] (Though terribly destructive, the actual Blitz was not quite that apocalyptic.) Churchill's warnings about Germany's growing air power were meant to spur British rearmament, but many of his listeners drew the conclusion that Hitler had to be placated at all costs.

On 25 March 1935 Anthony Eden (as Lord Privy Seal) and John Simon (the Foreign Secretary) went to Berlin to consult with Hitler, who told them that the Luftwaffe had attained "parity" with the RAF. This was a gross exaggeration, another instance of Hitler's use of theatrics to intimidate, but it appeared to vindicate Churchill and discredit Baldwin's assurances that Britain enjoyed, and would continue to enjoy, air superiority. On 2 May Churchill warned Parliament:

> When the situation was manageable it was neglected, and now that it is thoroughly out of hand, we apply too late the remedies which then might have effected a cure. There is nothing new in the story. It is as old as the Sibylline books. It falls into that immense dismal category of the fruitlessness of experience and the confirmed unteachability of mankind. Want of foresight, unwillingness to act when action would be simple and effective, lack of clear thinking, confusion of counsel until the emergency comes, until self-preservation strikes its jarring gong – these are the features which constitute the endless repetition of history.[57]

There was indeed nothing new in the story, which Churchill had seen in *The English Rose*. Baldwin and Chamberlain closely resembled the stolid, blinkered English gentleman of that drama, Sir Philip Kingston, who fails to see the villain's machinations, with fatal consequences. Blindness in the face of evil was a core theme of Victorian melodrama.

"THE ENGLISH ROSE," AT THE ADELPHI THEATRE.

1 Churchill's favorite Irish melodrama, *The English Rose* (*Penny Illustrated Paper*, 9 August 1890).

2 Churchill was in the audience for Jules Verne's spectacular melodrama *Michael Strogoff*, which portrayed an invasion of Russia a half-century before Operation Barbarossa.

SHE PRAYED FOR THE VICTORY OF THE REBEL SHE LOVED OVER HER HUSBAND, THE PRESIDENT.

[*p.* 105.

3a and 3b From a 1908 illustrated paperback edition of *Savrola*.

ANTONIO MOLARA LAY ON THE THREE LOWEST STEPS OF THE ENTRANCE OF HIS PALACE.

Frontispiece.] [*p.* 114.

4 A highly romanticized contemporary newspaper cartoon imagines Churchill's exploits in the Boer War.

5 The Siege of Sidney Street – which in a sense was the reenactment of Savrola.

6 Self-portait in self-doubt, around 1920.

7 David Low imagines Churchill as a British dictator commanding all authors to serve his cult of personality (*Evening Standard*, 19 July 1928).

8 *The Churchill–Wells Controversy*, pencil and wash drawing by Max Beerbohm, 1920. Churchill: "You were only 14 days in Russia!" Wells: "Your mother's an American!"

9 The Will Dyson cartoon that so upset Joseph Goebbels and Lord Halifax (*Daily Herald*, 1938).

TRIAL OF A NEW MODEL

10 David Low on pro-appeasement censorship, with Duff Cooper, Anthony Eden, and Churchill casting a cold eye (*Evening Standard*, 14 October 1938).

11 After the surrender of the Belgian Army, David Low meant to ridicule Hitler's prophesies of victory, but this cartoon may have had the opposite effect on British morale (*Evening Standard*, 30 May 1940).

12 Young John F. Kennedy autographs his early assessment of Churchill, *Why England Slept*, for actor Spencer Tracy, November 1940.

Chamberlain was quite capable of seeing through phony theatrics in democratic politics, as in the case of Rosevelt's New Deal. In October 1933 the Prime Minister asked him

> to give the Cabinet an "appreciation" of the Rooseveltian policy as several of them did not understand it. So I made a rather humorous story of it by representing the Yanks as a barbarous tribe and Roosevelt as a medicine man whose superiority over other medicine men consisted in the astonishing agility with which when one kind of Mumbo Jumbo failed, he produced another. The N.R.A. [National Recovery Administration] was put forward as a means of raising the prices of commodities. Unfortunately the tiresome things went back whereupon the backwoodmen from the Middle West beat their tom toms and prepared to march upon the capital. But the medicine man without losing a moment broadcast a new plan even more infallible than the last by which prices would surely be put up just where he wanted them. After which they would stay there for generations. And it was all to be done by buying & selling GOLD which still has a magic significance. . . . Now I see he has begun to buy gold and the dollar is *rising* and prices are *falling*

All this, Chamberlain concluded, had given Roosevelt "a sort of fictitious self-confidence."[58] In February 1937, after Walter Runciman (President of the Board of Trade) reported on a visit to Washington, Chamberlain concluded that Roosevelt was still impersonating a decisive chief executive. "I gather there was a great deal of what you might call showing off," he told his sister Ida. "The President asked Walter if he would like to see 'how we do business over here' and sat him in a chair for hours while he summoned lieutenants and gave orders about the measures to be taken in connection with the Ohio floods, exactly in the manner of the staccato hero on the stage."[59] He was therefore skeptical when Roosevelt, on 5 October, publicly called for "quarantining aggressors." For Chamberlain, this was playing to the gallery without substance:

> What did it really mean? It sounded very fierce but when one examined it carefully it was contradictory in parts & very vague in essentials. What does he mean by "putting them in quarantine"? And seeing that patients suffering from epidemic diseases do not usually go about fully armed is there not a difference here and something lacking in his analogy.

Chamberlain concluded that "the President's pronouncement was intended to sound out the ground & see how far his public opinion was prepared to go but that he himself had thought nothing out and in any case had no present intention of doing anything that wasn't perfectly safe." The Opposition argued that the Americans were prepared to join with Britain in imposing economic sanctions to deter Japanese aggression in China, but Chamberlain pointed out that with Hitler and Mussolini "in a thoroughly nasty temper we simply cannot afford to quarrel with Japan and I very much fear that after a lot of ballyhoo the Americans will somehow fade out & leave us to carry all the blame & odium."[60]

Chamberlain had good reason to think that Roosevelt, Lloyd George, and Churchill were prone to theatrics. But when the fascist dictators staged their performances, he was hopelessly credulous. In September 1937 he complained that the Foreign Office persisted "in seeing Musso only as a sort of Machiavelli putting on a false mask of friendship in order to further nefarious ambitions."[61] "Both Hitler & Goering said repeatedly & emphatically that they had no desire or intention of making war and I think we may take this as correct at any rate for the present. . . . The atmosphere in Berlin is decidedly clearer and even Goebbels has promised to be a better boy in the future," he concluded on 26 November. "Of course they want to dominate eastern Europe," as well as Austria and the Sudetenland and some African colonies, but Chamberlain believed that with the right set of concessions Hitler could be induced to rejoin the League of Nations and agree to arms limitations. He was convinced that "the League would exercise a far greater influence if it were not expected to use force but only moral pressure" – what would now be called "soft power."[62] He was unfazed when, less than three weeks later, Mussolini withdrew Italy from the League, attributing this to "a request from the Germans who appear to be trying to accumulate as many cards as possible for the game they will presently be playing with us. It's all rather childish I think but anyway I see no reason to be disturbed by it."[63] Chamberlain was baffled by Ribbentrop, who (he innocently wondered) "has always professed the strongest desire to come to an understanding with us, but his actions never appeared to be quite in keeping with his professions."[64] On 4 February 1938 Hitler had appointed Ribbentrop as Foreign Minister in place of the more cautious Constantin von Neurath, and purged Field Marshal Werner von Blomberg and General Werner von Fritsch from the Army leadership, thus removing three key opponents of his aggressive foreign policy. But Chamberlain's interpretation of these events was complacent: "For the time being the German power to strike is weakened and to that extent her neighbours breathe more freely."[65]

On 12 March 1938, Hitler invaded Austria. "Well it is all very disheartening and discouraging," Chamberlain sighed, "but I am relieved that at any rate so far there seems to have been no bloodshed." Now at last he conceded that "force is the only argument Germany understands and that 'collective security' cannot offer any prospect of preventing such events until it can show a visible force of overwhelming strength backed by determination to use it."

Then he proceeded to the inevitable conclusion: "if that is so is it now obvious that such force and determination are most effectively mobilized by alliances which don't require meetings at Geneva and resolutions by dozens of small nations who have no responsibilities?"[66] On 14 March Churchill called for just such a "Grand Alliance" on the floor of the House of Commons. Despite Churchill's support – or perhaps because of it – Chamberlain backed away from the idea by 20 March:

> As a matter of fact the plan of the "Grand Alliance" as Winston calls it had occurred to me long before he mentioned it. I was thinking about it all last week end – I talked about it to Halifax and we submitted it to the Chiefs of Staff and the F.O. experts. It is a very attractive idea; indeed there is almost everything to be said for it until you come to examine its practicability. From that moment its attraction vanishes. You have only to look at the map to see that nothing that France or we could do could possibly save Czecho-Slovakia from being over-run by the Germans if they wanted to do it. The Austrian frontier is practically open; the great Skoda munitions works are within easy bombing distance of the German aerodromes, the railways all pass through German territory, Russia is 100 miles away. Therefore we could not help Czecho-Slovakia – she would simply be a pretext for going to war with Germany. That we could not think of unless we had a reasonable prospect of being able to beat her to our knees in a reasonable time and of that I see no sign. I have therefore abandoned any idea of giving guarantees to Czecho-Slovakia or to France in connection with her obligations to that country.

Instead, Chamberlain proposed to approach Hitler and "say something like this":

> We gave you fair warning that if you used violence to Austria you would shock public opinion to such an extent as to give rise to the most disagreeable repercussions. Yet you obstinately went your way & now you can see for yourselves how right we were. Incidentally it has made it quite impossible for us in present circumstances to continue talking over colonies.
>
> But it is of no use crying over spilt milk & what we have to do now is to consider how we can restore the confidence you have shattered. Everyone is thinking that you are going to repeat the Austrian coup in Czecho-Slovakia. I know you say you aren't, but nobody believes you. The best thing you can do is to tell us exactly what you want for your Sudeten Deutsch. If it is reasonable we will urge the Czechs to accept it and if they do you must give assurances that you will let them alone in the future.[67]

It all sounds like a weak parent trying to reason with a berserk adolescent. Like many rigorously rational individuals, Chamberlain could not understand irrational people, nor could he see the method in their madness. He also made the mistake of defining "rational" and "theatrical" as antonyms, when in fact many of the most effective political strokes are both. Hitler wanted to shock public opinion, recognizing that such bombshells had an intimidating effect. He suffered no seriously disagreeable repercussions from the Anschluss. He was not interested in re-acquiring African colonies. He did plan to repeat the Austrian coup in Czechoslovakia, and did not care if the British and French governments knew it, because that knowledge would sap their will to resist. And now Chamberlain was planning to offer him more concessions, having ruled out an anti-Nazi alliance and any kind of meaningful guarantee to the Czechs, and was willing to settle for assurances of future good behavior. When Hitler stirred up another crisis over Czechoslovakia in September, Chamberlain could only explain it as the act of a "lunatic."[68] But if rationality is defined as the efficient pursuit of one's goals, for good or evil, who was the rational actor? As Hugh Dalton confided to his diary in the days leading up to the Munich Agreement, "The best that can be said of the P.M. is that, within the limits of his ignorance, he is rational, but I am appalled how narrow these limits are. . . ."[69] And on the other side Ernst von Weizsäcker, State Secretary at the German Foreign Office, who hoped to achieve the dissolution of Czechoslovakia without war, later admitted "I too much wanted to apply the art of the possible and underestimated the value of the irrational."[70]

CHAPTER 16

Blackout

In "You Get It in Black and White," published in the American magazine *Collier's* on 28 December 1935, Churchill offered a concise and remarkably sophisticated survey of media history, from prehistory to the present. Drums (he began) were the first medium for transmitting news, and were still "the surest and speediest means of communication" in parts of the British Empire. Wandering through ancient Greece, Homer "was probably welcomed no less for his gossip of neighbouring cities than for his tales of Troy." Then Churchill leapt forward to the newsletter writers of Stuart England, who reported Marlborough's victories. He emphasized the power of newspapers to effect political change, including the ratification of the United States Constitution. *The Federalist Papers*, "which is still accounted one of the world masterpieces of political literature, is nothing more or less than . . . eighty-five articles, reprinted from the files of an old newspaper." William Lloyd Garrison's *Liberator* energized the abolitionist movement, and Harriet Beecher Stowe's *Uncle Tom's Cabin* was so influential largely because the *National Era* published the novel as a serial. Churchill was familiar with Soviet propaganda films and (in spite of his militant anti-Communism) he granted that some of the early ones "attain high quality," though the more recent Stalinist movies were dismally sloganeering: "Movie propaganda is most effective where it creates atmosphere and certainly ineffective where it trumpets catchwords."

Today, Churchill concluded, newspapers, radio, and the newsreel "divide the Empire of Publicity," with television on the horizon. Would print be rendered obsolete by newer modes of communication? Churchill recognized that in some cases new media had driven out the old, for example, the telegraph and the Pony Express. But he doubted that newspapers would disappear any time soon, because they possessed many advantages over wireless and film: they could convey far more information, they could be read selectively, and at any time convenient to the reader. The essential point here is that

Churchill thought seriously and perceptively about the media, and understood how it functioned in society.

As a close friend of Lord Beaverbrook, Churchill discounted fears that big newspaper conglomerates and mass-market advertisers might limit freedom of expression. "A Press combine must, as a matter of business, delegate a large measure of responsibility for policy to its editors," he assured his readers, "and a great editor stamps his own personality upon the paper which he controls; and no newspaper can afford to suppress important news which its rivals will print." As for advertisers, "It was the development of commercial advertising that first enabled the Press to stand on its own feet, without relying on subsidies from governments or politicians, and revenue from this source is still the bulwark of its independence today. Advertisers are businessmen – they pay to have their announcements placed before the largest possible public, and they ought to know that permanent circulations can only be secured by honest news and honest opinion."[1]

That, however, was for public consumption. Privately Churchill knew well that, even in democratic societies, the media can be manipulated and effectively censored. The previous June (1934) he had been the guest of honor at the first organizational meeting of what became the Focus, a group that would campaign against appeasement and Nazi aggression. They met secretly at a West End hotel and, after making sure that no one was eavesdropping, Churchill said:

> You will understand that this meeting is private; no notes are to be taken and no information whatsoever must be given to the press. . . . At present the British public and press are very much the victims of the Nazi Ministry of Information and its lies; it has collared the press, the radio and every other instrument for spreading news. The task of this assembly is thus as difficult as it is indispensable and urgent. We must make an all-party effort, create a source from which unbiased and objective information will constantly flow to the government and to the whole country. . . . This task is made more difficult on account of the most regrettable pro-Nazi attitude of a considerable section of the national press.[2]

This was not paranoia. Even as the Focus was being organized, Norman Ebbutt, *The Times* correspondent in Berlin, had said much the same to the American journalist William L. Shirer. "Of late he has complained to me in private that the *Times* does not print all he sends, that it does not want to hear too much of the bad side of Nazi Germany and apparently has been captured by the pro-Nazis in London," Shirer wrote in his diary.[3] By the middle of 1935, twenty-seven foreign correspondents had been forced or persuaded to leave

Nazi Germany, starting with the celebrated American newspaperwoman Dorothy Thompson. Those who remained had to exercise some degree of self-censorship.[4]

From its first public meeting, at the Albert Hall in London on 3 December 1936, the activities of the Focus would be largely blacked out by Britain's national newspapers. (It received much more extensive and sympathetic coverage in the *Christian Science Monitor, New York Times*, and *Montreal Star*.) To take one example, in late 1937 the *Financial Times* ran a seven-part series painting a rosy picture of the German economy, but it refused to publish a response from the Focus, which offered a more critical set of facts and figures.[5] In the years leading up to the Second World War, Churchill and his allies had to run a journalistic blockade promoted by the Conservative government in Britain and Nazi Germany in Europe.

Martin Moore has claimed that the Labour government of 1945–51 was the first to develop peacetime machinery for manipulating the media,[6] but actually "the origins of modern spin" can be traced back to the interwar period. Traditionally, correspondents covering Whitehall had been free to interview ministers and MPs and had scouted out stories on their own. Then in 1929 Ramsay MacDonald created the 10 Downing Street Press Office, which throughout the 1930s became an increasingly effective tool for co-opting reporters. George Steward, the permanent Press Officer, organized twice-daily press briefings at Number 10, effectively controlling the flow of information to the media. At first journalists were suspicious, but soon they fell in with the new regime, which required less legwork and allowed them to think that they had access to the corridors of power. Neville Chamberlain inherited this system and developed it to a high level of efficiency. In addition to his general news briefings, he favored a few particularly loyal reporters with individual interviews and special leaks. The journalists themselves were fully complicit: as one of them recalled, they enjoyed being treated as "honorary members of a power establishment and ex-officio members of a political system . . . as allies, legmen and buddies." And if any of them questioned the wisdom of appeasement, the Prime Minister would express his surprise "that such an experienced journalist was susceptible to Jewish-Communist propaganda."[7]

Still more insidious tactics were used to promote Chamberlain's press agenda. Sir Joseph Ball, former chief of the investigation branch of MI5, had been recruited in 1924 to run a private intelligence agency for the Conservative Party. He applied the skills he had used in his previous job to spy on Labour Party headquarters, often securing advance copies of Labour literature before the party leadership did.[8] In 1930 Ball was chosen to head the new Conservative Research Department, in which capacity he became Chamberlain's most trusted and loyal lieutenant. He established the National Publicity Bureau to campaign for the government in the 1935 general election, and he ghostwrote articles for ministers to publish in newspapers. Later he would wiretap anti-appeasement MPs and journalists. In 1936 he secretly acquired control of *Truth*, the same weekly that had attacked Churchill forty years earlier.[9] Under its new management, *Truth* was once again anti-Churchill and anti-Jewish, fiercely assaulting Chamberlain's opponents until well after Britain had entered the war.[10] The other political weeklies – the *Spectator*, the *Economist, Time & Tide*, the *New Statesman*, the *Observer*, the *Tablet*, the *British Weekly*, the *New English Weekly*, the *Saturday Review*, and *Tribune* – were more independent and ranged across the ideological spectrum, but they were generally pro-appeasement.[11]

Several press lords enjoyed cozy relationships with Conservative leaders: Lord Beaverbrook (*Daily Express* and *Evening Standard*) with Samuel Hoare; Lord Kemsley (the *Sunday Times, Daily Sketch*) and Lord Astor (the *Observer*) with Neville Chamberlain. Geoffrey Dawson, editor of *The Times*, met almost daily with Lord Halifax after he became Foreign Secretary in February 1938. As Richard Cockett concluded, "Dawson was privy to more Cabinet thinking and secrets than most members of the government." One exception was Lord Camrose, who was more friendly with Churchill: his *Daily Telegraph* was the only national Conservative daily that took a somewhat skeptical stance towards Chamberlain's foreign policy.[12] Churchill had a column in the *Evening Standard*, where he regularly denounced appeasement, but on 25 February 1938 Beaverbrook's *Daily Express* warned that he was "unwittingly lending himself to the most violent, foolish, and dangerous campaign to drive this country into war since he drove us into it himself against Russia in 1919." On 24 March the *Evening Standard* ended Churchill's contract, though he swiftly found a new platform with the *Daily Telegraph*.[13]

In March 1936 a Cabinet Committee had resolved "to ask the BBC to refrain from arranging for independent expressions of views" on European affairs. Although in principle an autonomous corporation, the BBC was susceptible to pressure from Whitehall. Henceforward it would effectively ban anti-Nazi views from the airwaves and mostly limit its coverage of foreign crises to repeating anodyne government pronouncements. The following January a supporter urged Churchill to rouse the country with an extended speaking tour, but Churchill pointed out that he would get no media coverage. "One poor wretch may easily exhaust himself without his even making a ripple upon the current of opinion," he wrote. "If we could get access to the broadcast some progress could be made. All that is very carefully sewn up over here." When Chamberlain's appeasement of Mussolini drove Anthony Eden to resign as Foreign Secretary on 21 February 1938, the government swiftly "took every possible step to secure the London papers," Oliver Harvey (Eden's private secretary) noted in his diary, and "the BBC was told to say nothing that night about Germany and Italy." As Eden's successor, Lord Halifax tried to reach an agreement with Germany that would involve the return of some of her colonies, and the BBC was advised to cancel a series of talks on that sensitive subject. When Lord Reith asked "pointblank whether HMG wished him to stop them," Halifax (according to Harvey) said "that was so but he would deny it if challenged in public."[14]

The Foreign Office had its own News Department, headed since 1935 by Rex Leeper, a determined anti-appeaser. Up to a point, his operation was a rival and counterweight to Joseph Ball's. Leeper had a stable of collaborative journalists and through them he disseminated the Foreign Office view of events, which in its own way could be slanted and manipulative. In 1935 he leaked exaggerated reports of Germany's build-up of warplanes, though that was double-edged propaganda: it appeared to vindicate Churchill, but was also used by appeasers to argue that war would mean the destruction of Britain's cities. On 24 April 1936 Leeper met with Churchill at Chartwell and urged him to build a coalition of anti-appeasers, which ultimately took the form of the Focus in Defence of Freedom and Peace Group.[15]

But there were limits to Leeper's influence. Conservative papers generally welcomed Chamberlain's move to 10 Downing Street because they hoped for a new understanding with Germany, even if that meant serious concessions in Eastern Europe and Africa. The appointment of arch-appeaser Nevile Henderson as ambassador to Germany set off alarm bells with Vernon Bartlett, correspondent of the Liberal *News Chronicle*, who in July 1937 wrote an article warning that Henderson was preparing to sell out to Hitler. But Charles Peake, Leeper's lieutenant at the Foreign Office News Department, sternly advised the *News Chronicle* that publication would be "prejudicial to the public interest." That was enough for Bartlett's editor, who spiked the report. Even the *News Chronicle*, a solidly anti-Nazi paper, was prepared to exercise self-censorship on request, and the appeasers (Henderson especially) took ruthless advantage of that weakness.[16]

In November 1937 Lord Halifax visited Germany. "He told me he liked all the Nazi leaders, even Goebbels, and he was much impressed, interested and amused," wrote Chips Channon, an American-born pro-appeasement MP, though Halifax granted that the regime was "perhaps . . . too fantastic to be taken seriously."[17] Halifax conferred with Hitler and found that, while the Chancellor "was on the whole very quiet and restrained," he exploded at the very mention of the Soviet Union or British newspapers, evidently regarding them as equivalent threats. Hitler insisted that Britain's "licentious press" was the greatest obstacle to peace: "Nine tenths of all tension was produced simply and solely by it." Halifax "agreed with the Chancellor's remarks as to the dangerous influence of the Press," and on the 21st he told the British press corps in Berlin that they "had to create the right atmosphere if any real advance were to be made towards a better understanding." Later that day he met with Joseph Goebbels, who focused the discussion exclusively on the press. "Its power to mould public opinion was greater even than was realized, and if public opinion was moulded wrong incalculable harm could be done," Goebbels remarked. He singled out the "spiteful taint" of *Times* reports filed by Norman Ebbut, who had been expelled the previous August. Appealing to Halifax's sense of fairness, Goebbels noted that no German journalist would dream of attacking King George VI. In the spirit of even-handedness, could not something "be done to put a stop in the British Press to personal criticism of Hitler"? After he returned home, Halifax wrote to Henderson to say that he was optimistic about Anglo-German relations, "if only we can get the press in both countries tame."[18]

Halifax began by scolding Lord Southwood, part-owner of the *Daily Herald*, for publishing a Will Dyson cartoon that portrayed Europa offering to buy peace by sacrificing her colonized peoples to a villainous Hitler: "Take my child, but spare, oh spare me!" This Halifax thought "malevolently and I think unjustly cruel." (He was alluding to the cartoon, not Nazism.)[19] Goebbels had also singled out the anti-Hitler caricatures of David Low in the *Evening Standard*, and back in London Halifax advised Low over lunch that his cartoons were threatening the tranquility of Europe. "Do I understand you to say that you would find it easier to promote peace if my cartoons did not irritate the Nazi leaders personally?" Low asked. When Halifax answered affirmatively, Low felt obliged to tone down his drawings, but he sharpened them again after the German takeover of Austria in March 1938. For that he found himself attacked as a threat to peace by right-wing papers, left-wing papers, and even (speaking at the Newspaper Society's annual dinner) by the Prime Minister himself. The *Church Times* considered his lampoons of Hitler insensitive and inappropriate: "Good taste . . . forbids joking concerning subjects which are held sacred by others."[20]

On 8 March 1938 (just before the Anschluss) Halifax warned a press delegation that, while Britain was "a free country with a free press," any "unguarded criticism of other countries especially . . . the Heads of States" would amount to "needless provocation." Ambassador Henderson shared these remarks with Hitler, the clearest possible signal to the Nazis that their pressure to muzzle the British media was working. Meanwhile, Henderson repeatedly wired the Foreign Office urging an end to the "vilification of Germany in the foreign press." He reported that the Germans were particularly upset by the *News Chronicle* and the *Manchester Guardian*, which they considered "Jewish newspapers with journalists connected in one way or another with Soviet Bolshevism." Charles Peake reassured Henderson that the publishers of the

Manchester Guardian were "entirely Aryan", and the *News Chronicle* "free from all Jewish influences."[21] But had the Germans consulted Beaverbrook they would have found support for their worst suspicions. "The Jews have got a big position in the press here," he wrote in a private letter in December 1938. "I estimate that one third of the circulation of the *Daily Telegraph* is Jewish," which might have been true if every Jew in the United Kingdom had bought a copy. "The *Daily Mirror* may be owned by Jews. The *Daily Herald* is owned by Jews. And the *News Chronicle* should really be the *Jews Chronicle*. Not because of ownership but because of sympathy. The Jews may drive us into war. They do not mean to do it. But unconsciously they are drawing us into war. Their political influence is drawing us in that direction."[22]

Several newspaper proprietors convinced themselves that the recession of 1937–38 – and the resulting loss of advertising – had been caused by war jitters. If playing down international crises and promoting good Anglo-German relations encouraged investors and stimulated the economy, then appeasement made good business sense. Papers on the left, especially the *Daily Herald* (partly owned by the Trades Union Congress) and the Liberal *News Chronicle*, were particularly susceptible to this kind of logic.[23]

In this climate, even Churchill pulled his punches on at least one occasion. In May 1935 Reeves Shaw asked him to write an article on "The Truth About Hitler" for the *Strand Magazine*. "I should like you to be as outspoken as you possibly can in your appraisement of Hitler's personality and ambitions," Shaw urged, "and absolutely frank in your judgment of his methods." Churchill delivered. He wrote that Hitler had driven "the patriotic [former Chancellor Heinrich] Brüning, under threat of murder, from German soil." He luridly recounted the "Night of the Long Knives," denounced "this horrible blood-bath," and asked: "Can we really believe that a hierarchy and society built upon such deeds can be entrusted with the possession of the most prodigious military machinery yet planned among men?" Published in November, the article was roundly attacked by the German Foreign Ministry and press.[24] In July 1937, when he was planning to reprint the article in *Great Contemporaries*, Churchill secretly consulted the British Foreign Office, which expressed grave reservations. He therefore made some judicious cuts, which (in the words of a relieved Foreign Office official) "would certainly take a great deal of the sting out."[25] The *Great Contemporaries* version had a more ambiguous title, "Hitler and His Choice," and it omitted all of the inflammatory material mentioned above.

The oligopolistic newspaper press could be manipulated by the government and advertisers, but it was practically impossible to control the less concentrated book industry, which did not depend on advertising. As Dan Stone has shown, plenty of anti-Nazi books were published in Britain in the 1930s, and some of them sold quite well:

> The first Penguin Special, Edgar Mowrer's *Germany Puts the Clock Back*, sold its first print-run of 50,000 copies in a week. The next two, G. T. Garratt's *Mussolini's Roman Empire* and Geneviève Tabouis' *Blackmail or War*, both broke records for new books with first print-runs of 50,000. Emily Lorimer's *What Hitler Wants* was used by teachers with their sixth-formers, distributed to every member of parliament in Britain, Canada, Australia, New Zealand, South Africa, Eire and the United States, and the author herself received many letters of congratulation. Over the weekend it appeared (ten days after being completed!) Shiela Grant Duff's *Europe and the Czechs* sold 50,000 copies and orders were taken for 78,000 more copies.[26]

Chamberlain was familiar with some of this literature. In January 1938 he read Stephen Henry Roberts's devastating and much debated book *The House that Hitler Built*. Professor of Modern History at the University of Sydney, Roberts explicitly warned that "Hitlerism cannot achieve its aims without war; its ideology is that of war." Even before Kristallnacht (9–10 November 1938) he predicted "a campaign of annihilation" against the Jews, "a pogrom of the crudest form, supported by every State instrument."[27] Eden admired the book, which "said no more than the Foreign Office had been saying for months," and noticed that it seemed to break through the Prime Minister's complacency. "As we talked of it, Chamberlain even went so far as to suggest that if we could not reach agreement, we might have to aim at the encirclement of Germany and a possible alliance with Russia."[28] Chamberlain admitted that the book was "extremely clever & well informed," but ultimately he refused to allow it to change his mind: "If I accepted the author's conclusions I should despair but I don't & wont."[29]

One book that both Churchill and Chamberlain read, but read very differently, was Margaret Mitchell's *Gone with the Wind* (1936). It was hugely popular in Britain, the most frequently mentioned American book in a 1942 survey.[30] When a 1948 Gallup Poll asked "What's the best book you've ever read?" it was very near the top of the list, on a par with Charles Dickens and just behind the Bible.[31] For Chamberlain the novel was interesting mainly as social history, a document of a vanished world and Negro dialect.[32] But for Churchill it was "a terrific book," and in the wake of the Anschluss, the story of the downfall of a genteel civilization had immediate political relevance: "If mortal catastrophe should overtake the British Nation and the British Empire, historians a thousand years hence will still be baffled by the mystery of our affairs. They will never understand how it was that a victorious nation, with everything in hand, suffered themselves to be brought low, and to cast away all that they had gained by measureless sacrifice and absolute victory—gone with the wind!"[33]

On 3 June 1938 a *Times* leader proposed that the Sudeten Germans and other minorities in Czechoslovakia should have a plebiscite on self-determination. "The rulers of Czechoslovakia might in the long run be the gainers in having an homogenous and contented people," *The Times* soothingly suggested, though a much more likely result would be the dismemberment of the country. The Foreign Office immediately disavowed the article, but the press officer at the German Embassy told Berlin that it was "based on Chamberlain's interview with representatives of the British Press" on 1 June, and he correctly added that "no part of the article has been disavowed" by the Prime Minister.[34]

On 19 July the *Daily Herald* broke the story of secret conversations at the Foreign Office between Halifax and Captain Wiedemann, a close associate of Hitler. Outraged, Chamberlain effectively ordered Rex Leeper to silence the Foreign Office News Department. Diplomatic correspondents were now cut off from inside sources of government information other than the Prime Minister and his allies.[35] The result was a growing gulf between the British newspapers (which mostly supported appeasement) and their reporters and readers, many of whom were losing confidence in the credibility of the government and the press. One measure of that distrust was the growing combined circulation of dissident newsletters such as Claud Cockburn's *The Week, The Arrow, Whitehall News Letter*, and *King-Hall's News Letter*.[36] In 1940 Mass Observation, the social survey organization, identified at least sixty-six such newsletters, with a total circulation of 100,000.[37] Precursors to the Internet blog, they printed reports on the European situation that mainstream papers did not publish. But reading those newspapers, Chamberlain smugly concluded that public opinion was behind him and his policies, conveniently forgetting that he and his agents had orchestrated that chorus of approval.

Meanwhile, Churchill was trying to disseminate his dissenting views as widely as possible, with the help of an indispensable agent. Emery Reves was a Hungarian Jew who in 1930 launched the Cooperation Press Service. Based in Berlin, he distributed articles by prominent politicians to publications outside their home countries. Within two years he had about a hundred political writers in his stable (Austen Chamberlain, Bertrand Russell, Herbert Samuel, Arthur Henderson, Hugh Dalton, Paul Reynaud, Leon Blum, Count Sforza), publishing them in 400 newspapers in 70 nations. "Naturally the organization was rather profitable," he recalled. He even went to Moscow to arrange "for a regular exchange of articles between the Russian and Western press. Unfortunately, four months after my departure from Moscow, all the leaders with whom I negotiated were executed." On 1 April 1933 Nazi stormtroopers attacked Jewish businesses throughout Germany, and Reves took the night train to Paris, where he opened a new office on the Champs-Elysées.

Reves was keen to recruit Churchill, and Austen Chamberlain set up a meeting on 25 February 1937 in Churchill's London flat at Morpeth Mansions.

Having just emerged from his bath, Churchill was as skeptical as he was naked, so Reves handed him a fat folder of Austen's clippings. Promptly telephoning Lord Beaverbrook's office, Churchill was dismayed to learn that "Chamberlain's articles are much more widely distributed than mine." In June Churchill and Reves signed a contract, and the latter became the conduit for distributing Churchill's jeremiads against Hitler to Europe, the British Empire, and the United States. A senior Foreign Office official urged Reves to stop – for in fact he was enabling Churchill to run around Neville Chamberlain's media blockade, with some assistance from the latter's half-brother. "He was really in the political doghouse," Reves remembered. "Through my service he got on the front pages of the newspapers in twenty-five languages, with up to a fifteen, even twenty million circulation."[38]

Churchill was already known as a writer on the European Continent. *The World Crisis* had been brought out in French, German, Italian, Russian, Danish, Czech, Finnish, Norwegian, Swedish, and Spanish; *My Early Life* in French, German, Italian, Danish, Norwegian, and Swedish.[39] In 1937 Churchill published no fewer than sixty-four articles, mostly on politics, but also some potted histories, literary pieces, and prognostications of future technology. His main platform was Beaverbrook's *Evening Standard*, followed by the *News of the World*. Both paid very well, but Churchill had lost many of his outlets in the American press, as well as the *Daily Mail*.[40] Thanks to Reves, his article "A Plain Word to the Nazis," published in the *Evening Standard* on 20 August 1937, earned £45 for the author and £24 18s for the agent. Under the less provocative title "Anglo-German Relations," it was republished in Paris, Copenhagen, Stockholm, Oslo, Trondheim, Brussels, Rotterdam, Helsinki, Tallinn, Kaunas, Prague, Zurich, Geneva, Warsaw, Budapest, and Buenos Aires.[41] If Hitler had stuck pins on a map, he would have seen that he was surrounded by newspapers publishing Winston Churchill.[42]

The German press was outraged, Reves reported on 31 August. At a meeting of the Organization of German Residents Abroad in Stuttgart, Churchill's column was denounced by the Deputy Führer Rudolf Hess and Foreign Minister Constantin von Neurath. "It seems that the article was most useful," Reves concluded.[43] But a few weeks later German propagandists effectively sabotaged another Churchill article, "Friendship with Germany." Just hours after it appeared in the *Evening Standard* but before continental newspapers could republish it, a selective 400-word condensation was broadcast by German radio and distributed throughout Europe by a German wire service. As Reves warned Churchill:

> It is a most able and diabolical work, which carries the sign of the methods of Dr. Göbbels. They extracted phrases of your article in such a manner that

> the effect of this comment is exactly contrary to that of the whole article! It reads as a tribute to Herr Hitler, as a kind of "Mea Culpa" after your previous article. And in those countries where this has appeared, we cannot publish anymore the integral text of the article![44]

The *Evening Standard* took steps to protect its copyright, and the damage was apparently controlled for the time being.[45] By 1 January 1938 Reves had contracts with an array of newspapers throughout the British Dominions and Empire.[46] Eventually he placed Churchill's articles in every continental European country except Germany, Italy, the Soviet Union, Spain, Portugal, Bulgaria, and Albania.

But a steep political price was paid for that journalistic success. In the months leading up to the Munich Agreement in September 1938, Churchill was churning out articles on the European crisis, completing his biography of Marlborough, and starting *A History of the English-Speaking Peoples*. All of them were propaganda against appeasement, but they involved so much labor that he could spend little time on the floor of Parliament. There was a group of Tory MPs, perhaps forty in all, who were prepared to challenge Chamberlain's foreign policy, but they could not be effective without a leader, and the two obvious candidates for that role were unavailable: Anthony Eden had no stomach for that kind of fight, and Churchill was busy writing at Chartwell. After Munich most of those Tory rebels met frequently with Eden to plot strategy, but they did not invite Churchill, who had not shaken off his reputation as an erratic *littérateur*.[47]

By 19 May 1938, British, French, and Czech intelligence received reports that Germany was preparing to attack Czechoslovakia on the 22nd. The Czechs mobilized their own forces, and Britain and France issued warnings to Hitler. It was in fact a false alarm, and when no attack materialized, it seemed that Hitler had backed down in the face of Western pressure. The Führer was enraged at this international humiliation, especially when British and French newspapers gloated over their apparent victory. As Nevile Henderson told Halifax, "What Hitler could not stomach was the triumphant outcry of the foreign press, and particularly the British, to which above all he is susceptible." On the 22nd Halifax spoke to "all the British press" and made it clear that they were not to goad Hitler by reporting "that the present corner had been turned owing to British firmness." "Because of Germany's self-restraint," one German army officer recorded, Hitler had "suffered a loss of prestige which he is not willing to suffer again," and he immediately ordered an acceleration of preparations for an actual attack on Czechoslovakia. When Chamberlain, Halifax, and Henderson warned British journalists that negative coverage of Germany might provoke Hitler to launch a new war, they may have been craven, but they were not wrong as a matter of fact.[48]

On 7 September *The Times* ran its notorious leader that proposed "making Czechoslovakia a more homogeneous state by the secession of alien populations who are contiguous to the nation to which they are united by race," a line inserted by Dawson himself. Again the Foreign Office repudiated the article – and again everyone, including the Germans, correctly concluded that it represented the views of Chamberlain and Halifax. Even Chips Channon, who worshiped Chamberlain and found anti-Nazis tiresome, was stunned by *The Times* leader. A few days later he learned "that Lord Halifax dined with Geoffrey Dawson, my informants say, on Monday night, the 5th, and that 'The Times' article was definitely inspired, a ballon d'essai, to see how the public would react."[49]

On 10 September the press conveyed the impression that the British government had finally acquired some spine – and Chamberlain was outraged. "The Daily Mail's positive announcement yesterday – splashed even louder in its Paris edition – that 'at midnight' we had taken 'the dramatic step' of sending Hitler an ultimatum to the effect that if he used force we should at once declare war, was the most gratuitously mischievous of all," he complained. "I had to send urgent telegrams to Paris Prague & Berlin to deny it." Harold Temperley, the Master of Peterhouse College, Cambridge, had sent the Prime Minister a copy of his book *The Foreign Policy of Canning*, which he read keenly: "Again and again Canning lays it down that you should never menace unless you are in a position to carry out your threats."[50]

For Chamberlain, dramatic midnight ultimatums were far too Churchillian, but he was already contemplating an uncharacteristically theatrical stroke of his own. Desperate to find a way out of the crisis, "I thought of one so unconventional and daring that it rather took Halifax's breath away," he wrote on 3 September.[51] The code name could have been lifted from a spy thriller: "Plan Z." At a 12 September Nuremberg Rally Hitler charged that the Czechs aimed to "annihilate" the Sudeten Germans and vowed that Germany would stand by no longer. The impact on his audience was stunning, and not just in Germany: more than a hundred American radio outlets broadcast the speech, and the BBC cut into their regular programs three times to broadcast direct from Nuremberg.[52] The next morning intelligence services informed the Prime Minister and the Cabinet that German embassies had been forewarned that an attack on Czechoslovakia would begin on 25 September. Late in the evening of the 13th, without consulting the Cabinet or the French government beforehand, Chamberlain put Plan Z into effect: he telegraphed Hitler that he would immediately fly to Germany to negotiate a peace settlement.

He was probably stealing from the Führer's own playbook. Hitler loved to travel by air and make a Wagnerian entrance, swooping down from the clouds, most famously in *Triumph of the Will*. It was the first time a British Prime Minister had inserted himself into a foreign crisis so audaciously. A few days later Chamberlain explained to his sister Ida the stagecraft involved: it had to be "a complete surprise," sprung at the last possible moment, in order for the "coup" to have maximum "dramatic force." His initial plan called for flying into Nuremberg without prior notice, but the possibility that Hitler might refuse to see him put paid to that.[53] As it was, Chamberlain congratulated himself on upstaging Hitler, as the latter seemed to acknowledge when they met: "Afterwards I heard from Hitler himself and it was confirmed by others who were with him, that he was struck all of a heap," and even considered pre-empting Chamberlain by coming to London.[54] It is more likely that Hitler gloated, recognizing that Chamberlain's stroke was in fact a capitulation. The démarche won applause in the British press and among most Conservatives, Liberals, and Labourites alike, as well as 70 percent approval in a Mass Observation survey. But many of those who hailed Chamberlain hoped that he would at last read Hitler the riot act. Churchill and Eden were outraged, while Mussolini recognized that this meant "the liquidation of British prestige."[55]

Chamberlain conferred with Hitler at Berchtesgaden on 15 September. According to Chamberlain's account, Hitler "said if I could assure him that the British Government accepted the principle of self determination (which he had not invented) he was prepared to discuss ways & means." Chamberlain replied that he would have to consult his Cabinet, and Hitler promised not to attack Czechoslovakia in the meantime. Afterwards Chamberlain recorded that Horace Wilson (his closest advisor and a determined appeaser) felt sure that Hitler

> had been very favourably impressed. I have had a conversation with a *man*, he said, & one with whom I can do business & he liked the rapidity with which I had grasped the essentials. In short I had established a certain confidence which was my aim and on my side in spite of the hardness & ruthlessness I thought I saw in his face I got the impression that here was a man who could be relied on when he had given his word.[56]

The day before Chamberlain flew to Berchtesgaden, Halifax had advised the Cabinet that "it was of the utmost importance that steps should be taken to ensure that the press received the news of Plan Z correctly . . . it might be necessary that the newspaper proprietors and editors should be seen instead of the lobby and diplomatic correspondents." The Home Secretary Samuel Hoare took care of the press moguls, and coverage of the meeting was overwhelmingly positive.[57] Chamberlain secured the agreement of the British and French Cabinets to Hitler's demands, and the Czechoslovaks were forced to acquiesce.

On 22 September Churchill went to Paris to stiffen French resolve, without success. "Everybody was against him," Emery Reves recalled. César Campinchi, the Minister of Marine, denounced him as a "war monger." On the way back to Le Bourget airport, Churchill told Reves that he had one weapon left in his arsenal: "The articles I write are much more important than my speeches in Parliament. The press print one or two short paragraphs from the speeches, and that is all."[58]

That day Chamberlain met Hitler at Bad Godesberg, confident that he had a rational solution to the crisis in hand. He was appalled when Hitler escalated his demands once again, insisting on the immediate occupation of the Sudetenland by German forces. Even this Chamberlain was prepared to swallow, but his Cabinet, the French government, British public opinion, and the British newspaper press revolted.[59] The *Listener* noticed that the BBC was not broadcasting much more than Chamberlain's recorded pronouncements: "Surely, though, it should be possible to broadcast even one talk explaining, as simply as possible, the facts about the Czechoslovakian problem." Two respected journalists, A. J. Cummings (*News Chronicle*) and Wickham Steed (Churchill's ally on the Focus), said on a Paramount newsreel "Germany is marching to a diplomatic triumph ... Our people have not been told the truth," to general applause from cinema audiences. It was difficult to apply pressure to Paramount, a US corporation, but Halifax secured the withdrawal of the newsreel through the good offices of the American ambassador, Joseph P. Kennedy.[60]

War now seemed inevitable, but on 25 September Emery Reves proposed to Churchill "something which might stop Hitler and change the situation at once." His idea was an immediate conference between the French, British, and Soviet war ministers: Edouard Daladier, Leslie Hore-Belisha, and Marshal Kliment Voroshilov. "This would be an even greater sensation than the flight of Mr. Chamberlain to Hitler. . . . It would make a tremendous impression in Germany, and frighten them more than any Anglo-French declaration. . . . I believe that such a demonstration would be 'a lightning in the night', to use Hitler's own words."[61] Reves understood well Hitler's methods, but Chamberlain had no intention of involving the Soviets. Instead, he sent precisely the opposite message in a BBC broadcast on the 27th: "How horrible, fantastic, incredible it is that we should be digging trenches and trying on gas masks here because of a quarrel in a far-away country between people of whom we know nothing."

Chamberlain spoke to public anxieties that had been screwed up to breaking point. The 1936 H. G. Wells film *Things to Come* depicted an air attack on Britain, terrifyingly like the actual Blitz four years later, except that the movie graphically anticipated the use of poison-gas bombs and biological weapons, which would precipitate a total collapse of civilization. The Italian

Air Force had actually used gas bombs against Ethiopia, and the conventional bombing of Shanghai and Guernica was horrific enough. In 1937 British experts predicted that Germany would begin hostilities with a sixty-day bombing campaign that would kill 600,000 people. Mass Observation found that more than a few people were considering killing family members in the event of war ("I'd sooner see kids dead than see them bombed like they are in some places").[62]

On the morning of 28 September, Chamberlain sent final appeals to Hitler and Mussolini for a negotiated settlement. Meanwhile, Hitler's generals and advisors (with the sole exception of Ribbentrop) were pressing him to avoid war, at least at this point. That afternoon the House of Commons listened in depressed silence while Chamberlain recapitulated his so far unsuccessful efforts to preserve the peace. After he had spoken for more than an hour, he was handed a note and, with just a flicker of a smile, announced: "I have now been informed by Herr Hitler that he invites me to meet him at Munich tomorrow morning. He has also invited Signor Mussolini and M. Daladier. Signor Mussolini has accepted and I have no doubt M. Daladier will also accept. I need not say what my answer will be."[63]

"I felt sick with enthusiasm," wrote Chips Channon, "the House rose and in a scene of riotous delight, cheered, bellowed their approval. We stood on our benches, waved our order papers, shouted – until we were hoarse – a scene of indescribable enthusiasm – Peace must now be saved, and with it the world."[64] Chamberlain was treated to a five-minute ovation, including the Labour benches. According to Labour MP George Muff, Joseph Kennedy violated protocol by leading cheers from the Visitors' Gallery.[65] The scene was such breathtaking theatre that some suspected it was staged. It was not, but as Chamberlain wrote to his sister Hilda, "That the news of the deliverance should come to me in the very act of closing my speech in the House was a piece of drama that no work of fiction ever surpassed."[66] "Never again did I expect to be entertained in a theater after being here when the Prime Minister first made his flight to Germany and also being present at the finish of this dramatic speech in Parliament," exulted Ambassador Kennedy.[67] It was indeed "the most dramatic scene of all," Churchill admitted in the *News of the World* a few months later. "*I have never seen the House so strangely shaken as it was by the conclusion of his speech*" [Churchill's emphasis].[68] It was greeted like a last-minute reprieve from a death sentence – a common denouement in Victorian melodrama. And it had all been performed before the largest audience in history up to that moment, 100 million radio listeners.

At Munich Chamberlain, Hitler, Daladier, and Mussolini agreed that the German takeover of the Sudetenland should be phased in over ten days

(1–10 October), though Hitler actually gained more territory than he had demanded at Bad Godesberg. There was an alternative to caving in. The Siegfried Line, protecting Germany's western border, was far from completed and seriously undermanned. A commander on the spot warned Hitler that it could not be held in the face of a French attack. Germany's generals were terrified by the prospect of war. Admiral Horthy, Hungary's dictator, refused to join in attacking Czechoslovakia, even when offered the bribe of recovering territories lost after the First World War. He frankly told Hitler that Britain would "inevitably win" a new war.

If Britain and France had joined with the Soviet Union to stand behind Czechoslovakia, there would have been three possible outcomes. First, Hitler might have backed down. Second, he might have been overthrown by his generals. Third, he would have gone to war and crushed Czechoslovakia in a matter of weeks, inflicting serious suffering on the Czech people but also incurring some German military losses. Meanwhile, as the French General Maurice Gamelin had promised, his troops could have moved across the lightly defended Western Wall and occupied enough of the Rhineland to block the strike through the Ardennes that Germany launched in May 1940.[69] British air defenses were far from ready, but neither was the Luftwaffe prepared to conduct a sustained bombing campaign against Britain from German bases. Even if the Russians gave the Czechs no concrete military assistance, they would have cut off trade with Germany and never signed the Nazi-Soviet Pact. Germany would have found herself without allies, hemmed in on all sides, blockaded by the British fleet, and deprived of essential raw materials. Instead of a global conflagration there would have been only a local conflict that Germany could not win. Most of Europe would have been spared war, most of Eastern Europe would have escaped Nazi or Soviet domination, nearly all of the European Jews would have survived, and Japan probably would have avoided a confrontation with the United States.

Except for *Reynolds News* (a left-wing Sunday paper) and the *Daily Worker*, all British national papers supported the Munich Agreement. Nevertheless, in early November a *News Chronicle* poll found that 86 percent of the public did not believe that Hitler would make no further territorial demands. The editor, Walter Layton, did not publish that result, not "because I have any doubt that they faithfully reflect British opinion," he told Chamberlain, "but because I fear that so blunt an advertisement of the state of British opinion on this matter would exacerbate feelings in Germany."[70]

On 5 October Churchill delivered a lengthy, unsparing, and famous denunciation of the Munich accords. Certain rhetorical flourishes from it are often quoted: "A total and unmitigated defeat"; "the German dictator, instead of snatching his victuals from the table, has been content to have them served to him course by course"; "Silent, mournful, abandoned, broken, Czechoslovakia recedes into the darkness"; "Thou art weighed in the balance and found wanting." But one of the speech's most salient points, made towards the end, is not usually emphasized. Churchill affirmed that the core of his implacable resistance to Nazism was essentially literary. Not only would Hitler dominate continental Europe, he would also suppress the autonomy of the author in Britain, something Churchill absolutely could not tolerate:

> What I find unendurable is the sense of our country falling into the power, into the orbit of and influence of Nazi Germany, and of our existence becoming dependent upon their good will or pleasure. It is to prevent that that I have tried my best to urge the maintenance of every bulwark of defence – first the timely creation of an Air Force superior to anything within striking distance of our shores; secondly, the gathering together of the collective strength of many nations; and thirdly, the making of alliances and military conventions, all within the Covenant, in order to gather together forces at any rate to restrain the onward movement of this Power. It has all been in vain. Every position has been successively undermined and abandoned on specious and plausible excuses. We do not want to be led upon the high road to becoming a satellite of the German Nazi system of European domination. In a very few years, perhaps in a very few months, we shall be confronted with demands with which we shall no doubt be invited to comply. Those demands may affect the surrender of territory or the surrender of liberty. I foresee and foretell that the policy of submission will carry with it restrictions upon the freedom of speech and debate in Parliament, on public platforms, and discussions in the Press, for it will be said – indeed, I hear it said sometimes now – that we cannot allow the Nazi system of dictatorship to be criticized by ordinary, common English politicians. Then, with a Press under control, in part direct but more potently indirect, with every organ of public opinion doped and chloroformed into acquiescence, we shall be conducted along further stages of our journey.[71]

It was the same fear that George Orwell expressed in "Inside the Whale" (1940), that the independent author was facing extinction, crushed between big press conglomerates and totalitarian censors. Given the climate of the times, and the news blockade Churchill faced, such anxieties were far from groundless.

Arms and the Covenant, a collection of Churchill's speeches on the growing threat of war, was published by Harrap on 24 June 1938 at 18s. in a 5,000-copy edition. It would never be reprinted in Britain: the remainders were repackaged as a cheap edition in June 1940. For the first time, Churchill sold better in the United States. Putnam's brought out two printings (totaling 7,500 copies) in 1938, and two more in October 1940 and September 1941 (1,000 each). The publication date could not have been more perfectly timed: 30 September, the day the Munich Agreement was announced and Czechoslovakia capitulated.[72] The recycled speeches, familiar to British readers, were fresher for Americans, and in place of the dull British title Putnam's had hit on something far more gripping: *While England Slept*. It resonated with the American perception of the United Kingdom as a decadent society unwilling to defend its own Empire – yet it also began the rehabilitation of Churchill in American eyes, establishing his public image as a heroic fighting Englishman. "When it comes to proving the gift of prophecy there is no denying the amazing prescience which foresaw in '34 and '36 the fearful crisis of '38," Ellery Sedgwick wrote in the *Atlantic Monthly*.[73] "Churchill's speeches . . . will have a place in history as a noble expression of the British democracy when it was preparing for the decisive battle against fascism abroad and defeatism at home," predicted the *Nation*, though the reviewer warned that the British establishment was still "pro-fascist."[74] The *New York Times* noted that the book was particularly "well-timed, and it can hardly fail to stir the emotions of democracies, already deeply aroused."[75]

Sales of the book may well have been boosted by Churchill's 16 October radio address to the United States, though Chamberlain considered it counterproductive: "The very worst thing you can do with the U.S.A. is to lecture them on their duty to come to the assistance of the British Empire. Winston's broadcast disconcerted all our friends over there – not least the President himself – and made it practically impossible for them to help."[76] That was unfair to Churchill, who never mentioned the Empire in his talk, focusing instead on arguments that had more appeal for Americans. He denounced fascist imperialism in China and Ethiopia, and alluded to a semi-fascist regime taking root in Brazil. He emphasized the common traditions of liberty upheld by the English-speaking peoples, but warned, "I do not know how long such liberties will be allowed. The stations of uncensored expressions are closing down; the lights are going out; but there is still time for those to whom freedom and Parliamentary government mean something, to consult together."[77]

Meanwhile, Churchill was working "double shifts" to finish his big project to secure an American alliance: *A History of the English-Speaking Peoples*. Over four months, from August to November, straight through the Czech crisis, he had written the first section, totaling 136,000 words. However, he was far from finishing, and he ruefully admitted that writing limited his participation in parliamentary debates during these critical months.[78]

In *Collier's* on 3 September, Churchill still held out hope that "The most severe censorship cannot altogether prevent foreign newspapers, especially from Switzerland and Scandinavia, circulating among thinking people in Germany."[79] But in the wake of the Munich accord, the press blackout spread to the rest of Europe. On 4 November Reves warned Churchill that Nicolai Blædel, the anti-Nazi foreign editor of Copenhagen's *Berlingske Tidende*, had been effectively furloughed:

> A few days after the Munich agreements the German Minister has paid a visit to the Danish Foreign Minister and spoke to him about it in the following terms: As you will understand, the situation is completely changed now. Germany has got Czechoslovakia, her influence in Hungary, Rumania, Yugoslavia is growing every day, so that Germany can get all food and raw materials she wants from those "friendly countries". Germany has no need anymore to buy anything in Denmark and she will probably stop importations from that country. However, should the Danish government wish to continue selling their goods in Germany, and then came the conditions, mostly of a political nature, among them that Mr. Blaedel should leave his newspaper.
>
> In Sweden a few days after the Munich agreement the socialist Prime Minister has written personal letters to all the newspaper editors asking them to be extremely careful not to criticize Germany and not to publish anything which might hurt the German government.
>
> I have received similar information last week from Norway, from the President of the Storting, Mr. Hambro, who is also leader of the Conservative Party.
>
> As you see, the terror is spreading all over Europe. This complete change of the situation in the Scandinavian countries is a direct consequence of the Munich agreements. Until that modern peace treaty the Scandinavian countries were courageous fighting against Nazism, now they are helpless and have to capitulate. Direct German intervention is an accomplished fact.[80]

Speaking at a Press Club luncheon on 22 November, Churchill affirmed that Britain still had a free press, but then qualified that by noting some "restraints." There was the "misuse and abuse of the Official Secrets Act" – which Churchill himself had rushed through Parliament back in 1911. And there were:

> Some people [who] say how much better it would be if they were as in the totalitarian States. In those States they conduct foreign policy on the basis that the Press say nothing but what it is told, and immediately say what it is told. . . . It might be very convenient, no doubt, if we could suppress public

> opinion here, and everything was allowed to go on quietly without our knowing what was going on outside. A lot of platitudes would be uttered and lots of soothing, reassuring statements made, and lots of sanguine forecasts unfolded from time to time. But one of these days there would be an uncomfortable awakening.

What Churchill posed as hypothetical was approaching the reality of British mainstream journalism in 1938. He explained that there were three traditional bulwarks of free speech in Britain: Parliament, the press, and the public platform. But "The decay of the parliamentary system, or in these days the eclipse of the parliamentary system of criticism, and the abeyance of the party system where matters are hacked out clearly have thrown on the Press and journalists and leaders of the Press what is in some ways an undue burden." This was a diplomatic way of saying that the same Chamberlainite machine had stifled criticism both in Parliament and in the newspapers. In that case only one leg of the libertarian triad remained: the press had to be "corrected and if necessary resisted by a wide use of the public platform." Churchill concluded by affirming the value of a democratic free press ("We cannot change now!"), but why was it necessary to affirm that if a genuinely free press was not already under threat?[81]

In February 1939 Reves began to penetrate the American market, starting with the *New York Herald Tribune*. He passed up the *New York Times* because it "is owned by Jews, and today this would have meant that many Americans would have become suspicious that we are making 'European propaganda'." The *Herald Tribune* was owned by the Anglo-Saxon Reid family, "and nobody can suspect them that they are undertaking something which is 'un-American'."[82] The paper also ran a syndication service for widely read columnists such as Walter Lippmann and Dorothy Thompson, and through this Reves won contracts with fourteen major American newspapers, for a total of £50 per article.[83] "I am indeed sorry to hear that the net is closing round our activities, through fear of Germany," Churchill wrote. "Luckily, you have already called in the New World to redress the balance of the Old."[84]

In 1934 Churchill had warned the House of Commons that an air war would be apocalyptic, but now he sent his American audience a different message. In the 17 June 1939 *Collier's* he published an article proclaiming "Bombs Don't Scare Us Now." He used the examples of Spain and China to show that bombing of civilians, though indeed horrific, only stiffened the will to resist, and he outlined Britain's plans for meeting a German air assault. "Of these grievous events the people of the United States may soon, perhaps, be the spectators," he warned. "But it sometimes happens that the audience becomes infuriated by a revolting exhibition. In that case we might see the spectators leaving their comfortable seats and hastening to the work of rescue and retribution."[85] Twentieth-century theatregoers were expected to remain decorously in their seats, regardless of what horrors were enacted upon the stage. In contrast, Victorian melodrama encouraged vocal audience participation, especially to protest injustice. When Simon Legree thrashed Uncle Tom, spectators sometimes had to be forcibly restrained from intervening. Now that there was a real and immediate prospect of bombs falling on London, Churchill became increasingly convinced that the spectacle would be enough to bring the United States into the war.

Reves also secured a monthly radio broadcast with NBC for £100 each.[86] The first went out over the air on 8 August, and Churchill made sure to include a literary allusion that his listeners would appreciate: he cheered on the Chinese people for defending "the soil, the good earth, that has been theirs since the dawn of time."[87] (Pearl Buck's *The Good Earth* had topped the US bestseller list in 1931 and 1932, and in 1938 she had won the Nobel Prize in Literature.)

As late as 9 March 1939, Neville Chamberlain had offered reporters (on a not-for-attribution basis) an exceedingly optimistic briefing on the prospects for European peace, and the next day all the dailies repeated the same sunny predictions in indistinguishable articles. The spell was only broken on 15 March, when German troops marched into Prague.[88] Then the daily and weekly papers swung against appeasement, with the exception of *Truth*, which continued to assure its readers that "no appreciative section of British opinion desires to reconquer Berlin for the Jews."[89]

As Hitler advanced from triumph to triumph, Churchill's European newspaper outlets were snuffed out one by one. In a long and revealing letter (31 May 1939) to Reginald Leeper, Emery Reves explained in detail a mostly successful Nazi campaign to stifle press criticism in neighboring nations. The Austrian and Czech papers were the first to go, but the media in a given country could be controlled without actually invading it. Normally a vigorous protest from the German ambassador was enough to get articles suppressed and journalists fired. In Rumania all newspaper advertising was controlled and directed by the pro-German Undersecretariat for Press and Propaganda, with obvious consequences. Following the Italian occupation of Albania in March, the Greek government blocked the publication of articles by British and French politicians. In 1934 Germany and Poland had signed a Press Agreement promising that each government would suppress publications hostile to the other, which meant a virtual ban on Churchill. The fact that Britain had recently guaranteed the independence of Rumania, Greece, and Poland had no effect on press policies. The attitude of these countries was, as Reves paraphrased it, "We must be agreeable to the Germans until the very last moment, when we shall ask England and France to make war for us."

While the Eastern European press was all but closed to Churchill, the climate in Western Europe was not much better. The Danish journalist Nikolai Blaedel "has been forced to spend several months abroad in consequence of German protests against his pro-English and pro-democratic policy," Reves wrote. On 10 March the Cooperation News Service had begun sending Churchill's articles to American newspapers via an Amsterdam wireless station. But within three weeks the Dutch Foreign Minister and Minister of the Interior had shut down these transmissions, on the grounds that such "one-sided propaganda" was "dangerous for the neutrality of Holland." German firms such as Bayer, Opel, and Telefunken were major advertisers throughout Europe, and they withheld their business from non-cooperative newspapers. As Reves reported, "The Editor of a leading Swedish newspaper who recently denounced our contract for Mr. Anthony Eden's articles and said that he could only publish articles by Mr. Winston Churchill on 'non-political subjects' told me quite openly that he must do so as his shareholders are expecting dividends." Reves asked Leeper to keep all this confidential: if the information were made public, governments would deny it and the journalists mentioned would face further retaliation.[90]

The dissemination of Churchill's 8 June 1939 article "Triple Bulwark of Peace," which advocated an alliance with the Soviet Union, suggests that Reves was not exaggerating. It was placed in only a handful of European newspapers, in Paris, Brussels, Copenhagen, Stockholm, Bergen, Luxembourg, and Kaunas. In Poland it appeared only in *Hajnt*, a Yiddish daily, which was charged no publication fee.[91]

About eighty of Churchill's political articles were reprinted in *Step by Step*. Published by Thornton Butterworth in June 1939, it rapidly ran through four printings. *Time* reported that the Duke of Windsor had it in his car, while the Duchess drove.[92] The Putnam edition in the United States was once again perfectly timed, appearing on 25 August, just days before the outbreak of the war, though there was an incongruous blurb for Neville Chamberlain's *In Search of Peace* on the back flap of the dust jacket. "It proves him so inveterately right . . . that one wonders why he was not taken into the Government sooner," concluded the *Christian Science Monitor*.[93] "It is partly due to his crusading that [British] defenses are now in a comparatively formidable state," declared the *Nation*,[94] while *Foreign Affairs* called the book "amazingly coherent and sagacious."[95] The *New York Times* was more grudging, noting that the author had been wrong about intervention in Russia, India, and Edward VIII.[96] The book was translated into Danish by Gyldendal and into German by the émigré Netherlands-based publisher Allert de Lange, shortly before those countries were invaded by Nazi Germany.[97] The volume particularly impressed another unsuccessful novelist: "This man is a strange mixture of heroism and cunning," Joseph Goebbels recorded in his diary. "If he had come to power in 1933, we would not be where we are today [8 May 1941]. And I believe that he will give us a few more problems yet. . . . He is not to be taken as lightly as we usually take him."[98]

In Britain the newspaper war finally swung in Churchill's favor. On 23 April 1939 the lead article in the *Sunday Pictorial* called for his inclusion in the government. The reader response was unprecedented: 2,400 letters, all but 3 percent of them favorable.[99] When Churchill's contract with the *Daily Telegraph* expired in May he was taken on by the *Pictorial*'s sister paper, the *Daily Mirror*. It had a large circulation, 1.4 million copies daily, though it was a working-class tabloid that favored the Labour Party, not an effective vehicle for addressing Britain's conservative establishment. By July the *Daily Telegraph*, the *News Chronicle*, the *Daily Mirror*, the *Daily Mail*, the *Evening News*, the *Observer*, the *Manchester Guardian*, the *Yorkshire Post*, and even the *Daily Worker* all wanted Churchill in the Cabinet.[100] That mirrored a broader shift in public opinion recorded in the Gallup Poll: in May the public strongly favored Churchill's inclusion in the Cabinet (56 to 26 percent); in June they overwhelmingly endorsed his demand for an alliance with France and Russia (84 to 9 percent); and by July they were willing to fight for Poland over Danzig (76 to 13 percent).[101]

As he had done before the First World War, Churchill outlined a future history of the next impending conflict. On 24 July 1939 he told General Ironside that the war would begin with:

(i) The crippling or annihilation of Poland.
(ii) The employment of Italy to create diversions. Mussolini has sold his country for his job.
(iii) The capture of Egypt, chiefly by Italian forces.
(iv) A pressing on to the Black Sea *via* Roumania.
(v) An alliance with Russia, when the latter sees how the land lies.[102]

Except that the capture of Egypt was only attempted, the forecast was accurate. As Churchill predicted, Hitler authorized the Nazi-Soviet Pact, signed on 24 August just after midnight. Thus he neutralized a formidable adversary and (through trade agreements) ensured his supply of raw materials, canceling the effects of a British blockade. He calculated that if Britain and France realized that the USSR would not fight for them, they would abandon Poland as they had Czechoslovakia. The pact would be the *coup de théâtre* that would transform the drama: "That will hit like a bombshell," he gloated. But the surprise was dampened by the advance announcement, late in the evening on the 21st, that Ribbentrop was flying to Moscow to negotiate the treaty. The Poles, the

French government, and the British Cabinet (meeting on the 22nd) all concluded that the pact made no difference, and Nevile Henderson was dispatched to deliver a personal letter from Chamberlain to Hitler stating that Britain would stand by Poland. When Henderson arrived at the Berghof on the afternoon of the 23rd, Hitler treated him to another of his theatrical tirades. Once the ambassador departed, the Chancellor immediately dropped his act, slapped his thigh, and gloated that Chamberlain's government would fall that evening. When it did not, he summoned Henderson to another meeting at the Chancellery on the afternoon of the 25th. This time Hitler was more conciliatory, but when it became clear that he was getting nowhere, he concluded by saying that, after this Polish business was behind him, he intended to retire from politics and take up art – though in his mind there was never a clear distinction between the two.[103] The late period of Hitler's artistic career was cut short when Germany invaded Poland, early in the morning of 1 September. Sixty hours later, Britain and France declared war. Chamberlain, who had always feared that inviting Churchill into the government would provoke Hitler, at last brought him back to the Admiralty.

Given the determined and largely successful Nazi campaign to block Churchill's newspaper outlets, it is remarkable that a German translation of *My Early Life*, published in 1931 as *Weltabenteuer im Dienst* by Paul List Verlag of Leipzig, remained in print long after Hitler's seizure of power. As late as July 1939 Churchill received a royalty statement, which showed that he had not earned back his advance of £100.[104] As of 31 December 1938 a German translation of *Great Contemporaries*, which included his diatribe against Hitler, was the only one of Churchill's books that was banned in Germany.[105] By 1942 all of his works would be on the Nazi blacklist, along with those of G. K. Chesterton, Agatha Christie, John Cleland, Samuel Taylor Coleridge, Wilkie Collins, Joseph Conrad, James Fenimore Cooper, Noël Coward, and Stephen Crane. (The Propaganda Ministry strongly suspected that Crane had Jewish blood.)[106] Nevertheless, the Paris publisher Payot would continue to sell translations of *The World Crisis* and *My Early Life* throughout the war: they were never banned or confiscated by Occupation authorities.[107] Though it was ultimately responsible for destroying as many as 100 million volumes throughout Europe, Nazi censorship could be ludicrously inefficient.[108]

CHAPTER 17

The Loaded Pause

On the morning of Sunday 3 September 1939, John Colville, a young diplomat, attended church and then went to the Foreign Office. There he was assigned to the Ministry of Economic Warfare, which was supposed to be supervising the blockade on Germany: "On reporting to this new and bewildering organisation I was given an empty desk and nothing whatever to do." At 11.15 a.m. he heard Chamberlain declare war on the wireless, and then the air-raid sirens sounded, which reminded him and all the other idling civil servants in the office of a terrifying movie: "It was widely believed that London would be reduced to rubble within minutes of war being declared, as recently depicted to an alarmed populace in the film of H. G. Wells' book called *Things to Come*; and it seemed that this was about to happen." Many others made that connection.[1] "Of course we were afraid," remembered Shirley Annand. "We were absolutely terrified. We had all read H. G. Wells so we knew what it would be like. Bombs raining down, fires everywhere, gas, hundreds of thousands dead."[2] "It would be impossible to convey the sense of utter panic with which we heard the first air raid warning ten minutes after the outbreak of war," wrote a clerk George Beardmore. "We had all taken *The Shape of Things to Come* too much to heart, also the dire prophecies of scientists, journalists and even politicians of the devastation and disease that would follow the first air raid. We pictured St. Paul's in ruins and a hole in the ground where the Houses of Parliament stood."[3] The Wells film convinced pacifist Edward Blishen that the next war would bring immediate apocalypse: "The endless fleets of bombers throbbing into our skies, the cities exploding, the instant anarchy. Life would become an instant horror film. They wouldn't know how to bury the dead."[4] *The Shape of Things to Come* was only the best known of a slew of novels anticipating another war, and this time they did not portray plucky Englishmen foiling a German invasion. Their titles tell their stories: *The Gas War of 1940, The Poison War, War upon Women, Menace, Air Reprisal, Four Days' War*. Evelyn

Waugh's *Vile Bodies* (1930) and Aldous Huxley's *Brave New World* (1932) also presumed that a catastrophic war was in the offing.[5] That fear was the irresistible force behind appeasement. As General Edmund Ironside noted at the end of 1937, "The Cabinet . . . are terrified now of a war being finished in a few weeks by the annihilation of Great Britain."[6] Churchill's own warnings about the growing strength of the Luftwaffe may well have contributed to that panic.[7]

Awaiting the apocalypse on that Sunday, Colville retired with his co-workers to a shelter to play bridge. In this case, life did not follow art: the siren was a false alarm. He returned to his virginal desk and sat there until lunch, after which he "went home reflecting that we seemed remarkably ill-prepared for Armageddon," and played a round of golf. "A few days afterwards I went to the Foreign Office and pleaded, successfully, to be restored to my familiar and reasonably busy occupation in its Eastern Department." Even then, "reasonably busy" could mean arriving for work around 11.00 a.m. and drafting "a few dreary letters to the Colonial Office about Palestine."[8]

Colville soon grew impatient with what became known as the Phony War. Chamberlain's strategy of wearing down Germany through blockade, he observed in his diary, "will be dangerous because it will be boring; and in wartime boredom is certain to breed discontent at home." On 22 September he received a list of talking points explaining why Britain was doing nothing to help the Poles, the gist of which was that offensive action at this point would be mere theatrics: "To have devoted hundreds of British planes to bombing raids in Germany would have meant spectacular successes, but the inevitable loss of machines which will be used more effectively on the Western Front."[9] So he spent the weekend at Stansted Park with Lord and Lady Bessborough. On Sunday morning, while Warsaw was besieged, "as I lay in bed turning the pages at random of a sentimental novel, and contemplating the charm of my surroundings, I felt blissfully contented." A few days later Warsaw capitulated: it was "a heroic defence," Colville granted, but he concluded that the Germans should be offered generous peace terms, allowing them to keep the Sudetenland and Danzig.[10] A month later, on 31 October, he read a Government White Paper on German concentration camps and found it stomach-churning, but recommended that it not be published: "after all most of the evidence is produced from prejudiced sources, and it is in any case undesirable to arouse passions before the war has begun in earnest."[11]

This sums up the public and governmental inertia that Churchill had to overcome. On 26 September Chamberlain spoke before the House of Commons, with the port and mien of an undertaker, as Harold Nicolson observed: "He is dressed in deep mourning relieved only by a white handkerchief and a large gold watch-chain. One feels the confidence and spirits of the House dropping inch by inch." Then Churchill rose to speak:

> Greeted by a loud cheer from all the benches. . . . He began by saying how strange an experience it was for him after a quarter of a century to find himself once more in the same room in front of the same maps, fighting the same enemy and dealing with the same problems. His face then creases into an enormous grin and he adds, glancing down at the Prime Minister, "I have no conception how this curious change in my fortunes occurred." The whole House roared with laughter and Chamberlain had not the decency even to raise a sickly smile. He just looked sulky.
>
> The effect of Winston's speech was infinitely greater than could be derived from any reading of the text. His delivery was really amazing and he sounded every note from deep preoccupation to flippancy, from resolution to sheer boyishness. One could feel the spirits of the House rising with every word. It was quite obvious afterwards that the Prime Minister's inadequacy and lack of inspiration had been demonstrated even to his warmest supporters. In those twenty minutes Winston brought himself nearer to the post of Prime Minister than he has ever been before. In the Lobbies afterwards even Chamberlainites were saying, "We have now found our leader." Old Parliamentary hands confessed that never in their experience had they seen a single speech so change the temper of the House.

Churchill was able to hit so many notes, assume so many voices, and fascinate his audience largely because he had spent so many evenings at the theatre – and at the music hall. In one passage, which he unfortunately excised, he alluded to a British naval attack on a U-boat, "and all that thereafter was seen of the vessel was a large spot of oil and a door which floated up to the surface bearing my initials."[12] It was Churchill's dramatic talents that appealed to the British people, according to George Beardmore, who (on 28 September) complained that the Ministry of Information

> dishes out information the public already knows in the dullest way possible. Of course, the public is longing to hear about sensational exploits by air, sea, and land, of batteries wiped out and woods occupied and air squadrons engaged over enemy lines, our gallant airmen emerging infinitely superior. What we get is one sentence to the effect that a German sortie has been repelled with loss, that the Saarbrucken salient has undergone nightlong bombardment, and that enemy aircraft were seen over the Dutch border. Churchill, bless him, gave a splendid account of the navy the day before yesterday – so much contraband seized in excess of tonnage sunk, so many submarines disposed of and so many merchantmen preserved. One or two fine literary asides about the reliance to be placed on hostile accounts of fabulous engagements in which our capital ships are sunk. He is very popular

> indeed, notwithstanding that on the 18th the aircraft carrier *Courageous* was sunk by torpedo with the loss of just over half the crew of 1100-odd.[13]

And it was Churchill's theatrical flair that reinforced the distrust of some Chamberlainites, notably Chips Channon:

> The PM made his usual dignified statement: unfortunately he was followed by Winston who executed a tour-de-force, a brilliant bit of acting and exposition, in describing in detail the work of the Admiralty. He amused, and impressed the House. . . . He must have taken endless trouble with his speech, and it was a great contrast, which was noticed, to the PM's colourless statement. I am sure Winston is angling for the Premiership, convinced of it. . . .[14]

On 1 October Colville heard Churchill speak on the radio, with the same mixed emotions:

> He certainly gives one confidence and will, I suspect, be Prime Minister before this war is over. Nevertheless, judging from his record of untrustworthiness and instability, he may, in that case, lead us into the most dangerous paths. But he is the only man in the country who commands anything like universal respect, and perhaps with age he has become less inclined to undertake rash adventures.[15]

Colville's misgivings were not groundless. Upon his return to the Admiralty, Churchill promptly tried to revive his First World War plan for a surprise amphibious assault on Germany through the Baltic. It was, as Richard Holmes concludes, "wildly impractical even in 1914 and frankly insane in 1939, when the Luftwaffe would have sunk every ship."[16]

On 10 October Colville began work as one of Chamberlain's Assistant Private Secretaries. Here he came into contact with Churchill, and as he later recalled, "Many of his colleagues, and most senior civil servants, regarded him with suspicion, an attitude reflected by the staff at 10 Downing Street and one to which I was daily subjected."[17] Colville fell in with this view: Churchill was no doubt a great orator but a fireball of "unco-ordinated energy," always recklessly calling "for 'action' in any form and at all costs."[18]

Churchill recorded his thoughts, queries, and commands in minutes, thousands of them issued every year. Early in his premiership he established the rule that his orders should only be taken seriously if they were written.[19] He had enforced a similar policy during the First World War, accumulating the documents that made up *The World Crisis*.[20] Unlike most other Cabinet ministers, he personally read all telegrams sent to him.[21] This policy effectively collapsed the distinction between politics and art: everything he did and wrote, as First Lord and Premier, was potential material for his next book. Just days after he returned to the Admiralty in September 1939 there were grumblings to that effect. "He is writing his new memoirs," one official said to Samuel Hoare (Lord Privy Seal). "Why did he not bring his 'World War'?" asked Oliver Stanley (President of the Board of Trade).[22] On 17 September Chamberlain recorded that his dealings with Churchill were more harmonious than he had expected, except

> that he continually writes me letters many pages long. As we meet every single day in the War Cabinet this would seem unnecessary, but of course I realise that these letters are for the purpose of quotation in the Book that he will write hereafter. Hitherto I haven't answered them, but the one I got yesterday was so obviously recording his foresight and embodied warnings so plainly for purposes of future allusion that I thought I must get something on the record too which would have to be quoted in the Book.[23]

In fact both Churchill's letter and Chamberlain's reply were reproduced in *The Second World War*, even though they reveal that the Prime Minister was more prescient. To meet the anticipated German onslaught in the west, Churchill proposed strengthening static defenses and deploying mothballed First World War artillery, while Chamberlain gave top priority to strengthening the RAF.[24] Churchill's habit of writing memoranda on matters outside his department (such as land warfare) for the sake of including them in "the Book" finally drove Chamberlain to demand a stop to it. The First Lord vowed to forbear,[25] but evidently this promise did not apply to commenting on issues within the purview of the Admiralty, broadly derived. "It's one more for the book!" Halifax commented on Churchill's 15 January 1940 memorandum on Scandinavia, which was indeed quoted in *The Second World War*.[26] In contrast, Hitler was notoriously averse to putting anything in writing, though according to Goebbels he talked about writing his own history of the war – after he had won it.[27]

Just weeks after the war broke out, Thornton Butterworth proposed that, once it was all over, Churchill should publish a history of it.[28] John Colville recorded that as early as December 1940 Churchill told him he planned to "write a book on the war, which he had already mapped out in his mind chapter by chapter."[29] It was an astonishing example of premature advance planning: at that point actual events had not quite reached the end of the second volume of his future six-volume history. But for Churchill, even the Second World War was a matter of artistic composition. A few weeks later before the House of Commons he described it in precisely those terms: "Far be it from me to paint a rosy picture of the future. Indeed, I do not think we should be justified in using any but the more sombre tones and colours while our people, our Empire and indeed the whole English-speaking world are passing through a dark and deadly valley."[30]

While he was thinking of his next book, Churchill had yet to finish his last. At the outbreak of the war *A History of the English-Speaking Peoples* was a sprawling manuscript of 530,000 words, considerably more than the 400,000 called for in his contract. On 10 September 1939 he gave G. M. Young (one of the historians retained to assist with the manuscript) instructions for wrapping up the book. Certainly there should be more emphasis on Chatham (Pitt the Elder), "a man who from a private station compelled a sluggish, all-powerful Government to capitulate, and thereafter in four brilliant years gained the Seven Years' War, and completed the building of 'The first British Empire'." The overall focus was overwhelmingly English, with one conspicuous exception: its last chapter told the story of the American Civil War, concluding with Lincoln's assassination. Churchill conceded that this section was disproportionately large, "but this book is intended to appeal to the United States and it is necessary to emphasize their dramatic struggle. I took great pains about this part." He noted "the extreme pressure of the times," hoping to have a complete draft ready for a final reading by 15 November. His clear intention was to publish *A History of the English-Speaking Peoples* soon enough to affect the course of the current war, to inspire and unite the whole anglophone world.[31] In a 1 October broadcast he made explicit the connection between the two great conflicts:

> . . . I look back upon the history of the past to find many sources of encouragement. Of all the wars that men have fought in their hard pilgrimage, none was more noble than the great Civil War in America nearly eighty years ago. Both sides fought with high conviction, and the war was long and hard. All the heroism of the South could not redeem their cause from the stain of slavery, just as all the courage and skill which the Germans always show in war will not free them from the reproach of Nazism, with its intolerance and its brutality. We may take good heart from what happened in America in those famous days of the nineteenth century. We may be sure that the world will roll forward into broader destinies. We may remember the words of old John Bright after the American Civil War was over, when he said to an audience of English working folk: "At last after the smoke of the battlefield had cleared away, the horrid shape which had cast its shadow over the whole continent had vanished and was gone for ever."[32]

The same quotation from Bright would conclude that section of *A History of the English-Speaking Peoples*.

On 12 September another historiographical assistant, Alan Bullock, was summoned to the Admiralty to supply some modern history:

> . . . after warning the duty officer that we were not to be disturbed "unless the German High Seas Fleet is brought to battle" [Churchill] took me off to the Board Room where he had his desk. For well over an hour I was treated to a monologue of which to my eternal shame I failed to make a record. All that I recall was his insistence over and over that the great feature of his own time had been "the death grapple between these two great nations, the British and the German".[33]

But how could the book address that if it concluded before German unification? The logical end point for such a narrative was 11 November 1918, when the anglophone nations were at last united in victory.

Churchill more or less held to his schedule and delivered a complete draft to Desmond Flower at Cassell's on 16 December.[34] But Flower objected "that we are alarmed by the abrupt manner in which the work finishes." Anxious to get the book out as soon as possible, Churchill offered to dash off a quick 10,000-word epilogue, but Flower rejected that as wholly inadequate. Ending the book in 1865 meant giving short shrift to the Dominions, and Flower insisted on thorough coverage of the following fifty years, finishing with "the Relations of the English Speaking Races on the eve of the Great War." Unless that was supplied, he warned, "we cannot regard the contract as having been filled."[35] In February, Churchill invited Flower to the Admiralty to tell him that he could not carry forward work on the book while serving as one of the King's ministers, a decision Flower accepted.[36] Yet Churchill continued to write as late as 27 April 1940,[37] as William Deakin, his research assistant and sometime ghostwriter, recalled:

> . . . while conducting the grave affairs of the Royal Navy during the North Sea battles of the Norwegian campaign, [he would] spend an hour or so in the afternoon or in the early morning hours completing his chapters on the Norman Conquest and mediaeval England. Naval signals awaited attention, admirals tapped impatiently on the door of the First Lord's room, while on one occasion talk inside ranged around the spreading shadows of the Norman invasion and the figure of Edward the Confessor who, as Churchill wrote, "comes down to us faint, misty, frail". I can still see the map on the wall, with the dispositions of the British Fleet off Norway, and hear the voice of the First Lord as he grasped with his usual insight the strategic position in 1066. But this was no lack of attention to current business. It was the measure of the man with the supreme historical eye. The distant episodes were as close and real as the mighty events on hand.[38]

Churchill could not possibly finish this vast history in time to influence the war, but in the meantime he had other creative irons in the fire. On 24 September he proposed that the Admiralty recruit three prominent authors (their names have not been preserved) to observe the Fleet in action and produce patriotic articles that would be circulated to the press, much as Rudyard Kipling had done in the First World War. Churchill suggested that Sir William Nicholson be authorized to paint the ships at Scapa Flow: "The lights were very beautiful when I was there last week. Such pictures would be an artistic record, and care would be taken that the backgrounds revealed nothing of military interest."[39] According to Admiral J. H. Godfrey, Director of Naval Intelligence, the First Lord conducted his radio broadcasts with a fine sense of public relations: "Good news was made to seem better; bad news was toned down, delayed or sometimes suppressed. Any particularly spicey bit of news might be held up for three or four days until it could be included in the First Lord's broadcast and no one was more conscious than Mr. Churchill of the popularity of the bringer of good tidings."[40] When the Germans announced that they could win the war with their magnetic mines, Churchill entertained Parliament with a tale of British counter-measures, "a detective story written in a language of its own."[41] He still described himself as a "journalist" and the House of Commons as a "theatre."[42]

Just weeks after Churchill returned to the Admiralty, Scribner's brought out a new edition of *My Early Life*. Featuring prominently was a new and militantly pro-Churchill introduction by Dorothy Thompson, another popular anti-Nazi newspaper columnist. The "Author's Preface" was expanded to include more background on Churchill's American forebears. Scribner's would reprint the book seven times between 1939 and 1945: the total print run could not have been much less than 10,000.[43]

Stefan Lorant recalled that Churchill asked him to devote a special issue of his popular magazine, *Picture Post*, to the United States, "presenting life there in a popular style, and show what America and the Americans were really like. Sooner or later – so he said – they would have to join England in the war, thus it would be of some help if *Picture Post* would present a better image of our future fighting ally."[44] However, Churchill's habit of withholding bad news did not endear him to American journalists, who once again smelt British propaganda. He did not report that the battleships HMS *Nelson* and HMS *Barham* had both been seriously damaged in December 1939. "I think Winston has made a fool of himself," sighed Lord Lothian (the ambassador to Washington) on 22 March 1940. "He is always doing these things. That is why he never becomes Prime Minister."[45]

As early as 23 September, Chamberlain realized that the Phony War was sapping morale: all Hitler had to do was sit tight and then offer a peace settlement.[46] The literary scholar Ifor Evans quit the Ministry of Information in October, warning that "If there is no major action on the Western Front and the war of what may be called the 'mental blackout' proceeds, the enemy will attempt to destroy our morale at home in many ways."[47] In a 3 November letter from Washington, Lothian reported to Samuel Hoare "the present boredom with the stalemate war—amounting in places almost to resentment that the expected 'drama' of world war is not after all going to be played."[48] "There is no real war," Chips Channon observed on 4 November. "Hitler is indeed shrewd. Is he trying to bore us into peace?"[49]

George Bernard Shaw called for peace in the 7 October 1939 *New Statesman*. In the next issue he was supported by seventeen intellectuals, including John Middleton Murry, Vera Brittain, and Clive Bell. On 13 March 1940 Lord Halifax and R. A. Butler discussed the possibility of a truce with open minds. The National Peace Council also urged Chamberlain to consider a negotiated settlement, in a petition signed by G. D. H. Cole, John Gielgud, Sybil Thorndike, and Cyril Joad.[50] It was a position supported by Lloyd George, the press barons Rothermere and Beaverbrook, and some MPs on the right wing of the Conservative Party as well as the pacifist wing of the Labour Party.[51]

Just after the war began in early September, the Gallup Poll found overwhelming opposition to considering German peace proposals, 77 to 17 percent, but by February the numbers had slipped to 61/29.[52] In January 1940 arch-appeaser Arthur Bryant published *Unfinished Victory*, an apologia for Germany that echoed the main points of Nazi anti-Semitic propaganda and criticized the war as "barren and profitless." The publisher was anti-appeaser Harold Macmillan: as a matter of family tradition, the proprietors of the firm never allowed their personal beliefs to interfere with business. The reviews in the press were mostly favorable, raising the question of how the British media would have reacted if the government had reached a truce with Hitler.[53] By February–March, Mass Observation found that women were especially weary of the war (one called it "*poisonously boring*") but also that "People are longing for war to begin. . . . Increasingly they are in favour of getting on with it at once. Their patience is exhausted."[54]

Churchill recognized the danger. "He loved . . . the excitements and the tense situations which war always brings in its train," recalled Geoffrey Shakespeare, Parliamentary Secretary to the Admiralty. "'What a dull naval war this will be,' he said to me once with a spark of prophetic intuition. 'We have only Germany to fight. Now if we fought Germany, Italy and Japan together, that would be much more interesting.'"[55] Churchill did seem eager to pick fights for the sake of drama. On 20 January he suggested to the Cabinet that British pilots shooting down Russian airplanes on the Finnish front might do wonders for morale, without considering whether it might result in war with the USSR.[56] In addition to interdicting iron ore supplies to Germany, the same motive may have been behind his eagerness to intervene in Norway and Sweden. When John Colville and Chips Channon got wind of that scheme, they both thought of Gallipoli, while Alexander Cadogan (the crusty Permanent Under-Secretary at the Foreign Office) dismissed it as another "Winston stunt."[57]

Before the fall of France in the summer of 1940 Allied propaganda stressed their superior military and economic power. On a poster the French Prime Minister Paul Reynaud's ill-considered boast "Nous vaincrons parce que nous sommes les plus forts" ("We will win because we are strongest") was blazoned across a map of the world, where tiny Germany was hemmed in by the vast British and French empires. For a time Churchill indulged in such braggadocio, vowing that the huge populations (white and otherwise) of the Allies and their "inexhaustible resources will steadily and surely, through command of the seas, be brought to bear upon the evil things whose wickedness has cast its shadow upon mankind and seeks to bar its forward march."[58] One Canadian warned that Churchill's broadcasts were only contributing to Allied complacency: "Propaganda of the complete confidence in the collapse of Germany was discouraging Canadians from making any sacrifice and Americans from bothering about the war at all."[59]

Nevertheless, Churchill's literary gifts were a tonic for morale during the static Phony War. By 1 February 1940 Lord Lothian was convinced that the "façade of isolationism" was cracking: "There is the rising feeling that the United States is playing an unworthy part in one of the greatest dramas of history, and is in danger of losing her soul unless she shoulders her share of the burden."[60] In March the *New York Times* reported that theatre attendance had fallen by half in blacked-out London, but was always boosted by "a speech from Winston Churchill. Each time he has informed us that the Germans will never sing 'Deutschland Uber Alles' there has been a characteristic rise at the box office."[61] In April, Mass Observation quoted an Army man's report that "Churchill is far and away the most liked member of this government. Indeed his was the only talk I have heard a barrack room listen to on the wireless."[62] And over February–May 1940, Mass Observation found that, among newsreel audiences, Churchill was by far the most frequently applauded public figure – indeed the only applauded figure apart from the King and Queen.[63]

On 4 April Chamberlain assured a Conservative Party meeting that Allied defenses in the west were now strong enough to contain Hitler: "One thing is certain: he missed the bus." But just two days later he wrote to his sister Hilda, "We are getting the usual information from 'reliable sources' that something prodigious is imminent but I remain sceptical as I can't think any offensive on a large scale will pay the Boche as well as keeping quiet & developing relations with Russia." Given the choice between a very risky offensive and carrying on with *sitzkrieg*, "I know which I would choose & therefore can't help believing that he will choose the same."[64] Once more Chamberlain made the fatal error of assuming that Hitler's mind worked like his own and would follow the most rational strategy – when in fact military rationale dictated a much more audacious tactic. If the Germans had stayed put, the British and French would have gradually built up their forces to the point where Hitler would have indeed "missed the bus." Moreover, the German Army High Command initially planned to attack through Belgium around Liège, essentially a repeat of their First World War strategy. In that case, Allied mobile forces were prepared to advance into central Belgium and block the offensive. As he was boxing in the Germans, it did not occur to Chamberlain that Hitler (quite rationally) would resort to an unconventional strategy to break out of that box.[65] Working independently, he and General Erich von Manstein hit on the idea of a panzer thrust through the Ardennes and towards the Channel, cutting off Allied forces as they rolled into Belgium. And Hitler ordered that the plan be prepared under maximum secrecy, for the sake of dramatic surprise.[66]

On 9 April the Germans struck at Denmark and Norway. The Royal Navy was able to inflict heavy losses on the German surface fleet, which lost three of its eight cruisers and ten of its twenty destroyers. But Allied efforts to support the Norwegians on the ground were bungled. "Honestly, it does look as if it's coming to H. G. Wells' *Things to Come*" said one young London wife.[67] John Colville worried that "'Time and again we have 'missed the boat' (e.g. Finland, Norway) owing to excessive deliberation and fear of unnecessary extravagance." But Churchill seemed to fall into the opposite error: "his verbosity and restlessness make a great deal of unnecessary work, prevent any real practical planning from being done and generally cause friction. . . . The country believes that Winston is the man of action who is winning the war and little realise how ineffective, and indeed harmful, much of his energy is proving to be."[68]

Colville was right about that much: whatever his managerial failings, Churchill's dramatic performances had certainly enraptured and encouraged the general public. "How we look forward to the Churchill broadcasts!" exclaimed George Beardmore on 19 April. "Everyone adores him, if only because he warned us of the German threat years ago," but also because he stood out as a magnificent actor in a depressingly dull Cabinet: "He contrives to endow the word 'Nazi' with supreme contempt, and his literary phrases, such as when he spoke of the Dutch being 'penned in the same cage as the tiger', put new life into the news. 'We have no naval successes in the North Sea,' he says, 'because we have not been able to find any enemy ships.' As well as the dramatic content of his speeches there is often an item of brand-new information" – that is, he knew how to keep the plot advancing – and "that's what we are starved of – information."[69]

"It was a marvel," Churchill wrote in a draft of *The Second World War*. "I really do not know how – I survived and maintained my position in public esteem while all the blame was thrown on poor Mr. Chamberlain."[70] Yet on 27 April Colville foresaw that Churchill would be catapulted into the premiership by the Norwegian fiasco, even if he were largely responsible for it. For that he could thank Adolf Hitler, who had made "Winston Public Enemy Number One, because this fact has helped to make him Public Hero Number One at home and in the U.S.A."[71] Already the Second World War had become a grand melodrama with a good old hero and splendid villain. For that reason, "Hitler never failed to delight Churchill," his bodyguard Walter Thompson recalled. Hitler was enraged by his adversary, but Churchill relished the drama of it all:

> He had translations of [Hitler's] speeches played on the gramophone for himself, and never allowed the technician to cut out any of the cheers and screams. He loved to listen to the German hordes dismembering him (Churchill) and would lean forward in his seat, rich in the images that fled past. Hitler was now threatening, in his frequent spiels in the Reichstag, to drop one hundred bombs for each British bomb dropped on the Reich, until Britain got rid of Churchill. The Prime Minister liked to play back the parts where Hitler mentioned him by name.[72]

On 7 May the House of Commons began to debate an adjournment motion – which became, in effect, a motion of no confidence in the government. Now the deputy Labour Party leader Arthur Greenwood turned Churchill's literary reputation against him, accusing him of using his rhetorical skills to mislead the British people in a desperate hour:

> Mr. Greenwood: . . . is it not the case that the Norwegian episode – inadequately and, if I may say so, unconvincingly explained to the House by the Prime Minister – has profoundly shocked the people in every constituency in Great Britain? They have been misled by optimistic speeches. I have no doubt that the right hon. Gentleman the First Lord tomorrow night, with a debating power which I myself shall never attain, will be able to explain; but is it not the fact that the Prime Minister and the First Lord have led the people to believe the impossible about this adventure which was never thought out and which was never taken to the end? Is it not the case that, through lack of direction by the Government . . . the Press led the public to believe that day by day we were winning magnificent victories, when those people who looked at the map and thought about the situation knew that those things could not be? The right hon. Gentleman today told us that south

> of Trondheim and north of Trondheim we had succeeded, by a masterly policy, in evacuation with no losses. Wars are not won on masterly evacuations. . . . I remember the First Lord's statement, and I thought that it was not quite up to his literary style. . . . In that speech he led this House, the country and the neutrals to believe that victory, swift, certain, was bound to come.
>
> Mr Churchill: No.
>
> Mr Greenwood: I know what the right hon. Gentleman said in intervening this afternoon. Whatever, with all his great artistry, he had at the back of his mind, what he definitely conveyed to this House and to the public is clear. It was that he, the man trusted with the King's Navy . . . did undoubtedly create the impression that we were on top. . . . We have had a great reverse. It is no good minimising it.[73]

In the face of such attacks, Chips Channon noted on 8 May:

> the doubt was in everybody's mind, would Winston be loyal? He finally rose, and one saw at once that he was in a bellicose mood, alive and enjoying himself, relishing the ironical position in which he found himself: i.e. that of defending his enemies, and a cause in which he did not believe. He made a slashing, vigorous speech, a magnificent piece of oratory. . . . Winston told the story of the Norwegian campaign, justified it, and trounced the Opposition. . . . How much of the fire was real, how much ersatz, we shall never know, but he amused and dazzled everyone with his virtuosity.[74]

Either way, it was a breathtaking performance. As Harold Nicolson observed, Churchill was faced with an extraordinary dilemma: he had to defend the armed forces and leave no doubt of his loyalty to Chamberlain while subtly dissociating himself from the fiasco. "One felt that it would be impossible to do this after the debate without losing some of his own prestige, but he manages with extraordinary force of personality to do both these things with absolute loyalty and apparent sincerity, while demonstrating by his brilliance that he really has nothing to do with this confused and timid gang."[75] If Channon and Nicolson could not tell whether Churchill was performing or sincere, then obviously, like any great actor, he was both – exactly as he had argued in "The Scaffolding of Rhetoric." And if he were a great actor, then clearly (in the eyes of his audience) he stood apart from the rest of Chamberlain's plodding Cabinet, and could not be held responsible for their failures.

The vote, late in the evening of 8 May, was 281 for the government and 200 against, with 41 government supporters voting with the Opposition and about 40 abstaining. In peacetime that margin of victory would have been more than sufficient, but at a moment of national emergency it was fatal for Chamberlain.

A wartime coalition government was now a necessity, and the Labour Party refused to serve with him. On the afternoon of the 9th, Chamberlain invited Halifax and Churchill to 10 Downing Street to discuss the succession. Halifax's account of that momentous meeting, entered in his diary the following morning, was matter-of-fact:

> The PM, Winston, David Margesson [the Chief Whip] and I sat down to it. The PM recapitulated the position, and said that he had made up his mind that he must go, and that it must be either Winston or me. He would serve under either. . . .
>
> I then said that I thought for all the reasons given the PM must probably go, but that I had no doubt at all in my own mind that for me to take it would create a quite impossible position. Quite apart from Winston's qualities as compared with my own at this particular juncture, what would in fact be my position? Winston would be running Defence, and in this connection one could not but remember how rapidly the position had become impossible between Asquith and Lloyd George, and I should have no access to the House of Commons. The inevitable result would be that being outside both these vital points of contact I should speedily become a more or less honorary Prime Minister, living in a kind of twilight just outside the things that really mattered. Winston, with suitable expressions of regard and humility, said that he could not but feel the force of what I had said, and the PM reluctantly, and Winston evidently with much less reluctance, finished by accepting my point of view.[76]

Halifax also spoke with Alexander Cadogan, who recorded essentially the same account in his diary, except that it makes more explicit that Chamberlain spoke in favor of Halifax.[77] But Churchill's version of this meeting is vastly more dramatic, even if every reader knows the outcome. Chamberlain, he begins:

> told us that he was satisfied that it was beyond his power to form a National Government. The response he had received from the Labour leaders left him in no doubt of this. The question therefore was whom he should advise the King to send for after his own resignation had been accepted. His demeanour was cool, unruffled, and seemingly quite detached from the personal aspect of the affair. He looked at us both across the table.
>
> I have had many important interviews in my public life, and this was certainly the most important. Usually I talk a great deal, but on this occasion I was silent. Mr. Chamberlain evidently had in his mind the stormy scene in the House of Commons two nights before, when I had seemed to be in such

> heated controversy with the Labour Party. Although this had been in his support and defence, he nevertheless felt that it might be an obstacle to my obtaining their adherence at this juncture. I do not recall the actual words he used, but this was the implication. His biographer, Mr. Feiling, states definitely that he preferred Lord Halifax. As I remained silent a very long pause ensued. It certainly seemed longer than the two minutes which one observes in the commemorations of Armistice Day. Then at length Halifax spoke. He said that he felt that his position as a Peer, out of the House of Commons, would make it very difficult for him to discharge the duties of Prime Minister in a war like this. He would be held responsible for everything, but would not have the power to guide the assembly upon whose confidence the life of every Government depended. He spoke for some minutes in this sense, and by the time he had finished it was clear that the duty would fall upon me – had in fact fallen upon me. Then for the first time I spoke. I said I would have no communication with either of the Opposition parties until I had the King's Commission to form a Government. On this the momentous conversation came to an end, and we reverted to our ordinary easy and familiar manners of men who had worked for years together and whose lives in and out of office had been spent in all the friendliness of British politics.[78]

Then Churchill, according to his own account, returned to the Admiralty to find shell-shocked ministers of the Dutch government, who had just flown to London in the wake of the German invasion of their country. But this was a serious error, indeed a howler, on his part. According to *The Second World War*, he conferred with Chamberlain and Halifax on the late morning of 10 May, after the Germans had attacked the Low Countries. In fact the meeting took place at 1.30 p.m. on 9 May, just *before* the storm broke. Moreover, Churchill's version erases David Margesson completely, and it underplays and excuses Chamberlain's stated preference for Halifax.

How can we explain these discrepancies; can we get at the truth; and does it matter? The answer to that last question is certainly affirmative. If Halifax immediately turned down the premiership, then Churchill's ascension to 10 Downing Street was inevitable. But if Halifax hesitated while Churchill remained silent, there was a real possibility that the former might have come around to accepting Chamberlain's offer. That probably would have been catastrophic. Halifax was a poor speaker and leader, gentle to the point of being ineffectual, and not well versed in military affairs. The prospect of being Prime Minister in such a time of crisis literally made him sick to his stomach: throughout the 9 May meeting he suffered acute indigestion. He had been an appeaser until Bad Godesberg, when Hitler's intransigence stiffened his spine temporarily. But as a member of Churchill's Cabinet when the Western Front was crumbling, he would argue for exploring the possibilities of a compromise peace, even if that meant territorial concessions to Hitler and Mussolini. Had he been Prime Minister when France surrendered, it is likely that he would have accepted a truce offer from Hitler, provided Britain was allowed to retain her Empire (for the time being). That would have freed Hitler to concentrate all his forces (including the aircraft he actually lost in the Blitz) on defeating the Soviets, who probably would have received no aid from Britain or the United States. At relatively low cost, Hitler could have achieved his dream of a vast Nazi Empire dominating the Eurasian land mass, self-sufficient in natural resources and practically invulnerable to attack. That is why the drama of 9 May matters.

Andrew Roberts has collated and evaluated several not entirely compatible accounts of that meeting.[79] He writes that William Deakin, who assisted in writing *The Second World War*, "chivalrously" accepted the blame for getting the date wrong and omitting Margesson, but Deakin could have been covering up for his boss, who may have had sound artistic reasons for these alterations. Editing out Margesson made sense as dramatic compression, reducing the scene to its three essential characters. And the tension could be heightened if the Wehrmacht were already storming into the Low Countries while Halifax hesitated, even if that meant fiddling with the sequence of events. Deakin claimed that Churchill was "hamming up" the interview, and a December 1947 diary entry suggests that Churchill would have been the first to agree, that he aimed at art rather than documentary. At the time he was in Marrakesh with Lord Moran, his physician, writing his war memoirs and reading chapters aloud. "What did he think was most vivid and arresting?" Moran wondered, and then pointed to a chapter that "will grip the most casual reader. It tells how Chamberlain resigned and Churchill was invited to form a Government. Winston called his account a proem. He did not want to alter it. He could add a lot more detail, but it was better as it stood."[80]

As for that long silence, Churchill was a master of "The Loaded Pause," the title he gave to a 1936 speech and a chapter in *The Second World War*.[81] Margesson said that there was no long pause, and it is not mentioned in the diaries of either Halifax or Cadogan, though Halifax did include it in a retelling one year after the fact. Brendan Bracken and Kingsley Wood (who would serve under Churchill as Minister of Information and Chancellor of the Exchequer, respectively) each claimed that before the meeting they advised Churchill not to say anything if Chamberlain proposed Halifax for the premiership.[82]

According to three other retellings – by Alexander Cadogan, Malcolm MacDonald (Colonial Secretary under Chamberlain), and Randolph Churchill, all recorded in August 1942 – Winston was more assertive in staking a claim to Number 10 than either he or Halifax made out. The same is suggested by the diary of Joseph P. Kennedy, who visited Chamberlain on 19 October 1940. According to Kennedy, Chamberlain "wanted to make Halifax P.M. and said he would serve under him. Edward [Halifax] as [is] his way, started saying 'Perhaps I can't handle it being in H of Lords' and Finally Winston said 'I don't think you could'. And he wouldn't come and that settled it."[83] On 23 January 1942 John F. Kennedy discussed the incident with Halifax, and according to his notes Churchill was not reticent: after Halifax explained why he should not be Prime Minister, "Churchill said he was interested to hear what Halifax had said because he was inclined to agree with him. (He was the man for the job.)"[84] Given Churchill's fierce ambition, it is fairly plausible that, when the fate of civilization hung in the balance, and the ultimate prize was within his grasp, he would have reached out and seized it without much hesitation.

Obviously Halifax did not want the job: he said as much in an earlier meeting with Chamberlain on the morning of the 9th. But Chamberlain had not given up and again proposed Halifax at the afternoon meeting with Churchill. All accounts indicate that Halifax, for all his reluctance, did not categorically refuse. Instead, he listed reasons why he would not be suitable for the position. Chief among them was that, as a peer, he could not lead the government in the House of Commons, but Chamberlain and the King had already found ways around that difficulty. (Exceptions could be arranged in a time of national emergency.) In his morning meeting with Chamberlain, Halifax granted that if the Labour Party would only agree to serve in a coalition headed by himself, "we should all no doubt have to boil our broth again." In their afternoon meeting Chamberlain could have tried to address Halifax's concerns and persuade him to change his mind. In that case, knowing he was the first choice of Chamberlain, the King, most of the Parliamentary Conservative Party, many Labour Party leaders, the House of Lords, the City, *The Times*, the senior civil service – in short, the British establishment – Halifax might have accepted out of an aristocratic sense of duty.[85] According to some accounts, Churchill (very fortunately) spoke up before that could happen.

Those of us who were not present cannot know with certainty what actually happened that afternoon at Number 10. But it is entirely possible that, pause or no pause, Halifax hesitated to close the door – until Churchill slammed it shut. If that were true, and if he had portrayed that in *The Second World War*, he would have appeared rudely pushy, shoving Halifax off the stage of history. On the other hand, Andrew Roberts may be right to conclude that Halifax promptly bowed out, with no one nudging him – but then the scene would have had no drama. In any case, Churchill crafted a riveting interlude that allowed all three players to emerge as gentlemen.

CHAPTER 18

The Hour of Fate and the Crack of Doom

In February 1939 the Ministry of Information commissioned the Royal Institute of International Affairs to suggest guidelines for war propaganda. The Institute envisioned a top-down effort, where elites would spread authorized rumors down to the British people, who were assumed to be unintelligent and easily led. As various internal memoranda put it, "Our masses dislike and distrust argument." They are "idealistic and illogical in temperament," not receptive "to such abstract concepts as Freedom," having "never consciously fought for an ideal in the 'Liberty, Equality, Fraternity' sense." But given that they are "at least averagely susceptible to propaganda," the "oblique shepherding of opinion" is possible as long as the authorities stick to "simple facts, anecdotes, descriptions and so forth." This mentality, amounting to a collection of upper-class prejudices, produced an early – and breathtakingly inept – war propaganda poster. It commanded the British people:

YOUR COURAGE

YOUR CHEERFULNESS

YOUR RESOLUTION

WILL BRING US VICTORY

as one might order a servant to bring cocktails.[1] In contrast to this poster and to Hitler (who preferred the first-person singular), Churchill usually spoke in the first-person plural ("We shall fight on the beaches . . .", "Let us go forward together"). It was the rhetorical device he had first outlined in *Savrola*, to make the audience feel that they were players in a great drama, and it worked brilliantly, at least in 1940–41. BBC surveys suggest that his radio audience was huge: 77 percent of potential listeners in 1941, falling to 65.4 percent in February 1942.[2]

"I have nothing to offer but blood, toil, tears and sweat." Churchill spoke those words twice on 13 May 1940, first to his ministers meeting in Admiralty House, then in his first address to the House of Commons as Prime Minister, but he had been working on the phrase (adapted from Garibaldi) for more than forty years. He first drafted it when he was imprisoned by the Boers, assuring his captors that a British victory "is only a question of time and money expressed in terms of blood and tears."[3] In the final volume of *The World Crisis* he described the pointless sacrifice of millions of men on the Eastern Front: "Their sweat, their tears, their blood bedewed the endless plain."[4] In *Marlborough*, speaking to the contemporary issue of rearmament, he denounced English parliamentarians for rapidly demobilizing their armies after the Peace of Ryswick in 1697: "they were only too soon to redeem their follies in blood and toil."[5] And in February 1939, at the conclusion of the Spanish Civil War, he mourned the "blood, sweat and tears" it had cost.[6]

The 13 May speech struck the dominant chords of melodrama. It promised a struggle against absolute evil ("a monstrous tyranny, never surpassed in the dark, lamentable catalogue of human crime"). That war would be a terrible ordeal, but ultimate victory was certain. "I feel sure that our cause will not be suffered to fail among men." It was all framed within a Victorian vision of progress: without victory, there could be "no survival for the urge and impulse of the ages, that mankind will move forward towards its goal."[7]

As Richard Overy has observed, British social commentators in the 1930s had been obsessed with "the survival of civilization as it was popularly understood," and that discourse too had been framed in melodramatic terms. "In this great melodrama Hitler's Germany was the villain; democratic civilization the menaced heroine; the many forces of progressive thinking the simple-minded but courageous hero; Soviet Communism the hero's bold but not altogether trustworthy accomplice."[8] That is how Will Dyson portrayed the Führer in the cartoon that so distressed Lord Halifax. Wyndham Lewis, an early Nazi sympathizer, was by 1939 urging the British people to "*keep hissing*. Herr Hitler is a villain who, if he is not sufficiently hissed, becomes really dangerous."[9] He even looked the part of a stage villain, who was invariably dark-haired and moustachioed. (In the 1880s, one English actor tried to play a blond Aryan villain, but angry audiences would have none of it.) In fact Hitler and Mussolini together played perfectly what Michael Booth identified as melodrama's "two main kinds of villains: the grim, determined, immensely evil; and the shifty, cowardly, half-comic."[10]

Victorian melodrama tended to treat evil as an individual moral failing rather than as something inherent in a political or economic system. Capitalists might corner markets and exploit laborers, aristocrats might seduce honest working girls, Europeans might not always deal justly with Africans and

Indians. But these only represented the actions of wicked men: there was nothing intrinsically wrong with capitalism, the class system, or imperialism.[11] This was the premise of the play *The English Rose*: if it were not for a nefarious land agent, there would be no Anglo-Irish problem. Churchill was eager to kill Hitler and a few dozen high-ranking Nazis after the war, but was genuinely horrified by suggestions that the German people should suffer mass executions and deportations. He wanted post-war Germany disarmed but readmitted to the concert of nations and not burdened with reparations.[12]

John Charmley (among others) has asked why Churchill pursued a war that would inevitably lead to the exhaustion of the British Empire and Soviet domination of half of Europe. The answer is that Churchill was dedicated to the preservation of the Empire and the containment of Communism, but these were not his first wartime priorities. On 10 August 1940 he wrote that proposals on "the post-war position of the British Empire are far too airy and speculative to be useful at the present moment, when we have to win the war in order to survive." He had "only one aim, to destroy Hitler."[13] Neville Chamberlain's stated war aim had been subtly but significantly different: to destroy "Hitlerism," that is, the German determination to dominate Europe by force of arms. That implied Chamberlain was prepared to make peace with a German government that renounced aggression, or even with Hitler himself, if he would only cease to be Hitlerian.[14] It was a slogan that held out the illusory hope of a truce, but it was not designed to rouse the nation to implacable resistance. Churchill mobilized the passion to fight by making the war personal, concentrating public attention on a single evildoer. As he assured the French government when they were close to capitulation, "Everything is subordinated to the British determination to destroy Hitler and his gang."[15]

As the only important British politician who had written a melodrama, Churchill was uniquely capable of framing the world conflict in such terms. And in 1940 melodrama was the only mode of rhetoric capable of sustaining British morale. As Clement Attlee readily admitted, "Without Churchill, Britain might have been defeated. I do not say we would have been defeated. But we might have been. He was so perfectly suited to fill a particular need; the need was so vital; and the absence of anybody of his quality was so blatant that one cannot imagine what would have happened if he had not been there."[16]

Richard Overy identifies the prevailing cultural mood of the 1930s – the mood that Churchill inherited – as despair. Socialists pronounced that capitalism had failed, eugenicists worried that the gene pool was deteriorating, psychologists determined that modern man was hopelessly unhappy and neurotic, progressives warned that fascism was on the march, and pacifists pleaded that another war would mean the end of everything. It all added up to a modernist sense that it was closing time for Western Civilization, as predicted by Oswald Spengler and Arnold Toynbee. Communists and fascists agreed on this much, each imagining themselves the vanguard of a new and virile culture that would sweep away the old. At the end of what W. H. Auden called "a low, dishonest decade," Joseph Goebbels recorded that he had come "to know the inner rottenness of English society by reading [Somerset] Maugham. This society will collapse if it is pushed hard enough. And we shall make sure of that."[17]

That pessimism fed into appeasement and the apathy of the Phony War. But Churchill still retained his nineteenth-century confidence in progress. Like modernism, melodrama portrayed the world as an arena of crisis, but unlike modernism, it promised happy endings. No matter how terrible the odds or how long the struggle, good would triumph in the end. Churchill dealt with public fears not through bland assurances (the great error of the Phony War) but by confirming and even amplifying those fears – and then promising ultimate victory. It was an obsolescent Victorian theatrical device, which would have been ridiculed a few years earlier, but in the crisis of 1940 it worked brilliantly. Through such alchemy was the Age of Anxiety transmuted into Their Finest Hour.

Churchill also echoed a speech by the younger Pitt, which he would quote in *A History of the English-Speaking Peoples*:

> [Mr. Fox] defies me to state, in one sentence, what is the object of the war. I know not whether I can do it in one sentence, but in one word I can tell him that it is "security"; security against a danger, the greatest that has ever threatened the world. It is security against a danger which never existed in any past period of society. It is security against a danger which in degree and extent was never equalled; against a danger which threatened all the nations of the earth; against a danger which has been resisted by all the nations of Europe, and resisted by none with so much success as by this nation, because by none has it been resisted so uniformly and with so much energy.[18]

Churchill called this great oratory: in fact it is flaccid, wordy, and redundant. "Security" is a notoriously weak noun, more appropriate to insurance salesmen, and if Churchill had used it he would have left the door open to a truce with Hitler. He therefore translated Pitt's words into the theatre of crisis:

> You ask, what is our policy? I will say: It is to wage war, by sea, land and air, with all our might and with all the strength that God can give us; to wage war against a monstrous tyranny, never surpassed in the dark, lamentable catalogue of human crime. That is our policy. You ask, what is our aim? I can answer in one word: It is victory, victory at all costs, victory in spite of all

> terror, victory, however long and hard the road may be; for without victory, there is no survival. Let that be realized; no survival for the British Empire, no survival for all that the British Empire has stood for, no survival for the urge and impulse of the ages, that mankind will move forward towards its goal.[19]

The Labour benches cheered, though Conservatives still treated Churchill with some reserve. Robert Rhodes James would become one of his sharpest critics, but he confirmed that this speech

> was a real turning point. It stirred the Commons to its depths. It came to the British people as a call to service and sacrifice. It rang round the world, and thrilled the many friends of Western civilization with the realization that Britain was going to fight. There were those in 1940 who believed that Britain should seek a negotiated settlement with Hitler: perhaps it was, technically, the wisest thing to do. But, after that first, unforgettable speech, such arguments lost whatever appeal they might have had. Here was the authentic voice of leadership and defiance. It was Churchill's outstanding quality as a war leader that he made the struggle seem not merely essential for national survival, but worthwhile and noble. No one – not even a child, as I was – who was in England in the summer of 1940 will ever forget the *cheerfulness* of the people. It was not even a gallows-humour mood. One caught Churchill's infectious spirit that this was a great time to be alive in; that Destiny had conferred a wonderful benefit upon us; and that these were thrilling days to live through. Of course, this mood could not be permanent, and the reality of sacrifice was a very different thing to the prospect. But the horror of war was to a remarkable extent exorcized by the exhilaration of the struggle, and I have no doubt that it was this that brought the British people through their ordeal.[20]

As John Colville remembered, "Churchill arrived on the scene like a jet-propelled rocket," imparting to a languid Whitehall bureaucracy the kind of dynamism usually (and wrongly) attributed to fascist regimes:

> The pace became frantic and totally unfamiliar methods had to be adopted. . . . The hours expanded from early morning till long after midnight. Telephones of various hues were installed in every nook and cranny. . . . Labels marked "Action This day" or "Report in Three Days" were attached to the ceaseless flow of minutes, dictated straight on to a typewriter, which poured out of the Prime Minister's bedroom, the cabinet room or even the Bath Room. The Chiefs of Staff, the Secretary to the cabinet, Ministers of all

kinds and dozens of almost unidentifiable characters came and went with bewildering speed. Replies were expected within minutes of questions being asked, staid officials actually took to running and bells rang continuously. Whitehall was galvanized and the office at No. 10 was pandemonium. We realised that we were at war.[21]

At 7.30 a.m. on 15 May Churchill was awakened by a telephone call from the French Premier Paul Reynaud. "We have been defeated," he said, in English. "We are beaten; we have lost the battle." Churchill was stunned: "Surely it can't have happened so soon?" German armor had broken through near Sedan, and was surging through a fifty-mile gap in the French defences. Churchill flew to Paris the next day. At the Quai D'Orsay General Gamelin briefed the British party on the military situation, with apparently unstoppable German columns racing toward the Channel:

The General talked perhaps five minutes without anyone saying a word. When he stopped there was a considerable silence. I then asked. "Where is the strategic reserve?" and, breaking into French, which I used indifferently (in every sense): "*Où est la masse de manœuvre?*" General Gamelin turned to me and, with a shake of the head and a shrug, said: "*Aucune.*"

There was another long pause. Outside in the garden of the Quai D'Orsay clouds of smoke arose from large bonfire, and I saw from the window venerable officials pushing wheel-barrows of archives on to them. Already therefore the evacuation of Paris was being prepared.

One is immediately struck by Churchill's skills as a playwright. He understood the impact of the astonishing reversal of fortune, the loaded pause, the wordless and tragic tableau. Most devastating of all is his deployment of the one-word line, which by itself illuminates the tragedy of France:

"*Aucune.*" I was dumbfounded. What were we to think of the great French Army and its highest chiefs? It had never occurred to me that any commanders having to defend five hundred miles of engaged front would have left themselves unprovided with a mass of manœuvre.[22]

Gamelin insisted that he said not *aucune* ("there are none") but *qu'il n'y en avait plus* ("there are no more") – that is, there had been a reserve, but it had already been committed elsewhere.[23] But both men had a motive for rewriting reality: saving face for Gamelin, transfixing the audience for Churchill.

At 9.00 p.m. on 16 May Churchill telegraphed "the mortal gravity of the hour" to the War Cabinet, and urged that the RAF provide the fighter and bomber cover that the French were requesting. He acknowledged that French resistance was crumbling, that papers were being burned at the Quai d'Orsay, and that "results cannot be guaranteed." But he was already looking ahead to the history books: "It would not be good historically if their requests were denied and their ruin resulted."[24] Later that night John Colville was thinking along similar lines as he dashed off an entry in his diary, knowing well that the events of the day "will be in every history book of the future." The Cabinet met at 11.00 p.m., and Colville rushed in each section of Churchill's telegram as it was decrypted. When they came to the phrase "the mortal gravity of the hour," Arthur Rucker muttered "he is still thinking of his books." One might expect that from Chamberlain's private secretary, but even Eric Seal, Churchill's secretary, grew impatient with his "blasted rhetoric."[25] Initially the Cabinet agreed to the French request, but when the Prime Minister returned from France and met them the following morning, he emphasized that he would only commit the aircraft if the French did everything possible to rally their forces. And that was not happening.

On 15 May Churchill had sent Franklin Roosevelt his first message as Prime Minister. He opened with a dramatic flourish ("the scene has darkened swiftly") and then assumed the classic posture of the melodramatic hero, with his back to the wall: "The enemy have a marked preponderance in the air. . . . The small countries are simply smashed up, one by one, like matchwood. . . . Mussolini will hurry in to share the loot of civilization. We expect to be attacked here ourselves, both from the air and by parachute and air borne troops in the near future. . . ." He followed this with a request for desperately needed aid: "forty or fifty of your older destroyers . . . several hundred of the latest types of aircraft . . . anti-aircraft equipment and ammunition," as well as steel and other supplies. "We shall go on paying dollars for as long as we can," he promised, "but I should like to feel reasonably sure that when we can pay no more, you will give us the stuff all the same." He conjured up all this blood and thunder to impress the President with the gravity of the situation, but it may well have been counterproductive. Churchill affirmed that "If necessary, we shall continue the war alone," implying that France could soon surrender, and then he suggested that Britain too might go under: "You may have a completely subjugated, Nazified Europe established with astonishing swiftness, and the weight may be more than we can bear."[26] If the crack of doom had arrived for Europe, then Roosevelt might have understandably concluded that he should keep his war materiel at home, to build up America's grossly unprepared defenses. He sent a noncommittal reply, which did not absolutely rule out loaning old destroyers to Britain, but gave numerous reasons why such a deal was not practical at the present time. Any requests for aid, he added, had to be assessed "in the light of our own defense needs and requirements."[27] Nevertheless, on the 19th Winston assured his son Randolph that he had a plan for victory: "I shall drag the United States in."[28] Of course he only dragged the Americans halfway in; the Japanese accomplished the rest.

At this point Roosevelt did not know Churchill well, and he had reason to doubt that Britain would prosecute the war vigorously. In February 1939 Lord Lothian had advised him that the Americans must now assume Britain's responsibilities as "the guardians of Anglo-Saxon civilisation." "I got mad clear through, and told him that just so long as he or Britishers like him took that attitude of complete despair, the British would not be worth saving anyway," Roosevelt exclaimed. "What the British need today is a good stiff grog, inducing not only the desire to save civilisation, but the continued belief that they can do it. In such an event, they will have a lot more support from their American cousins – don't you think so?"[29] His skepticism about British resolve might have been reinforced by Churchill's *While England Slept*, which he had recently received as a gift, though it is not clear that he had read it.[30] Nor can we be sure that he read *The World Crisis*, though he owned a copy[31] and had discussed H. M. Tomlinson's evisceration of the book with Supreme Court Justice Felix Frankfurter.[32] In his first wartime letter to Churchill, on 11 September 1939, Roosevelt said that he "much enjoyed reading" *Marlborough*, that very long tale of English resistance to a European tyrant, which Churchill had sent him as the volumes were published. But given that he misspelled the name ("Marlboro") this may have been a polite lie.[33] "I always disliked him," Roosevelt told Joseph P. Kennedy, ever since he had somehow been slighted by Churchill when he visited England during the First World War. "I'm giving him attention now [March 1940] because of his possibilities of being P.M. and wanting to keep my hand in. . . . I'm willing to help [the British] all I can but I don't want them to play me for a sucker."[34] The ambassador did not argue that point: "Mr. President, there is no doubt in my mind that Churchill has no particular love for the U.S. nor in his heart for you."[35]

On 17 May, as German armored spearheads approached the Channel, Cecil Beaton noted in his diary that "A mood of panic was gripping upper-class circles."[36] That included General Ironside, now Chief of the Imperial General Staff. "We stand faced by a completely Nazified Europe," he confided to his diary. "What chance have we in reality of continuing the struggle by ourselves with the French knocked out? . . . It seems hard to think that we are up against the crashing of the Empire. And yet we are most surely. Nothing could be more certain."[37] The following day he told Anthony Eden quite openly, and almost casually, "This is the end of the British Empire." As Eden later confessed, "militarily I did not see how he could be gainsaid."[38] And on the 19th his private secretary Oliver Harvey also noticed "Defeatism in London among the richer classes."[39] This was partly a function of the governing elite knowing better how desperate the military situation was: the full scope of the disaster was not always immediately reported by the press or the BBC. As one Ministry of Information officer put it later that month, "The whiter the collar the less the assurance."[40]

On 18 May the Ministry of Information issued the first in a series of Home Intelligence Reports, which found that public morale was shaky. "The Norwegian defeat staggered people," it concluded. "People came not to believe anything. The BBC suffered less than political leaders and the press, but all suffered," given that all of them (including Churchill) assured the public that the German threat had been contained. And then, on top of that shock:

> . . . came the invasion of Holland and Belgium. It must be remembered that the defence of the Low Countries had been continually built up in the press. . . . Not one person in a thousand could visualise the Germans breaking through into France. A certain amount of wishful thinking was still at work, and a relieved acceptance of Mr. Churchill as Prime Minister allowed people to believe that a change of leadership would, in itself, solve the consequences of Mr. Chamberlain. . . .

But with German armored columns tearing across northern France, "Reports sent in yesterday afternoon and this morning show that disquiet and personal fear has returned."[41] In another MOI memorandum that same day, a staffer proposed that the following propaganda line could restore public confidence: "This is not the battle of England alone but the battle of civilisation. It does not matter even if, at the worst, Britain herself is crushed. The empire is still there and it will go on arming and fighting until Germany is finally crushed."[42] This proposal was rejected, perhaps because the Ministry was not quite ready to entertain the possibility of the conquest of Britain. But it is striking that these three sentences read like a précis of the "Never Surrender" and "Finest Hour" speeches, delivered 4 and 18 June, respectively, when the military situation was still more desperate.

One of the most revealing dimensions of literary scholarship is the study of audience response. In addition to the MOI Home Intelligence Reports, Mass Observation conducted daily surveys of the popular mood, which together allow us to gauge how effective Churchill's speeches were amidst the vicissitudes of war in May–July 1940. They show that morale was highly volatile, depressed by bad news from the front and then boosted (up to a point) by Churchill's tonics. They also suggest that if Number 10 had been occupied by Halifax, a dismal public speaker, morale would have likely collapsed, especially in the face of the French surrender, in which case the government probably would have been ready to accept a compromise peace with Hitler. Given their applause for the Munich Agreement and (more recently) for Arthur

Bryant's *Unfinished Victory*, it is disturbingly probable that most of the press would have supported such a deal.

On 16 May Mass Observation reported that the public was becoming more anxious, but they "haven't begun to consider that we might be actually beaten. It just hasn't occurred to most people that we *can* be beaten. The old complacency has been shaken, but it persists. If suddenly shattered, there will be a morale explosion."[43] Three days later "people remain confident that we will win in the long run, but today still shows plenty of implicit or unconscious defeatism, and a few open references to German victory."[44]

In this climate of fragile morale, Churchill made his first radio broadcast as Prime Minster on 19 May, using some of his favorite literary devices. As French resistance crumbled, he held out the hope that the Allies might yet effect "a sudden transformation of the scene". He poetically summed up the conflict as an exalted aesthetic experience:

> If this is one of the most awe-striking periods in the long
> history of France and Britain
> it is also beyond all doubt the most sublime.
> Side by side,
> unaided except by their kith and kin in the great Dominions,
> and by the wide Empires which rest beneath their shield,
> the British and French people have advanced
> to rescue not only Europe only but mankind
> from the foulest and most soul-destroying tyranny
> which has ever darkened and stained the pages of history.[45]

"Unaided" evokes the melodramatic image of the underdog fighting against overwhelming odds, though in reality it was Germany that was fighting a broad coalition without allies of her own – and winning. When Duff Cooper disparaged the Italian Army in a 10 June broadcast, Churchill advised that "it is a well-known rule of war policy to praise the courage of your opponent which enhances your victory when gained," a principle he followed when he was fighting Field Marshal Rommel.[46]

By 20 May German Panzers reached the English Channel at Abbeville, cutting off the British Expeditionary Force (BEF), the Belgian Army, and some French Army units. Two days later Mass Observation reported that public confidence had been seriously shaken by the German breakthrough, but "The result of the speeches given in the last few days by Churchill and Duff Cooper is to engender a feeling of relief, not because the situation is not serious, but because the people feel they know the worst, which is a new experience for them."[47] By May 23 there was

> A noticeable increase in cheerfulness and general calm, a distinct decrease in pessimism and extreme nervousness . . . for the time being. The intense gloom which affected many in London yesterday, mainly among the middle-classes, but also some of the working-classes, is not conspicuous today.
>
> The feeling that a big effort is going to be required and that our leaders are capable of asking for it . . . is growing. The feeling had a big value in liberating people from the general feeling of apathy, inactivity, and ineffectiveness which seriously depressed and worried a large number. . . . The new feeling is frequently reflected in verbatim material today, comments like "We'll soon be doing something." "I'm prepared to do anything." "Well, everyone's in it now."[48]

Now the British people wanted their government to mobilize them fully for the war effort. Anthony Eden issued a radio appeal for the Local Defence Volunteers on 14 May, and by late June half a million had signed up. In war industries workers commonly accepted seven-day workweeks and 10–12 hour shifts without government diktats, and strike activity fell to its lowest level on record.[49]

But the public mood could fluctuate radically from day to day. On 24 May, when it was apparent that a British counterattack at Arras had failed to break the German encirclement, Mass Observation reported the following overheard conversation among trade unionists:

> "I've never seen the working-class change so much in such a short time. Absolutely down, they are."
>
> "Weren't they always?"
>
> "No, not like this. Up till now, they've been cheerful. They've said, 'Oh, we'll pull through all right in the end.' But now, – they don't care. They simply don't care. Do you know, our women went round canvassing for the Housewives Union, and some of them, especially some of the younger housewives they talked to – have got to the stage when they would more or less welcome Hitler here. They say it couldn't be worse, and they'd at least have their husbands back."
>
> "That's right. You see, they think to themselves well it'd be something to have a good night's rest, and be able to switch on the lights when they chose, and so on. They say it can't be worse, so what's the good of fighting? I can see that if the morale goes on the decline as steep as it is at the moment, there won't be much resistance to him, when he does come."[50]

A secret document issued by the Ministry of Information on 25 May reported that "Although there seems to be general confidence about the ultimate outcome of the war, there is considerable confusion in most of the Regions about the present military situation in France." The report warned that morale would sink if a planned French counterattack did not begin soon. (It never materialized.) "The effect of Lord Haw Haw [William Joyce, former deputy leader of the British Union of Fascists, now broadcasting propaganda for the Germans] is considered to be extremely insidious," the report continued, "and this danger is underestimated by the BBC and the Government, who do not fully appreciate to what extent this propaganda is believed." On the same day, Mass Observation confirmed that:

> Depression is quite definitely up. . . . A large number of people today are finding themselves unable to express any opinion or to know what to think. . . . On the whole, the quality of optimism has violently declined, and the quality of pessimism deepened. The public mind is in a chaotic condition and ready to be plunged into the depths of an utterly bewildered, shocked, almost unbelieving dismay. The whole structure of national belief would seem to be rocking gently.[51]

On 27 May Mass Observation found a pervasive "undercurrent of anxiety present," as well as "a growing section of women who say that they prefer not to think about it, and deliberately refrain from listening to the wireless." In parts of the country "there was an increased reluctance to express an opinion." The British people still did not entirely identify with the war effort, though "this identification and general realisation of the situation has been rapidly growing since Mr. Churchill became Prime Minister." The Germans had involved their own population in the war drama "with a vivid technique of frequent broadcast news bulletins including vivid despatches, eye-witness and participant accounts direct from the front. . . . The effect of this is to identify the mass of civilian listeners with the armed conflict, to make them feel the excitements and tensions and successes, personally." Except for reports of RAF successes, there was little of this in Britain, where the government and the media preferred to deal with bad news by providing no news.[52]

In contrast, Churchill's broadcasts were effective precisely because "he breaks every accepted rule of broadcasting," observed BBC reporter Richard Dimbleby. "He drops his voice where he should raise it, he alters the recognized system of punctuation to suit himself (some of his scripts were virtually unintelligible to anyone else), he speaks much of the time with anything but clarity." And yet he commanded "a silent and appreciative audience of millions, following every word and phrase with relish." Like every modern artist, Churchill arrested his audience by violating aesthetic canons. Had he spoken with the usual BBC polish, the effect would have been soporific, but his own idiosyncratic voice created an air of authenticity. The very lack of clarity forced listeners to pay close attention. He had adopted a method of madness similar to Stanley Baldwin's, an apparent artlessness that was in fact meticulously artistic. His recording engineer told Dimbleby "that he had never met anyone who worked so hard on his script beforehand as the Prime Minister. Nor had anyone been more willing to persevere until a recording was exactly right."[53]

On 26 May Churchill asked John Martin (one of his Private Secretaries) to look up a morale-boosting quotation in George Borrow's *The Bible in Spain*. It was: "Fear not the result, for either shall thy end be a majestic and an enviable one, or God shall perpetuate thy reign upon the waters." Note that it does not promise victory; it guarantees only a beautiful ending.[54] And Alexander Cadogan still thought the Prime Minister was "too rambling and romantic and sentimental and temperamental."[55]

The following day the War Cabinet debated a French suggestion that Mussolini be asked to mediate a possible peace settlement, which was supported by Halifax. Churchill warned that "The approach proposed was not only futile, but involved us in a deadly danger," insofar as Germany and the world would interpret it as a sign of Allied weakness. After promising nothing less than victory just two weeks earlier, Churchill realized that even to hint at a truce would destroy public confidence. "If the worst came to the worst," he asserted, "it would not be a bad thing for this country to go down fighting for the other countries which had been overcome by the Nazi tyranny." Halifax countered that a decision to fight on would mean "that the future of the country turned on whether the enemy's bombs happened to hit our aircraft factories. He was prepared to take that risk if our independence was at stake; but if it was not at stake he would think it right to accept an offer which would save the country from avoidable disaster."[56] As Halifax later confided to his diary:

> At the 4:30 Cabinet we had a long and rather confused discussion about, nominally, the approach to Italy, but also largely about general policy in the event of things going really badly in France. I thought Winston talked the most frightful rot, also Greenwood, and after bearing it for some time I said exactly what I thought of them, adding that if that was really their view, and if it came to the point, our ways must separate. Winston, surprised and mellowed, and, when I repeated the same thing in the garden, was full of apologies and affection. But it does drive me to despair when he works himself up into a passion of emotion when he ought to make his brain think and reason.[57]

A few days later Chips Channon "reflected on Halifax's extraordinary character; his high principles, his engaging charm and grand manner," but also noted "his eel-like qualities and, above all, his sublime treachery which is never deliberate, and, always to him, a necessity dictated by a situation. Means are nothing to him, only ends."[58] Early drafts of *The Second World War* stated that Halifax was prepared to "buy off" Mussolini, even suggesting to the Italian ambassador (in a 25 May conversation) that Gibraltar, Malta, and Suez were bargaining chips.[59] Of the five members of the War Cabinet, only Churchill firmly refused negotiation: Chamberlain, Attlee, and Arthur Greenwood all tried to strike a middle position, opposing negotiation at the present moment but not ruling it out in the future.[60]

On May 28 the Belgian Army surrendered. Recalling this crisis in *The Second World War*, Churchill wrote "It was a severe experience for me, bearing so heavy an overall responsibility, to watch during these days in flickering glimpses this drama in which control was impossible."[61] That day, speaking to ministers outside the War Cabinet, Churchill delivered one of the great monologues of his career. As Hugh Dalton (Minister of Economic Welfare) recorded it, he dismissed out of hand any talk of peace negotiations. The evacuation from Dunkirk was only beginning, but Churchill may have already seen the dramatic potential of such a miraculous escape: "If we could get 100,000 away, that would be a magnificent performance," though that may be Dalton's paraphrase rather than an exact quotation. "It would of course be said, and with some truth, that what was now happening in Northern France would be the greatest British military defeat for many centuries." But even if France surrendered, the spectacle of Britain fighting on alone would generate "an immense wave of feeling, not least in the USA which, having done nothing much to help us so far, might even enter the war." At the very worst, he was fully prepared for a grand finale: "We shall go on and we shall fight it out, here or elsewhere, and if at last the long story is to end, it were better it should end, not through surrender, but only when we are rolling senseless on the ground." Here Dalton ostensibly quoted Churchill directly, but later he wrote a yet more stirring version in the margins of the page, a version that sounds more like Churchill: "If this long island story of ours is to end at last, let it end only when each one of us lies choking in his own blood upon the ground."[62]

This was standard melodrama. In 1893 an outnumbered British company was wiped out by the Matabele, and two years later the battle was commemorated by Drury Lane Theatre in *Cheer, Boys, Cheer*. "My men, you see how it is with us," declaims the stage commander, "we've got to die – and we're going to do it like Englishmen and sell our lives as dearly as we can. Our fathers have died that our country might be great – it's our turn to-day."[63]

In contrast, Churchill's own version of his remarks, in *The Second World War*, was far more matter-of-fact: "Then I said quite casually, and not treating it as a point of special significance: 'Of course, whatever happens at Dunkirk, we shall fight on.' " Then the ministers cheered wildly:

> Quite a number seemed to jump up from the table and come running to my chair, shouting and patting me on the back. There is no doubt that had I at this juncture faltered at all in the leading of the nation I should have been hurled out of office. I was sure that every Minister was ready to be killed quite soon, and have all his family and possessions destroyed, rather than give in. In this they represented the House of Commons and almost all the people. It fell to me in these coming days and months to express their sentiments on suitable occasions.[64]

Leo Amery's diary confirms Dalton's more histrionic account,[65] but Churchill recognized that only bad playwrights focus exclusively on the hero. He could not emphasize his own role in keeping Britain in the fight without revealing the existence of faint hearts in the public at large and in his own government. He always insisted that he only gave voice to the patriotic fervor of the British people.[66] Therefore, the supporting players in *The Second World War* were always cheering him on.

On 29 May, when the newspapers reported that the British Expeditionary Force was nearly surrounded with little chance of escape, Mass Observation found that "whereas before people were more confident in victory, without a glimmering of what the struggle for victory might mean, now they realise to a considerable extent what they are up against."[67] Already 40,000 men had been evacuated, but Cadogan still feared that "the end will be awful. . . . WSC rather theatrically bulldoggish. . . . That is Winston's fault – theatricality."[68]

In his efforts to keep France in the war, Churchill was flamboyantly theatrical. On 31 May he told the Supreme War Council (a body representing the British and French premiers and anyone they chose to bring with them), "It would be better far that the civilisation of Western Europe, with all its achievements, should come to a tragic but splendid end, than that the two great Democracies should linger on, stripped of all that made life worth living."[69] General Edward Spears (Churchill's personal representative to Reynaud) noted that this speech was only "heard by a tiny audience of men who, with one or two exceptions, were already half enemies." True, "they were moved," but "perhaps it was only [their] artistic sense that had been impressed, for it had been a grand performance."[70] And two days earlier Churchill had assured the War Cabinet that "Never Surrender" was not meant to imply "that troops which were cut off from hope of relief and were without food or without water or without ammunition should attempt to continue the struggle."[71]

By Sunday 2 June the Dunkirk evacuation was nearly complete and far more successful than anyone had dared hope. Even Alexander Cadogan, who had faulted Churchill's "theatricality" the previous Wednesday, allowed himself to indulge in dramatics: "come the 4 corners of the world in arms!"[72]

Or as Nella Last, a housewife from Barrow, recorded: "I felt as if deep inside me was a harp that vibrated and sang. . . . The story made me feel part of something that was undying and never old."[73] Churchill would unleash a full complement of theatrical metaphors ("Suddenly the scene has cleared . . .") and literary allusions in his 4 June "Dunkirk speech" to the House of Commons. He seized and used the verbal weapon that Arthur Greenwood had used against him in the Norway debate: "Wars are not won by evacuations." He compared RAF airmen to the knights of Tennyson's "Morte d'Arthur":

> When every morning brought a noble chance,
> And every chance brought out a noble knight.

There were suggestions of the threat of yet-to-be-imagined Wellsian super-weapons:

> We are assured that novel methods will be adopted, and when we see the originality of malice, the ingenuity of aggression, which our enemy displays, we may certainly prepare ourselves for every kind of novel stratagem and every kind of brutal and treacherous manoeuvre. I think that no idea is so outlandish that it should not be considered and viewed with a searching, but at the same time, I hope, with a steady eye.

He concluded with a very old but potent dramatic stratagem. "Claptrap" was defined earlier in this book as a speech where the hero, with his back to the wall, hurls defiance in the face of the villain to general applause. Churchill saw it used in Jules Verne's *Michael Strogoff* and probably other melodramas, and used it himself in his March 1914 Bradford speech on the Irish crisis. Here is a better known example, and note the foreshadowing of the ultimate reversal of fortunes:

> Even though large tracts of Europe and many old and famous States have fallen or may fall into the grip of the Gestapo and all the odious apparatus of Nazi rule, we shall not flag or fail. We shall go on to the end. We shall fight in France, we shall fight on the seas and oceans, we shall fight with growing confidence and growing strength in the air, we shall defend our island, whatever the cost may be. We shall fight on the beaches, we shall fight on the landing grounds, we shall fight in the fields and in the streets, we shall fight in the hills; we shall never surrender, and even if, which I do not for a moment believe, this island or a large part of it were subjugated and starving, then our Empire beyond the seas, armed and guarded by the British Fleet, would carry on the struggle, until, in God's good time, the new world, with all its power and might, steps forth to the rescue and the liberation of the old.[74]

Just a few days earlier he had privately vowed that, if Britain were overrun by the Wehrmacht, the Cabinet would die fighting in the last ditch. But these last lines now suggested a more sensible strategy: carrying on the struggle from abroad, as other Allied governments-in-exile were doing. (In fact, in July he instructed Eden to ask Army commanders if their soldiers would obey an order to evacuate to Canada: they concluded that many would refuse.)[75] On 4 June, when popular morale was fragile, Churchill had to promise ultimate victory, and his timing was perfect: he spoke on the 125th anniversary of Waterloo. Even Chips Channon was won over:

> . . . he was eloquent, and oratorical, and used magnificent English; several Labour members cried. . . . How the atmosphere has changed from only a few weeks ago when idiotic MPs were talking academic nonsense about our restoring independence to Warsaw and Prague.
>
> Jock Colville tells me that the Admiralty is fantastic now; people who were at each other's throats a few weeks ago are now intimate and on the best of terms. Winston darts in and out, a mountain of energy and good-nature. . . .[76]

Harold Nicolson called it "the finest speech that I have ever heard."[77] His wife Vita Sackville-West fervently agreed, though she (like nearly all of the British people) never heard Churchill deliver it: the BBC only broadcast excerpts read by an announcer. "Even repeated by the announcer it sent shivers (not of fear) down my spine," she told Harold. "I think that one of the reasons why one is stirred by his Elizabethan phrases is that one feels the whole massive backing of power and resolve behind them, like a great fortress: they are never words for words' sake."[78] Nicolson knew that French ground forces were now demoralized and outnumbered more than two to one, but "even if they lose Paris, it is not the end in so far as France is concerned. I feel so much in the spirit of Winston's great speech that I could face a world of enemies."[79] One veteran later recalled his narrow escape from Dunkirk, where:

> the Nazis kicked my unit to death. We left everything behind when we got out; some of my men didn't even have boots. They dumped us along the roads near Dover, and all of us were scared and dazed, and the memory of the Panzers could set us screaming at night. Then he got on the wireless and said that we'd never surrender. And I cried when I heard him. . . . And I thought to hell with the Panzers, WE'RE GOING TO WIN.[80]

Again, he had not actually heard Churchill, who disliked radio as a medium and only broadcast five times between May and December 1940.[81] But this was the effect that claptrap is designed to produce on an audience, and in Parliament Churchill had just delivered the finest claptrap ever uttered.

Nevertheless, the following day both a Ministry of Information survey and Mass Observation independently noted a mood of growing public pessimism. MO reported:

> Churchill's speech has been mentioned frequently and spontaneously this morning. There does not appear to have been a great deal in it which was unexpected, but its grave tone has again made some impression, and may be in part the cause of the depression.
>
> Some people think that the end of his speech was a suggestion that France might make a separate peace. Some said that he was preparing us for another undefined blow. A few say that he always takes a gloomy view. A general and rather vague effect of the speech is to increase an already existing suspicion about our association with France.[82]

Those listeners were not wrong to read doubts about France into the speech. The 13 May and 4 June speeches recalled a series of defiant statements Georges Clemenceau had issued in 1918: "*Politique intérieure, je fais la guerre; politique étrangère, je fais la guerre. Je fais toujours la guerre.*" "We will fight them on the Loire, then on the Garonne if we have to, and even on the Pyrenees. And if, finally, we are chased out of the Pyrenees we will continue the war overseas, but as for making peace, never!" As the Allies reeled before the Summer 1918 German offensive, Clemenceau personally told Churchill, "I will fight in front of Paris; I will fight in Paris; I will fight behind Paris."[83] Churchill's stirring phrases of 1940 were not plagiarisms, they were allusions: he deliberately echoed Clemenceau's words in the hope of stiffening French resistance.[84] In a 10 June telegram to Franklin Roosevelt requesting American aid, Paul Reynaud affirmed that he would fight in front of and behind Paris, but spoiled the effect by leaving out any mention of fighting *in* Paris, which would be declared an open city.[85]

That day the French government abandoned Paris and Italy entered the war. "There has never been such a flourish of trumpets to announce a grand entry," Colville wryly commented, "but the Italians have a sense of the melodramatic."[86] On 11–12 June Churchill and his entourage were in Briare, on the Loire, for a meeting of the Supreme War Council. It was clear that most members of the French government had given up, and responded to Churchill's demands for further resistance with apathy bordering on resentment. RAF bombers based in southern France were ready to strike at northern Italy, but the French blocked the runways, fearing retaliation from the legendary Aeronautica Regia. The allies could only agree on a plan to send British units to hold Brittany. General H. L. Ismay (Churchill's chief staff officer) knew that this was madness, that if anything the British had to begin evacuating their remaining forces in France. But when he suggested at least delaying reinforcements to Brittany, Churchill was indignant: "Certainly not. It would look very bad in history if we were to do any such thing."[87] From the vantage of today, it looks very bad that Churchill was allowing "the verdict of history" to drive military policy and risk a second Dunkirk. It would have looked much worse if General Alan Brooke, then a BEF commander, had not persuaded Churchill to begin the evacuation.[88]

On the 13th Churchill flew to Tours to consult with the French government in a meeting of the Supreme War Council – its final meeting. Reynaud began with an announcement that stunned the British delegation: General Maxime Weygand, the French supreme commander, "had declared the preceding evening that the situation of the army was desperate, and that an armistice should be asked for at once." He added that "The majority of the Cabinet had not endorsed this view, but if Paris fell, and this seemed inevitable, the question would have to be raised again." France could only continue the fight if President Roosevelt promised to aid her. Confronted with this ultimatum, Churchill deployed his last remaining weapon: words. He worked himself into a oratorical fury, again hurling back at the French the heroic phrases of Clemenceau: "We must fight, we will fight, and that is why we must ask our friends to fight on. . . . We ask you to fight on as long as possible, if not in Paris, at least behind Paris, in the provinces, down to the sea, then, if need be, in North Africa."[89]

The Supreme War Council agreed to appeal once more to Roosevelt. As the meeting broke up, Churchill noticed Charles de Gaulle. The French general had supported waging guerrilla war against the Germans, and Edward Spears had assured Churchill that he "was completely staunch." At one point Churchill had hoped that Reynaud would give de Gaulle command of the French armies. Now, "Greeting him, I said in a low tone, in French: '*L'homme du destin.*' "[90]

That, at least, is what he wrote in his memoirs. Neither de Gaulle nor his aide-de-camp, who was standing by him, remembered any such words. Years later, when the discrepancy was pointed out to him, de Gaulle shrugged, saying: "You know, Churchill is a romantic type."[91] It may well have been a dramatic embellishment, inspired by Churchill's Bonapartist fixation and perhaps specifically by George Bernard Shaw's Napoleon play, *The Man of Destiny*. In any event, de Gaulle significantly shared his predilection for dramatic metaphors, and drew on one to describe the conference at Tours: "The courtyard and corridors of the prefecture were filled with a crowd of members of Parliament, civil servants, and journalists whom the news had attracted and who formed, as it were, the tumultuous chorus of a tragedy nearing its catastrophe."[92]

Then Churchill flew home to Hendon airport, while Reynaud drove to the nearby Château de Cangey to meet with his Cabinet. The day before Reynaud had promised his ministers that Churchill would speak with them when he next visited France, but he did not mention that to Churchill, and the meeting never took place. When the Cabinet learned that Churchill had already left France, they were thoroughly demoralized. "A terrible mistake had been made," General Spears recalled:

> I sensed that all these Frenchmen were looking to Churchill for a lead. I knew the formidable impact his eloquence and will always had on his auditors. I felt he might have carried them with him in his determination to fight on. He was the leader they really recognised and looked to. They would have feared his scorn and been glad to lay some at least of the responsibility they found so irksome on his broad shoulders.
>
> Something perhaps irreparable had happened. An opportunity that might not recur had been missed.[93]

On 11 and 12 June Churchill had warned Roosevelt that France might drop out of the war, and urged him "to strengthen Reynaud to the utmost you can and try to tip the balance in favor of the best and longest possible French resistance."[94] On the 13th, before leaving for France, he dashed off a quick message warning Roosevelt that the "crisis has arrived. . . . Anything you can say or do to help them now may make a difference." He even suggested that an American naval squadron be sent to Berehaven, one of the "treaty ports" that the United Kingdom had handed over to Eire in 1938, but Roosevelt was hardly going to antagonize Irish-American voters in an election year.[95] He did send a message to both Reynaud and Churchill, which Churchill and the War Cabinet read as an American promise to join the fight against Germany.

It was nothing of the sort. Roosevelt offered only platitudes ("The magnificent resistance of the French and British armies has profoundly impressed the American people"), concluding with a clear refusal to commit the US Navy to anything.[96] But Churchill seized on it and urged Roosevelt to publish it at once, "in order that it may play the decisive part in turning the course of world history. It will I am sure decide the French to deny Hitler a patched-up peace with France."[97] Roosevelt refused. He emphasized that his previous message "was in no sense intended to commit and did not commit the Government to Military participation in support of Allied governments," patiently reminding Churchill that the United States Constitution gave the President no such authority.[98] At this time the Gallup Poll reported that, when asked who was likely to win the war, American public opinion was equally divided between Britain, Germany, and Don't Know.[99]

Reynaud's appeal to Roosevelt had backfired among the British public, who interpreted it (correctly) as a sign of desperation. A Ministry of Information survey of morale found "a guilty admiration for Hitler's fulfilment of his prophecies" alongside growing impatience with the government's "inefficient and inadequate preparedness. . . . Phrases like 'We will never surrender'; 'We will fight in the streets; on the hills ------' are being criticized in the light of inadequate mobilization of men and materials."[100]

The German Army marched into Paris on 14 June. The following day, with the French war effort collapsing, Churchill dispatched several messages to his present and prospective allies – messages which reveal that, in his mind, only strokes of drama could save the situation. One was sent to the Dominion prime ministers, who were promised that even if France surrendered, the United Kingdom would continue the fight and ultimately prevail. The Germans might well bomb and invade Britain, but "I personally believe that the spectacle of the fierce struggle and carnage in our Island will draw the United States into the war."[101] That evening Churchill sent Roosevelt two more messages, less than two hours apart. First, as if Roosevelt's earlier refusal had not registered in his mind, Churchill once again insisted that "A declaration that the United States will, if necessary, enter the war might save France."[102] In his second message he explained that he was immediately requesting not actual soldiers or weapons, but a theatrical gesture:

> When I speak of the United States entering the war I am, of course, not thinking in terms of an expeditionary force, which I know is out of the question. What I have in mind is the tremendous moral effect that such an American decision would produce, not merely in France but also in all the democratic countries of the world, and, in the opposite sense, on the German and Italian peoples.[103]

When Colville told him that the French were drifting toward capitulation, Churchill warned that they would be punished in the history books: "If they surrender without consulting us we shall never forgive. We shall blacken their name for a thousand years!" Ambassador Kennedy then telephoned, and according to Colville the Prime Minister "poured into his ears a flood of eloquence about the part that America could and should play in saving civilisation. Referring to promises of industrial and financial support, he said such an offer 'would be a laughing-stock on the stage of history.' "

"It was at once the most dramatic and fantastic evening I have ever spent," Colville recorded in his diary. Churchill "was in high spirits, repeating poetry, dilating on the drama of the present situation." The BEF had abandoned all its heavy equipment at Dunkirk: the only weapons Churchill had left were literary. Obviously the telegrams sent to Roosevelt were divorced from reality. Edward R. Murrow and other American journalists who reported the Blitz did increase American willingness to aid Britain,[104] but the spectacle of London in flames did not bring the United States into the war. In June 1940 Americans were still overwhelmingly isolationist, and in any case, as Churchill conceded, they did not yet have an army remotely capable of fighting in Europe. Nevertheless, he presumed that the spectacle of Britain besieged would irresistibly induce the Americans to gallop to the rescue, something that often occurred in Victorian melodramas – for example, *Michael Strogoff*. A declaration of war signed by President Roosevelt would turn the tide of battle, even if it was a scrap of paper backed by no armed force. If Roosevelt refused even that, he would be hooted off the stage in the great world drama now unfolding. And if the French surrendered, Britain would retaliate by humiliating them in the history books. As Churchill remarked to Colville that day, "If words counted, we should win this war."[105]

Roosevelt did not respond. Over the next two months, in Britain's direst hour, he did not write to Churchill at all.

With hope of American intervention fading, Churchill seriously considered a yet more dramatic and desperate stroke. Britain and France had already established a number of joint ventures to coordinate their warmaking efforts: the Supreme War Council; an Anglo-French Coordinating Committee, chaired by Jean Monnet, for economic cooperation; an Anglo-French Industrial Council; joint purchases from the United States; financial collaboration, including a sterling-franc link; talks between the colonial ministers of the two countries; and exchange of scientific information, including nuclear research.[106] On both sides of the Channel, there were voices calling for a closer Anglo-French union as a bulwark against German aggression, and the British Foreign Office was seriously studying the possibilities. Over lunch on 13 June, Monnet told Leo Amery that (in Amery's paraphrase) "If France is to sustain the terrible ordeal of continued struggle in her own country and then carry on outside if necessary we must make it clear that we stand in with her in making good her losses afterwards and in fact that we are for the war and afterwards in effect one country. A clear promise to do this coupled with some dramatic gesture emphasising our unity would help a lot."[107] The following day Amery sent a memorandum to the War Cabinet insisting that victory was only possible if France continued to fight and the United States joined the Allies – and that required a "dramatic and spectacular" gesture. Britain and France must immediately proclaim "the real, complete, immediate and enduring unity of the two countries, acting as one, without regard to separate interests," with a joint Cabinet and some kind of joint Parliament.[108]

On 15 June the War Cabinet considered the memorandum. At first the ministers were skeptical, Churchill especially. But as the discussion progressed, he recalled:

> I was somewhat surprised to see the staid, solid, experienced politicians of all parties engage themselves so passionately in an immense design whose implications and consequences were not in any way thought out. I did not resist, but yielded easily to these generous surges which carried our resolves to a very high level of unselfish and undaunted action.

It was a reversal of the usual order of things: Churchill's practical misgivings were overcome by the dramatic fervor of his Cabinet colleagues. "In these days," as he later wrote, "the War Cabinet were in a state of unusual emotion."[109]

On the morning of 16 June de Gaulle arrived at London's Hyde Park Hotel, where the French ambassador André Corbin and Jean Monnet offered their astounding proposal:

> It has occurred to us that some sensational stroke, by throwing a new factor into the situation, might be what is needed to change the state of mind and, in any case, to strengthen M. Paul Reynaud in his intention to go to Algiers. We have therefore worked out with Sir Robert Vansittart, [formerly] Permanent Undersecretary at the Foreign Office, a plan which does seem striking. It would consist of a proposal for the union of France and England. . . . The two countries would decide on the fusion of their administrations, the pooling of their resources and losses – in short, a complete linking of their respective destinies. In face of such a proposal, made in such circumstances, it is possible that our Ministers may wish to think again and, at least, postpone surrender. But we still have to get the plan adopted by the British government. You alone can obtain that from Mr. Churchill.

De Gaulle realized that the plan was wholly impractical – but he understood that, as a *coup de théâtre*, it might rescue his country from seemingly inevitable defeat:

> It was clear to me at once that the grandeur of the thing in any case made its rapid realization impossible. It was obvious that one could not, by an exchange of notes, even in principle fuse England and France together, including their institutions, their interests, and their Empires, supposing this were desirable. Even the points in the proposal that were capable of being settled practically – for instance, the sharing of war damage – would demand complex negotiations. But the offer addressed by the British government to

> ours did involve a manifestation of solidarity which might take on a real significance. Above all, I thought, like M. Corbin and M. Monnet, that the proposal was of a nature to provide M. Paul Reynaud, in the supreme crisis in which he was plunged, with an element of comfort and, vis-à-vis his ministers, an argument for tenacity. I consented, therefore, to do what I could with Mr. Churchill to get him to adopt it.[110]

De Gaulle made exactly that argument when he met Churchill over lunch at the Carlton Club. When the Prime Minister warned "it's an enormous mouthful," the General granted the practical difficulties, but emphasized that the "gesture" was essential, and Churchill was ultimately persuaded.[111]

Even John Colville, the cautious civil servant, was carried away by this "stupendous" stroke. "I am not clear about the details of this epoch-making idea; but . . . it sounded inspiring, something which will revive the flagging energies of the French and invigorate our own people. It is a historic document and its effects will be more wide-ranging than anything that has occurred this century – and more permanent?" The War Cabinet met at 3.00 p.m. to discuss "some dramatic announcement which might strengthen M. Reynaud's hand." Robert Vansittart, together with de Gaulle, Monnet, and René Pleven (the last two would be future architects of European integration), had already drafted a proclamation. "It was recognised that such a proclamation raised some very big questions with which it was difficult to deal at such short notice" – a crashing understatement. The mind staggers at the thought of the complications. What would the new federation be called? Would it adhere to English Common Law or the Napoleonic Code? Who would command the combined armed forces? (De Gaulle's name was on everyone's lips, including Churchill's.) Who would head the common War Cabinet? (Churchill evidently suggested Reynaud.) How could the two national legislatures be merged, and in which language would they deliberate? What would be the position of the King, who, as Colville noted, "does not know what is being done to his Empire."[112] (Chamberlain was dispatched to tell him.) And how could all this be worked out in a few days, while the Wehrmacht was dashing across France? The answer is that many leading men in the French and British governments were convinced that nothing could save them from catastrophe but a coup that left their national audiences gasping. As the minutes recorded: "The Prime Minister said that his first instinct had been against the idea, but in this grave crisis we must not let ourselves be accused of a lack of imagination. Some dramatic announcement was clearly necessary to keep the French going."[113]

At 3.55 p.m. the Cabinet learned that the French Council of Ministers would meet at 5.00 to decide whether to seek an armistice. Reynaud had told de Gaulle over the telephone that if the British endorsed the union plan by that deadline, he could persuade his colleagues to fight on. Their minds concentrated wonderfully, the King's ministers swiftly wrapped up their deliberations and agreed on a declaration "that France and Great Britain shall no longer be two nations, but one Franco-British Union," with common citizenship and shared responsibility for repairing war damage within their borders. They would create "joint organs of defence, foreign, financial, and economic policies," thus greatly accelerating the process of intergovernmental coordination that was already under way. Command of the armed forces would be entrusted to a combined War Cabinet, which would "govern from wherever it best can" – a realistic but unhappy choice of words, given that the French Cabinet was currently fleeing the Germans. And the document vaguely asserted that "The two Parliaments will be formally associated," with no further details.[114] Obviously, as a working constitution it left a great deal to be worked out, but as theatre it was electric. "That rough Cabinet," Churchill later recalled, "... was carried off its feet. It was like a religious revival."[115]

De Gaulle read the text over the telephone to Reynaud, who scribbled it down with growing excitement. "This sensational turn of events could only fill me with joy," Reynaud later wrote, precisely the dramatic effect the British Cabinet had hoped for. But most of the French ministers dismissed it as at best hopelessly unrealistic, or at worst a plot to reduce France to a British colony. Convinced that Britain would soon capitulate, Marshal Philippe Pétain called it "fusion with a corpse." Without putting the proposal to a vote, Reynaud resigned. At 11.30 p.m. a new Cabinet was formed under Pétain, which met for ten minutes and decided to seek an armistice from Germany.

The union plan was conceived as theatre and failed as theatre. "At the purely tactical level," explained the historian Avi Shlaim, "the idea relied on an element of surprise in order to make a dramatic impact." General Weygand had Reynaud's telephone line tapped, so he had advance warning of the plan and lobbied the ministers against it before the Cabinet met. As Georges Mandel, one of Reynaud's strongest supporters, put it, "it was like pressing the trigger and the cartridge not going off." Shlaim has argued that if the British proposal had come just three days earlier, before the collapse of French morale, it might have succeeded. In that case, the governments-in-exile of the occupied countries could have joined in, and the result might well have been a European Union created in 1940 led by Great Britain.[116]

As a 20 June retrospective by Mass Observation explained, during the Phony War the government and the press had lulled the public into believing that Germany would be contained by the allied fleets and the Maginot Line. That complacency was shattered by lightning German victories in Scandinavia, the Low Countries, and France – and Hitler exploited those triumphs as only a master dramatist could. "Hitler, whose devilish powers of deception in the execution of his schemes would have made Caesar Borgia green with envy, time and again announced beforehand with amazing audacity what he intended doing – and did it," recalled Edward Spears. "It seems to have been one of his mental traits to challenge providence and opponents he despised by writing chapters of history before they occurred and then ensuring that events conformed with his forecasts."[117] The same terrifying device was employed by Shakespeare's Richard III, Marlowe's Tamburlaine, and Victorian melodramatic villains, who invariably revealed their schemes in asides to the audience. As Mass Observation concluded:

> The effect of all this was, by late May, enormously to heighten the prestige of Hitler, and by no means only in the eyes of enemies or neutrals. This was particularly so among women, and for many he has become a secret and somewhat mystical astrological figure. Whatever he said he would do, he would do it. Low's cartoon in the *Evening Standard* of May 30, showing Hitler in a charabanc looking across the channel, and on the side of the machine "LONDON, AUGUST 18", on the back, a list of other capitals and dates, each successfully ticked. Apparently intended to make Hitler look ridiculous, the unconscious effect on ordinary people was precisely the opposite.
>
> Throughout morale investigations in late May, innumerable unconscious tributes to Hitler, and innumerable expressions of an inferiority feeling towards Germany, were obtained. It is, of course, the deliberate object of German propaganda to attain exactly this end. The propaganda of events backed by the propaganda of words has been very successful in this respect, and has been enormously assisted by the failure of our own propaganda to provide any protective answers or alternative philosophies. In this connection, a noticeable new type of rumour is the one in which Lord Haw-Haw is said to predict events which subsequently happen, a few hours later, in this country. He never makes such predictions, but this type of rumour is persistent and has increased. . . .
>
> Moreover, and most important of all, Hitler took Paris one day ahead of his predicted schedule. His prediction had been given the widest publicity, in Low Cartoons and Astrological Columns in popular papers and street-corner joke sheets. This success was the last straw in the long record of Hitler's efficiency. It finally proved, to the enormous number of people with superstitious minds, that here was someone who always did what he said and couldn't be stopped. This effect was, of course, largely underlying and unconscious. . . .
>
> Here is an unprecedented situation in British civilization. Here is something that demands immediate dramatic solution. Yet the authorities, the

> Minister of information, the Military, are still treating the mass of people as they have always treated them. If that goes on much longer, the mass of people will inevitably take control. They may take control by overthrowing the status quo but more probably they will take control ably assisted by Hitler's propaganda in the negative form. That is to say, a feeling of hopelessness, bewilderment and frustration, the feeling that nothing can be done, which leads straight to panic and chaos, widescale defeatism and the feeling that it doesn't make any difference who is in charge. As we have seen, at least people feel that Hitler is efficient, correct and a man of action.

This pessimism was more pronounced among social elites than the working classes, and deeper in London than in the provinces – but decisions concerning war and peace would be made by the metropolitan governing classes.[118]

"Today depression and pessimism are again almost universal," Mass Observation reported on the morning of 17 June, with the French surrender expected imminently. "The momentum which Churchill gained with his new leadership has heavily declined. . . . Home morale is still being bungled and . . . there is a danger of complete feeling of futility growing dramatically over night."[119] The capitulation, reported that day on the 1.00 p.m. news, brought to a head a crisis in confidence that had been brewing for weeks. The Ministry of Information found that the general reaction was "confusion and shock, but hardly surprise. From all parts come reports of great anxiety. . . . The public are ready and determined to follow the Prime Minister if he gives the word, but if that word is not given there are signs that morale may change rapidly for the worst. Some reports express fear that our Government may go abroad" – which, after all, was one possible reading of the "We Shall Fight" speech – "others that the Government may itself give in. A few feel all is over." The report strongly advised that Churchill speak out on "what can be done to save the country." Failing that, "it is certain that a defeatist attitude will gain ground, and the divorce of feeling between the people and the Government will be gravely accentuated."[120]

A quick poll conducted by MOI on the afternoon and evening of 17 June, immediately after the announcement of the French surrender, found that just half the population faced with confidence the prospect of fighting alone; a quarter were doubtful; and another quarter deeply discouraged. Those results were dismal enough, but they may have been skewed by a desire to appear patriotic and avoid defeatist talk, which was considered almost treasonable.[121] Mass Observation simultaneously conducted an intensive study of Bolton, based on overheard or casual conversations, and their findings were considerably bleaker:

"Oh everyone is going round looking as though they want to put their heads in a gas oven. They are morbid as hell. . . . There's one chap who . . . always says that Hitler always does that what he says he'll do. He's right this time too."

"I can't see what we can do now. If the French navy gets away there might be a chance – a very slight one. But if not I can't see that we can do anything but give in."

"It'll just be panic when the planes come over in their thousands. And he'll have the chance to do what he likes with us. And I don't think he'll let us get away with it like we did Germany in 1918. I think he's got it in for us now, and he's now in the position he wants to be in. I guess there's nothing you can do about it."

"Father said 'The buggers will be here in a few days'."

"It won't be long now. We are in a bad way. . . . You heard what Winston Churchill said – we would fight on even if it came to street fighting and if the country was swimming in blood. That will be nice won't it?"

"There is no doubt that we shall be exterminated."

"What will become of our army? Are they trapped out there? It's no use hoping that things will come out all right. We don't seem to have a chance."

"If France and England can't do it together I don't see what we can do alone. . . . It looks as though all we can do is give up. It's no use throwing away a lot of lives when there is no hope. We have a good navy and a good air force but they can't last out against him."

"I bet the King and the Queen are packing to go – if they've not gone already. I bet the damn government's getting ready to fly to. They'll all leave us as usual. We shall probably be on the trek by the end of the week."

"He's got us now – he's massing millions of men."

"Well, what are we going on fighting for?"[122]

"Everyone around me was convinced we were 'done'," a neighbor confided to Nella Last, who secretly recorded in her diary the despair she would have been ashamed to speak aloud:

> There will be no Dunkirk this time. . . . My head felt as if it was full of broken glass instead of thoughts, and I felt if I could only cry – or better still scream and scream – it would have taken the sharp pain away. . . . Never have I felt so naked, never so alone. I've often said we were only "grains of sand on the sands of time," but today I knew what the words meant, and for the first time in my life I was unable to "ask" for courage and strength with the certainty I would receive it. . . . My husband came in and we looked at one another silently, and then I said, "bad – very bad". . . . He leaned against me and looked up at me, and I saw the terror bogey looking out of his eyes.[123]

In this atmosphere, on 18 June, Churchill delivered his "Finest Hour" speech to the House of Commons. (He then reread it – reluctantly and very poorly – over the radio.) It was laden with literary constructions designed to address the crisis. He first had to explain why the French and British forces had been routed, but he glossed over that in one paragraph and then closed the subject, suggesting that in any event the history of the last few weeks, when it would be written, would be a selective and constructed narrative: "Now I put all this aside. I put it on the shelf, from which the historians, when they have time, will select their documents to tell their stories." He asked the British people not only to resist Hitler, but to do so with a sense of high drama, following the words of Andrew Marvell: "He nothing common did, or mean, / Upon that memorable scene." As John Colville noted, Churchill had been repeating that line "consistently and often irrelevantly for the past fortnight." Given that it alludes to Charles I on the day of his execution, it may have been a poetic recognition of Britain's desperate situation. But in closing, consistent with his belief in the indeterminacy of history, Churchill sketched out two possible alternative futures:

> The Battle of Britain is about to begin. Upon this battle depends the survival of Christian civilisation. Upon it depends our own British way of life and the long continuity of our institutions and our Empire. The whole fury and might of the enemy must very soon be turned on us. Hitler knows that he will have to break us in this island or lose the war. If we can stand up to him, all Europe may be free, and the life of the world may move forward into broad, sunlit uplands; but if we fail, then the whole world, including the United States, and all that we have known and cared for, will sink into the abyss of a new dark age made more sinister, and perhaps more protracted, by the lights of a perverted science.[124]

The inspiration for that last sentence is sometimes attributed to Paul Reynaud, who on 6 June had said, "It would be the Middle Ages again, but not illuminated by the mercy of Christ."[125] In fact the fear that civilization might revert to a Dark Age was commonplace among the British intelligentsia in the 1930s.[126] Churchill had long regarded Nazism as an atavism, anathema to his faith in progress. It "leaps out upon us from the Dark Ages," he said in a 16 October 1938 broadcast to the United States: "This combination of mediaeval passion, a party caucus, the weapons of modern science and the blackmailing power of air-bombing, is the most monstrous menace to peace, order and fertile progress that has appeared in the world since the Mongol invasions of the 13th century."[127] As early as June 1935 he had warned that Nazi Germany and militarist Japan were "advancing upon the modern world in the full buccaneering spirit of the Dark Ages." Churchill had in mind Gibbon and his Romans ("They and all they stood for perished as may yet be our own fate") but also a more modern writer on the collapse of civilizations:

> A sense of the helplessness of Man amid the current of Destiny steals numbingly over the mind. Our vaunted progress – why should it continue? What grounds have we for assuming that the voyage of mankind will improve; that as we turn the bend as each new reach of river is opened, there will be calmer waters, wider channels, easier navigation, the assurance of a landing upon more fertile and hospitable shores? How many times, perhaps long before the dawn of history, has humanity attained a high development and the consciousness of glorious possibilities? How many times has it been swept back into chaos, so that everything has had to grow up again, slowly, painfully, blindly, from the beginning? That vivid modern philosopher Mr. H. G. Wells, for twenty years past heard but unheeded, has uttered these warnings in a popular style.[128]

In *The Discovery of the Future* (first published in 1902) Wells had used similar language, promising that the "uplands of the future are still more gracious and splendid than we can either hope or imagine."[129] But he always insisted that progress was not inevitable. Intelligently used, science could open the doors to utopia, but it could just as easily be corrupted and lead to horror. In *The Shape of Things to Come* education and science come to a halt as a post-apocalyptic world dissolves into fiefdoms ruled by petty warlords. Churchill likewise recognized that technology could be employed in the service of barbarism. Real progress had to include ethical progress, which he regarded as a basic Darwinian force: "How would the race of men have risen above the apes . . . how would they have ever evolved the moral theme, how would they have marched forward across the centuries to broad conceptions of compassion, of freedom, and of right?"[130] This was the philosophical question he had posed forty years earlier in *Savrola*, and now he was fully prepared for its practical application.

In conclusion, Churchill reminded his listeners that they were all actors in the grandest and longest historical drama of all: "Let us therefore brace ourselves to our duty and so bear ourselves that if the British Commonwealth and Empire lasts for a thousand years, men will still say, 'This was their finest hour.' "[131] Virginia Woolf granted that it was "not all claptrap" – suggesting that some of it was, and that she recognized Churchill's favorite stage device. "Now," she wrote, "we're fighting alone with our backs to the wall," the situation in which melodramatic heroes customarily delivered such rhetoric.[132] Mass Observation reported that the speech "was well received as regard subject matter, and has certainly had some settling effect. But his delivery was frequently criticized. Some suggested that he was drunk, others that he did not himself feel the confidence he was proclaiming. A few thought he was tired. It would seem that the delivery to some extent counteracted the contents of the speech." MO nevertheless concluded "that on the whole people have *more* confidence in Churchill now than they had before he became Prime Minister."[133] The Ministry of Information agreed: Churchill's speech "was considered courageous and hopeful and . . . welcomed for its frankness," but there was also "widespread comment on his delivery."[134]

That somewhat mixed response suggests an unsettling question: even if Churchill had delivered the most stirring words in the English language, were words enough? Without some kind of action, the stimulus they gave to morale quickly wore off. Just two days after the speech General Ironside (now in charge of preparing British defenses against a German invasion) recorded that Will Spens (the Master of Corpus Christi College, Cambridge) "told me that there were many intellectuals who were already defeatists. . . . His own attitude was he hoped the Government was not continuing out of pride or fear of telling the House that there was no chance." Ironside indignantly insisted that "we could defeat the Germans given stout hearts," but he had taken the precaution of sending his diaries to Canada.[135] In late June the Ministry of Information reported "pockets of defeatism" mainly among the lower middle classes ("suppose we do lose the war, what difference will it make to us; we could not be any worse off under Hitler; it's the bosses he's after"). Much more common was increasing discontent, especially among skilled workers and younger businessmen, with the government's slowness to involve civilians in the war effort.[136] Some went so far as to draw parallels with the new Vichy government in France: "That appreciation has now penetrated the popular mind and the effect of it is to bring to the front those doubts about our own leadership which have been finding expression in criticisms of Government action. There is no escaping the tenor of our reports: leadership is in jeopardy."[137]

Then on 27 June Mass Observation reported that some minor British commando raids in occupied France (which accomplished next to nothing) had sharply boosted public spirits, having "shown people that we are active in the conduct of the war. Some people mentioned that it made them feel more cheerful whilst claiming that the reaction was unreasonable."[138] The Ministry of Information also concluded that "The news of British landings on the French coast spread with amazing rapidity and had a very stimulating effect on morale: 'There's plenty of kick left in us', 'At last we're showing them', 'most heartening'." However, the same report noted that "There is still great uneasiness about the French Fleet" – would it be taken over by the Axis? – and there was still a "demand for more energetic leadership."[139]

It is likely (though not certain) that Churchill read the Ministry of Information report, and in any case he well understood this psychology, which was behind the destruction of the French fleet at Oran on 3 July. It has been argued that the action was carried out for hard-headed and inescapable military reasons: Britain could not risk having those ships fall into Axis hands. But the assault could have driven the French back into the war on the Axis side, with more awful consequences than the surrender of some warships to the Germans. Moreover, French ships could have been given the option of being disarmed in colonial ports. On 26 June the Cabinet (in Churchill's absence) had endorsed that policy, only to be reversed by the Prime Minister the following day. Against his wishes, the bloodless neutralization of French ships in Alexandria harbor would be secured on 7 July. Admiral Marcel Gensoul, who commanded the squadron at Oran, offered similar terms at the last minute, but Churchill insisted that French warships either join the British fleet or sail to British-controlled ports, something few if any French commanders could agree to.[140]

The decisive motive for launching "Operation Catapult" was not so much naval as dramatic. Churchill had to convince his people, the world, and especially the Americans that Britain would fight and defeat the Axis by any means necessary. If there was any doubt about that, Roosevelt would not send Britain the military materiel he needed to build up his own armed forces. On the same day as the attack, Churchill ordered all government and military leaders "to report, or if necessary remove, any officers or officials who are found to be consciously exercising a disturbing or depressing influence, and whose talk is calculated to spread alarm and despondency."[141] But ultimately defeatism could only be defeated by a shocking *coup de théâtre*. Whether it influenced his decision is impossible to say, but a week before the attack Churchill received this letter from a playwright he admired:

Dear Prime Minister,

Why not declare war on France and capture her fleet (which would gladly strike its colours to us) before AH recovers his breath?

Surely that is the logic of the situation?

Tactically,

G. Bernard Shaw[142]

Around midnight on 2 July, Churchill met with Beaverbrook, Sir Dudley Pound (the First Sea Lord), and A. V. Alexander (First Lord of the Admiralty) in the Cabinet Room to reach the agonizing decision. Pound favored an attack and eventually persuaded a more reluctant Alexander, but Churchill's Francophilia still held him back from anything so ruthless. Without much of a surface navy of his own, Hitler could not have reached across the Mediterranean to grab the French ships, and in any case he did not have the sailors to man them. Beaverbrook later claimed that it was he who persuaded Churchill, warning that the Germans would demand the French fleet and then resort to blackmail, "threatening to burn Bordeaux the first day the French refuse, the next day Marseilles, and the third day Paris." This was more melodramatic than realistic, and perhaps for that reason Churchill swung around and at once ordered an attack. Then, Beaverbrook recalled, Churchill grabbed his arm and hustled him out to a dark-and-stormy-night scene in the 10 Downing Street garden: "There was a high wind blowing. He raced along, I had trouble keeping up with him. And I had an attack of asthma. Churchill declared that there was no other decision possible. Then he wept."[143]

Admiral Andrew Cunningham at Alexandria, Admiral Dudley North at Gibraltar, and Admiral James Somerville (who carried out the attack) were all extremely reluctant to do anything so ruthless. Churchill later admitted that he had "to give them the most precise orders."[144] General Ismay was horrified, worrying that it would provoke Vichy to re-enter the war on the German side.[145] There was the precedent of the pre-emptive seizure of the Danish fleet in 1807, which Churchill defended in *A History of the English-Speaking Peoples*,[146] but Denmark had then been a neutral power. At Oran, for the first time, Britain attacked an ally, killing more than 1,250 French sailors. Speaking to the House of Commons on 4 July, Churchill made his dramatic motives explicit:

> The action we have already taken should be, in itself, sufficient to dispose once and for all of the lies and rumours which have been so industriously spread by German propaganda and Fifth Column activities that we have the slightest intention of entering into negotiations in any form and through any

> channel with the German and Italian Governments. We shall, on the contrary, prosecute the war with the utmost vigour by all the means that are open to us until the righteous purposes for which we entered upon it have been fulfilled.[147]

Chips Channon was thrilled by this "stirring story" of a "great naval victory," noting only in passing that it involved attacking an ally.[148] Even Alexander Cadogan, who never spared Churchill criticism, called the speech a "triumph."[149] "The scene at the end was quite awe-inspiring," Eric Seal told his wife, "the whole crowded House rose, & cheered for a full two minutes." For the first time, the Tories cheered as loudly as the Labour members, and Churchill's eyes welled up with tears. "What it was all about I still really don't know," Seal wondered. "The speech was good, but no better than the others; & the occasion – the outbreak of hostilities with our old ally – hardly one for rejoicing." He concluded that it was the sheer drama of the stroke that touched a nerve: "There was general relief that such vigorous action had been taken." And, he added, "The reception in America seems to have been good, too." On 26 May Roosevelt had warned Reynaud and Edouard Daladier (who had represented France at the Munich Conference) not to allow their navy to fall into German hands, and shortly before the attack he assured Lord Lothian that Americans would approve the seizure of the French fleet. Later, in January 1941, John Colville recorded that Harry Hopkins, Roosevelt's closest advisor, "believed that Oran had been the turning-point in our fortunes: it made the world realize that we were in earnest in our intentions to carry on." The Viceroy of India and the ambassador to Spain likewise reported that those countries were properly impressed. So were Marshal Pétain and Admiral Darlan: except for a token air raid on Gibraltar, Vichy took no armed action against the British.[150] In January 1939 Mussolini had assured Count Ciano, his Foreign Minister, that Chamberlain and his government "are not made of the same stuff as the Francis Drakes and the other magnificent adventurers who created the empire. These, after all, are the tired sons of a long line of rich men and they will lose their empire."[151] But now the action at Oran left Ciano stunned and worried: "It proves that the fighting spirit of His British Majesty's fleet is quite alive, and still has the aggressive ruthlessness of the captains and pirates of the seventeenth century."[152]

The day before the assault, Mass Observation had reported that the public needed just such a stimulant:

> People are still in a state of *expectancy*, but without a clear knowledge of what to expect. They long to know how to orientate their minds. Some are forming their own opinions again about the future. Others find an outlet in

> increased irritability. In general analysis suggests that the general underlying tension is piling up. This is mainly due to natural fears which are not being offset by adequate leadership and propaganda or sympathetic treatment from above. The gulf between the leaders and the people continues to widen, and no attempt appears to have been made from above to bridge it strongly. In particular, the feeling of frustration, of inadequate outlets for the desire to act and produce, is having an immense and subtle effect. . . . The absence of any statement from the Prime Minister this week has not helped the people.[153]

When the attack came, it was greeted with "great relief" by the British people, who did not question the necessity of firing on their allies. "And it has given people something to shake them up so that the gradual drift previously noted is likely to be checked for the time being," Mass Observation concluded.[154] The Ministry of Information agreed: "All regions express widespread approval at our action against the French fleet . . . and they welcome this evidence of our initiative." Reactions to Churchill's speech were "universally and strongly favourable."[155] Phrases commonly heard included "the turn of the tide," "hitting hard," "Well, we've shown what we can do," and "That'll give Hitler a surprise for a change."[156] Harold Nicolson had been deeply depressed by the first news of "this odious attack," but by 10 July he was elated:

> Hitler seems to be funking the great attack upon England. All our reports from abroad (I see the Foreign Office telegrams) show that he is not now quite so sure. . . . If we can stick it, we really shall have won the war. What a fight it is! What a chance for us! Our action against the French Fleet has made a tremendous effect throughout the world. I am as stiff as can be.[157]

Mass Observation noted a similar response among the general population:

> The effect of the French Fleet incident seems to have been to jog people out of their anxiety drift, and to have established a new attitude at a higher level of cheerfulness which has been constant for several days. People are saying more than before that "he's always got what he wants up to now, but he won't find it so easy this time." This attitude has been greatly helped by the facts that one of Hitler's many prophecies foretold that he would invade us before this, and his infallibility is not quite so much a bogey as it was before. If, by August 15th, the most mentioned date, we do not look like collapsing, and if the present frame of mind continues till then, it is likely that there will be a sudden leap in morale. . . .[158]

In fact the leap happened sooner. On 3 July Mass Observation found that pessimists outnumbered optimists by almost 2 to 1, but by the middle of the month the ratio had flipped to 1 to 5.[159] From the Beer Hall Putsch of November 1923 up to this point Hitler had always seized the initiative. Like any melodramatic villain, he had driven the drama forward with one shock after another, constantly unnerving his adversaries. Churchill could only turn that around with a yet more staggering bolt from the blue. French sailors paid a terrible price, but Churchill had won a psychological battle that Britain – and France – could not afford to lose. In *Savrola* and at Gallipoli he had tried to transform the drama with a surprise naval bombardment. Now, for the first time, the device worked.

CHAPTER 19

This Different England

There is no doubt that Hitler made preparations to invade Britain in 1940. Whether his plan (Operation Sealion) could have succeeded, or was seriously meant to be carried out, is another question.[1] Even if the Luftwaffe had gained air dominance, Germany's minimal surface fleet would have had to deal with the Royal Navy, which that summer could have deployed in or near the Channel two aircraft carriers, three battleships, two battlecruisers, eight heavy cruisers, twenty light cruisers, and seventy-six destroyers. The Kriegsmarine, having suffered heavy losses in the Norway campaign, had one heavy cruiser, three light cruisers, seven destroyers, and no capital ships.[2] Was such a force really capable of escorting and securely supplying an army large enough to subdue a hostile island of 45 million people? In 1973 British and German officers played a war game at Sandhurst based on the actual plan for Sealion, and the result was a disaster for the Germans.[3] Peter Fleming concluded that, while the British people energetically prepared for the invasion, they did not actually believe it would happen. They were like spectators at a play gripping their seats when it appeared that the villain had triumphed, though they knew he would be defeated in the end: "The extreme and disheartening bleakness of their long-term prospects was obscured by the melodramatic nature of the predicament in which . . . the fortunes of war had placed them."[4]

Even after the fall of France (as David Edgerton has shown), Britain could still rely on the limitless resources of her Empire, as well as vast industrial and technological establishments at home. Churchill's dispatch of tanks to the Middle East in August 1940 was not the high-risk gamble it is often made out to be: in fact he had enough armor to deal with Sealion, with some to spare.[5] The people and leaders of France had suffered a collapse of morale in June.[6] Hitler could only win by similarly demoralizing the British, at least to the point where they would agree to a compromise peace. This was a battle that Churchill was singularly well-equipped to fight.

On 26 June the Prime Minister asked for copies of the German invasion scenarios he drafted in 1913.[7] But by 12 July he privately confided that he considered an invasion unlikely, a view increasingly shared by the public. Nevertheless, the "invasion scare" was good theatre insofar as it mobilized the British people to action, and Churchill did everything he could to encourage that useful illusion. He told John Colville that "Human beings don't require rest; what they require is change or else they become bloody-minded."[8] Colville himself worried about "the film-fed public's insatiate longing for sensation. It has often been said that the Dictators could only survive if they took some dramatic action every six months, and now the British public, drugged by Hollywood and by the stirring events of recent months, seems to need incessant change and excitement."[9] There would be no shortage of that over the next few months.

On 30 June General Alfred Jodl, as head of the Wehrmacht Operations Staff, had submitted a plan to invade Britain, but only as a final resort. The prime objective of the invasion preparations, he argued, would be to frighten the British away from any offensive operations elsewhere, thus freeing Hitler to pursue his ultimate objective, an attack on the Soviet Union. Hitler approved the plan. The German Navy considered Sealion impractical, and agreed to it only if full air superiority was achieved, something they knew was virtually impossible.[10] Hitler had planned to deliver a Reichstag speech on 8 July offering Britain one last chance to make peace, but the British attack on Oran five days earlier made him hesitate. He postponed the speech three times. On 16 July he signed a directive authorizing planning for an invasion, but it was hedged with so many ifs ("if need be . . . if necessary") that it communicated irresolution to his commanders. The Navy probably went along with the business of amassing invasion barges because they did not think they would ever be used. General Günther von Blumentritt, who was assigned to plan the invasion, later recalled that "we did not regard this order very seriously. . . . The resources available to me were ridiculous," and significantly "neither Hitler nor any of his personal staff seemed to take any interest in the operation or the plans." According to Blumentritt, around 1 August Hitler told Field Marshal Gerd von Rundstedt that he would not execute Sealion, and by the end of that month the invasion barges were already being quietly dispersed. Army staff officers planned Sealion "academically rather than zealously – much as a map-problem or peacetime theoretical exercise." More exactly, it was theatre, designed to intimidate the British or at least force them to concentrate their forces at home. The massed troops, barges, and supplies were all quite real, but as Blumentritt explained, "a bluff can succeed only when everything is done as if the operation were meant seriously and when all the staffs and units believe implicitly in its execution."[11]

Hitler finally spoke to the Reichstag on 19 July, for two and a quarter hours. The speech mainly reviewed German military victories and extolled German military strength. Hitler, observed William L. Shirer, was "so wonderful an actor, so magnificent a handler of the German mind, that he mixed superbly the full confidence of the conqueror with the humbleness which always goes down so well with the masses when they know a man is on top. . . . His oratorical form was at its best. . . . I've often admired the way he uses his hands, which are somewhat feminine and quite artistic. Tonight he used those hands beautifully, seemed to express himself almost as much with his hands – and the sway of his body – as he did with his words and the use of his voice."[12] Only at the very end did he briefly warn that the British faced destruction, unless they heeded his "appeal to reason," though no specific peace terms were offered. When the British government promptly rejected the overture, Count Ciano noted, "a sense of ill-concealed disappointment spreads among the Germans," including Hitler himself.[13] The Ministry of Information reported that the British public was growing confident and even complacent, interpreting Hitler's speech as "a sign of weakness" and discounting the possibility of invasion.[14]

Unsure of his next step, Hitler began to explore the possibility of attacking the Soviet Union, working on the assumption Churchill was only staying in the fight in the hope that Russia would eventually join the war against Germany. If that prospect were eliminated, the British presumably would at last see reason and sue for peace. But this strategy only made sense if Sealion were a non-starter. The actual air war against Britain did not begin until 13 August. The switch from attacking military targets to terror-bombing London on 7 September was a tacit admission that Sealion would never take place, that Britain could only be defeated through a collapse of morale. Barring such a collapse, the Luftwaffe, according to its own internal assessments, lacked the capacity to score a decisive victory in the skies. By 13 September Admiral Erich Raeder admitted that the Blitz had not succeeded and Sealion was too risky, but insisted that the stage set should not be dismantled: "The British must be kept insecure. Cancellation of the landing would take a great deal of pressure off England." Hitler indefinitely postponed the invasion on 17 September, but he never formally canceled it: even in January 1944 he still treated it as a future possibility.[15] Sealion was yet another example of his "Politik des Bluffs und Theatrecoups," with the emphasis on bluff – and Churchill called it.

Thus alongside the desperate air battles of "Spitfire Summer" two expert political actors were engaged in a dramatic duel, which was crucial to the ultimate outcome of the war. At this point no quick military decision was possible: Britain alone could not hope to defeat Germany, but the Channel was an insuperable barrier to a final German victory. Therefore, everything now depended on morale, which in turn depended on theatre. Churchill had to convince the British people and the larger world that he would never surrender, by means of such vivid dramatic devices as his speeches and the destruction of a French naval squadron. Hitler's aim was to sap the British will to fight. His stage tricks included his histrionic performance before the Reichstag as well as the Potemkin village preparations for Sealion.[16]

Hitler did persuade the British that an invasion was imminent, but that only heightened the drama. On 20 July Harold Nicolson recorded his expectation of a German landing, backed by 6,000 aircraft (a vast overestimate). "How strange it all is!" he wrote in his diary. "We know that we are faced with a terrific invasion. We half-know that the odds are heavily against us. Yet there is a sort of exhilaration in the air. If Hitler were to postpone invasion and fiddle about in Africa and the Mediterranean, our morale might weaken. But we are really proud to be the people who will not give way."[17] One Eleanor Silsby, a Londoner writing to an American friend on 23 July, affirmed that "we are proud to have the honour of fighting alone for the things that matter much more than life and death. It makes me hold my chin high to think, not just of being English, but of having been chosen to come at this hour for this express purpose of saving the world."[18] "It's hard to describe how much England has changed," David Ben-Gurion (head of the Jewish Agency in Palestine) wrote to his wife from London on 8 August. "Since Churchill inherited Chamberlain's place, the silent and confident bravery beating in every Englishman's heart is the fruit of this exchange."[19]

Visiting Chequers in the summer of 1940, de Gaulle found Churchill shaking his fist at the sky because the Luftwaffe was not yet bombing civilian targets in Britain. "Are you in such a hurry to see your towns smashed to bits?" The Prime Minister explained that "the bombing of Oxford, Coventry, Canterbury, will cause such a wave of indignation in the United States that they'll come into the war!" He had said much the same thing to Joseph P. Kennedy,[20] and he would not be dissuaded, even when de Gaulle gently noted that the attack on France had not induced the Americans to abandon isolationism.[21] The German air assault on London, broadcast by Edward R. Murrow and covered extensively in US newspapers, did have a profound effect on American public opinion. A Gallup poll in late September found 52 percent approval of aid to Britain, a shift that helped Franklin Roosevelt secure the passage (in March 1941) of the Lend-Lease Act, which eventually supplied $31.4 billion in war materiel to Britain.[22] But neither the Blitz nor the invasion of Russia brought the United States into the war.

Churchill did communicate to the British people that they were now all players in a great national drama, in stark contrast to the passivity of the

Phony War. The coinage of the term "People's War" is often attributed to Tom Wintringham, and its popularization to J. B. Priestley, but Churchill laid out the essential concept in a 14 July radio broadcast:

> This is no war of chieftains or of princes, of dynasties or national ambition; it is a War of peoples and of causes. There are vast numbers not only in this island but in every land, who will render faithful service in this War, but whose names will never be known, whose deeds will never be recorded. This is a War of the Unknown Warrior. . . .[23]

BBC audience research estimated that 64.4 percent of the adult population listened in to this broadcast, compared with 59.8 percent for the "Finest Hour" speech of 18 June.[24] It was a theme Churchill returned to again and again, for instance in this 27 April 1941 broadcast:

> This ordeal by fire has even in a certain sense exhilarated the manhood and womanhood of Britain. The sublime but also terrible and sombre experiences and emotions of the battlefield which for centuries had been reserved for the soldiers and sailors, are now shared, for good or ill, by the entire population. All are proud to be under the fire of the enemy. Old men, little children, the crippled veterans of former wars, aged women, the ordinary hard-pressed citizen or subject of the King, as he likes to call himself, the sturdy workmen who swing the hammers or load the ships; skilful craftsmen; the members of every kind of ARP service, are proud to feel that they stand in the line together with our fighting men, when one of the greatest of causes is being fought out, as fought out it will be, to the end. This is indeed the grand heroic period of our history, and the light of glory shines on all.[25]

In October 1940 Mass Observation cited the revealing results of a *Sunday Dispatch* competition, in which readers were invited to send in their favorite movie fadeouts on postcards. The endings most admired by the British public were not Senator Smith vanquishing a corrupt Washington politician, or Dorothy returned to her Kansas homestead, or the Marx Brothers bombarding Margaret Dumont with rotten fruit, or any other kind of upbeat finale. The most frequently mentioned were, in descending order:

Three Comrades: Two of the comrades, already dead, beckon the third to join them. Arm in arm the three comrades march through the skies.

Dark Victory: The heroine walks slowly upstairs to die bravely and alone.

Goodbye Mr. Chips: Mr. Chips in his old age murmurs the names of the boys that he has known, as he dies.

Wuthering Heights: The hero climbs the hill, faithful to a tryst with a lover who is dead.

A Tale of Two Cities: Carton says "It is a far, far better thing" etc. The camera pans as the guillotine knife falls, and shows the clear sky. Then a scripture text.

"Here we see down into the secret heart of stolid old British emotion," Mass Observation concluded. "The tragic ending wins every time, provided it looks into the future and brings some message of heroic hope. It is because Winston Churchill" – an avid movie fan – "feels like the *Sunday Dispatch* readers that he is able to call out so much in British people that Chamberlain, Halifax, or Attlee could never command."[26]

In *The Second World War* Churchill acknowledged that the Battle of Britain had been won not just by "The Few," but also by their many support personnel. Aircraft workers, the Ministry of Supply, Anti-Aircraft Command, the Observer Corps, and the staff of Fighter Command "All played their part."[27] This became his favorite theatrical metaphor, which he used relentlessly to reinforce the sense that all were actors in a grand global drama. He resorted to it when celebrating the alignment of the great anglophone powers at the 1941 Placentia Bay conference ("even the most sceptical person must have the feeling that we all have the chance to play our part and to do our duty in some grand design, the end of which no mortal can foresee"); or promising the United States Congress that resistance movements would flare up in occupied Europe ("the masses of the people of all classes and creeds await the hour of liberation, when they too will be able once again to play their part and strike their blows like men"); or rallying the people to fight a People's War ("The mine, the factory, the dockyard, the salt sea waves, the fields to till, the home, the hospital, the chair of the scientist, the pulpit of the preacher – from the highest to the humblest tasks, all are of equal honour; all have their part to play").[28] Or, most famously, in his 29 October 1941 address to the boys of his old school, Harrow:

> Do not let us speak of darker days; let us speak rather of sterner days. These are not dark days: these are great days – the greatest days our country has ever lived: and we must all thank God that we have been allowed, each of us according to our stations, to play a part in making these days memorable in the history of our race.[29]

In *The Second World War* it becomes practically a verbal tic, applied dozens of times to a vast cast of characters, including baby aircraft carriers, the fighting Poles, British gunners at El Alamein in 1942, the Italian Fleet (when it went over to the Allies in 1943), Canadian arms factories, the Germans in the Battle of the Bulge in 1944, American isolationists, and finally, in his Victory Broadcast of 13 May 1945, the whole British people.[30] In this epic of "the world stage,"[31] his other favorite tropes were *drama*[32] and *tragedy*[33] – the "Greek tragedy" of the French fleet at Oran,[34] the "squalid tragedy" of Mussolini's puppet government at Salo in northern Italy,[35] "Renaissance tragedy" when he executed his son-in-law Ciano,[36] "a tragedy within a tragedy" when Partisans and Cetniks betrayed each other in occupied Yugoslavia.[37]

Following the attack on Oran in July 1940, Churchill sought other opportunities for a dramatic stroke, often divorced from reality. General James Marshall-Cornwall remembered a 27 July "Mad Hatter's Dinner Party" at Chequers, where he reported that he was training his III Corps for offensive action only. Churchill was delighted, and was set to order the unit into action immediately, only to become enraged when he was told that it was desperately short of equipment. Then he asked Professor Lindemann to show the startled guests a new kind of hand grenade he had invented, and ordered it to be put into production at once. Perhaps it was more efficient than the standard Mills Bomb, but as General John Dill attempted to explain, one could hardly ask the munitions factories to stop and retool while the Germans might invade at any moment. Then Churchill produced a map of the Red Sea, pointed to the Eritrean port of Massawa, and instructed Marshall-Cornwall to come up with a plan for capturing it from the Italians. With virtually no knowledge of Massawa and no chance to prepare, the general could only suggest some of the practical difficulties. "You soldiers are all alike," Churchill harrumphed, "you have no imagination."[38]

He meanwhile urged the Chiefs of Staff to launch an amphibious assault behind the Italian army in Libya, cutting off the coastal road that was their sole supply route. "We had not of course at that time proper tank landing craft," he later conceded, but all the same he was sure something could have been improvised. He was unable to understand why his generals never tried this sort of maneuver. "It was not until Anzio in 1944 that I succeeded in having this experiment tried," he concluded, without fully acknowledging that the results may have vindicated his cautious commanders.[39]

Churchill's imagination then turned to other targets. On 6 August he invited Charles de Gaulle to the Cabinet Room, spread out maps, and graphically illustrated his plan to swoop down on Dakar in Senegal. With a hint of bemusement, the French general realized that he was dealing with an aesthete:

> Mr. Churchill, colouring his eloquence with the most picturesque tints, set to work to paint for me the following picture: "Dakar wakes up one morning, sad and uncertain. But behold, by the light of the rising sun, its inhabitants

> perceive the sea, to a great distance, covered with ships. An immense fleet! A hundred war or transport vessels! These approach slowly, addressing messages of friendship by radio to the town, to the navy, to the garrison. Some of them are flying the Tricolour. The others are sailing under the British, Dutch, Polish, or Belgian colours. From this Allied force there breaks away an inoffensive small ship bearing the white flag of parley. It enters the port and disembarks the envoys of General de Gaulle. These are brought to the Governor. Their job is to convince him that if he lets you land the Allied fleet retires, and that nothing remains but to settle, between him and you, the terms of his cooperation. On the contrary, if he wants a fight, he has every chance of being crushed."
>
> And Mr. Churchill, brimming over with conviction, described and mimed, one by one, the scenes of the future, as they spurted up from his desire and his imagination.

It was terribly melodramatic, but "Stripping Mr. Churchill's idea of the seductive ornaments added to it by his eloquence, I recognized, on reflection, that it was based on certain solid data."[40] Although the assault on Dakar would end in failure, Churchill credited the commanders on the spot for audacity. "It was one of my rules that *errors toward the enemy* must be lightly judged," he emphasized. "They were quite right to try." In *The Second World War* he even tried to spin the fiasco as a psychological success, insofar as it encouraged Free French forces in the rest of Africa.[41]

De Gaulle shared Churchill's sense of drama but not his hunger for publicity. Even posing for a photograph struck him as undignified: "I do not want to be made a film star by the press." He ruefully predicted that "Churchill will launch me like a new bar of soap" – and, in fact, on 18 July His Majesty's Government commissioned Richmond Temple, an advertising agent, to make "the name of General de Gaulle thoroughly well-known throughout the world and particularly in Great Britain and the British Empire." On 9 August Churchill minuted the Minister of Information: "It is important to keep General de Gaulle active in French on the broadcast, and to relay by every possible means our French propaganda in Africa." "*Quel grand artiste!*" was de Gaulle's usual response to Churchill's grand gestures.[42]

It was after witnessing the Operations Room of Fighter Command in mid-August that Churchill coined his most famous epigram, "Never in the field of human conflict has so much been owed by so many to so few."[43] Like most immortal phrases, it was a rephrase. Earlier in his career Churchill had used similar locutions on several occasions.[44] *Henry V* is usually identified as the ultimate source, and George VI had used the phrase "we few, we happy few" in a June radio address.[45] Words to that effect can be found in any number of nineteenth-century military melodramas, where a small band of British brothers were inevitably pitted against vastly superior numbers of Frenchmen (under Napoleon), Russians (during the Crimean War), rebellious Africans, or treacherous Indians.[46] Andrew Roberts finds a more exact parallel in General Sir John Moore on the conquest of Corsica in 1793: "Never was so much done by so few men."[47] A still more likely source was Sir Thomas Gower's sardonic comment on the Battle of Newburn in August 1640, when a Scottish army utterly routed the English: "Never so many ran from so few with less ado," which is quoted in *A History of the English-Speaking Peoples*.[48] Churchill took England's most ignominious defeat and, by rearranging a few words, celebrated Britain's most glorious victory.

The sentence also appears in the latter part of a speech he delivered to the House of Commons on 20 August 1940, and it profits from being read in context. Churchill had to begin by addressing two obvious and deeply disturbing questions: the shock of the French collapse, and explaining why the same fate would not befall Britain. "We have seen great countries with powerful armies dashed out of coherent existence in a few weeks," he bluntly acknowledged, and then, far from softening the blow, he hammered home the fact that "We have seen the French Republic and the renowned French Army beaten into complete and total submission with less than the casualties which they suffered in any one of half a dozen of the battles of 1914–18." How could this catastrophe be explained? Churchill attributed it to the cold-blooded mechanization of war – meaning not the internal combustion engine, but the direction of war from remote offices, deploying divisions by electronic communication following preordained tactics: "Moves are made upon the scientific and strategic boards, advantages are gained by mechanical means, as a result of which scores of millions of men become incapable of further resistance, or judge themselves incapable of further resistance, and a fearful game of chess proceeds from check to mate by which the unhappy players seem to be inexorably bound." Until fairly recently in history soldiers at all levels had to exercise initiative on the battlefield: now even the generals, trapped by their own machinery of command, had lost any real sense of free will, and were helpless when their plans went awry. But the Battle of Britain, Churchill promised, was being fought on radically different terms:

> The whole of the warring nations are engaged, not only soldiers, but the entire population, men, women and children. The fronts are everywhere. The trenches are dug in the towns and streets. Every village is fortified. Every road is barred. The front line runs through the factories. The workmen are soldiers with different weapons but the same courage. These are great and distinctive changes from what many of us saw in the struggle of a quarter

> century ago. There seems to be every reason to believe that this new kind of war is well suited to the genius and the resources of the British nation and the British Empire; and that, once we get properly equipped and properly started, a war of this kind will be more favourable to us than the sombre mass slaughters of the Somme and Passchendaele. If it is a case of the whole nation fighting and suffering together, that ought to suit us, because we are the most united of all the nations, because we entered the war upon the national will and with our eyes open, and because we have been nurtured in freedom and individual responsibility and are the products, not of totalitarian uniformity but of tolerance and variety. If all these qualities are turned, as they are being turned, to the arts of war, we may be able to show the enemy quite a lot of things that they have not thought of yet.[49]

From his earliest schooldays, Churchill had fought for individualism and against regimentation – and until 1940, it appeared to be a losing battle. War, like politics, had become ever more totalitarian, with masses of men herded into combat according to plans and timetables decided at the top. Now Churchill proposed a new strategy, relying on small groups exercising initiative and improvisation. Thus "scores of millions of men" who had been reduced to chess pieces could be defeated by "the Few." Churchill specifically associated that word with the pilots of Fighter Command, but he also gave it a broader meaning, taking in any kind of local team that mobilized itself for the war effort: Home Guard units, farmers digging tank traps, workers organizing overtime production, Women's Institute ladies making jam, kids collecting scrap metal. "The Few" included everyone.

Now that civilians felt they were playing a real role, "confidence is increased, opinion is stiffer and there is a feeling of growing exhilaration," the Ministry of Information concluded.[50] "Reports from raided areas show that morale remains very high, and seems to rise in proportion to the number of raids."[51] The 20 August speech "was received extremely well" throughout the United Kingdom: "It is the most forceful and heartening he has yet made" (Northern Ireland); "It has created a strong feeling of confidence" (Newcastle); "Everyone feels now that, come what will, we are top dogs" (Bristol).[52] Even Count Ciano found the rhetoric "definite and forward-looking. One can feel that behind the façade of beautiful words and strong affirmations there is a will and a faith."[53] The Wartime Social Survey found that between 23 and 28 August Churchill's radio speeches were mentioned 166 times in 551 interviews; Anthony Eden ran a distant second with 76 mentions.[54] On 14 August Churchill had told Joseph Kennedy that "the only thing that disturbed him was that Hitler might not invade," ending the drama with an anticlimax. "He said the British soldiers would probably want their money back, because they won't be satisfied with the show."[55] As he put it to Hugh Dalton on 3 September, "the public will stand everything except optimism."[56]

On 7 September German bombers broke through for the first big raid on London, hitting the East End and killing around three hundred people. "What is threatening this ancient and magnificent City?" wondered Colin Perry, a young office clerk. "You read novels, of the unknown, like H. G. Wells and his Martian invasions, and you feel we must be one too." But on the 10th his spirits vaulted when he saw Churchill touring the ruins around Mansion House Station, as he wrote in his diary:

> I cheered, I yelled. . . . He looked invincible, which he is. Tough, bulldogged, piercing. . . . As he made his way through the smoke, through the City, workers all crying "Good old Winston" – "Give 'em socks" – "Good Luck" – and the culminating cry of "Are we downhearted?" to the heaven-rising response of "Noooooo" which echoed round the City, round the world indeed. And warmed the "cockles of our British hearts" and of all free men in the world. It was magnificent, tremulous, stirring, dramatic.

It was, Perry added, every bit as dramatic as Sidney Street, but what had then been played as farce was now something intensely heroic, "the records of which will find space in every future book of history."[57] When Samuel Battersby, an official censor, visited the bombed-out streets of London:

> The familiar figure of Churchill was there dabbing at his eyes from time to time with a large white handkerchief clutched in one hand. It was a harrowing sight, with the ARP and other officials digging out from the ruins injured people and bodies. From one forlorn little group alongside the remains of their home an old woman shouted "When are we going to bomb Berlin, Winnie?" Instinctively – without time for thought – Winston swung round, waving his fist clutching his handkerchief and, I think, an ebony, silver topped stick, and growled with menacing emphasis "you leave that to me"! Morale rose immediately; everyone was satisfied and reassured. "By God we're going to knock the hell out of them for this" was doubtless the general feeling. It was certainly mine.
>
> Afterwards I pondered the incident and have done so countless times since. What could a Prime Minister at that time and in such desperate conditions say that was not pathetically inadequate – or even downright dangerous? "When are we going to bomb Berlin?" "As soon as we are able to" . . . "In a year or two when we have built up a striking force" . . . "Not just yet – you must be patient" . . . Almost anything – except what he did say – would have been wrong.

> The incident typifies the uniquely unpredictable magic that was Churchill. Transformation of the despondent misery of disaster into a grimly certain stepping stone to ultimate victory.[58]

Hitler was an electrifying performer in staged political rallies, but he conspicuously avoided touring bombed German cities, undermining German morale in the long term.

In a radio address on 11 September Churchill enlisted all his listeners as fellow players in this grand historical drama, which was now at its climax:

> It ranks with the days when the Spanish Armada was approaching the Channel, and Drake was finishing his game of bowls; or when Nelson stood between us and Napoleon's Grand Army at Boulogne. We have read all about this in the history books; but what is happening now is on a far greater scale and of far more consequence to the life and future of the world and its civilization than these brave old days of the past. Every man and every woman will therefore prepare himself to do his duty, whatever it may be, with special pride and care.

And he reminded them that they were performing in front of a global audience: "All the world that is still free marvels at the composure and fortitude with which the citizens of London are facing and surmounting the great ordeal to which they are subjected, the end of which or the severity of which cannot yet be foreseen."[59] A week later he authorized a new medal, the George Cross, to honor civilians for conduct that was both heroic and dramatic, such as disarming unexploded bombs. As he put it, it "will be for the few outstanding deeds of *éclat*."[60]

Mass Observation reported that the 11 September radio address "was well received," though a number of listeners thought Churchill sounded tired and "suggested that his morale was considerably worse than ordinary people's! . . . Some people are feeling almost cheerful about the prospect of a straight, tough fight with German troops."[61] At the height of the bombing, American consulates throughout Britain reported on local morale, and the military attaché Raymond E. Lee summed it up: "What was striking was that the spirit among the workers in the industrial districts which have been frequently bombed was the best of all. It was high everywhere and no consul but thought that the people would see the thing through. . . . By every test and measure I am able to apply, these people are staunch to the bone and won't quit."[62] When bombs damaged her house in Mecklenburgh Square, even Virginia Woolf found her Bloomsbury hauteur melting. "Churchill cheered me up" when he compared the present conflict with the arrival of the Spanish Armada. "What touched and indeed raked what I call my heart in London was the grimy old woman at the lodging house at the back, all dirty after the raid, and preparing to sit out another," she wrote to the composer Ethel Smyth. "We, after all, have at least been to Italy and read Shakespeare. They haven't: dear me, I'm turning democrat," she exclaimed, surprised by her own reaction.[63] "What I'm finding odd and agreeable and unwonted is the admiration this war creates – for every sort of person: chars, shopkeepers, even much more remarkably, for politicians – Winston at least, and the tweed wearing sterling dull women here, with their grim good sense: organising First aid, putting out bombs for practise, and jumping out of windows to show us how. . . . I'd almost lost faith in human beings, partly owing to my immersion in the dirty water of artists envies and vanities while I worked at [my biography of Roger Fry]. Now hope revives again."[64]

"This island race is extraordinary," Chips Channon wrote on 12 September, "everyone I have seen today was in the highest spirits. They are all convinced that an English victory now lies just around the corner, and that our Air Force is actually superior, not only in quality but in numbers, to the Germans." R. A. Butler, formerly a defeatist, now compared the German Dornier bombers to Hannibal's elephants and looked forward to certain triumph.[65] And another Conservative MP, Victor Cazalet, noted on 10 October:

> I am amazed at the morale and spirit of the people. Of course one has always been proud to be English, but really these last weeks have made me feel that if I had been out of England I should have missed seeing a very wonderful side of the British character. Whatever may happen in the future, I would never have missed the experience of the last few weeks for anything in the world. . . .
>
> We do not know, of course, what is in store for us, but I have a feeling that whatever it is we shall not only survive but that certain and overwhelming victory will ultimately be ours.[66]

As *Time* magazine commented, Americans had once associated Britain with Stanley Baldwin's campaign against Mrs. Simpson, and Neville Chamberlain's appeasement: "But the country they ruled has changed. This England is different." Churchill might be "a Tory, an imperialist, and has been a strike-breaker and Red-baiter; and yet, when he tours the slums of London, old women say: 'God bless you, Winnie.' "[67]

On 15 September the Luftwaffe launched its climactic attack, which Churchill compared to Waterloo. But unlike the Duke of Wellington, he did not directly observe the fighting. This confronted him with a narrative problem: in the twentieth century, when battles were directed from offices by telecommunication, how could thrilling war literature be written? As he had protested in "Mass Effects in Modern Life":

> We see the modern commander entirely divorced from the heroic aspect by the physical conditions which have overwhelmed his art. No longer will Hannibal and Caesar, Turenne and Marlborough, Frederick and Napoleon, sit their horses on the battlefield and by their words and gestures direct and dominate between dawn and dusk the course of a supreme event. No longer will their fame and presence cheer their struggling soldiers. No longer will they share their perils, rekindle their spirits and restore the day. They will not be there. They have been banished from the fighting scene, together with their plumes, standards and breast-plates. The lion-hearted warrior, whose keen eye detected the weakness in the foeman's line, whose resolve outlasted all the strains of battle, whose mere arrival at some critical point turned the tide of conflict, has disappeared. Instead our Generals are to be found on the day of battle at their desks in their offices fifty or sixty miles from the front, anxiously listening to the trickle of the telephone for all the world as if they were speculators with large holdings when the market is disturbed.[68]

In *The World Crisis* Churchill had to describe engagements and hot pursuits on the high seas while he himself remained at the Admiralty War Room. He was able to generate dramatic tension by simply reproducing the telegrams sent to the Admiralty, an ingenious literary innovation, though one that focused attention on himself rather than the men in the fighting ships:

> There can be few purely mental experiences more charged with cold excitement than to follow, almost from minute to minute, the phases of a great naval action from the silent rooms of the Admiralty. Out in blue water in the fighting ships amid the stunning detonations of the cannonade, fractions of the event unfold themselves to the corporeal eye. There is the sense of action at its highest; there is the wrath of battle; there is the intense, self-effacing, physical or mental toil. But in Whitehall only the clock ticks, and quiet men enter with quick steps laying pieces of pencilled paper before other men equally silent who draw lines and scribble calculations, and point with the finger or make brief subdued comments. Telegram succeeds telegram at a few minutes' interval as they are picked up and decoded, often in the wrong sequence, frequently of dubious import; and out of these a picture always flickering and changing rises in the mind, and imagination strikes out around it at every stage flashes of hope or fear.[69]

Churchill used this device to recount the 15 September air battle, which he monitored from fifty feet underground, in the Operations Room of No. 11 Fighter Group in Uxbridge. He brought Clementine with him, as if it were a matinee. In fact it "was like a small theatre," and "we took our seats in the Dress Circle." Below them was a large map where discs marked the position of enemy aircraft, and "covering the entire wall, where the theatre curtain would be, was a gigantic blackboard divided into six columns with electric bulbs, for the six fighter stations." The bulbs indicated whether the fighter squadrons were refueling, ready, in the air, engaged with the enemy, or flying home. On each side of the stage there was "a kind of glass stage-box," where officers processed visual reports of approaching enemy aircraft and monitored anti-aircraft guns. Air Vice-Marshal Keith Park, in command of the center, at first told them that everything was quiet, but within minutes reports of German bomber groups filtered in. The fighters were ordered into the air, though the dispatchers had to husband their reserves and ensure that not too many squadrons were refueling at the same time, when they could be destroyed on the ground. Ultimately every fighter squadron was committed, and Churchill anxiously asked Park the same question he had asked General Gamelin four months earlier, and received the same chilling answer:

> "What other reserves have we?"
> "There are none."

Churchill had to ramp up the tension, even though his audience knew the outcome, and here he resorted to the device of dramatic echo. Early in the play a portentous line is spoken, followed by terrible consequences, and then the line is repeated much later, suggesting that the tragedy is about to repeat itself. It usually doesn't, but until that relief the audience is brought to the edge of their seats: "The odds were great; our margins small; the stakes infinite." In this case most of the British fighters were refueling and vulnerable to attack, but soon it became clear that the Germans were flying home. Churchill returned to Chequers for a very long nap, "tired by the drama of No. 11 Group."[70]

Many reviewers pointed to this as the most electrifying scene of *Their Finest Hour*, the second volume of *The Second World War*.[71] It was one episode of the war that Churchill returned to again and again with Lord Moran: "You see, Charles, it was very nearly the end of everything." Moran noted the cinematic style of Churchill's narratives:

> Winston sees everything in pictures. I could feel the tension in the operation room, fifty feet underground. I could see Park walking up and down giving his orders. And then, as more of our fighting squadrons were put in, more of

the little electric bulbs on the great blackboard glowed red. All the bulbs were red now, all our squadrons were in the air.

But Moran offered a different version of the climactic exchange between Churchill and Park: "How many more have you got?" "I am putting in my last."[72] Of course it is possible that Moran's second-hand account (set down five years after the event) is not absolutely accurate, and that General Gamelin rewrote the dialogue of May 1940 to cover up his own incompetence. But it could be that they were both telling the truth, and that Churchill, for the sake of drama, doctored their script.

Melodramatic heroes were always brought to the very brink of defeat before their ultimate (and inevitable) victory. This is why Churchill's habit of telling the British people the worst had the counterintuitive effect of lifting their spirits. As Harold Nicolson noted on 5 November:

> The Prime Minister makes a statement after Question-time. He is rather grim. He brings home to the House as never before the gravity of our shipping losses and the danger of our position in the Eastern Mediterranean. It has a good effect. By putting the grim side foremost he impresses us with his ability to face the worst. He rubs the palms of his hands with five fingers extended up and down the front of his coat, searching for the right phrase, indicating cautious selection, conveying almost medicinal poise. If Chamberlain had spoken glum words such as these the impression would have been one of despair and lack of confidence. Churchill can say them and we all feel, "Thank God that we have a man like that!" I have never admired him more.[73]

Alexander Cadogan, in his customary end-of-the year review, wrote in his diary:

> I haven't much to say tonight – except that worse things have happened during this year than we could have expected. But one thing is much better than anyone could have hoped – and that is the British spirit. I am amazed at the courage of my fellow-countryman. I am rather a physical coward, and I can't say how much I admire the courage all round me. . . . Everything – on paper – is against us, but we shall live. I don't frankly, see how we are going to win, but I am convinced that we shall not lose. And if you hang on – like a bull-dog – it's funny what things do happen. The enemy is a very good façade. But if it cracks, it will crack suddenly and cataclysmically.[74]

Home Intelligence and Mass Observation both found that especially heavy raids could produce bouts of despair and defeatism, notably in London,

Coventry, and Southampton. But these were exceptional and temporary.[75] It has been argued that those surveyed suppressed their real anxieties when questioned by pollsters, for fear of "letting the side down." And one could say that in his "Finest Hour" speech Churchill urged the British people to do precisely that. But when he fought on the Northwest Frontier more than forty years earlier, Churchill had understood that all soldiers are actors, putting on a show of bravery to impress – and he knew that in war there is no practical difference between theatrical courage and "real" courage. When journalists reported the "performance" of Londoners, who could "take it" and were "carrying on," they established a role that everyone in Britain could play, with Churchill directing as the dramaturge-in-chief.[76] Mass Observation concluded, from the vantage point of 1948, that "we tend today to think of the 'Dunkirk spirit' as a spontaneous growth from innate British characteristics. In point of fact, as diaries and overheard conversations demonstrate, *private* defeatism was widespread at first. The current was changed, principally by leadership from without, before private feeling had time to translate itself into public mood."[77]

Paradoxically, Churchill's success in bolstering the morale of the British people and leading them through "Spitfire Summer" would ultimately erode his charisma. As early as October 1940, the Postal Censorship Centre in Inverness reported that Churchill was now mentioned in letters only one-tenth as frequently as a few months earlier, even if the remarks were almost unanimously positive. "Whereas in June people seemed to feel that only Churchill stood between them and disaster, now the ordinary people of England have shown that they too could play just as stubborn and important a part."[78] That confidence in themselves, which Churchill had done so much to inspire, may have convinced them that they could do without him in the General Election of 1945.

The high spirits of 1940 could not be maintained indefinitely, and would come under severe strain in 1941 and 1942, as the war became an ever longer and grinding routine. But a more immediate threat was escalating losses to German submarines. Germany was incapable of invading Britain or bombing her into submission, but the U-boats came frighteningly close to choking off vital imports of food and raw materials. "The P.M. tells me that 640,000 tons of merchant shipping have been sunk in the last two months in what he calls 'American waters'," Moran noted in his diary. "Wherever he goes he carries in his head the monthly figures of all sinkings, though he never talks about them. . . . He knows that we may lose the war at sea in a few months and that he can do nothing about it."[79] By 6 March 1941 shipping losses had become so severe that Churchill decided the war could only be won by rebranding it. "We have got to lift this business to the highest plane, over everything else," he told Admiral Pound. "I am going to proclaim 'the Battle of the Atlantic'." As he explained in *The Second World War*, "This, like featuring 'the Battle of Britain' nine months earlier, was a signal intended to concentrate all minds and all departments concerned upon the U-boat war."

The Battle of the Atlantic involved a host of coordinated practical strategies, including fighters launched from ships by catapult, reorganization of convoys, diversion of anti-aircraft guns to the Admiralty, priority for repairing damaged merchant vessels, and more efficient turnaround at the docks. But there were also literary weapons: "Strong propaganda . . . run locally at the ports and yards, in order that all engaged may realise the vital consequences of their work."[80] After the euphoria of Spitfire Summer, war fatigue was beginning to set in. Though the Blitz continued, the most crucial battle was now being fought not in the skies above Britain, where everyone could see it and feel a part of it, but far out at sea. Something had to be done to keep morale at a high pitch, even if Churchill sometimes sounded like an adman, convinced that a winning campaign depended on the right slogan. On 19 May the War Cabinet minutes recorded that, on top of the huge shipping losses, "it was difficult to see in what precise way the Battle of the Atlantic could be dramatized."[81] The British people were told next to nothing about this theatre of war, for fear of damaging morale and leaking vital information to the Germans.[82] Eden and Beaverbrook wanted to give American journalists free rein to report on this life-and-death struggle, hoping it would encourage the United States to enter the war, but Churchill feared that it would have the opposite effect.[83]

"The Battle of the Atlantic was the dominating factor all through the war," Churchill wrote in retrospect. "Never for one moment could we forget that everything happening elsewhere, on land, at sea, or in the air, depended ultimately on its outcome." The problem for the historian and the war propagandist was that, for the ordinary seamen and airmen, it was a long monotonous struggle only occasionally "lighted by incident and drama." Thus, in proportion to its importance, it is relatively neglected in histories of the war, though Churchill tried to redress that balance in his own memoir.[84]

He continued to express faith (on 27 March 1941) in "the sentiment aroused in American breasts at the spectacle of courage and devotion shown by simple and ordinary folk of this country in standing up to the fire of the enemy."[85] That confidence was not entirely misplaced. In February Cassell had brought out *Into Battle*, a collection of Churchill's war-related speeches and broadcasts. It was a great success in Britain, with 30,000 copies in print before publication and a total of eleven printings before the end of the war. But the impact in America (where it was published by Putnam's under the title *Blood, Sweat, and Tears*) was enormous. It was released on 14 April after a twelve-week publicity blitz that a Putnam executive called "one of the most satisfactory campaigns we ever had." (It overlapped with the Lend-Lease Act, signed by President Roosevelt on 11 March.) The Book of the Month Club edition alone probably accounted for at least 120,000 in sales. At last, Churchill had an American bestseller – fourth place on the *Publishers Weekly* non-fiction list for 1941. All told, the book earned him more than £12,000 by 1 June 1942.[86]

More importantly, the volume fixed in the minds of the American reading public an indelibly heroic image of Churchill. Once regarded as a crafty and dishonest imperialist, now he became a bulwark of freedom and the greatest contemporary master of English prose. According to Raymond Daniell, London bureau chief for the *New York Times*, the book made "plain what Mr. Churchill and the people he leads and represents are fighting for with all their might . . . for if one thing shines clear through all these addresses it is the profound conviction that a truce with Nazism means the ultimate death of freedom."[87] "A historical and human document of the first order," proclaimed Smith College historian Hans Kohn in the *Nation*, "one of the great classics of statesmanship."[88] As book review editor for the *New Yorker*, Clifton Fadiman stressed two points: "The first is that these speeches, viewed now in retrospect, prove Churchill was right nine times out of ten in his judgment of the varying phases of the world crisis. The second is that much of this book is literature."[89] And the paeans continued in the *Boston Evening Transcript* ("These speeches are among the greatest works ever penned"), the *Christian Science Monitor* ("To stress the power of Mr. Churchill's language would be superfluous"), and the *New York Herald Tribune* ("This is the voice of a great leader and a great fighter for democracy, standing in one of the greatest crises in the history of the world").[90] Most of the *Time* review simply quoted his most memorable epigrams, with the brief comment: "In their simple eloquence they mirror (and helped cause) the reawakening of a people's faith."[91] "I don't like to use superlatives, but Churchill has earned the right to be called the best public speaker in the world today," wrote Malcolm Cowley in the *New Republic*. "He not only makes laws for his people but writes their songs as well, in the sense that his speeches are battle cries, dirges for the fallen and hymns of victory."[92] The *New Republic* had been so hostile to British imperialism that John Maynard Keynes quit writing for it.[93] But Cowley was one of many American leftists who had been bitterly disillusioned by the Nazi-Soviet Pact. It was not lost upon them that now Churchill, not Stalin or Roosevelt, was actually fighting fascism.

Churchill's irresistible impulse to launch offensive coups, even when Britain (and her Empire) were fighting alone, inspired Britons and impressed Americans, but that policy of action at all costs often drove experienced bureaucrats and generals to despair. "We are in that awful period when everything is going wrong and those in authority feel they have got to *do* something," protested Alexander Cadogan on 28 April. He cornered Anthony Eden (now Foreign Secretary) for a moment and pleaded with him: "Please don't do anything for the sake of *doing* something! Don't throw in small packets here and there to get chewed up. I know it's disappointing and humiliating to look forward to another year of the defensive, but *don't* squander the little you've got." Eden gave the appearance of agreeing, but (Cadogan sighed) "will o' the wisps have a fatal attraction for him and Winston."[94] As Clement Attlee shrewdly observed a few months after the end of the war, Churchill "was always looking around for 'finest hours,' and if one was not immediately available, his impulse was to manufacture one."[95]

When Mussolini invaded Greece in October 1940, Churchill immediately demanded that "maximum possible" assistance be dispatched to the Greeks. This strategy did not have much to recommend it. True, Chamberlain had promised to defend Greece in March 1939, but on their own the Greeks managed to hurl the Italian army back into Albania. General Archibald Wavell was building up his army in Egypt to repel a much larger Italian force attacking from Libya, and could hardly afford to spare men and equipment. If Mussolini insisted on frittering away his forces on several fronts, the British had no good reason to emulate him. When Wavell, General Dill, and Eden all protested, Churchill composed his rebuttal with all the concentration of an artist, as John Colville noted:

> He lay there in his four-post bed with its flowery chintz hangings, his bed-table by his side. Mrs. Hill [his stenographer] sat patiently opposite while he chewed his cigar, drank frequent sips of iced soda-water, fidgeted his toes beneath the bedclothes and muttered stertorously under his breath what he contemplated saying. To watch him compose some telegram or minute for dictation is to make one feel that one is present at the birth of a child, so tense is his expression, so restless his turnings from side to side, so curious the noises he emits under his breath. Then comes out some masterly sentence and finally with a "Gimme" he takes the sheet of typewritten paper and initials it or alters it with his fountain-pen, which he holds most awkwardly halfway up the holder.

Churchill dismissed Eden's warnings that such a diversion would weaken Wavell's planned offensive.[96] In December 1940 Wavell's stunning victory over a much larger Italian army seemed to vindicate Churchill, but the offensive bogged down halfway across Libya. And the forces sent to Greece proved wholly insufficient to repel the German invasion in April 1941. Ever since historians have debated whether, if Churchill had not drained Wavell's army, it might have secured all of Libya and wrapped up the North African war two years before El Alamein. Even at the time, as Colville recorded, Churchill indulged in counterfactual history:

> He said we had taken the right course: we had risked sending troops and material to Egypt when still under the threat of invasion at home, and we had sent substantial air assistance to Greece in spite of the fact that we were preparing for a "Spring of the Lion" in North Africa. But if events had taken a different course, as they might have, what would history have said? He quoted dramatically from a mythical history book of the future, denouncing the criminal gambler who sent overseas the divisions which might have turned the scale against the German invasion at home, or the vacillators who sent to Greece the aeroplanes which could have turned the North African fiasco into a success.[97]

By 26 May 1941 the news from all fronts was particularly dismal. The Germans were overrunning Crete, the *Bismarck* had sunk the *Hood* and had so far eluded British carrier aircraft. Most of the Cabinet favored publishing demoralizing statistics of convoy losses, but Churchill browbeat them into submission. Then he argued melodramatically in favor of extending conscription to Ulster ("to back down now, in face of clamour, would show that the mainspring of resolution was broken &c. &c."), but the Cabinet blocked that. "Poor Winston," sighed Cadogan. "Tonight he was almost throwing his hand in. But there is a bit of the histrionic art in *that*."[98]

If that Cabinet meeting resembled a dress rehearsal where everything went wrong, it all came magically together in the House of Commons the following day. Churchill began by admitting naval losses in the battle for Crete, but then proceeded to weave a gripping sea yarn about the *Bismarck*. "He does it beautifully," wrote Harold Nicolson:

> He builds up the whole picture from the moment when we heard that the *Bismarck* and the *Prinz Eugen* were driving westwards against our convoys to the moment when we came into contact with them and the *Hood* was sunk. After paying a tribute to the loss of these men, he passed on to the further pursuit. The *Prinz Eugen* had disappeared, but the *Bismarck* was followed closely and bombed. This bombing slowed down her escape, which by then was evidently directed towards some French port. Further arrangements were made to intercept her, but then the weather changed and visibility diminished, and by a sudden change of course the *Bismarck* managed to elude our vigilance. The whole House felt at that moment that Winston was about to break to us that the ship had escaped. There was a hush of despair. At dawn next morning (Winston continued) we again resumed

> contact. He told us how the Fleet Air Arm fired torpedoes at the ship, destroying her steering gear and forcing her to go round and round in immense circles in the ocean. From all sides our fleet approached to destroy her. Such is the innate sporting feeling of the House that we all began to feel sorry for the *Bismarck*. The P.M. went on to say that our ships had established contact, that they had begun to fire; that their shells had not made any effect; and that the only hope was to fire torpedoes. "The process", he said, "is in action as I speak."

At this point Churchill (who knew how to make an audience wait) coolly digressed to the issue of conscription in Northern Ireland, leaving "the House with a sense of *coitus interruptus*," as Nicolson put it. Then, after an interval, he received a slip of paper from Brendan Bracken (one of his closest advisors) and rose to announce, to thunderous cheers, "I have just received news that the *Bismarck* has been sunk."[99] It was a strictly factual report, yet it brilliantly deployed all the devices of adventure fiction. Two weeks later he candidly explained his narrative method to the House of Commons: "The British nation is unique in this respect. They are the only people who like to be told how bad things are, who like to be told the worst, and like to be told that they are very likely to get much worse in the future and must prepare themselves for further reverses." Ultimately, though, "The only answer to defeat is victory. If a Government in time of war gives the impression that it cannot in the long run procure victory, who cares for its explanations? It ought to go. . . "[100]

Churchill's backs-to-the-wall performances discouraged the Germans as much as they elated the British. In April 1941 an infuriated Joseph Goebbels protested that "everywhere among the German public one can now hear the offensive phrase: 'The British are tougher than us! Just suppose we had to go through what the British are now standing up to.' "[101] By 7 December he was compelled to admit that "Churchill did the right thing when . . . he promised the British 'blood, sweat and tears.' "[102] That rhetoric of adversity secured Churchill "in a position that makes him totally immune from attack," Goebbels complained after the surrender of Singapore on 15 February 1942. "He is like a doctor who prophesies that his patient will die and who, every time the patient's condition worsens, smugly explains that, after all, he prophesied it."[103] On 19 February the Propaganda Minister was driven to protest that "The German press is still publishing biographies, pictures and stories of Churchill which are too favourable and tend to make Churchill popular among the German people."[104]

Conversely, Nazi triumphalism backfired badly. In September–October 1940 William L. Shirer noted that attempts to play down the damage done by RAF raids on Berlin (which in fact was not yet very serious) undermined the credibility of the German media. Many Berliners tossed aside their evening papers and turned off radio news bulletins with a disgusted "*Quatsch!*" "I'll never believe another thing they say," Shirer was told. "If they've lied about the raids in the rest of Germany as they have about the ones in Berlin, then it must have been pretty bad there."[105] Later, when the tide of war turned at Stalingrad and in North Africa, in 1942–43, Goebbels urged his propagandists to do what "Churchill did after Dunkirk," but at the same time (contradictorily) he forbade them "to explain or even mention defeats."[106] Groping for a slogan to match "blood, sweat and tears," he finally came up with "No more crises!", which was pathetic.[107] Goebbels never quite fathomed that Churchill had roused the British people precisely by dwelling on defeats, and that crisis is the energy that drives drama.

Churchill had anticipated the German invasion of the Soviet Union on 21 June 1941, the day before it actually began. Even then, John Colville recorded, he was prepared to "go all out to help Russia." When Colville brought him news of the invasion the following morning, he immediately resolved to broadcast that evening at 9.00 p.m., without consulting his Cabinet.[108] He began the radio address by describing the invasion as the fourth great coup of the war, following the fall of France, the defeat of the Luftwaffe over Britain, and the Lend-Lease Act. He then briefly acknowledged his own long-standing hostility to the Soviet Union, reiterating that Nazism "is indistinguishable from the worst features of Communism. . . . No one has been a more consistent opponent of Communism than I have for the last twenty-five years. I will unsay no word that I have spoken about it." Then how could he explain his volte-face? Again he resorted to the devices of melodrama. In *The Second World War*, he established the mood of this episode by referring to an intelligence report he had read at the end of March, which revealed that the Germans were concentrating their panzer divisions in Cracow: "To me it illuminated the whole Eastern scene like a lightning-flash. The sudden movement to Cracow of so much armour needed in the Balkan sphere could only mean Hitler's intention to invade Russia in May."[109] Then, in his 22 June broadcast, he resorted to similar stage imagery:

> But all this fades away before the spectacle which is now unfolding. The past, with its crimes, its follies and its tragedies, flashes away.
>
> I see the Russian soldiers standing on the threshold of their native land, guarding the fields which their fathers have tilled from time immemorial. I see them guarding their homes where mothers and wives pray—ah, yes, for there are times when all pray—for the safety of their loved ones, the return of the bread-winner, of their champion, or their protector. I see the ten thousand villages of Russia where the means of existence was wrung so hardly

> from the soil, but where there are still primordial human joys, where maidens laugh and children play. I see advancing upon all this in hideous onslaught the Nazi war machine, with its clanking, heel-clicking, dandified Prussian officers, its crafty expert agents fresh from the cowing and tying down of a dozen countries. I see also the dull, drilled, docile, brutish masses of the Hun soldiery plodding on like a swarm of crawling locusts.[110]

"I see. . . . I see. . . . I see. . . . I see. . . . I see. . . ." In fact Churchill had seen it all, fifty years earlier, on the London stage. Jules Verne's *Michael Strogoff* had portrayed an invasion of Russia, with the Russian people (including even Siberian exiles) rallying to her defense and employing the same kind of patriotic speeches:

> Are you no longer children of old Siberia? . . . Have not the Tartars invaded the whole of the provinces? . . . Is it not an army of barbarians who have entered our villages? . . . For as far as one can see there is nothing but villages in flames. . . . Our own rivers are flowing in blood. . . . Resist – resist to the end and die, if need be. . . . Every hour gained gives Russia time to rally herself. . . . My friends, listen to the old Siberian's voice, who wants to die with you to defend her country. . . . Courage, my friends! Let each one of us die bravely – not for the safety, but for the honour of Russia. . . . Hurrah for Russia![111]

Eden, unhappy that he had not been asked about Churchill's broadcast beforehand, argued that Britain should keep the USSR at arm's length. They should be co-belligerents rather than allies, cooperating solely in the military sphere. As Colville paraphrased it, "Politically Russia was as bad as Germany and half the country would object to being associated with her too closely. The PM's view was that Russia was now at war; innocent peasants were being slaughtered; and we should forget about Soviet systems and extend our hand to fellow human beings in distress. The argument was brilliant and extremely vehement."[112]

Churchill realized that cold realpolitik alone would satisfy no one – neither pro-Soviet Britons nor anti-Soviet Britons nor the Soviets themselves. The day before the invasion, as Colville noted, he concluded that "Hitler is counting on enlisting capitalist and right-wing sympathies in this country and the US."[113] Churchill could only bring the right and the left together in a common anti-Nazi front through melodrama. In his broadcast, he acknowledged ideological differences only to sweep them aside and conjure up in the mind's eye a series of theatrical/cinematic images. Victorian melodrama commonly employed dramatic tableaux, where the action momentarily halted and the actors froze in heroic postures.[114] *Michael Strogoff* used just such a device: in fact the play apparently pioneered a new technique for staging tableaux.[115] Later, any number of Hollywood movies would do something similar: at a moment of crisis, dialogue is suspended and, against a background of climactic orchestral music, a succession of grippingly emotional scenes fade in and out. A classic example comes from a movie Churchill had seen just a few months earlier, Charlie Chaplin's *The Great Dictator*, when Hynkel's stormtroopers invade Osterlich and rampage through the Jewish quarters.[116]

According to the Ministry of Information's Home Intelligence Report, the listening public received the speech with "warm approval," because it appealed to them as both pragmatic and dramatic. It was "generally accepted as both a practical and logical move," and it was acknowledged that Churchill "discharged a difficult task well when he spoke of our support for Russia, after he had for many years voiced his contempt, and at times his abhorrence, for the Bolshevik regime." At the same time, and on the other hand, "His use of the word 'guttersnipe' appealed to almost all classes."[117] Never loath to give an adversary his due, Count Ciano, speaking "objectively," readily acknowledged that the speech "carries the mark of a great orator."[118]

CHAPTER 20

The War Poet

In August 1941 General Ismay explained to General Claude Auchinleck (the newly appointed commander of British forces in the Middle East) that Churchill was a creative genius who, like any modern artist, kicked against mechanical rules and bureaucratic limits:

> Churchill could not be judged by ordinary standards; he was different from anyone we had ever met before, or were ever likely to meet again. As a war leader, he was head and shoulders above anyone that the British or any other nation could produce. He was indispensable and completely irreplaceable. . . . He was a child of nature. He venerated tradition, but ridiculed convention. . . . When the spirit moved him, he could be a *gamin*. . . . At the same time, he did not fully realize the extent to which mechanization had complicated administrative arrangements and revolutionized the problems of time and space; and he never ceased to cry out against the inordinate "tail" which modern armies required. "When I was a soldier," he would say, "infantry used to walk and cavalry used to ride. But now the infantry require motor-cars, and even the tanks have to have horse boxes to take them to battle."[1]

As Churchill expressed it in a March 1943 memorandum: "An operation of war cannot be thought out like building a bridge; certainty is not demanded, and genius, improvisation and energy of mind must have their parts."[2] "Without imagination not much can be done," he said at Harrow, in October 1941. "Those people who are imaginative see many more dangers than perhaps exist, certainly many more than will happen; but then they must also pray to be given that extra courage to carry this far-reaching imagination."[3] For Churchill, literary and strategic creativity were inseparable: "You cannot expect to have the genius type with a conventional copy-book style."[4] He insisted that every military officer should read Plutarch's *Lives*: "The present trouble was that officers were admirably versed in weapon training but had little stimulus to use their imagination and look at military problems with a broad view," as John Colville summed it up.[5] Churchill's style of command was therefore more aesthetic than scientific, following literary models rather than administrative structures. It could be highly imaginative and creative; it could also ignore the mundane imperatives of global strategy and logistics.

As a political artist, he would have been more at home in France. He was fascinated by the "blood-curdling political drama" of the Third Republic in the age of Clemenceau.[6] So was Charles de Gaulle, even if he was more skeptical about the histrionics: "As an adolescent, the fate of France, whether as the subject of history or as the stake in public life, interested me above everything. I was therefore attracted, but also severely critical, towards the play which was performed, day in, day out, in the forum; carried away as I was by the intelligence, fire, and eloquence lavished upon it by countless actors, yet saddened at seeing so many gifts wasted in political confusion and national disunity."[7] De Gaulle commonly characterized the Second World War as a "drama",[8] "the worst drama in all our history," as he put it in a 1943 Bastille Day speech.[9] His memoirs, like Churchill's, were a deliberately literary production, acutely conscious of political theatre, laced with stage metaphors and allusions to Goethe's *Faust* and Shakespeare's *Macbeth*.[10] Mussolini made himself "a great star of the international stage" with his parades and pageantry and "dramatic gestures," though it all ended in a "Roman *coup de théâtre*."[11] At a Moscow summit in December 1944, de Gaulle noticed that "Stalin began playing an extraordinary scene," conspicuously bullying his own generals and commissars in a "tragicomic" effort to intimidate the French delegation. It resembled a "well-made play, in which the plot remains unsolved while the peripeties mingle and multiply until the moment of denouement."[12]

De Gaulle and Churchill worked together as well as they did because they understood and respected each other as equally gifted actors. "This exceptional artist was certainly conscious of the dramatic character of my mission," the general recalled:[13]

> . . . he was fitted by his character to act, take risks, play the part out-and-out and without scruple. . . . Whatever his audience – crowd, assembly, council, even a single interlocutor – whether he was before a microphone, on the floor of the House, at table, or behind a desk, the original, poetic, stirring flow of his ideas, arguments, and feelings brought him an almost infallible ascendancy in the tragic atmosphere in which the poor world was gasping. Well tried in politics, he played upon that angelic and diabolical gift to rouse the heavy dough of the English as well as to impress the minds of foreigners. The humour, too, with which he seasoned his acts and words, and the way

> in which he made use now of graciousness, now of anger, contributed to make one feel what a mastery he had of the terrible game in which he was engaged. . . . Winston Churchill appeared to me, from one end of the drama to the other, as the great champion of a great enterprise and the great artist of a great history.

True, "harsh and painful incidents . . . often arose between us," but even these de Gaulle attributed to "the friction of our two characters," as if it were the necessary dramatic conflict that drove the story forward.[14] The wartime tensions between the British government and the Free French were legion, but they never led to a breakdown in relations, largely because de Gaulle recognized they were theatre following a predictable script. Typically the British officials would open by making demands that they thought perfectly reasonable. De Gaulle would then adamantly refuse (he felt a need to compensate for the spinelessness of the Third Republic) and the British would respond first with chilling silence, to heighten the dramatic tension:

> Then would come the decisive attack. A solemn Franco-British meeting would take place unexpectedly. At it, all means would be brought to bear; all the arguments produced; all the complaints given utterance; all the tunes chanted. Although among the responsible British there were different degrees of dramatic skill, each one of them played his part like an artist of distinction. For hours on end heart-rending and alarming scenes followed one another. It would break up on a solemn warning of what would happen if we did not yield.
>
> A little while more and there would come the epilogue. Various British sources would give out signals for an easing of tension. Intermediaries would come and say that there had doubtless been a misunderstanding. Suitable people would ask how I was. Some benevolent paragraph or other would appear in the newspapers. Thereupon there would arrive a British proposal for accommodation over the disputed question, with a good deal of resemblance to what we ourselves had proposed.[15]

Much like Churchill, de Gaulle was a literary determinist, who believed that texts were motors of history. "There would have been no Arab invasion without the Koran," he asserted. "No crusades without the Gospels. The *ancien régime* in Europe rose against France when the Assembly proclaimed, 'Men are born free and equal by law.' "[16] He recognized the crucial role of print in the Resistance: the underground newspapers, literary magazines, and publishing operations such as the Éditions de Minuit.[17] Even pulp literature, de Gaulle insisted, played its part: "Between the two wars the young had shown a marked taste for stories of the Deuxième Bureau, secret service, detection, and even sabotage and conspiracy. Books, newspapers, the theatre, and the cinema had devoted themselves largely to the adventures of more or less imaginary heroes who were prodigal of shadowy exploits in the service of their country. This psychology was destined to make recruitment for special missions easier," though it also involved some "risk of introducing into them romanticism, irresponsibility, and sometimes fraud."[18]

During the first few months of the war Neville Chamberlain indulged heavily in escapist literature: books about the Elizabethans and Jacobeans, Regency aristocrats, and a Swiss gaucho, short stories by H. E. Bates, Francis Steegmuller's *Flaubert and Madame Bovary*, and Shakespeare's comedies. "One must have something to take one's mind off these perpetual war problems and the unending nagging of the Press & House of Commons," he groaned, suggesting that he was not fully focused on the job at hand.[19] In contrast, Churchill loved novels and films that were directly relevant to the current conflict, especially those that drew analogies to Britain's 1793–1815 struggle with France. C. S. Forester's *Captain Hornblower RN* he "found vastly entertaining." And when he saw *That Hamilton Woman* for the fifth time the final scene, Nelson's triumphant death at Trafalgar, still brought tears to his eyes. It was screened on board HMS *Prince of Wales*, which had recently participated in sinking the *Bismarck*: "Gentlemen, I thought this Film would interest you, showing great events similar to those in which you have been taking part." In 1942, when it appeared that Hitler might march through Spain to capture Gibraltar, Churchill and Roosevelt both studied Wellington's Peninsular campaign.

Churchill thoroughly enjoyed "*Pimpernel*" *Smith*, in which Leslie Howard updated the role he played in *The Scarlet Pimpernel* (1934).[20] In this 1941 revision of Baroness Orczy's melodrama (staged as a play in 1903 and novelized in 1905), the Pimpernel rescues concentration camp inmates in Nazi Germany. (The same film may have inspired another key figure in the war: when Raoul Wallenberg saw it, his sister recalled, "he told me this was the kind of thing he would like to do," and he appears to have copied Leslie Howard's tactics in his efforts to rescue Hungarian Jews.)[21] Earlier, when France fell in the summer of 1940, Churchill had suggested creating a "Scarlet Pimpernel organization" to spirit pro-de Gaulle soldiers and technicians out of the country.[22] He later commended to Franklin Roosevelt General d'Astier de la Vigerie, who was organizing resistance inside France, as a "remarkable man of the Scarlet Pimpernel type."[23] Still later he praised the Yugoslav Partisans by adapting Orczy's catchphrase: "They were here, they were there, they were everywhere."[24]

In May 1941 Churchill had a cinema installed at Chequers, where films became a regular ritual.[25] For him movies were a stimulant to strategic thinking rather than an escape. A "sort of a mental liberation was granted him when looking at the cinema," his bodyguard Walter Thompson recalled. "Churchill could sit for two hours looking at a film, know in some detail what he'd looked at, but come away from the session with a brand-new, full blown revolutionary war plan in his mind. He would then take it directly to one of his secretaries and set it down in detail while its images were as sharp edged and clean surfaced as shells on a sandbar."[26]

He could just as readily find war strategies in novels. John Steinbeck's *The Moon is Down* (1942) was set in an unidentified occupied country, where the inhabitants ask the British to airdrop weapons that they can use against the Germans. This encouraged Churchill's passion for "setting Europe ablaze": "In addition to being a well-written story, it stresses, I think quite rightly, the importance of providing the conquered nations with simple weapons, such as sticks of dynamite, which could easily be concealed and are easy in operation."[27] Lord Selborne, the head of the Special Operations Executive, advised him that such a rash policy at the present time would only expose civilians to German reprisals.[28]

"Where are the war poets?" was the question posed by every serious reader in the Second World War, when there seemed to be no obvious successors to Rupert Brooke, Wilfred Owen, or Siegfried Sassoon. Some pointed to RAF Squadron Leader John Pudney ("Do not despair / For Johnny-head-in-air . . ."),[29] but another possible answer was "At Ten Downing Street." Churchill seemed to have a poetic epigram for every crisis, defeat, or victory When in April 1939 Mussolini seized Albania, while the scattered British Mediterranean Fleet was caught unawares, he quoted Byron's *Childe Harold's Pilgrimage*: "A thousand years scarce serve to form a State, / An hour may lay it in the dust."[30] In September, after his return to the Admiralty, he wondered whether it would all end in a second Gallipoli, and remembered the words of the Irish poet Thomas Moore:

> I feel like one
> Who treads alone
> Some banquet-hall deserted,
> Whose lights are fled,
> Whose garlands dead,
> And all but he departed![31]

On 1 November 1940, as Churchill was discussing the prospect of bombing Rome, *Childe Harold* again came to mind ("When falls the Coliseum Rome shall fall . . .).[32] In December he urged General Wavell, after defeating the Italians at Sidi Barrani, to pursue them relentlessly: "The poet Walt Whitman says that from every fruition of success, however full, comes forth something to make a greater struggle necessary."[33] And in February 1941, with Mussolini routed in Libya and Greece, Byron's "Ode to Napoleon Buonaparte" seemed appropriate: "Those Pagod things of sabre-sway / With fronts of brass, and feet of clay."[34] That spring, as the Americans were increasingly assisting the British in the Battle of the Atlantic, he cited Arthur Hugh Clough:

> And not by eastern windows only,
> When daylight comes, comes in the light,
> In front the sun climbs slow, how slowly,
> But westward, look, the land is bright.[35]

On 19 March, in the midst of a particularly spectacular air raid, Tennyson's "Locksley Hall" naturally came to mind:

> Heard the heavens fill with shouting, and there rain'd a ghastly dew
> From the nations' airy navies grappling in the central blue.[36]

By September, with Britain's position not quite so desperate as it had been a year earlier, Churchill could close a speech to the House of Commons with W. E. Henley's "Invictus",[37] and sing the unsung victories of minesweepers with a favorite Kipling poem:

> Mines reported in the fairway,
> Warn all traffic and detain.
> Send up Unity, Claribel, Assyrian, Stormcock, and Golden Gain.[38]

And when, in January 1942, Franklin Roosevelt proposed that the Allies adopt the title "United Nations," Churchill referred him back once again to *Childe Harold's Pilgrimage*: "Here, where the sword united nations drew, / Our countrymen were warring on that day!"[39]

One of young Randolph's military friends, David Stirling, reminded him of Byron's *Don Juan*: "the mildest mannered man that ever scuttled ship or cut a throat."[40] A minute planning the invasion of Italy concluded with Shakespeare's *Julius Caesar* ("There is a tide in the affairs of men . . .").[41] Even when his secretaries drafted his messages, as they sometimes did, they learned to lace them with Churchillian literary allusions. When John Colville wrote up the Prime Minister's proclamation honoring Greek Independence Day, he made sure to mention Byron. "Although Mr. Churchill at his best was beyond plagiarism, it was possible to imitate his style fairly closely on matters which were not of supreme importance and I reached the stage where I could draft most of his shorter compositions without his correcting them," Colville recalled when he published his diaries.[42] Toward the end of the Second World War he wondered "how difficult it will be for future historians to know what is 'genuine Churchill' and what is 'school of'. We [his secretaries] are all fairly good imitators of his epistolary style now. . . ."[43]

When Churchill and the Australian Prime Minister Robert Menzies met in March 1941, the latter noted that it was Churchill's ability to (mis)quote Wordsworth that kept up morale, his own and that of the British people:

> The PM in conversation will steep himself (and you) in gloom on some grim aspect of the war (tonight shipping losses to Focke Wulf planes and U-boats – the supreme menace of the war . . .) only to proceed to fight his way out while he is pacing the floor with the light of battle in his eyes.
>
> In every conversation he inevitably reaches a point where he positively enjoys the war: "Bliss in that age it was to be alive".
>
> "Why do people regard a period like this as 'years lost out of our lives' when beyond question it is the most interesting period of them? Why do we regard history as of the past and forget we are making it?"

But Menzies saw the potential danger here: though Churchill had an "amazing grasp of detail . . . his real tyrant is the glittering phrase – so attractive to his mind that awkward facts have to give way."[44]

Even as morale boosters, the glittering phrases could only accomplish so much for so long. The *Washington Post* was deeply impressed when Churchill addressed Congress in December 1941, shortly after the attack on Pearl Harbor: "A consummate actor, who carefully times his speech so that each word and each syllable is given the exact emphasis it should have, Mr. Churchill also pauses at the proper time for applause."[45] Back home, reported the Ministry of Information, praise for the speech was "almost unanimous and it is regarded by many as the best he has ever made," a "great historic utterance" that would "knit the British Empire and the United States more closely together, not only for the duration of the war but for a long time to come."[46] However, Moran observed that the applause in Washington depended on the notes struck: when Churchill denounced Japan, "Congress rose as one man and stood cheering as if they would never stop," but they were far less enthusiastic when he spoke of Anglo-American unity.[47] That old distrust of Britain persisted. A spring 1942 survey conducted by the US Office of War Information (OWI) found that many Americans still regarded the British as "arrogant" exploitive imperialists who did not pay their war debts and had deceptively lured the United States into the last war. They granted that the British people had courage and that it was in America's interest to assist them, but hardly anyone favored a post-war Anglo-American alliance.[48] A July 1942 OWI poll asked which country was making the greatest effort to win the war: just 6 percent of Americans named Britain, far behind Russia (30 percent) and China (14 percent).[49]

Moreover, Churchill still had to explain a continuing series of humiliating reverses. On 23 April 1942 the House of Commons met in secret session to hear him speak bluntly about the sinking of the *Repulse* and the *Prince of Wales*, the disabling of the *Queen Elizabeth* and *Valiant* in Alexandria Harbour, the fall of Singapore, the serious shipping losses in the Atlantic. "It is a long and utterly remorseless catalogue of disaster and misfortune," wrote Harold Nicolson:

> And as he tells us one thing after another, gradually the feeling rises in the packed House. "No man," Members begin to feel in their hearts, "no man but he could tell us of such disaster and increase rather than diminish confidence." He has the psychological force of a supreme specialist who tells one that there are signs of tuberculosis, that one may become very ill, but that cure is certain. And as this feeling rises, there rises with it a feeling of shame at having doubted him. He ends without rhetoric, but with a statement about our aircraft production which is encouraging. The House gives him a great ovation and the debate thereafter peters out.[50]

And on 2 July, after the fall of Tobruk, Chips Channon noted that:

> for over an hour we had all the usual Churchillian gusto. . . . But his magic had no magic for me, we might as well have Macaulay or even Caruso as Prime Minister. He skated around dangerous corners, and by clever evasion managed to ignore the question as to whether he had ordered Tobruk to be held. Nevertheless he had his usual effect of intoxicating his listeners.[51]

The government defeated a No Confidence vote by a healthy margin of 475 to 25. Churchill's tactic of building morale by painting a grim picture was still working, but for how much longer? Even in melodrama, the happy reversal cannot be postponed indefinitely. The coup at last arrived more than three years into the war: on 11 November, Chips Channon wrote, Churchill offered the House of Commons "a dramatic treat," announcing the victory at El Alamein and the American landings in North Africa. "It was an admirable performance. . . . Indeed, events just now seem to happen with such dramatic celerity and frequency, that we are breathless." Churchill was clearly "enjoying himself and seemed to be relishing the unexpected turn of events."[52]

From the beginning of the war, Churchill had grasped at every opportunity (however far-fetched) to effect just such a *coup de théâtre*. Again and again he strove to repeat the mistake he made in *Savrola* and at Gallipoli: proposing a surprise naval attack without thinking two steps ahead. As early as February 1940 General Alan Brooke protested that, even after the disasters of the First World War, there was "now the same tendency to start subsidiary theatres of war, and to contemplate wild projects!! We shall apparently never apply the lessons of one war to the next."[53] He had repeatedly to argue down Churchill's impractical plan to recapture northern Norway. Not only would there be inadequate air cover, the objective was also a dead end. "Why he wanted to go back and what he was going to do there, even if he did succeed in capturing Trondheim, we never found out. The only reason he ever gave was that Hitler had unrolled the map of Europe starting with Norway, and he would start rolling it up again from Norway." Of course that rationale made no sense – except as a line in a play.[54] After his elevation to Chief of the Imperial General Staff in December 1941, Brooke complained that "Winston was never good at looking at all the implications of any course of action which he favoured! In fact, he frequently refused to look at them."[55]

And yet there was some method in this madness. On 3 June 1940, the day the Dunkirk evacuation was completed, Churchill was already insisting on offensive action to boost British spirits and rattle the Axis. "How wonderful it would be if the Germans could be made to wonder where they were going to be struck next instead of forcing us to try to wall in the Island and roof it over," he wrote to General Ismay. "An effort must be made to shake off the mental and moral prostration to the will and initiative of the enemy from which we suffer." He seized Hitler's most effective weapon, the *theatrecoup*, and turned it against him.[56] Starting in the fall of 1941, British double agents fed the Germans false reports of a planned assault on Norway, compelling them to divert forces that might otherwise have reinforced the Russian front or North Africa.[57] The August 1942 Dieppe Raid (an early rehearsal for D-Day) has generally been accounted a failure, but it could have aggravated Hitler's fears that Churchill might choose to pounce anywhere, and compelled him to disperse his forces. On 30 September the Führer complained that his adversary was not fighting fairly:

> Had I in front of me a serious opponent I could figure out where the second front would come. But with these military idiots one never knows where they will attack. The maddest enterprise may be launched and – this is the only disagreeable thing – one never knows what next when faced with such lunatics and drunkards. Of course, we must prepare everywhere.[58]

Churchill realized that Pearl Harbor meant ultimate victory for Britain and national suicide for Japan, but he also half-recognized that it resembled his own preferred method of waging war. The attack on 7 December 1941 was so dramatic in its irrationality that it threw Japan's adversaries off balance and allowed her to overrun Southeast Asia and the western Pacific. "Madness," he concluded, is "an affliction which in war carries with it the advantage of SURPRISE."[59]

Far from being reluctant to launch a cross-Channel invasion in 1943, Churchill's June 1942 plan for "Operation Round-Up" called upon the Allies to attack just about every sector of Hitler's "Atlantic Wall." First would come "Jupiter," the seizure of northern Norway, followed by no fewer than six "heavy disembarkations" elsewhere. Diversionary attacks would strike everywhere from Denmark to the mouth of the Gironde in southwestern France. In the first wave he would send ashore ten or more armored brigades, which "must accept very high risks in their task of pressing on deeply inland, rousing the populations, deranging the enemy's communications, and spreading the fighting over the widest possible areas." The objective was to create "confusion and disorder," to take full advantage of the fact "The enemy cannot be ready everywhere."[60] True enough, but could the Allies?

Churchill never fired a commander simply for disagreeing with him. Brooke granted that, as long as he was persistent, he could ultimately make the Prime Minister see reason, though it "required superhuman efforts and was never entirely successful in so far as he tended to return to these ideas again and again."[61] In the face of opposition Churchill could emote like Sarah Bernhardt: "We then find him adopting the attitude that he was the only one trying to win the war, that he was the only one who produced any ideas, that he was quite alone in all his attempts, no one supported him. Indeed, instead of supporting him all we did was provide and plan difficulties etc. etc. Frequently in this oration he worked himself up into such a state from the woeful picture he had painted, that tears streamed from his face!"[62] Any audacious coup necessarily involved a radical change of strategy, and Churchill's flexibility was not always a military asset, as Brooke complained:

> I had the greatest difficulty in making him realize that strategy was a long term process in which you could not frequently change your mind. He did not like being reminded of this fact and frequently shook his fist in my face and said, "I do not want any of your long term projects, all they do is cripple initiative." I agreed that it might possibly cripple initiative but all I wanted was to know when he would put his left foot down after having put down his right, and that I refused to look upon that as a "long term project".[63]

In May 1943, en route to Washington, Churchill drafted a paper proposing a landing somewhere on the eastern shores of the Bay of Bengal: "The surest way to make a successful landing is to go where you are not expected."[64] Surprise is important in both drama and war, but the least expected attack is the one that makes no military sense whatsoever, and this scheme was wholly impractical. Churchill devoted considerable space in *The Second World War* to justifying "the Sumatra project, which I compared, in its promise of decisive consequences, with the Dardanelles operation of 1915." He could never quite understand why his Chiefs of Staff found this comparison unpersuasive.[65] When he met with Roosevelt at the White House, with the American and British Chiefs of Staff, he seemed unable to focus on any one front, calling at one point or another for dramatic action on all them. "Thinks one thing at one moment and another at another moment," Brooke grumbled:

> At times the war may be won by bombing and all must be sacrificed to it. At others it becomes essential for us to bleed ourselves dry on the Continent because Russia is doing the same. At others our main effort must be in the Mediterranean, directed against Italy or Balkans alternatively, with sporadic desires to invade Norway and "roll up the map in the opposite direction to Hitler"! But more often than all he wants to carry out ALL operations simultaneously irrespective of shortages of shipping![66]

Brooke realized that Churchill was fighting the war as a romantic artist rather than as a methodical military planner, more concerned with éclat than tedious logistics, and hence "temperamental like a film star":

> I wonder whether any historian of the future will ever be able to paint Winston in his true colours. It is a wonderful character – the most marvellous qualities and superhuman genius mixed with an astonishing lack of vision at times, and an impetuosity which if not guided must inevitably bring him into trouble again and again. . . . He is quite the most difficult man to work with that I have ever struck, but I should not have missed the chance of working with him for anything on earth![67]

Those qualities left Churchill's commanders awestruck and exasperated. Admiral J. C. Tovey warned the Prime Minister that sending Arctic convoys to Russia in the long daylight of summer would lead to catastrophe, and he was proved right by events. War strategy, Tovey protested to Admiral Cunningham, amounted to a diffuse collection of "bright ideas without any real governing policy behind it. WC as Prime Minister is magnificent and unique, but as a strategist and tactician he is liable to be most dangerous. He loves the dramatic and public acclamation," and to achieve that he "put up some wild schemes."[68]

In the face of American opposition, in September 1943 Churchill launched an ill-planned and disastrous thrust into the eastern Aegean, aiming at Rhodes, Leros, and Kos. "This is the time to think of Clive and Peterborough, and of Rooke's men taking Gibraltar," he urged grandiosely. The cost was 1,500 British dead, 3,000 taken prisoner, 113 aircraft and several warships lost or damaged. And just days after the British force on Leros surrendered, Churchill urged the Combined Chiefs of Staff (then meeting in Cairo) to attack Rhodes. When the US General George C. Marshall resisted, Churchill literally grabbed him by the lapels and emoted, "His Majesty's Government can't have its troops standing idle. Muskets must flame." Marshall's answer was no less melodramatic: "Not one American soldier is going to die on [that] goddam beach."[69]

On another beach in another part of the Mediterranean, the Americans were more willing to gamble. Following the landings at Salerno on Italy's west coast in September 1943, Allied forces had secured the southern part of the country but were then stymied halfway between Naples and Rome. General George Patton had twice successfully outflanked Axis forces in Sicily with amphibious American attacks, and General Dwight Eisenhower now planned to break the Italian stalemate by a landing at Anzio about 56 miles south of Rome. Here Churchill's support was crucial: without it the American Joint Chiefs of Staff would never have approved the plan. "I had of course always been a partisan of the 'end run', as the Americans call it, or 'cat-claw', which was my term," Churchill recalled.[70] The landing on 22 January 1944 was a total surprise for the Germans, but Field Marshal Albert Kesselring swiftly recovered and bottled up four British and American divisions on the beach-head, where they were exposed to relentless artillery barrages. "To an extraordinary degree," Max Hastings concludes, Allied "commanders failed to think through a plan for what was to happen once the troops got ashore"[71] – exactly the error that Churchill habitually made in his endless quest for a strategic coup. When the Anzio attack bogged down, Churchill bitterly acknowledged – in a nod to Gallipoli – that it had become "Sulva Bay all over again."[72]

Naturally Churchill wanted to be onstage for what he called "the supreme climax of the war." He planned to observe the bombardment of Normandy from the cruiser HMS *Belfast* and then "make a short tour of the beaches, with due regard to the unswept mine areas." George VI initially offered to accompany him but then sensibly decided that neither of them should go, lest a German shell simultaneously dispose of both the monarch and his chief minister. In his memoirs Churchill did not hide his disappointment. "A man who has to play an effective part in taking, with the highest responsibility, grave and terrible decisions of war may need the refreshment of adventure," suggesting that the Second World War served the same purposes as a Robert Louis Stevenson novel. "I thought my view and theme of the war were sufficiently important and authoritative to entitle me to full freedom of judgment as to how I discharged my task in such a personal matter."[73] Of course "view" and "theme" are aesthetic factors, properly decided by independent artists and authors, and Churchill still conducted himself as a war correspondent as well as a Prime Minister.

The day before the invasion Goebbels was with Hitler at the Berghof. "We talked about problems of the theatre and opera, film, literature and heavens knows what else," the Propaganda Minister recorded in his diary. By 10 p.m. German intelligence informed them that radio signals revealed a probable Allied invasion in the morning, but their only response was to continue to "talk a lot about film, opera and theatre matters."[74] These episodes highlight one more crucial contrast between Hitler the artist and Churchill the author. Hitler treated the war as a distraction from his vital interest in the arts, and his bohemian inattention to administrative matters was one factor that cost him victory. Churchill was a writer, but he treated the Second World War as his greatest literary work. He produced memoranda, speeches, and even military campaigns with his big book in mind. His impulse to perform on the stage of history often misled him. But unlike Hitler, Churchill was able to make his aesthetic and militaristic impulses work together, and therefore remained thoroughly focused on the prosecution of the war at least until victory was assured.

Though the weather was far from ideal, Eisenhower gave the green light for the Normandy invasion to begin on 6 June 1944. It was a gamble, but as Churchill noted in hindsight, it helped to secure "the precious advantage of surprise." German commanders expected the main invasion to come at the Pas de Calais, and in any case their meteorologists advised them that no attack would be possible under such conditions as existed at the time. At last, the Gallipoli strategy worked.[75] Four days later General Bernard Montgomery allowed Churchill a visit to the front, which he enjoyed tremendously. Observing an Allied naval bombardment on board the destroyer *Kelvin*, he asked the commander to fire off a few shots of his own, which was done – the only time Churchill ever participated in combat on a naval vessel. "We were of course well within the range of their artillery," he assured his readers. "Altogether it had been a most interesting and enjoyable day."[76]

However, once that adventure was accomplished, Churchill could not concentrate on the more mundane business of deciding upon a strategy for assaulting the Japanese Empire. The Chiefs of Staff had a plan worked out: an amphibious assault on Rangoon and the capture of Burma combined with naval and air operations in the western Pacific launched from Australia. But Churchill kept bringing up Sumatra and avoiding the larger issue. "Winston gets more and more prosy relating all his old reminiscences when holding various Cabinet appointments, none of which have any bearing on the points under discussion," Brooke observed on 28 July.[77] Churchill was rehearsing his next book, but accomplishing little else. When the Prime Minister left for Italy two weeks later, Brooke marveled at how much work he was able to get done: "I feel that we have now reached the stage that for the good of the nation and for the good of his own reputation it would be a godsend if he could disappear out of public life."[78]

Churchill's next scheme was yet another pointless peripheral attack, this time against the Istrian peninsula at the head of the Adriatic. "Without him England was lost for a certainty," Brooke moaned, "with him England has been on the verge of disaster again and again."[79] As Keith Sainsbury recognizes, an attack in the eastern Mediterranean was "something of an obsession" with Churchill. "It reappears again and again in his strategic appreciations, like a recurring decimal. . . . In one form or another – an attack on the Dodecanese, British use of Turkish air bases, a landing in Greece, on the Dalmatian coast, in Trieste – it continued to occupy his thoughts, and consequently to raise dire suspicions in the minds of Marshall, [US War Secretary, Henry] Stimson and, more and more as time went by, of Roosevelt himself." Sainsbury considers the various explanations historians have offered for this fixation. Did Churchill aim to re-establish British hegemony in the eastern Mediterranean, or prove to the world that he had been right about the Dardanelles, or avoid a war of attrition in Western Europe? But a modest diversionary assault east of Italy would not accomplish any of these goals, especially if it resulted in a humiliating defeat.[80] When all rational explanations for human behavior have been eliminated, we must look to the irrational. Churchill was aiming at a literary stroke in the region where *Savrola* had been set. It had not worked particularly well in the novel, but he hoped it would create more of a splash in his next book.

For all the ill-feeling it created, the constant friction between Churchill and his military chiefs helped Britain win the war. He and Brooke represented opposite personality types – creative versus regimented, poetic versus pragmatic, improvisational versus methodical, visionary versus careful, dramatic versus dispassionate – that checked and balanced each other. Hitler and Mussolini were in their own ways imaginative unconventional politicians whose daring strokes often produced dazzling successes but ultimately led to catastrophe. Unlike Churchill, they did not allow their more cautious generals to rein them in. The creative tension between Churchill and his commanders produced a war strategy that for the most part struck the right balance between audacity and practicality. That model of dual leadership may offer a successful formula for all kinds of enterprises: businesses, universities, religious denominations, political movements, as well as countries at war.

Churchill and Hitler both embodied what Max Weber identified as the defining tension of the modern world: the struggle between the bureaucratic and the charismatic. They both habitually violated Weber's definition of bureaucracy: "the principle of fixed and official jurisdictional areas, which are generally ordered by rules."[81] They worked outside the educational machine that produces a disciplined governing class: neither flourished in secondary school, neither attended university, neither was much good at taking tests. Given that mainstream political parties are also bureaucratized, charismatic politicians must either create their own revolutionary parties (as did Hitler) or, in the case of Churchill, shuttle between two parties and stand out as a maverick in both. As Churchill told Lloyd George in May 1940, "Like you I have no Party of my own";[82] and speaking with the historian A. L. Rowse shortly after his 1955 retirement, he always referred to his fellow Conservatives as "they".[83] "You have never been a real Tory," George Bernard Shaw assured him in 1946. "A foundation of American democracy, with a very considerable dash of author and artist and the training of a soldier, has made you a phenomenon that the Blimps and Philistines and Stick-in-the-muds have never understood and always dreaded."[84]

Weber posited that "As a permanent structure with a system of rational rules, bureaucracy is fashioned to meet calculable and recurrent needs by means of normal routine." But moments of crisis offer an opening to the charismatic leader, who "gains and maintains authority solely by proving his strength in life. If he wants to be a prophet, he must perform miracles; if he wants to be a war lord, he must perform heroic deeds." Hence Churchill and Hitler strove to achieve opposing political goals through similarly bold strokes. Although Weber mostly envisioned charismatic leaders as warlords or religious prophets, he allowed that they could also be artists.[85] Hitler and Churchill played all three of these roles, dazzling their followers with monumental creative works: one built (or planned) gargantuan architectural projects, the other wrote multi-volume histories. And as John Colville recognized, Churchill was a highly idiosyncratic artist rather than a predictable administrator:

> A Private Secretary who works intimately with his master over a long period can usually say with little risk of error what the reaction to a given proposition is likely to be. With Winston this was impossible, as even his wife found and admitted. I was often asked what the Prime Minister would feel about something and there were occasions on which I thought I knew the answer

> for a certainty. Sometimes I was right, but just as often I was wrong. There were none of his associates who would have claimed to do better. This was due to some strange intuitive power which he held and which might induce him to take a line contrary, as it appeared, to logic and contrary to the normal mental workings of everybody else. . . .
>
> He always retained unswerving independence of thought. He approached a problem as he himself saw it and of all the men I have ever known he was the least liable to be swayed by the views of even his most intimate counsellors.[86]

As Lord Moran noted, although the public schools and the army were machines for producing conformity, nevertheless Winston always "devoted more time to self-expression than self-discipline."[87] In an undated entry in his diary, probably written late in the war, when Churchill's powers were failing, he asked:

> Is Winston's impressionable nature itself a source of weakness in war? The idea is, of course, far from novel. That a man's imagination may run riot in battle is indeed as old as the literature of war. "More life," wrote Thomas Hardy, "may trickle out of a man through thought than through a gaping wound." . . . If it should happen that a man of action, exercising supreme power, is also an artist, then God help him. He will have to change his nature to survive.[88]

That, Moran concluded, explained Churchill's fascination with T. E. Lawrence and *Seven Pillars of Wisdom*. "He tells us that Lawrence had never been, in time of peace, 'in complete harmony with the normal.' Winston knew what that meant. He knew more than most what happens to a man who is different from other people; the penalty exacted from those who do not conform. In the years before the war he had come to realize that he had no real friends in any of the three parties; he could not remember a time when he was sure of his own reception in the country. He felt his isolation."[89] He looked for other solitary geniuses, notably General Orde Wingate, hoping that he would be a second Lawrence. "The P.M. is not at all conventional, and his open mind has been a valuable asset in this war," wrote Moran; "no idea was too improbable, too absurd to be given a trial. But when he came to select men he was somehow less successful – the incipient genius rescued from obscurity was apt to prove a disappointment."[90] There he resembled a well-off bohemian who patronizes an array of artists, writers, and gurus, most of whom never achieve anything memorable.

Churchill was wordier than Ernest Hemingway, but they shared a similar passion for experiencing combat and transforming it into literature. The

Prime Minister spent much of the Second World War visiting anti-aircraft batteries and enjoying the fireworks, sailing out on warships and hoping to exchange fire with the enemy, flying to the front and often sitting in the pilot's seat, practicing his marksmanship with a view toward personally shooting Germans. Steaming across the Atlantic in the *Queen Mary* in May 1943, he was warned that a submarine might intercept the ship. He had a machine gun mounted in his lifeboat so that, if the worst happened, he could engage in a shoot-out with the U-boat. "The finest way to die is in the excitement of fighting the enemy," he told an appalled Averell Harriman. "You must come with me in the boat and see the fun."[91]

Those who criticize *The Second World War* for embellishing the truth, neglecting fronts where the British did not fight and being mainly about Winston, are missing the point. In his 1948 introduction to the first volume, Churchill insisted that it was not a conventional history, but rather something like Daniel Defoe's *Memoirs of a Cavalier*, "in which the author hangs the chronicle and discussion of great military and political events upon the thread of the personal experiences of an individual."[92] *The Second World War* belongs to the same genre as Churchill's early writings on colonial wars, T. E. Lawrence's *Seven Pillars of Wisdom*, and George Orwell's *Homage to Catalonia*, insofar as they all represented artists' impressionistic accounts of combat. Flying from Gibraltar to Egypt in 1942, Churchill once again observed, experienced, and reported from the same front he had covered back in 1898:

> It was my practice on these journeys to sit in the co-pilot's seat before sunrise, and when I reached it on this morning of August 4 there in the pale, glimmering dawn the endless winding silver ribbon of the Nile stretched joyously before us. Often had I seen the day break on the Nile. In war and peace I had traversed by land or water almost its whole length, except the "Dongola Loop", from Lake Victoria to the sea. Never had the glint of daylight on its waters been so welcome to me.
>
> Now for a short spell I became "the man on the spot". Instead of sitting at home waiting for the news from the front I could send it myself. This was exhilarating.[93]

Attending Churchill's September 1943 speech at Harvard University, Lord Moran was struck by the bohemian melange of his outfit: a bow tie, a "quaint black velvet hat," and "a pair of rather inadequate grey flannel trousers" under a magnificent scarlet Oxford DCL robe. "But Winston would not be Winston if he was strictly conventional," wrote Moran. Churchill concluded with the words "And here let me say how proud we ought to be, young and old, to live in this tremendous, thrilling, formative epoch in the human story," and

Moran immediately recognized that he had recast, in his own words, one of the most famous poems in the language:

> "Now, God be thanked Who has matched us with His hour," sang Rupert Brooke at the Dardanelles, and this old tough, so near to seventy years of age, throws up his hat that he is alive to play a part.[94]

CHAPTER 21

Victory?

In February 1943, after the Casablanca conference, Churchill reflected: "It would be a pity to have to go out in the middle of such an interesting drama without seeing the end. But it wouldn't be a bad moment to leave – it is a straight run-in now, and even the cabinet could manage it."[1] The crises that demanded heroic leadership and great performances were behind him. Now eventual victory was simply a matter of the wise application of overwhelming force, which his ministers and generals could carry out, perhaps better than he could. Had he died at this point, his historical reputation would have been even greater than it is. As it was, by October 1943 Alexander Cadogan noticed that Churchill had already become the "worst chairman of a Cabinet imaginable."[2] "At times of crisis, when big issues had to be settled promptly, Churchill was always superb and most businesslike," Edward Bridges (the Cabinet Secretary) explained. "The essential points and arguments would be quickly brought to the surface. They would be searchingly discussed and decisions taken." But now he often came to Cabinet meetings unprepared. Rather than stick to the agenda, he indulged in rambling monologues, like an over-the-hill author at his favorite café going on about his next book.[3]

In December 1943 Churchill was in Tunisia recovering from pneumonia. He resisted his doctors' instructions that he forget about the war and rest, but ultimately he allowed his daughter Sarah to read him *Pride and Prejudice*. Churchill generally preferred contemporary books that spoke to contemporary issues, but now he needed some respite from the war, and Jane Austen was wonderfully irrelevant: "What calm lives they had, those people! No worries about the French Revolution, or the crashing struggle of the Napoleonic wars. Only manners controlling natural passion so far as they could, together with cultured explanations of any mischances."[4] He also read R. H. Gronow's *Reminiscences of Regency and Victorian Life 1800–1865*[5] and, later, Jane Austen's *Emma*.[6] On board the *Queen Mary* in September 1944, Churchill seemed to spend most of his time with Anthony Trollope's *Phineas Finn* and *The Duke's Children*.[7] This was not necessarily a good sign. For the first time in his life, Churchill was indulging in escapist reading, as Neville Chamberlain had done during the Phony War, and in the final phase of the Second World War he often seemed distracted from the job at hand.

Even if the war was effectively won, there was still pressing business to attend to, especially the question of building a new Britain. Churchill might be reluctant to face that issue, but the voters felt differently. By-elections were running against the government. Opinion poll results depended largely on the phrasing of the question. When the British people were asked whether they approved of Churchill's performance as Prime Minister, his ratings hovered close to 90 percent. In June 1944, when asked who should lead the country after the war, 67 percent named Churchill.[8] (No Labour politician scored higher than 3 percent.) But when they were asked which party they intended to vote for in the next general election, the results (from 1943 on) pointed to a Labour victory.[9]

The Beveridge Report, published in December 1942, promised a comprehensive system of social insurance that would allow no one to fall below a "national minimum." The Ministry of Information Home Intelligence division reported that public approval of the plan was not far short of universal. In a 21 March 1943 broadcast Churchill warned that after years of fighting an enormously costly war there was only so much that Britain could afford. He did propose a somewhat less ambitious "four-year plan" which would ultimately provide "cradle to the grave" social insurance, full employment through Keynesian methods, some measure of "State ownership and enterprise," housing construction, better educational opportunities, and improved health services.[10] Privately, however, he preferred raw urban melodrama to the brave new world envisioned by the Labour Party. "Ah, yes," he sighed in the Cabinet Room, toward the end of the war. "All this stuff about planning and compensation and betterment. Broad vistas and all that. But give to me the eighteenth-century alley, where foot-pads lurk, and the harlot plies her trade, and none of this new fangled planning doctrine."[11]

In something of a contradiction, Churchill enthusiastically promoted a planning doctrine for the English language, which eliminated such delicious words as "foot-pad" and "harlot". As early as 1909 he had expressed the "hope that our language will continue to exert an ever-increasing dominion over the whole world, that it will exert a powerful influence upon the growth of the human race."[12] Churchill found a means to that end in "Basic English," invented by the Cambridge linguist C. K. Ogden. Ogden reduced the English language to a core vocabulary of 850 words, and made its grammatical rules far simpler and more consistent. It was so elementary that non-anglophones could easily master and use it as a universal tongue. Assuming that he was still a fan of H. G. Wells, Churchill would have encountered Basic English in his 1933 novel *The Shape of Things to Come*, on which the 1936 film *Things to Come* was based. Wells predicted that a new world war would begin with a confrontation between Germany and Poland over Danzig (he missed the actual starting date by just a few months), but out of the wreckage of war emerges yet another Wellsian benevolent world dictatorship, which adopts Basic English as its lingua franca. *The Shape of Things to Come* includes some sniping at *The World Crisis* ("There one finds all the stereotyped flourishes and heroisms of nineteenth-century history from the British point of view; the 'drama of history' in rich profusion, centred upon one of the most alert personalities in the conflict"), but assuming there were no hard feelings, it might have planted an idea.

On 11 July 1943 Churchill told Edward Bridges that Basic English "would be a gain to us far more durable and fruitful than the annexation of great provinces. It would also fit in with my ideas of closer union with the United States by making it even more worthwhile to belong to the English-speaking club."[13] At the next day's Cabinet meeting he proposed that the BBC offer daily instruction, and that he himself would promote it on the radio. "In Basic English?" came the inevitable query. A Cabinet committee chaired by Leo Amery was charged with producing a feasibility study, but in late September Churchill was "shocked" to learn that the committee had never met. The official excuse was the demands of other responsibilities, though one cannot rule out the possibility that the ministers hoped the PM would forget about what they considered a daft idea. Meanwhile, Alexander Cadogan had drafted a proposal of his own:

> **Bar-Ji English**
>
> **Preliminary Report of the Lord President's Committee.**
>
> Much thought was being devoted to the debasement of English to the point where it could serve as a medium of communication between Anglo-Saxons and other races (o.r.). For this purpose – of Keeping the Foreigner in his Place – was required a limited range of forceful and easily memorized admonitions.
>
> Considerable research has convinced us that this purpose would be best served by the standardisation and widest possible adoption (by Anglo-Saxons) of the colloquialisms employed by the barge-workers of this country. . . . Many cases have been reported to us of Anglo-Saxon functionaries of no great linguistic attainment or education, such as Embassy butlers in Turkey, China and other countries, who, with a comparatively elementary

> equipment of Bar-Ji English, can reduce the o.r. of those countries to a condition of docility bordering on panic.
>
> Prolonged experimentation with what may be called the raw material of Bar-Ji English shows that the number of nouns can be reduced to 1163 and the adjectives to 1. A considerable number of verbs would have to be retained (together with their participles) but . . . the less said about some of these verbs, the better. . . . For instance, when the French porters come on board at Calais, all [one] will have to say is "Nah then, yah bloody nigger, drop that!". . . . We feel confident that a little further study will result in producing a suitable medium for the dissemination, and enforcement, of Anglo-Saxon culture throughout both hemispheres.[14]

Cadogan saw that non-anglophones might regard Basic English as linguistic imperialism – and Churchill's handling of the issue guaranteed that they would. Accepting his honorary degree from Harvard University on 6 September 1943, Churchill again affirmed the importance of close Anglo-American cooperation, during and after the war. Both nations had a common enemy: "Tyranny is our foe, whatever trappings or disguise it wears, whatever language it speaks. . . ." Americans and Britons shared a common sense of decency and fair play, "a stern sentiment of impartial justice, and above all the love of personal freedom." Most important was the "gift of a common tongue" which could eventually become the basis of shared citizenship. But Churchill went still further: he proposed "to spread our common language even more widely throughout the globe." He revealed his plans and hopes for Basic English, noting President Roosevelt had expressed an interest in it, and that I. A. Richards (a key proponent of Basic) was currently based at Harvard. He commended the Harvard Commission on English Language Studies for promoting Basic in South America, in Boston high schools, and in citizenship classes for immigrants. His enthusiasm warming, Churchill predicted that as a universal language Basic would preserve world peace. "Let us have another Boston Tea Party about it," which would presumably undo the damage done by the first. "Such plans offer far better prizes than taking away other people's provinces or lands or grinding them down in exploitation," he argued. "The empires of the future are the empires of the mind." In conclusion, Churchill reminded his audience to "remember that we are on the stage of history, and that whatever our station may be, and whatever part we have to play, great or small, our conduct is liable to be scrutinized not only by history but by our own descendants."[15]

Clearly Churchill considered this a very important speech: he asked Brendan Bracken (now Minister of Information) for "a tabular report of the reactions of all important American newspapers to my Harvard statement, showing which are for and which against."[16] The Cabinet committee finally reported in December, and recommended that key works of literature should be translated into Basic, which should be promoted by the British Council, the Colonial Office, the Ministry of Information, and the BBC. Churchill sent Roosevelt and the Secretary of State Cordell Hull that report the following April: "My conviction is that Basic English will then prove to be a great boon to mankind in the future and a powerful support to the influence of the Anglo-Saxon peoples in world affairs."[17] Roosevelt hoped that Basic "would soon take the place of French as the so-called 'language of diplomacy,' " and he urged Hull to find a "sympathetic" congressional committee to assess the issue.[18] But, he asked Churchill, "I wonder what the course of history would have been if in May 1940 you had been able to offer the British people only 'blood, work, eye water and face water', which I understand is the best that Basic English can do with five famous words."[19]

Roosevelt had put his finger on the problem. Translation into Basic would strip the poetry from every important literary work – except the Bible, where the result is a stark minimalist beauty. In April 1944 a *Punch* spoof (probably by A. P. Herbert) rendered Hamlet's soliloquy in Basic: there was no difficulty with the first line, but then it descended into "If it is best in the mind to undergo the stone-sending chords and sharp-pointed air going instruments of unkind chance . . ." After Churchill was voted out of office in 1945, the Labour government dropped the scheme. With obvious relief, the Director General of the BBC minuted his subordinates that Basic English had been "put on a high shelf in a dark corner."[20]

In fairness, no one ever intended that Basic should replace standard English. It was always meant to be only an English as a Second Language tool, and as such I.A. Richards had generated some genuine interest among the Chinese. But Churchill's public endorsement was "the kiss of death," as the literary critic William Empson confessed.[21] Now indelibly tainted with the odor of anglophone hegmony, Richards' wife Dorothea warned that Basic would raise the hackles of:

> All sorts of French Canadians with different slants from extreme Nationalism who see nothing in Basic but [an effort] to deprive them of their own language. Then the Latin Americans fear U.S. cultural aggression and want Spanish to be the world language. Others are afraid of an Anglo-American bloc and linguistic imperialism. Then there are our friends the [Chinese Communist] comrades who think – because Churchill was in favour of it – they must damn it.[22]

Basic English would be damned forever in *Nineteen Eighty-Four*, where it was satirized as Newspeak. As a BBC broadcaster, George Orwell had initially taken an interest in Basic, but soon realized that radically limiting the English vocabulary to a kind of texting would make impossible the expression of such Churchillian concepts as *democracy* and *freedom*. The broadcast on Basic that he commissioned was beamed at India, so he understood all too well its imperialist implications.[23] In *Nineteen Eighty-Four* English has been imposed everywhere in Oceania, including Latin America.

In moments of crisis, Churchill swiftly recovered his old energies and ability to focus. He was thrilled whenever science fiction became reality, and he found himself confronting Wellsian superweapons. On 19 June 1944, at a meeting to discuss the V-1 threat, Alan Brooke discovered that "Winston was in very good form, quite 10 years younger, all due to the fact that the flying bombs have again put us into the front line!!"[24] Leo Amery observed the same rejuvenation: "The excitement of the new menace has been absolute champagne to him and he looked years younger and bubbling over with mischievous humour as we discussed the subject up and down."[25] But the V-2 would drive Churchill seriously to consider, in a 6 July minute, the use of poison gas against the Germans.[26]

The following day, 7 July 1944, Churchill was informed about the full horror of Auschwitz. As early as 18 July 1941, less than a month after the Nazi invasion of the USSR, British intelligence had picked up and decrypted reports from the Waffen SS detailing massacres of Jews. A broadcast by Churchill a few weeks later reported that Hitler had turned to outright "mass murder" on the Russian front:

> As his armies advance, whole districts are being exterminated. Scores of thousands – literally scores of thousands – of executions in cold blood are being perpetrated by the German police-troops upon the Russian patriots who defend their native soil. Since the Mongol invasions of Europe in the sixteenth century, there has never been methodical, merciless butchery on such a scale, or approaching such a scale. And this is but the beginning. Famine and pestilence have yet to follow in the bloody ruts of Hitler's tanks. We are in the presence of a crime without a name.[27]

In fact he had named it in 1929, when he applied the word "holocaust" to the Armenian genocide. (It was not commonly attached to the Jewish genocide until after 1945.)[28] In his 1941 broadcast Churchill did not mention the Jews, perhaps to avoid tipping off the Germans that their codes had been broken.[29] But on 16 December 1939 *The Times* had reported that the Germans were deporting Jews to an area in Poland "for gradual extermination." In May 1942 the Jewish Labor Bund (an Eastern European socialist party) reported that more than a million Jews had already been killed. That report was headlined in the *Daily Telegraph, The Times*, the *Daily Mail*, and the *Manchester Guardian*.

(The *New York Times* relegated it to page 6.) On 25 June 1944 the *Manchester Guardian* specifically reported that Hungarian Jews were being exterminated at Auschwitz, and two days later the Foreign Office received a telegram confirming that, which was immediately passed on to the War Cabinet. "What can be done? What can be said?" Churchill minuted Anthony Eden. A fuller report reached the Foreign Office on 4 July. It noted that Poles, Russians, homosexuals, professional criminals, and dissident Christians were imprisoned at Auschwitz, but made clear that the primary purpose of the camp was to kill Jews, at least 1.5 million of them by April 1944. It described the gas chambers in detail and briefly mentioned the hideous medical "experiments."[30]

The Jewish Agency in Palestine urged the bombing of the railway lines then being used to transport Hungarian Jews to the death camp. Eden urged Churchill to seriously consider bombing the railways or the camp itself. "Get anything out of the Air Force you can," Churchill ordered Eden on 7 July, "and invoke me if necessary." On the 11th he wrote to Eden again:

> There is no doubt that this is probably the greatest and most horrible crime ever committed in the whole history of the world, and it has been done by scientific machinery by nominally civilized men in the name of a great State and one of the leading races in Europe. It is quite clear that all concerned in this crime who may fall into our hands, including the people who only obeyed orders by carrying out the butcheries, should be put to death after their association with the murders has been proved.[31]

The V-1, the V-2, and now this confirmed his worst premonitions about "perverted science." In a sense, both Wells and Churchill had anticipated the Island of Doctor Mengele.

As Air Minister, Archibald Sinclair investigated the issue and told Eden (but not Churchill) that the camp and the railways leading to it were too remote for a night attack by the RAF. The United States Army Air Corps might conduct that kind of precision bombing by daylight, "but it would be a costly and hazardous operation." Sinclair was willing to broach the idea to the Americans, but he doubted that they would agree. The US War Department had already dismissed the proposal as impractical. The British Foreign Office was no more enthusiastic.[32] Churchill's war memoir would publish the 11 July minute but not his earlier demand to despatch RAF bombers. The 7 July note would have once again vindicated Churchill as a prophet of the horrors of Nazism, but it might have also raised uncomfortable questions about the inaction of the British and American air commands. Michael Cohen discovered a pair of identical unpublished letters sent by Churchill on 11 July to the Archbishop of Canterbury and the Jewish industrialist Lord Melchett. "There is no doubt in my mind that we are in the presence of one of the greatest and most horrible crimes ever committed," Churchill wrote, but "the principal hope of terminating it must remain the speedy victory of the Allied Nations." This suggested that he had, on second thoughts, rejected the idea of bombing Auschwitz or the connecting railways.[33]

Military historians, who are far more familiar with the technical problems involved in air warfare than Holocaust historians, have shown that bombing the camps was in fact not realistic.[34] But those, like Churchill, who demanded action may have been performing a kind of theatre. In a memorandum of 11 July 1944 to the Foreign Office, Moshe Shertok, chief of the Political Department of the Jewish Agency in Palestine, conceded that an air attack on Auschwitz could at best only delay the extermination of the inmates, and might immediately kill some of them. But it would have an unforgettable impact on the world audience:

> It would mean, in the first instance, that the Allies waged direct war on the extermination of the victims of Nazi oppression – today Jews, tomorrow Poles, Czechs, or whatever race may become the victim of mass murder during the German retreat and collapse. Secondly, it would mean the lie to the oft-repeated assertions of Nazi spokesmen that the Allies are not really so displeased with the work of the Nazis in ridding Europe of the Jews. Thirdly, it would go far towards dissipating the incredulity which still persists in Allied quarters with regard to the report of mass extermination perpetrated by the Nazis. Fourthly, it would give weight to the threats of reprisals against the murderers, by showing that the Allies are taking the extermination of the Jews so seriously as to warrant the allocation of aircraft resources for this particular operation, and thus have a deterrent effect. Lastly, it would convince the German circles still hopeful of Allied mercy of the genuineness of Allied condemnation of the murder of the Jews, and possibly result in some internal pressure against a continuation of the massacres.[35]

In short, bombing Auschwitz would be a dramatic stroke. It would accomplish everything that a *coup de théâtre* is designed to do: rivet the attention of the spectators, expose what had hitherto been ambiguous or hidden, illuminate the true intentions of the characters, clarify starkly the moral issues at stake, bring the action to a gripping climax, and point toward a denouement where justice will triumph. This interpretation of events presumes that the historian William Rubinstein was essentially right to conclude that rescuing the Jews of Nazi-occupied Europe was impossible, that nothing would have deterred Hitler from completing his project of mass murder. Given that, only one course of action was open to those who wanted to help the concentration camp inmates: they should perform dramatic gestures because they could do nothing else. Rubinstein cites a fifteen-point plan of "action" proposed by the American Jewish Congress, including a "Day of Universal Mourning," public processions, one day work stoppages, professorial lectures, newspaper advertisements, proclamations, radio programs, and a warning to Dr. Mengele that he was in violation of the Hippocratic Oath. Impatient with such impotent pronouncements, the militant Bergson group staged a protest pageant at New York's Madison Square Garden, "We Will Never Die!", produced and performed by an array of Hollywood notables – but that too saved no Jews.[36]

Churchill was a master of the theatrical gesture in politics, and his impulsive order to bomb Auschwitz has to be understood in this context. He did not initially think through the practical considerations. In melodrama every threatened heroine must be rescued at any cost, preferably at the last minute, and this time the RAF would play the role that, on the Victorian stage, was usually assigned to the Royal Marines. Confronted by the Holocaust, such gestures had an understandable appeal for people who were powerless to stop it, including the Prime Minister of Great Britain.

Meanwhile, Churchill was confronting another human catastrophe halfway around the world. Bombing Auschwitz and the Bengal Famine have generated agonizingly complicated moral debates. To what extent and when was the government in London aware of these disasters, and how much (in the midst of fighting a global war) it could have done to stop them?[37] The answers are far from obvious, but in both cases Churchill's response was importantly conditioned by literature.

His passionate philo-Semitism contrasted with his increasingly bitter prejudices towards Indians, which came to the fore during the "Quit India" campaign, launched by Congress on 8 August 1942. Mahatma Gandhi called once again for nonviolent resistance, but the British authorities promptly arrested him and other Congress leaders. Many Indian workers went on strike, and there were some cases of bombing, arson, attacks on Europeans, and sabotage of electric and railway lines. In one part of Uttar Pradesh locals overthrew British authorities and briefly asserted their independence. Subhas Chandra Bose, who was organizing an Indian National Army to fight alongside the Japanese, praised the revolt over Axis radio. The British soon re-established control, but only after killing hundreds and arresting more than 100,000 people. This only confirmed Churchill's conviction that Gandhi and the Congress were Fifth Columnists, and it inspired some of his worst racial outbursts. "I hate Indians," he spat. "They are a beastly people with a beastly religion." On 10 September he told the House of Commons that while Indian soldiers had remained loyal:

> The Congress Party has now abandoned in many respects the policy of nonviolence which Mr. Gandhi has so long inculcated in theory, and has come into the open as a revolutionary movement designed to paralyse the comunications by rail and telegraph and generally to promote disorder, the looting of shops and sporadic attacks upon the Indian police, accompanied from time to time by revolting atrocities—the whole having the intention or at any rate the effect of hampering the defence of India against the Japanese invader who stands on the frontiers of Assam and also upon the eastern side of the Bay of Bengal. It may well be that these activities by the Congress Party have been aided by Japanese fifth-column work on a widely extended scale and with special direction to strategic points.[38]

A draft of *The Second World War* went even further, absurdly and libelously claiming that Gandhi "was willing to join hands with the Germans in return for Japanese military aid to hold down the Moslems." That passage was removed at the urging of General Ismay and Cabinet Secretary Norman Brook.[39] "If we ever have to quit India," Churchill vowed, "we shall quit it in a blaze of glory, and the chapter that shall be ended then will be the most glorious chapter of that country, not merely in relation to the past but equally in relation to the future, however distant that may be."[40] A stage hero, attacked by hordes of natives, might die courageously, but he would never agree to a peaceful transfer of power.

In September 1942 the humiliations of Singapore and Tobruk were stinging and recent wounds. The Battle of Stalingrad and the North African war still hung in the balance. Japan's navy dominated the Pacific, and U-boats were strangling sea lanes in the Atlantic. Viewing the war through his melodramatic lens, Churchill saw the Allies with their backs to the wall, and now betrayed by native treason. (One of his most vivid childhood memories was John Tenniel's *Punch* cartoon on the Sepoy Mutiny, in which the British Lion pounced on a treacherous Bengal Tiger.)[41]

In October a cyclone devastated Bengal's crops. Much of what remained was sent to feed Indian soldiers in other theatres. The rice crop was also hit by a fungal epidemic that has been compared to the Irish potato blight of the 1840s. By summer 1943, mass starvation had set in. Famines can be as deadly as genocides, but assigning human responsibility for failing to deal with them can be diabolically complicated.[42] In the case of Bengal, there was plenty of blame to share around. The Japanese embargoed rice imports from occupied Burma, and British Army efforts to deny food supplies to the Japanese also disrupted supplies for many Bengalis. Harvest reports were grossly inaccurate. The response of unelected British officials and elected Bengali politicians alike was usually negligent and incompetent. Wealthy Indians did little to organize private relief efforts, British demand for war-related goods produced in India fueled inflation, Indian speculators hoarded rice and further drove up prices, and other Indian provinces (which now enjoyed local self-rule under the 1935 Government of India Act) were slow to share their food surpluses. As a moral question, the Bengal Famine resembles J. B. Priestley's *An Inspector Calls*: a crime where none of the suspects can be convicted, but everyone is implicated.

As Secretary of State for India, Leo Amery at first was inclined to follow a Malthusian policy of laissez-faire for the "overpopulated" subcontinent. But as the crisis deepened he pleaded with the War Cabinet to provide some relief, and he was not afraid to confront the Prime Minister over this issue. The Churchill that emerges from Amery's diaries was not wholly indifferent to the calamity, even though he might be stubborn and irascible. On 4 August 1943 Amery's demand for 500,000 tons of food was treated with great skepticism by the Cabinet, including Baron Leathers (the Minister for War Transport) and Professor Lindemann: they felt that India could do more to make hoarders disgorge their stores. According to Amery, however, Churchill was truly sympathetic: "For once I think Winston realizes the strength of my case more than he has on previous occasions, and he was really quite friendly," though ultimately Amery had to settle for just 150,000 tons, with the option of asking for more if the situation deteriorated.[43] Amery raised the issue again on 24 September, and again it was Leathers who resisted, allowing only another 50,000 tons of food. "Winston was prepared to admit that something should be done but very strong on the point that Indians are not the only people who are starving in this war," and Amery granted that Churchill was right to point out the competing demands of famine-wracked Greece.[44] On 10 November Amery asked the Cabinet for another 150,000 tons over three months. "Winston, after a preliminary flourish on Indians breeding like rabbits," deferred to Leathers, who only promised 100,000 tons. When Amery pointed out that Canada was ready to send a shipload of wheat from Vancouver, Churchill and Leathers refused, on the grounds that the shipping was needed elsewhere. "I cannot see that the war transport situation is so hopeless that the extra month involved in the case of this one ship would really upset things," Amery protested. "The trouble is that Winston so dislikes India and all to do with it that he can see nothing but the mere waste of shipping space involved in the longer journey."[45]

Field Marshal Wavell, who had become the Indian Viceroy in September 1943, swiftly recognized the catastrophe and asked for 500,000 tons of food. On 12 February 1944 Amery met with Sir David Monteath, Permanent Under-Secretary of State for India and Burma, to discuss the famine: "He also told me that Winston was sufficiently stirred by Wavell's telegrams . . . to say that Leathers and Co. must try to do something for India."[46] The Chiefs of

Staff endorsed sending 200,000 tons immediately and more later, but when the Cabinet met on 20 March "Winston was obviously very annoyed with the Chiefs' of Staff recommendation. . . . As usual he indulged in a few monologues on the subject of the wholly worthless and possibly even dangerous Indian Army." Churchill again deferred to Leathers, "who made out as negative a case as he could," and when Amery attempted a rebuttal the Prime Minister repeatedly interrupted him. But the Cabinet ultimately agreed to dispatch 200,000 tons of food at once, with the possibility of arranging another 150,000 tons.[47] Wavell promptly mobilized his armed forces to move food from other parts of India (where there were surpluses) to Bengal. That broke the back of the famine, though only after as many as three million people had died. And Wavell had to face down Churchill, who, he complained, "seemed to regard sending food to India as an 'appeasement' of Congress."[48]

At a Cabinet meeting on 24 April, specifically devoted to the food crisis, Churchill (according to Amery) "had great difficulty in holding himself in and came very near to suggesting that we really could not let Indian starvation or multiplying too fast interfere with operations." The Prime Minister only agreed to send a wire to Roosevelt requesting 40,000 to 50,000 tons of grain for India.[49] (Roosevelt refused.)[50]

On 4 August Amery finally exploded at Churchill in front of the Cabinet: "I lost patience and couldn't help telling him that I didn't see much difference between his outlook and Hitler's which annoyed him no little. I am by no means sure whether on this subject of India he is quite sane." Amery was responding to Churchill's proposal to (in Amery's paraphrase) "carry out a great regeneration of India based on extinguishing landlords and oppressive industrialists and uplift the peasant and untouchable, probably by collectivization on Russian lines."[51] These daydreams were obviously divorced from a horrific present reality. But then, just after the war in Europe ended, Churchill flipped once again. On 18 May 1945 Amery asked the Cabinet for more wheat for India, and again was opposed by Leathers, but he was surprised when "For once Winston took up my side."[52]

Overall, Amery portrayed Churchill as cranky and erratic, a view that agrees with everything we know about the Prime Minister in the final two years of the war. On the specific issue of food aid for India, Churchill was consistently inconsistent: sometimes growling grossly callous remarks, sometimes grudgingly allowing shipments, and sometimes urging that more must be done. His ambivalence may have been a product of his early reading, which included Malthus, but he seems to have been more powerfully influenced by the prime directives of Victorian imperial melodrama. In his imagination, the hero (Churchill) had to protect good natives (the Indian lower castes) against wicked natives (the Japanese) and treacherous natives (Gandhi and Congress), and the result was an incoherent food relief policy, alternately generous and punitive. One of Churchill's greatest failings was that he viewed twentieth-century India through the prism of bad nineteenth-century plays. As Amery observed back in 1929, "I have always said that the key to Winston is to realize that he is Mid Victorian, steeped in the politics of his father's period, and unable ever to get the modern point of view."[53]

Of course, it was not simply a question of Victorian literary tastes. One has to avoid the smugness of hindsight and appreciate the real competing pressures that Churchill faced. He was fighting a global war where transportation resources were stretched to the limit, and beyond. The Battle of the Atlantic had nearly choked Britain, forcing the government to economize on shipments of military goods to the East. In the fourth quarter of 1942 and the first quarter of 1943, imports to Britain were barely 30 percent of pre-war levels. In March 1943 Lindemann warned Churchill that German submarine deployments might rise by as much as a third in the coming months. We now know that the tide of battle turned dramatically in favor of the Allies in April and May, but at the time there was no telling whether the U-boats would stage a deadly comeback. Ships were needed for the planned invasions of Italy and France, and food had to be set aside to feed liberated Europe, where shortages were terrible. Moreover, Britain did ship food to India: 300,000 tons in 1943, 639,000 tons in 1944, 870,000 tons in 1945.[54] (Meanwhile, up to 35,000 tons a month was sent to occupied Greece, but only a total of 4,500 tons via the Red Cross to concentration camp inmates from fall 1943 to 1945.)[55] Today the rich countries are much richer, they have far more sophisticated "famine early warning systems," and they are not distracted by a world war, but still, as I write, Oxfam and Save the Children report that governments failed to respond promptly to a famine in the Horn of Africa, at a cost of up to 100,000 lives.[56]

Even after making all allowances, however, one has to conclude that Churchill could have done more and obstructed less. Portraying him as the prime and unambiguous villain of the piece (as Madhusree Mukerjee does)[57] is far too simple, but clearly his racial attitudes were anachronistic, and sometimes downright poisonous. As Lord Moran wrote in 1943, to Roosevelt "China means four hundred million people who are going to count in the world of tomorrow, but Winston thinks only of the colour of their skin; it is when he talks of India or China that you remember he is a Victorian."[58] In early 1945 Churchill read Beverley Nichols's book *Verdict on India*, given to him by John Colville. It portrayed Gandhi as a fraud, a wholly false friend of the Untouchables, a master of "evasion, duplicity, and false implication." As for Congress, it was "the only 100 per cent, full blooded, uncompromising example of undiluted Fascism in the modern World." Nichols was less far-fetched when he compared caste oppression to Nazi anti-Semitism. But he saw nothing of value in Indian art, architecture, films, religion, journalism, music, or folk medicine.[59] *Verdict on India* was part of a largely successful British propaganda effort to counter sympathy for Indian nationalism in the United States, where the book was published by Harcourt Brace and a condensation appeared in the February 1945 *Reader's Digest*.[60] Colville found that Churchill warmly shared Nichols's prejudices: "The PM said the Hindus were a foul race 'protected by their mere pullulation from the doom that is their due' and he wished Bert Harris could send some of his surplus bombers to destroy them."[61]

In September 1943, when Axis forces still occupied much of the USSR, Churchill minuted the Chiefs of Staff about heading off a Communist takeover in Greece. He proposed to send "five thousand troops with armoured cars and Bren gun carriers into Athens. . . . Their duty would be to give support at the centre to the restored lawful Greek government." A few months later he warned Eden that "we are approaching a showdown with the Russians about their Communist intrigues in Italy, Yugoslavia, and Greece." On 31 May 1944 Churchill told Roosevelt that he was seeking an agreement with the Russians that would secure British control of Greece, assuring him that "We do not of course wish to carve up the Balkans into spheres of influence."[62]

Meeting in Moscow on 9 October, Churchill and Stalin agreed to do precisely that. In their negotiations, they performed one of the most memorable scenes in *The Second World War*. "Let us settle about our affairs in the Balkans," Churchill proposed, immediately proceeding to business. "Your armies are in Roumania and Bulgaria. We have interests, missions, and agents there. Don't let us get at cross-purposes in small ways." He then sketched out on a half-sheet of paper the following arrangement:

Roumania	
Russia	90%
The others	10%
Greece	
Great Britain	90%
(in accord with USA)	
Russia	10%
Yugoslavia	50-50%
Hungary	50-50%
Bulgaria	
Russia	75%
The others	25%

I pushed this across to Stalin, who had by then heard the translation. There was a slight pause. Then he took his blue pencil and made a large tick

> upon it, and passed it back to us. It was all settled in no more time than it takes to set down. . . .
>
> After this there was a long silence. The pencilled paper lay in the centre of the table. At length I said, "Might it not be thought rather cynical if it seemed we had disposed of these issues, so fateful to millions of people, in such an offhand manner? Let us burn the paper." "No, you keep it," said Stalin.[63]

This raises in the mind of the audience a host of questions, none of which reflect well upon the author. The first and foremost is: Did this scrap of paper mean anything at all? Normally, formal diplomatic agreements are fairly detailed and signed in ink, and the signers usually keep copies for their own records. In checking this vague list of fractions, Stalin may have simply been indicating that he read it without taking it too seriously. Churchill and most historians have interpreted his silent gesture to mean *Da*, but it might be more accurately translated as *Whatever*. The official British record of the meeting did not even bother to mention the percentages. After all, how could the complicated and delicate business of assigning zones of occupation be decided in such a shallow deal, which overlooked Albania (among many other issues)? In practical terms, if British and Soviet occupation officers found themselves at loggerheads in Sofia, what would 25 percent of Bulgaria amount to? In May Anthony Eden had informally agreed with the Russian ambassador, Feodor Gusev, that the Soviets should occupy post-war Romania while the British should control Greece. That deal made sense: Churchill knew that "the Russians will take all they want in Roumania whatever we say," and he realized that it was essential to secure Greece, which was vulnerable to a Communist uprising and commanded vital Mediterranean sea lanes. But the hazy percentages deal astonished Eden (who was not consulted beforehand) and upset the Foreign Office. On 11 October Churchill drafted a letter in which he attempted to explain the percentages to Stalin, but it clarified nothing, and he never sent it. The War Cabinet demanded to know what was going on, so Churchill assured them that "The system of percentage is not intended to prescribe the numbers sitting on commissions for the different Balkan countries." But in that case, what did it prescribe in concrete terms? He added that in "the case of Yugoslavia, the numerical symbol 50-50 is intended to be the foundation of joint action and an agreed policy between the two Powers," without explaining what would happen if they disagreed or the Yugoslavs objected.[64] (Marshal Tito was outraged when he heard of the deal.) The US diplomat Averell Harriman, who was keeping an eye on the negotiations, was baffled. "I don't understand now," he recalled, "and I do not believe I understood at the time, just what Churchill thought he was accomplishing by these percentages." Over the week following 9 October there was some pointless dickering over these numbers, which were adjusted in the Soviets' favor, but the real negotiations fleshed in the details, outlining in much more specific terms the rights of the two occupying powers. As Eden assured the Foreign Office on 12 October, "Too much attention should not be paid to percentages which are of symbolic character and bear no exact relation to number of persons of British or Soviet nationality to be employed" in any given context.

And was not Churchill admitting, in *The Second World War*, that he handed over millions of Eastern Europeans to Soviet domination? Having denounced the "Iron Curtain," he now left the impression that it was his idea in the first place. He might protest that he meant only to address "immediate war-time arrangements," but his deal with Stalin had no expiry date. In a war ostensibly fought for democracy and national self-determination, this was old-fashioned cynical spheres-of-influence horse-trading. Churchill professed to be so embarrassed by the agreement that he offered to destroy all documentary evidence of it – and then, in a stunning contradiction, his memoir gave maximum publicity to his offer to burn the paper. He even proposed to reproduce a facsimile of the agreement in *The Second World War*. Ever since, this episode has baffled historians.[65] As diplomacy, it was amateurish.

But as theatre, it was brilliant. If the agreement seems simplistic, that was a matter of dramatic compression. A playwright portraying the negotiation of a treaty would of course use some kind of shorthand to summarize it rather than list all its tedious details (such as Albania). Churchill once again dissolved the boundary between theatre and reality: his script was his negotiating strategy, and to some extent he was more concerned with playing a role than with securing a workable agreement. In dramatic terms this scene was expertly constructed, a virtual monologue in which the ever-eloquent Churchill beguiles the audience with his grand bargain. There are perfectly timed loaded pauses, the longest when the whole cast and the audience gaze guiltily at the incriminating paper on the table. The laconic despot has nothing to say at all – except the mordant curtain line. He quietly waits for Churchill to walk into a trap of his own devising, which is sprung with devastating effect: the playwright understood the impact of a simple silent gesture. And the whole interlude foreshadows terrible conflicts to come.[66] The following April, in the final days of the war in Europe, finds Churchill pleading with Stalin:

> There is not much comfort in looking into a future where you and the countries you dominate, plus the Communist Parties in many other States, are all drawn up on one side, and those who rally to the English-speaking nations and their associates or Dominions are on the other. It is quite obvious that their quarrel would tear the world to pieces and that all of us

> leading men on either side who had anything to do with that would be shamed before history.[67]

So if Churchill wrote *The Second World War* to vindicate himself to history, why did he spotlight a scene that was, in more ways than one, shameful? Perhaps, in performing it in 1944 and in writing it out years later, he was more concerned with creating dramatic art in which he and Stalin were the "leading men" (a telling choice of words on Churchill's part)? "For five years he has tried to justify to posterity in the six volumes of his book all that he did in the war," Lord Moran observed in 1953. "But have there been black hours when he has not been so sure?" Was he capable of rationalizing or dismissing from his mind all the costly mistakes and terrible decisions he had made? "Does the artist, for that is what Winston is, really escape so lightly?"[68] Or was he a prima donna, willing to play an unattractive role as long as he was center stage? Reviewing his diary entry for the Moscow meeting, Alan Brooke commented, "I had frequently noticed that he liked the limelight to concentrate on him."[69]

On 12 October 1944 the Germans pulled out of Athens, and two days later 5,000 British troops under General Ronald Scobie moved in. On 3 December the Greek Communist resistance groups EAM and ELAS began their revolt, and two days after that Churchill ordered Scobie "to hold and dominate Athens. It would be a great thing for you to succeed in this without bloodshed if possible, but also with bloodshed if necessary." He flew to Athens on Christmas Day and met with the opposing parties, assuring them that he only wanted the Greeks to work out a democratic solution for themselves, but it was an assurance backed up by British armed force. In effect he treated Greece as a colony, where he aimed to install a "responsible" government and bring back King George II, who was pro-British but deeply unpopular with his own people.[70]

Churchill's motives were strategic and imperial, but also literary. As Harold Macmillan recognized in his diary, the Prime Minister had come to Greece partly because, "as a good journalist," he wanted to witness and ultimately report on a revolution in progress. "He was in good form and had been taken by [General Alexander] to an 'observation post' from which he could see the whole city and get an idea of the fighting. Of course this affair is a sort of 'super Sidney Street', and he quite enjoyed having the whole problem explained to him by a master of the military art."[71] Even more than Sidney Street, the Greek affair made real the climactic chapters of *Savrola*, where a country in southeastern Europe, after liberating itself from tyranny, succumbs to a civil war between moderate and radical revolutionaries. But Churchill insisted on projecting the black-and-white morality of his third-rate novel upon the very complicated realities of Greek politics. Earlier Eden had prudently suggested keeping the Greek King out of the country for the time being and establishing a regency under Archbishop Damaskinos of Athens, but Churchill dismissed him as a potential "dictator who may very likely become the champion of the extreme Left." Only after he arrived in Athens did Churchill grasp the depths of anti-royalist sentiment and allow Damaskinos to form a non-Communist government. On 11 January 1945, the Communists agreed to a ceasefire.[72] At last, *Savrola* had a happy ending.

But Churchill paid a price for his intervention, which might have affected the result of the next General Election. A Gallup poll reported that the British public was deeply divided on his Greek policy, with 43 percent approving and 38 percent disapproving.[73] Mass Observation found widespread public revulsion, with a shocking number of interviewees comparing Churchill's methods to Hitler's.[74] The Prime Minister had to face down attacks in the House of Commons; he was vociferously criticized by many British and most American newspapers; and Roosevelt was deeply unhappy. But there were no protests from Stalin, and Churchill remained silent when the Soviets imposed a pro-Communist regime on Romania in February 1945: both leading men kept to their agreement.

The Greek crisis had focused Churchill's mind once more, but after it was settled he again sunk into a disorganized state. On 19 January 1945 Clement Attlee took the extraordinary step of composing a 2,000-word protest, typing it himself so as not to embarrass the Prime Minister in the eyes of any third party. Cabinet committees (which Attlee frequently chaired) labored to produce reports reflecting a cross-party consensus, but the Cabinet was very slow to consider them. Even when they found a place on the agenda, the Prime Minister usually neglected to read them beforehand. And then "Not infrequently a phrase catches your eye which gives rise to a disquisition on an interesting point only slightly connected with the subject matter"[75] – like an Edwardian man of letters writing a rambling causerie for a Sunday paper. Churchill's only response was contemptuous indignation.

In Berlin, Hitler had a scale model of his planned reconstruction of the Austrian city of Linz installed in his bunker. During the final weeks of the war he spent hours studying it, admiring its classical proportions while Germany was being blasted to ruins.[76] He and Goebbels were fervent devotees of Thomas Carlyle's biography of Frederick the Great, and now they found inspiration in the story of the Prussian king who, facing near-certain defeat in the Seven Years War, was miraculously rescued by the demise of his arch-enemy, the Czarina Elizabeth. "We must be as Frederick the Great and act as he did," Goebbels wrote in his diary. "Why should not we also hope for a similar wonderful turn of fortune!"[77] The death of Franklin Roosevelt on 12 April momentarily convinced Hitler that life would once again follow literature, and he proclaimed to his remaining troops that "the turning point in this war had been decided."[78]

When that final hope was dashed, the only question that remained was how Hitler would make his exit. On 8 April Churchill had privately suggested a dramatic gesture like that of Rudolf Hess, flying to England and proclaiming a melodramatic cliché: "I am responsible; wreak your vengeance on me but spare my people."[79] But Hitler was determined to bring his people down with him. As he told Goebbels on the 25th, "If we leave the world stage in disgrace, we'll have lived for nothing."[80] Goebbels was of a similar mind: on an earlier occasion he had called suicide in the face of defeat "A heroic decision. A drama that arouses pride and sadness."[81] Now, at the Propaganda Ministry, he told his staff that their last days would be celebrated in some future movie: "Everybody now has a chance to choose the part which he will play in the film a hundred years hence. I can assure you that it will be a fine and elevating picture."[82] As the Red Army closed in on the capital, Albert Speer countermanded orders to arm the musicians of the Berlin Philharmonic for a final battle, judging that they could achieve the same artistic effect by performing, in their last concert, the finale to Wagner's *Götterdämmerung*.[83] Clifford Geertz has described the self-immolation of his Balinese theatre state, performing to the end as it was overrun by a Dutch colonial army. "It expired as it had lived: absorbed in a pageant,"[84] and the final act of the Third Reich may be understandable only in those terms. As Hitler thundered in his last will and testament, he had to choose between two theatrical denouements, and one was absolutely unthinkable: "I do not want to fall into the hands of enemies who for the delectation of the hate-riddled masses require a new spectacle promoted by the Jews." The Nuremberg Trials would be the most devastating courtroom drama ever staged. What would it have been if Hitler had been captured alive?

On several occasions in 1940–41 Churchill remarked that he did not expect to maintain his popularity after the war, and would therefore retire to write his memoirs.[85] A November 1942 Mass Observation survey detected widespread public distrust of "leaders," and the obvious candidate for that role was the Prime Minister.[86] In a February 1944 poll 62 percent did not want Churchill to stay on as a peacetime PM, with only 28 percent in favor.[87] But when the moment arrived for a General Election, he was determined to stand again – and he began the campaign with a staggering blunder. In his election broadcast of 4 June 1945 he warned:

> I declare to you, from the bottom of my heart, that no Socialist system can be established without a political police. . . . No Socialist government conducting the entire life and industry of the country could afford to allow free, sharp, or violently-worded expressions of public discontent. They would have to fall back on some kind of Gestapo, no doubt very humanely

> directed in the first instance. And this would nip opinion in the bud; it would stop criticism as it reared its head, and it would gather all the power to the supreme party and the party leaders, rising like stately pinnacles above their vast bureaucracies of civil servants, no longer servants and no longer civil.

The socialist state, he declared, would prescribe for every individual "where they are to work; what they are to work at; where they may go and what they may say; what views they are to hold and within what limits they may express them; where their wives are to go to queue up for the State ration; and what education their children are to receive to mould their views of human liberty and conduct in the future." He conceded that many of these restrictions had been instituted by his own government during wartime, when a large measure of state regulation was necessary. But he insisted that these were only temporary war emergency measures, which must not be extended into peacetime.[88] And he issued similar warnings in his political broadcast of 21 June, even if he avoided the word "Gestapo."[89]

"It would be difficult to exaggerate the disappointment and genuine distress aroused by this speech," reported Mass Observation, which cited any number of hostile voter comments:

> "I am astounded at his overnight change from National Leader to Party Leader. The whole speech seems to have been in bad taste. No one but the veriest baby in politics would believe his assumption that the Labour Leaders are potential Gestapo officials."

> "Everyone I meet angry and resentful and glad all at once – angry that he dare speak such lying statements into the microphone, resentful that he can make such allegations against his own countrymen, and glad that he has shown up Tory tactics, and that by one speech of abuse he shows that he has no real policy."

> "The most used expressions about him to-day were 'wicked' and 'lying'."

> "I think there's a lot of men in the forces see through him now that didn't before. . . . I know my husband's changed his views a lot since he went away, and I think there's a lot like him."

> "Churchill's first speech did not make a good impression. I did not hear one favourable remark about it. But many adverse ones. Attlee's speech the following night was very well received. I heard a woman whom I regard as a

> staunch Tory saying that if she had only those two speeches on which to base her judgement, she would not have the slightest hesitation in voting Labour."

Even a Conservative wine butler had to admit that "It was a lot of whitewash really." But when Londoners were directly asked "Which speeches on the wireless or in the papers did you like best?" Churchill was mentioned more often than any other politician. Those respondents did not admire him because they thought that Clement Attlee would be a British Himmler. Rather, they continued to be enthralled by the aesthetics of his oratory, regardless of the content: "Because I like listening to Mr. Churchill. Not because of what he says, but because of him speaking." Contrast that with the words voters consistently used to describe the broadcasts by Attlee and other Labour politicians: "Sensible", "Straightforward", "Grown-up", "Calm", "Clear", "Sound", "Decent", "To the point", "Reasonable", "Factual", "Constructive", "Definite". "We must remember . . . the psychological background to the election," Mass Observation concluded. "After six years of emotion, of glory, of tragedy, of heights and depths of feeling, one gets the impression that people were weary of being roused to any kind of emotion whatever; that the very mediocrity of some of the speeches was a relief to a people worn out with reacting to great events and world-shaking announcements." When voters discussed the issues that were most important to them, most mentioned hard economic issues that were Labour's strong points: Housing (48 percent), Employment (15 percent), and Social Security (9 percent). Only 5 percent mentioned Controls, the one issue that might have worked in Churchill's favor.[90] The Conservatives actually narrowed the polling gap somewhat in the weeks leading up to the election on 5 July, but the result was still a landslide for the Labour Party, which won 393 seats to 213 for the Tories.

Churchill later claimed that he entered the election campaign "deeply distressed at the prospect of sinking from a national to a party leader."[91] In that case, he should have declined to sink. An April 1945 poll found that while Labour was well ahead of the Tories (40 to 24 percent), 43 percent wanted to continue the all-party coalition government into peacetime.[92] Election surveys also revealed widespread apathy and cynicism among voters, who profoundly disliked politicians engaging in partisan slanging matches. Churchill's Gestapo speech earned a 69 percent disapproval rating in the Gallup poll.[93] He would have been far better advised to call magnanimously for continued cooperation among the parties. And he should have adopted a radio style more like Attlee's. He had done that in a broadcast on 21 March 1943, where he addressed post-war reconstruction issues, including the Beveridge Report and his own Four Year Plan. It was generally received well by London listeners: 53 percent favorable, 25 percent unfavorable, 22 percent no opinion.

Churchill deliberately shelved his high oratory in favor of a more conversational tone, and that too was approved by a ratio better than two-to-one. As Mass Observation concluded:

> His rhetoric, so very highly appreciated during the Battle of Britain, has become a more and more frequent source of criticism and irritation. The "fireside manner" so successfully used by Sir Stafford Cripps in his radio talk after his return from Russia, in which people feel that they are being talked to rather than addressed, seems to be more appropriate to present circumstances. At present people suspect "talk", and want precise, clear statement, rather than an emotion-rousing approach. It seems probable that the success of this speech, despite its controversial elements, depended partly on this new manner.[94]

As Richard Toye has recently reminded us, in the years leading up to the "Gestapo speech," similar epithets were commonly hurled back and forth by both Labour and Tory politicians. In 1945 Attlee did not respond to Churchill in kind, but in 1937 he had publicly characterized the policies of Ramsay MacDonald as "essentially fascist," and Michael Foot's acid review of *The Gathering Storm* in *Tribune* (8 October 1948) would be headlined "Churchill's 'Mein Kampf'."

As for literary sources of inspiration, the economist Friedrich Hayek later claimed responsibility: "I am afraid there can be little doubt that Winston Churchill's somewhat unfortunately phrased Gestapo speech was written under the influence of *The Road to Serfdom*." In 1944 Hayek had twice arranged to send Churchill his book. There is no hard evidence that the Prime Minister read it, but given that it was widely debated in British newspapers, he must have been familiar with its main arguments. Conservative Party Chairman Ralph Assheton was a fervent admirer of Hayek, and no doubt Churchill absorbed some of his enthusiasm. Assheton cited Hayek in an April 1945 speech which he sent to Churchill, who wrote back "I read your speech and think it very good." The Conservative Central Office was willing to sacrifice 1.5 tons of its precious paper ration to publish an abridged edition of the book, though it appeared too late to influence the 1945 General Election. In any case, *The Road to Serfdom* gave the Conservative Party the theme it needed to fight the election, though Labour was quite happy to engage the Tories on that ground. In his radio rebuttal Attlee said "I shall not waste time on this theoretical stuff, which seems to me to be a secondhand version of the academic views of an Austrian professor – Friedrich August von Hayek – who is very popular just now with the Conservative Party." Thus in one sentence Attlee deftly dismissed the economist as (1) Teutonic, (2) an abstract theoretician divorced from solid British common sense, and (3) an aristocrat, though the "von" had been dropped from Hayek's name in 1919. But the word "second-hand" suggested that Churchill had not actually read *The Road to Serfdom*, and in fact he nowhere mentioned it.[95]

He definitely read a book with a similar message: Sinclair Lewis's dystopian novel *It Can't Happen Here* (1935). To drive home the reality of totalitarianism to his comfortable American audience, Lewis employed the same strategy that George Orwell would use: he imagined his readers' homeland, where democracy seemed secure, transformed into a dictatorship in the near future, simply by extrapolating current political trends. Lewis's dictator, Buzz Windrip, closely resembled the Louisiana demagogue Huey Long. His political manifesto reads like *Mein Kampf* translated into down-home straight-talking no-bunk American. He takes power by promising a radical redistribution of wealth, but then creates a network of prison camps run by the Minute Men, or MM, his version of the SS. Dissidents are driven into Canadian exile, with H. L. Mencken becoming a kind of American Solzhenitsyn.

In a 24 April 1935 article, Churchill had warned the readers of the *Daily Mail* that Long was a real threat to American democracy, a rabblerouser howling "war-cries of hate and prejudice."[96] When Long was shot and killed in September of that year, Churchill gloated over the demise of "the most clownish of the Dictator tribe."[97] Then on 22 August 1936 he recommended *It Can't Happen Here* to the readers of *Collier's* magazine. The article was devoted to the larger issue of whether constitutional government could survive a severe economic downturn. In Germany

> discontent about the inequalities of wealth . . . made the Weimar Constitution "a scrap of paper". . . . In the United States, also, economic crisis had led to an extension of the activities of the Executive and to the pillorying, by irresponsible agitators, of certain groups and sections of the population as enemies of the rest. There have been efforts to exalt the power of the central government and to limit the rights of individuals. . . .
>
> It is when passions and cupidities are thus unleashed and, at the same time, the sense of public duty rides high in the hearts of all men and women of good will that the handcuffs can be slipped upon the citizens and they can be brought into entire subjugation to the executive government. Then they are led to believe that, if they will only yield themselves, body, mind and soul, to the State, and obey unquestioningly its injunctions, some dazzling future of riches and power will open to them, either – as in Italy – by the conquest of the territories of others, or – as in America – by a further liberation and exploitation of the national resources.

In this context Churchill praised *It Can't Happen Here*. "Such books render a public service to the English-speaking world" – that is, not just the United States. "When we see what has happened in Germany, Italy and Russia we cannot neglect their warning. This is an age in which the citizen requires more, and not less, legal protection in the exercise of his rights and liberties."[98] In any number of speeches delivered in the 1920s he had warned that a Labour government would mean stifling regimentation.[99] That raw nerve was hit when Clement Attlee advocated a New Deal for Britain. He had nothing in common with Huey Long's loudmouthed populism except a demand to redistribute the wealth, but that was enough for Churchill.

Bear in mind also that wartime Britain, while still a democracy, was hemmed in by a vast web of restrictions characteristic of totalitarian societies – rationing, blackout regulations, conscription, direction of labor, internment of aliens, pervasive official surveillance, and sanctions against political extremists and "careless talk." The raw police statistics might suggest that there was a wartime crime wave, but many of the criminals were normally law-abiding people who had carelessly or inadvertently done things that were perfectly legal in peacetime. And if one openly protested that Britain was turning fascist, one could be accused of disloyalty. "Restrictions, discomforts, official supervision that smacks of Fascism – these we suffer but do not enjoy," the *Spectator* protested in April 1943. "Nor do we discuss them. But they are felt."[100] *Nineteen Eighty-Four* would be largely an extrapolation of England in 1944, but before Orwell published it (in 1949) there were many fictional imaginings of a fascist Britain: in MOI pamphlets (*What Would Happen if Hitler Won*); BBC radio plays (*They Call It Peace, It Might Happen Here*); films (*Went the Day Well?, The Silent Village*); Robin Maugham's 1943 short story "The 1946 MS"; and Noël Coward's 1947 play *Peace in Our Time*.[101]

The lightning German victories of spring 1940 had been widely attributed to the malign work of "Fifth Columnists." There was the real example of Vidkun Quisling in Norway, but in a British context these fears were fanciful, a revival of the "spy scares" of the First World War. The day after Churchill became Prime Minister, his government moved to intern all male enemy aliens aged sixteen to sixty (most of them refugees, many of them Jewish) who were living on England's vulnerable southern and eastern coasts. However, once the initial panic had passed, his libertarian instincts reasserted themselves: by January 1941 he was protesting "the witch-finding activities of MI5."[102] In the first volume of *The Second World War* he still asserted that "There were known to be twenty thousand organized German Nazis in England" at the beginning of the war.[103] That sounds like something out of a paranoid Edwardian invasion novel, and it was contradicted by what Churchill wrote in his second volume: "No Fifth Column existed in Britain."[104]

Regulation 18b permitted imprisonment without trial for Axis sympathizers. Indeed, in their negotiations to join Churchill's coalition, the Labour Party had insisted on internment for British fascists. By the end of 1940 more than one thousand people had been detained, including the fascist leader Oswald Mosley. At that point Churchill was urging Herbert Morrison, the Home Secretary, to ameliorate conditions for detainees, feeling somewhat guilty for compromising his own libertarian ideals: "Naturally I feel distressed at having to be responsible for action so utterly at variance with all the fundamental principles of British liberty, *Habeas Corpus* and the like. The public danger justifies the action taken, but that danger is now receding."[105] By November 1943 Churchill had decisively turned against "the totalitarian idea of the right of the Executive to lock up its political opponents or unpopular people."[106] He released Mosley in spite of protests from many quarters, including the National Council for Civil Liberties. It was a courageous and profoundly unpopular decision, supported by barely 10 percent of people surveyed by Mass Observation.[107] Churchill wanted to abolish Regulation 18b altogether, but was blocked by MI5 and Labour members of the coalition government – a point he probably had in mind when he made his "Gestapo speech." He succeeded in stopping a plan to unify all British intelligence agencies, fearing that it might expand the powers of MI5 beyond ministerial control. "Look what has happened to the liberties of this country during the war," he protested in a newspaper article. "Men of position are seized and kept in prison for years without trial . . . a frightful thing to anyone concerned about British liberties." Privately he went further: "The power of the Executive to cast a man into prison is in the highest degree odious and is the foundation of all totalitarian government whether Nazi or Communist."[108] As the war drew to a close, there were many others who worried that secret police agencies and restrictions on civil liberties, which were perhaps a necessary evil in wartime, might become permanently institutionalized. Even Stewart Menzies, head of MI6, warned against the possibility of an "internal Gestapo." Clement Attlee also feared "a British Comintern," and as Prime Minister he would take steps to rein in MI5.[109]

Churchill the author had always been a passionate defender of freedom of expression, but the war brought with it the spectre of censorship. The Emergency Powers Act of 1939 gave the government potentially unlimited scope for restricting liberties. At its outbreak, Churchill declared that the war was being fought "to establish, on impregnable rocks, the rights of the individual, and . . . to establish and revive the stature of man." He conceded that war inevitably involved the suspension of some freedoms, but these measures would be temporary: "Surely and confidently we look forward to the day when our liberties and rights will be restored to us, and when we shall be able to share them with the peoples to whom such blessings are unknown."[110] Duff

Cooper, as Minister of Information, tried to recruit "silent columns," volunteers who would eavesdrop on and report defeatist conversations. They were swiftly dubbed "Cooper's Snoopers" and were devastatingly satirized in *Nineteen Eighty-Four*. Responding at "Question Time" on 25 July 1940, Churchill admitted that this was a rum idea:

> I have asked the Home Secretary to have every sentence imposed by the courts for loose or defeatist talk carefully and immediately reviewed, and that it should be reduced or remitted whenever it is clear that there was no evil wish, or systematic purpose to weaken the National Defence in the persons concerned. His Majesty's Government have no desire to make crimes out of silly vapourings which are best dealt with on the spur of the moment by verbal responses from the more robust members of the company. They desire only to curb, as it is their duty to do, propaganda of a persistent, organized and defeatist character.

Note that Churchill did not renounce censorship powers, he simply promised not to use them against everyday bellyaching.[111]

Churchill opposed prison sentences for the mere expression of pro-Axis opinion "not accompanied by conspiracy,"[112] but in February 1941 he did urge some restrictions on publishing sensitive war information.[113] The *Daily Worker* was banned for eighteen months in 1941–42. When the *Sunday Pictorial* published a blistering attack on his conduct of the war on 26 October 1941, he seriously considered suppressing the paper.[114] And in March 1942 threats of suppression from Churchill and Herbert Morrison were enough to persuade the *Daily Mirror* to tone down its criticisms. Churchill even endorsed the withdrawal of John Masefield's book about Dunkirk, *Twenty-Five Days*, because it made the evacuation seem too chaotic.[115] In the course of the war he tried to interfere with only four films, including the politically innocuous *Life and Death of Colonel Blimp*, but all four were released with scarcely any infringement of freedom of expression.[116]

To sum up, Churchill's record on censorship and civil liberties was blemished but reasonably good considering the temper of the times. He was neither alone nor completely irrational in his fear that the war might lead to a British Gestapo, a fear aroused by both his reading and his inside knowledge of how far the government's police powers had expanded. Given its intransigence on the issue of internment without trial, the Labour Party was certainly open to criticism on this point, but Churchill's electioneering rhetoric had been too extreme. If he had focused more on the entirely legitimate issue of preserving liberty in the face of growing state power, and less on vilifying his political opponents, he might have left a much better impression on the voters – and on history.

CHAPTER 22

The Summit

On the morning of 23 July 1945 at the Potsdam Conference – where Churchill, Stalin, and US President Harry Truman were deciding the fate of defeated Germany – Lord Moran dropped in on his patient while he was having breakfast. The Prime Minister hustled his valet out of the room and revealed an awful secret:

> I am going to tell you something you must not tell to any human being. We have split the atom. The report of the great experiment has just come in. A bomb was let off in some wild spot in New Mexico. It was only a thirteen-pound bomb, but it made a crater half a mile across. People ten miles away lay with their feet towards the bomb; when it went off they rolled over and tried to look at the sky. But even with the darkest glasses it was impossible. It was the middle of the night, but it was as if seven suns had lit the earth; two hundred miles away the light could be seen. The bomb sent up smoke into the stratosphere.

Moran immediately saw the horror. "It is H. G. Wells stuff," he exclaimed. "Exactly," said Churchill, who went on to say that it would be dropped on Japanese cities rather than strictly military targets. "It has just come in time to save the world."[1] A decade later Moran recalled that what shocked him about Churchill's reaction was that "he saw the scene as an artist," dwelling on the hellish aesthetics of the explosion. The Prime Minister recognized the literary connection with Wells, who had predicted nuclear weaponry in his 1914 novel *The World Set Free*. But though Wells realized that the atomic bomb could mean mutual assured destruction, Churchill "had not yet grasped what it meant to the world. It had not occurred to him then that it might in the long run mean the end of everything on which he sets store."[2]

At lunch that day Churchill related the earth-shattering news to Field Marshal Brooke, who recorded the Prime Minister's dreadful enthusiasm in his diary:

> We now had something in our hands which would redress the balance with the Russians! The secret of this explosive, and the power to use it, would completely alter the diplomatic equilibrium which was adrift since the defeat of Germany! Now we had a new value which redressed our position (pushing his chin out and scowling), now we could say if you insist on doing this or that, well we can just blot out Moscow, then Stalingrad, then Kiev, then Kuibyshev, Karkhov . . .

Who was "we"? Churchill talked as if the Bomb were Britain's to use, or at least controlled by his projected English-speaking confederation, which so far existed only in the form of a very long unfinished historical manuscript. As Brooke recalled, "He had at once painted a wonderful picture of himself as the sole possessor of these bombs and capable of dumping them where he wished, thus all powerful and capable of dictating to Stalin!"[3] In fact Churchill had urged Truman to have a "showdown" with the Soviet Union as early as 11 May,[4] well before the Bomb was tested, and now he thought he had been dealt an unbeatable card.

Throughout the Cold War Western leaders debated three possible strategies for dealing with the Soviet Union: confrontation (aggressively rolling back communism, even at the risk of war); containment (allowing the Soviets to dominate Eastern Europe, but resisting any further encroachments); and conciliation (negotiating arms control and a general reduction of tensions). Churchill at various points embraced all three of these positions, and in each case his foreign policy reflected an important literary influence, as well as a compelling desire to place himself at the center of the world stage once again.

In 1939 Churchill had contracted with Harrap to write a book on "Europe Since the Russian Revolution," but its thrust would have been the crimes and political instability that followed the Bolshevik takeover, and the war put paid to that project. By 1944 he was looking forward to a "Twenty Years' Alliance with Russia."[5] But even before the war ended in Europe, Churchill worried that a new barrier was dividing the Continent, using metaphors that grew ever more ominous and theatrical. On 16 March 1945 he had warned Roosevelt that "An impenetrable veil has been drawn across the scene" in Soviet-occupied Poland.[6] On 1 April he asked Stalin "why a veil of secrecy should thus be drawn over the Polish scene."[7] The words took their final form in a secret communication to Truman on 12 May,[8] and publicly before the House of Commons on 16 August: "It is not impossible that tragedy on a prodigious scale is unfolding itself behind the iron curtain which at the moment divides Europe in twain."[9]

The phrase was not original to Churchill. Patrick Wright and other historians have invested considerable detective work in tracking down its origins. It was first applied to Russia almost immediately after the Bolshevik seizure of power by the philosopher Vasily Rozanov in *Apocalypse of Our Time* (1918): "With a rumble and a roar, an iron curtain is descending on Russian history." Then it was introduced to Western readers by Ethel Snowden, an Independent Labour Party activist, in *Through Bolshevik Russia* (1920). However, it had been used even earlier by the peace agitator Vernon Lee (1917) and Queen Elisabeth of Belgium (1915) to describe a Europe riven by the First World War, and still earlier (1904) by H. G. Wells in *The Food of the Gods*. But when asked in 1951 if he was familiar with any of these earlier usages, Churchill replied, "No. I didn't hear of the phrase before – though everyone has heard of the 'iron curtain' which descends in a theatre."[10]

Once again, he had resorted to a dramatic metaphor. In *My Early Life* Churchill recalled that, as a child in Dublin, he had missed seeing the pantomime *Ali Baba* because the theatre burned down, a fairly common hazard of the Victorian stage.[11] Iron curtains were therefore installed as a safety device, lowered to protect the audience in the event of a fire.

Another previous use of the term was in February 1924, when the French occupation of the Ruhr had created an international crisis. Viscount D'Abernon, the British ambassador to Berlin, wrote to the new Prime Minister, Ramsay MacDonald, proposing to defuse the situation by demilitarizing the Rhineland. He compared such a buffer zone to "an iron curtain between a stage and an auditorium," which would "considerably reduce the danger of a conflagration." D'Abernon's basic concept would be embodied in the Locarno Treaty of 1925.[12] Later, Robert Vansittart and General J. H. Morgan would label D'Abernon an early advocate of "appeasement,"[13] but he favored appeasing a democratic Germany, a policy supported by Churchill at the time. The phrase "iron curtain" is now, of course, associated with the imprisonment of Eastern Europe and an opaque barrier cutting off communication between East and West, and no doubt that is what Churchill meant to convey – in part. But for him it was also a firewall, a metaphor of containment. It ended with an ominous clang the drama of the Second World War, but by stabilizing the division of the Continent, it also prevented a holocaust. After all, the title of Churchill's famous speech at Fulton, Missouri, was not "The Iron Curtain" but "The Sinews of Peace."

Even before this speech, given on 5 March 1946 at Westminster College, influential American newspapers and magazines had been urging a tougher line with the Soviets, closer Anglo-American cooperation, and attention to

Churchill's advice. That line was argued by the *New York Times*, the *Washington Star, Reader's Digest* ("Keep British-American Teamwork"), *Time, Fortune*, the *Saturday Evening Post, Harper's* ("We must back Britain"), and *Life* ("The Lives of Winston Churchill: The Last Truly Great Man of the Western World"), as well as columnists Walter Lippmann, Joseph Alsop, and Arthur Crock.[14] Truman himself was increasingly irritated by Soviet provocations and seriously considering a change in foreign policy, but he was not sure that the American public would support a departure from the wartime spirit of cooperation with Russia. On 10 February 1946 Churchill met him at the White House and outlined what he intended to say at Westminster College. Truman was obviously pleased, even if he could not publicly endorse the speech. At no political cost to the President, Churchill was conveniently sending up a trial balloon. If the reaction to the speech was negative, Truman could disown it; if positive, he could join Britain in a common front against the USSR. Just two days later, on the 12th, Secretary of State James F. Byrnes suddenly became markedly less accommodating toward the Soviets than he had so far been, raising objections to their conduct in Bulgaria, Rumania, Albania, and Austria. This was before the receipt on the 22nd of George F. Kennan's "long cable," which is often credited with inspiring the Cold War policy of containment. Throughout the Second World War Churchill had overestimated his ability to influence American policy with words, but now the political climate was exactly right.[15]

In his Fulton speech[16] Churchill advocated a "special relationship" between the United States and the British Commonwealth, strong enough to inspire respect and good behavior among the Soviets. Here he paralleled his 1930 counterfactual essay on the consequences of a Confederate victory at Gettysburg, where he had argued that an Anglo-American alliance would have forestalled German aggression in 1914. In 1946 he avoided the word "alliance", which might have set off alarm bells among American audiences, but he did call for a "fraternal association of the English-speaking peoples" that would involve "the continuance of the intimate relationship between our military advisers, leading to common study of potential dangers, similarity of weapons and manuals of instruction, and to the interchange of officers and cadets at technical colleges." Churchill specifically proposed that the existing Permanent Defense Agreement between the United States and Canada be enlarged to include the British Empire, and he held out the prospect of "common citizenship" at some point in the far future. After all, "the English-speaking world" was united by its "joint inheritance": constitutional government based on the rule of law, "freedom of speech and thought," trial by jury, free elections by secret ballot, and an independent judiciary. He pointed out that mutual defense pacts were not inconsistent with United Nations membership, and he favored continued "mutual assistance and collaboration" with Russia. To preserve the peace, he proposed the creation of an international air force under UN command, though he warned against UN control of nuclear technology at least until some remote future utopia, "when the essential brotherhood of man is truly embodied and expressed in a world organization with all the necessary practical safeguards to make it effective." And he spoke vaguely but fervently of collective efforts to raise the living standards of the masses.

So far there was much here that would have found favor with the left wing of the Labour Party or the fellow-traveling partisans of Henry Wallace in the United States. Churchill emphasized his

> strong admiration and regard for the valiant Russian people and for my wartime comrade, Marshal Stalin. There is deep sympathy and goodwill in Britain – and I doubt not here also – towards the peoples of all the Russias and a resolve to persevere through many differences and rebuffs in establishing lasting friendships. We understand the Russian need to be secure on her western frontiers by the removal of all possibility of German aggression. We welcome Russia to her rightful place among the leading nations of the world. We welcome her flag upon the seas. Above all, we welcome constant, frequent and growing contacts between the Russian people and our own people on both sides of the Atlantic.

But then, more than halfway through the speech, he dropped his bombshell: "From Stettin in the Baltic to Trieste in the Adriatic, an iron curtain has descended across the Continent." Though he prefaced that remark with extended peacemongering, it was bound to shock his audience, which for years had viewed the Soviets as allies, and were now warned to treat them as potential adversaries.

The initial response was deeply polarized. American newspapers in the isolationist Midwest were unsurprisingly hostile, though those on the East and West coasts were more favorable. The British Consulate in New York analyzed about a thousand letters and telegrams they received and reported that nearly all expressed forceful opinions, but just 18 percent were clearly negative, and their "marked similarity of wording made the sudden spate of abuse seem anything but spontaneous."[17] The speech revived long-standing American fears that "Anglo-American unity" meant in practice inveigling the United States into propping up British imperialism under "enlightened Anglo-Saxon atomic bomb auspices," as Henry Wallace put it. On the left, Pearl S. Buck warned that "we are nearer war tonight than we were last night." On the right, the *Wall Street Journal* stuck to isolationism: "The United States wants no alliance, or anything that resembles an alliance with any other nation." And yet the Fulton speech marked the beginning of a sea change on both sides of the American political spectrum. The non-communist left, which was itself becoming increasingly critical of the USSR, found it difficult to dismiss entirely Churchill's warnings about Soviet conduct. The right began to realize that it would have to choose between its traditional isolationism and an alliance to contain communism, and in particular the Hearst newspapers warmly endorsed Churchill's call for vigilance and rearmament.[18]

American public opinion, which at the end of the war had strongly favored post-war cooperation with the Soviet Union, was rapidly shifting. Just before the speech, in January 1946, the Gallup poll asked which nation was seeking to achieve global hegemony: 26 percent said the USSR, compared with 13 percent for the United Kingdom.[19] (It is remarkable that, even at this late date, a significant portion of the American people believed that a bombed-out exhausted Britain still aimed to control the world.) A poll conducted just after the speech found that, of those who knew it, 40 percent disapproved and 22 percent approved. But when asked what they thought of Soviet foreign policy, 71 percent were critical and just 7 percent approved. Another poll immediately after the speech reported that only 18 percent supported a US-UK alliance, but a month later the numbers had shot up to 85 percent.[20] Before the year was out, public opinion in the United States and Britain would catch up with Churchill. In March 1946 British responses to the speech were deeply divided (34 percent approved, 39 percent disapproved, 16 percent no opinion), but two years later 62 percent felt that the government was not tough enough with the Soviet Union, whereas just 6 percent wanted a more conciliatory policy.[21] Mass Observation concluded that Churchill had revived something of the "Dunkirk spirit," crystallizing increasing public distrust of the Soviet Union.[22]

Churchill drew comparisons between Nazi Germany and Soviet Russia, insofar as both were expansionist and dangerous totalitarian regimes. In both cases, he warned, appeasement could only lead to war. But he also suggested crucial differences between the two cases. While his criticisms of Stalin's Russia were sharp, they were considerably less vitriolic than his denunciations of Hitler's Germany – or of Lenin's Russia, for that matter. The USSR in 1946 was aggressive, but not so recklessly aggressive as Germany had been in 1938–39. "I do not believe that Soviet Russia desires war," he explained. "What they desire is the fruits of war and the indefinite expansion of their power and doctrines." And the atomic bomb meant that any third world war would end in a Wellsian apocalypse, far worse than the present devastation of Europe and Japan: "The dark ages may return, the Stone Age may return on the gleaming wings of science, and what might now shower immeasurable material blessings upon mankind may even bring about its total destruction."

Churchill predicted the eventual collapse of Communism as early as 1920 and as late as 1957, but he said nothing to suggest that in "The Sinews of Peace." Nor did he advocate (in this speech, at any rate) a protracted Cold War. He argued that world peace could "only be achieved by reaching now, in 1946 – this year, 1946 – a good understanding on all points with Russia under the general authority of the United Nations Organization, and by the maintenance of that good understanding through many peaceful years, by the world instrument, supported by the whole strength of the English-speaking world and all its connections." The Western democracies would have to stand firm and united against Soviet tresspasses, but as soon as the Russians understood that, détente and peaceful coexistence would follow – before New Year's Day 1947. In the weeks following the speech the Soviets further encroached on Iran, moving their tanks to within 20 miles of Tehran, but then they pulled back in the face of American pressure. They could not have done more to vindicate Churchill in the eyes of Americans. As Robert Gellately recently concluded from a study of the Soviet archives, that was indeed Stalin's post-war strategy: to advance as far as he could but retreat when confronted with superior Western power.[23]

The Fulton speech, however, never made clear how far the West should go in pressuring the USSR, except that it seemed to rule out nuclear war. Yet in private Churchill's Cold War strategy was more specific and far more confrontational. The newspaper publisher Lord Camrose recalled that in a conversation the day after the 6 August bombing of Hiroshima, Churchill voiced

> the opinion that, with the manufacture of this bomb in their hands, America can dominate the world for the next five years. If he had continued in office he is of the opinion that he could have persuaded the American Government to use this power to restrain the Russians. He would have had a show-down with Stalin and told him he had got to behave reasonably and decently in Europe, and would have gone so far as to be brusque and angry with him if needs be. If the President and his advisors had shown weakness in this policy he would have declared his position openly and feels certain that the American people would have backed the policy on the grounds that it would have been carrying out the Atlantic Charter.[24]

In August 1946 he suggested to Lord Moran that the Americans could eliminate half of the USSR's motor vehicle plant by dropping one bomb on Moscow: "It might mean wiping out three million people, but they would think nothing of that. They think more of erasing an historical building like the Kremlin."[25] In the late 1940s he proposed to some Western leaders – including Mackenzie King, Jan Christian Smuts, and General Dwight Eisenhower – that the USSR should be presented with an ultimatum backed up by the explicit threat of a nuclear attack. The precise terms of that demand were not entirely clear, but Churchill seems to have been thinking of a Soviet withdrawal from Eastern Europe. He apparently presumed that the threat would not have to be carried out, because the Soviets would bow to pressure. He never made this threat explicit in public, but at the October 1948 Conservative Party conference he argued that "the Western nations would be far more likely to reach a lasting settlement, without bloodshed, if they formulated their just demands while they had the atomic power and before the Russians had it too." *The Times* realized what he was suggesting and warned "It is unreasonable to suppose that Russia will willingly negotiate on the division of the world under the threat of nuclear bombardment."[26]

A policy of containment was one thing, but the idea that the Red Army would pull back to its borders in the face of nuclear threats was dangerously delusional. The United States still possessed only a handful of atomic warheads and no means of delivering them to the Russian heartland, while the USSR had a huge preponderance of conventional ground forces in Europe. Stalin could have simply refused to budge, leaving the Western nations to choose between a humiliating climbdown and launching an aggressive apocalyptic war. Happily, no Western leader took Churchill's proposal seriously. "In terms of influence," concludes David Carlton, "he was again in a certain sense as much in the wilderness as he had been during the 1930s."[27]

The literary source of this mad daydream appears to have been Harold Nicolson's *Public Faces* (1932), a political novel set in the near future, whose cast of characters included both real and fictional politicians. Churchill considered it "a very remarkable book,"[28] perhaps because he appeared in it. Nicolson accurately predicted that Neville Chamberlain would become Prime Minister, followed by Churchill, whose government would begin research on a British atomic bomb and then lose a general election. The next government, though committed to a pacific foreign policy, is appalled to discover that the bomb is on the verge of being tested. They recoil from using such a ghastly weapon, but they recognize that France, Germany, Russia, and the United States are all casting covetous eyes on Britain's Empire. They also fear that, if they renounce the bomb, Churchill will use that issue to bring down the government. In *Public Faces* the United Kingdom controls all the fissionable material in the world, which might explain why the actual Churchill talked as if Britain had a nuclear monopoly: in the novel, she has. Even the fictional Foreign Secretary, a peace-loving man, recognizes that if the other powers gang up on him he can say: "Unless by midnight on Thursday we receive an unconditional demand for an armistice our air forces will before dawn on Friday destroy Detroit, Tourcoing, Halle, and Magnetogorsk."[29] It sounds frighteningly like what Brooke reported Churchill saying after Alamogordo: ". . . if you insist on doing this or that, well we can just blot out Moscow, then Stalingrad, then Kiev, then Kuibyshev, Karkhov . . ."

Nicolson's novel is a black comedy of dithering politicians and incompetent diplomats who bring the world to a nuclear flashpoint. (Imagine *Dr. Strangelove* written by Anthony Trollope.) A not entirely authorized test of the bomb is conducted in the North Atlantic, too close to the American coastline, and the resulting tidal waves kill 80,000 people in the Carolinas. With the Americans threatening war and the Russians encroaching on Persia, the ineffectual males of the Cabinet are at a complete loss. The only real man in the government is Jane Campbell, the smart and sexy Parliamentary Under-Secretary of State (designated "P.U.S.S." in official documents), who realizes that the one way out of the crisis is blackmail. On her advice, an ultimatum is issued proclaiming that the test has demonstrated the destructive power of the bomb, and that unless "all other Powers pledge themselves unreservedly to abandon all forms of aerial and submarine warfare, and to suppress their existing fleets of aeroplanes and submarines . . . the British Government will reluctantly be obliged to resort to progressive means of compulsion."[30] The other powers swiftly agree to negotiations, the Russians withdraw from Persia, and a Pax Britannica ensues.

The actual Churchill evidently expected the actual Russians to capitulate to nuclear threats just as readily. In the Fulton speech he did not specify the terms he would lay down to the Soviets or the threats he would use, but he did say that they would see reason and back off, whereupon (in a matter of months) East and West could resume friendly and peaceful relations. That was the script of *Public Faces*. We cannot know whether Churchill would have favored dropping the bomb if the Soviets had called his bluff. He did not think that far ahead, and the novel did not consider that possibility.

As early as 1943 Churchill feared that the Soviets would someday be capable of nuclear blackmail, recognized that the only deterrent would be a bomb with a Union Jack on it, and therefore pressed the Americans (with very limited success) to share their atomic research with Britain.[31] Lord Halifax, Professor Lindemann, Jan Smuts, the Danish physicist Niels Bohr, the Royal Society President Sir Henry Dale, and Sir John Anderson (the wartime Chancellor of the Exchequer, who as a chemistry student had written a thesis on uranium) all had influence on Churchill, and before Hiroshima all of them urged him to support the international control of atomic weapons. But he was absolutely closed-minded on the subject, to the point of rudeness.[32] In *Public Faces* all the other great powers want a piece of the nuclear action, but Britain prudently keeps the bomb to herself.

Churchill completely dropped the idea of pre-emptive nuclear threats after the Soviets tested an atomic bomb in 1949, which drove home the reality that Britain was a very small and vulnerable island with no deterrent of its own. In a 14 February 1950 General Election speech in Edinburgh he coined the term "a parley at the summit." War, he warned, was no longer a romance: it could only result in mass extermination "by the hideous force of perverted science."[33] That Wellsian concept, which Churchill had first applied to the Nazis, he now attached to nuclear war. Labour Foreign Secretary Ernest Bevin pointed out that Munich had been a summit conference and dismissed the proposal as a "stunt,"[34] but with Churchill there was no clear boundary between a stunt and a serious diplomatic initiative.

Here Churchill was drawing on Wells's 1914 novel *The World Set Free* (which he had quoted in a 1931 article).[35] Unlike Nicolson, Wells realized the dangers of nuclear proliferation. In his future history, an atomic war reduces great urban centers to radioactive wastelands, and civilization is brought to the brink of collapse. But then a sudden epidemic of common sense breaks out amongst the world's leaders. They meet at a hastily arranged conference, where they effortlessly agree to end the war and establish secure international machinery for the control of all nuclear weapons and fissionable materials. Then they all selflessly surrender their national sovereignties and proceed to build yet another practically perfect Wellsian world state. Much of Churchill's thinking on international relations implied a world state as a very remote goal, but by October 1950 he was much more urgent on this point: "The creation of an authoritative, all-powerful world order is the ultimate aim towards which we must strive. Unless some effective world super-Government can be set up and brought quickly into action, the prospects for peace and human progress are dark and doubtful." And like Wells, Churchill envisioned a European union as an essential step toward world union.[36] As for the origins of the term "summit conference," Wells set his fictional conference on a mountaintop in the Italian Alps, and then, in the final chapter, moved the action to the Himalayas, "to the culminating summits of our globe, to Dhaulagiri and Everest."[37] In his headier utopian moments, Wells was very fond of that word. In *Men Like Gods* (1923) he put it into the mouth of none other than Rupert Catskill/Winston Churchill, who proclaims that the Utopians "have reached a summit – and passed it."[38]

In the concluding volume of *The World Crisis* Churchill had offered a Wellsian "dream", imagining what the Versailles Conference would have produced if all the participants had put aside blinkered nationalism. In this alternative history, the great powers easily sweep aside the Bolsheviks and restore democracy to Russia. Reparations are determined by a mathematical formula which Churchill never specifies, but he assures us that all parties accepted it as equitable, and that it might even provide the basis of an eventual world currency. There is also a League of Nations including "all the dominating races of the world," which is not quite a world state, but does preserve the peace through its own international air force and a monopoly on chemical weapons.[39] Churchill often shared with Wells (and many newspaper columnists) the delusion that thorny diplomatic issues could be easily settled if world leaders simply parleyed together like reasonable men. A nuclear arms control agreement, with trustworthy inspection and verification machinery, would have been practically impossible with Stalin and very difficult to achieve with his successors. In any case, it would require years of research and negotiation by armies of experts and diplomatic staffers. Churchill imagined that it could be achieved at one dramatic stroke, with himself at center stage. On 21 October 1944, just after his "percentages deal," Churchill wrote to Stalin saying that "This memorable meeting in Moscow has shown us that there are no matters that cannot be adjusted between us when we meet together in frank and intimate discussion."[40] That was probably a motive for revealing the potentially embarrassing agreement in *The Second World War*. "You see," he explained to Lord Moran, it would show that "the people at the top can do these things, which others can't do."[41]

In the General Election of October 1951, at the age of nearly seventy-seven, Churchill was finally returned to power with a narrow parliamentary majority. Labour had won fewer seats but more votes: no party led by Churchill ever secured a plurality of ballots cast. But he may well have been helped by his summit conference idea, which was overwhelmingly popular among the electorate, approved by 83 to 5 percent in a December 1951 Gallup poll.[42]

At an 11 December Cabinet meeting Churchill announced that he would visit the United States with the objective of strengthening Anglo-American relations. But in Washington in January 1952 he found that Britain carried less weight than ever. He tried to persuade the Americans to appoint a British admiral to head NATO naval forces, and when all else failed he resorted to melodrama:

> For centuries England has held the seas against every tyrant, wresting command from Spain and then from France, protecting our hemisphere from penetration by European systems in the days of our weakness. Now, in the plenitude of our power, bearing as we did the awful burden of atomic command and responsibility for the final word of peace or war, surely we could make room for Britain to play her historical role "upon that western sea whose floor is white with the bones of Englishmen."

The performance impressed Secretary of State Dean Acheson, but plain-spoken Harry Truman preferred to enjoy the plenitude of American power.[43]

Churchill met with Eisenhower in New York City in January 1953, and it was actually the President-Elect who broached the idea of meeting with Stalin – just the two of them. Churchill reacted coolly, offering no objections in principle, but advising Eisenhower to wait. Clearly the Prime Minister did not want to be cut out of what could be a great moment in diplomacy. After Stalin died on 5 March, the new Soviet leadership promptly launched a "peace offensive." Churchill saw his opening: on 10 March he urged the president to call for a three-power summit. Now it was Eisenhower's turn to be cautious: he warned that the Soviets might use the meeting as yet "another propaganda mill." First, he advised, the United States, Britain, and "probably France" should confer on a common strategy for dealing with the USSR.[44]

By 3 May Churchill was seriously discussing the possibility of an Anglo-Soviet summit, though his own Foreign Office warned him that such a move would alienate the French and damage his "special relationship" with the Americans. Eisenhower sent him a sharp rebuke on 5 May, but Churchill argued back that he hoped to repeat the success (if it can be called that) of his October 1944 "Percentages Deal." On 11 May Churchill formally proposed a summit conference on the floor of the House of Commons, without consulting the Cabinet beforehand. He insisted that the meeting "should not be overhung by a ponderous or rigid agenda, or led into mazes and jungles of technical details, zealously contested by hordes of experts and officials drawn up in a vast, cumbrous array." It was a fine sentiment, but without a clear agenda, without experts to supply data, and without officials to work out details, what did he hope to accomplish? Like Wells, Churchill talked airily about nuclear arms control without seriously thinking through inspection and verification, an inevitable stumbling block when dealing with a society as secretive as the USSR.

"It must be long in history since any one speech did so much damage to its own side," sighed Anthony Eden, back as Foreign Secretary.[45] Except for Premier Georgy Malenkov, the Soviet leadership was never very receptive to Churchill's appeals for a summit, and did not believe that Britain, a declining power, could do much to restrain the United States.[46] But the American Embassy had to admit that this was "perhaps Churchill's greatest performance since the war."[47] The Gallup poll found that the British people approved of his initiative by 77 to 4 percent. But when asked whether they expected the summit to accomplish anything, they were less optimistic: 47 percent Yes, 16 percent No, 37 percent Don't Know.[48]

After dinner on 23 June 1953, Churchill suffered a stroke. Over the next few days near total paralysis set in, and Lord Moran advised Buckingham Palace that the newly crowned Queen Elizabeth should stand ready to appoint a new

Prime Minister.[49] Churchill would make a remarkable recovery, but he knew that time was running out. On 20 October John Colville told Moran, "You know, he is always acting a part, but I am sure he was not acting last night after dinner when he suddenly said: 'I think, Jock, we are near the end of the road.' "[50] His comeback may well have been driven by the desire for what Moran called the "dramatic curtain" of a summit conference: "It was the old hankering for a romantic role. War had been his hobby. Nothing had been to him so consistently stimulating. But that was gone and done with. And now, with his life running out, it was in his mind to end as a maker of peace among men; in this, his final role, he would appear before the world as, perhaps, the only hope of breaking the cold war."[51]

By 3 November, Churchill was capable of delivering to the House of Commons what Chips Channon called.

> one of the speeches of his lifetime. Brilliant, full of cunning and charm, of wit and thrusts, he poured out his Macaulay-like phrases to a stilled and awed house. It was an Olympian spectacle. A supreme performance which we shall never see again from him or anyone else. In 18 years in this honourable House I have never heard anything like it. . . . then he sought refuge in the Smoking Room and, flushed with pride, pleasure, and triumph sat there for two hours sipping brandy and acknowledging compliments. He beamed like a schoolboy.[52]

The speech addressed the terrifying prospect of the hydrogen bomb, but Churchill offered his audience the reassurance that the specter of mutual annihilation made war less likely: "It may be that . . . when the advance of destructive weapons enables everyone to kill everybody else nobody will want to kill anyone at all." He concluded by offering two possible futures: humanity could choose either "mass destruction" or, "as an alternative, what many of them might prefer, namely, the swiftest expansion of material well-being that has ever been within their reach, or even within their dreams. . . . We, and all nations, stand, at this hour of human history, before the portals of supreme catastrophe and of measureless reward. My faith is that in God's mercy we shall choose aright."[53] One Labour MP was moved to tears, and urged Lord Moran to keep the Prime Minister alive.[54] By 2 December the doctor had concluded, "Where people are concerned Winston Churchill exists in an imaginary world of his own making. Sometimes his ideas, too, have no roots in reality; the supposed change of heart in Russia may be one of them."[55] But here Churchill was more in step with British public opinion: according to a September 1954 Gallup poll, 59 percent believed that peaceful coexistence with the Soviet Union was possible, and just 22 percent expected a major war.[56]

Churchill paid his final visit to Washington as Prime Minister between 25 and 29 June 1954. As Lord Moran noted: "He has always felt that the future of the world is bound up with the union of the English-speaking races. Now, at the end of the long day, nothing else seems to matter. He is going to America – he thinks it may be his last visit to his mother's native land – to see if anything can be done to narrow the rift about Moscow that is opening up between the two countries. . . ."[57] Eisenhower noticed that "The Prime Minister has moments when he does not seem to be entirely aware of everything that is going on. It is merely old age, but it is becoming increasingly more noticeable." The President often had to shout when speaking with the increasingly deaf Churchill. The Prime Minister once again raised the prospect of a summit, and then misinterpreted Eisenhower's conciliatory manner as indicating approval.[58] Literally wide-eyed, he told Moran, "This may lead to results which will be received by the world with a gasp of relief and amazement," the inevitable conclusion of any melodrama. And then he added, revealingly, "It's my show entirely."[59]

On 4 July Churchill sent the Soviets an invitation to a summit, after consulting with Eden (who had grave misgivings) but not with the rest of the Cabinet. Oddly, the invitation was sent to Foreign Minister Vyacheslav Molotov rather than Churchill's counterpart, Premier Malenkov. Molotov's reply seemed encouraging, but the British Cabinet and the American President were exasperated.[60] There was a fraught exchange of messages between a testy Eisenhower and an apologetic Churchill. On 12 July Eisenhower (who could be cruel) wrote that most Americans would consider the summit initiative "as Hoover is supposed to have said of Prohibition, 'a noble experiment.' "[61] Then he tried one last stratagem to divert Churchill. The previous November Winthrop Aldrich, the US ambassador to Britain, had advised the State Department that Churchill was "imaginative, unpredictable, firm in [his] belief in his own genius, and apparently determined to attempt one last crowning act on [the] world stage."[62] On 22 July Eisenhower appealed directly to that flair for drama:

> I am certain that you must have a very deep and understandable desire to do something special and additional in your remaining period of active service that will be forever recognized as a milestone in the world's tortuous progress towards a just and lasting peace. Nothing else could provide such a fitting climax to your long and brilliant service to your sovereign, your country and the world.
>
> I am sure that some such thought of your conscious or subconscious mind must be responsible for your desire to meet Malenkov and to explore, so far as is possible, the purposes of his heart and the designs of his brain.

Churchill, who had always been dismissive of modern psychology, did not care to have his subconscious psychoanalyzed, certainly not by Dwight Eisenhower. The suggestion that his summit proposal was motivated by an underlying desire to score a final theatrical coup was galling, all the more because it was true. Eisenhower insisted that there was no point in talking with Soviet leaders, but as an alternative he proposed an equally dramatic initiative: a joint Anglo-American effort to promote independence for the colonized peoples of the world. The President readily agreed that many of them were "not yet ready for self-rule and that any attempt to make them now responsible for their own governing would be to condemn them to lowered standards of life and probably to communistic domination." But he recognized that "Colonialism is on the way out as a relationship among peoples. The sole question is one of time and methods. I think we should handle it so as to win adherents to Western aims." He urged Churchill to deliver a major address – "no other could so well do it as you" – announcing a vast program supported by the "great nations in the Western World to bring educational opportunities to all peoples we are able to reach," training them in the arts of self-government. If he could throw into the speech "A good bit of cold war campaigning," so much the better. The issue of imperialism, which had so long divided Britain and America, would now unite them in a common purpose, and they would frustrate communist schemes to infiltrate the Third World. Moreover, "If you could say that twenty-five years from now, every last one of the colonies (excepting military bases) should have been offered a right to self-government and determination, you would electrify the world. More than this, you could be certain that not a single one of them would, when the time came, take advantage of the offer of independence. Each would cling more tightly to the mother country and be a more valuable part thereof."[63]

The Prime Minister reacted with the resentment of an old man who knows that he is being patronized. "I am not looking about for the means of making a dramatic exit or of finding a suitable Curtain," he shot back. As for educating colonized peoples, Churchill testily replied that the British had been "bringing forward backward races" for quite some time. "I was brought up to feel proud of much that we had done. Certainly in India, with all its history, religion and ancient forms of despotic rule, Britain has a story to tell which will look quite well against the background of the coming hundred years." Besides, he confessed, "I am a bit skeptical about universal suffrage for the Hottentots."[64] As it was, both leaders underestimated the global demand for self-government: in ten years, not twenty-five, the British Empire would be all but liquidated.

Churchill resigned the premiership on 5 April 1955. His final words to his junior ministers were "Man is spirit" and "Never be separated from the

Americans."[65] That July the summit he had worked for was at last convened: his successor Eden, Eisenhower, Soviet Premier Nicolai Bulganin, and Premier Edgar Faure of France met in Geneva. It did not accomplish much, and Churchill greeted it with indifference ("I am quite cool about it all") tinged with some jealousy and resentment. Eden and Eisenhower, who had always resisted the idea of a summit, had now stolen his limelight.[66] One of the last novels Churchill read (twice) was *On the Beach*, Nevil Shute's poignant but nightmarish vision of the world after a nuclear holocaust. He proposed to have it translated into several languages and sent to all the world's leaders, except perhaps Eisenhower: "It would be a waste of money," he snorted.[67]

CHAPTER 23

The Last Whig

One of the first things Churchill did after losing the 1945 General Election was to attend Noël Coward's *Private Lives*, where the audience treated him to two lengthy standing ovations.[1] A few weeks later Lord Moran noted that, "as he confessed tonight, he had found the solution of his troubles in his paint-box, just as he had thirty years ago when he was thrown out over the Dardanelles."[2] In October 1945 he returned to another artistic outlet, resuming work on *A History of the English-Speaking Peoples*.[3] And by 1947 he had a contract for the American rights to *The Second World War* – the book, newspaper and magazine serialization – for $2.25 million, the most ever paid at that time for a work of non-fiction in the United States.[4] Once more, Churchill would find in artistic creativity a form of therapy for a deep psychological wound, a means of communicating his political vision, a vehicle for permanently validating his role in history, and an exceptionally lucrative stream of royalties in an era of confiscatory income taxes. Out of power, he was free to complete two of his largest and most widely read literary projects, and freer (up to a point) to treat politics as a literary art.

In a 4 January 1947 article in *Collier's*, Churchill called for a United States of Europe, and cited as a source of inspiration Victor Hugo who, during the Franco-Prussian War, had extended his hand to his enemy:

> . . . we shall be but one united people, but one single family, but one Republic. I will demolish my fortresses. You will demolish yours. My vengeance, it is fraternity. No more frontiers, the Rhine for all! Let us be the same Republic! Let us have the United States of Europe, let us have Continental federation, let us have European freedom![5]

The idea might have also owed something to Gibbon. In a speech planned in March 1943 but never delivered, Churchill lamented the break-up of the

Roman Empire, which led to "an unending succession of bloody and devastating wars, of which we are at present passing through the latest," and he looked forward to "some sort of central residing power" that would once again make the Continent whole and united.[6] But Churchill's vision of European unity stopped at Dover: he never meant to include Great Britain. When he returned to power in 1951, his government did not embrace the 1950 Schuman Plan, the nucleus of what would become the European Union.[7]

On 31 January 1947 Churchill spoke to the House of Commons about dealing with Irgun terrorism in Palestine. He deplored these "detestable outrages" but emphasized that they were limited to a "small, fanatical desperate minority" and warned against resorting to reprisals. He then turned to the case of Dov Gruner, who had served in the British Army during the war but then joined the Irgun and participated in an attack on a Ramat Gan police station, in which an Arab policeman was killed. Sentenced to death, Gruner refused to ask for a pardon, since that would have involved an admission of guilt. "The fortitude of this man, criminal though he be, must not escape the notice of the House," Churchill proclaimed.[8]

With violence escalating out of control in Palestine, no politician was likely to win votes by saluting a Jewish terrorist on the floor of the House of Commons. The Conservative MP Robert Boothby recalled that he and Labour's Richard Crossman were then practically the only vocal Zionists left in Parliament, and they found themselves "being cut left, right, and centre."[9] For all Churchill's sympathy with Zionism, he had been deeply embittered when the Stern Gang assassinated his friend Lord Moyne two years earlier. Yet there was a precedent and a rationale for his astonishing statement. In 1909 a Hindu nationalist studying in England, Madan Lal Dhingra, had shot and killed Curzon Wyllie, aide to the Secretary of State for India, as well as a Parsi doctor who tried to protect the Englishman. "I am proud to lay down my life for my country," Dhingra told the court after he was tried and sentenced to death. "But remember we shall have our time in the days to come." According to Wilfred Scawen Blunt, Churchill predicted that Dhingra "will be remembered 2000 years hence, as we remember Regulus and Spartacus and Plutarch's heroes," and quoted from memory his speech, "the finest ever made in the name of patriotism." (That said, he insisted that Dhingra hang.)[10]

We can only reconcile these paeans with Churchill's arch-imperialism by looking, again, to the Victorian theatre. Melodramatic heroes invariably chose death over dishonor. Even when they were wrongly condemned to the scaffold, they scorned opportunities to save themselves. "The idea of martyrdom," observes Richard Allen Cave, "the transformation of physical defeat into moral victory (which is how melodrama heroes face the crises that beset them), was also a traditional aspect of [Irish] nationalist rhetoric, much fuelled by Catholic piety, that was to reach its apogee in [Patrick] Pearse's thinking at the time of the Easter Rising in 1916."[11] In *The English Rose*, Harry O'Mailley is falsely convicted for killing an Englishman. His brother, a Catholic priest, has discovered the real murderer in confession, but Harry sternly commands him (in the Act III curtain line), "You cannot break your sacred vows! I would not have you utter one word, even to save me from a felon's death. My brother! My brother! Pray for me! (Bows his head) *But keep your oath to God.*"[12]

Harry O'Mailley, Dick Dudgeon (in Shaw's *The Devil's Disciple*), Dov Gruner, and Madan Lal Dhingra all represented colonized peoples in struggle with the British Empire, and all four were willing to play the same role. Late in life Churchill seriously suggested that the Germans should have dealt with nurse Edith Cavell not by executing her, but by upstaging her: "What a chance of immortality the German officer commanding the firing-squad missed! He could have stood in front of her and commanded the soldiers to shoot him first."[13]

On 26 January 1949 Churchill criticized Ernest Bevin for his continuing hostility to the Jewish state, which Britain had yet to recognize eight months after it had proclaimed its independence. Bevin argued that, as in the case of the recently proclaimed Republic of Indonesia, a new nation should firmly establish its legitimacy before it deserved recognition, but Churchill again swept aside short-term political considerations in favor of embracing a very long view of history:

> Whether the right hon. Gentleman likes it or not, and whether we like it or not, the coming into being of a Jewish State is an event to be viewed in the perspective, not of a generation or a century, but in the perspective of a thousand, two thousand or even three thousand years. That is a standard of temporal values or time values which seems very much out of accord with the perpetual click-clack of our rapidly-changing moods and of the age in which we live. This is an event in world history.

To those who compared the Zionist project to slicing off Scotland from the rest of Britain and introducing a foreign race there, Churchill noted (correctly) that Jews and Arabs "have lived in Palestine for thousands of years side by side."[14] And he argued that the condition of the Arab war refugees could only be ameliorated by a peace settlement followed by mutual economic development, of the kind he had seen in Rishon le-Zion in 1921.[15]

The first volume of *The Second World War* was published in the United States by Houghton Mifflin on 21 June 1948, and by Cassell in London on 4 October. Noël Coward immediately recognized it as the work of a great playwright. He wrote to compliment Churchill on "your impeccable sense of theatre which kept bubbling up at unexpected moments. Your 'curtain' line after your description of Ribbentrop – at lunch in 1938 – 'that was the last time I saw him before he was hanged' was quite wonderful."[16] "Mr. Churchill's true genius is not epic but dramatic," commented *The Times* on the fourth volume, *The Hinge of Fate*. "The essence of tragedy lies in reversal of fortune. So does that of comedy, and Mr. Churchill, with the youthful zest which has carried him unfatigued through half a century of public life, here misses no opportunity of picking out the little comic things in the midst of the sorrows and terrors of war."[17]

The Second World War is indeed a work of theatre, starting with the title of the first volume: *The Gathering Storm* is straight out of blood-and-thunder melodrama. The fact that Churchill did not invent the title is irrelevant. He planned to call it "Downward Path," but Emery Reves telegraphed to say that Houghton Mifflin thought that "sounds somewhat discouraging." Reves proposed a "more challenging title indicating crescendo events," and Churchill adopted his suggestion.[18] A good literary agent often understands better than the author himself how to find his authentic voice, eliminate distractions, and achieve the effects he desires. Having read a late draft of the volume, Reves recognized that Churchill was striving for drama and had largely succeeded: "I do not think there is anything like it in the literature of history writing," he wrote on 22 December 1947. But, he added, there were still patches where the action ground to a halt, where Churchill was telling rather than showing:

> There are too many documents, letters and quotes from speeches in the text. Not as if every one of them would not be of importance and interest. But the narrative is so dramatic, so exciting, that one resents the many interruptions, and the average reader will certainly skip most of the documents for the simple reason that he will be anxious to continue reading the narrative. I very much hope that it will be possible for you to absorb the greatest part of the documents into the narrative, and either to eliminate the original documents or relegate them to the Appendix.[19]

Churchill wired that he was open to "suggestions for cutting documents and speeches," but he was clearly wounded. What the agent meant as a helpful criticism, the author read as an invalidation of his distinctive historical method, "to tell the tale from current authentic documents where possible."[20] Churchill had composed his letters and memoranda as works of literature, with a view toward eventual publication, and now he was told that they should be cut or shunted to the back of the book. Reves immediately wrote back "I was very happy indeed . . . to see that you agree with my suggestions" (he had not agreed) and went on to report that the first volume had been assessed by a kind of focus group consisting of "the highest literary authorities in the United States." These were the five judges of the Book of the Month Club – Henry Seidel Canby, Dorothy Canfield Fisher, Christopher Morley, John P. Marquand, and Clifton Fadiman. They were leading arbiters of middlebrow taste, and each one came to Reves's office to read the draft while he gauged their reactions. "They were completely absorbed," he told Churchill, "but they all skipped the documents and speeches, and said exactly what I indicated to you in my last letter."[21]

"I hate to see you pale & no longer happily preoccupied," Sarah Churchill wrote to her father. She was herself a professional actress, who would experience some success (and much heartbreak) on the stage, the screen, and television. And she said what one theatre person always says to another in the face of bad reviews or directorial criticism:

> Don't listen to too many critics. . . . The work is yours from deep within you – and its success depends on it flowing from you in an uninterrupted stream. . . . It is your story, as you moved through, what will one day be history.
>
> You are the best historian – the best journalist – the best poet – shut yourself up and only listen to a very few, and even then, write this book from the heart of yourself – from the knowledge you have – and let it stand or fall by that – it will stand – everyone will listen to your story.[22]

Her advice was probably reassuring and certainly wrong. Many of the greatest authors have profited from the attentions of scrupulous editors – D. H. Lawrence and Edward Garnett, Thomas Wolfe and Maxwell Perkins, Jack Kerouac and Malcolm Cowley. Churchill was no exception, and telling him to listen only to his own inner voice was not helpful. Reves told him what he needed to hear, especially regarding the third volume, which (more than the others) got bogged down in technical details and unimportant telegrams. Reves insisted on more grand strategy, more high politics, more episodes that were "characteristic and dramatic, like the sinking of the Bismarck." *The Second World War* was published as a serial, as Victorian novels were, and like Charles Dickens and Wilkie Collins, Churchill had to end each installment with a cliffhanging climax or risk losing his audience:

> Volume I was excellent. Volume II was better. Volume IV is superb. There is no reason why Volume III should not be a step in this crescendo. It would be dangerous for the future volumes to leave it weaker than the first two. Please forgive my mentioning the "bloody public", but I am the Sales

> Department in this enterprise and it is my duty to draw the attention of the Production Chief to the problems of marketing. It has always been difficult to keep up public interest in a work of many volumes issued at intervals. The only way to overcome this psychological difficulty is to make each volume more interesting than the previous one. If Volume III is not more exciting than the first two volumes were, it will be extremely difficult, if not impossible, to revive interest again for the subsequent volumes.[23]

Frequently Churchill accepted his agent's advice, but what is remarkable is how often he resisted it, even when it was clear that Reves knew how to design a play. "The arrival of Montgomery and your first meeting with him should be described in more detail," was a typical constructive suggestion. "Just as when you first met Eisenhower in Washington, a leading actor of acts to come appears for the first time on the scene. He needs proper introduction, a short portrait, an appreciation." But Churchill did nothing to flesh out his introduction of either general: *The Second World War* would have only one leading actor. Reves also proposed a detailed account of the devastating Cologne air raid in 1942, which was only mentioned briefly in the final version. And though he argued that the Battle of Stalingrad in 1942–43 might deserve at least half a dozen pages, Churchill allowed only a page plus some passing references to this "tremendous drama."[24]

The Second World War was mainly about Winston, but that was not entirely the author's fault. While Churchill was generally free to include his own documents, Clement Attlee (as Prime Minister) would subsequently block the use of most other government papers. The occasion for Attlee's intervention is revealing: Churchill wanted to publish parts of a paper by the Chiefs of Staff criticizing his plans for Norway in 1940. There is much self-justification in *The Second World War*, but in this case (and others) Churchill wished to include material that would not reflect well on him. Attlee worried that publishing such documents promiscuously might prove "most embarrassing," especially if they dealt with such fiascos as the capture of Singapore in 1942. Norman Brook, the Cabinet Secretary, protested that "Mr. Churchill quotes so many of his own documents that there is some danger of his creating the impression that no one but he ever took an initiative."[25]

In the United States, *The Gathering Storm* ranked seventh on the *Publishers Weekly* non-fiction bestseller list for 1948, not far behind the Kinsey Report.[26] By November 1949 the Book of the Month Club had sold 366,000 copies of *The Gathering Storm* (their July 1948 selection) and 247,500 copies of the more recently published *Their Finest Hour*, and both volumes were still shipping several hundred copies a month. These figures did not include the trade edition published by Houghton Mifflin: by July 1951 total sales of the first four volumes of *The Second World War* stood at 319,801, with another 1,118,750 sold by the Book of the Month Club. In Britain Cassell printed 221,000 copies of *The Gathering Storm* in October 1948 and had another 210,000 in print by February 1950, not counting the Book Society edition. At the end of 1953 a Gallup poll asked British readers to name the best book they had read that year, and *The Second World War* ranked fourth (just ahead of *Wuthering Heights*). In Churchill's lifetime, it would be published in Croatian, Danish, Dutch, French, German, Hebrew, Italian, Japanese, Norwegian, Portuguese, Serbian, Spanish, and Swedish, as well as incomplete editions in Russian and Turkish.[27]

As an author, Churchill had somehow struck a special chord in Sweden: the only country to publish translations of *The River War, Marlborough*, and *Thoughts and Adventures* before the outbreak of the war; the first country to translate *Great Contemporaries* and *While England Slept*, and the only country ever to translate *Lord Randolph Churchill* (in 1941). The Stockholm firm Skoglund may have been the first publisher to explore the prospects of translating *A History of the English-Speaking Peoples*, as early as February 1941, and it brought out a Swedish version in 1956–59. There had been several Swedish editions of *My Early Life*, perhaps encouraged by a 1936 abridgment in the original language, published by Albert Bonniers Förlag for teaching English to schoolchildren. All that may have been a factor in the decision to award Churchill the Nobel Prize in Literature in 1953. It is often assumed that he won it for *The Second World War*, but in his presentation speech the eminent Swedish author Sigfrid Siwertz never mentioned that work. Though Skoglund had begun to publish it in 1948, the subject matter was somewhat embarrassing for neutral Sweden.[28] Instead Siwertz extolled *My Early Life* as "one of the world's most entertaining adventure stories," a fast-moving tale that "even a very youthful mind can follow with the keenest pleasure."[29]

Whatever his literary achievements, there is no denying that Churchill had by this time become a political anachronism. "He put on a great show" was Roy Jenkins's summation of his second government:

> Indeed there is a constant feeling that he was asking all his interlocutors, the new Queen, President Eisenhower, his ageing crown prince Anthony Eden, the members of the House of Commons, and various insecure Prime Ministers of the Fourth French Republic to live up to a role which they thought was a little over the top for the beginning of the second half of the twentieth century. . . . There was even an element of play-acting about it. The most vivid moments of the second premiership were in the bustle of his returning to office: putting together the government, summoning officials, re-creating his staff, sending or acknowledging greetings all over the world.

> It was at least as much a pageant to commemorate the great days of the first government as it was a realistic preparation for a new period of office.[30]

Churchill adored the young Queen because, like the first Elizabeth, she played her role so well: "Lovely, inspiring. All the film people in the world, if they had scoured the globe, could not have found anyone so suited to the part."[31] But now he was an over-the-hill actor playing his younger self, and the setting was all wrong. He continued to orate as he had in 1940, recalled John Colville, but "The difference lay in the situation: there could be no call to fight on the beaches, no tribute to the Few. Poetry which danger evokes in speakers and writers of the English language is out of place and even absurd in a peacetime ministerial statement. What was magic in 1940 would have been melodrama in 1955."[32] As many post-war British politicians learned painfully, we can only conjure up "the spirit of Dunkirk" when we face an actual Dunkirk. (That was driven home to me on 11 September 2001, when I saw pleasure boats evacuating office workers from lower Manhattan.)

In 1952 Churchill frankly admitted, "When you learn to think of a race as inferior beings it is difficult to get rid of that way of thinking; when I was a subaltern the Indian did not seem to me equal to the white man."[33] But something of his old benevolent imperialism remained. On 10 December 1954 he discussed the Mau Mau revolt with a white settler representative, who found him surprisingly sympathetic to the rebels. He granted that he "did not really think that black people were as capable or as efficient as white people," but he also condemned the detention camps and brutal methods used to crush the rebellion. "It's the power of a modern nation being used to kill savages. It's pretty terrible," he said, again echoing Macaulay's words about "the strength of civilisation without its mercy." He urged a policy of negotiation and magnanimity, the same approach that in 1922 had solved (up to a point) the Irish problem. In practice he left Kenya policy to others in the government and did little to rein them in, but by then he was very elderly and very tired.[34]

When another old controversy cropped up, Churchill's libertarian instincts at least flickered. In January 1954 the highly publicized arrests of journalist Peter Wildeblood and Baron Montagu of Beaulieu for homosexual offenses sparked a public debate, and on 24 February the Cabinet discussed the issue. What clearly emerges from the Cabinet Secretary's notes is that Churchill favored liberalization in principle but felt constrained to act according to political pressures. "Tory Party won't want to accept responsibility for makg. law on homosexuality more lenient," the notes read, but he went on to propose limiting media publicity of prosecutions and offering medical treatment as an alternative to prison. "Otherwise, I wdn't touch the subject," though he held out the "hope of a more united public pressure for some amendment." As he reminded the Cabinet, "Remember that we can't expect to put the whole world right with a majority of 18," implying that decriminalization would indeed be the right thing.[35] In 1957 the Wolfenden Report would recommend the legalization of private homosexual acts. The Gallup poll found the public opposed to that by 48 to 25 percent, but in 1967 the law used to convict Oscar Wilde would be repealed.[36] So Churchill was correct about the current state of public opinion – and correct in predicting that attitudes would eventually shift. His later comments on Guy Burgess and the Cambridge spies could be construed as remarkably sympathetic: if homosexuals were security risks, he reasoned, it was because they felt marginalized by society, much like black people in a white-majority nation. And there was distinctly Wildean humor in his comment on the left-wing Labour MP Tom Driberg: "That's the fellow who brought sodomy into disrepute."[37]

Starting in 1953 Churchill began to immerse himself in nineteenth-century literature to the neglect of government business: Anthony Trollope's parliamentary novels, *Jane Eyre, Wuthering Heights*, Thomas Hardy's *The Dynasts*, Walter Scott's *Quentin Durward*, Disraeli's *Coningsby*, and Balzac's *Père Goriot*. He confessed that he read *The Reason Why*, Cecil Woodham-Smith's history of the Crimean War, for eight hours at a stretch: "I get bitten by books nowadays." And when Lord Woolton asked whether he could afford the time, "I explained that I didn't bother much about other things as much as I used to do."[38]

But not all of the fiction he read was escapist and historical: much of it was intensely political, relevant to the contemporary world, and profoundly troubling. In a parliamentary speech on 12 November 1946, Churchill had urged that the defeated German people should be treated with magnanimity and understanding. "Everyone is not a pastor Niemöller or a martyr, and when ordinary people are hurled this way and that, when the cruel hands of tyrants are laid upon them and vile systems of regimentation are imposed and enforced by espionage and other forms of cruelty, there are great numbers of people who will succumb." And then he suggested a disturbing counterfactual: "I thank God that in this island home of ours, we have never been put to the test which many of the peoples of Europe have had to undergo." How would the British people have conducted themselves if they actually had been persecuted by some kind of Gestapo?[39] George Orwell was already working on that thought experiment, and Churchill would read *Nineteen Eighty-Four* twice.[40] Throughout the 1950s he was enthralled by novels of totalitarianism: *Spark of Life* (Erich Maria Remarque's account of a German concentration camp), *Brave New World, One Day in the Life of Ivan Denisovitch, Doctor Zhivago*.[41] With Orwell and many other intellectuals of that decade, he wondered whether a new technology would abolish the individual even in the Western democracies: in one of his last "Question Time" sessions he denounced "the TV age, in which I fear mass thought and actions will be taken too much charge of by machinery, both destructive and distracting."[42]

After his 1953 stroke, Churchill again resumed work on *A History of the English-Speaking Peoples*, assisted by Alan Hodge, editor of *History Today*. Hodge's marching orders were simple: emphasize "famous dramatic events" and construct "a lively, continuous narrative."[43] Maurice Ashley estimated that it went through a dozen drafts.[44] Here, in contrast to *The Second World War*, Churchill was able to construct a gripping story uninterrupted by documents. "I am convinced that this is going to be considered your greatest literary work," Emery Reves wrote after reading the first volume. "One cannot stop reading it, the narrative is more dramatic than any fiction and the language sometimes evokes great paintings, sometimes lovely music. . . . Reading the description of events one would swear that you had been a war correspondent at the time of Julius Caesar."[45] In a sense, every important book that Churchill wrote was war reportage.

The first chapter relied heavily on Caesar's *Conquest of Gaul*. It is possible that this, like the *War Memoirs of U. S. Grant* and *Seven Pillars of Wisdom*, offered Churchill a model for an "author and commander," but given his boyhood hatred of the classics, it seems likely that he only read it late in life. The translation he cited here, by S. A. Handford, was published in 1951. In any case, Churchill noted in conclusion that Caesar won nothing lasting in Britain, except self-publicity.[46]

Again Churchill lavishly laid on theatrical tropes. Claudius planned a "dramatic" conquest of Britain, but he was upstaged when one of his generals won an early victory, which "marred the stage-management of the campaign." Later legions would sometimes leave the backwater province undefended as they attempted to seize power in Rome: "They left the local scene for the supreme theatre, like players who wish to quit the provinces for the capital." And when they departed for good, "the curtain fell between Britannia and the Continent."[47] He conjured "the sense of drama" surrounding the trial and execution of Charles I, when he played "the truly magnificent and indisputable role of the champion of English – nay, British, for all the Island was involved – rights and liberties."[48] The elder Pitt, after whom he clearly modeled himself, was "a born actor" who appealed "to the imagination of the country" from the floor of Parliament, "a stage on which his gifts could be displayed and his foibles indulged." Or, to put it more cinematically, "his policy was a projection on to a vast screen of his own aggressive, dominating personality."[49] And the American Civil War was precipitated largely by a woman who knew how to deploy all the devices of melodrama, which Churchill catalogued in detail:

> Harriet Beecher Stowe . . . presented to her readers a succession of simple, poignant incidents inseparable from a system of slavery: the breaking up of the Negro's home and family, the parting of husband and wife, the sale of the baby from the breast of its mother; the indiscriminate auction of the slaves on the death of a good employer; the impotence of the virtuous slave-owner, the cruelties of the bad, the callous traffic of the slave-dealers, and the horrors of the remote plantations, the whipping establishments to which fine ladies sent their maids for chastisement for minor faults; the aggravated problem of the quadroon and the mulatto; the almost-white slave girl sold and resold for lust; the bringing into the world of slave children indistinguishable in their colour from the dominant race – all these features of the life of a civilised, educated, modern Christian community, occupying enormous fertile regions of the earth, were introduced with every trapping of art and appeal into her pages.[50]

And yet Churchill did not use theatre history to illuminate English cultural history: there are only a few passing allusions to Shakespeare and the Elizabethan stage. His historical methodology was still stuck in the nineteenth century. He grudgingly conceded that modern researchers had forced some modest revisions in the Victorians' narrative – "Their dramas have been modified or upset. . . . Nevertheless the broad story holds, for it is founded in a dominating simplicity."[51] Robert Rhodes James called it "the last of the Whig histories",[52] and that is true insofar as Churchill's narrative is about the love of liberty, which (he suggests) is in the genes of the English, going back to the crossbreeding of the Danes and Anglo-Saxons: "All through English history this strain continues to play a gleaming part."[53]

But in an important sense Churchill overturned Whig historiography. Rather than portray history as an inexorable march toward ever greater liberty, he contrasted the relative freedom of medieval England with the nightmare of modernity. Thomas Becket and Thomas More were heroic opponents of the totalitarian state, who put to shame the appeasers of 1938.[54] Magna Carta might read like a laundry list of feudal grievances or (in the words of an unidentified writer) "a monument of class selfishness," but it did in fact become a bulwark against state attempts "to ride roughshod over the rights or liberties of the subject."[55] Simon de Montfort failed to consolidate his grip on power because he did not dare "proceed in the brutal manner of modern times in several European countries by the wholesale slaughter of all who were in his power."[56] Churchill furiously denounced the persecutions of the Albigensians, the Jews, and the Lollards, but he noted that even if Edward I invoked the anti-Semitic "propaganda of ritual murder and other dark tales," these are also "the commonplaces of our enlightened age."[57] He clearly sympathized with the villeins who, having survived the Black Death, took advantage of the resulting labor shortage to flee their masters, comparing them to runaway slaves in antebellum America. And though the Peasants' Revolt of 1381 was suppressed with a total of 150 executions, this "was nothing like the savagery we have seen in many parts of Europe in our own times."[58] Brushing aside revisionist historians, Churchill insisted that Richard III had in fact murdered the princes in the tower, but more significant than the crime itself was the public reaction to it: "Although accustomed to the brutalities of the long civil wars, the English people of those days still retained the faculty of horror; and once it was excited they did not soon forget." That healthy medieval outrage compared favorably with the Orwellian present: "A modern dictator with the resources of science at his disposal can easily lead the public on from day to day, destroying all persistency of thought and aim, so that memory is blurred by the multiplicity of daily news and judgment baffled by its perversion. But in the fifteenth century the murder of the two young princes by the very man who had undertaken to protect them was regarded as an atrocious crime, never to be forgotten or forgiven."[59]

Maurice Ashley wrote the first draft of the chapter on Oliver Cromwell, "for which I was handsomely paid." Yet when he read the published version, "I was astonished to find some of my facts and phrases embedded in it, but the whole draft had been stood completely on its head. For Churchill was convinced that Cromwell was a dictator of the stamp of Adolf Hitler. . . ."[60] Victorian Whigs (as Churchill noted) tended to treat Cromwell indulgently: though the Lord Protector had been ruthless, in the long run the Puritan Commonwealth was a good thing, given that it led ultimately to the freedoms of the nineteenth century. But they could believe that only so long as they believed in progress. Viewed in the context of modern dictatorships, Cromwell's atrocities in Ireland began to look like the first in a long escalating series of holocausts:

> Men thought such scenes were gone for ever, and that while moving into a broad age of peace, money-making, and debatings they could afford to pay their tributes to the rugged warriors who had laid the foundations of a liberal society. The twentieth century has sharply recalled its intellectuals from such vain indulgences. We have seen the technique of "frightfulness" applied in our own time with Cromwellian brutality and upon a far larger scale. We know too much of despots and their moods and power to practise the philosophic detachment of our grandfathers. It is necessary to recur to the simpler principle that the wholesale slaughter of unarmed or disarmed men marks with a mordant and eternal brand the memory of conquerors, however they may have prospered.

Before the Easter Rebellion of 1916, like many Englishmen of his generation, Churchill dismissed as bores Irishmen who were still going on about Cromwell. Now, after Hitler, he understood their anger. That very English terror had poisoned relations between the two islands and created "a potent obstacle to the harmony of the English-speaking peoples throughout the world. Upon all of us there still lies 'the curse of Cromwell.' "[61]

Churchill despised the Puritan Commonwealth, with its ubiquitous fines and restrictions, its repression of innocent amusements, its sumptuary laws, its replacement of feast days with fast days, its armies of snoopers and informers, its soldiers everywhere, its "numberless and miserable petty tyrannies." Very likely it reminded him of Britain during the Second World War. Yet Churchill realized that Cromwell fell well short of the modern Hitler/Stalin model. He did not establish a one-party state or a cult of personality. With some exceptions and limitations, there was religious freedom, respect for private property, and habeas corpus. It was precisely because Cromwell ruled with some restraint that traditional English liberties swiftly returned after the Restoration.[62]

In the United States, *A History of the English-Speaking Peoples* matched *The Second World War* in terms of sales and critical acclaim. It became a staple of the Book of the Month Club: that edition alone ran through twenty-two printings between 1956 and 1962, in addition to eight printings of the Dodd, Mead trade edition.[63] But as a monument of middlebrow history it belonged to a genre that readers, who were now more likely to be college-educated, increasingly perceived as simplistic, obsolete, and (said the *New Republic*) "too conventional."[64] "There are only the sketchiest references to science, religion, economics, ideology, literature, and art," protested Charles Rolo in the *Atlantic*. "There is a certain childishness in the way Churchill dismisses a Darwin or a Marx in a few sentences while lavishing space on battle after battle. . . . Actually, it is the brand of history I was taught as a schoolboy."[65] Reviewing the Tudor-Stuart volume in the *Nation*, George Dangerfield found it "odd to read about an England in which, so far as the author is concerned, there appears to have been no drama, no poetry, no music, no philosophy and no science. (Or, for that matter – since this book is innocent of social history – no English-speaking peoples.)"[66] Even *Time* noticed that Churchill was still relying on melodramatic devices, building his story around memorable villains (for example, Richard III) and "the strong and resolute hero who brings order out of a moment of historic chaos and crisis" (for instance, Alfred the Great and Richard I).[67] It was also decidedly Anglocentric, with one striking exception: nearly 10 percent of the four-volume two-millennium narrative was devoted to Churchill's favorite historical subject, the American Civil War, including its causes and reconstruction. That section was long enough to publish as a stand-alone book in 1961, in time for the centenary.

A History of the English-Speaking Peoples concluded with a vague and brief paragraph, expressing the hope that, in the face of yet another threat to liberty, the English-speaking peoples would once again unite, even if the author could not "define precisely the exact terms of ultimate union."[68] In fact, drawn together by Churchill's literary legacy, the United States and the United Kingdom would soon collaborate in a crisis as grave as anything they had confronted in 1940.

CHAPTER 24

The Terrible Ifs

In the 1930s, when Churchill was a failed writer in the United States, he had at least two young and passionate fans in the precincts of Cambridge, Massachusetts. One was the son of a notorious Irish-American Anglophobe. To impress his children with the futility of war in general and the senselessness of fighting for the British Empire in particular, Joseph P. Kennedy sternly, graphically, and repeatedly told them the story of the Battle of the Somme, where a generation had been herded to slaughter "for nothing." But his son John (Jack) loved the heroic in English literature: the King Arthur stories, Walter Scott's *Ivanhoe*, Macaulay's *Lays of Ancient Rome*, Robert Louis Stevenson. And, confined to a hospital in October 1932, he read *The World Crisis* closely. Churchill argued that the war was the avoidable result of diplomatic miscalculations, but he also insisted that military strength and explicit warnings to potential aggressors were essential to keeping the peace. And while he granted that the Somme was a costly disaster, he sang the gallantry of the men who died there. One of them was Raymond Asquith, the first son of the Prime Minister, celebrated in *Great Contemporaries*: "The War which found the measure of so many never got to the bottom of him, and when the Grenadiers strode into the crash and thunder of the Somme, he went to his fate cool, poised, resolute, matter-of-fact, debonair."[1] John F. Kennedy memorized and frequently recited that passage, whatever his father might think.

Jack would follow Churchill's career religiously in the *New York Times*, and a few weeks later he read Churchill's first parliamentary speech denouncing German rearmament. On 10 November Stanley Baldwin expressed a willingness to release Germany from the disarmament clauses of the Versailles Treaty, and warned the British public that "The bomber will always get through." Churchill replied on 23 November, warning that rearmament would only lead to German aggression (Hitler was not yet Chancellor, but power was almost within his grasp).

Churchill's influence on John F. Kennedy was profound (as Barbara Leaming has shown),[2] but it was also ambiguous, not simply a matter of avoiding "another Munich." Kennedy deliberately and successfully used the Churchillian legacy to propel himself to the White House, but he did not always read Churchill as the American public read him, and those different reader responses would have momentous political consequences.

In February 1933, just after Hitler's rise to power, the Oxford Union approved its notorious resolution "That this House will in no circumstances fight for its King and Country." Churchill warned at the time that this would only encourage Britain's enemies, and repeated the claim in *The Gathering Storm*.[3] In fact the Nazi leadership, which at the time was preoccupied with consolidating control over Germany, scarcely noticed the brouhaha: there is no record of Hitler ever mentioning it, nor did it figure in Nazi propaganda. Mussolini apparently alluded to it on a few occasions, and the Italian press cited it as evidence that Britain would not seriously resist the invasion of Ethiopia.[4] But the resolution clearly impressed John F. Kennedy, if only because it contrasted so starkly with the patriotism of Churchill and other British authors he loved. Given that Churchill was in the political wilderness and out of step with public opinion, Jack could only conclude that Britain had become "decadent," unwilling to defend its Empire.[5]

On 4 March 1938 Joe Kennedy, the newly arrived American ambassador, gave Neville Chamberlain his "assurance that the United States must not be counted upon to back Great Britain in any scrape, right or wrong." Chamberlain, who never had any faith in American aid, accepted that with equanimity.[6] Hitler invaded Austria on the 12th, and on the 18th Kennedy spoke at London's Pilgrims Club. Rather than the usual bromides about Anglo-American fellowship that previous ambassadors had offered, he bluntly told "our British cousins that they must not get into a mess counting on us to bail them out." (This was after Franklin Roosevelt and Cordell Hull, rattled by the Anschluss, had urged him to tone down his isolationism.)[7] Two months before the Munich Agreement, which his father warmly endorsed, Jack predicted that Britain would not fight for Czechoslovakia.[8]

On 6 October 1939, just after the fall of Poland, Hitler offered the Allies peace on his conditions, which would have allowed him to keep his conquests. Three days later Jack Kennedy published his first essay in political commentary, an unsigned article in the *Harvard Crimson*, urging the British to accept that they could not defeat Hitler and to agree to his terms, even if that meant reducing Poland to a puppet state, handing over some colonies, and allowing German economic domination of Eastern Europe.[9] It reflected his father's defeatist views at the time; it went much further in the direction of appeasement than even Chamberlain was prepared to go; and it was frighteningly close to what Hitler himself had just proposed.

Jack wrote his Harvard senior honors thesis, "Appeasement at Munich," during the Phony War, between January and March 1940. He insisted that "To blame one man, such as Baldwin, for the unpreparedness of British Armaments is illogical and unfair," given the widespread opposition to rearmament among the British people.[10] That was too much even for his father, who wrote on 20 May (as German panzers were overrunning France) that he had shown the manuscript to a number of people, who "think you are letting Baldwin off too easily." They argued – and Joe Kennedy evidently agreed – that Baldwin should have used some of his considerable political capital to alert the voters to the danger of Hitler.

> I think you had better go over the material to make sure that, in pinning it on the electorate, you don't give the appearance of trying to do a complete whitewash of the leaders. I know that in a Democracy a politician is supposed to keep his ear to the ground; he is also supposed to look after the national welfare, and to attempt to educate the people when, in his opinion, they are off base. It may not be good politics but it is something that is vastly more important – good patriotism. I do not see how we can take any other line if we hope to make Democracy work.[11]

Over the following weeks, as French resistance disintegrated, Jack revised the manuscript, assisted by his father's speechwriter and *New York Times* reporter Arthur Krock. A new title was suggested by Krock, "Why England Slept": a nod to Churchill's *While England Slept*, which the thesis frequently cited. But it was not much less charitable toward the appeasers than the first draft. After Munich "Americans simplified the issue, compared it to a game of poker, and decided that Chamberlain had played his cards badly and had been outbluffed," Kennedy wrote. "But they did not examine the cards he held."[12] Kennedy insisted that Britain was not prepared, militarily or psychologically, to go to war in September 1938. Public anti-war sentiment was still deeply ingrained. Churchill's demands for more rapid rearmament were not economically realistic, and were supported at first only by "extremists of the right."[13] His 1936 call for the creation of a Ministry of Supply, in effect a demand for "industrial conscription," was premature. By commandeering export industries for the war effort, such a dictatorial agency would ruin Britain's balance of payments and undermine her ability to finance a sustained global war.[14] Kennedy noted that Churchill was capable of exaggerating German arms expenditures.[15] He quoted the *Economist*, which in the 1930s dismissed Churchill "as our brilliant but erratic *enfant terrible. Once again he has displayed an unerring instinct for hitting on the worst possible policies.*" That events had vindicated Churchill was a point Kennedy granted, but rather grudgingly:

> No one has ever questioned his ability or his dynamic energy. But these very qualities, which now cause Britain to consider him the only man who can carry through a successful war policy, have in times of peace caused him to be considered "dangerous," and a little uncomfortable to have around. Then, too, Churchill has always represented the extreme viewpoint. He has never stood on middle ground – he went "all out" for anything he advocated, with the result that his opinions have always been taken advisedly by most British leaders.[16]

On 12 November 1936 Baldwin had admitted in Parliament that he had delayed rearmament too long, but offered this excuse:

> Supposing I had gone to the country and said that Germany was rearming and that we must rearm, does anybody think that this pacific democracy would have rallied to that cry at that moment? I cannot think of anything that would have made the loss of the election from my point of view more certain.

"I have never heard such a squalid confession from a public man as Baldwin offered us yesterday," Churchill shot back. Before the First World War, "the most insulting charge which could be made against a Minister . . . short of actual malfeasance, was that he had endangered the safety of the country . . . for electioneering considerations," he wrote in the *Evening Standard*, but Baldwin seemed to treat that kind of expediency as "a canon of political virtue."[17] Even Joe Kennedy was sharply critical (at least in 1940), but Jack offered apologetics. He thought that Churchill was "making a political football out of a poor choice of words." Baldwin probably did not mean to suggest that "he had put his party's welfare above his country's welfare;" he was simply making a point about the depth of public anti-war sentiment. And, Jack insisted, Baldwin at the time did not see a pressing need to rearm: he was shortsighted, perhaps, but not dishonest.[18]

Jack gave Chamberlain credit for accelerating rearmament after Munich, and faulted the Labour Party for opposing conscription.[19] And he reminded Americans "that we are in no position to criticize blindly" the British appeasers. In May 1940 US military unpreparedness was as bad as Britain's had been in 1936, and Americans too might blanch at the cost of rearmament. "Like England, we have general commitments that we may not be able to fill. For example, we have warned the Japanese to stay out of the Dutch East Netherlands," Jack noted, "yet, if they seized it, would the cry, 'Are the Dutch East Indies worth a war,' go up, strangely familiar to the old cry in England at the time of Munich, 'Are the Sudeten Germans worth a war?' "[20] It was the first time, but certainly not the last, that Kennedy would apply the Munich analogy to Southeast Asia.

In one important respect *Why England Slept* was tougher, more Churchillian, than Jack's senior thesis. In his conclusion, he acknowledged that Britain might be defeated, and in that case America would have to mobilize its military resources to match the dictator powers, regardless of cost. As he wrote, "while the menace is there, all groups must be prepared to sacrifice many of the particular group interests for the national interests" – a foreshadowing of "Ask not what your country can do for you. . . ." And if Chamberlain had been forced to capitulate at Munich because he lacked the arms to resist Hitler, America could not repeat that mistake:

> We must always keep our armaments equal to our commitments. Munich should teach us that; we must realize that any bluff will be called. We cannot tell anyone to keep out of our hemisphere unless our armaments *and the people behind these armaments* are prepared to back up the command, even to the ultimate point of going to war. There must be no doubt in anyone's mind, the decision must be automatic: if we debate, if we hesitate, if we question, it will be too late.[21]

"Appeasement at Munich" did not contain that passage. The context was the current fear that Nazi Germany might establish beachheads in Latin America, but one cannot read that conclusion today without thinking of the Cuban Missile Crisis.

Published in America in late July and in Britain in October 1940, *Why England Slept* sold about 12,000 copies in the US edition,[22] and it was selected by the Book of the Month Club. Henry Luce, a friend of Joe Kennedy, supplied a preface to the book that emphasized the importance of military preparedness, and he reviewed it glowingly in his *Time* magazine.[23]

The fall of Singapore in February 1942 confirmed John F. Kennedy's long-standing perception of British decadence. "It has come time to write the obituary of the British Empire," he wrote to his sister Kathleen. Churchill roused a nation when he looked forward to the day when "the new world, with all its power and might, steps forth to the rescue and the liberation of the old," but Kennedy put a very different construction on those words: "Any time the Prime Minister of a country will admit to his own people that another country is going to save them – it's on the toboggan."[24] Yet already Kennedy was drawing a distinction between Churchill the politician, whom he treated skeptically, and Churchill the performance artist, who fascinated him. It took some time and effort for Kennedy to develop an effective speaking style, and early on he looked to Churchill as a model. His friend Charles Spalding recalled that, when Churchill delivered his December 1941 speech to the United States Congress:

> Jack and I were in a hotel room, listening to this thing, wrapped in it. He just hovered over that radio. In the elevator afterwards, we were still going through the speech and he was imitating it, asking me, "What do you think of this gesture, Charlie?" It was just as though he had gone to a Wagnerian opera, and he was trying to recapture it with all its implications. He did it in such a strangely classy way . . . like a beautiful ice skater or dancer . . . with such graceful moves. . . .[25]

In April 1948 the serial publication of *The Gathering Storm* began in the *Daily Telegraph*, the *New York Times*, and *Life* magazine. The book was released by Houghton Mifflin on 21 June, by which date the first printing of 75,000 copies had already sold out.[26] Three days later, the Soviets imposed a blockade on West Berlin, and Congressman John F. Kennedy sailed for Europe on a fact-finding trip. On the 26th Churchill publicly drew the Munich analogy, insisting that only firm resistance to Stalin could prevent a third world war, and on the same day the Berlin Airlift began. In London Jack found everyone talking about Churchill's memoir and the parallels with 1938, and he made a point of scheduling a side trip to Berlin. On 9 October, when it was clear that the airlift was working, Churchill told the Conservative Party conference that only the American nuclear monopoly prevented the conquest of Europe by the Soviets, who might become still more aggressive once they acquired the bomb. He quoted Luke 23 – "If these things are done in the green wood, what will be done in the dry?" Kennedy would use the same epigram in his 1960 presidential campaign, to emphasize the importance of negotiating from a position of nuclear strength.[27] Though he had been something of an apologist for Baldwin and Chamberlain, Kennedy readily assumed a Churchillian resolve vis-à-vis the Soviets. His largely Catholic constituents were loyal Democrats but also fiercely anti-Communist. Many of them came to admire another prominent Irish-American politician, Senator Joseph McCarthy, about whom Kennedy himself occasionally had positive things to say.[28]

Jack was narrowly elected to the Senate in 1952, and was a serious contender for the Democratic Vice Presidential nomination in 1956. By then the Munich analogy pervaded American political discourse. When President Eisenhower flew back from the 1955 Geneva Summit, he spoke from the airport tarmac in the rain, pointedly without an umbrella, which might have recalled the ghost of Neville Chamberlain.[29] The launch of Sputnik on 4 October 1957, followed by a humiliating string of failed American missile launches, embarrassed the Eisenhower administration and opened up a political opportunity for Cold

War Democrats, who could now outflank the Republicans on the right. In a 14 August 1958 speech Kennedy warned that the USSR was about to overtake the US in the deployment of nuclear-armed missiles, and he repeatedly echoed Churchill:

> These were the vital years, the years the locusts have eaten, and it is quite obvious we obtained economic security at the expense of military security, and that this policy will bring us into great danger within the next few years. . . . in the words of Sir Winston Churchill in a dark time of England's history: "Come then – let us to the task, to the battle and the toil – each to our part, each to our station. . . . Let us go forward together in all parts of the [land]. There is not a week, nor a day, nor an hour to be lost."

Kennedy had found his issue, and that November it won him re-election to the Senate by an unprecedented landslide. He was now ideally positioned for a presidential campaign in 1960, and he would run, as Harold Macmillan once put it, "on the Churchill ticket."[30]

There were important differences between the two cases. In the 1930s Britain had fallen dangerously behind Germany in the arms race, whereas the "missile gap" was imaginary. And where Churchill had risked his political career to deliver timely warnings, Kennedy was telling Americans exactly what they wanted to hear. Jack was much more like Stanley Baldwin, too shrewd to buck mainstream public opinion. But in his Pulitzer Prize-winning book *Profiles in Courage* (1955), Kennedy had successfully cast himself as a fearless Churchillian truth-teller. Only once did the book directly quote Churchill ("Democracy is the worst form of government – except all those other forms that have been tried from time to time"),[31] but it followed Churchill's style of historiography: middlebrow, patriotic, easy to read, uplifting rather than debunking, and focusing solely on great men and high politics. It was modeled on *Great Contemporaries*, where Churchill had written that "Courage is rightly esteemed the first of human qualities, because . . . it is the quality which guarantees all others."[32] That was echoed in Kennedy's opening line: "This is a book about that most admirable of human virtues – courage."[33] And yet none of the eight American politicians that Kennedy chose to profile could be called "Churchillian," if that term is taken to mean waging implacable war against tyranny. Three of them (Daniel Webster, Thomas Hart Benton, Sam Houston) bent every effort to head off a civil war, even if that meant compromising with slavery. Two were notorious isolationists: George Norris (who filibustered Woodrow Wilson's proposal to arm American merchant ships against German submarines) and Robert A. Taft (who denounced the Nuremberg Trials). Only John Quincy Adams, who in 1807 opposed "appeasement of Great Britain"[34] and supported Jefferson's Embargo Bill, came close to the Churchillian model, and even he (Kennedy suggested) "should have realized that the Embargo would ruin New England but hardly irritate the British."[35] In his first and final chapters, Kennedy somewhat undercut the message of the book by arguing the virtues of compromise, flexibility, and attending to the interests of one's local constituents. In the end, he endorsed the skeptical pragmatism of the Whig statesman Lord Melbourne, "who, when irritated by the criticism of the then youthful historian T. B. Macaulay, remarked that he would like to be as sure of anything as Macaulay seemed to be of everything."[36] Compared with Churchill, Kennedy was far less willing to jeopardize his political career by acting on his convictions. Perhaps for that reason, one Churchill epigram, found in a draft of *Profiles in Courage*, did not make it into the final text: "Politicians who cannot face unpopularity are really not worth having – they look like it for a time but afterwards you will find that you have had the worst of the deal."[37]

On 14 January 1960 Kennedy proclaimed that "We will need in the sixties a president who is willing and able to summon his national constituency to its finest hour." He prepared for the campaign by listening to a record of Churchill's war oratory, introduced by the sonorous words of Edward R. Murrow: "Now the hour had come for him to mobilize the English language and send it into battle," a phrase Kennedy would later borrow.[38] In his 1960 speeches Kennedy frequently quoted Churchill, drew on what he had read in *While England Slept*, and ran against Stanley Baldwin, to whom he repeatedly compared Richard Nixon.[39] (Nixon had stuck the "appeaser" label on Adlai Stevenson, the last Democratic standard-bearer. This time Kennedy struck first and struck often.) After attacking Nixon's past sins in his acceptance speech to the Democratic Party Convention, Kennedy professed to put aside partisan bickering and offer a high-minded forward vision of a "New Frontier": "As Winston Churchill said on taking office some 20 years ago: if we open a quarrel between the present and the past, we shall be in danger of losing the future."[40] The Vice President's ideology, he charged, was me-tooism, telling everyone what they wanted to hear, an impression reinforced by Nixon's performance in their television debates, where the Munich analogy was bandied back and forth. Both candidates agreed that the United States should defend the Chinese Nationalist regime on Taiwan, but should that guarantee also extend to Quemoy and Matsu, tiny offshore islands under the guns of the Communists? Kennedy said they were unimportant and indefensible, but Nixon equated them with the Sudetenland, whereupon Kennedy (equally absurdly) charged that Nixon "never really protested the Communists seizing Cuba."[41]

The title of Kennedy's volume of campaign speeches, *The Strategy of Peace*, obviously echoed Churchill's speech "The Sinews of Peace." It outlined essentially the same approach to dealing with the Russians and often quoted him. Advocating a medical care program for the elderly before an audience of Detroit auto workers, Kennedy cited Churchill the Edwardian social reformer, who challenged Parliament to confront the evils of poverty.[42] Promising federal aid to stimulate the depressed economy of West Virginia, he repeated Churchill's plea for Lend-Lease: "Give us the tools – and we will finish the job."[43] Campaigning in the Western states, Kennedy naturally recited the poetic line "But westward, look, the land is bright" – yet instead of quoting Arthur Hugh Clough directly, he quoted Churchill quoting Clough.[44]

Nine days before the presidential election, a confidential internal campaign memorandum advised Kennedy that, according to the polls, he and Nixon were at a "stand-off" when they debated the issues – but when Kennedy assumed a Churchillian tone, he opened up a significant lead. In their fourth and final television debate, when the candidates confronted "the question of prestige, of rallying the American people to look the hard truth in the eye and face the facts, Senator Kennedy scored through most decisively. He won this 62 38 per cent. In the volunteered remarks of voters in state after state following Debate #4, the issue of American prestige abroad became the dominant foreign policy issue." Accordingly, the memorandum urged Kennedy, in the closing days of the campaign, to get tough with Fidel Castro, support anti-Castro Cubans, and speak out against the "Communist military build-up in Cuba."[45]

Kennedy was familiar with the Churchill of the 1920s, who warned against war by miscalculation, and the Churchill of the 1950s, who advocated nuclear arms control. For the 1960 campaign he could therefore offer a two-pronged foreign policy: he would secure nuclear superiority over the USSR but then, from that position of strength, negotiate an atomic test ban treaty. And he had at hand Churchill's pithy formula: "We arm – to parley."[46] Thus he simultaneously outmaneuvered the Republicans on both the right and the left, held together a Democratic Party divided between hawks and doves, and in either case portrayed himself as a more dynamic agent of change than the exhausted Eisenhower administration.

Most American readers, however, only knew the Churchill of the 1930s and the 1940s, and as the 1950s drew to a close the American mass media amplified and broadcast the image of the great man who had stood up to the dictators, reaching ever larger audiences. In 1959 two abridged editions of *The Second World War* were published, by Houghton Mifflin and Time-Life. In *The Gathering Storm* Churchill had warned against the simplistic habit of treating every international conflict as another Munich:

> No case of this kind can be judged apart from its circumstances. . . . Those who are prone by temperament and character to seek sharp and clear-cut

> solutions of difficult and obscure problems, who are ready to fight whenever some challenge comes from a foreign Power, have not always been right. On the other hand, those whose inclination is to bow their heads, to seek patiently and faithfully for peaceful compromise, are not always wrong. On the contrary, in the majority of instances they may be right, not only morally but from a practical standpoint. How many wars have been averted by patience and persisting good will! . . . How many wars have been precipitated by firebrands! How many misunderstandings which led to wars could have been removed by temporising![47]

Kennedy would quote from that paragraph in a November 1961 speech[48] – but it had been cut from both of the 1959 editions of *The Second World War*. Instead an epilogue on the post-war world had been added in which Churchill (writing just after the crushing of the 1956 Hungarian revolt) took a tougher line on the Soviet Union. He reproduced key sections of the "Iron Curtain" speech, and concluded that "half Europe had merely exchanged one despot for another."[49] He highlighted all the landmarks of the Cold War – the Berlin Blockade, NATO, the Korean War – insisting that "It was in the American possession or preponderance of nuclear weapons, that the surest foundation of our hopes for peace lay." And while he briefly alluded to summitry, he foreswore disarmament, insisting that there "could not be . . . any relaxation of the comradeship and preparations of the free nations, for any slackening of our defence efforts would paralyse every beneficial tendency toward peace."[50]

At one point in the epilogue Churchill offered an astounding recollection: in an earlier phase of the Cold War, "It even occurred to me that an announced but peaceful aerial demonstration over the main Soviet cities, coupled with the outlining to the Soviet leaders of some of our newest inventions, would produce in them a more friendly and sober attitude."[51] Apparently it did not occur to him that the men of the Kremlin would take measures against Western warplanes that were rattling their windows. If one asks where Churchill got such a lunatic idea, the answer once again appears to be Harold Nicolson's *Public Faces*: in the novel, as soon as Britain acquires the Bomb, supersonic RAF bombers are sent to buzz all the major capitals of the world, to impress rival powers.

The Time-Life edition was a vast coffee-table book containing barely one-sixth of the original text, but it was vividly illustrated with the kind of large, striking photographs that distinguished *Life* magazine. It concluded with two awesome full-color images of mushroom clouds: one was a full-page photo of a hydrogen explosion, the other was a two-page poster-sized spread of the Bikini Atoll atomic test of 1946. Across the latter ran a brief quotation from Churchill's epilogue: "When war is itself fenced about with mutual extermination it seems likely that it will be increasingly postponed."[52] In the same postscript, Churchill correctly predicted that the Hungarian revolt would be only the first of a series of shocks that would eventually bring down the Soviet Empire. The message of this edition was actually reassuring: as long as the West remained strong and vigilant, nuclear war would be avoided, and the USSR would ultimately be done in by its own internal contradictions. It was in this format that I discovered the writings of Winston Churchill, in a school library, my teacher having told the class that, were it not for the great man, we would all be wearing swastika armbands.

His career in American television began on 15 November 1956, when NBC broadcast a version of *Savrola* – live, in color, compressed into 37 minutes (not counting commercials), and starring Sarah Churchill as Lucile.[53] *Time* reported that she "looked pretty, proper, and bored," and concluded that the dialogue was even more excruciating than the original novel ("All's fair in love and war." "And this?" "This is both.")[54] Winston vetted the script in advance and objected that Molara was played too much like the great twentieth-century despots, which seemed anachronistic. "The particular political type of political dictator which has dominated our lives" had not yet been invented in 1900, he protested. Instead, he recommended that the story be staged as it was written – as "a thorough-going rip-roaring melodrama."[55]

But producers and viewers wanted the Churchill who had vanquished tyrants. That image was confirmed in the minds of Americans by *Winston Churchill: The Valiant Years*, a serialization of *The Second World War* produced by the ABC television network. As ABC told its writers, "we must make it a cardinal principle of this series that Winston Churchill is our leading man, and every creative and dramatic device must be used to bring him to life." The story would be cast in a form that closely resembled melodrama, but was more familiar to Americans: "It will be like a Western; Winston Churchill hiding behind rocks as a sharpshooter or leading the charge down the valley. We have a good leading man and a good heavy."[56] (Westerns were ABC's forte.)

The Valiant Years was an attempt to repeat the success of *Victory at Sea* (1952–53), NBC's critically acclaimed Second World War documentary. The latter underplayed Britain's role in the war, and when it was rebroadcast by the BBC many viewers (Churchill especially) were outraged.[57] The fact that, by 1960, American television was producing an Anglocentric retelling of the war story reflected a major cultural shift, as well as Churchill's canonization in the United States. Britain was no longer regarded as an imperialist rival for world power, but a valued ally in an epic struggle against totalitarianism.

At this time ABC was still the "third network," well behind CBS and NBC in terms of ratings, advertising revenues, affiliates, and critical respect. *The Valiant Years* represented a major investment in prestige, assembled by a staff of almost 250, including such distinguished journalists as Quentin Reynolds and William L. Shirer. There was background music by Richard Rodgers, who had scored *Victory at Sea*. Churchill's words were recited by Richard Burton. In 1953 Burton had been performing *Hamlet* at the Old Vic when the house manager brought him the unnerving news that Churchill was in the audience. According to *Time* magazine:

> As Burton spoke his first line – "A little more than kin, and less than kind" – he was startled to hear deep identical mutterings from the front row. Churchill continued to follow him line for line, a dramaturgical beagle, his face a thunderhead when something had been cut. "I tried to shake him off," remembers Burton. "I went fast and I went slow, but he was right there." Churchill was right there to the end, in fact, when Burton took 18 curtain calls and Churchill told a reporter that "it was as exciting and virile a performance of Hamlet as I can remember." Years later, when *Winston Churchill – The Valiant Years* was under preparation for television, its producers asked Sir Winston who he thought should do the voice of Churchill. "Get that boy from the Old Vic," said the old man.[58]

The first episode was broadcast on 27 November 1960, just after the election of John F. Kennedy to the White House. (The outcome of the vote would not have mattered: Richard Nixon was an equally fervent admirer of Churchill.) The episode in which, just after the Fall of France, Churchill braces Britain for a possible German invasion, was aired five days before Kennedy's inauguration on 20 January 1961. Even the title seemed to echo *Profiles in Courage*, at a time when that quality was actually valued in politicians. The series won two Emmy awards, for Rodgers's music and "Outstanding Writing Achievement in the Documentary Field." Critics were generally impressed, with Gilbert Seldes in *TV Guide* calling it "one of the few programs that does honor to television." "Excellent . . . graphic . . . unforgettable," raved *Time*, it was Churchill's "Finest Half-Hour."[59] In a 9 May 1961 speech, Federal Communications Commission chairman Newton Minow famously denounced American television as "a vast wasteland" but applauded *The Valiant Years* as a glorious exception. The ratings were somewhat disappointing: the premiere episode was less than half as popular as *What's My Line?* on CBS.[60] Even so, 9.3 percent of all American households with television sets were tuned into Churchill, an audience vastly larger than for any of his books.

This was the cultural context in which Kennedy drafted his inaugural address, which his staff referred to as "blood, sweat and tears." Though it never exactly quoted or mentioned Churchill, it packed several Churchillian allusions into a brief space (1,364 words in 14 minutes). In its cadences one could hear the resolute Churchill ("we shall pay any price, bear any burden, meet any hardship, support any friend, oppose any foe to ensure the survival and the success of liberty") but also Churchill's Wellsian vision of the future as a choice between utopia and apocalypse ("man holds in his mortal hands the power to abolish all forms of human poverty and all forms of human life"). What Churchill called "perverted science," Kennedy called "the dark powers of destruction unleashed by science," and the President explicitly called for nuclear arms control. "Let us never negotiate out of fear, but let us never fear to negotiate" concisely summed up Churchill's approach to diplomacy. There was a passage that could be read as an endorsement of the "special relationship" with Britain: "To those old allies whose cultural and spiritual origins we share, we pledge the loyalty of faithful friends. United, there is little we cannot do in a host of cooperative ventures." Kennedy warned the new nations emerging from colonialism not to be tempted by the "far more iron tyranny" of communism: "Remember that, in the past, those who foolishly sought power by riding the back of the tiger ended up inside." That was the closest he came to directly quoting Churchill, who in the post-Munich parliamentary debate had said, "Dictators ride to and fro upon tigers which they dare not dismount. And the tigers are getting hungry." (That speech was reprinted in *While England Slept*.) Twenty years earlier Churchill had told the boys of Harrow, "These are not dark days: these are great days – the greatest days our country has ever lived: and we must all thank God that we have been allowed, each of us according to our stations, to play a part in making these days memorable in the history of our race."[61] And now Kennedy gave his audience the same sense of playing a uniquely heroic role in history: "In the long history of the world, only a few generations have been granted the role of defending freedom in its hour of maximum danger. I do not shrink from this responsibility. I welcome it. I do not believe that any of us would exchange places with any other people or any other generation."

During the campaign Harold Macmillan had not been impressed with either candidate: "one looked like a convicted criminal and the other looked like a rather engaging young undergraduate." After the President stumbled badly at the Bay of Pigs and the Vienna Summit, the Prime Minister mournfully concluded that "Kennedy is going to fail to produce any real leadership. . . . We may drift to disaster over Berlin – a terrible diplomatic defeat or (out of sheer incompetence) a nuclear war." But he was pleasantly surprised to discover that Kennedy was well read in British political history, and not just Churchill. He had also studied William Pitt, Charles James Fox, and Lord Melbourne as political models. He particularly admired David Cecil's *The Young Melbourne* (1939) and, as David Ormsby-Gore later noted, he shared with Melbourne an "ability to stand back from the battle and appraise coolly what was happening," a useful talent during the Cuban Missile Crisis.[62]

Macmillan's hope that Britain could play Greece to America's Rome, supplying wise guidance to a new and inexperienced empire, is never cited today without a roll of the eyes. There were certainly many points of friction between Macmillan and Kennedy, of which the cancellation of the Skybolt missile system was only the most conspicuous. And given that the United States spent ten times as much on defense as Britain, any "partnership" between the two was bound to be unequal.[63] But Ormsby-Gore, now the British ambassador to Washington, had been a friend of JFK since 1938, and he enjoyed a genuinely special relationship, with far greater access to the White House than any other foreign diplomat.[64] And communication between the President and the Prime Minister was facilitated by a shared Churchillian frame of reference. Kennedy listened to Macmillan, who could be a steadying influence. When they met in Key West in March 1961 to discuss Communist encroachments on neutral Laos, they both drew the analogy with the remilitarization of the Rhineland, though Macmillan restrained American plans to commit substantial military forces to the region. Bullied by Nikita Khrushchev at the June 1961 Vienna summit, Kennedy adapted Churchill's words to the effect that he would not preside over the dissolution of America's global alliances. Shaken by that confrontation, Kennedy was reassured by Macmillan. The Prime Minister was concerned about Khrushchev's threats against West Berlin and acknowledged that this could be "a Danzig," a point where the West would have to fight, but he also suggested that the Soviet leader might have been engaging in another episode of shoe-banging theatrics, not to be taken too seriously.[65] (To the Queen, Macmillan confided that Kennedy's experience in Vienna "reminded me in a way of Lord Halifax or Mr. Neville Chamberlain trying to hold a conversation with Herr Hitler.") Ultimately, it was largely thanks to Macmillan's persistent nudging that the superpowers agreed to a ban on atmospheric nuclear testing.[66] And where American and British policies clashed, Kennedy had a ready Churchill quotation at hand: "The history of any alliance is the history of mutual recrimination among the various people."[67]

Nikita Khrushchev was not Adolf Hitler, but he ominously resembled Wilhelm II. He was an authoritarian though not a mass murderer. As the leader of the world's second superpower, he deeply resented the first superpower, engaging his rival in an arms race while also wishing for some kind of accommodation. He had expansionist aims; he freely resorted to threats and tirades; he took ruthless advantage of perceived weaknesses in opponents. His foreign policy was dangerously erratic and impulsive, more *gefuhlspolitik* than realpolitik, and sometimes resembling the theatre of the absurd. He commanded a vast military machine and aimed to project power on a global scale, though his country did not really have the resources to support such an ambitious policy. For all these reasons, he was quite capable of blundering into a war. "We knew where we stood much better with Stalin," commented one Foreign Office person, but Khrushchev brought to the nuclear age what "we have always most feared . . . audacity and adventurism."[68] His placement of missiles in Cuba was as reckless as any of Hitler's coups, though he was terrified when the prospect of nuclear war became real. Under extreme time pressures, US and UK leaders struggled to discern the Soviet leader's motives and objectives, which fifty years later are still debated among historians. Frank Roberts, the British ambassador to the Kremlin, probably came closest to the truth when he pointed to "Khrushchev's well-known proclivity for setting out on courses of action without correctly foreseeing where they could lead him."[69]

In his anxiety to avoid war by miscalculation, Kennedy was haunted by two different types of mistakes that had led to two catastrophic wars. The first, as his brother Robert recalled, was the blunder committed by Europe's leaders in 1914: "They somehow seemed to tumble into war, he said, through stupidity, individual idiosyncrasies, misunderstandings, and personal complexes of inferiority and grandeur." At the same time, the Kennedy brothers also "talked about the miscalculation of the Germans in 1939 and the still unfulfilled commitments and guarantees that the British had given to Poland."[70] Chamberlain's error had been to send mixed signals, selling out Czechoslovakia in 1938 and guaranteeing Poland in 1939. The first persuaded Hitler not to take the second seriously, and thus he stumbled into a war with Great Britain, a war he did not plan for. Kennedy had good reason to fear that if he did not respond decisively to the missiles in Cuba, an emboldened Khrushchev might press his luck by moving on West Berlin, leading to nuclear war via a different route. The Munich analogy was thrown around too loosely during the Kennedy era, but it was by no means entirely wrong.

During this particularly treacherous phase of the Cold War, Kennedy's reading of Churchill served him well. Because he knew the whole Churchill oeuvre, he was aware that it was more than just denunciations of Munich. At points throughout his political life Churchill had deployed the whole spectrum of diplomatic strategies: implacable resistance, resistance allowing a face-saving retreat, magnanimous concessions, horse trading, spheres-of-influence deals, arms reduction, and (where appropriate) appeasement. That model gave Kennedy considerable freedom of maneuver in dealing with the volatile and difficult-to-read Soviet leader. When he announced the blockade of Cuba, he warned the American people that "The 1930s taught us a clear lesson. Aggressive conduct, if allowed to grow unchecked and unchallenged, ultimately leads to war." But when opportunities for negotiation appeared, Kennedy also liked to (mis)quote Churchill's "It is better to jaw-jaw than to war-war."[71]

Kennedy absorbed a similar lesson from *The Guns of August*, Barbara Tuchman's study of the origins of the First World War. Published in January 1962, it received an immediate boost from front-page coverage in the *New York Times Book Review*, and remained on the newspaper's bestseller list for forty-two weeks.[72] Like *Profiles in Courage* and *A History of the English-Speaking Peoples*, *The Guns of August* was middlebrow history: irresistibly readable, with a strong and simple narrative line, not grounded in current scholarship, and not much respected among academic specialists. One of those experts, Harvard Professor Sidney Fay, concluded that "she has got the history wrong, but historians need to write like Tuchman or we will be out of business."[73] Kennedy read the book in April and was profoundly impressed. On 16 August, before the Cuban crisis blew up, he recommended it to retired General Douglas MacArthur, and asked:

> I was wondering, having read that, whether in reading some other things—whether you thought the leadership by the British and the French was wholly incompetent, and left, particularly in '17 Passchendaele and all these tremendous casualties for 8, 9, 10 miles – from what – June till October, November? Was there any alternative action by the allies? Do you think they had to continue those assaults on those trenches, or was there anything else they could have done?[74]

But *The Guns of August* contains no description of Passchendaele or any of the other grinding static battles on the Western Front. Tuchman focuses solely on the opening phase of the conflict, when it was still a war of rapid movement. Here Kennedy apparently conflated her book with *The World Crisis*, which includes an unsparing account of the horrors of Passchendaele:

> In six weeks at the farthest point we had advanced four miles. Soon the rain descended, and the vast crater field became a sea of choking fetid mud in which men, animals and tanks floundered and perished hopelessly. . . . [The Germans] always took nearly two lives for one and sold every inch of ground with extortion. . . . It was not until the end of November that the final failure was accepted.

Tuchman denounced the pig-headedness of generals who refused to change their battle plans, but Churchill had been no less scathing:

> They tried their sombre experiment to its conclusion. They took all they required from Britain. They wore down alike the manhood and the guns of the British Army almost to destruction. They did it in the face of the plainest

> warnings, and of arguments which they could not answer. . . . [As Sir William Robertson wrote,] "I confess I stick to it more because I see nothing better, and because my instinct prompts me to stick to it, than because of any good argument by which I can support it." These are terrible words when used to sustain the sacrifices of nearly four hundred thousand men.[75]

Kennedy evidently linked Churchill and Tuchman in his mind, and together they only reinforced his distrust of "brass hats" and his determination not to sacrifice another generation on the battlefield. He badgered his military men to read *The Guns of August*, recalled Maxwell Taylor, Chairman of the Joint Chiefs of Staff: "[He] frequently turned to me and commented on the dull generals who never had more than one solution and hence governments were bound to call a levee en masse – massive mobilization – and depend on the execution of a single war plan at the time of the outbreak of World War I."[76] At a White House luncheon he gave a copy to Macmillan and launched into a deep discussion of the issues Tuchman raised. David Ormsby-Gore, who was present, recalled that though Macmillan had not yet read it, nevertheless this meeting of minds over a book "really set the seal on their friendship," to the point where "a kind of complete family atmosphere had developed between them."[77] When Macmillan read the book he was (according to Alistair Horne) "profoundly affected" and drew "from it the same cautionary conclusions on the political miscalculations that had precipitated the First World War."[78] On 13 October, as the Cuban crisis was heating up, US diplomat Chester Bowles met with Soviet ambassador Anatoly Dobrynin and recommended that he read *The Guns of August*, "in which he would see a pattern of politico-military action and counter-action that could be repeated in the next six months. In July 1914, men of intelligence in Russia, Germany, Austria-Hungary, France and England, all quite conscious of the forces which were feeding the approaching holocaust, found themselves enmeshed in internal pressures, commitments and precedents which left them powerless to avoid the inevitable. It would be the greatest folly in history if we were to repeat this insane process in the nuclear age."[79] Tuchman had argued that the momentum of general mobilization had driven the European nations to war in August 1914, and it was quite possibly this lesson that impelled Macmillan to resist placing NATO forces on alert in October 1962.[80]

The story of the role of *The Guns of August* in the Cuban Missile Crisis is familiar. What should be better known is the role of Winston Churchill in shaping Barbara Tuchman as a historian. Her first serious work of scholarship was her 1933 senior honors thesis at Radcliffe College (just across from Harvard), a study of moral justifications for imperialism in late Victorian Britain, which relied importantly on *The River War* and *Lord Randolph Churchill*.[81] In the two books Tuchman wrote before *The Guns of August*, Churchill significantly had the final word. *Bible and Sword: England and Palestine from the Bronze Age to Balfour* (1956) concluded with his 1920 prediction of "the creation in our lifetime by the banks of the Jordan of a Jewish State under the protection of the British Crown," and his condemnation of the 1939 White Paper restricting Jewish immigration into Palestine.[82] (She was as passionate a Zionist as he was.) *The Zimmerman Telegram* (1958), her study of the trigger that brought the United States into the First World War, ended with Churchill's observations on the role of chance and accident in history.[83] And in the book that followed *The Guns of August, The Proud Tower* (1966), Churchill would again play a starring role, as one of the most flamboyant politicians of the Edwardian era.

For Tuchman, history was a literary art, as creative as the novel or poetry – and, she asked rhetorically, was Churchill "less of an artist in words . . . than William Faulkner or Sinclair Lewis?"[84] Above all, she treated history as theatre, and "The first month of the First World War, as Winston Churchill said, was 'a drama never surpassed.' "[85] They both understood the dramatic potential of a high-speed naval chase: where Churchill breathlessly described the hunting down of Admiral von Spee in the southern seas, Tuchman devoted a full chapter to the pursuit of the cruiser *Goeben* across the Mediterranean. She aimed to write history that reached a mass audience, and there she explicitly placed herself in the company of H. G. Wells, Will Durant, Lytton Strachey, William L. Shirer, Samuel Eliot Morison, Arthur Schlesinger, Jr., and Winston Churchill.[86] And she wrote with the knowledge that Victorian confidence in historical progress had been shattered by what Churchill (in 1949) called "this terrible twentieth century."[87] Tuchman readily admitted that *The Guns of August* drew heavily on the first volume of *The World Crisis*, "the single most important book among English sources by a person holding key office at the outbreak."[88] And lest anyone miss the point of her book, she opened it with Churchill's epigram on the unpredictability of human conflict: "The terrible Ifs accumulate."

A reader opening *The World Crisis* in the early 1960s would have found a description of the First World War as horrific as anything expected from a nuclear exchange:

> Every outrage against humanity or international law was repaid by reprisals often on a greater scale and of longer duration. No truce or parley mitigated the strife of the armies. The wounded died between the lines: the dead mouldered into the soil. Merchant ships and neutral ships and hospital ships were sunk on the seas and all on board left to their fate, or killed as they swam. Every effort was made to starve whole nations into submission without regard to age or sex. Cities and monuments were smashed by artillery. Bombs

> from the air were cast down indiscriminately. Poison gas in many forms stifled or seared the soldiers. Liquid fire was projected upon their bodies. Men fell from the air in flames, or were smothered, often slowly, in the dark recesses of the sea. . . . When it was over, Torture and Cannibalism were the only two expedients that the civilised, scientific, Christian States had been able to deny themselves: and these were of doubtful utility.[89]

Churchill always recognized that causation was the most difficult and complicated dimension of history, never more so than in August 1914. "Was there any man of real eminence and responsibility whose devil heart conceived and willed this awful thing?" he asked:

> One rises from the study of the causes of the Great War with a prevailing sense of the defective control of individuals upon world fortunes. It has been well said, "there is always more error than design in human affairs." The limited minds even of the ablest men, their disputed authority, the climate of opinion in which they dwell, their transient and partial contributions to the mighty problem, that problem itself so far beyond their compass, so vast in scale and detail, so changing in its aspect.

All these factors hemmed in and shackled the most powerful political actors. Thus events "got on to certain lines, and no one could get them off again."[90]

But what lines specifically, and why were Europe's leaders incapable of changing course? Given his lifelong presumption that men could steer history, Churchill could not pursue far the idea that the war was the product of inexorable forces. He argued that the European balance of power had been destabilized by Germany's decision, in 1900, to build the world's second most powerful navy, which amplified international tensions and drove Britain to join forces with Japan, France, and Russia.[91] A reader might conclude that any attempt by a secondary power to catch up with and challenge a primary power – such as the Soviet effort to overcome American nuclear superiority – is terribly dangerous.

Moreover, as John Maynard Keynes read *The World Crisis*, "Mr. Churchill's principal thesis amounts to the contention that, broadly speaking, in each country the professional soldiers, the 'brass hats,' were, on the great questions of military policy, generally wrong—wrong on the weight of the argument beforehand and wrong on the weight of the evidence afterward – whilst the professional politicians . . . were generally right."[92] Could war have been averted if Sir Edward Grey, the Foreign Secretary, had made it more clear to the Germans that Britain would fight to defend France and Belgium? Churchill pointed out the political constraints Grey faced: had he issued such an ultimatum before Belgium was actually invaded, "I am certain that . . . the Cabinet would have broken up, and . . . the House of Commons would have repudiated his action."[93] Naturally Churchill was reluctant to criticize a government of which he had been a member.

Barbara Tuchman had no such inhibitions. "Grey had perfected a manner of speaking designed to convey as little meaning as possible; his avoidance of the point-blank, said a colleague, almost amounted to a method." That evasiveness was a function of his distaste for diplomacy, a serious handicap in a Foreign Secretary. He much preferred trout fishing to studying European affairs.[94] Churchill, focusing mainly on Britain, argued that all the war contingency plans drafted before 1914 worked with marvelous efficiency when set in motion, especially his own plan for transporting the British Expeditionary Force to France. "If everything had not been prepared, if the plan had not been perfected, if it had not been the only plan, and if all military opinion had not been industriously marshalled around it – who shall say what fatal hesitancy might not have intervened?"[95] But in *The Guns of August* it was precisely Germany's Von Schlieffen Plan, France's Plan XVII, and all the other inflexible timetables, which the commanders could not or would not change, that dragged the belligerents into a stalemated and mutually destructive war. It was all determined by "the inherent ifs, errors, and commitments of the first month. . . . The nations were caught in a trap, a trap made during the first thirty days out of battles that failed to be decisive, a trap from which there was, and has been, no exit."[96] These two books did not agree on every point, but together they offered Kennedy some clear lessons: In times of crisis, politicians had to pay attention, speak plainly, be flexible, treat skeptically the advice of "brass hats," and above all never allow the unchecked momentum of events to sweep them into war.

The difficulty was that most Americans had a far less nuanced view of Churchill. Hundreds of thousands of them had read *The Second World War*, millions had seen *The Valiant Years*, but hardly anyone besides John F. Kennedy and Barbara Tuchman knew or remembered *The World Crisis*, which had been a failure when it was first published. In 1949 Scribner's had reprinted 3,050 copies of the abridged edition, which took nine years to sell out, and it would not reissue the complete first volume until February 1963.[97] At the height of the Churchill cult, which Kennedy had done so much to promote, only the Churchill who had stood up to Hitler was known well in the United States, and that one-sided image often pressured Kennedy to be more hawkish than he really cared to be. Moreover, he was always vulnerable to the charge that he was his father's son. "I was never any Chamberlain umbrella policy man," Lyndon Johnson had thundered while battling Kennedy for the Democratic presidential nomination. "I never thought Hitler was right."[98]

When East Germany began construction of the Berlin Wall in August 1961, and at first Kennedy appeared to do nothing, West Berlin mayor Willy Brandt publicly warned against a repeat of the remilitarization of the Rhineland and "a new Munich," and some West German students sent Kennedy a Chamberlainesque umbrella.[99] If it had been known at the time that Jack Kennedy had written that 1939 *Harvard Crimson* article calling for peace with Hitler, his political career would have been wrecked.

On 27 August 1962 Republican Senator Homer Capehart charged that the Soviets had based troops in Cuba and called for an invasion of the island. At a news conference two days later Kennedy dismissed the allegation ("We've no evidence of troops"), but at that moment a U-2 spy plane was taking the first photographs of Russians building anti-aircraft missile bases around Mariel in the north of the island, which raised the question of what those missiles were designed to protect. After the story broke, Kennedy worried that a lack of toughness would hurt the Democrats in the 1962 congressional elections. Was he coming to resemble a complacent Stanley Baldwin, the man he had defended in 1940 and denounced in 1960? On 16 October Kennedy was supplied with another set of U-2 photos, confirming that the Soviets were installing medium range ballistic missiles in Cuba. By the 19th he was leaning toward a blockade of the island, but the Joint Chiefs of Staff considered that a halfway measure would lead to a Russian attack, and insisted that US forces strike first against the missile bases. "This is almost as bad as the appeasement at Munich," warned General Curtis LeMay, an outburst followed by a loaded pause.[100] "Well, I guess Homer Capehart is the Winston Churchill of our generation," Kennedy remarked the following evening. "We are very, very close to war. And there's not room in the White House bomb shelter for all of us."[101] At this historical moment, it was very fortunate that Barbara Tuchman had put the warnings voiced in *The World Crisis* back into circulation.

The closest historical parallel to the Cuban Missile Crisis was not September 1938 or August 1914 but the Second Moroccan Crisis, when Europe went to the brink of war and drew back. On 1 July 1911 the German gunboat *Panther* arrived at the Moroccan port of Agadir, in response to French intervention in Morocco. The British and French were both alarmed, fearing that the Germans aimed to threaten their sea lanes by establishing a naval base on the Atlantic, perilously close to Gibraltar. The episode is only mentioned in passing in *The Guns of August*, but it merited a full (and highly dramatic) chapter in *The World Crisis*. Here Churchill outlined a three-pronged strategy for minimizing the chances of war in a tense international confrontation: (1) make clear to one's adversary that certain lines must not be crossed, and (2) prepare for war, but (3) remain open to concessions that would allow a face-saving retreat. First, Lloyd George threw down the gauntlet in his Mansion House speech of 21 July, affirming that Britain would fight rather than be humiliated. Second, Churchill described in breathless detail a secret Committee of Imperial Defence meeting on 23 August, where the Army and Navy laid out their plans for war. But third, by November the French had persuaded the Germans to abandon Morocco in return for some territory in central Africa, largely swampland infested with sleeping sickness. In this context Churchill was an avowed appeaser: "If aiding Germany in the Colonial sphere was a means of procuring a stable situation, it was a price we were well prepared to pay." He recognized that Agadir was a close-run thing, in which "one violent move by any party would rupture and derange the restraints upon all, and plunge Cosmos into Chaos." He knew that a weak response by Britain would have only encouraged the Germans to press their advantage to the point of war, which could only be averted by a precise balance of firmness, preparation, and flexibility. True, in 1911 the Great War was only postponed, but, Churchill concluded, "a war postponed may be a war averted."[102]

It is not difficult to see Kennedy using similar tactics in the Cuban crisis: (1) announcing on nationwide television that he would not tolerate Soviet missiles in Cuba and would impose a quarantine on offensive weapons, (2) making very serious preparations for bombing Russian installations in Cuba and invading the island, but (3) effectively agreeing to remove obsolete American missiles from Turkey (which could easily be replaced by submarine-based Polaris missiles) in return for the withdrawal of Soviet bombers and missiles in Cuba. When some of his advisors objected that giving up the missiles in Turkey might be perceived as appeasement, Kennedy responded with a sardonic Churchillian allusion: "We can't very well invade Cuba, with all this toil and blood it's going to be, when we could have gotten them [the Soviet missiles] out by making a deal on the same missiles in Turkey. If that's part of the record, then I don't see how we'll have a very good war."[103] The tape recordings of Kennedy's meetings with his more hawkish civilian advisors and his still more belligerent generals reveal that he was cautious, flexible, and careful to think through all the possible consequences of a given decision. These are not qualities often associated with the word "Churchillian", but Kennedy owed them to his reading of Churchill.

Like Churchill, Kennedy made political decisions with a view toward how they would look in history books, and there *The Guns of August* hit home. "I am not going to follow a course which will allow anyone to write a comparable book about this time, *The Missiles of October*," he told his brother Robert. "If anybody is around to write after this, they are going to understand that we made every effort to find peace and every effort to give our adversary room to move."[104] His Secretary of State, Dean Rusk, likewise advised everyone present to "remember the guns of August where certain events brought about a general situation in which at the time none of the governments involved really wanted." Allowing Khrushchev an opportunity to step back gracefully might not work, "But at least it will take that point out of the way for the historical record, and just might have in it the seeds of prevention of a great conflict."[105]

Those who scoff at the notion of an Anglo-American "special relationship" argue that, during the missile crisis, Macmillan never persuaded Kennedy to do anything important that he would not have otherwise done. But he never had to, because they both shared a common approach to international politics, based on the Churchillian model. During the crisis Kennedy consulted with Macmillan frequently, far more often than with any other foreign leader. The Prime Minister played an important role as a sounding board and a source of support for Kennedy, assuring him that his policy was basically right, promising that the Western alliance would not come apart, validating his cautious instincts in the face of more aggressive advisors. After the crisis was behind them, the two leaders congratulated each other on their close cooperation. Privately, Macmillan expressed the hope that Kennedy now saw him as something more than a caricature out of *Beyond the Fringe*.[106] As Kennedy put it in his last (18 October 1963) message to Macmillan, "I believe that the world is a little more safe and the future of freedom more hopeful than when we began."[107]

They had both been on the same page, a page written by Winston Churchill. Between them, Kennedy, Macmillan, and Tuchman had drawn upon Churchill's books to create a discourse of caution, which enabled the President to navigate an interval of extreme danger. The methodology employed in this chapter is known as "reception history," which involves studying how given readers read and use given texts. Historians find it a useful means of measuring the cultural climate of an era, or tracking the booms and busts of authors' reputations on the literary stock exchange. And occasionally it can help us understand how to avoid nuclear war.

In March 1962 Kennedy had offered to name a Polaris nuclear submarine after Churchill. (Churchill seems to have been genuinely touched, but evidently did not accept.)[108] In April 1963 Kennedy conferred honorary United States citizenship on Churchill, a distinction that Congress had first offered back in 1958. In his note of thanks, Churchill (probably irked by the cancellation of Skybolt) somewhat testily insisted that he represented "a great sovereign state . . . for I reject the view that Britain and the Commonwealth should now be relegated to a tame and minor role in the world."[109] This marked the zenith of the "special relationship," when the two nations were brought together by reciprocal admiration of each other's leaders, each of whom seemed to supply what the other country lacked. Americans were not sure how to handle their newfound global power and the anxieties of the Cold War, and Churchill offered experienced mentorship in combating totalitarianism. Kennedy offered youth, vigor, and vision, qualities conspicuously missing in the British political establishment at that time. In October 1961 his approval rating in Britain (61 to 10 percent) was considerably better than Macmillan's (55 to 33 percent). A full 75 percent endorsed Kennedy's handling of the Cuban Missile Crisis – at least after it was over.[110] The British people subconsciously treated Kennedy as their President too, only becoming fully aware of their attachment when he was gone. Noël Coward, reduced to tears, called the assassination "a lethal blow to the future."[111] "We have lost our champion," mourned the *Daily Mirror*. "Beyond doubt President Kennedy was the man the British people would have chosen if they had had the right to choose," affirmed the *Sunday Times*. In 1969 the Gallup poll asked UK respondents to name "The Man of the Decade," and Kennedy was the clear winner, with Churchill a distant second.[112] Like Churchill, Kennedy had planned to compose a history of his own administration, relying on ghostwriters and researchers (Theodore Sorensen and Arthur Schlesinger), and again like Churchill, he said that history would treat him well "because I intend to write it!"[113] The Kennedy family's first choice for an author to chronicle the life of JFK was Randolph Churchill, who was then working on his father's vast biography, but he died well before he could start the one project or finish the other.[114]

In old age Churchill continued to attend the theatre, even when he could no longer hear the lines. Just months before his last illness, he enjoyed watching Sarah perform on stage in Ernest Vajda's *Fata Morgana*. When he fell into his final coma, she recalled, he remained an artist to the end: "Sometimes his hand would begin to move in painting gestures, and we would know that he was happy. Needless to say, we wondered what particular scene was crossing his mind."[115]

As every observer noted, Churchill's state funeral on 30 January 1965 was his greatest performance, the kind of spectacle usually reserved for royalty. Breaking precedent, the Queen and the royal family were in attendance. With some show business friends, Noël Coward watched the whole four-hour pageant on television, "in floods of proud tears most of the time. No other race could have done so great a tribute with so little pomposity and so much dignity."[116] Though Coward did not say it, it was also the grand finale of the British Empire. In that performance Churchill won what he had always sought: it was watched by the largest American television audience up to that point in history, larger even than John F. Kennedy's funeral in 1963.[117] In his condolence note to the Queen, Charles de Gaulle chose exactly the right epitaph: "In the great drama he was the greatest of all."[118]

Following his death, Churchill's legacy in American political discourse became more complicated and mixed. The Munich Analogy was still frequently invoked, but (in the wake of *The Guns of August*) so too was the Sarajevo

Analogy. As the Vietnam War escalated, President Lyndon Johnson told a press conference, "I don't want to repeat Mr. Churchill's phrase of 'blood, sweat, and tears,' " – but he did warn that "it is not going to be easy, and it not going to be short." By 1968 Churchill's V-sign had been adopted by anti-war activists and redoubled by Richard Nixon, the latter waving both hands at once. Now it was Nixon's turn to run "on the Churchill ticket," comparing his surprising political comeback to the "return from the Wilderness." Nixon admired Churchill's war writings, which he compared to Tolstoy's, but in Vietnam neither he nor Johnson ever pursued a Churchillian victory-at-all costs policy. It was actually Churchill's advocacy of détente with the Soviets that Henry Kissinger thought worth emulating.[119]

Churchill was less frequently invoked during the relatively placid intervals between the end of the Vietnam War (1975) and the Soviet invasion of Afghanistan (1979), and again between the First Iraq War (1990–91) and 9/11, but his myth remained potent. Though the SALT II treaty of 1979 represented what Churchill had yearned for in the 1950s, after he signed it Jimmy Carter insisted on walking in the rain, rather than using a Chamberlainesque umbrella. And when the Russians rolled into Afghanistan, Carter would once again point to Munich. In his first term Ronald Reagan compared his promotion of "Star Wars" to Churchill's support for radar, and indeed they did share a fascination with futuristic military technology. But in his second term, when he was negotiating an end to the Cold War with Mikhail Gorbachev, Reagan more often cited Churchill the summiteer and parleyer. During the First Iraq War the first President Bush often compared Saddam Hussein to Hitler, though one could argue that Bush himself had committed the folly of appeasement. (Eight days before the invasion of Kuwait, US ambassador April Glaspie told the Iraqi dictator that Bush wanted to improve relations and took no position on his border dispute with Kuwait.)

The second President Bush inevitably echoed Churchill in his 20 September 2001 speech declaring war against Al-Qaeda. His advisor Karen Hughes had a Churchillian quotation ("I was not the lion, but it fell to me to give the lion's roar") posted near her desk. At the time (reported the *New York Times*) the President's speechwriters were in the dark about the enemy and the administration's battle plans, and "knowing little increased their natural tendency to sound like Churchill, whose writing they all liked. . . . The computer screen filled with rolling triads."[120] After 9/11 any number of American politicians compared Tony Blair to Churchill – and probably did him no favor. When Condoleezza Rice worried that Blair's support for the Second Iraq War was making him unpopular at home, President Bush could not believe that the British people would vote out a Prime Minister who had led them to victory. "Remember Churchill," she gently noted.[121]

While everyone quoted Churchill, the New York Mayor, Rudolph Giuliani, stood out as the American political figure who most closely modeled himself after the great Briton, and he may have understood him better than most. Giuliani studied Churchill's books as carefully as Kennedy had, and he adopted a very similar persona – flamboyant, iron-willed, hyperbolic, combative, often impulsive and (hence) often wrong, but ultimately redeemed by a superb performance in a moment of extreme crisis. "I also thought about him a lot when I went for mayor back in 1993," he recalled in February 2002, "the way he had revived the spirit of the British people when it was down, and I used that for what I had to do. New York was floundering under too much crime and dirt. I knew the press thought it was over-dramatising the situation, to compare it to Britain during the war," and in retrospect Giuliani granted that New York in 1993 was not quite as dangerous as London in 1940. Nevertheless, "I used Churchill to teach me how to reinvigorate the spirit of a dying nation, and after the [11 September] attack, I'd talk to him. During the worst days of the Battle of Britain, Churchill never stepped out of Downing Street and said: 'I don't know what to do', or, 'I'm lost'. He walked out with a direction, a purpose, even if he had to fake it."[122] Giuliani grasped Churchill's prime insight, outlined in "The Scaffolding of Rhetoric" – that the most effective politics is the theatre of sincerity, where one believes absolutely in the role one is playing, even if it involves exaggeration for effect.

So Churchill, who modeled his politics on literature, has become the prime literary model for politicians on both sides of the Atlantic, probably more so in the United States. We must also recognize that his individual artistic vision, when applied to public policy, gave him the ability to be brilliantly right when everyone else was wrong and astoundingly wrong when everyone else was right. That, perhaps, is the definition of genius. His life demonstrates that literature matters, more than we think and in more ways than we imagine. Every important political decision Churchill made was influenced by literary imperatives. What he read and what he wrote made all the difference in two moments of ultimate global peril, when everything was at stake. It mattered enormously that John F. Kennedy was a dedicated reader of Winston Churchill – and that Franklin Roosevelt was not. And Churchill should provoke us to ask an unsettling question about ourselves: When we engage in politics, are we thinking rationally, or are we performing some story, remembered or forgotten, that we read long ago?

Notes

Abbreviations

This book relies so much on the comprehensive biographical series by Randolph S. Churchill and Martin Gilbert, *Winston S. Churchill* (Boston, MA: Houghton Mifflin, 1966–), that references to it simply give the volume and page numbers: e.g. 3:487. The companion volumes of documents are referenced thus: 5C2 would be the second companion volume of the fifth volume of the biography. Works by Winston Churchill have these abbreviations:

CE *The Collected Essays of Sir Winston Churchill*, ed. Michael Wolff (London: Library of Imperial History, 1976).
CS *Winston S. Churchill: His Complete Speeches, 1897–1963*, ed. Robert Rhodes James (New York: Chelsea House, 1974).
GC *Great Contemporaries* (New York: G. P. Putnam's Sons, 1937).
HESP *A History of the English-Speaking Peoples* (New York: Dodd, Mead, 1956–58).
IHM *Ian Hamilton's March* (London: Longmans, Green, 1900).
LLP *London to Ladysmith via Pretoria* (London: Longmans, Green, 1900).
LRC *Lord Randolph Churchill* (London and New York: Macmillan, 1906).
M *Marlborough* (Chicago, IL: University of Chicago Press, 2002).
MAJ *My African Journey* (London: Hodder and Stoughton, 1908).
MEL *My Early Life* (New York: Charles Scribner's Sons, 1958).
PR *The People's Rights* (London: Jonathan Cape, 1970).
RW *The River War* (London: Longmans, Green, 1899).
S *Savrola* (New York: Longmans, Green, 1900).
SBS *Step by Step, 1936–1939* (London: Thornton Butterworth, 1939).
SMFF *The Story of the Malakand Field Force* (London and Bombay: Longmans, Green, 1901).
SWW *The Second World War* (Boston, MA: Houghton Mifflin, 1985).
TA *Thoughts and Adventures* (London: Thornton Butterworth, 1932).
WC *The World Crisis* (New York: Charles Scribner's Sons, 1923–29).
WES *While England Slept* (New York: G. P. Putnam's Sons, 1938).
WP *The Churchill War Papers*, ed. Martin Gilbert (New York and London: W. W. Norton, 1985–).

The Churchill Archives Centre at Churchill College Cambridge is divided into the Chartwell Papers (up to the end of his first term as Prime Minister, 26 July 1945) and the Churchill Papers (thereafter), designated CHAR and CHUR. Other archives consulted include:

CSS Charles Scribner's Sons Archives, Manuscripts Division, Department of Rare Books and Special Collections, Princeton University Library, NJ.
HGW H. G. Wells Papers, Rare Book and Manuscript Library, University of Illinois, Urbana-Champaign.

HIR Ministry of Information, *Home Intelligence Reports on Opinion and Morale, 1940–1944* (Brighton: Harvester Microform, 1979).
JFK John F. Kennedy Presidential Library and Museum, Boston, MA.
MO *The Tom Harrisson Mass-Observation Archive* (Brighton: Harvester Microform, 1983).

Preface: A Literary History of Politics

1. R. James Woolsey, "Where's the Posse?" *Wall Street Journal*, 25 February 2002, p. A20.
2. Denis MacShane, "Une entente (pas très) cordiale," *Financial Times*, 28–29 February 2004, p. W5. Philip Delves Broughton, "Monsieur Triple Espresso," *Wall Street Journal*, 10 June 2005, p. A8.
3. Manfred Weidhorn, *Sword and Pen: A Survey of the Writings of Sir Winston Churchill* (Albuquerque, NM: University of New Mexico Press, 1974). Paul K. Alkon, *Winston Churchill's Imagination* (Lewisburg, PA: Bucknell University Press, 2006). David Reynolds, *In Command of History: Churchill Fighting and Writing the Second World War* (London: Penguin, 2004). Peter Clarke, *Mr. Churchill's Profession* (London: Bloomsbury, 2011).
4. Kevin J. Hayes, *The Road to Monticello: The Life and Mind of Thomas Jefferson* (Oxford: Oxford University Press, 2008).
5. Ruth Clayton Windscheffel, *Reading Gladstone* (Houndmills: Palgrave Macmillan, 2008).
6. Timothy W. Ryback, *Hitler's Private Library: The Books That Shaped His Life* (New York: Knopf, 2008). s
7. Peter Catterall, "The Prime Minister and His Trollope: Reading Harold Macmillan's Reading," *Cercles*, Occasional Paper No. 1 (2004).
8. John D. Fair, "The Intellectual JFK: Lessons in Statesmanship from British History," *Diplomatic History* 30 (January 2006), 119–42.
9. James T. Kloppenberg, *Reading Obama: Dreams, Hope and the American Political Tradition* (Princeton, NJ: Princeton University Press, 2011).
10. Mark Feeney, *Nixon at the Movies: A Book about Belief* (Chicago, IL: University of Chicago Press, 2004).

1 The Theatre Rage

1. 1C:152–56, 159.
2. A. E. Wilson, *Penny Plain Two Pence Coloured: A History of the Juvenile Drama* (London: George G. Harrap, 1932), 26, 72.
3. CHAR 1/54/92; 1/69/25; 1/92/5; 1/106/57, 84, 125, 147; 1/110/32, 107, 126; 1/116/61, 69, 84; 1/122/113; 1/311/5–13; 1/334/1–3; 1/336/108–11.
4. 1C:101–04, 128–30, 143, 145, 147, 166, 172–75, 853. Lady Randolph Churchill to Lord Randolph Churchill, 13 February 1885, CHAR 28/99/34–36.
5. John S. Churchill to Lord Randolph Churchill, 23 October 1887, CHAR 28/29/3.
6. Ralph G. Martin, *Jennie: The Life of Lady Randolph Churchill* (Englewood Cliffs, NJ: Prentice-Hall, 1969–71), 1:10–12.
7. CHAR 28/4/32–33; 28/6/28; 28/10/9; 28/12/46, 49A; 28/94/15–16, 81–86, 95–97; 28/96/29–31, 34–35, 58–60; 28/99/7–9, 38–40; 28/101/5–6, 24–25.
8. Martin, *Jennie*, 2:332–36.
9. *The Diary of Beatrice Webb*, eds. Norman and Jeanne MacKenzie (Cambridge, MA: Harvard University Press, 1983), 2:122, 30 July 1897.
10. Max Beerbohm, "1880," in *The Works of Max Beerbohm* (New York: Dood, Mead, 1922), 46–54.
11. R. F. Foster, *Lord Randolph Churchill: A Political Life* (Oxford: Clarendon Press, 1981), 76–78.
12. Robert Rhodes James, *Lord Randolph Churchill* (London: Weidenfeld and Nicolson, 1959), 102–06.
13. Foster, *Randolph Churchill*, 107.
14. Ibid., 413.
15. James, *Randolph Churchill*, 115–17.
16. Ibid., 136–38.
17. Ibid., 247.
18. Foster, *Randolph Churchill*, 174, 219–20.
19. James, *Randolph Churchill*, 190.
20. John Beattie Crozier, *Lord Randolph Churchill: A Study of English Democracy* (London: Swan Sonnenschein, Lowrey, 1887), esp. chs. 5 and 8.
21. James, *Randolph Churchill*, 159.
22. LRC 1:276–77.
23. LRC 1:332.

24. LRC 1:375.
25. J. M. Barrie, *Better Dead* (London: Swan Sonnenschein, Lowrey, 1888), ch. 8.
26. Lady Randolph Churchill to Lord Randolph Churchill, 10 January 1883, CHAR 28/98/34.
27. Lady Randolph Churchill to Lord Randolph Churchill, 2 January 1885, CHAR 28/99/27–29.
28. 1C:200.
29. Foster, *Randolph Churchill*, 299–320.
30. 2C1:436.
31. MEL 32.
32. MEL 46–48.
33. Walter Henry Thompson, *Assignment: Churchill* (New York: Farrar, Straus and Young, 1955), 94.
34. Elaine Hadley, *Melodramatic Tactics: Theatricalized Dissent in the English Marketplace, 1800–1885* (Stanford, CA: Stanford University Press, 1995), esp. ch. 3.
35. Michael R. Booth, *English Melodrama* (London: Herbert Jenkins, 1965), 14–18. This convention was spoofed in the animated cartoon character Dudley Do-Right, a noble but dim Canadian Mountie who is unfailingly oblivious to the obvious evildoing of his nemesis, Snidely Whiplash.
36. Booth, *English Melodrama*, 45–46, 62–63.
37. Wilson, *Penny Plain*, 17–19.
38. Peter Brooks, *The Melodramatic Imagination: Balzac, Henry James, Melodrama, and the Mode of Excess* (New Haven, CT, and London: Yale University Press, 1976), 47.
39. 1C:208.
40. *The Times* (4 August 1890), p. 10.
41. Richard Allen Cave, "Staging the Irishman," in *Acts of Supremacy: The British Empire and the Stage*, ed. J. S. Bratton (Manchester: Manchester University Press, 1991), 99–100.
42. Bratton, *Acts of Supremacy*, 40, 57, 90.
43. 1C:668–69.
44. Bernard Shaw, *Complete Plays with Prefaces* (New York: Dodd, Mead, 1962), 2:914. GC 40.
45. 1C: 976. Also WSC to Ivor Guest, 25 October 1898, Malcolm S. Forbes Collection.
46. Robert Rhodes James, *Victor Cazalet: A Portrait* (London: Hamish Hamilton, 1976), 129.
47. 1C:1041.
48. Bernard Shaw, *Our Theatres in the Nineties* (London: Constable, 1954), 1:283.
49. That Churchill was familiar with *The Devil's Disciple* is not certain but very probable, given his admiration for Shaw as a playwright.
50. MEL 45. Joseph Donohue, *Fantasies of Empire: The Empire Theatre of Varieties and the Licensing Controversy of 1894* (Iowa City, IA: University of Iowa Press, 2005), 50–56.
51. John M. Mackenzie, *Propaganda and Empire: The Manipulation of British Public Opinion, 1880–1960* (Manchester: Manchester University Press, 1984), ch. 2. Booth, *English Melodrama*, 146–47.
52. Mahatma Gandhi, *Collected Works* (Delhi: Publications Division, Ministry of Information and Broadcasting, Government of India, 1958–94), 17:79, 86.
53. For the conventions of the genre, see Michael Booth, "Soldiers of the Queen: Drury Lane Imperialism," in Michael Hays and Anastasia Nikolopoulou, eds., *Melodrama: The Cultural Emergence of a Genre* (New York: St. Martin's Press, 1996), 3–20.
54. 1C:301.
55. Jules Verne, *Michael Strogoff* (London and New York: Samuel French, n.d.), 49.
56. *Pall Mall Gazette* (4 August 1890).
57. Shaw, *Theatres in the Nineties*, 1:94.
58. Ibid., 1:206.
59. These types are outlined in Michael R. Booth, *Theatre in the Victorian Age* (Cambridge: Cambridge University Press, 1991), 150–69.
60. 1C:527–28.
61. MEL 50–59. For a complete history of the controversy, see Donohue, *Fantasies of Empire*.
62. 1C:526, 530, 532–33.
63. Vyvyan Holland, introduction, *The Complete Works of Oscar Wilde* (New York: Harper & Row, 1989), 11.
64. Lady Randolph Churchill to Oscar Wilde, 6 May 1888, Harry Ransom Research Center, Oscar Wilde Papers 2/10.
65. Jennie Churchill, *The Reminiscences of Lady Randolph Churchill* (New York: Century, 1908), 280–83.
66. Thompson, *Assignment: Churchill*, 252.
67. WC 4:30.
68. GC 38.
69. 1C:625–29.
70. *Truth* 39 (21 May 1896):1276–78; (11 June 1896):1494–96; (18 June 1896):1565–66.

71. *Truth* 39 (25 June 1896):1629–31.
72. *Truth* 40 (23 July 1896):209; (30 July 1896):275; (10 September 1896):637; (1 October 1896):824–26; (8 October 1896):890–93; (15 October 1896):941–42; (22 October 1896):1023–26; (29 October 1896):1080; (19 November 1896):1302–03.
73. *Truth* 40 (23 July 1896):210.
74. *Truth* 40 (3 September 1896):594–96.
75. *Truth* 46 (23 November 1899):1251.
76. CS 2010.
77. CS 7665.
78. 1C:816–21.
79. Oscar Wilde, "The Decay of Lying," in *The Soul of Man under Socialism and Selected Critical Prose*, ed. Linda Dowling (London: Penguin, 2001), 174.
80. Ibid., 179–83.
81. 1C:813.
82. Margaret D. Stetz, "The Love That Dared Not Speak *His* Name: Literary Responses to the Wilde Trials," in *Bound for the 1890s: Essays on Writing and Publishing in Honor of James G. Nelson*, ed. Jonathan Allison (High Wycombe: Rivendale Press, 2006), 45–63.

2 An Uneducated Man

1. Violet Bonham Carter, *Winston Churchill: An Intimate Portrait* (New York: Harcourt, Brace & World, 1965), 210.
2. MEL 13, 23.
3. CS 904.
4. CS 7745.
5. MEL 38.
6. MEL 41–42.
7. MEL 38–39, 113.
8. John Charmley, *Churchill: The End of Glory* (London: Hodder & Stoughton, 1993), 55.
9. Dwight D. Eisenhower, "Churchill as an Ally in War," in *Churchill by his Contemporaries*, ed. Charles Eade (London: Hutchinson, 1953), 197.
10. Ralph G. Martin, *Jennie: The Life of Lady Randolph Churchill* (Englewood Cliffs, NJ: Prentice-Hall, 1969–71), 1:15–16. Anne Sebba, *American Jennie: The Remarkable Life of Lady Randolph Churchill* (New York and London: W. W. Norton, 2007), 14–15.
11. LRC 1:44.
12. Lord Moran, *Winston Churchill: The Struggle for Survival 1940–1965* (London: Constable, 1966), 440. TA 25.
13. 1C:147.
14. LRC 2:60–71.
15. 1C:218.
16. 1C:666.
17. 1C:922.
18. 5C1:652. Shane Leslie, *The End of a Chapter* (New York: Charles Scribners' Sons, 1916), 122–25.
19. Ulysses S. Grant, *Personal Memoirs of U. S. Grant* (New York: Century, 1903), 2:391–92.
20. RW 2:168, see also 2:349–50.
21. WSC to Milner, 14 March 1901, quoted in Paul Addison, *Churchill on the Home Front 1900–1955* (London: Pimlico, 1993), 18.
22. CS 66.
23. MEL 301.
24. 1C:669.
25. 4C:1849–50, 1853, 1857.
26. WP 3:1651.
27. 7:1073–74.
28. 5C2:912.
29. MEL 109–13, 116.
30. 1C:776.
31. Addison, *Churchill on the Home Front*, 414–15.
32. Edward Gibbon, *The Decline and Fall of the Roman Empire* (New York: Modern Library, n.d.), 8.
33. Ibid., 36–50.
34. Thomas Babington Macaulay, *Warren Hastings* (London: Macmillan, 1893), 9–10.
35. Ibid., 25–31.
36. MEL 115.

37. CE 2:80.
38. Winwood Reade, *The Martyrdom of Man* (Honolulu: University Press of the Pacific, 2004), 412–14.
39. WSC, "Foreword to the Biographical Dictionary of the British Empire," undated TS, CHAR 8/556/14–16.
40. MEL 113–15.
41. 1:151. The quotation is from Benjamin Disraeli, *Endymion* (London: Longmans, Green, 1880), 3:135.
42. 1C:711–12.
43. 1C:712–14.
44. MEL 115.
45. 1C:724–25.
46. 1C:907.
47. 1C:759–60, 1031.
48. 2C:xxvi–xxvii.
49. MEL 115–16.
50. Jonathan Rose, *The Edwardian Temperament 1895–1919* (Athens, OH: Ohio University Press, 1895), esp. ch. 1.
51. MEL 115–17.
52. 1C:726, 728.
53. 1C:996. See also 1C:688, 691, 731, 738, 1002.
54. Algernon West, *Private Diaries of the Rt. Hon. Sir Algernon West, G.C.B.*, ed. Horace G. Hutchinson (New York: E. P. Dutton, 1922), 344.
55. Madhusree Mukerjee, *Churchill's Secret War: The British Empire and the Ravaging of India during World War II* (New York: Basic Books, 2010), 204; and Arthur Herman, *Gandhi and Churchill* (New York: Bantam, 2009), 108.
56. SMFF 139.
57. CE 4:473–74, 490.
58. G. R. Searle, *Eugenics and Politics in Britain 1900–1914* (Leyden: Noordhoff International Publishing, 1976). Richard A. Soloway, *Demography and Degeneration: Eugenics and the Declining Birthrate in Twentieth-Century Britain* (Chapel Hill, NC, and London: University of North Carolina Press, 1990).

3 A Pushing Age

1. Lord Moran, *Churchill: The Struggle for Survival 1940–1965* (London: Constable, 1966), 123.
2. 1C:413–14.
3. 1C:499–500.
4. MEL 12–13, 77.
5. Robert Rhodes James, *Lord Randolph Churchill* (London: Weidenfeld and Nicolson, 1959), 319.
6. 1C:253–54.
7. 1C:619–22.
8. Richard Ellmann, *Oscar Wilde* (New York: Knopf, 1988), 158.
9. CS 6031.
10. GC 35–38, see also CS 686–87.
11. Philip Waller, *Readers, Writers, and Reputations: Literary Life in Britain 1870–1918* (Oxford: Oxford University Press, 2008), 348–56.
12. Kevin Barnhurst and John Nerone discuss this point in "US Newspaper Types, the Newsroom, and the Division of Labor, 1750–2000," *Journalism Studies* 4:4 (2003), 435–49.
13. Karen Roggenkamp, *Narrating the News: New Journalism and Literary Genre in Late Nineteenth-Century American Newspapers and Fiction* (Kent, OH, and London: Kent State University Press, 2005), ch. 2.
14. Michael Schudson, *Discovering the News: A Social History of American Newspapers* (New York: Basic Books, 1978), 89.
15. Roggenkamp, *Narrating the News*, xii–xvi. Though Schudson and Roggenkamp focus on American newspapers, the New Journalism was also a very British phenomenon: see Andrew Griffiths, "Winston Churchill, the *Morning Post*, and the End of the Imperial Romance," *Victorian Periodicals Review* 46 (Summer 2013), 163–83.
16. 1C:675–76.
17. 1C:754–56.
18. 1C:781.

19. 1C:796–97.
20. 1C:784.
21. 1C:808–09.
22. 1C:811–14.
23. 1C:824.
24. 1C:833–34.
25. 1C:839–40.
26. Frederick Woods, ed., *Young Winston's Wars: The Original Despatches of Winston S. Churchill, War Correspondent, 1897–1900* (New York: Viking, 1973).
27. CE 1:23.
28. 1C:906.
29. SMFF 142.
30. SMFF vii.
31. SMFF 4.
32. SMFF 14.
33. SMFF 43.
34. SMFF 47–49.
35. SMFF 172.
36. 1C:864.
37. Paul Fussell, *The Great War and Modern Memory* (London: Oxford University Press, 1975), ch. 6.
38. Glenn R. Wilkinson, *Depictions and Images of War in Edwardian Newspapers, 1899–1914* (Basingstoke: Palgrave Macmillan, 2003), ch. 5.
39. SMFF 299–300.
40. 1C:792–93.
41. SMFF 140–41.
42. Woods, *Young Winston's Wars*, 16.
43. Edward Ziter, *The Orient on the Victorian Stage* (Cambridge: Cambridge University Press, 2003), 1–3.
44. Michael Booth, "Soldiers of the Queen: Drury Lane Imperialism," in *Melodrama: The Cultural Emergence of a Genre*, ed. Michael Hays and Anastasia Nikolopoulou (New York: St. Martin's Press, 1996), 9–10.
45. SMFF 223.
46. RW 1:18–19.
47. SMFF 6–7.
48. Woods, *Young Winston's Wars*, 149.
49. SMFF 40–41.
50. SMFF 123.
51. SMFF 139.
52. In *The Yearbook of Railway Literature* (Chicago, IL: Railway Age, 1897), preface.
53. 1C:851–52.
54. 1C:862.
55. 1C:880.
56. 1C:874.
57. 1C:863–64.
58. 1C:893–900.
59. 1C:913–14.
60. 1C:881–82.
61. MEL 154–56.
62. 1C:922, 927.
63. 1C:971.
64. MEL 161–67.
65. 1:378–79.
66. 1C:950–51.
67. MEL 161–62.
68. H. John Field, *Toward a Programme of Imperial Life: The British Empire at the Turn of the Century* (Westport, CT: Greenwood Press, 1982), 169.
69. 1C:856.
70. 1C:807.
71. 1C:788.
72. 1C:810–11.

4 War of the Worlds

1. Frederick Woods, ed., *Young Winston's Wars: The Original Despatches of Winston S. Churchill, War Correspondent, 1897–1900* (New York: Viking, 1973), 69.
2. Ibid., 84.
3. Ibid., 78.
4. Ibid., 101.
5. Ibid., 120.
6. RW 2:142.
7. Woods, *Young Winston's Wars*, 109.
8. Ibid., 112, 121.
9. Ibid., 122–23.
10. Ibid., 131.
11. Ibid., 124–28.
12. Ibid., 139–40.
13. Ibid., 137–38.
14. SMFF 36–37.
15. Woods, *Young Winston's Wars*, 95.
16. Ibid., 128–29.
17. See Aaron L. Friedberg, *Weary Titan: Britain and the Experience of Relative Decline, 1895–1905* (Princeton, NJ: Princeton University Press, 2010).
18. Woods, *Young Winston's Wars*, 133.
19. RW 1:18–19.
20. MEL 6.
21. Richard Toye, *Churchill's Empire: The World That Made Him and the World He Made* (New York: Henry Holt, 2010), 16–25.
22. 5C1:211.
23. Shane Leslie, *Long Shadows* (London: John Murray, 1966), 18.
24. Shane Leslie, *The End of a Chapter* (New York: Charles Scribner's Sons, 1916), 120.
25. 5C2:465.
26. H. Rider Haggard, *King Solomon's Mines* (London: Cassell, 1907), 13–16, 210.
27. Robert Fraser, *Book History through Postcolonial Eyes* (New York: Routledge, 2008), 174–76.
28. RW 1:25.
29. RW 1:26–28.
30. RW 1:65.
31. RW 1:31–36.
32. 1C:1002.
33. RW 1:36–56.
34. RW 1:118–19.
35. RW 1:148–50.
36. RW 1:169.
37. RW 2:161–62.
38. Ronald I. Cohen, *Bibliography of the Writings of Sir Winston Churchill* (London and New York: Thoemmes Continuum, 2006), 35–39.
39. MAJ 125.
40. RW 2:195.
41. RW 2:196–97.
42. RW 2:174.
43. RW 2:195–215.
44. RW 2:394–95.
45. 2C:xxv–xxvi.
46. Toye, *Churchill's Empire*, 55–59.
47. Bernard Porter, *Critics of Empire: British Radical Attitudes to Colonialism in Africa 1895–1914* (London: Macmillan, 1968).
48. Richard Fulton, "The Sudan Sensation of 1898," *Victorian Periodicals Review* 42 (Spring 2009), 37–63.
49. Cohen, *Bibliography*, 1:47–64.
50. MEL 171.
51. MAJ 84–85.
52. MAJ 62–63.
53. MAJ 204–07.
54. MAJ 86–92.

55. Lytton Strachey, *Eminent Victorians* (London: Penguin, 1986), 209–13.
56. CE 3:73–75.

5 A Portrait of the Artist

1. 1C:779.
2. 1C:931.
3. 1C:913.
4. S 47.
5. Lord Moran, *Churchill: The Struggle for Survival 1940–1965* (London: Constable, 1966), 328.
6. S 117.
7. S 29.
8. S 14.
9. S 166.
10. S 238.
11. S 332.
12. S 278.
13. S 241.
14. S 313–14.
15. S 307.
16. S 88.
17. 1C:825.
18. S 146; 1C:825.
19. S 87–89.
20. Anthony Hope, *The Prisoner of Zenda* (Champaign, IL: Book Jungle, n.d.), 63, 64, 94.
21. Ibid., 106, 107, 119.
22. GC 103.
23. S 154–55.
24. *New York Times Book Review* (10 February 1900), 2.
25. 1C:990.
26. S 188.
27. Maurice Ashley, *Churchill as Historian* (London: Secker & Warburg, 1968), 36–38.
28. WSC to Greenhaugh Smith, 12 July 1916, CHAR 8/33.
29. Quoted in Ronald I. Cohen, *Bibliography of the Writings of Sir Winston Churchill* (London and New York: Thoemmes Continuum, 2006), 66.
30. MEL 154.
31. MEL 212–13.
32. 1:497–500.
33. 2C1:181.
34. LRC 2:130.
35. 5C:856–57.
36. MEL 201.
37. Ernest Rhys to WSC, 23 June 1906, CHAR 8/24.
38. 1C:776.
39. 1C:877.
40. 3C2:1151.
41. Shane Leslie, *The End of a Chapter* (New York: Charles Scribner's Sons, 1916), 78.
42. Ibid., 112–13.
43. CHAR 8/7/3–4.
44. S 106–11.
45. 1C:815.
46. Cohen, *Bibliography*, 1292–93.
47. A. P. Watt to WSC, 28 April 1908, CHAR 8/28.
48. Cohen, *Bibliography*, 71–80.
49. This edition is not listed in Cohen's bibliography. It is described in Robert Compton, "A Study of the Translations of Lin Shu, 1852–1924" (PhD diss., Stanford University, 1971), 401–02. Compton did not recognize it as Churchill's book, since the author is transliterated as "Cecixiluo" and the title is "Can chan ye sheng lu." But the plot summary and the identification of the author as an English MP confirm that it is *Savrola*. The Chinese title is a poetic allusion to a cicada who flits from branch to branch – that is, a woman who is unfaithful to her husband and will soon be swept away by events, which fairly sums up Lucile. I thank Christopher Reed, James Soren Edgren, and Bai Di for illuminating these points.

50. S 118–19.
51. S 119–20.
52. S 115–16.
53. S 114–15, 123.
54. George Orwell, "Prophecies of Fascism," in *The Collected Essays, Journalism and Letters of George Orwell*, ed. Sonia Orwell and Ian Angus (New York: Harcourt, Brace & World, 1968), 2:30–33.

6 Publicity Capital

1. 1:437.
2. Lionel James, *High Pressure* (London: John Murray, 1929), 87–88.
3. G. W. Steevens, "The Youngest Man in Europe," in *Churchill by His Contemporaries*, ed. Charles Eade (London: Hutchinson, 1953), 64.
4. 1C:1050–51, 1054–55.
5. LLP 8.
6. MEL 59.
7. MEL 242–44.
8. J. B. Atkins, *Incidents and Reflections* (London: Christophers, 1947), 127–30.
9. Aylmer Haldane, *A Soldier's Saga* (Edinburgh and London: Blackwood, 1948), 147.
10. Violet Bonham Carter, *Churchill: An Intimate Portrait* (New York: Harcourt, Brace & World, 1965), 36–37.
11. 1:461–67.
12. MEC 259–60.
13. LLP 157.
14. 1C:1101–02.
15. Frederick Woods, ed., *Young Winston's Wars: The Original Despatches of Winston S. Churchill, War Correspondent, 1897–1900* (New York: Viking, 1973), 178.
16. 1:468–69.
17. MEL 263–67.
18. 1:470–74.
19. Karen Roggenkamp, *Narrating the News: New Journalism and Literary Genre in Late Nineteenth-Century American Newspapers and Fiction* (Kent, OH, and London: Kent State University Press, 2005), ch. 4.
20. Martin Meisel, *Shaw and the Nineteenth-Century Theater* (Princeton, NJ: Princeton University Press, 1963), 191–94.
21. Quoted in Brian Roberts, *Churchills in Africa* (New York: Taplinger, 1970), 241.
22. MEL 273, CE 4:221.
23. MEL 290.
24. Woods, *Young Winston's Wars*, 187–88.
25. MEL 296, 298.
26. LLP 247.
27. MEL 352.
28. 1C:1158.
29. 1C:1159.
30. 1C:1176.
31. 1C:1184.
32. 1C:1189–90.
33. Philip Waller, *Readers, Writers, and Reputations: Literary Life in Britain 1870–1918* (Oxford: Oxford University Press, 2008), 12, 635.
34. Shane Leslie, *Long Shadows* (London: John Murray, 1966), 23–24.
35. MEL 213.
36. Andrew Horrall, *Popular Culture in London c.1890–1918: The Transformation of Entertainment* (Manchester and New York: Manchester University Press, 2001), 2–4.
37. Sarah Churchill, *A Thread in the Tapestry* (New York: Dodd, Mead, 1967), 71.
38. Richard Toye, *Churchill's Empire: The World That Made Him and the World He Made* (New York: Henry Holt, 2010), 74.
39. Waller, *Readers, Writers, and Reputations*, ch. 25.
40. 1C:1204.
41. 1C:1206.
42. CS 74–75.
43. 1C:1070, Churchill's emphasis.

7 Things to Come

1. R. F. Foster, *Lord Randolph Churchill* (Oxford: Clarendon Press, 1981), 294.
2. Roy Jenkins, *Churchill* (New York: Farrar, Straus & Giroux, 2001), 20–21.
3. Violet Bonham Carter, *Winston Churchill: An Intimate Portrait* (New York: Harcourt, Brace & World, 1965), 5.
4. 5C2:266–67.
5. CE 3:53.
6. 1C:878.
7. H. G. Wells, *Anticipations* (New York and London: Harper & Brothers, 1901), 303.
8. WSC to H. G. Wells, 17 November 1901, C-238-3, HGW.
9. 2C:98–99.
10. WSC to H. G. Wells, 20 November 1901, C-238-4, HGW.
11. WSC to H. G. Wells, 9 October 1906, C-238-2, HGW.
12. WSC to Clementine Churchill, 25 March 1926, in *Winston and Clementine: The Personal Letters of the Churchills*, ed. Mary Soames (Boston, MA: Houghton Mifflin, 1999), 298.
13. 2C:777–81.
14. CE 1:304.
15. TA 181.
16. 3:591–93.
17. 4C:90–92.
18. 4:74.
19. 4C:105–06.
20. 4C:131.
21. WSC to H. G. Wells, 1 October 1916, C-238-7, HGW.
22. WC 2:69–70.
23. 4C:886–93.
24. 4C:1044.
25. CE 2:79–84.
26. H. G. Wells, *Men Like Gods* (New York: Macmillan, 1927), 97–104.
27. 5C2:273.
28. 5C1:148.
29. TA 269–80.
30. 5C1:140, 146.
31. TA 250–51.
32. RW 1:142.
33. RW 1:235.
34. For a survey and critique of this genre, see Martin Bunzl, "Counterfactual History: A User's Guide," *American Historical Review* 109 (June 2004), 845–58.
35. For example, M 2:240, 336, 382–84, 683–85.
36. CE 4:73–84.
37. 8:494.
38. CE 4:397.
39. CE 4:410–26.
40. CE 3:53.
41. 6:158–59. David Edgerton, *Britain's War Machine: Weapons, Resources, and Experts in the Second World War* (Oxford: Oxford University Press, 2011), 89–92, 257–61.
42. 6:165.
43. R. Stuart Macrae, *Winston Churchill's Toyshop* (New York: Walker, 1971), esp. 167–68. See also Gerald Pawle, *The War and Colonel Warden* (New York: Knopf, 1963), 97–102.
44. SWW 2:339–41.
45. CE 1:394.
46. Robert Rhodes James, *Churchill: A Study in Failure, 1900–1939* (New York and Cleveland, OH: World Publishing, 1970), 268.
47. Ibid., 276–77.
48. Lord Moran, *Winston Churchill: The Struggle for Survival 1940–1965* (London: Constable, 1966), 729.
49. Ibid., 74–75.
50. 4C:1253–55.
51. CE 1:396.
52. CE 1:388–90.
53. CE 1:421–27.

54. Peter Carpenter, "Churchill and His 'Technological' College," *Journal of Educational Administration and History* 17 (September 1985), 69–75.

8 Comédie Anglaise

1. Maurice Baring, *The Puppet Show of Memory* (Boston, MA: Little, Brown, 1922), 71.
2. 1:63.
3. 1:109–10.
4. Shane Leslie, *Long Shadows* (London: John Murray, 1966), 21.
5. 5:787–88.
6. 1C:733, 757. CE3:169.
7. 1C:1083.
8. CS 109–10.
9. 2C:9–21.
10. CE 2:427.
11. Robert Rhodes James, ed., *Chips: The Diaries of Sir Henry Channon* (Harmondsworth: Penguin, 1984), 507.
12. William George, *My Brother and I* (London: Eyre & Spottiswoode, 1958), 211.
13. G. K. Chesterton, *Heretics* (London: John Lane, The Bodley Head, 1909), 54–55.
14. Denis Judd, *Radical Joe: A Life of Joseph Chamberlain* (London: Hamish Hamilton, 1977), 242.
15. 1C:916–20.
16. Michael R. Booth, *Theatre in the Victorian Age* (Cambridge: Cambridge University Press, 1991), 164–67.
17. Richard Schickel. *D. W. Griffith and the Birth of Film* (London: Pavilion, 1984), 345
18. 2C:205.
19. CE 3:272–73.
20. CE 4:16–25.
21. *Liberal Magazine* 10 (1902), 609.
22. CS 233–35.
23. 2C:105–11.
24. CS 151.
25. CS 262.
26. CS 293.
27. CS 380–82, 384; 2:88–90.
28. CS 384.
29. CS 671–77.
30. CS 1030.
31. Beatrice Webb to Mary Playne, 2 February 1908; Sidney Webb to Beatrice Webb, 21 February 1908; Beatrice Webb to Mary Playne, 22 February 1908; Beatrice Webb to H. G. Wells, [October 1908], in *The Letters of Sidney and Beatrice Webb*, ed. Norman Mackenzie (Cambridge: Cambridge University Press, 1978), 2:281, 285, 287, 318.
32. CS 993.
33. Chesterton, *Heretics*, 282–84.
34. *Daily Mail*, 5 January 1906, quoted in Violet Bonham Carter, *Winston Churchill: An Intimate Portrait* (New York: Harcourt, Brace & World, 1965), 100–02.
35. Philip Waller, *Readers, Writers, and Reputations: Literary Life in Britain 1870–1918* (Oxford: Oxford University Press, 2008), ch. 15.
36. "Cartoons and Cartoonists", in TA 23–35.
37. H. A. Taylor, *Jix: Viscount Brentford* (London: S. Paul, 1933), 61–62.
38. 5C2:217–18.
39. John Gross, *The Rise and Fall of the Man of Letters* (New York: Macmillan, 1969), ch. 4.
40. Bonham Carter, *Winston Churchill*, 162.
41. *Saturday Review* (29 February 1908), 269. See also Brad Kent, "Censorship and Immorality: Bernard Shaw's *The Devil's Disciple*," *Modern Drama* 54 (Winter 2011), 511–33.
42. Wilfrid Scawen Blunt, *My Diaries* (New York: Knopf, 1921), 3 April 1910, 2:298.
43. Ibid., 31 October 1903, 2:74–75.
44. 2C:441.
45. CS 903–04.
46. CS 905.
47. Ronald Hyam, *Elgin and Churchill at the Colonial Office 1905–1908* (London: Macmillan and New York: St. Martin's Press, 1968), 58.
48. Ibid., 84–89, 95–97. *Hansard*, "Adjournment: Chinese in the Transvaal," 15 November 1906.

49. Hyam, *Elgin and Churchill*, 239–53.
50. Ibid., 491–99.
51. Edward Marsh, *A Number of People* (New York and London: Harper, 1939), 149–50. (Churchill's emphasis.)
52. Paul Addison, *Churchill on the Home Front 1900–1955* (London: Pimlico, 1993), 111–20.
53. 2C:1148–53, 1187–91.
54. WSC to Hermon Ould, 26 October 1933, and accompanying documents, CHAR 2/576A/30–44.
55. 2:374–79.
56. CS 1591–98.
57. CE 4:460.
58. Bonham Carter, *Winston Churchill*, 151.
59. CE 4:460.
60. WSC to François Le Lann, 9 January 1945, CHAR 20/193A/30.
61. Addison, *Churchill on the Home Front*, 123–26. G. R. Searle, *Eugenics and Politics in Britain 1900–1914* (Leyden: Noordhoff International Publishing, 1976), ch. 9.
62. Blanche E. C. Dugdale, *Arthur James Balfour* (London: Hutchinson, 1936), 2:70. (Balfour's emphasis.)
63. J. A. Spender and Cyril Asquith, *Life of Herbert Henry Asquith, Lord Oxford and Asquith* (London: Hutchinson, 1932), 1:329–31.
64. Blunt, *My Diaries*, 3 April 1910, 2:298.
65. CE 4:278–79.
66. Robert Rhodes James, *Churchill: A Study in Failure, 1900–1939* (New York and Cleveland, OH: World Publishing, 1970), 42–43.
67. Lucy Masterman, *C. F. G. Masterman* (London: Frank Cass, 1968), 140–41.
68. 2:393–95, 2C:1032–33.
69. Masterman, *Masterman*, 184.
70. TA 65–72.
71. Masterman, *Masterman*, 165–66.
72. Quoted by Robert Rhodes James, "The Politician," in *Churchill Revised: A Critical Assessment* (New York: Dial Press, 1969), 71.
73. A. G. Gardiner, *Pillars of Society* (London: James Nisbet & Co., 1913), 56.
74. George Dangerfield, *The Strange Death of Liberal England 1910–1914* (New York: G. P. Putnam's Sons, 1961), 88.
75. Gardiner, *Pillars of Society*, 56–58.
76. Ibid., 59.
77. TA 15–18.
78. Gardiner, *Pillars of Society*, 63.

9 On the Stage of History

1. Jan Rüger, *The Great Naval Game: Britain and Germany in the Age of Empire* (Cambridge: Cambridge University Press, 2007), chs. 1–2.
2. Ibid., p. 238.
3. WC 1:63–64.
4. CS 56–58.
5. Niall Ferguson, *The Pity of War: Explaining World War I* (New York: Basic Books, 1999), 1–15.
6. WC 5:370, SWW 2:263.
7. WC 1:125–28.
8. 2:594–608.
9. A. J. Marder, *From the Dreadnought to Scapa Flow: The Royal Navy in the Fisher Era, 1904–1919* (London and New York: Oxford University Press, 1961–70), 1:352–53.
10. Ferguson, *Pity of War*, 87.
11. 3:63–64. (Fisher's emphasis.)
12. David French, "Spy Fever in Britain, 1900–1915," *Historical Journal* 21 (1978), 355–70.
13. David Stafford, *Churchill and Secret Service* (Woodstock, NY: Overlook Press, 1998), ch. 2.
14. "My Spy Story", in TA 87–88.
15. H. H. Asquith to Venetia Stanley, 28 July 1914, in *H. H. Asquith: Letters to Venetia Stanley*, ed. Michael and Eleanor Brock (Oxford and New York: Oxford University Press, 1982), 129.
16. WSC to Clementine Churchill, 28 July 1914, in *Winston and Clementine: The Personal Letters of the Churchills*, ed. Mary Soames (Boston, MA, and New York: Houghton Mifflin, 1999), 96.
17. 3C:850.
18. 3:480.
19. 3C:52.

20. Edward David, ed., *Inside Asquith's Cabinet: From the Diaries of Charles Hobhouse* (New York: St. Martin's Press, 1978), 183.
21. Ibid., 189.
22. WC 2:5.
23. 3:47–51.
24. E. Alexander Powell, *Fighting in Flanders* (New York: Charles Scribner's Sons, 1914), 181–84.
25. Ibid., 184–88.
26. Ibid., 214–15.
27. H. H. Asquith to Venetia Stanley, 13 October 1914, *Letters to Venetia Stanley*, 275–76.
28. 3C:178.
29. David, *Inside Asquith's Cabinet*, 203.
30. Frances Stevenson, *Lloyd George: A Diary*, ed. A. J. P. Taylor (New York: Harper & Row, 1971), 6 (23 October 1914).
31. 3C:177–78.
32. 3C:191.
33. A. J. Marder, ed., *Portrait of an Admiral: The Life and Papers of Sir Herbert Richmond* (Cambridge, MA: Harvard University Press, 1952), 121.
34. 3C:217.
35. 3C:284. (Margot Asquith's emphasis.)
36. Marder, *Dreadnought to Scapa Flow*, 2:178–82.
37. Marder, *Portrait of an Admiral*, 96.
38. Ibid., 98–99.
39. Robert Rhodes James, *Gallipoli* (New York: Macmillan, 1965), 12. Robert Rhodes James, *Churchill: A Study in Failure, 1900–1939* (New York and Cleveland, OH: World Publishing, 1970), 76–79.
40. 3C:341–42.
41. 3C:344–45.
42. Marder, *Dreadnought to Scapa Flow*, 2:187.
43. 3C:346.
44. 3C:354–55.
45. Lord Hankey, *The Supreme Command 1914–1918* (London: George Allen and Unwin, 1961), 265–66.
46. 3:220, 3C:81–83.
47. 3C:95.
48. 3:233.
49. 3C:367, 380.
50. Marder, *Portrait of an Admiral*, 134–35.
51. Robin Prior, *Churchill's World Crisis as History* (Beckenham: Croom Helm, 1983), 51–61.
52. 3C:397.
53. 3:246.
54. Stevenson, *Lloyd George*, 50 (15 May 1915).
55. 3:306–11.
56. 3:314.
57. Violet Bonham Carter, *Winston Churchill: An Intimate Portrait* (New York: Harcourt, Brace & World, 1965), 295.
58. Ibid., 296.
59. Kenneth Harris, *Attlee* (New York and London: W. W. Norton, 1982), 36–37.
60. 3:321–24.
61. WC 2:229.
62. 3C:770.
63. 3C:782.
64. 3C:806.
65. 3C:814.
66. S 147.
67. Bonham Carter, *Churchill: An Intimate Portrait*, 312.
68. Paul Fussell, *The Great War and Modern Memory* (London: Oxford University Press, 1975), 21–23.
69. Gilbert Murray, *Faith, War and Policy: Addresses and Essays on the European War* (Boston, MA, and New York: Houghton Mifflin, 1917), 91–92.
70. 3C:817.
71. George Riddell, *Lord Riddell's War Diary 1914–1918* (London: Ivor Nicholson & Watson, 1933), 82.

72. Quoted in James, *Study in Failure*, 88.
73. 3C:862.
74. 3C:885.
75. 3C:888.
76. Stevenson, *Lloyd George*, 50 (15 May 1915).
77. Riddell, *War Diary*, 89.
78. 3C:976.
79. Cynthia Asquith, *Diaries 1915–1918*, ed. E. M. Horsley (New York: Knopf, 1969), 31 (27 May 1915).
80. WC 2:428.
81. 3C:1081.
82. 3C:850.
83. 3C:1081.
84. CS 2388.
85. 4:895.
86. 3C:1220–24, 1242.
87. 3C:1190.
88. 3C:1329–30.
89. 3C:1334.
90. 3C:1373.
91. 3C:1395–96.
92. 3C:1402.
93. 3C:1479.
94. 3C:1546–47.
95. 3C:1551.
96. Shane Leslie, *The End of a Chapter* (New York: Charles Scribner's Sons, 1916), 120–25.
97. 3C:1553–57.
98. 3C:1530.
99. 3C:1578.
100. 3C:1583.
101. 1:124. Celia Sandys, *From Winston with Love and Kisses: The Young Churchill* (London: Sinclair-Stevenson, 1994), 71.
102. 1C:580, 623–24.
103. 1C:817.
104. "Painting as a Pastime," in TA 306–12.
105. Thomas Bodkin, "Churchill the Artist," in *Churchill by His Contemporaries*, ed. Charles Eade (London: Hutchinson, 1953), 416.
106. 8:1152–54.
107. 3:657–59.
108. Frederic Spotts, *Hitler and the Power of Aesthetics* (Woodstock and New York: Overlook Press, 2009).
109. Bonham Carter, *Churchill: An Intimate Portrait*, 382.
110. 8:142.
111. 4:139–40.
112. Siegfried Sassoon, *Siegfried's Journey 1916–1920* (New York: Viking, 1946), 115–19.
113. GC 38–39.
114. For the neo-Hegelian influences on Shaw, see Robert F. Whitman, *Shaw and the Play of Ideas* (Ithaca, NY, and London: Cornell University Press, 1977).
115. 4C:373. See also his laudatory comments on Philip Gibbs's 1920 account *Realities of War*, which scathingly criticized Douglas Haig and other commanders: "very impressive and terrible, also extremely well written. If it is monotonous in its tale of horror, it is because war is full of inexhaustible horrors." (4C:1058.)
116. CE1:273–74.
117. For instance, Fussell, *Great War*, 21.
118. Cynthia Asquith, *Diaries*, 170.
119. 4C:64.

10 What Actually Happened

1. 4C:50–52.
2. 1C:90–96.
3. 1C:146, 155.

4. 1:110, 113; 1C:175.
5. 1C:726, 730.
6. 1C:835.
7. 2C:71.
8. 1C:903–06.
9. SMFF 36.
10. 1C:933.
11. Maurice Ashley, *Churchill as Historian* (London: Secker & Warburg, 1968), 18.
12. Leslie Howsam, *Past into Print: The Publishing of History in Britain 1850–1950* (London: British Library and Toronto: University of Toronto Press, 2009), 7–8, 26–28.
13. J. R. Seeley, *The Expansion of England* (Cambridge: Cambridge University Press, 1883), 174–75.
14. Howsam, *Past into Print*, 87–88.
15. P. J. Waller, "Robert Ensor, Edwardian Rationalist," *History Today* 37 (January 1987).
16. Herbert Butterfield, *The Historical Novel* (Cambridge: Cambridge University Press, 1924), 15–21.
17. C. Y. McIntire, *Herbert Butterfield: Historian as Dissenter* (New Haven, CT, and London: Yale University Press, 2004), ch. 2.
18. Ashley, *Churchill as Historian*, 22–24.
19. 4C:1562–63.
20. For a detailed account of the distortions, see Robin Prior, *Churchill's "World Crisis" as History* (London: Croom Helm, 1983), esp. chs. 6–10.
21. 5C1:1448–49.
22. 8:274.
23. 8:315.
24. Susan A. Brewer, *To Win the Peace: British Propaganda in the United States during World War II* (Ithaca, NY, and London: Cornell University Press, 1997), 51.
25. HESP 1:66, 432–33, 476; CS 454.
26. CE 1:310.
27. For a rare reference to the workers, "skilled and unskilled, men and women alike, [who] stood to their lathes and manned the workshops under fire as if they were batteries in action – which indeed they were," see SWW2:299–300.
28. 5C3:1456–57.
29. 5C3:1511–12.
30. 5C3:1513–14.
31. TA 255–56.
32. Lord Moran, *Churchill: The Struggle for Survival 1940–65* (London: Constable, 1966), 127.
33. CE 1:365–72.
34. F. W. Deakin, *Churchill the Historian* (Zurich: Schweizerischen Winston Churchill Stiftung, 1969), 1.
35. Gordon A. Craig, "Churchill and Germany," in Robert Black and W. Roger Louis, eds., *Churchill* (New York: Norton, 1993), 22.
36. HESP 1:21, 206, 400–09, 2:iii, 178, 192–93, 225, 291, 378. See also references to Ranke in CE3:294–95.
37. WC 1:513.
38. M 1:310.
39. M 1:111.
40. M 1:296.
41. M 1:116, 135, 372.
42. 5C2:721.
43. 5C2:723–24.
44. Natalie Zemon Davis, "On the Lame," *American Historical Review* 93 (June 1988), 575.
45. Michael Bentley, *Modernizing England's Past: English Historiography in the Age of Modernism, 1870–1970* (Cambridge: Cambridge University Press, 2006), 115.
46. Ibid., 221.
47. Robert Finlay, "The Refashioning of Martin Guerre," *American Historical Review* 93 (June 1988), 553–71.
48. Ashley, *Churchill as Historian*, 26–27, 236.
49. SWW 1:xiii, 33, 150, 281, 541; 2:101, 123, 176, 212, 251, 512; 3:xiii, 5, 215, 232, 237, 252, 382, 401, 478, 724; 4:210, 273, 342, 344, 348, 360, 459, 565, 614, 728; 5:xiii–xiv, 10, 21, 29, 103, 118, 213, 231, 289, 301, 434, 437, 556, 635; 6:xiii, 43, 85, 155, 180, 195–96, 319, 363, 400, 418, 478, 522, 552, 578, 580.
50. Quoted in David Reynolds, *In Command of History: Churchill Fighting and Writing the Second World War* (London: Allen Lane, 2004), 495.

51. Deakin, *Churchill the Historian*, 14–15.
52. Bentley, *Modernizing England's Past*, 199.
53. Ashley, *Churchill as Historian*, 19–20.
54. WP 2:1081.
55. M 1:27, 210, 245, 473–74. Adrian Jones, *The Nature of the Book: Print and Knowledge in the Making* (Chicago and London: University of Chicago Press, 1998).
56. M 1:131.
57. M 1:84, 88.
58. M 2:86–87.
59. 3C:840–41.
60. 3C:1290, 1310, 1321, 1371, 1383–84, 1455, 1458–59.
61. 4:3.
62. 4:10–11.
63. WC 3.1:246–53.
64. M 2:183–88, 654, 793–96, 868–69, 891–92, 917, 968–69.
65. M 1:18.
66. Violet Barbour, "A review of *Malborough: His Life and Times, Vol IV*," *American Historical Review* 41 (January 1936), 332–34.
67. 5C3:784.
68. Blanche E. C. Dugdale, *Arthur James Balfour* (London: Hutchinson, 1936), 2:337.
69. 5C2:659–60.
70. M 1:228–29.
71. 5C3:1445.
72. SWW 1:545.
73. SWW 3:514.
74. CS 5653.
75. HESP 4:113.
76. WC 4:232–33.
77. WP 1:697.
78. SWW 5:470–71.
79. Will Swift, *The Kennedys Amidst the Gathering Storm: A Thousand Days in London, 1938–1940* (New York: HarperCollins, 2008), 224–25.

11 Revolutionaries

1. David Stafford, *Churchill and Secret Service* (Woodstock, NY: Overlook Press, 1998), 112–20.
2. GC 103.
3. GC 105.
4. WC 4:68.
5. Graham Robb, Introduction to *Victor Hugo: Ninety-Three*, trans. Frank Lee Benedict (New York: Carol & Graf Publishers, 1988).
6. GC 104.
7. 4:220.
8. 4:278. See also 4:318, 375.
9. 4:365.
10. GC 109.
11. Christopher Hassall, *Edward Marsh* (London: Longmans 1959), 448.
12. 4:330, 341–43, 351; 4C:659, 673, 677.
13. 4:915.
14. Archibald Sinclair to WSC, 29 November 1919, in Ian Hunter, ed., *Winston and Archie: The Letters of Sir Archibald Sinclair and Winston S. Churchill 1915–1960* (London: Politico's, 2005), 117–18.
15. 4C:993.
16. 4C:1010–12.
17. CE 4:26–30.
18. Martha F. Lee, "Nesta Webster: The Voice of Conspiracy," *Journal of Women's History* 17 (Fall 2005), 81–104.
19. 5C1:51.
20. 2C:355–58.
21. CS 684–85.
22. Martin Gilbert, *Churchill and the Jews* (New York: Henry Holt, 2007), 11, 19–23.
23. 2C:495–96.
24. 8:723–24.

25. Gilbert, *Churchill and the Jews*, 24–30.
26. Michael Makovsky, *Churchill's Promised Land: Zionism and Statecraft* (New Haven, CT, and London: Yale University Press, 2007), 117–23. But compare Michael J. Cohen, *Churchill and the Jews*, 2nd ed. (London and New York: Routledge, 2013), who is more skeptical of Churchill's commitment to Zionism.
27. 4:574–75.
28. Gilbert, *Churchill and the Jews*, 72.
29. Ibid., 58–61.
30. Albert S. Lindemann, *Esau's Tears: Modern Anti-Semitism and the Rise of the Jews* (Cambridge: Cambridge University Press, 2000), 248.
31. Benjamin Disraeli, *Tancred* (Teddington: Echo Library, 2007), chs. 32–33, 53. Disraeli reiterated some of these themes in *Coningsby* (Teddington: Echo Library, 2007), ch. 10.
32. Ronald Sanders, *The High Walls of Jerusalem* (New York: Holt, Rinehart & Winston, 1984), 8–13.
33. H. H. Asquith to Venetia Stanley, 28 January 1915, *H. H. Asquith: Letters to Venetia Stanley*, ed. Michael and Eleanor Brock (Oxford and New York: Oxford University Press, 1982), 406.
34. Disraeli, *Tancred*, ch. 29.
35. MEL 201.
36. L. S. Amery, *My Political Life* (London: Hutchinson, 1953), 2:115.
37. Martin Gilbert, "Lawrence of Judea," *Azure* 38 (Autumn 2009), 56–62.
38. CE 2:170.
39. 4C:1648.
40. GC 132–39.
41. Anthony Montague Browne, *Long Sunset* (London: Cassell, 1995), 201–02.
42. T. E. Lawrence, *Seven Pillars of Wisdom* (Harmondsworth: Penguin, 1979), 495, 684.
43. Ibid., 283.
44. 5C2:912.
45. 5C2:913.
46. SBS 127.
47. 5C3:605.
48. 5C3:615.
49. Mary C. Bromage, *Churchill and Ireland* (Notre Dame, IL: University of Notre Dame, 1964), 14–17. This and the following paragraphs draw from Bromage's sympathetic account, Ian Chambers's more cynical "Winston Churchill and Irish Home Rule, 1899–1914," *Parliamentary History* 19 (2000), 405–21, and Richard Toye's perceptive " 'Phrases Make History Here': Churchill, Ireland and the Rhetoric of Empire," *Journal of Imperial and Commonwealth History* 38 (December 2010), 549–70, as well as Andrew R. Muldoon's "Making Ireland's Opportunity England's: Winston Churchill and the Third Irish Home Rule Bill," *Parliamentary History* 15 (1996), 309–31.
50. 2C3:1377–78.
51. Robert Rhodes James, *Churchill: A Study in Failure, 1900–1939* (New York and Cleveland, OH: World Publishing, 1970), 47–56.
52. CS 2222–2233.
53. *Manchester Guardian*, 7 December 1942.
54. 2:463–67.
55. Anthony Montague Browne, *Long Sunset: Memoirs of Winston Churchill's Last Private Secretary* (London: Cassell, 1995), 203–04.
56. WC 1:204–05.
57. Martin Meisel, *Realizations: Narrative, Pictorial, and Theatrical Arts in Nineteenth-Century England* (Princeton, NJ: Princeton University Press, 1983), 184–86.
58. WC 4:292–93.
59. Bromage, *Churchill and Ireland*, ch. 3.
60. Nevil Macready, *Annals of an Active Life* (New York: George H. Doran), 2:615.
61. WC 4:365–68.
62. Bromage, *Churchill and Ireland*, ch. 4.
63. Bricriu Dolan, "Clare Sheridan, an Adventuress and Her Childen," *Journal of Irish Literature* 19 (May 1990), 22–23.
64. WC 4:226–27.
65. 5C2:196–97.
66. Ian Kershaw, *Making Friends with Hitler: Lord Londonderry, the Nazis and the Road to World War II* (New York: Penguin, 2004), 28–35. Brigitte Granzow, *A Mirror of Nazism: British Opinion and the Emergence of Hitler 1929–1933* (London: Victor Gollancz, 1964).
67. Ernst Hanfstaengel, *Hitler: The Missing Years* (London: Eyre & Spottiswoode, 1957), 184–87.
68. "Moses: The Leader of a People," in TA 283–94.

69. Browne, *Long Sunset*, 238.
70. Gilbert, *Churchill and the Jews*, 95.
71. 8:557.

12 The Chancellor's Star Turn

1. Robert Self, ed., *The Neville Chamberlain Diary Letters* (Aldershot: Ashgate, 2000–05), 1:328.
2. Lord Riddell, *Lord Riddell's Intimate Diary of the Peace Conference and After 1918–1923* (New York: Reynal & Hitchcock, 1934), 259–60, 1 January 1921.
3. Lord Beaverbrook, *Politicians and the War 1914–1916* (London: Collins, 1960), 78.
4. Frances Stevenson, *Lloyd George: A Diary*, ed. A. J. P. Taylor (New York: Harper & Row, 1971), 31, 43, 269–70.
5. Self, *Chamberlain Diary Letters*, 1:332.
6. Ibid., 1:20.
7. John Colville, *Winston Churchill and His Inner Circle* (New York: Wyndham Books, 1981), 22–25, 146–47.
8. Peter Stansky, *Sassoon: The Worlds of Philip and Sybil* (New Haven, CT, and London: Yale University Press, 2003), 89, 105, 118–19, 151, 154, 158, 160–62, 178, 219.
9. *Selected Letters of James Joyce*, ed. Richard Ellmann (New York: Viking, 1976), 280–81.
10. "Painting as a Pastime," in TA 315.
11. Self, *Chamberlain Diary Letters*, 1:359; 2:295; 4:71, 121, 211.
12. Ibid., 4:70.
13. David Dilks, *Neville Chamberlain* (Cambridge: Cambridge University Press, 1984), 1:388. Self, *Chamberlain Diary Letters*, 2:388, 404.
14. Self, *Chamberlain Diary Letters*, 4:178.
15. Ibid., 2:212, 321; 4:173.
16. Ibid., 2:283–84.
17. Ibid., 4:164.
18. Ibid., 1:378.
19. Ibid., 1:354.
20. Winifred Holtby, *Letters to a Friend* (London: Collins, 1937), 246.
21. 5:69–70.
22. Robert Rhodes James, *Churchill: A Study in Failure, 1900–1939* (New York and Cleveland, OH: World Publishing, 1970), 194.
23. PR 133–34, 142–43, 154.
24. 5C1:411–12.
25. Paul Addison, *Churchill on the Home Front 1900–1955* (London: Pimlico, 1993), 244–50.
26. Lord Moran, *Churchill: The Struggle for Survival 1940–65* (London: Constable, 1966), 303–04.
27. Self, *Chamberlain Diary Letters*, 2:282.
28. Ibid., 2:285.
29. Ibid., 2:287–88.
30. 5C1:472–73.
31. 5C1:499.
32. 5C1:533–34.
33. Self, *Chamberlain Diary Letters*, 2:316.
34. 5C1:693–96.
35. 5C1:702.
36. 5C1:712.
37. 5:159–60.
38. 5C1:713.
39. 5C1:715–16.
40. James, *Study in Failure*, 188–93.
41. This according to the diary of Thomas Jones, quoted in Addison, *Churchill on the Home Front*, 263–64.
42. Self, *Chamberlain Diary Letters*, 2:363.
43. 5C1:744–45.
44. 5C1:776–78.
45. 5C1:809.
46. 5C1:819–20.
47. Self, *Chamberlain Diary Letters*, 2:393.
48. Philip Williamson, *Stanley Baldwin* (Cambridge: Cambridge University Press, 1999), 108–21, 251, 253.

49. Lucy Masterman, *C. F. G. Masterman* (London: Frank Cass, 1968), 355.
50. Williamson, *Baldwin*, ch. 2.
51. British Film Institute, ref. no. 21594.
52. Williamson, *Baldwin*, 226–27.
53. Viscount Templewood, *Nine Troubled Years* (London: Collins, 1954), 32–33.
54. 5C1:984–86.
55. 5C1:987.
56. 5C1:1202.
57. 5C1:1050.
58. Self, *Chamberlain Diary Letters*, 2:434–35.
59. Ibid., 3:77.
60. Ibid., 3:81.
61. Leo Amery, *The Leo Amery Diaries 1896–1929*, ed. John Barnes and David Nicholson (London: Hutchinson, 1980), 542 (24 April 1928).
62. 5C1:1327–29; 5:297.
63. Robert Self, *Neville Chamberlain* (Aldershot: Ashgate, 2006), 128–32.
64. WSC to Clementine Churchill, 7 November 1928, *Winston and Clementine: The Personal Letters of the Churchills*, ed. Mary Soames (Boston, MA: Houghton Mifflin, 1999), 330.
65. CE 2:431.
66. Amery, *Amery Diaries 1896–1929*, 590 (27 February 1929).
67. Self, *Chamberlain Diary Letters*, 3:133–34.
68. 5C1:1462.
69. 5C1:1463.
70. U. K. Hicks, *The Finance of the British Government 1920–1936* (London: Oxford University Press, 1938), 7.
71. Moran, *Churchill*, 530.
72. Sir Frederick Maurice, "Mr. Churchill as a Military Historian," *Foreign Affairs* 5 (July 1927), 663–74.
73. H. M. Tomlinson, *War Books* (Cleveland, OH: Rowfant Club, 1930), 13–16.
74. WC 3.1:229.
75. Herbert Read, *English Prose Style* (London: G. Bell, 1928), 191–92.
76. Herbert Read, *English Prose Style* (New York: Pantheon, 1980), 171–73.
77. Isaiah Berlin, *Mr. Churchill in 1940* (Boston, MA: Houghton Mifflin, n.d.), 7–9.
78. Ibid., 39.

13 That Special Relationship

1. WSC, "Success in Journalism," *The Inlander* 11 (February 1901), 170.
2. 1C:597.
3. 1C:598.
4. 1C:599–600.
5. 1C:937–38.
6. 1C:947.
7. 1C:862.
8. Ronald I. Cohen, *Bibliography of the Writings of Sir Winston Churchill* (London and New York: Thoemmes Continuum, 2006), 4–5.
9. Ibid., 34–35, 43.
10. Ibid., 88–93.
11. Philip Waller, *Readers, Writers, and Reputations: Literary Life in Britain 1870–1918* (Oxford: Oxford University Press, 2008), ch. 16.
12. 1C:1218–19. Martin Gilbert, *Churchill and America* (New York: Free Press, 2005), ch. 5.
13. CS 550. See also 2C1:183; CS 318.
14. Waller, *Readers, Writers, and Reputations*, 659.
15. Cohen, *Bibliography*, 122–31.
16. Frederick Macmillan to WSC, 16 May 1907, CHAR 8/27.
17. Cohen, *Bibliography*, 133.
18. Ibid., 154, 159–60.
19. 3C:1292, 1325.
20. 5C1:296.
21. 4C:337.
22. 4C:442–43.
23. 4C:1352–53. See also 5:301, 307–08.

24. Thornton Butterworth to Charles Scribner, 7 January 1921, CSS, Box 50, File 1. In this correspondence it is sometimes unclear which Charles Scribner is writing or being written to. For the most part Churchill worked with Charles Scribner III, who joined the company in 1913, but this early correspondence may have been handled by his father Charles Scribner II, who died in 1930.
25. Cohen, *Bibliography*, 215–18.
26. Thornton Butterworth to WSC, 29 March 1923, CHAR 8/50.
27. 5C2:276.
28. 5C1:49–50.
29. Cohen, *Bibliography*, 216–62.
30. Charles Scribner to WSC, early September 1929, CSS, Box 50, File 2.
31. Charles Scribner to WSC, 19 June 1931, CSS, Box 50, File 4.
32. Cohen, *Bibliography*, 265–74.
33. Thorton Butterworth to Miss Penman, 31 January 1939, CHAR 8/636/19.
34. Edward Breck, review of *The World Crisis, American Historical Review* 20 (October 1923), 137–40. His review of the second volume was equally critical: *American Historical Review* 32 (July 1927), 876.
35. Review of *The World Crisis, American Political Science Review* 21 (August 1927), 689.
36. Ellery Sedgwick, "Atlantic's Bookshelf," *Atlantic Monthly* (June 1927), n.p.
37. Carlton J. H. Hayes, review of *The World Crisis*, vol. 1, *New Republic* 35 (6 June 1923), 48.
38. Theodore Collier, *American Historical Review* 35 (Janaury 1930), 365; Walter Millis, *Books* (24 March 1929), 3; *Christian Science Monitor* (1 May 1929), 14; Leon Whipple, *Survey* 62 (1 June 1929), 315; *Nation* 128 (24 April 1929), 498; Herschel Brickell, *North American Review* 227 (May 1929), n.p.; *Springfield Republican* (28 April 1929), 7; "Winnie the Poohbah," *Time* 13 (22 April 1929), 47; Lillian Rogers, *New York Evening Post* (6 April 1929), 11; P. W. Wilson, *New York Times* (17 March 1929), 1.
39. Nicholas John Cull, *Selling War: The British Propaganda Campaign Against "Neutrality" in World War II* (New York and Oxford: Oxford University Press, 1995), 9–10.
40. WC4:135–37.
41. WC4:118–19.
42. 5:348–49.
43. 5C2:89.
44. 5:424–26.
45. Cohen, *Bibliography*, 326, 334, 338–39. Charles Scribner to WSC, 19 December 1930, CSS, Box 50, File 3.
46. T. R. Ybarra, *New York Times* (30 November 1930), 5; C. G. Bowers, *New York World* (7 December 1930), 3; *Nation* 132 (18 February 1931), 194.
47. Thornton Butterworth to WSC, 16 December 1932, CHAR 8/312/151. Thornton Butterworth to WSC, 29 December 1932, CHAR 8/312/161.
48. Cohen, *Bibliography*, 378–97.
49. Ellery Sedgwick, *Atlantic Monthly* (June 1935), 8; Edwin Noble, *Boston Transcript* (11 November 1933), 1; E. E. Kellett, *Christian Science Monitor* (7 October 1933), 6; William MacDonald, *Nation* (27 December 1933), 738; P. W. Wilson, *New York Times* (12 November 1933), 3; R. M. Lovett, *New Republic* (7 August 1935), 369; A. L. Cross, *Saturday Review of Literature* (16 March 1935), 545.
50. Charles Scribner to WSC, 20 November 1933, CHAR 8/337/32.
51. Cohen, *Bibliography*, 1:402–03, 424–35. Charles Scribner to J. H. H. Gaute, 6 December 1949, CSS, Box 255, File 9.
52. James L. W. West III, "The Divergent Paths of British and American Publishing," *Sewanee Review* 120 (Fall 2012), 503–13.
53. Paul Delany, *Literature, Money and the Market from Trollope to Amis* (Basingstoke and New York: Palgrave, 2002), 115–19.
54. Charles Scribner to WSC, 19 April 1932, CSS, Box 51, File 5.
55. WSC to Charles Scribner, 22 June 1937, CSS, Box 51, File 6.
56. Charles Scribner to WSC, 13 July 1937, CSS, Box 51, File 6.
57. Thornton Butterworth, royalty statement for *Great Contemporaries*, 4 October to 31 December 1937, and letter to WSC, 1 January 1938, CHAR 8/605/2–3. In 1938 Churchill belatedly added a chapter on Franklin Roosevelt, but that edition was not published in the United States.
58. Waller, *Readers, Writers, and Reputations*, 646–68.
59. Compiled in www.booksofthecentury.com.
60. A. Scott Berg, *Max Perkins: Editor of Genius* (New York: Berkley, 2008), 116, 376.
61. Charles Scribner to WSC, 16 June 1931, CSS, Box 50, File 4.
62. Waller, *Readers, Writers, and Reputations*, 659.

63. Roger Burlingame, *Of Making Many Books: A Hundred Years of Reading, Writing and Publishing* (New York: Charles Scribner's Sons, 1946), 140.
64. *Punch*, 23 December 1925.
65. WSC to Charles Scribner, 30 June 1931, CSS, Box 50, File 4.
66. Charles Scribner to WSC, 15 January 1930, CSS, Box 50, File 3.
67. 4:50.
68. Berg, *Max Perkins*, 377; Desmond Flower, *Fellows in Foolscap: Memoirs of a Publisher* (London: Robert Hale, 1991), 148; Cohen, *Bibliography*, 921–22.
69. 8:255.
70. Charles Scribner, Jr., *In the Web of Ideas: The Education of a Publisher* (New York: Charles Scribner's Sons, 1993), 24. Charles Scribner to Alan C. Collins, 28 March 1941, CS, Box 51, File 6.
71. William Palmer, "On or About 1950 or 1955 History Departments Changed: A Step in the Creation of the Modern History Department," *Journal of the Historical Society* 7 (September 2007), 385–86.
72. CE 4:435–42.
73. Charles Scribner to WSC, 19 June 1930, CSS, Box 50, File 3.
74. Susan A. Brewer, *To Win the Peace: British Propaganda in the United States during World War II* (Ithaca, NY, and London, 1997), 11–28.
75. David Reynolds, *The Creation of the Anglo-American Alliance, 1937–41* (London: Europa, 1981), 17.
76. Lawrence Spinelli, *Dry Diplomacy: The United States, Great Britain, and Prohibition* (Lanham, MD: Rowman & Littlefield, 2008), 5, 25.
77. 5C1:1033.
78. John E. Moser, *Twisting the Lion's Tail: American Anglophobia between the World Wars* (New York: New York University Press, 1999), chs. 1–2, pp. 82, 97, 100, 118, 128–29.
79. B. J. C. McKercher, *Transition of Power: Britain's Loss of Global Pre-Eminence to the United States 1930–1945* (Cambridge: Cambridge University Press, 1999), esp. 109.
80. Robert Self, ed., *The Neville Chamberlain Diary Letters* (Aldershot: Ashgate, 2000–05), 4:99–100.

14 The Apple Cart

1. 4:409.
2. Arthur Herman, *Gandhi and Churchill* (New York: Bantam Dell, 2009), 253–58.
3. 4C:1986.
4. Herman, *Gandhi and Churchill*, 277–81.
5. 4C:1190.
6. WSC to Clementine Churchill, 12 and 15 September 1918, *Winston and Clementine: The Personal Letters of the Churchills*, ed. Mary Soames (Boston, MA: Houghton Mifflin, 1999), 214–15.
7. 4C:1561.
8. Robert Self, ed., *The Neville Chamberlain Diary Letters* (Aldershot: Ashgate, 2000–05), 2:65–66.
9. 5C1:1042, 1054.
10. Richard Toye, *Churchill's Empire* (New York: Henry Holt, 2010), 178–79.
11. CS 4915.
12. Edward Gibbon, *The Decline and Fall of the Roman Empire* (New York: Modern Library, n.d.), 8.
13. Ibid., 36–50.
14. Ibid., 560.
15. Ibid., 1086–87.
16. Ibid., 1149.
17. MEL 103–04.
18. *New York Times* (30 November 1930), 5.
19. *Spectator* 145 (25 October 1930), 599.
20. Robert Rhodes James, *Memoirs of a Conservative: J. C. C. Davidson's Memoirs and Papers, 1910–1937* (London: Weidenfeld and Nicolson, 1969), 355.
21. 5C1:1452.
22. 5C2:232–33.
23. CS 5226–27.
24. CS 5004.
25. Herman, *Gandhi and Churchill*, 392–93.
26. Quoted in Heidi J. Holder, "Melodrama, Realism and Empire on the British Stage," in J. S. Bratton et al., *Acts of Supremacy: The British Empire and the Stage* (Manchester: Manchester University Press, 1991), 141.
27. Toye, *Churchill's Empire*, 272.

28. Duff Cooper, *The Duff Cooper Diaries 1915–1951*, ed. John Julius Norwich (London: Weidenfeld & Nicolson, 2005), 142 (3 May 1921).
29. CE 3:82–89.
30. 5C3:1405.
31. Wilfred Scawen Blunt, *My Diaries* (New York: Knopf, 1921), 2:270.
32. Glenn R. Wilkinson, *Depictions and Images of War in Edwardian Newspapers, 1899–1914* (Basingstoke and New York: Palgrave Macmillan, 2003), 5, 37–38.
33. Thomas Babington Macaulay, *Warren Hastings* (London: Macmillan, 1893), 18–19.
34. Herman, *Gandhi and Churchill*, 375–80, 445–46.
35. Ibid., 229–30.
36. 5C2:199. Churchill's first mention of the word "appeasement" in a foreign policy context had been in July 1921, when he argued for friendly relations with Germany: "The aim is to get an appeasement of the fearful hatreds and antagonisms which exist in Europe and to enable the world to settle down." It was a sensible policy at the time, when Germany was a struggling new democracy. Martin Gilbert, *Churchill* (New York: Henry Holt, 1991), 439.
37. 5C2:592–93, 595–96.
38. 5C2:713.
39. 5C2:258–59.
40. 5C2:350–52, 355–56.
41. CE 3:76–78.
42. CE 3:79–81.
43. Herman, *Gandhi and Churchill*, 398–401.
44. Viscount Templewood, *Nine Troubled Years* (London: Collins, 1954), 102.
45. *Hansard*, 14 March 1933.
46. Quoted in Robert Rhodes James, *Churchill: A Study in Failure, 1900–1939* (New York and Cleveland, OH: World Publishing, 1970), 5.
47. Soames, *Winston and Clementine*, 399.
48. GC 182–83.
49. 5C3:438–39.
50. 5C3:439–40.
51. Cooper, *Diaries*, 234 (30 November 1936).
52. 5C3:455–56. Stanley Weintraub, "King Magnus and King Minus: A Play and a Playlet," *The Annual of Bernard Shaw Studies* 27 (2007), 11–27.
53. 5C3:457–59.
54. 5C3:459–60.
55. 5C3:461.
56. Robert Rhodes James, ed., *Chips: The Diaries of Sir Henry Channon* (Harmondsworth: Penguin, 1984), 107, 116–17. Robert Rhodes James, *Victor Cazalet* (London: Hamish Hamilton, 1976), 187. Charles Stuart, ed., *The Reith Diaries* (London: Collins, 1975), 191. L. S. Amery, *The Empire at Bay: The Leo Amery Diaries 1929–1945* (London: Hutchinson, 1988), 431.
57. 5C3:462.
58. 5C3:463.
59. 5C3:747.
60. Susan Williams, *The People's King: The True Story of the Abdication* (New York and Basingstoke: Palgrave Macmillan, 2003).
61. Amery, *Empire at Bay*, 432.
62. Edward Winterton, *Orders of the Day* (London: Cassell, 1953), 223.
63. 5C3:465. (Baldwin's emphasis.)
64. Harold Nicolson, *Diaries and Letters 1930–1939*, ed. Nigel Nicolson (New York: Atheneum, 1966), 284.
65. Self, *Chamberlain Diary Letters*, 4:228.
66. Graham Stewart, *Burying Caesar: The Churchill-Chamberlain Rivalry* (Woodstock, NY: Overlook Press, 2001), 264–69.
67. 5:829.
68. Williams, *People's King*, 183.
69. 5C3:499.
70. 5C3:917.
71. "Mass Effects in Modern Life" (1925), TA 255–66.
72. 5C2:725.
73. K. D. Williams and S. A. Nida, "Ostracism: Consequences and Coping," *Current Directions in Psychological Science* 20, 2 (2011), 71–75.
74. SWW 1:180.

15 The Producer

1. CS 5888.
2. Jan Rüger, *The Great Naval Game: Britain and Germany in the Age of Empire* (Cambridge: Cambridge University Press, 2007), 114–15.
3. Frederic Spotts, *Hitler and the Power of Aesthetics* (Woodstock, NY: Overlook Press, 2003), ch. 4.
4. George L. Mosse, *The Nationalisation of the Masses: Political Symbolism and Mass Movements in Germany from the Napoleonic Wars through the Third Reich* (New York: Howard Fertig, 1975), esp. chs. 4–5. Peter Fritzsche, *Rehearsals for Fascism: Populism and Political Mobilization in Weimar Germany* (Oxford: Oxford University Press, 1990).
5. Spotts, *Hitler and the Power of Aesthetics*, ch. 10.
6. Ibid., ch. 1.
7. Joachim Fest, *Hitler*, trans. Ralph Manheim (Boston, MA: Houghton Mifflin, 1974), 677.
8. Spotts, *Hitler and the Power of Aesthetics*, 25–27.
9. Ibid., chs. 18–20. Albert Speer, *Inside the Third Reich*, trans. Richard and Clara Winston (New York: Macmillan, 1970), 177–86, 298–99.
10. Spotts, *Hitler and the Power of Aesthetics*, 56.
11. Ian Kershaw, *Hitler 1889–1936: Hubris* (New York and London: Norton, 2000), 200–19.
12. Spotts, *Hitler and the Power of Aesthetics*, 55–56.
13. Kershaw, *Hitler 1889–1936*, 581–82.
14. Ibid., 280–81. Steven F. Sage, *Ibsen and Hitler* (New York: Carroll & Graf, 2006), makes an elaborate argument that the dictator was influenced by the Norwegian playwright. But given that there is no record of Hitler ever mentioning Ibsen's name, the evidence behind this theory is highly circumstantial.
15. Kershaw, *Hitler 1889–1936*, 401, 546; Ian Kershaw, *Hitler 1936–1945: Nemesis* (New York and London, Norton, 2001), 755.
16. SWW 4:560.
17. Adolf Hitler, *Mein Kampf*, trans. Ralph Manheim (Boston, MA: Houghton Mifflin, 1971), 476–77.
18. Roderick Macleod and Denis Kelly, eds., *Time Unguarded: The Ironside Diaries 1937–1940* (New York: David McKay, 1963), 50.
19. Ibid., 77–78.
20. Kershaw, *Hitler 1936–1945*, 13–18.
21. Spotts, *Hitler and the Power of Aesthetics*, 43.
22. Klemens von Klemperer, *German Incertitudes, 1914–1945: The Stones and the Cathedral* (Westport, CT: Praeger, 2001), 114.
23. Günter Berghaus, ed., *Fascism and Theatre: Comparative Studies on the Aesthetics and Politics of Performance in Europe, 1925–1945* (Providence, RI, and Oxford: Berghahn, 1996).
24. Clifford Geertz, *Negara: The Theatre State in Nineteenth-Century Bali* (Princeton, NJ: Princeton University Press, 1980), 11–13.
25. See Jeffrey Brooks, *Thank You, Comrade Stalin! Soviet Public Culture from Revolution to Cold War* (Princeton, NJ: Princeton University Press, 2000); Stephen Kotkin, *Magnetic Mountain: Stalinism as a Civilization* (Berkeley, CA: University of California Press, 1995); Sheila Fitzpatrick, *Tear Off the Masks: Identity and Imposture in Twentieth-Century Russia* (Princeton, NJ: Princeton University Press, 2005); and Julie A. Cassady, *The Enemy on Trial: Early Soviet Courts on Stage and Screen* (DeKalb, IL: Northern Illinois University Press, 2000).
26. Simonetta Falasca-Zamponi, *Fascist Spectacle: The Aesthetics of Power in Mussolini's Italy* (Berkeley, CA: University of California Press, 1997), chs. 1 and 5.
27. Brian Regal, "Madison Grant, Maxwell Perkins, and Eugenics Publishing at Scribner's," *Princeton University Library Chronicle* 65 (Winter 2004), 317–41.
28. Timothy W. Ryback, *Hitler's Private Library: The Books That Shaped His Life* (New York: Knopf, 2008), pp. xi–xiv, 50–51, 109–19, chs. 6–7.
29. GC ix.
30. Biographies of Roosevelt, Charles Stewart Parnell, and Robert Baden-Powell were added to the second edition of *Great Contemporaries* (London: Thornton Butterworth, 1938).
31. GC 10.
32. GC 49.
33. GC 68.
34. GC 157.
35. GC 196.
36. GC 79.
37. GC 148.
38. GC 214–15.

39. WSC, *Great Contemporaries*, 2nd ed., 358–59.
40. Ibid., 363, 365.
41. GC 266–67.
42. GC 273.
43. GC 167–68, 173.
44. GC 21–31.
45. GC 232.
46. Robert Self, ed., *The Neville Chamberlain Diary Letters* (Aldershot: Ashgate, 2000–05), 3:296.
47. Ibid., 3:387.
48. Ibid., 4:52.
49. Ibid., 4:81.
50. Ibid., 4:123.
51. Ibid., 4:181.
52. Ibid., 4:219–20.
53. GC 230.
54. SWW 1:50.
55. CE 3:53.
56. WES 142–43.
57. *Hansard*, Commons, 2 May 1935.
58. Self, *Chamberlain Diary Letters*, 3:409–11.
59. Ibid., 4:234.
60. Ibid., 4:273.
61. Ibid., 4:270.
62. Ibid., 4:286–87.
63. Ibid., 4:292.
64. Ibid., 4:300.
65. Ibid., 4:301–02.
66. Ibid., 4:304–05.
67. Ibid., 4:306–07.
68. Ibid., 4:344.
69. Quoted in David Faber, *Munich, 1938* (New York: Simon and Schuster, 2008), 304.
70. Quoted in Kershaw, *Hitler 1936–1945*, 105.

16 Blackout

1. CE 4:316–23.
2. Eugen Spier, *Focus: A Footnote to the History of the Thirties* (London: Oswald Wolff, 1963), 19–23.
3. William L. Shirer, *Berlin Diary* (New York: Knopf, 1941), 41 (18 June 1935).
4. John Maxwell Hamilton, *Journalism's Roving Eye: A History of American Foreign Reporting* (Baton Rouge, LA: Louisiana State University Press, 2011), 271–72.
5. Spier, *Focus*, 10–11, 74, 101, 124, 130–32.
6. Martin Moore, *The Origins of Modern Spin: Democratic Government and the Media in Britain, 1945–51* (Basingstoke and New York: Palgrave Macmillan, 2006).
7. Richard Cockett, *Twilight of Truth: Chamberlain, Appeasement and the Manipulation of the Press* (New York: St. Martin's Press, 1989), 3–8.
8. Robert Rhodes James, ed., *Memoirs of a Conservative: J. C. C. Davidson's Memoirs and Papers, 1910–1937* (London: Weidenfeld and Nicolson, 1969), 272.
9. Claire Hirshfield, "Labouchere, Truth and the Uses of Antisemitism," *Victorian Periodicals Review* 26 (Fall 1993), 134–42.
10. Cockett, *Twilight of Truth*, 9–12.
11. Benny Morris, *The Roots of Appeasement: The British Weekly Press and Nazi Germany during the 1930s* (London: Frank Cass, 1991).
12. Cockett, *Twilight of Truth*, 12–13. For a survey of the mostly pro-appeasement stance of the national newspapers, see Franklin Reid Gannon, *The British Press and Germany 1936–1939* (Oxford: Clarendon Press, 1971).
13. 5:906, 928.
14. 5:835. Anthony Adamthwaite, "The British Government and the Media, 1937–1938," *Journal of Contemporary History* 18 (April 1983), 281–85.
15. Cockett, *Twilight of Truth*, 16–24.
16. Ibid., 25–32.
17. Robert Rhodes James, *Chips: The Diaries of Sir Henry Channon* (Harmondsworth: Penguin, 1984), 177.

18. Cockett, *Twilight of Truth*, 39–41.
19. R. A. C. Parker, *Chamberlain and Appeasement: British Policy and the Coming of the Second World War* (New York: St. Martin's Press, 1993), 127–28.
20. David Low, *Low's Autobiography* (New York: Simon and Schuster, 1957), 278–79, 312–13.
21. Cockett, *Twilight of Truth*, 41–54.
22. Letter to Frank Gannett, 9 December 1938. Quoted in David Faber, *Munich, 1938* (New York: Simon and Schuster, 2008), 190.
23. Cockett, *Twilight of Truth*, 59–62.
24. 5C2:1175.
25. Clifford J. Norton to Violet Pearman, 7 July 1937; Violet Pearman to Clifford J. Norton, 8 July 1937; Clifford J. Norton to Violet Pearman, 9 July 1937, CHAR 8/548/28, 33, 36.
26. Dan Stone, *Responses to Nazism in Britain, 1933–1939: Before War and Holocaust* (Basingstoke: Palgrave Macmillan, 2003), 5.
27. Stephen Henry Roberts, *The House that Hitler Built* (London: Methuen, 1937), 361–63.
28. Anthony Eden, *Facing the Dictators* (Boston, MA: Houghton Mifflin, 1962), 648.
29. Robert Self., ed., *The Neville Chamberlain Diary Letters* (Aldershot: Ashgate, 2000–05), 4:300.
30. MO, "Opinion of America," 16 March 1942, p. 17.
31. George H. Gallup, ed., *The Gallup International Public Opinion Polls: Great Britain 1937–1975* (New York: Random House, 1976), 174.
32. Self, *Chamberlain Diary Letters*, 4:245.
33. 5C3:957, 1405; see also SWW 1:311.
34. Cockett, *Twilight of Truth*, 68.
35. Ibid., 66–68.
36. Ibid., 101–03, 124–25.
37. MO, "What People Think About the Press," 12 August 1940, p. 25.
38. Martin Gilbert, ed., *Winston Churchill and Emery Reves: Correspondence 1937–1964* (Austin, TX: University of Texas Press, 1997), 1–9.
39. Ronald I. Cohen, *Bibliography of the Writings of Sir Winston Churchill* (London: Thoemmes Continuum, 2006), 220, 257, 273, 279, 328–30.
40. Roy Jenkins, *Churchill* (New York: Farrar, Straus and Giroux, 2001), 508.
41. Cooperation News Service to WSC, 20 August 1937, in Gilbert, *Churchill and Reves*, 54–55.
42. Such a map is published in ibid., xvi.
43. Emery Reves to WSC, 31 August 1937, in Gilbert, *Churchill and Reves*, 56.
44. Emery Reves to WSC, 20 September 1937, ibid., 63–64.
45. Violet Pearman to Emery Reves, 26 September 1937, ibid., 65–66.
46. Cooperation News Service to WSC, 1 January 1938, ibid., 92.
47. Lynne Olson, *Troublesome Young Men: The Rebels who Brought Churchill to Power and Helped Save England* (New York: Farrar, Straus and Giroux, 2007), 108–09, 177–79, 185.
48. Faber, *Munich*, 177–85. Parker, *Chamberlain and Appeasement*, 148–49.
49. James *Diaries*, 203, 205.
50. Self, *Chamberlain Diary Letters*, 4:344.
51. Ibid., 4:342.
52. Faber, *Munich*, 265–67.
53. Ibid., 273–74.
54. Self, *Chamberlain Diary Letters*, 4:345–46.
55. Faber, *Munich*, 283–85.
56. Self, *Chamberlain Diary Letters*, 4:348.
57. Adamthwaite, "British Government and the Media," 287–88.
58. Gilbert, *Churchill and Reves*, 144.
59. Daniel Hucker, *Public Opinion and the End of Appeasement in Britain and France* (Farnham and Burlington, VT: Ashgate, 2011), 48–49.
60. Adamthwaite, "British Government and the Media," 288–91.
61. Gilbert, *Churchill and Reves*, 145.
62. Angus Calder, *The People's War* (New York: Ace Books, 1969), 23–25.
63. Faber, *Munich*, 378–99.
64. Channon, *Diaries*, 213.
65. Kathleen Kennedy to the Kennedy family, 22 February 1944, JFKPP-004-035.
66. Self, *Chamberlain Diary Letters*, 4:349.
67. Joseph P. Kennedy to Cordell Hull, 28 September 1938, in Amanda Smith, ed., *Hostage to Fortune: The Letters of Joseph P. Kennedy* (New York: Viking, 2001), 289.
68. CE 2:432–33.
69. Faber, *Munich*, 217–18, 222–26, 233, 275.

70. Cockett, *Twilight of Truth*, 101.
71. CS 6011–12.
72. Cohen, *Bibliography*, 491–97.
73. *Atlantic Monthly* (January 1939).
74. Arthur Rosenberg, *Nation* 147 (29 October 1938), 455–56.
75. P. W. Wilson, *New York Times* (9 October 1938), 8.
76. Self, *Chamberlain Diary Letters*, 4:361.
77. CS 6015.
78. 5C3:1316–17, 1340; 5:1024.
79. CE 1:418.
80. Emery Reves to WSC, 4 November 1938, in Gilbert, *Churchill and Reves*, 153–54.
81. CS 6030–32.
82. Emery Reves to WSC, 10 February 1939, in Gilbert, *Churchill and Reves*, 167–69.
83. Emery Reves to WSC, 9 May 1939, ibid., 184.
84. WSC to Emery Reves, 8 May 1939, ibid., 183.
85. CE 1:447–53.
86. Emery Reves to WSC, 11 July 1939, in Gilbert, *Churchill and Reves*, 202–03.
87. 5:1099.
88. Cockett, *Twilight of Truth*, 104–07.
89. Morris, *Roots of Appeasement*, ch. 7.
90. Emery Reves to Reginald Leeper, 31 May 1939, in Gilbert, *Churchill and Reves*, 187–92.
91. Cooperation News Service to WSC, 8 June 1939, ibid., 199–200.
92. *Time* (25 September 1939), 24.
93. E. B. H., *Christian Science Monitor* (9 September 1939), 16.
94. Keith Hutchison, *Nation* (23 September 1939), 325–26.
95. Robert Gale Woolbert, *Foreign Affairs* 18 (January 1940), 368.
96. P. W. Wilson, *New York Times Book Review* (3 September 1939), 5.
97. Cohen, *Bibliography*, 500–04.
98. Fred Taylor, trans. and ed., *The Goebbels Diaries 1939–1941* (New York: G. P. Putnam's Sons, 1983), 354.
99. 5C3:1475.
100. Graham Stewart, *Burying Caesar: The Churchill-Chamberlain Rivalry* (Woodstock, NY: Overlook Press, 2001), 369–71.
101. George H. Gallup, ed., *The Gallup International Public Opinion Polls: Great Britain 1937–1975* (New York: Random House, 1976), 18, 20, 21.
102. Roderick Macleod and Denis Kelly, eds., *Time Unguarded: The Ironside Diaries 1937–1940* (New York: David McKay, 1963), 83–84.
103. Quoted in Ian Kershaw, *Hitler 1936–1945: Nemesis* (New York: W. W. Norton, 2001), 211–13.
104. Cohen, *Bibliography*, 329.
105. *Liste des schälichen und unerwünschten Schrifttums* (Leipzig: Ernst Hedrich Nachf., 1939), 21. The translation was produced by the émigré Amsterdam publisher Allert de Lange in 1938.
106. Reichsministerium für Volksaufclärung und Propaganda, *Verzeichnis englischer und nordamerikanischer Scriftsteller* (Leipzig: Verlag des Börsenvereins der Deutschen Buchhändler, 1942), 12–13.
107. Editions Payot to Macmillan and Co., 10 January 1945, CHAR 8/716/25.
108. For the Nazi destruction of books, see Jonathan Rose, ed., *The Holocaust and the Book: Destruction and Preservation* (Amherst, MA: University of Massachusetts Press, 2001). For Nazi censorship – and a sense of how much could slip past the authorities – see Jan-Pieter Barbian, *Literaturpolitik im NS-Staat: Von der "Gleichschaltung" bis zum Ruin* (Frankfurt am Main: Fischer Taschenbuch Verlag, 2010); Jan-Pieter Barbian, *Die vollendete Ohnmacht? Schriftsteller, Verleger und Buchhändler im NS-Staat* (Essen: Klartext, 2008); Jan-Pieter Barbian, "Die doppelte Indizierung: Verbote US-amerikanischer Literatur zwischen 1933 und 1941," in Julius H. Schoeps and Werner Tress, eds., *Verfemt und Verboten: Vorgeschichte und Folgen der Bücherverbrennungen 1933* (Hildesheim: Georg Olms Verlag, 2010); and Ine van Linthout, *Das Buch in der nationalsozialistischen Propagandapolitik* (Berlin: De Gruyter, 2011).

17 The Loaded Pause

1. For example, Colin Perry, *Boy in the Blitz* (London: Leo Cooper, 1972), 123, 131.
2. Juliet Gardiner, *Wartime: Britain 1939–1945* (London: Headline, 2005), 9.
3. George Beardmore, *Civilians at War: Journals 1938–46* (Oxford: Oxford University Press, 1986), 34.

4. Edward Blishen, *A Cackhanded War* (London: Thames and Hudson, 1972), 11.
5. Robert Mackay, *Half the Battle: Civilian Morale in Britain during the Second World War* (Manchester: Manchester University Press, 2002), ch. 1.
6. Roderick Macleod and Denis Kelly, eds., *Time Unguarded: The Ironside Diaries 1937–1940* (New York: David McKay, 1963), 42–43.
7. Wesley K. Wark makes that argument in *The Ultimate Enemy: British Intelligence and Nazi Germany, 1933–1939* (Oxford: Oxford University Press, 1986), esp. ch. 3.
8. John Colville, *The Fringes of Power: 10 Downing Street Diaries 1939–1945* (New York and London: Norton, 1985), 19–21, 25.
9. Ibid., 25.
10. Ibid., 27–28.
11. Ibid., 46.
12. Harold Nicolson, *Diaries and Letters* (New York: Atheneum, 1966–68), 2:37–38, 26 September 1939.
13. Beardmore, *Civilians at War*, 40.
14. WP 1:160.
15. Colville, *Diaries*, 29.
16. Richard Holmes, *In the Footsteps of Churchill: A Study in Character* (New York: Basic Books, 2006), 118.
17. Colville, *Diaries*, 36.
18. Ibid., 75, 88, 115.
19. 6:893–94.
20. WC 1:vii.
21. 6:157.
22. 6:15.
23. Robert Self, ed., *The Neville Chamberlain Diary Letters* (Aldershot: Ashgate, 2000–05), 4:448.
24. SWW 1:409–10.
25. Self, *Chamberlain Diary Letters*, 4:457.
26. David Reynolds, *In Command of History: Churchill Fighting and Writing the Second World War* (London: Allen Lane, 2004), 111–12. SWW 1:498–99.
27. Entry for 22 January 1940, Fred Taylor, trans. and ed., *The Goebbels Diaries 1939–1941* (New York: G. P. Putnam's Sons, 1983), 101.
28. Thornton Butterworth to WSC, 28 September 1939, CHAR 8/636/13.
29. Colville, *Diaries*, 310.
30. 6:1004.
31. WP 1:67–69.
32. WP 1:195.
33. WP 1:86.
34. WP 1:526–27.
35. WP 1:577, 611.
36. Desmond Flower, *Fellows in Foolscap: Memoirs of a Publisher* (London: Robert Hale 1991), 171.
37. 6:56, 274.
38. F. W. Deakin, *Churchill the Historian* (Zurich: Schweizerischen Winston Churchill Stiftung, 1969), 15.
39. WP 1:144–45.
40. David Reynolds, "1940: The Worst and Finest Hour," in Robert Blake and William Roger Louis, eds., *Churchill* (New York and London: Norton, 1993), 242.
41. WP 1:810.
42. WP 1:830, 833.
43. Ronald I. Cohen, *Bibliography of the Writings of Sir Winston Churchill* (London and New York: Thoemmes Continuum, 2006), 342–47.
44. WP 1:245–46.
45. Nicholas John Cull, *Selling War: The British Propaganda Campaign Against American "Neutrality" in World War II* (New York and Oxford: Oxford University Press, 1995), 40–41.
46. Self, *Chamberlain Diary Letters*, 4:451.
47. Mackay, *Half the Battle*, 51–56.
48. Viscount Templewood, *Nine Troubled Years* (London: Collins, 1954), 411.
49. Robert Rhodes James, ed., *Chips: The Diaries of Sir Henry Channon* (Harmondsworth: Penguin, 1984), 276.
50. WP 1:875. Julian Jackson, *The Fall of France: The Nazi Invasion of 1940* (Oxford: Oxford University Press, 2003), 204.

51. Ian Kershaw, *Making Friends with Hitler: Lord Londonderry, the Nazis and the Road to World War II* (New York: Penguin, 2004), ch. 7.
52. George H. Gallup, ed., *The Gallup International Public Opinion Polls: Great Britain 1937–1975* (New York: Random House, 1976), 22, 30.
53. Richard Griffiths, "The Reception of Bryant's *Unfinished Victory*: Insights into British Public Opinion in Early 1940," *Patterns of Prejudice* 38 (2004), 18–36.
54. Olivia Cockett, *Love and War in London: A Woman's Diary, 1939–1942* (Waterloo, ON: Wilfred Laurier University Press, 2005), 47–51, 66–68.
55. Geoffrey Shakespeare, *Let Candles Be Brought In* (London: Macdonald, 1949), 68–69.
56. WP 1:667.
57. Colville, *Diaries*, 104, 108. David Dilks, ed., *The Diaries of Sir Alexander Cadogan 1938–1945* (New York: G. P. Putnam's Sons, 1972), 255.
58. WP 1:696.
59. D. J. Wenden, "Churchill, Radio, and Cinema," in Blake and Louis, *Churchill*, 222.
60. Templewood, *Nine Troubled Years*, 417.
61. "Blackouts and the Theatre," *New York Times*, 24 March 1940.
62. John Ramsden, *Man of the Century: Winston Churchill and His Legend* (New York: Columbia University Press, 2002), 57.
63. MO, "News Reel Report," 27 May 1940.
64. Self, *Chamberlain Diary Letters*, 4:514–15.
65. Adam Tooze, *The Wages of Destruction: The Making and Breaking of the Nazi Economy* (New York: Viking, 2007), 315–25.
66. Ian Kershaw, *Hitler 1936–1945: Nemesis* (New York and London: W. W. Norton, 2001), 289–91.
67. Cockett, *Love and War in London*, 70–71.
68. Colville, *Diaries*, 108.
69. Beardmore, *Civilians at War*, 49–50.
70. Reynolds, *In Command of History*, 126.
71. Colville, *Diaries*, 112.
72. Walter Henry Thompson, *Assignment: Churchill* (New York: Farrar, Straus and Young, 1955), 220.
73. WP 1:1219–20.
74. James, *Channon*, 301–02.
75. Nicolson, *Diaries and Letters*, 2:79, 8 May 1940.
76. Andrew Roberts, *"The Holy Fox": A Life of Lord Halifax* (London: Papermac, 1992), 205.
77. Dilks, *Cadogan*, 280.
78. SWW 1:596–98.
79. Roberts, *"The Holy Fox"*, 203–07.
80. Lord Moran, *Churchill: The Struggle for Survival 1940–1965* (London: Constable, 1966), 322–23.
81. SWW 1:186–201.
82. Moran, *Churchill*, 322–23. Anthony Eden, *The Reckoning* (Boston, MA: Houghton Mifflin, 1965), 110–11.
83. Joseph P. Kennedy, diary, 19 October 1940, in Amanda Smith, ed., *Hostage to Fortune: The Letters of Joseph P. Kennedy* (New York: Viking, 2001), 476.
84. JFK, "Talk with Lord Halifax," 23 January 1942, JFKPP-011-016.
85. Roberts, *"Holy Fox"*, 1–2, 198–203.

18 The Hour of Fate and the Crack of Doom

1. Ian McLaine, *Ministry of Morale: Home Front Morale and the Ministry of Information in World War II* (London: George Allen & Unwin, 1979), 20–21, 31.
2. John Ramsden, *Man of the Century: Winston Churchill and His Legend since 1945* (New York: Columbia University Press, 2002), 65–68.
3. LLP 77.
4. WC 5:17.
5. M 1:428–30.
6. SBS 319.
7. WP 2:22.
8. Richard Overy, *The Twilight Years: The Paradox of Britain between the Wars* (New York: Viking, 2009), 313.
9. Wyndham Lewis, *The Hitler Cult* (London: Dent, 1939), vii, 132.
10. Michael Booth, *English Melodrama* (London: Herbert Jenkins, 1965), 18–20, 199.

11. See Marvin Carlson, "He Never Should Bow Down to a Domineering Frown: Class Tensions and Nautical Melodrama"; Jeffrey N. Cox, "The Ideological Tack of Nautical Melodrama"; Harrmut Ilsemann, "Radicalism in the Melodrama of the Early Nineteenth Century"; and Julia Williams and Stephen Watt, "Representing a 'Great Distress': Melodrama, Gender, and the Irish Famine," in *Melodrama: The Cultural Emergence of a Genre*, ed. Michael Hays and Anastasia Nikolopoulou (New York: St. Martin's Press, 1996), 147–207, 245–65.
12. John Colville, *The Fringes of Power: 10 Downing Street Diaries 1939–1955* (New York and London: W. W. Norton, 1985), 312–13.
13. Ibid., 215.
14. Guy Nicholas Esnouf, "British Government War Aims and Attitudes Towards a Negotiated Peace, September 1939 to July 1940," Ph.D. diss. King's College London, 1988, chs. 1–6.
15. Edward Spears, *Assignment to Catastrophe* (New York: A. A. Wyn, 1954), 2:205–07.
16. Charles Eade, ed., *Churchill by his Contemporaries* (London: Hutchinson, 1953), 35.
17. Entry for 26 December 1939, Fred Taylor, trans. and ed., *The Goebbels Diaries 1939–1941* (New York: G. P. Putnam's Sons, 1983), 75.
18. HESP 3:296.
19. WP 2:22.
20. Robert Rhodes James, "The Politician," in *Churchill Revised: A Critical Assessment* (New York: Dial Press, 1969), 121–22.
21. John Colville, *Footprints in Time* (London: Century, 1986), 75–76.
22. SWW 2:38–43.
23. David Reynolds, *In Command of History: Churchill Fighting and Writing the Second World War* (London: Allen Lane, 2004), 205–06.
24. WP 2:61–62.
25. Colville, *Diaries*, 132.
26. Warren F. Kimball, ed., *Churchill & Roosevelt: The Complete Correspondence* (Princeton, NJ: Princeton University Press, 1984), 1:37–38.
27. Ibid., 1:38–39.
28. Martin Gilbert, *Churchill and America* (New York: Free Press, 2005), 186.
29. David Cannadine, *In Churchill's Shadow: Confronting the Past in Modern Britain* (Oxford: Oxford University Press, 2003), 197.
30. Elliott Roosevelt, ed., *F.D.R.: His Personal Letters 1928–1945* (New York: Duell, Sloan and Pearce, 1950), 793.
31. Kimball, *Churchill & Roosevelt*, 1:23.
32. Max Freedman, ed., *Roosevelt and Frankfurter: Their Correspondence 1928–1945* (Boston, MA: Little, Brown, 1967), 37–38.
33. Kimball, *Churchill & Roosevelt*, 1:24.
34. Joseph P. Kennedy, diary, 28 March 1940, in Amanda Smith, ed., *Hostage to Fortune: The Letters of Joseph P. Kennedy* (New York: Viking, 2001), 411.
35. Ibid., 1 December 1940, p. 496.
36. Angus Calder, *The People's War* (New York: Ace, 1972), 106.
37. Roderick Macleod and Denis Kelly, eds., *Time Unguarded: The Ironside Diaries 1937–1940* (New York: David McKay, 1963), 316.
38. Anthony Eden, *The Reckoning* (Boston, MA: Houghton Mifflin, 1965), 123.
39. Esnouf, "British Government War Aims," 90.
40. HIR, 27 May 1940.
41. McLaine, *Ministry of Morale*, 61–62.
42. Ibid., 73.
43. MO, "Morale Today," 16 May 1940.
44. MO, "Morale Today," 19 May 1940.
45. WP 2:83–90.
46. McLaine, *Ministry of Morale*, 139.
47. MO, "Morale Today," 22 May 1940.
48. MO, "Morale Today," 23 May 1940.
49. Robert Mackay, *Half the Battle: Civilian Morale in Britain during the Second World War* (Manchester: Manchester University Press, 2002), 61.
50. MO, "Morale Today," 24 May 1940.
51. John Lukacs, *Five Days in London: May 1940* (New Haven, CT, and London: Yale University Press, 2001), 100–03.
52. MO, "Morale: Sunday and Monday, May 26th and 27th, 1940," 27 May 1940.
53. Richard Dimbleby, "Churchill the Broadcaster," in Eade, *Churchill by His Contemporaries*, 409–10.

54. 6:406.
55. David Dilks, ed., *The Diaries of Sir Alexander Cadogan 1938–1945* (New York: G. P. Putnam's Sons, 1972), 290.
56. WP 2:166–69.
57. WP 2:170.
58. Robert Rhodes James, ed., *Chips: The Diaries of Sir Henry Channon* (Harmondsworth: Penguin, 1984), 313.
59. Reynolds, *In Command of History*, 171–72.
60. Christopher Hill, *Cabinet Decisions on Foreign Policy: The British Experience October 1938–June 1941* (Cambridge: Cambridge University Press, 2002), ch. 6.
61. SWW 2:86, 136–37.
62. WP 2:182–84.
63. Quoted in Michael Booth, "Soldiers of the Queen: Drury Lane Imperialism," in Hays and Nikolopoulou, *Melodrama*, 13–15.
64. SWW 2:88.
65. Leo Amery, *The Empire at Bay: The Leo Amery Diaries 1929–1945* (London: Hutchinson, 1988), 28 May 1940, p. 619.
66. Lord Ismay, *The Memoirs of General Lord Ismay* (New York: Viking, 1960), 155.
67. MO, "Morale Today," 1 June 1940.
68. Cadogan, *Diaries*, 292.
69. WP 2:218.
70. Spears, *Assignment to Catastrophe*, 1:314.
71. 6:423.
72. Cadogan, *Diaries*, 293.
73. Richard Broad and Suzie Fleming, eds., *Nella Last's War: A Mother's Diary 1939–1945* (Bristol: Falling Wall Press, 1981), 62.
74. WP 2:240–47.
75. Miles Hudson, *The Extraordinary Life of Charles Hudson VC: Soldier, Poet, Rebel* (Stroud: Sutton, 2007), 178–80.
76. Channon, *Diaries*, 314.
77. Harold Nicolson to Victoria Sackville-West, 4 June 1940, in Harold Nicolson, *Diaries and Letters* (New York: Atheneum, 1967), 2:93.
78. Victoria Sackville-West to Harold Nicolson, 5 June 1940, ibid., 2:93.
79. Harold Nicolson to Victoria Sackville-West, 6 June 1940, ibid., 2:94.
80. Howard LeFay, "Be Ye Men of Valour," *National Geographic* 128 (1965), 159.
81. Paul Addison, *Churchill on the Home Front 1900–1955* (London: Pimlico, 1993), 334–35.
82. MO, "Morale Today," 5 June 1940. HIR 5 June 1940.
83. GC 273.
84. Spears, *Assignment to Catastrophe*, 2:205–07.
85. Ibid., 2:136.
86. Colville, *Diaries*, 152.
87. Ismay, *Memoirs*, 143.
88. Lord Alanbrooke, *War Diaries 1939–1945* (Berkeley, CA: University of California Press, 2001), 81–82.
89. François Kersaudy, *Churchill and De Gaulle* (New York: Atheneum, 1982), 58–60.
90. SWW 2:142–62.
91. Kersaudy, *Churchill and De Gaulle*, 64.
92. Charles de Gaulle, *The Complete War Memoirs* (New York: Simon and Schuster, 1972), 68.
93. Spears, *Assignment to Catastrophe*, 2:225–26.
94. Kimball, *Churchill & Roosevelt*, 1:43–44.
95. Ibid., 1:45.
96. Ibid., 1:45–46.
97. Ibid., 1:46–47.
98. Ibid., 1:47–48.
99. Peter Fleming, *Operation Sea Lion* (New York: Simon and Schuster, 1957), 91.
100. HIR 14 June 1940.
101. WP 2:339–41.
102. Kimball, *Churchill and Roosevelt*, 1:49–51.
103. Ibid., 1:51–52.
104. Nicholas John Cull, *Selling War: The British Propaganda Campaign Against American "Neutrality" in World War II* (New York and Oxford: Oxford University Press, 1995), 97–115.
105. Colville, *Diaries*, 157–58, 163.

106. David Edgerton, *Britain's War Machine: Weapons, Resources, and Experts in the Second World War* (Oxford: Oxford University Press, 2011), 43.
107. Amery, *Empire at Bay*, 13 June 1940, p. 622.
108. Avi Shlaim, "Prelude to Downfall: The British Offer of Union to France, June 1940," *Journal of Contemporary History* 9.3 (July 1974), 27–44.
109. SWW 2:180–81.
110. De Gaulle, *War Memoirs*, 74–75.
111. Ibid., 77.
112. Colville, *Diaries*, 159–60. Paul Reynaud, "Churchill and France," in Eade, *Churchill by his Contemporaries*, 321.
113. WP 2:347–49.
114. SWW 2:183–84.
115. Lord Moran, *Winston Churchill: The Struggle for Survival 1940–65* (London: Constable, 1966), 259–60.
116. Shlaim, "Prelude to Downfall," 49–65. Paul Reynaud, *In the Thick of the Fight, 1930–1945* (New York: Simon and Schuster, 1955), 539–41. SWW 2:182–89. Spears, *Assignment to Catastrophe*, 2:315.
117. Spears, *Assignment to Catastrophe*, 1:68.
118. MO, "General Points in Morale," 22 June 1940.
119. MO, "Morale Today," 17 June 1940.
120. HIR, 17 June 1940.
121. HIR, 18 June 1940.
122. MO, "Capitulation Talk in Worktown," 19 June 1940.
123. Broad and Fleming, *Nella Last's War*, 63–65.
124. WP 2:360–68.
125. Spears, *Assignment to Catastrophe*, 2:101.
126. Overy, *Twilight Years*, 1–3, 25–27, 51, 83, 273.
127. 5C3:1220–22.
128. CE 1:347–49.
129. H. G. Wells, *The Discovery of the Future* (New York: B. W. Huebsch, 1914), 52–53.
130. WP 1:672–75.
131. WP 2:360–68.
132. Virginia Woolf, *The Diary of Virginia Woolf* (New York: Harcourt Brace Jovanovich, 1977–84), 5.297.
133. MO, "Morale Today," 19 June 1940.
134. HIR, 19 June 1940.
135. Macleod and Kelly, *Ironside Diaries*, 363, 367–68.
136. HIR, 20 June 1940.
137. HIR, 24 June 1940.
138. MO, "Morale Today and Yesterday," 26–27 June 1940.
139. HIR, 27 June 1940.
140. Phillipe Lasterle, "Could Admiral Gensoul Have Averted the Tragedy of Mers el-Kebir?" *Journal of Military History* 67 (July 2003), 835–44.
141. WP 2:464.
142. WP 2:421.
143. Kenneth Young, *Churchill and Beaverbrook* (New York: James H. Heineman, 1966), 153.
144. Moran, *Churchill*, 259.
145. Ismay, *Memoirs*, 150.
146. HESP 3:314–15.
147. WP 2:469–75.
148. Channon, *Diaries*, 319.
149. Cadogan, *Diaries*, 311.
150. 6:628–44. Kevin Jefferys, *The Churchill Coalition and Wartime Politics, 1940–45* (Manchester: University of Manchester Press, 1991), 47–48. Colville, *Diaries*, 335. Orville H. Bullitt, ed., *For the President Personal and Secret: Correspondence between Franklin D. Roosevelt and William C. Bullitt* (Boston, MA: Houghton Mifflin, 1972), 431–32, 488–89.
151. *The Ciano Diaries 1939–1943*, ed. Hugh Gibson (Garden City, NY: Doubleday, 1946), 11 January 1939, p. 10.
152. Ibid., 4 July 1940, p. 273.
153. MO, "Morale Today," 3 July 1940.
154. Ibid., 5 July 1940.
155. HIR, 5 July 1940.

156. HIR, 8 July 1940.
157. Harold Nicolson, diary, 4 June 1940, and letter to Victoria Sackville-West, 10 June 1940, in Nicolson, *Diaries and Letters*, 2:100.
158. MO, "Morale Today," 10 July 1940.
159. MO, "Fifth Weekly Morale Report," August 1940.

19 This Different England

1. For an overview of this debate, see Garry Campion, *The Good Fight: Battle of Britain Propaganda and The Few* (Basingstoke: Palgrave Macmillan, 2009), 1–6.
2. Peter Schenk, *Invasion of England 1940: The Planning of Operation Sealion*, trans. Kathleen Bunten (London: Conway Maritime Press, 1990), 334–45.
3. David Shears, "Could Sea Lion Have Worked?" in *No End Save Victory: Perspectives on World War II*, ed. Robert Cowley (New York: G. P. Putnam's Sons, 2001), 102–06.
4. Peter Fleming, *Operation Sea Lion* (New York: Simon and Schuster, 1957), 80, 307.
5. David Edgerton, *Britain's War Machine: Weapons, Resources, and Experts in the Second World War* (Oxford: Oxford University Press, 2011), ch. 3.
6. Julian Jackson, *The Fall of France: The Nazi Invasion of 1940* (Oxford: Oxford University Press, 2003), ch. 4.
7. WP 2:422.
8. Ian McLaine, *Ministry of Morale: Home Front Morale and the Ministry of Information in World War II* (London: Allen and Unwin, 1979), 66. John Colville, *The Fringes of Power: 10 Downing Street Diaries 1939–1955* (London: W. W. Norton, 1985), 192–93.
9. Colville, *Diaries*, 207.
10. Schenk, *Invasion of England*, 8–9.
11. Günther von Blumentritt, "Operation 'Sealion'," *An Cosantóir* 9 (January 1949), 644–50.
12. William L. Shirer, *Berlin Diary* (New York: Knopf, 1941), 19 July 1940, p. 454.
13. Hugh Gibson, ed., *The Ciano Diaries 1939–1943* (Garden City, NY: Doubleday, 1946), 19 and 20 July 1940, p. 277.
14. HIR, 27 July and 5 August 1940.
15. Ian Kershaw, *Hitler 1936–1945: Nemesis* (New York: W. W. Norton, 2001), 301–08. Schenk, *Invasion of England*, 350–55.
16. Fleming, *Operation Sea Lion*, chs. 6 and 8.
17. Harold Nicolson, *Diaries and Letters* (New York: Atheneum, 1967), 2:103, 20 July 1940.
18. Max Hastings, *Winston's War: Churchill 1940–1945* (New York: Knopf, 2010), 71–73.
19. Martin Gilbert, *Churchill and the Jews* (New York: Henry Holt, 2007), 175–76.
20. Joseph P. Kennedy, diary, 12 June 1940, in Amanda Smith, ed., *Hostage to Fortune: The Letters of Joseph P. Kennedy* (New York: Viking, 2001), 439.
21. Charles de Gaulle, *The Complete War Memoirs*, trans. Jonathan Griffin and Richard Howard (New York: Simon and Schuster, 1972), 104.
22. Campion, *The Good Fight*, 236–43.
23. WP 2:520.
24. John Lukacs, *The Duel: The Eighty-Day Struggle between Churchill and Hitler* (New Haven, CT, and London: Yale University Press, 1990), 170.
25. WP 3:549.
26. MO, "Social Research and the Film," 8 October 1940, pp. 15–16.
27. SWW 2:299–300.
28. WP 3:1100, 1688, 1712.
29. WP 3:1388.
30. SWW 2:448; 3:580; 4:241, 552, 554, 552; 5:103, 108; 6:43–44, 96, 129, 133, 134, 204, 238, 275, 347, 357, 359, 485, 543, 669.
31. SWW 3:175.
32. SWW 1:33; 2:86, 183; 3:172, 283; 4:637, 729; 5:6, 52, 104.
33. See also SWW 2:207, 264; 4:279; 5:360.
34. SWW 2:205.
35. SWW 5:170.
36. SWW 5:439.
37. SWW 5:409.
38. WP 2:580–82.
39. SWW 2:374.
40. De Gaulle, *War Memoirs*, 114–17.
41. SWW 2:436–37.

42. François Kersaudy, Churchill *and De Gaulle* (New York: Atheneum, 1982), 86, 120. SWW 2:579.
43. Lord Ismay, *The Memoirs of General Lord Ismay* (New York: Viking, 1960), 181–82.
44. Ronald Hyam, "Winston Churchill before 1914," *Historical Journal* 12 (1969), 172–73.
45. Campion, *The Good Fight*, 78–81.
46. J. S. Bratton, "British Heroism and the Structure of Melodrama," in Bratton et al., *Acts of Supremacy: The British Empire and the Stage, 1790–1930* (Manchester and New York: Manchester University Press, 1991), 25–27.
47. Andrew Roberts, *Hitler and Churchill: Secrets of Leadership* (London: Phoenix, 2004), 40.
48. HESP 2:210.
49. WP 2:687–97.
50. HIR, 17 August 1940.
51. HIR, 22 August 1940.
52. HIR, 21 August 1940.
53. Gibson, *Ciano Diaries*, 20 August 1940, p. 286.
54. HIR, 6 September 1940.
55. Joseph P. Kennedy, diary, 14 August 1940, in *Hostage to Fortune*, 461.
56. WP 2:765.
57. Colin Perry, *Boy in the Blitz* (London: Leo Cooper, 1972), 120–21, 131.
58. WP 2:788–89.
59. CS 6:276–77.
60. WP 2:717, 835.
61. MO, "Morale Today," 12 September 1940.
62. Robert Mackay, *Half the Battle: Civilian Morale in Britain during the Second World War* (Manchester and New York: Manchester University Press, 2002), 67–68, 75.
63. Virginia Woolf to Ethel Smyth, 12 September 1940, in *The Letters of Virginia Woolf*, ed. Nigel Nicolson and Joanne Trautmann (New York and London: Harcourt Brace Jovanovich, 1975–80), 6:431.
64. Virginia Woolf to Ethel Smyth, 25 September 1940, in ibid., 6:434–35.
65. Robert Rhodes James, ed., *Chips: The Diaries of Sir Henry Channon* (Harmondsworth: Penguin, 1984), 325.
66. Robert Rhodes James, *Victor Cazalet: A Portrait* (London: Hamish Hamilton, 1976), 241–42.
67. Hastings, *Winston's War*, 93.
68. TA 262.
69. WC 2:127–30.
70. SWW 2:293–97.
71. David Reynolds, *In Command of History: Churchill Fighting and Writing the Second World War* (London: Allen lane, 2004), 211.
72. Lord Moran, *Churchill: The Struggle for Survival 1940–1965* (London: Constable, 1966), 298.
73. Nicolson, *Diaries and Letters*, 2:125, 5 November 1940.
74. David Dilks, ed., *The Diaries of Sir Alexander Cadogan* (New York: G. P. Putnam, 1972), 345–46.
75. Mackay, *Half the Battle*, 76–80.
76. Ibid., 86.
77. MO, "Attitudes towards America and Russia," March 1948, pp. 3–4.
78. HIR, 14–21 October 1940.
79. Moran, *Churchill*, 32.
80. WP 3:315–17, 850; SWW 3:106–09.
81. WP 3:683.
82. Mackay, *Half the Battle*, 146.
83. Susan A. Brewer, *To Win the Peace: British Propaganda in the United States during World War II* (Ithaca, NY, and London: Cornell University Press, 1997), 34–35.
84. SWW 5:6.
85. WP 3:407.
86. Ronald I. Cohen, *Bibliography of the Writings of Sir Winston Churchill* (London and New York: Thoemmes Continuum, 2006), 548–63; www.booksofthecentury.com.
87. *New York Times* (13 April 1941), 1.
88. *Nation* (3 May 1941), 534.
89. *New Yorker* (19 April 1941), 88.
90. J. C. Skinner, *Boston Evening Transcript* (12 April 1941), 7; C. W. M., *Christian Science Monitor* (14 April 1941), 22; Walter Millis, *Books* (13 April 1941), 1.
91. "Hero & Hero Worship," *Time* 37 (14 April 1941), 99.
92. *New Republic* (21 April 1941), 537.
93. Robert Skidelsky, *John Maynard Keynes: Fighting for Freedom* (New York: Viking, 2000), 92.

94. Cadogan, *Diaries*, 374.
95. Quoted in Hastings, *Winston's War*, 102.
96. Colville, *Fringes of Power*, 283–87. For differing views, see Hastings, *Winston's War*, 104–14, and Walter Reid, *Churchill 1940–1945: Under Friendly Fire* (Edinburgh: Birlinn, 2008), ch. 12.
97. Colville, *Diaries*, 315.
98. Cadogan, *Diaries*, 380–81.
99. Nicolson, *Diaries and Letters*, 2:168, 27 May 1941.
100. WP 3:784–85.
101. Entry for 23 April 1941, in Willi A. Boelcke, ed., *The Secret Conferences of Dr. Goebbels: The Nazi Propaganda War 1939–43*, trans. Ewald Osers (New York: E. P. Dutton, 1970), 150.
102. Ibid., 192.
103. Entry for 16 February 1942, in Louis P. Lochner, trans. and ed., *The Goebbels Diaries 1942–1943* (Garden City, NY: Doubleday, 1948), 90.
104. Boelcke, *Conferences of Dr. Goebbels*, 213.
105. William L. Shirer, *Berlin Diary* (New York: Knopf, 1941), 1 September and 8 October 1940, pp. 493–94, 541–42.
106. Lochner, *Goebbels Diaries*, entries for 12 November 1942 and 24 January 1943, 298, 320–21.
107. Ibid., entries for 26 January, 5 and 13 March 1943, 322, 337, 342.
108. Colville, *Diaries*, 404–06.
109. SWW 3:319.
110. WP 3:835–38.
111. Jules Verne, *Michael Strogoff* (London and New York: Samuel French, n.d.), 30–33.
112. Colville, *Diaries*, 405–06.
113. Ibid., 404.
114. Martin Meisel, *Realizations: Narrative, Pictorial, and Theatrical Arts in Nineteenth-Century England* (Princeton, NJ: Princeton University Press, 1983), ch. 3.
115. "A new system of scenery has lately been introduced in pieces like 'Michael Strogoff' which consists of grouping living persons and bits of still life with pictorial background into a picture." Percy Fitzgerald, *The World Behind the Scenes* (London: Chatto & Windus, 1881), 79.
116. Colville, *Diaries*, 316.
117. HIR, 18–25 June and 25 June–2 July 1941.
118. Gibson, *Ciano Diaries*, 23 June 1941, p. 370.

20 The War Poet

1. Lord Ismay, *The Memoirs of General Lord Ismay* (New York: Viking, 1960), 269.
2. 7:355.
3. WP 3:1387.
4. John Colville, *The Fringes of Power: 10 Downing Street Diaries 1939–1955* (New York and London: W. W. Norton, 1985), 262.
5. Ibid., 273.
6. GC 266–67.
7. Charles de Gaulle, *The Complete War Memoirs*, trans. Jonathan Griffin and Richard Howard (New York: Simon and Schuster, 1972), 4.
8. Ibid., 306, 339, 682, 711, for example.
9. Ibid., 445.
10. Ibid., 713, 771.
11. Ibid., 452, 864–65.
12. Ibid., 744–52.
13. Ibid., 900.
14. Ibid., 57–58.
15. Ibid., 163–65.
16. Ibid., 773.
17. Ibid., 496–97.
18. Ibid., 150–51.
19. Robert Self, ed., *The Neville Chamberlain Diary Letters* (Aldershot: Ashgate, 2000–05), 4:459, 472–73.
20. 6:1155–58. David Dilks, ed., *The Diaries of Sir Alexander Cadogan 1938–1945* (New York: G. P. Putnam, 1972), 396–97. Elliott Roosevelt, ed., *F.D.R.: His Personal Letters 1928–1945* (New York: Duell, Sloan and Pearce, 1950), 1380.
21. Richard Raskin, "From Leslie Howard to Raoul Wallenberg: The Transmission and Adaptation of a Heroic Model," *P.O.V.* 28 (December 2009), 85–104.

22. WP 2:404.
23. Warren F. Kimball, ed., *Churchill & Roosevelt: The Complete Correspondence* (Princeton, NJ: Princeton University Press, 1984), 2:692.
24. SWW 5:420.
25. Ibid., 390.
26. Walter Henry Thompson, *Assignment: Churchill* (New York: Farrar, Straus and Young, 1955), 173.
27. SWW 4:774.
28. David Stafford, *Churchill & Secret Service* (Woodstock, NY: Overlook Press, 1998), 237–40, 256.
29. Angus Calder, *The People's War* (New York: Ace Books, 1969), 596–604.
30. 5C3:1436.
31. 6:32.
32. Colville, *Diaries*, 282.
33. WP 2:1224.
34. WP 3:193.
35. 6:1022, 1070.
36. Colville, *Diaries*, 366.
37. WP 3:1196.
38. CS 6483.
39. 7:35.
40. 7:169.
41. 7:442.
42. Colville, *Diaries*, 367.
43. Ibid., 553.
44. WP 3:300, 302.
45. Max Hastings, *Winston's War: Churchill 1940–1945* (New York: Knopf, 2010), 188–89.
46. HIR, 31 December 1941.
47. Lord Moran, *Churchill: The Struggle for Survival 1940–1965* (London: Constable, 1966), 15.
48. Susan A. Brewer, *To Win the Peace: British Propaganda in the United States during World War II* (Ithaca, NY, and London: Cornell University Press, 1997), 93–94.
49. Hastings, *Winston's War*, 240–45.
50. Harold Nicolson, *Diaries and Letters* (New York: Atheneum, 1967), 2:223–24, 23 April 1942.
51. Robert Rhodes James, ed., *Chips: The Diaries of Sir Henry Channon* (Harmondsworth: Penguin, 1984), 408.
52. Ibid., 417, 422–23.
53. Lord Alanbrooke, *War Diaries 1939–1945*, ed. Alex Danchev and Daniel Todman (Berkeley and Los Angeles, CA: University of California Press, 2001), 36, 38, 44–46.
54. Ibid., 187–91.
55. Ibid., 214.
56. Colville, *Diaries*, 146–47.
57. Ronald Lewin, *Churchill as Warlord* (New York: Stein & Day, 1973), 83–85.
58. Quoted in Charles Eade, ed., *Churchill by His Contemporaries* (London: Hutchinson, 1953), 214.
59. SWW 3:536.
60. 7:124.
61. Alanbrooke, *War Diaries*, 273.
62. Ibid., 324.
63. Ibid., 376.
64. SWW 4:703.
65. SWW 5:78–80.
66. Alanbrooke, *War Diaries*, 409–10.
67. Ibid., 450–51.
68. Stephen Roskill, *Churchill and the Admirals* (New York: William Morrow, 1977), 129–30.
69. Hastings, *Winston's War*, ch. 14.
70. SWW 5:378.
71. Hastings, *Winston's War*, 354–58.
72. 7:621, 667.
73. SWW 5:546–58.
74. Frederic Spotts, *Hitler and the Power of Aesthetics* (Woodstock, NY: Overlook Press, 2003), 14.
75. SWW 5:556–57.
76. SWW 6:10–12.
77. Alanbrooke, *War Diaries*, 570, 576.
78. Ibid., 580–81.

79. Ibid., 589–90.
80. Keith Sainsbury, *Churchill and Roosevelt at War: The War They Fought and the Peace They Hoped to Make* (New York: New York University Press, 1994), 36–38.
81. *From Max Weber: Essays in Sociology*, trans. and ed. H. H. Gerth and C. Wright Mills (London: Routledge & Kegan Paul, 1948), 196. For a Weberian analysis of Hitler, see Laurence Rees, *Hitler's Charisma: Leading Millions into the Abyss* (New York: Pantheon, 2012).
82. WP 2:195.
83. 8:1150.
84. 8:253.
85. Weber, *Essays in Sociology*, 245–49.
86. Colville, *Diaries*, 124–25.
87. Moran, *Churchill*, 67–68.
88. Ibid., 99–100.
89. Ibid., 106.
90. Ibid., 107–09.
91. 7:396–97.
92. SWW 1:xiii–xlv.
93. SWW 4:412.
94. Moran, *Churchill*, 116–17.

21 Victory?

1. Quoted in Max Hastings, *Winston's War: Churchill 1940–1945* (New York: Knopf, 2010), 295.
2. David Dilks, ed., *The Diaries of Sir Alexander Cadogan 1938–1945* (New York: G. P. Putnam, 1972), 564–65, 645, 647, 653, 689, 719–20, 759–60.
3. Lord Bridges, in *Action This Day: Working with Churchill*, ed. John Wheeler-Bennett (London: Macmillan, 1968), 231.
4. SWW 5:376–77.
5. Duff Cooper, *The Duff Cooper Diaries 1915–1951*, ed. John Julius Norwich (London: Weidenfeld & Nicholson, 2005),11 January 1944, 288.
6. Lord Moran, *Winston Churchill: The Struggle for Survival 1940–65* (London: Constable, 1966), 157.
7. John Colville, *The Fringes of Power: 10 Downing Street Diaries 1939–1955* (New York and London: W. W. Norton, 1985), 509–11.
8. George H. Gallup, ed., *The Gallup International Public Opinion Polls: Great Britain 1937–1975* (New York: Random House, 1976), 91.
9. Kevin Jefferys, *The Churchill Coalition and Wartime Politics, 1940–1945* (Manchester and New York: Manchester University Press, 1991), 18, 150–51.
10. Correlli Barnett, *The Audit of War* (London: Macmillan, 1986), 26–32.
11. Harold Wilson, *The Governance of Britain* (New York: Harper & Row, 1976), 54.
12. CS 1262.
13. SWW 5:571.
14. Cadogan, *Diaries*, 543–44.
15. CS 6823–27.
16. 7:492–95.
17. Warren F. Kimball, *Churchill & Roosevelt: The Complete Correspondence* (Princeton, NJ: Princeton University Press, 1984), 3:105.
18. Elliott Roosevelt, ed., *F.D.R.: His Personal Letters 1928–1945* (New York: Duell, Sloan and Pearce, 1950), 1513–14.
19. Kimball, *Churchill & Roosevelt*, 3:154.
20. K. E. Garay, "'Empires of the Mind'? C. K. Ogden, Winston Churchill and Basic English," *Historical Papers/Communications historiques* 23 (1988), 280–291.
21. John Paul Russo, *I. A. Richards: His Life and Work* (London: Routledge, 1989), 438–39.
22. Rodney Koeneke, *Empires of the Mind: I. A. Richards and Basic English in China, 1929–1979* (Stanford, CA: Stanford University Press, 2004), 186–88.
23. W. J. West, ed., *Orwell: The Lost Writings* (New York: Arbor House, 1985), 47–48, 62–63.
24. Lord Alanbrooke, *War Diaries 1939–1945* (Berkeley and Los Angeles, CA: University of California Press, 2001), 19 June 1944, 560.
25. Leo Amery, *The Empire at Bay: The Leo Amery Diaries 1929–1945*, ed. John Barnes and David Nicholson (London: Hutchinson, 1988), 19 June 1944, 989.
26. 7:840–42.
27. WC 3:1101–02.

28. WC 4:158, 428–32. The term had been used in an Armenian context since at least 1913. Jon Petrie, "The Secular Word HOLOCAUST: Scholarly Myths, History, and 20th-Century Meanings," *Journal of Genocide Research* 2 (March 2000), 31–63.
29. Michael Smith, "Bletchley Park and the Holocaust," *Intelligence and National Security* 19 (Summer 2004), 262–74.
30. Martin Gilbert, *Auschwitz and the Allies* (New York: Holt, Rinehart and Winston, 1981), 13–14, 39–44, 251–53, 262–65.
31. 7:846–47.
32. Bernard Wasserstein, *Britain and the Jews of Europe 1939–1945* (Oxford: Clarendon Press, 1979), 311–20.
33. Michael J. Cohen, "Churchill and Auschwitz: End of Debate?" *Modern Judaism* 26 (May 2006), 127–40.
34. James H. Kitchens III, "The Bombing of Auschwitz Re-examined," *Journal of Military History* 58 (April 1994), 233–66.
35. Quoted in Wasserstein, *Britain and the Jews of Europe*, 310.
36. William D. Rubinstein, *The Myth of Rescue: Why the Democracies Could Not Have Saved More Jews from the Nazis* (London and New York: Routledge, 1997), 89–99, 144–45.
37. David S. Wyman, *The Abandonment of the Jews: America and the Holocaust, 1941–1945* (New York: Pantheon, 1984), argues that anti-Semitism was an obstacle to the possible rescue of Jews.
38. Richard Toye, *Churchill's Empire* (New York: Henry Holt, 2010), 225–29. *Hansard*, House of Commons, 10 September 1942.
39. David Reynolds, *In Command of History: Churchill Fighting and Writing the Second World War* (London: Allen Lane, 2004), 337.
40. Nicholas Mansergh, ed., *The Transfer of Power 1942–7* (London: HMSO, 1970–83), 3:2.
41. TA 23–26.
42. For a sense of how complicated the case of Bengal is, see Cormac Ó Gráda, *Famine: A Short History* (Princeton, NJ: Princeton University Press, 2009), ch. 6; Mark B. Tauger, "Entitlement, Shortage and the 1943 Bengal Famine: Another Look," *Journal of Peasant Studies* 31 (October 2003), 45–72; and Lizzie Collingham, *The Taste of War: World War II and the Battle for Food* (New York: Penguin Press, 2012), 141–54.
43. Amery, *Empire at Bay*, 4 August 1943, 933–34.
44. Ibid., 24 September 1943, 943.
45. Ibid., 10 November 1943, 950–51.
46. Ibid., 12 February 1944, 968.
47. Ibid., 20 March 1944, 971–72.
48. Arthur Herman, *Gandhi and Churchill* (New York: Bantam, 2009), 512–15. Toye, *Churchill's Empire*, 234–36.
49. Amery, *Empire at Bay*, 13 April 1944, 979–80.
50. Ibid., 2 June 1944, 985–86.
51. Ibid., 4 August 1944, 992–93.
52. Ibid., 18 May 1945, 1042.
53. Ibid., 5 August 1929, 49–50.
54. For a defense of Churchill and Lindeman in connection with the Bengal Famine, written by an economist who worked with Lindeman, see Thomas Wilson, *Churchill and the Prof* (London: Cassell, 1995), ch. 7.
55. Wasserstein, *Britain and the Jews of Europe*, 354.
56. Hugo Slim, "Why East Africa's Famine Warning Was Not Heeded," *Guardian* (18 January 2012).
57. Madhusree Mukerjee, *Churchill's Secret War: The British Empire and the Ravaging of India During World War II* (New York: Basic Books, 2010).
58. Moran, *Churchill*, 131.
59. Beverley Nichols, *Verdict on India* (London: Jonathan Cape, 1944), esp. 157–77.
60. Gary R. Hess, *America Encounters India 1941–1947* (Baltimore, MD: Johns Hopkins Press, 1971), ch. 5.
61. Colville, *Diaries*, 563.
62. Kimball, *Churchill & Roosevelt*, 3:153–54.
63. SWW 6:197–98.
64. SWW 6:201–04.
65. Albert Resis, "The Churchill-Stalin Secret 'Percentages' Agreement on the Balkans, Moscow, October 1944," *American Historical Review* 83 (April 1978), 368–87; Panos Tsakaloyannis, "The Moscow Puzzle," *Journal of Contemporary History* 21 (January 1986), 37–55; P. G. H. Holdich, "A Policy of Percentages? British Policy and the Balkans after the Moscow Conference of October 1944," *International History Review* 9 (February 1987), 28–47; Reynolds, *In Command of History*, 458–61.

66. SWW 6:197–98.
67. SWW 6:433.
68. Moran, *Churchill*, 470.
69. Alanbrooke, *War Diaries*, 604–05.
70. Thanasis D. Skifas, " 'People at the Top Can Do These Things, Which Others Can't Do': Winston Churchill and the Greeks, 1940–45," *Journal of Contemporary History* 26 (April 1991), 307–22.
71. Harold Macmillian, *War Diaries: Politics and War in the Mediterranean, January 1943–May 1945* (New York: St. Martin's Press, 1984), 27 December 1944, 619–20.
72. Lord Ismay, *The Memoirs of General Lord Ismay* (New York: Viking, 1960), 367–71.
73. Gallup, *Gallup Polls*, 103.
74. MO, "Greece," December 1944.
75. Kenneth Harris, *Attlee* (New York and London: W. W. Norton, 1982), 241–43.
76. Frederic Spotts, *Hitler and the Power of Aesthetics* (Woodstock, NY: Overlook Press, 2003), xi.
77. Hugh Trevor-Roper, ed., *Final Entries 1945: The Diaries of Joseph Goebbels*, trans. Richard Barry, Entries for 27 February, 4, 11, 20, and 23 March 1945, (New York: G. P. Putnam's Sons, 1978), 1–2, 39, 102, 183, 215.
78. Timothy W. Ryback, *Hitler's Private Library* (New York: Alfred Knopf, 2008), 201–13.
79. Colville, *Diaries*, 585.
80. Ian Kershaw, *Hitler 1936–1945: Nemesis* (New York and London: W. W. Norton, 2001), 810–11.
81. Fred Taylor, trans. and ed., *The Goebbels Diaries 1939–1941*, Entry for 21 December 1939, (New York: G. P. Putnam's Sons, 1983), 71.
82. David Welch, *Propaganda and the German Cinema 1933–1945* (Oxford: Clarendon Press, 1983), 234.
83. Albert Speer, *Inside the Third Reich*, trans. Richard and Clara Winston (New York: Macmillan, 1970), 463.
84. Clifford Geertz, *Negara: The Theatre State in Nineteenth-Century Bali* (Princeton, NJ: Princeton University Press, 1980), 11–13.
85. 6:943, 1170, 1238; WP 3:1453; Colville, *Diaries*, 428–29; Anthony Eden, *The Reckoning* (Boston, MA: Houghton Mifflin, 1965), 885.
86. MO, "Sir Stafford Cripps and the Future," 5 November 1942.
87. MO, "N.Q. Extract," 8 February 1944.
88. CS 7171–73.
89. CS 7191–95.
90. MO, "A Report on the General Election, June–July 1945," October 1945.
91. SWW 6:512.
92. Gallup, *Gallup Polls*, 107.
93. Stephen Fielding, "What Did 'The People' Want?: The Meaning of the 1945 General Election," *Historical Journal* 35 (September 1992), 623–39.
94. MO, "Churchill's Reconstruction Speech," 10 April 1943.
95. Richard Toye, "Winston Churchill's 'Crazy Broadcast': Party, Nation, and the 1945 Gestapo Speech," *Journal of British Studies* 49 (July 2010), 655–80. Richard Cockett, *Thinking the Unthinkable: Think-Tanks and the Economic Counter-Revolution 1931–1983* (London: HarperCollins, 1994), ch. 2.
96. CE 2: 372.
97. 5C2:1258.
98. CE 2:386–93.
99. CS 3236, 3306–08, 3385–87, 3437, 3441–42, 3455, 3850, 4213–17.
100. Robert Mackay, *Half the Battle: Civilian Morale in Britain during the Second World War* (Manchester and New York: Manchester University Press, 2002), 106, 127–28.
101. Ibid., 170–72.
102. Wasserstein, *Britain and the Jews of Europe*, 84–107.
103. SWW 1:358.
104. SWW 2:246.
105. WP 2:1276–77.
106. 7:567.
107. MO, "Mosley and After," January 1944, 6.
108. A. W. Brian Simpson, *In the Highest Degree Odious: Detention without Trial in Wartime Britain* (Oxford: Oxford University Press, 1992), 389.
109. David Stafford, *Churchill and Secret Service* (Woodstock, NY: Overlook Press, 1998), 308–09.
110. WP 1:4.
111. WP 2:563–64.
112. WP 3:959.

113. WP 3:174, 176.
114. WP 3:1375.
115. WP 3:7–8.
116. D. J. Wenden, "Churchill, Radio, and Cinema," in *Churchill*, ed. Robert Blake and W. Roger Louis (New York and London: W. W. Norton, 1993), 233–35.

22 The Summit

1. Lord Moran, *Winston Churchill: The Struggle for Survival 1940–65* (London: Constable, 1966), 280–81.
2. Moran, *Churchill*, 634.
3. Lord Alanbrooke, *War Diaries 1939–1945* (Berkeley and Los Angeles, CA: University of California Press, 2001), 709–10.
4. WSC to Harry Truman, 11 May 1945, in G. W. Sand, ed., *Defending the West: The Truman Churchill Correspondence, 1945–1960* (Westport, CT, and London: Praeger, 2004), 71.
5. 7:949–50.
6. SWW 6:377.
7. SWW 6:383.
8. WSC to Harry Truman, 12 May 1945, in Sand, *Truman-Churchill Correspondence*, 75.
9. CS 7214.
10. Patrick Wright, *Iron Curtain: From Stage to Cold War* (Oxford: Oxford University Press, 2009), 17–18, 60–61, 80–82, 105, 152–53, 351–53. Henry B. Ryan, "Churchill's 'Iron Curtain' Speech," *Historical Journal* 22 (1979), 897–98.
11. MEL 16.
12. Wright, *Iron Curtain*, 220–25.
13. Lord Vansittart, *The Mist Procession* (London: Hutchinson, 1958), 276. J. H. Morgan, *Assize of Arms: Being the Story of the Disarmament of Germany and Her Rearmament (1919–1939)* (London: Methuen, 1945), 334.
14. Fraser J. Harbutt, *The Iron Curtain: Churchill, America, and the Origins of the Cold War* (Oxford: Oxford University Press, 1986), 155–56.
15. Ibid., 159–72.
16. Reproduced in James W. Muller, ed., *Churchill's "Iron Curtain" Speech Fifty Years Later* (Columbia, MI, and London: University of Missouri Press, 1999), 1–13.
17. John Ramsden, "Mr. Churchill Goes to Fulton," in Muller, *"Iron Curtain" Speech*, 25–27.
18. Harbutt, *Iron Curtain*, 197–201.
19. Ibid., 152.
20. Ibid., 204–08.
21. George H. Gallup, ed., *The Gallup International Public Opinion Polls: Great Britain 1937–1975* (New York: Random House, 1976), 128, 173.
22. MO, "Attitudes towards America and Russia," March 1948, 3–5.
23. Robert Gellately, *Stalin's Curse* (New York: Knopf, 2013).
24. 8:119.
25. Moran, *Churchill*, 315.
26. John W. Young, *Winston Churchill's Last Campaign: Britain and the Cold War 1951–5* (Oxford: Clarendon Press, 1996), 25–28. David Carlton, "Churchill and the Two 'Evil Empires'," in *Winston Churchill in the Twenty-First Century*, ed. David Cannadine and Ronald Quinault (Cambridge: Cambridge University Press, 2004), 180–81.
27. David Carlton, *Churchill and the Soviet Union* (Manchester and New York: Manchester University Press, 2000), 151–59.
28. Moran, *Churchill*, 573.
29. Harold Nicolson, *Public Faces* (London: Constable, 1932), 157.
30. Ibid., 330–32.
31. Barton J. Bernstein, "The Uneasy Alliance: Roosevelt, Churchill, and the Atomic Bomb, 1940–1945," *Western Political Quarterly* 29 (June 1976), 214–16.
32. Jacques E. C. Hymans, "Britain and Hiroshima," *Journal of Strategic Studies* 32 (October 2009), 769–97.
33. CS 7:936–44; 8:509–10.
34. Paul Addison, *Churchill on the Home Front 1900–1955* (London: Pimlico, 1993), 403.
35. TA 203, 209.
36. *The Times*, 12 October 1950, p. 4. For an analysis of Churchill's views on world government, see Kenneth W. Thompson, *Winston Churchill's World View: Statesmanship and Power* (Baton Rouge, LA: Louisiana State University Press, 1983), ch. 13.

37. H. G. Wells, *The World Set Free* (New York: E. P. Dutton, 1914), 265–66.
38. H. G. Wells, *Men Like Gods* (New York: Macmillan, 1927), 186.
39. WC 4:6–12.
40. Quoted in P. G. H. Holdich, "A Policy of Percentages? British Policy and the Balkans after the Moscow Conference of October 1944," *International History Review* 9 (February 1987), 42.
41. Moran, *Churchill*, 452.
42. Gallup, *Gallup Polls*, 259.
43. John Charmley, *Churchill's Grand Alliance* (San Diego, CA: Harcourt Brace, 1996), 256–57.
44. Daniel C. Williamson, *Separate Agendas: Churchill, Eisenhower, and Anglo-American Relations, 1953–1955* (Lanham, MD: Lexington Books, 2006), 11–16.
45. Ibid., 19–22.
46. Uri Bar-Noi, "The Soviet Union and Churchill's Appeals for High-Level Talks, 1953–54: New Evidence from the Russian Archives," *Diplomacy & Statecraft* 9 (1998), 110–33.
47. Young, *Churchill's Last Campaign*, 163.
48. Gallup, *Gallup Polls*, 300.
49. 8:846–53.
50. Moran, *Churchill*, 483–84.
51. Ibid., 446.
52. Robert Rhodes James, ed., *Chips: The Diaries of Sir Henry Channon* (Harmondsworth: Penguin, 1984), 582.
53. 8:904–08.
54. Moran, *Churchill*, 494.
55. Ibid., 501–02.
56. Gallup, *Gallup Polls*, 333.
57. Moran, *Churchill*, 559.
58. Klaus Larres, *Churchill's Cold War: The Politics of Personal Diplomacy* (New Haven, CT, and London: Yale University Press, 2002), 335–40.
59. Moran, *Churchill*, 561.
60. Williamson, *Separate Agendas*, 34–37.
61. Dwight Eisenhower to WSC, 12 July 1954, in Peter G. Boyle, ed., *The Churchill-Eisenhower Correspondence 1953–1955* (Chapel Hill, NC, and London: University of North Carolina Press, 1990), 161.
62. Quoted in Larres, *Churchill's Cold War*, 303.
63. Dwight Eisenhower to WSC, 22 July 1954, in Boyle, *Churchill-Eisenhower Correspondence*, 162–65.
64. WSC to Dwight Eisenhower, 8 August 1954, in ibid., 166–68.
65. 8:1123.
66. Moran, *Churchill*, 655. Carlton, *Churchill and the Soviet Union*, 195–96.
67. 8:1250–51; Moran, *Churchill*, 763; Ashley Montague Browne, *Long Sunset: Memoirs of Winston Churchill's Last Private Secretary* (London: Cassell, 1995), 157.

23 The Last Whig

1. Gerald Pawle, *The War and Colonel Warden* (New York: Knopf, 1963), 412–13.
2. Lord Moran, *Winston Churchill: The Struggle for Survival 1940–65* (London: Constable, 1966), 299.
3. 8:177, 180.
4. David Reynolds, *In Command of History: Churchill Fighting and Writing the Second World War* (London: Allen Lane, 2004), xxii.
5. CE 2:461–62.
6. Richard Toye, *Churchill's Empire* (New York: Henry Holt, 2010), 313.
7. John W. Young, "Churchill's 'No' to Europe: The 'Rejection' of European Union by Churchill's Post-War Government, 1951–1952," *Historical Journal* 28 (December 1985), 923–37.
8. 8:295–96.
9. Robert Boothby, *Boothby: Recollections of a Rebel* (London: Hutchinson, 1978), 208.
10. Arthur Herman, *Gandhi and Churchill* (New York: Bantam, 2009), 163–66. Wilfrid Scawen Blunt, *My Diaries* (New York: Knopf, 1921), 2:277–78.
11. Richard Allen Cave, "Staging the Irishman," in J. S. Bratton et al., *Acts of Supremacy: The British Empire and the Stage, 1790–1930* (Manchester and New York: Manchester University Press, 1991), 97.
12. G. R. Sims and Robert Buchanan, "The English Rose," TS, BL Add. Ms. 53456E, Act III, 23.

13. Anthony Montague Browne, *Long Sunset: The Memoirs of Winston Churchill's Last Private Secretary* (London: Cassell, 1995), 204.
14. For the Jewish presence in early medieval Palestine, see Moshe Gil, *A History of Palestine: 634–1099* (Cambridge: Cambridge University Press, 1997).
15. CS 7773–83.
16. 8:449.
17. 8:626.
18. Emery Reves to WSC, 7 January 1948, *Winston Churchill and Emery Reves: Correspondence 1937–1964*, ed. Martin Gilbert (Austin, TX: University of Texas Press, 1997), 284.
19. Emery Reves to WSC, 22 December 1947, ibid., 279–80.
20. WSC to Emery Reves, 4 January 1948, ibid., 281.
21. Emery Reves to WSC, 5 January 1948, ibid., 281–83.
22. Sarah Churchill to WSC, n.d., ibid., 283.
23. Emery Reves to WSC, 22 August 1949, ibid., 297–300.
24. Emery Reves to WSC, 22 August 1949, ibid., 301–04. SWW 4:637–38. David Reynolds, *In Command of History: Churchill Fighting and Writing the Second World War* (London: Allen Lane, 2004), 321.
25. Reynolds, *In Command of History*, 88–89.
26. www.booksofthecentury.com.
27. Ronald I. Cohen, *Bibliography of the Writings of Sir Winston Churchill* (London and New York: Thoemmes Continuum, 2006), 729–30, 738, 750, 753, 755, 759–64. George H. Gallup, ed., *The Gallup International Public Opinion Polls: Great Britain 1937–1975* (New York: Random House, 1976), 310.
28. Cohen, *Bibliography*, 41, 131, 330, 341–42, 383, 408, 470, 494, 730, 926.
29. http://www.winstonchurchill.org/learn/biography/redux/nobel-prize-for-literature/1953-nobel-prize-presentation-speech.
30. Roy Jenkins, "Churchill: The Government of 1951–1955," in Robert Blake and Wm. Roger Louis, eds., *Churchill* (New York and London: W. W. Norton, 1993), 492–93.
31. Moran, *Churchill*, 403.
32. John Colville, in *Action This Day: Working with Churchill*, ed. John Wheeler-Bennett (London: Macmillan, 1968), 72.
33. Moran, *Churchill*, 370.
34. Toye, *Churchill's Empire*, xi–xii, 293–300.
35. National Archives, CAB 195/11, C.C. 11(54), 24 February 1954.
36. Gallup, *Gallup Poll*, 487.
37. Browne, *Long Sunset*, 219–20.
38. Moran, *Churchill*, 413, 419–21, 427, 430, 432, 437, 443, 445, 457, 482–84, 486, 499, 507, 512–21, 532.
39. 8:284.
40. Moran, *Churchill*, 400.
41. 8:1220, 1258. WSC to Clementine Churchill, 21 September 1953 and 18 January 1958, *Winston and Clementine: The Personal Letters of the Churchills*, ed. Mary Soames (Boston, MA, and New York: Houghton Mifflin, 1999), 572, 622.
42. 8:1132.
43. 8:876–77, 891.
44. Maurice Ashley, *Churchill as Historian* (London: Secker & Warburg, 1968), 30.
45. Emery Reves to WSC, 14 June 1955, *Churchill and Reves*, 348–49.
46. HESP 1:3, 13–17.
47. HESP 1:19–20, 50, 54, 56.
48. HESP 2:276–81.
49. HESP 3:135–36, 149.
50. HESP 4:153–54.
51. HESP 1:47–48.
52. Robert Rhodes James, *Churchill: A Study in Failure 1900–1939* (New York and Cleveland, OH: World Publishing, 1970), 312. See also Peter Clarke, *Mr. Churchill's Profession* (London: Bloomsbury, 2012), 224–30.
53. HESP 1:110–11.
54. HESP 1:212, 2:64–65.
55. HESP 1:254–57.
56. HESP 1:278.
57. HESP 1:265–67, 289–90, 410–11.
58. HESP 1:369, 374.

59. HESP 1:487–90.
60. Ashley, *Churchill as Historian*, 33–34.
61. HESP 2:290–92.
62. HESP 2:311–16.
63. Cohen, *Bibliography*, 938, 942.
64. Arthur Bestor, "Sir Winston with Paint-Brush," *New Republic* 135 (20 August 1956), 20.
65. Charles Rolo, *Atlantic* 201 (April 1958), 90.
66. George Dangerfield, "Optimism of Winston Churchill," *Nation* 183 (1 December 1956), 480.
67. "Fact and Fiction," *Time* 67 (23 April 1956), 122.
68. HESP 4:387.

24 The Terrible Ifs

1. GC 114.
2. Barbara Leaming, *Jack Kennedy: The Education of a Statesman* (New York: W. W. Norton, 2006), 17–24, 56–57.
3. SWW 1:77, 150.
4. Martin Ceadel, "The 'King and Country' Debate, 1933: Student Politics, Pacifism and the Dictators," *Historical Journal* 22 (1979), 397–422.
5. Leaming, *Jack Kennedy*, 25.
6. Amanda Smith, ed., *Hostage to Fortune: The Letters of Joseph P. Kennedy* (New York: Viking, 2001), 239.
7. Ibid., 243–45.
8. Leaming, *Jack Kennedy*, 57–58, 71–72.
9. Nigel Hamilton, *JFK: Reckless Youth* (New York: Random House, 1992), 290–91.
10. John F. Kennedy, "Appeasement at Munich," 1940, TS in John F. Kennedy Presidential Library and Museum, preface, http://www.jfklibrary.org/Asset-Viewer/Archives/JFKPP-002-011.aspx.
11. Smith, *Hostage to Fortune*, 433–35.
12. John F. Kennedy, *Why England Slept* (New York: Wilfred Funk, 1961), xxvi–xxvii.
13. Ibid., 38–39.
14. Ibid., 134–38.
15. Ibid., 125.
16. Ibid., 65–66. (J.F. Kennedy's emphasis.)
17. SBS 87–90.
18. Kennedy, *Why England Slept*, 138–44.
19. Ibid., ch. 9.
20. Ibid., xxiv.
21. Ibid., 229–30. (J.F. Kennedy's emphasis.)
22. William Roulet to JFK, 30 November 1959, JFKPOF-129-018.
23. Thomas C. Reeves, *A Question of Character: A Life of John F. Kennedy* (New York: Free Press, 1991), 49–50.
24. Smith, *Hostage to Fortune*, 542–43.
25. Quoted in Ralph G. Martin, *A Hero for Our Time: An Intimate Story of the Kennedy Years* (New York: Macmillan, 1983), 204–05.
26. Ronald I. Cohen, *Bibliography of the Writings of Sir Winston Churchill* (London and New York: Thoemmes Continuum, 2006), 720.
27. JFK, interview at the National Press Club, 14 January 1960, JFKCAMP1960-1038-004.
28. Leaming, *Jack Kennedy*, 195–202.
29. Keith Eubank, "The Myth," in Dwight E. Lee, ed., *Munich: Blunder, Plot, or Tragic Necessity?* (Lexington, MA: D. C. Heath, 1970), 100.
30. Leaming, *Jack Kennedy*, 229–31.
31. John F. Kennedy, *Profiles in Courage* (New York: HarperCollins, 2006), 223.
32. GC 185.
33. Kennedy, *Profiles in Courage*, 1.
34. Ibid., 44.
35. Ibid., 240.
36. Ibid., 242.
37. JFK, draft of *Profiles in Courage*, JFKPP-035-004.
38. Thurston Clarke, *Ask Not: The Inauguration of John F. Kennedy and the Speech That Changed America* (New York: Henry Holt, 2004), 68.
39. For instance, the JFK speech at Lawrence Park Shopping Center, Pennsylvania, 29 October 1960, JFKCAMP1960-1033-004.

40. JFK, "The New Frontier," 15 July 1960, JFKPOF-137-003.
41. Leaming, *Jack Kennedy*, 246–57.
42. United Auto Workers press release on JFK's remarks at UAW rally in Detroit, 27 March 1960, JFKCAMP1960-1032-008.
43. JFK, speech in Beckley, West Virginia, 11 April 1960, JFKCAMP1960-1032-016.
44. JFK, Dave Epps Memorial Dinner, 1 August 1959, JFKCAMP1960-1028-030.
45. "Memorandum on the Last 9 Days of Campaigning," JFKCAMP1960-1076-007.
46. JFK, "An Investment for Peace," *Congressional Record*, 29 February 1960.
47. SWW 1:287.
48. JFK, address at the University of Washington centennial, 16 November 1961, JFKPOF-036-017.
49. WSC, *Memoirs of the Second World War* (Boston, MA: Houghton Mifflin, 1959), 1001.
50. Ibid., 1006, 1008.
51. Ibid., 1007.
52. WSC, *The Second World War* (New York: Time, 1959), 588–91.
53. William Hawes, *Filmed Television Drama, 1952–1958* (Jefferson, NC: McFarland, 2002), 47–49.
54. "The Spirit of '97," *Time* 68 (26 November 1956), 66.
55. Cohen, *Bibliography*, 82–83.
56. John Ramsden, *Man of the Century: Winston Churchill and His Legend since 1945* (New York: Columbia University Press, 2002), 203–04.
57. S. P. Mackenzie, "*War in the Air*: Churchill, the Air Ministry, and the BBC Response to *Victory at Sea*," *Contemporary British History* 20 (December 2006), 560–63.
58. *Time* (26 April 1963), 92–101.
59. *Time* (5 December 1960), 52.
60. James L. Baughman, *Same Time, Same Station: Creating American Television, 1948–1961* (Baltimore, MD: Johns Hopkins University Press, 2007), ch. 10, esp. 292.
61. WP 3.1388.
62. Donnette Murray, *Kennedy, Macmillan and Nuclear Weapons* (New York: St. Martin's, 2000), 21–25. John D. Fair, "The Intellectual JFK: Lessons in Statesmanship from British History," *Diplomatic History* 30 (January 2006), 119–42.
63. Nigel J. Ashton, "Harold Macmillan and the 'Golden Days' of Anglo-American Relations Revisited, 1957–63," *Diplomatic History* 29 (2005), 691–723.
64. David Nunnerley, *President Kennedy and Britain* (New York: St. Martin's Press, 1972), esp. ch. 4.
65. "Record of a Conversation at Admiralty House at 12:15 pm on Monday, June 5, 1961," JFKPOF-127-013.
66. Leaming, *Jack Kennedy*, 274–76, 312–15, 339, 405–06, 422–35. Richard Reeves, *President Kennedy: Profile of Power* (New York: Simon & Schuster, 1993), 165.
67. News conference, 14 February 1963, Howard W. Chase and Allen H. Lerman, eds., *Kennedy and the Press: The News Conferences* (New York: Thomas Y. Crowell, 1965), 240.
68. L. V. Scott, *Macmillan, Kennedy and the Cuban Missile Crisis: Political, Military and Intelligence Aspects* (Basingstoke: Macmillan, 1999), 5.
69. Ibid., 67, 159.
70. Robert F. Kennedy, *Thirteen Days: A Memoir of the Cuban Missile Crisis* (New York: W. W. Norton, 1971), 40.
71. News conference, 9 May 1962, in Chase and Lerman, *Kennedy and the Press*, 240. Speaking to US Congressional leaders on 26 June 1954, Churchill actually said "that meeting jaw to jaw is better than war," 8:1004–05.
72. Cyril Falls, *New York Times Book Review* (28 January 1962), 1.
73. Samuel R. Williamson, Jr., "Fifty Years On: *The Guns of August*, Always Popular, Always Flawed," *Sewanee Review* 121 (Winter 2013), 159–62.
74. Timothy Naftali, ed., *The Presidential Recordings: John F. Kennedy* (New York and London: W. W. Norton, 2001), 1:457.
75. WC 3.2:49–52.
76. Michael O'Brien, *John F. Kennedy* (New York: St. Martin's Press, 2005), 793.
77. Fair, "Intellectual JFK," 134–35.
78. Alistair Horne, *Macmillan 1957–1986* (New York: Viking, 1989), 383.
79. U.S. Department of State, *Foreign Relations of the United* States, *1961–1963*, vol. XI, Cuban Missile Crisis and Aftermath (Washington: United States Government Printing Office, 1996), 26–29.
80. Scott, *Macmillan, Kennedy and the Cuban Missile Crisis*, 137–40, 146–47.
81. Barbara Wertheim, "The Englishman Presents His Empire: A Study of the Moral Justification of British Imperialism in the Late Nineteenth Century," senior honors thesis, Radcliffe College (1933), Barbara Tuchman Papers, Yale University Library, MS 574 1/23, 15, 23–24, 66, 101, 106.

82. Barbara W. Tuchman, *Bible and Sword: England and Palestine from the Bronze Age to Balfour* (New York: Ballantine, 1984), 347–48.
83. Barbara W. Tuchman, *The Zimmermann Telegram* (New York: Macmillan, 1966), 200.
84. Barbara W. Tuchman, *Practicing History* (New York: Knopf, 1981), 45.
85. Ibid., 21.
86. Ibid., 56–57.
87. Ibid., 118–19.
88. Barbara W. Tuchman, *The Guns of August* (New York: Macmillan, 1962), 445.
89. WC 1:2–3.
90. WC 1:5–6.
91. WC 1:13–14.
92. John Maynard Keynes, "Mr. Churchill on the War," *New Republic* (23 March 1927).
93. WC 1:210–17.
94. Tuchman, *Guns of August*, 77–78, 116–17.
95. WC 1:248.
96. Tuchman, *Guns of August*, 436–40.
97. Cohen, *Bibliography*, 270–71, 293–95.
98. *New York Times*, 14 July 1960.
99. Reeves, *Question of Character*, 306.
100. Timothy Naftali and Philip Zelikow, eds., *The Presidential Recordings: John F. Kennedy* (New York and London: W. W. Norton, 2001), 2:583.
101. Richard Reeves, *President Kennedy: Profile of Power* (New York: Simon & Schuster, 1994), 344–46, 390.
102. WC 1:38–67, 95–96.
103. Philip Zelikow and Ernest May, eds., *The Presidential Recordings: John F. Kennedy* (New York and London: W. W. Norton, 2001), 3:481.
104. Kennedy, *Thirteen Days*, 105.
105. Naftali and Zelikow, *Presidential Recordings*, 2:523.
106. Nigel J. Ashton, *Kennedy, Macmillan and the Cold War: The Irony of Interdependence* (Houndmills and New York: Palgrave Macmillan, 2002), ch. 4.
107. Ibid., 226.
108. David Bruce to Captain Tazewell T. Shepard, Jr., 6 April 1962, JFKPOF-084-013.
109. WSC to JFK, 6 April 1963, JFKPOF-029-022.
110. George H. Gallup, ed., *The Gallup International Public Opinion Polls: Great Britain 1937–1975* (New York: Random House, 1976), 605, 657.
111. Entries for 24 November 1963 and 19 April 1964, in Graham Payn and Sheridan Morley, eds., *The Noël Coward Diaries* (Boston, MA: Little, Brown, 1982), 550–51, 563.
112. Nunnerley, *Kennedy and Britain*, chs. 16–17.
113. Reeves, *President Kennedy*, 278.
114. Ramsden, *Man of the Century*, 357.
115. Sarah Churchill, *Keep on Dancing* (New York: Coward, McCann & Geoghegan, 1981), 333–36.
116. Entry for 4 February 1965, in Payn and Morley, *Coward Diaries*, 591.
117. Ramsden, *Man of the Century*, 22.
118. François Kersaudy, *Churchill and De Gaulle* (New York: Atheneum, 1982), 428.
119. Henry Kissinger, *Diplomacy* (New York: Simon and Schuster, 1994), 512–14.
120. D. T. Max, "The Making of the Speech: The 2,988 Words That Changed a Presidency: An Etymology," *New York Times Magazine* (7 October 2001), 32–37.
121. John Dumbrell, "Winston Churchill and American Foreign Relations: John F. Kennedy to George W. Bush," *Journal of Transatlantic Studies* 3 (1S) 2005, 31–42.
122. *Daily Telegraph*, 12 February 2002.

Index

NOTE: Ranks and titles are generally the highest mentioned in the text